Textbook of Computational Biology and Bioinformatics

Textbook of Computational Biology and Bioinformatics

Edited by **Christina Marshall**

SYRAWOOD
PUBLISHING HOUSE
New York

Published by Syrawood Publishing House,
750 Third Avenue, 9th Floor,
New York, NY 10017, USA
www.syrawoodpublishinghouse.com

Textbook of Computational Biology and Bioinformatics
Edited by Christina Marshall

International Standard Book Number: 978-1-68286-234-6 (Hardback)

Printed in the United States of America.

Contents

Preface

The purpose of the book is to provide a glimpse into the dynamics and to present opinions and studies of some of the scientists engaged in the development of new ideas in the field from very different standpoints. This book will prove useful to students and researchers owing to its high content quality.

Bioinformatics aids the discipline of biology by developing tools and techniques to interpret and analyze all types of biological data through numerical and computational modeling. The focus of this book lies in the concepts of genome annotation, structural bioinformatics, comparative genomics, etc. It aims to bring forth the latest researches from across the globe to keep the readers updated with the progress of this field. This text is an apt reference material for students, academicians as well as professionals.

At the end, I would like to appreciate all the efforts made by the authors in completing their chapters professionally. I express my deepest gratitude to all of them for contributing to this book by sharing their valuable works. A special thanks to my family and friends for their constant support in this journey.

Editor

A top-down approach to classify enzyme functional classes and sub-classes using random forest

Chetan Kumar* and Alok Choudhary

Abstract

Advancements in sequencing technologies have witnessed an exponential rise in the number of newly found enzymes. Enzymes are proteins that catalyze bio-chemical reactions and play an important role in metabolic pathways. Commonly, function of such enzymes is determined by experiments that can be time consuming and costly. Hence, a need for a computing method is felt that can distinguish protein enzyme sequences from those of non-enzymes and reliably predict the function of the former. To address this problem, approaches that cluster enzymes based on their sequence and structural similarity have been presented. But, these approaches are known to fail for proteins that perform the same function and are dissimilar in their sequence and structure. In this article, we present a supervised machine learning model to predict the function class and sub-class of enzymes based on a set of 73 sequence-derived features. The functional classes are as defined by International Union of Biochemistry and Molecular Biology. Using an efficient data mining algorithm called random forest, we construct a top-down three layer model where the top layer classifies a query protein sequence as an enzyme or non-enzyme, the second layer predicts the main function class and bottom layer further predicts the sub-function class. The model reported overall classification accuracy of 94.87% for the first level, 87.7% for the second, and 84.25% for the bottom level. Our results compare very well with existing methods, and in many cases report better performance. Using feature selection methods, we have shown the biological relevance of a few of the top rank attributes.

1. Introduction

Recent advancements in sequencing technologies have seen an exponential growth in protein sequences, thus bringing to light new metabolic pathways. For many such newly found protein sequences, it is of prime interest to biologists to identify their biological function. In a biology lab, scientists conduct expensive and time consuming experiments to decipher the function of the sequences. One of the questions they often strive to address is whether the query protein is an enzyme or non-enzyme. Enzymes, as we all know catalyze biochemical reactions, but they perform this function differently using mechanisms depending on their bio-chemical properties. This has lead to the genesis of an interesting problem in Bioinformatics, i.e., given a protein sequence, how well can we classify it as an enzyme and accurately predict its function?

In light of the key biological role of enzyme proteins, the Enzyme Commission (EC) of the International Union of Biochemistry and Molecular Biology (NC-IUBMB) has created a hierarchical classification scheme based on the functional mechanism of enzymes [1]. Each enzyme is designated an EC number of the format X.Y.Z.W., where 'X' at the top of this scheme represents one of the six main classes (one-six), each further sub-divided to three levels in the hierarchy (Y.Z.W). The six main classes are Oxidoreductases (1), Transferases (2), Hydrolases (3), Lyases (4), Isomerases (5), and Ligases (6). Considering the costly experiments scientists conduct to know the enzyme mechanism, a need is felt for an automated method that can reliably predict the EC function class and thus significantly expedite experimental investigations on the query enzyme.

Enzyme function classification has engaged bioinformaticians for a considerable time now resulting in

* Correspondence: chetankumar.iisc@gmail.com
Department of Electrical Engineering and Computer Science, Northwestern University, Evanston, IL 60201, USA

different feature extraction methods to tackle this problem. There are three prominent approaches that have been widely experimented with: first, using sequence similarity between enzymes belonging to same functional class and second protein structure comparison [2,3]. These methods have been considered inefficient since enzymes belonging to same functional class are not necessarily similar in sequence and structure [4,5]. The third approach involves representing enzymes using their sequence and structure driven features that do not use similarity.

Studies that propose methods from the third category of approaches can be found in [6-10]. Features are chosen such that they capture the bio-chemical characteristics of a protein from its protein sequence and are represented in the form of vectors. References [6,7] established that support vector machine (SVM) is useful for protein function classification showing accuracy in the range of 84-96%. This study classifies protein sequences into classes like RNA-binding, homodimer, drug absorption, drug delivery, etc., using feature vectors like amino acids composition, hydrophobicity, polarizability, and secondary structure. It thus became clear that classification using sequence features and machine learning algorithms can be useful to predict functions of proteins. Reference [9] uses 36 features drawn from enzyme protein sequences, and employs a C4.5 classifier to build the classification model. This study classified enzymes into one of the six main EC classes, achieving precision and recall in the range of 86-92%. Reference [10] uses features to represent subtle distinctions in local regions of sequence along with features as used in [9]. It applies SVM to predict the main class and reports accuracy in the range of 66.02-90.78%.

There have been efforts to predict the enzyme function to the sub-class level as well. Reference [8] uses amino acid compositions derived from sequence and employs the covariant discriminant algorithm to classify oxidoreductases (enzymes belonging to class 1) into their sub-class. Although the results are promising, this study is limited only to the scope of oxidoreductases. Reference [11] introduces a technique that uses protein sequences to compute their functional domain and PSSM matrix. It proposes a three-layer predictor model built using the optimized evidence-theoretic *k*-nearest neighbor classifier, to predict enzyme main and sub-functional class. This study does not use sequence features and achieves an overall accuracy close to 90%.

In this article, we present a new approach to predict enzyme function class and sub-class using random forest. Random forest is an ensemble-based classification and regression algorithm, considered unsurpassable in accuracy among current data mining algorithms [12]. Random forest algorithms have been applied extensively in different applications ranging from network intrusion detection [12], probability estimation [13], information retrieval, and until recently in bioinformatics [14]. Our method is based on a three-tier predicting model which when given a query protein sequence, first classifies it into an enzyme or non-enzyme, and if an enzyme it predicts the main EC function class and sub-class. To the best of authors' knowledge, this is the first article that explores the use of random forest to this particular problem. Using a unique set of sequence-driven features extracted with the aid of online tools, our model reports an overall accuracy of 94.87% for the first level, 87.7% for the second, and 84.25% for the bottom level. We also report results from a direct single-step model to predict EC sub-class, which obtained an overall accuracy of 87%. The sequence features used in our study contain the dayhoffstat value for each of 20 amino acids, which is a unique aspect of this feature set. We find that the dayhoffstat features appear in the list of top ranked attributes thus suggesting that they are important to improving classification accuracy. We also provide an analysis of one of the top ranked features, composition of Cysteine in enzyme sequences.

2. Materials and methods

2.1. Random forest

Random forest is a classification algorithm developed by Leo Breiman that uses an ensemble of classification trees [14]. Each of the classification trees is built using a bootstrap sample of the data. At every node of the tree, a candidate set of features selected from a random subset of the entire feature set is used to calculate the feature with the highest information gain. This strategy turns out to perform very well as compared to many other classifiers, including discriminant analysis, SVMs, and neural networks [14]. Thus, random forest uses both bagging (a successful approach for combining unstable learners) and random variable selection for tree building. Once the forest is formed, every tree classifies the instances by voting for a particular class. The class that gets maximum votes is chosen as the final classification. Random forest has several characteristics that make it well suited for enzyme function classification: (a) It runs efficiently on large datasets with many features and does not require for data to be normalized. (b) It can handle missing values. (c) Because many trees are built and each tree is effectively an independent model, the model tends not to over-fit to the training dataset.

The error rate of a random forest depends on the correlation between any two trees and the strength of each tree in the forest [12]. The random variable selection procedure applied at every split of the classification trees contributes to the low correlation between the individual trees. The strength of the tree is determined by the error rate of the tree. Reducing the correlation between the trees and increasing the strength of each tree can decrease the overall error rate of the forest. The two parameters that can help achieve this are: *mtry*, size of random sub-set of features, and *ntree*, the number of trees in the forest. Random forest error is measured in terms of out-of-bag (OOB) estimate [15]. Increasing ntree reduces the OOB error rate of the forest as it decreases the correlation between individual trees and the possibilities of over-fitting. *mtry* should be a value much smaller than the total number of features. In most cases, an optimum value between *ntree* and *mtry* results in the lowest OOB error and higher accuracy.

To improve the classification accuracy, we have optimized the parameter values at every level of the model. In this article, we also present results obtained using a direct single-step model, in which a model built using random forest is trained on enzymes labeled with their sub-classes and tested on an independent set. The architecture of the two models is explained in the next section.

2.2. Model description

In this article, we focus on the three-tier top-down model to predict enzyme function till the sub-class level and also share results from a direct one-step approach to predict the same. The former model comprises of three layers: the first layer classifies enzymes and non-enzymes, the second predicts the main function class of the classified enzymes and the third layer predicts their sub-class. Each of the three layers is built using a random forest classifier with parameter values optimized to achieve highest accuracy possible. Figure 1 illustrates the design of the model with optimized parameter values at each level.

A diagram showing different components of the three-tier model. The first level classifies enzymes from non-enzymes. This model has been trained using a random forest with parameter values *mtry* = 25 and *ntree* = 200. Level 2 classifies enzymes into their main function class, while level three classifies the enzymes whose main class is predicted in level 2, into the sub-classes. There are six classifiers in level 3, each for the corresponding main class. The level three classifier is built using a random forest with parameter values identical to level 2, i.e., *mtry* = 7 and *ntree* = 200.

The second of the two models is a direct one-step approach to predict the sub-class function level (see Figure 2). This model was built by training random forest using instances of enzymes labeled with their sub-class. Once, the parameter values were optimized, the model was tested on an independent test set. Later sections discuss the comparison of results from the two approaches discussed above.

This model uses a query enzyme sequence and directly classifies into the sub-class. This model has been built using a random forest classifier with optimized parameter values, *mtry* = 7 and *ntree* = 200. These values correspond to the minimum OOB error rate obtained using this classifier.

2.3. Sequence extraction

We extracted protein sequences of enzymes from the enzyme repository of SWISS-PROT database [16]. Research in machine learning has proved that imbalance in class size can be an obstacle in building an accurately predicting model [17]. Hence, the number of sequences extracted from every main class was kept well balanced. Since, each main class has many sub-classes, we randomly extracted sequences such that they are well distributed over the latter. The next step was to remove identical sequences present in each main class. For this, we used CD-HIT, a program that removes redundant sequences, given a sequence identity threshold, which we set to 100% [18]. Table 1 summarizes the distribution of sequences across all the main classes and sub-classes. We selected sequences from only those sub-classes that contained significant number of sequences (> 200 sequences). The third column represents the sequences after removing all identical sequences.

2.4. Feature representation

To extract sequence-derived features, we used two online tools, EMBOSS-PEPSTAT: an online tool that generates a list of 61 feature values for a given sequence [19], and ProtParams: an online tool that computes values for 36 sequence features [20]. PEPSTATS generates values for features such as molecular weight, isoelectric point, amino acid composition, aliphatic amino acids, molar compositions of aromatic, polar, non-polar, charged, basic, and acidic amino acids. A unique aspect of this tool is that it provides the dayhoffstat value for every amino acid present in the sequence. As defined by EMBOSS, dayhoffstat is the amino acid's molar percentage divided by the dayhoff statistic. The dayhoff statistic is the amino acid's relative occurrence per 1000 amino acids normalized to 100 [19]. ProtParams, on the other hand, does not compute dayhoffstat values. However, it provides for feature values such as number of negatively or positively charged residues, number of carbon, hydrogen, nitrogen, oxygen and sulfur atoms, GRAVY, theoretical-pI, and aliphatic index. The use of these features is well reasoned and motivated in previous studies [21,22]. From our experiments, we find that a union of the features of ProtParams and PEPSTATS delivers better accuracy in comparison to using only one of the two

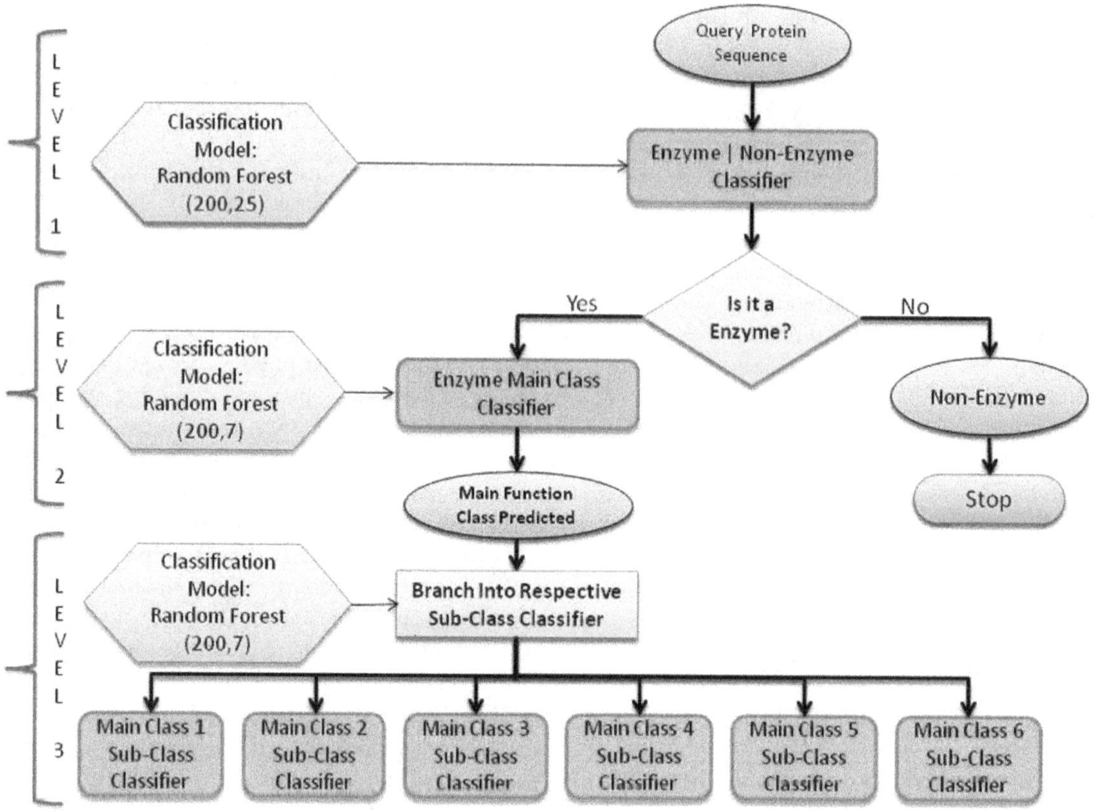

Figure 1 A flowchart diagram of the three-tier top down model (Model 1).

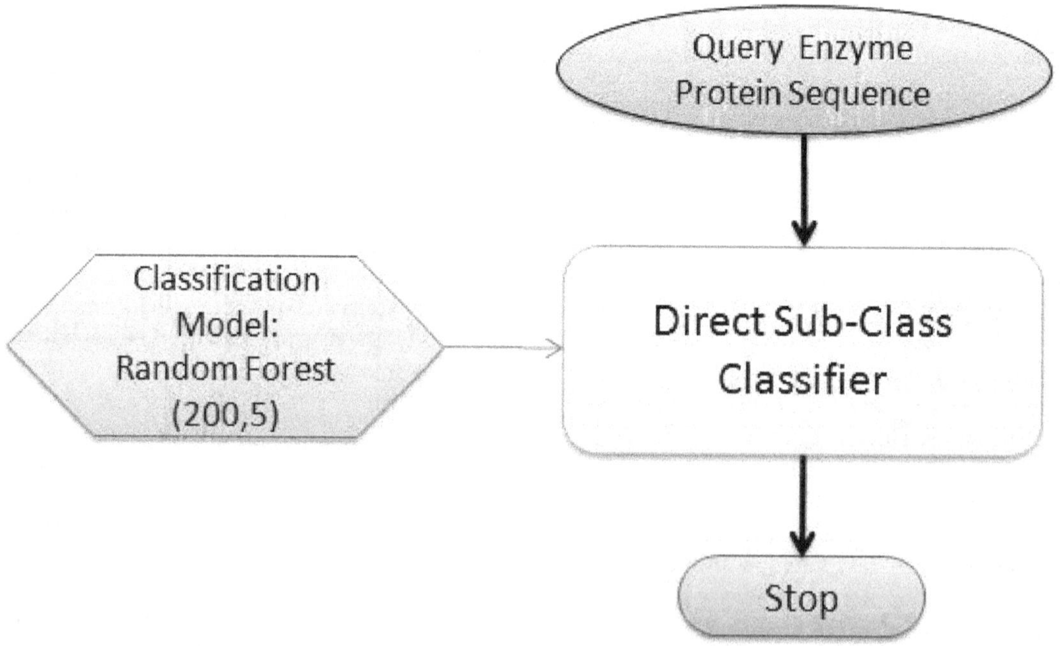

Figure 2 A flowchart diagram of direct sub-class level prediction model (Model 2).

Table 1 Distribution of sequences across different classes in training and test data combined together

Class	Sub-classes	Number of sequences
1 Oxidoreductases	1.1, 1.2, 1.3, 1.4, 1.5, 1.10, 1.16	986
2 Transferases	2.1, 2.2, 2.3, 2.4, 2.5, 2.6, 2.7, 2.8	734
3 Hydrolases	3.1, 3.2, 3.3, 3.4, 3.5, 3.6, 3.7, 3.8, 3.11	674
4 Lyases	4.1, 4.2, 4.3, 4.4, 4.6, 4.99	828
5 Isomerases	5.1, 5.2, 5.3, 5.4, 5.5	664
6 Ligases	6.1, 6.2, 6.3, 6.4	845

The sequences extracted from SWISS-PROT enzyme database are spread over a total of 40 sub-classes. Sequences have been extracted from the sub-classes having the largest bank of sequences. The number of sequences shown represent sequences with 100% reduced identity.

feature sets. Figure 3 presents a comparison of the OOB error and accuracy for three cases obtained using a random forest classifier with default settings (*mtry* = 7, *ntree* = 10). Unique features from both tools such as dayhoffstat and number of carbon atoms play a significant role in enhancing the classification accuracy. This is corroborated by the fact that they appear in our analysis of the top predicting attributes (Figure 4).

The classifier used is random forest with parameter values, i.e., *ntree* = 10, *mtry* = 7. PepStats, an online sequence analysis tool, computes values for 61 sequence features, while ProtParams computes for 36 features. The classification result obtained after taking a union of the features from the two tools is shown in the third bar. Some of the features that are unique to each tool help in improving the accuracy and reducing OOB error.

2.5. Dataset preparation and tools used

We selected a total of 2400 non-enzyme sequences and 4731 enzyme sequences. For level 1 experiment, we randomly selected 2400 enzyme sequences against an identical number of non-enzyme sequences. For levels 2 and 3 experiments, we divided the 4731 enzymes equally into training and test data, each containing 2366 and 2365 instances, respectively. The distribution of sequences across different classes was kept equivalent in both test and train data, as can be seen from Table 1. We did not normalize the feature values. WEKA, a widely used open source tool in machine learning was used to carry out all experiments [23]. We used Rattle, to perform feature selection using variable importance method [24].

3. Results

3.1. Results from experiments using model 1

First, experiments were carried out with different classifiers to identify the best classifier for our dataset. We carried out tenfold cross-validation experiments between LibSVM [25], NaiveBayes, C4.5 [26], and Random Forest, with default settings and parameters for all, as set by Weka. The experiment was performed at level-2, i.e., to predict the main class of the enzymes. Figure 5 illustrates the area under the ROC curve for the four different classifiers. Random forest out-performed all the remaining classifiers by recording the highest area under the curve.

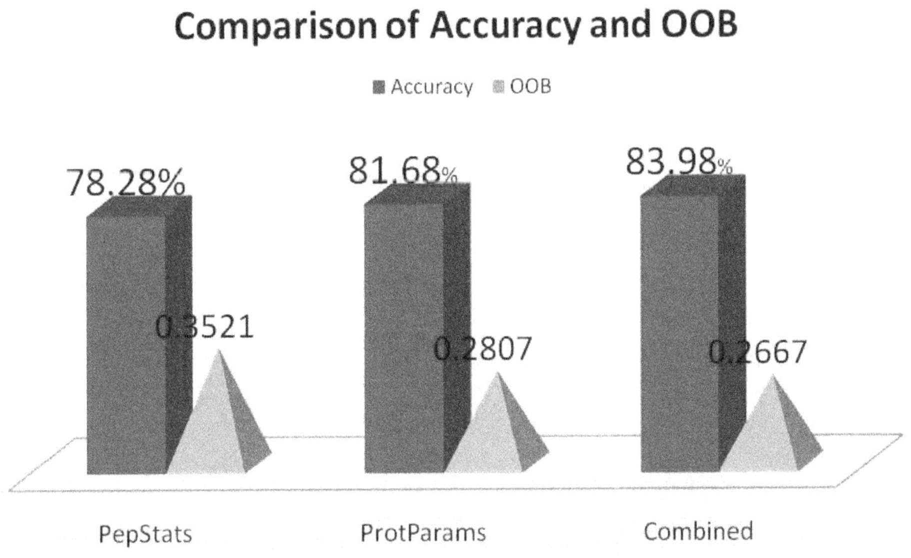

Figure 3 Accuracy and OOB error obtained using features from PepStats, ProtParams and combined features from the two tools.

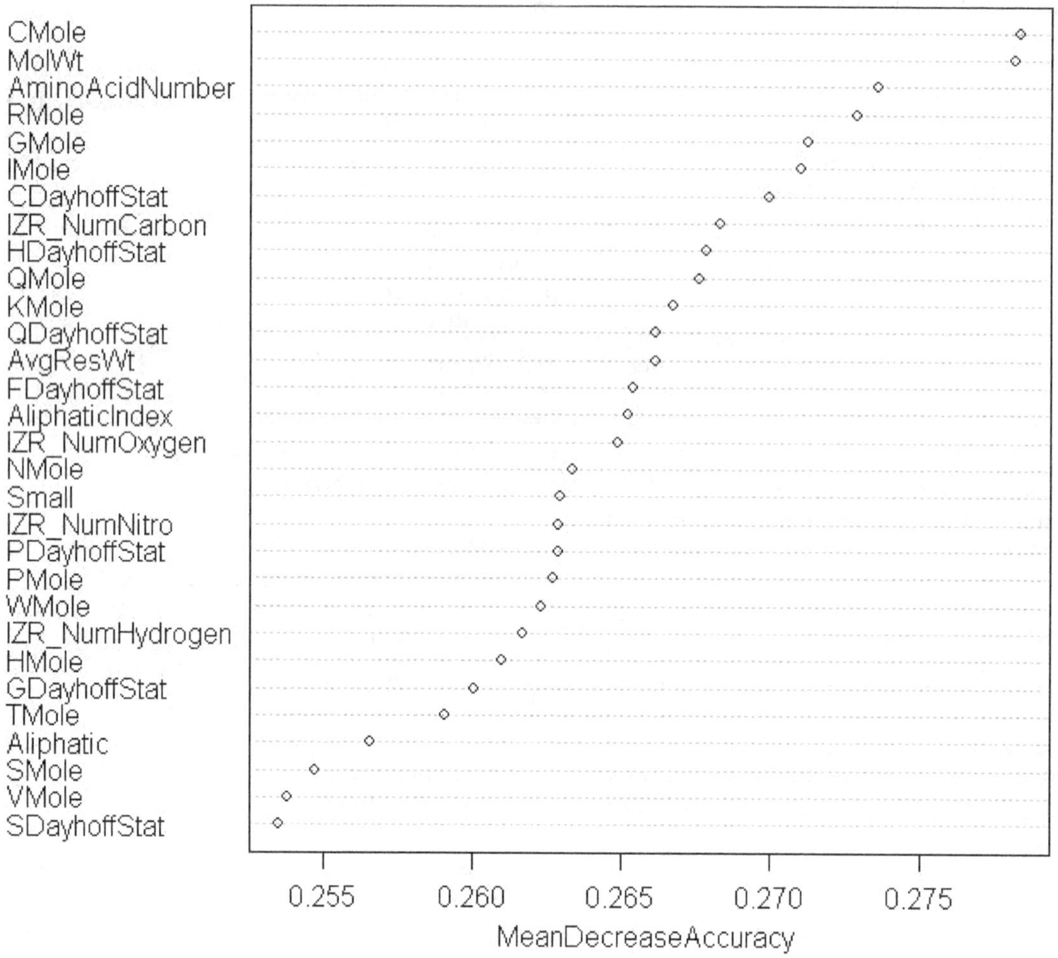

Figure 4 Mean decrease accuracy of top attributes for predicting main class of enzymes, computed using variable importance. Model 2 random forest classifier OOB error for different *ntree* and *mtry* values.

Figure 5 plots the area unde the ROC curve reported after running Weka on the different classifiers. The experiment was performed on enzyme sequences to predict their main class. Random forest recorded the highest area as compared to LibSVM, Naïve Bayes and C4.5.

3.2. Level 1: enzyme | non-enzyme classification

Level 1 of the model classifies enzyme protein sequences from non-enzyme protein sequences. We performed tenfold cross-validation experiments on a dataset containing values for all 73 features extracted from 2400

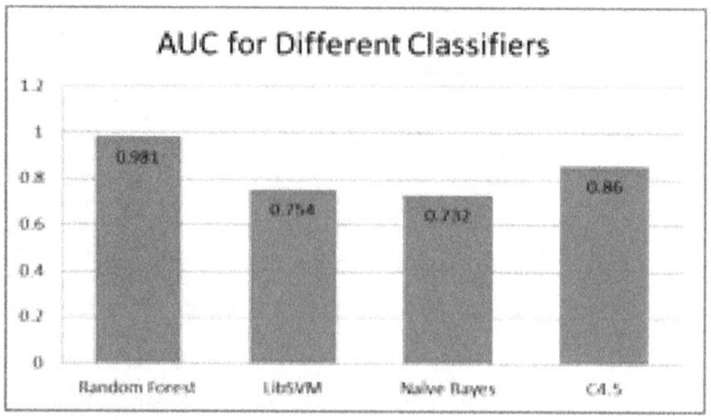

Figure 5 Area under the ROC curve for different classifiers to predict enzyme main class.

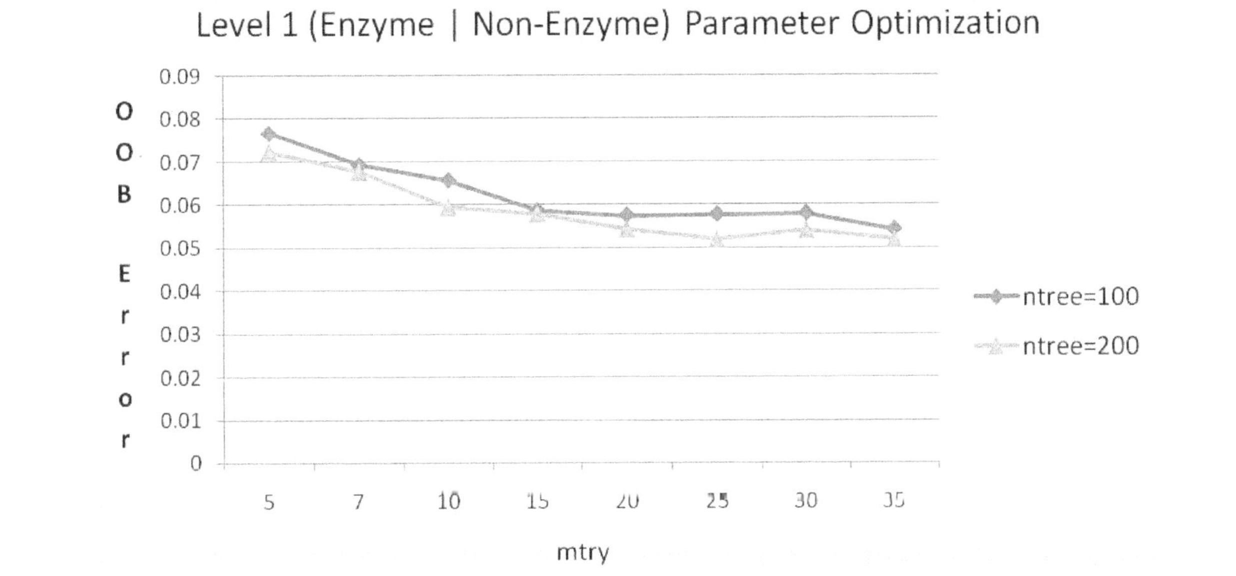

Figure 6 Level 1 OOB error for different values of *mtry* and *ntree*.

enzyme and non-enzyme protein sequences, a total of 4800 sequences. We first sought to optimize the two random forest parameters, *ntree* and *mtry*. Figure 6 provides OOB error estimates for varying values of *ntree* and *mtry*.

This graph shows OOB error obtained for different runs of the random forest classifier during its training phase. As the values of *mtry* and *ntree* are changed, the OOB error also varies. With increasing *mtry* and *ntree*, the error appears to decline till a certain value of *mtry*, i.e., 25 is reached. Hence, *mtry* = 25 and *ntree* = 200 are selected as values for the parameters for the level 1 classifier.

The least OOB error is obtained when *ntree = 200* and *mtry = 25*. We anchor these parameter values for level 1 classifier. Table 2 summarizes the results obtained from a tenfold cross-validation experiment. The overall accuracy obtained is 94.87%, with an OOB error of 0.056. This result compares quite favorably with other articles [11,27] that report an overall accuracy of approximately 75% (using neural network) and 91.3%, respectively.

Table 2 Tenfold cross-validation results obtained from experiment to classify enzyme and non-enzyme protein sequences

Protein type	Sequences	Correctly predicted	Precision	Recall	Accuracy
Enzyme	2399	2287	94.50%	95.30%	95.33%
Non - Enzyme	2399	2265	95.30%	94.40%	94.41%
Overall	4798	4552	-	-	94.87%

3.3. Level 2: enzyme main function class classification

Using a training and test data consisting of 2366 and 2365 instances, respectively, the second layer in the model classifies the test set of enzyme sequences into one of the six EC main function classes. We carried out several runs of the random forest classifier to obtain the optimal values of *ntree* and *mtry*, the results of which are shown as a graph in Figure 7. As can be seen in the figure, the lowest OOB error (approx. 0.117) is obtained when *ntree* = 200 and *mtry* = 7, respectively. Table 3 summarizes the classification results from level 2 classifier built using these parameter values.

Figure 7 shows OOB error obtained from different runs during training phase of the level 2 random forest classifier. The least value of OOB error is obtained when *mtry* = 7 and *ntree* = 200. Hence, these values are selected for the parameters for the level 2 classifier.

The overall classification accuracy achieved was 87.7%, with 2074 enzymes being correctly classified into their main function class out of a total of 2365 instances. This accuracy has been attained by a combination of 73 sequence driven features (union of PepStats and ProtParams features) and random forest classifier with optimal parameter values. In comparison to [9] that applies features from ProtParams and [10] which uses those from PepStats, respectively, this is a significant improvement in accuracy. Further, the dataset used in this study comprises of a total of 4731 enzyme sequences spread

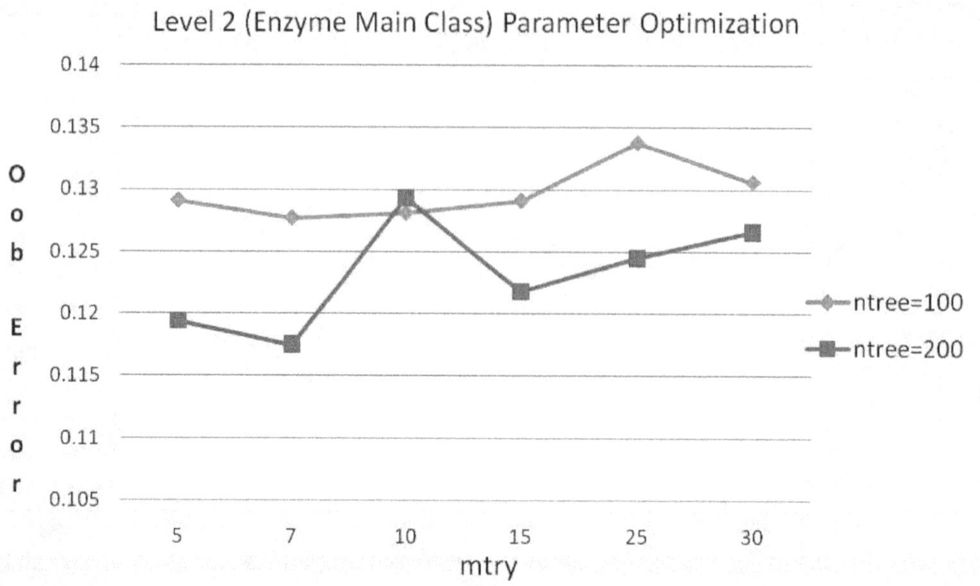

Figure 7 Level 2 OOB error for different values of *mtry* and *ntree*.

over 39 sub-classes. The dataset used in [9] contains 780 enzymes spread over 18 sub-classes. Random forest achieves a higher accuracy despite a wider distribution of enzyme proteins. These results substantiate the application of random forest to classification problems in bio-informatics.

Using random forest, we also carried out tenfold cross-validation experiments on all of the 4731 sequences with *mtry* = 7 and *ntree* = 200. We found 4171 or 88.16% of the sequences to be correctly classified into their main enzyme class, with an overall root mean squared error of 0.1992. Table 4 summarizes the results from this experiment.

The next step is to predict the sub-class for the enzymes. To do this, first we collected the enzymes classified into their respective main classes, into different files. For example, we took all enzymes classified as belonging to class 1, and used them as a test dataset for the level three classifier. We repeated this process for all six classes. The six level three classifiers were trained using corresponding main class instances from level two training data. As an illustration, the level three, sub-class 1 classifier was trained using main class 1 instances that were used for level two training, but are now labeled with their corresponding sub-class.

3.4. Level 3: enzyme sub-class function classification

In level three of the model, we classify enzymes whose main class has been predicted, into the sub-class that they might belong to. There are six random forest classifiers in this stage, each to predict the sub-class for enzymes under the corresponding main class. We used the same parameter values as used in level two for all six classifiers of level three, i.e., *ntree* = 200 and *mtry* = 7. This is because we did not see a big difference in OOB error even after varying values of *mtry* between 5 and 25.

The level two classifier also generates false positives, as shown in Table 3. If we consider class 1 only, false positives here are the enzymes that are classified as class

Table 3 Classification results on test data for main enzyme class classification using level 2 classifier

Class	Total enzymes	True positive	False positive	Precision (%)	Recall (%)	ROC area
1	493	436	57	88.40	88.40	0.94
2	367	302	49	86	82.30	0.92
3	337	297	66	81.80	88.10	0.95
4	414	371	53	87.50	89.60	0.95
5	332	281	32	89.80	84.60	0.94
6	422	387	34	91.90	91.70	0.96
Overall	2365	2074	291	87.70	87.70	0.94

Table 4 Results of tenfold cross-validation experiment performed using Model 1 to predict main enzyme class

Class	Total sequences	True positive	False positive	Precision rate (%)	Recall (%)
1	986	878	115	88.40	88.70
2	734	602	95	86.40	84.10
3	674	610	124	83.10	86.60
4	828	737	81	90.10	89.60
5	664	558	75	88.20	86
6	845	786	70	91.80	92.40
Overall	4731	4171	560	88.20	88.20

1 but actually belong to other classes like 2 or 3. As a result, as an example enzymes might get wrongly assigned a sub-class label of 1.2, which in reality is 2.2. Hence, we need to account for false positives as errors while reporting the classification accuracy of level three. Table 4 carries a column titled carry over false positives. These are the enzymes wrongly predicted as belonging to the respective main class. For class 1, there are 57 such enzymes that we need to account and distribute across the sub-classes of class 1. We factor the number of carry over false positives by the number of test sequences in each sub-class. For instance, sub-class 1.1 has 81 enzymes while 1.16 has 35 enzymes, hence number of carry over false positives to 1.1 is twice that for 1.16, i.e., 10 and 5, respectively. We calculate new values for precision by the addition *f* carry over false positives and false positives reported in the experiment. The formula we use is as follows:

$$\text{Precision} = \frac{\text{TruePositves}}{\text{TruePositves} + \text{FalsePositives} + \text{CarryOverFalsePositives}}$$

False negatives are instances of class 1, for example, that get wrongly classified as being in class 3, and hence the sub-class will also be wrongly identified, say 3.1 instead of 1.2. Just like precision, we calculate new values for recall that take into account the false negatives generated in level two. New recall values are calculated using the formula given below:

$$\text{Recall} = \frac{\text{TruePositves}}{\text{TruePositves} + \text{FalseNegatives} + \text{CarryOverFalseNegatives}}$$

Table 5 and Figure 8 provide a quantitative estimate of the performance of random forest in predicting the sub-class of the enzymes. The overall precision and recall when we do not account for carry over false positives and false negatives is 95.67 and 95.34%, respectively, and after incorporating these errors, the overall precision and recall falls to 83.01 and 82.67%, respectively. Precision and recall across all sub-classes ranges from 74.07 to 91.19% and 57.5 to 100%, respectively. From the results, we can deduce that at level 2, if the classifier correctly predicts the main class, there is 95% probability that level three will correctly identify the sub-class. However, if it does not predict the main class correctly, this probability drops to 83%. This deduction is also established by the correlation between the ROC area for the main class and the corresponding sub-classes. From Table 3 we can see that the ROC Area is highest for class 6 and lowest for class 2. When we look at the ROC area for their corresponding sub classes, in Table 5 we notice that the sub-classes of class 6 have higher ROC area as compared to sub-classes of class 6. Summarizing the results, it is clear that the three layer model has achieved highly promising results, with the capability to correctly predict till the sub-class level with 83% accuracy.

Precision and recall for most sub-classes is around similar range, besides seven sub-classes that have a higher recall. Minimum precision is 74.07% (sub-class 3.7) while minimum recall is 57.05% (sub-class 2.3).

3.5. Results from experiments using model 2

Model 2 (see Figure 2) is a direct single step approach to predicting the sub-class of enzymes. As in previous cases, we first sought to find optimal values of the random forest parameters. We carried out a tenfold cross-validation experiment. The random forest classifier reports the lowest OOB error when *mtry* = 5 and *ntree* = 200 (see Figure 9). Using these values, the results from the experiment are summarised in Table 6.

Figure 9 shows OOB error obtained from different runs of the random forest classifier during training phase. The least value of OOB error is obtained when *mtry* = 5 and *ntree* = 200.

The overall precision and recall obtained using Model 2 is 87.35 and 86.74%. Precision ranges from 60.94 to 95.24% while recall lies in the ranges 48.75-99.52%. We also tested model 2 by introducing 784 non-enzyme sequences into the dataset. For this, we conducted another tenfold cross-validation experiment using the same values for *mtry* and *ntree*, 5 and 200, respectively. Random forest correctly classified 86% of the sequences, where the precision and recall of the non-enzyme class was 87.4 and 86.6%, respectively. This is lower than the results from level-1 of model-1 which reported around 94% accuracy.

Table 5 Level 3 classification results for sub-classes of all six main classes

Class	Size	False positives	Carry over false positives	Precision	New precision	Recall	Carry over false negatives	New recall	ROC area
1.1	81	4	10	95.06	84.61	95.1	15	80.20	0.96
1.2	81	5	10	93.98	83.87	96.3	10	85.71	0.96
1.3	81	7	10	91.76	82.11	96.3	7	88.63	0.99
1.4	81	2	10	97.44	86.36	93.8	6	87.35	0.96
1.5	34	3	5	91.18	79.48	91.2	14	64.58	0.89
1.10	43	0	7	100	86	100	1	97.72	0.98
1.16	35	0	5	100	86.48	91.4	4	82.05	0.98
2.1	38	0	6	100	86	97.37	10	77.08	0.96
2.2	45	0	7	100	86.5	100	0	100.00	0.97
2.3	23	0	4	100	85.2	100	17	57.50	0.96
2.4	44	1	7	97.73	84.3	97.72	6	86.00	0.99
2.5	43	4	7	91.49	79.6	100	6	87.75	0.98
2.6	36	3	6	91.89	79.1	94.44	13	69.38	0.95
2.7	36	1	6	96.77	81.1	83.33	3	76.92	0.94
2.8	37	4	6	89.47	77.3	91.89	8	75.55	0.89
3.1	35	1	8	96.97	78.05	91.43	8	74.41	0.97
3.2	45	2	10	95.74	78.95	100		100.00	0.95
3.3	34	1	8	96.97	78.05	94.18	11	71.11	0.94
3.4	46	2	10	95.56	78.18	93.48	3	87.75	0.93
3.5	42	0	10	100	79.17	90.48	4	82.60	0.97
3.6	44	3	10	93.62	77.2	100	2	95.65	0.97
3.7	20	3	4	86.96	74.07	100	6	76.92	0.92
3.8	13	1	2	92.31	80	92.3	5	66.66	0.90
3.11	18	1	4	94.44	77.27	94.45		94.44	0.97
4.1	76	4	11	94.87	83.15	97.37	12	84.09	0.99
4.2	78	4	11	95	83.51	97.44	15	81.72	0.98
4.3	90	4	13	95.7	83.97	98.89	1	97.80	0.97
4.4	41	1	6	97.37	84.09	90.24	5	80.43	0.97
4.6	42	2	6	94.87	82.22	88.1	7	75.51	0.96
4.99	43	2	6	95.24	83.33	93.02	3	86.95	0.97
5.1	83	2	10	97.59	87.1	97.6	8	89.01	0.98
5.2	39	1	4	97.5	88.63	100	9	81.25	0.99
5.3	78	1	8	98.73	89.65	100	16	82.97	1.00
5.4	40	2	5	94.87	84.1	92.5	9	75.51	0.97
5.5	40	0	5	100	88.63	97.5	9	79.59	0.98
6.1	207	2	18	99.04	91.19	100	1	99.51	1.00
6.2	73	1	6	98.61	91.02	97.26	19	77.17	0.98
6.3	72	3	6	95.65	88	91.67	13	77.64	0.95
6.4	35	5	3	86.49	80	91.43	1	88.88	0.94
Overall	2072	82	290	95.67	83.01	95.34	287	82.670	0.96

Carry over false positives and negatives from level two classifier experiments are taken into account while calculating precision and recall in level three. The distribution of the carry over false positives is factored by the number of test sequences in the respective sub-classes, in order to conserve the sequence distribution

4. Discussion

Although both models 1 and 2 report promising results, comparing favorably well with other published studies [8-11], the precision and recall obtained using model 2 (87.35 and 86.74%, respectively) is higher in comparison to model 1. If we only look at the minimum precision and recall values, model 2 reports 60.94 and 48.75%, respectively, both for sub-class 2.3. Through model 1, the precision for the same class 2.3 is 85.2% while recall is 57.5%. Model 1 has the advantage that if we only consider the instances whose main class is predicted correctly, the precision for predicting the sub-class is very

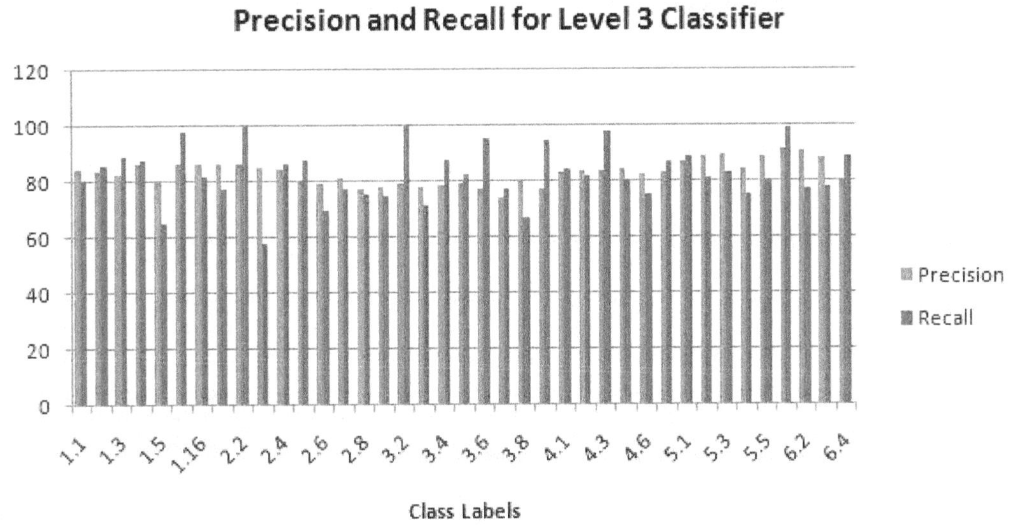

Figure 8 Graph showing precision and recall for all sub-classes obtained using level 3 random forest classifier.

high, almost 95%. This result leads us to reliably conclude that the set of features extracted from enzyme protein sequences capture rich information about the functional mechanism of the enzyme, down to the sub-class level. Further, model 1 is designed with the objective of segregating enzymes from non-enzymes, and subsequently predicting main and sub-class of the enzymes. It can hence be applied to any generic sequence. This could be helpful to biologists for they would first want to know whether a query protein sequence is an enzyme or not. Model 2 on the other hand proves to be more effective to sequences that are already known to be enzymes.

5. Ranking attributes

In a classification problem, ranking the features is often of interest as it tells us which features are strong predictors. Reference [17] has indicated that it is possible not all features from a protein sequence are strong predictors and hence many might contribute to noise. In random forest, importance of features is computed using a method called variable importance [15]. This method provides two indices to quantify which features are most informative, i.e., exhibit strong characteristics associated with enzyme function classes: mean decrease in accuracy and the gini index. Mean decrease in accuracy is

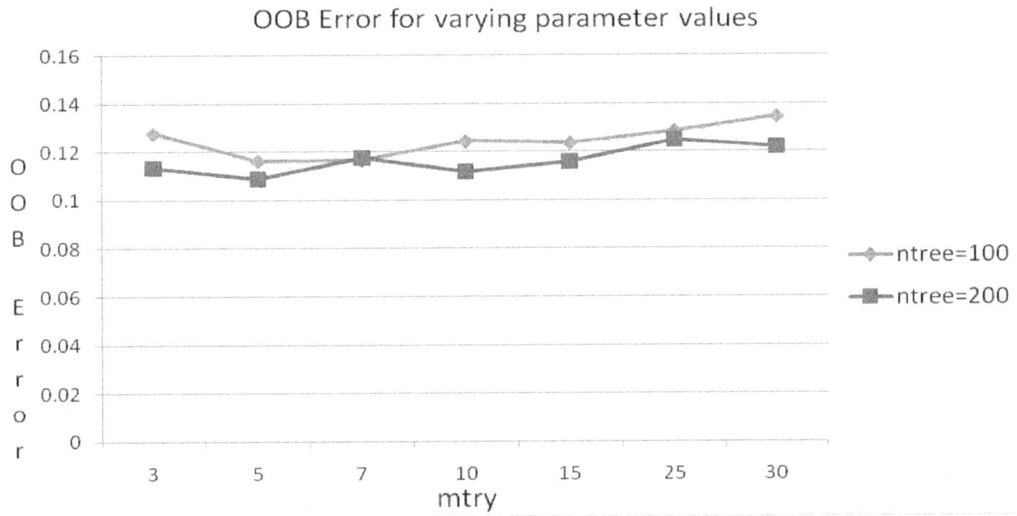

Figure 9 Model 2 random forest classifier OOB error for different *ntree* and *mtry* values.

Table 6 Performance of random forest classifier using Model 2, direct sub-class classification approach

Class label	Instances	True positive	Precision (%)	Recall (%)
1.1	192	157	83.51	81.77
1.10	88	87	93.55	98.86
1.16	74	65	89.04	87.84
1.2	179	169	88.02	94.41
1.3	176	162	94.74	92.05
1.4	175	162	94.74	92.57
1.5	97	78	81.25	80.41
2.1	96	80	95.24	83.33
2.2	91	90	70.87	98.9
2.3	80	39	60.94	48.75
2.4	98	83	91.21	84.69
2.5	97	86	88.66	88.66
2.6	96	82	82.83	85.42
2.7	110	68	93.15	61.82
2.8	93	74	94.87	79.57
3.1	87	71	77.17	81.61
3.11	36	33	80.49	91.67
3.2	89	85	86.73	95.51
3.3	87	76	87.36	87.36
3.4	95	86	94.51	90.53
3.5	91	85	91.4	93.41
3.6	92	88	92.63	95.65
3.7	55	43	91.49	78.18
3.8	36	31	79.49	86.11
4.1	172	159	90.34	92.44
4.2	185	147	89.63	79.46
4.3	183	180	91.84	98.36
4.4	91	77	91.67	84.62
4.6	97	85	91.4	87.63
4.99	93	87	92.55	93.55
5.1	179	168	85.28	93.85
5.2	96	86	83.5	89.58
5.3	188	154	84.15	81.91
5.4	98	77	92.77	78.57
5.5	99	84	85.71	84.85
6.1	418	416	93.91	99.52
6.2	183	156	81.68	85.25
6.3	170	151	87.79	88.82
6.4	82	70	80.46	85.37
Overall	4748	4190	87.35	86.74

considered more reliable and accurate than the gini index [12]. Hence, we used the former to report the strong predictors. Since WEKA does not provide the variable importance feature for random forest as yet, we used Rattle for this purpose, a data mining tool developed by Dr Graham Williams [24]. The experiment we performed was to compute the top predicting attributes for the enzyme main class by way of tenfold cross validation. Figure 4 lists the top features computed by the variable importance method.

Figure 4 shows the top predicting attributes in decreasing order of accuracy. CMole represents the Cysteine percentage composition in the protein sequences. MoltWt is the molecular weight. HDayhoff-Stat is dayhoffstat value for Histidine in the enzyme protein sequences.

From the figure we can see that Cysteine amino acid (CMole) has the highest prediction accuracy, followed by molecular weight and amino acid number. A box plot diagram in Figure 10 provides the relative distribution of cysteines in the six main function classes. Sequences that belong to class 3, i.e., hydrolases have the highest median composition of cysteines and highest upper quartile value. We verified this information with published studies and found that studies carried out in [28] report high conservation of cysteines in glycosyl hydrolase family, which are enzymes from class 3. Reference [29] has analyzed proteins from this family and also reports high cysteine conservation in glycoside hydrolases. Hence, results from this experiment might indicate that composition of cysteines is higher in hydrolases. This would however need to be validated and verified with biological experiments.

Figure 10 showing class 3, i.e., Hydrolases to have the highest median and upper quartile percentage composition of Cysteines.

We also noted the top predicting attributes for enzyme versus non-enzyme classification and sub-class level classification. First, for the enzyme versus non-enzyme classification: CMole was not quite the top predicting attribute, although its Mean Decrease Accuracy figure was about the same (0.26). Molecular weight (MolWt.) was the top predicting attribute for this experiment, with a mean decrease accuracy of 0.36. Next, for the enzyme sub-class level classification: CMole, AminoAcidNumber and MolWt were amongst the top four predictors, with the mean decrease accuracy ranging between 0.32 and 0.33.

6. Conclusions

Enzyme function classification is a challenging problem, and sequence features alone will not be enough to accurately predict enzymatic mechanisms. However, using a unique set of features extracted from sequence and an efficient classifier, random forest, we have demonstrated that sequence features do capture rich bio-chemical information about an enzyme and if coupled with structural characteristics, can contribute to a more robust and accurately predicting model. By using 73 different features extracted using EMBOSS PEPSTAT and Prot-Params tool, we have tried to highlight how existing

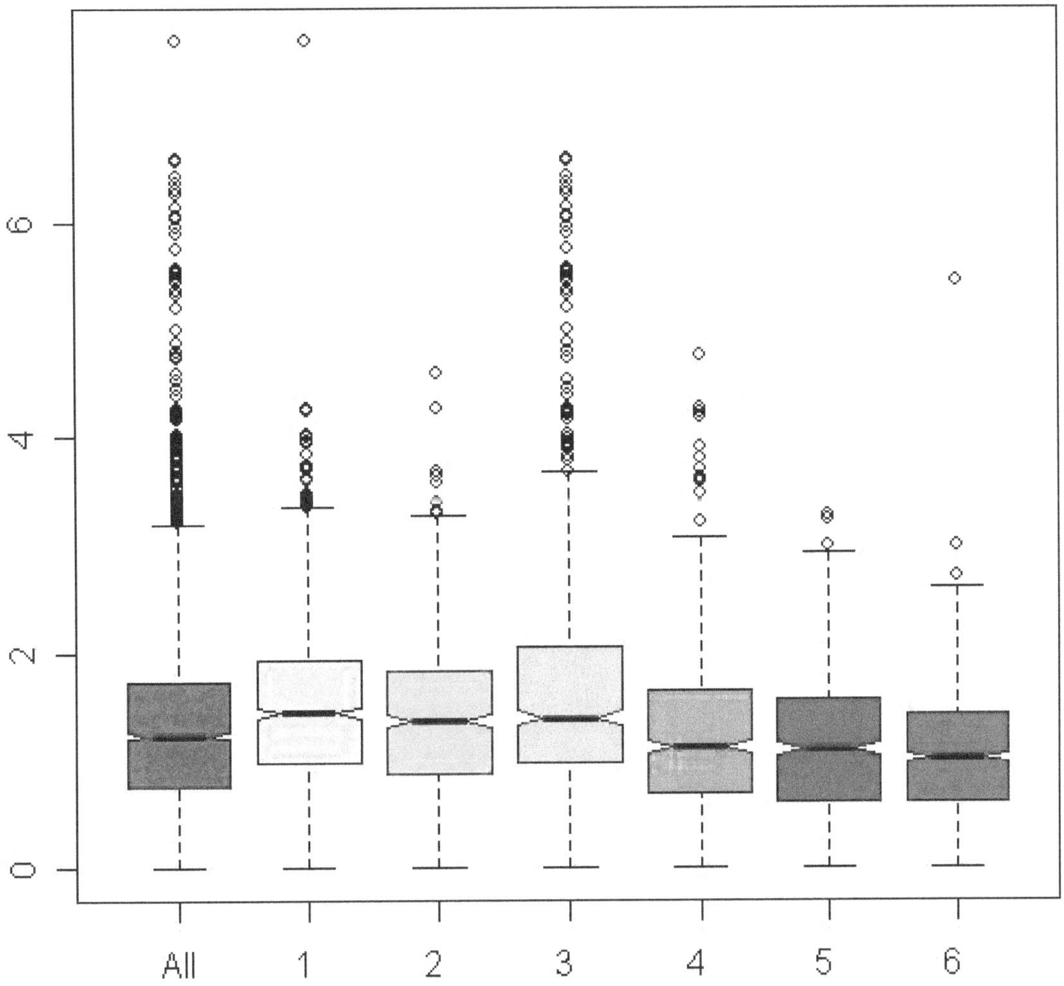

Figure 10 **Box plot diagram showing distribution of cysteines across the six main enzyme function classes**.

tools can be re-used and extended to address interesting problems in Bioinformatics. The results from the experiments demonstrate the useful application of random forest for multi-class problems like enzyme function classification. The random forest classifier achieved a high accuracy on a widely distributed and reasonably large dataset. Further, our analysis of top rank features suggests that percentage composition of cysteines can be important in enzyme function classification. The datasets are available online for other groups to experiment and could prove to be useful for extracting interesting information about enzymes, especially with regard to the features that we have used.

Acknowledgements
This study was supported in part by the NSF grants CNS-0551639, IIS-0536994, NSF HECURA CCF-0621443, and NSF SDCI OCI-0724599 and DOE SCIDAC-2: Scientific Data Management Center for Enabling Technologies (CET) grant DE-FC02-07ER25808 and DOE DE-FG02-08ER25848/A000.

Competing interests
The authors declare that they have no competing interests.

References

1. Enzyme-Nomenclature, Nomenclature Committee of the International Union of Biochemistry and Molecular Biology (NC-IUBMB) (Academic Press, NY)http://www.chem.qmul.ac.uk/iubmb/enzyme
2. HL Shah, Predicting enzyme function from sequence: a systematic appraisal. Proc ISMB. **5**, 276–283 (1997)
3. SF Altschul, TL Madden, AA Schaffer, J Zhang, Z Zheng, W Miller, Gapped BLAST and PSI-BLAST., *et al*, a new generation of protein database search programs. Nucleic Acids Res. **35**, 3389–3402 (1987)
4. X Wang, D Schroeder, D Dobbs, V Honaver, Automated data-driven discovery of motif-based protein function classifiers. Inf Sci. **155**, 1–18 (2003). doi:10.1016/S0020-0255(03)00067-7
5. S Umar, Y Golan, Enzyme function prediction with interpretable models. Comput Syst Biol. **541**, 373–420 (2009). doi:10.1007/978-1-59745-243-4_17
6. LY Han, CZ Cai, ZL Ji, ZW Cao, J Cui, YZ Chen, Predicting functional family of novel enzymes irrespective of sequence similarity. Nucleic Acids Res. **32**, 6437–6444 (2004). doi:10.1093/nar/gkh984

7. CZ Cai, WL Wang, LZ Sun, YZ Chen, Protein function classification via support vector machine approach. Math Biosci. **185**, 111–122 (2003). doi:10.1016/S0025-5564(03)00096-8
8. KC Chou, EW David, Prediction of enzyme family classes. J Proteome Res. **2**(2), 183–190 (2003). doi:10.1021/pr0255710
9. BJ Lee, HG Lee, JY Lee, KH Ryu, Classification of enzyme function from protein sequence based on feature representation. IEEE Xplore. **10**, 741–747 (2007)
10. BJ Lee, HG Lee, KH Ryu, Design of a novel protein feature and enzyme function classification, in *Proceedings of the 2008 IEEE 8th International Conference on Computer and Information Technology Workshops*, (Sydney, 2008), pp. 450–455
11. HB Shen, KC Chou, A top-down approach for predicting enzyme functional classes and subclasses. Biochem Biophys Res Commun. **364**, 53–59 (2007). doi:10.1016/j.bbrc.2007.09.098
12. J Zhang, M Zulkernine, A hybrid network intrusion detection technique using random forests, in *First International Conference on Availability, Reliability and Security (ARES'06)*, (Vienna, Austria, 2006), pp. 262–269. 20-22 April
13. TF Wu, C Lin, RC Weng, Probability estimates for multi-class classification by pairwise coupling. J Mach Learn Res. **5**, 975–1005 (2004)
14. R Diaz-Uriarte, S de Andres Alvarez, Gene selection and classification of microarray data using random forest. BMC Bioinf. **7**, 3 (2006). doi:10.1186/1471-2105-7-3
15. L Breiman, Random forests. Mach. Learn. **45**, 5–32 (2001)
16. A Bairoch, The ENZYME database in 2000. Nucleic Acids Res. **28**, 304–305http://www.expasy.ch/enzyme/ (2000). doi:10.1093/nar/28.1.304
17. A Al-Shahib, R Breitling, D Gilbert, Feature selection and the class imbalance problem in predicting protein function from sequence. Appl Bioinf. **4**, 195–203 (2005)
18. W Li, A Godzik, Cd-hit: a fast program for clustering and comparing large sets of protein or nucleotide sequences. Bioinformatics. **22**, 1658–1667 (2006). doi:10.1093/bioinformatics/btl158
19. P Rice, I Longden, A Bleasby, Emboss: the European Molecular Biology Open Software Suite. Trends Genetics. **16**, 276–282 (2000). doi:10.1016/S0168-9525(00)02024-2
20. E Gasteiger, C Hoogland, A Gattiker, S Duvaud, MR Wilkins, RD Appel, A Bairoch, in *Protein Identification and Analysis Tools on the ExPASy Server*, ed. by Walker JM (The Proteomics Protocols Handbook Humana Press, NY, 2005), pp. 571–607
21. PD Dobson, AJ Doig, Predicting enzyme class from protein structure without alignments. J Mol Biol. **345**, 187–199 (2005). doi:10.1016/j.jmb.2004.10.024
22. LJ Jensen, M Skovgaard, S Brunak, Prediction of novel archael enzymes from sequence-derived features. Protein Sci. **3**, 2894–2898 (2002)
23. H Ian, *Data Mining: Practical Machine Learning Tools and Techniques*, 2nd edn. (Morgan Kaufmann, San Francisco, 2005) http://www.cs.waikato.ac.nz/ml/weka/
24. G Williams, Rattle: a graphical user interface for data mining in R using GTK. R package version 2.4.10. http://rattle.togaware.com/ (2008)
25. VN Vapnik, *Statistical Leaning Theory* (Wiley-Interscience, New York, 1998)
26. R Quinlan, *C4.5: Programs for Machine Learning (Morgan Kaufmann Publishers, San Mateo, CA, 1993)*
27. PK Naik, VS Mishra, M Gupta, K Jaiswal, Prediction of enzymes and non-enzymes from protein sequences based on sequence derived features and PSSM matrix using artificial neural network. Bioinformation. **2**, 107–112 (2007). doi:10.6026/97320630002107
28. R Thangudu, M Manoharan, N Srinivasan, F Cadet, R Sowdhamini, B Offman, Analysis on conservation of disulphide bonds and their structural features in homologous protein domain families. BMC Bioinf. **8**(Suppl 55), 1–22 (2008)
29. O Markovic, S Janecek, Pectin degrading glycoside hydrolases of family 28: sequence-structural features, specificities and evolution. Protein Engineering Design and Selection. **14**(Suppl 9), 615–631 (2001)

2

Identification of CpG islands in DNA sequences using statistically optimal null filters

Rajasekhar Kakumani[1*], Omair Ahmad[1] and Vijay Devabhaktuni[2]

Abstract

CpG dinucleotide clusters also referred to as CpG islands (CGIs) are usually located in the promoter regions of genes in a deoxyribonucleic acid (DNA) sequence. CGIs play a crucial role in gene expression and cell differentiation, as such, they are normally used as gene markers. The earlier CGI identification methods used the rich CpG dinucleotide content in CGIs, as a characteristic measure to identify the locations of CGIs. The fact, that the probability of nucleotide G following nucleotide C in a CGI is greater as compared to a non-CGI, is employed by some of the recent methods These methods use the difference in transition probabilities between subsequent nucleotides to distinguish between a CGI from a non-CGI. These transition probabilities vary with the data being analyzed and several of them have been reported in the literature sometimes leading to contradictory results. In this article, we propose a new and efficient scheme for identification of CGIs using statistically optimal null filters. We formulate a new CGI identification characteristic to reliably and efficiently identify CGIs in a given DNA sequence which is devoid of any ambiguities. Our proposed scheme combines maximum signal-to-noise ratio and least squares optimization criteria to estimate the CGI identification characteristic in the DNA sequence. The proposed scheme is tested on a number of DNA sequences taken from human chromosomes 21 and 22, and proved to be highly reliable as well as efficient in identifying the CGIs.

Introduction

In the recent years, computational methods for processing and interpreting vast amount of genomic data, generated from genome sequencing, have gained a lot of scientific interest. Genomic sequences such as deoxyribonucleic acid (DNA) consist of biological instructions which are crucial for the development and normal functioning of almost all living organisms [1]. A DNA molecule has a complex double helix structure that involves two strands, consisting of alternating sugar and phosphate groups. Attached to these sugar groups of each DNA strand are one of the four chemical bases, namely, adenine (A), thymine (T), guanine (G), and cytosine (C). A unit comprising of base, sugar, and phosphate is referred to as a nucleotide. Hydrogen bonds between the nucleotides A and T (similarly between nucleotides G and C) from the opposite strands not only stabilize the DNA molecule, but also make the two strands complimentary. Nucleotides in a DNA strand exhibit short, recurring patterns (also called sequence motifs) that are presumed to have a biological function. Identification of these patterns helps in understanding the biological information hidden in a DNA sequence. A human DNA consists of about 3 billion nucleotides and completion of genome sequencing of numerous model organisms has further proliferated genomic databases. To completely decipher, the biological information in a DNA sequence is a daunting task and development of fast, efficient, and cost effective computational techniques for the same is a big challenge.

A sequence pattern that plays a crucial role in the analysis of genomes is CpG Island (CGI). A typical CGI consists high-frequency of CpG dinucleoetides, where 'p' refers to the phosphodiester bond between the adjacent nucleotides [1,2]. This bond is different from the hydrogen bond that exists between C and G across two strands in a DNA double helix. The length of a CGI varies from a few hundred to a few thousand base pairs (bp), but rarely exceeds 5000 bp. It is known that CpG Islands (CGIs) occur in and around the promoter regions of (50–60)% of human genes, including most housekeeping genes (the genes which are essential for general cell functions) [3]. Gene is a stretch

*Correspondence: r_kakuma@encs.concordia.ca
[1] Department of Electrical and Computer Engineering, Concordia University, 1455 de Maisonneuve Blvd. West Montreal, QC H3G1M8, Canada
Full list of author information is available at the end of the article

of DNA sequence which has biological information for the synthesis of a protein. The promoter region in a gene regulates its functionality [4-7]. Due to the association of CGIs with promoters, CGIs play an important role in promoter prediction and consequently in the prediction of genes [8,9]. CGIs also contribute significantly in discovering the epigenetic causes of cancer. CGIs located in the promoter regions of certain tumor suppressor genes are normally unmethylated in healthy cells. DNA methylation is a biochemical modification resulting from addition of a methyl group to cytosine nucleotide (C). In cancer cells, CGIs usually undergo a dense hypermethylation leading to gene silencing as shown in Figure 1. Owing to this, they can be used as candidate regions for aberrant DNA methylation, for early detection of cancer [10-14]. For these reasons, identification of CGIs has become indispensable for genome analysis and annotation.

Despite their accuracy, experimental methods employed by biologists for identification of CGIs are extremely time-consuming, simply because of the enormity of genomic data. On the other hand, computational methods can be much more attractive for the identification of possible CGIs. The results obtained from computational methods can be used by biologists to validate and further enhance the accuracy of identified CGI locations. There are several computational methods [15-26] reported in the literature for identification of CGIs in DNA sequences. In one of the first computational attempts [15], a CGI is defined as a DNA segment fulfilling the following three conditions: (i) length of segment is at least 200 bp, (ii) G and C contents are $\geq$ 50%, and (iii) observed CpG to expected CpG ratio (o/e) is $\geq$ 0.6. Observed CpG is the number of CpG dinucleoetides in a segment and expected CpG is calculated by multiplying the number of 'C's and the number of 'G's in a segment and then dividing the product by length of the segment. This method however falsely identifies the other G and C rich motifs, e.g., *Alu repeats*, as CGIs. In subsequent methods, these three conditions were made more stringent in order to reduce false identification at the expense of missing some true CGIs [24]. Sophisticated methods utilizing two Markov chain models [27,28], one for CGIs and the other for non-CGIs, are proposed [2,25,26]. These two Markov models differ in their respective model parameters which characterize the difference in transition probabilities between successive nucleotides in CGIs and non-CGIs, respectively. In these methods, a DNA segment is defined as CGI, if the log-score [2] computed using Markov model for a CGI is greater than that computed using Markov model for a non-CGI. Consequently, the model parameters used for CGIs and non-CGIs play a crucial role in identifying the CGIs. However, different methods employing such models from time-to-time produce inconsistent results. Another criterion based on the physical distance distribution of CpG dinucleoetides in a DNA segment has also been proposed [23]. Methods based on this criterion are dependent on nucleotide composition of a DNA sequence being analyzed and suffer from low identification specificity.

Recently, digital signal processing (DSP)-based algorithms have gained popularity for the analysis of genomic sequences since they can be mapped to numerical sequences. Digital filters have successfully been employed for identification of protein coding regions (exons) in DNA sequences and hot-spots in protein sequences [29-33]. Digital filters have also been used for identification of CGIs with considerable success [25,26]. These methods are similar to Markov chain methods but use digital filters to compute weighted log-score to identify CGIs. The method proposed in [25] employs a bank of IIR low-pass filters (about 40 filters, each with different bandwidth) to identify the CGIs by looking at the weighted log-scores of all the filters together. The CGI identification sensitivity of this method is affected by the tradeoff between responsiveness of filter and stability of the output. Moreover, this method may become computationally demanding as it makes use of a large number of filters in the bank. Another DSP based algorithm in [26] employs an underlying multinomial statistical model [34] to estimate its Markov chain parameters followed by an FIR filter with Blackman window to compute the weighted log-score.

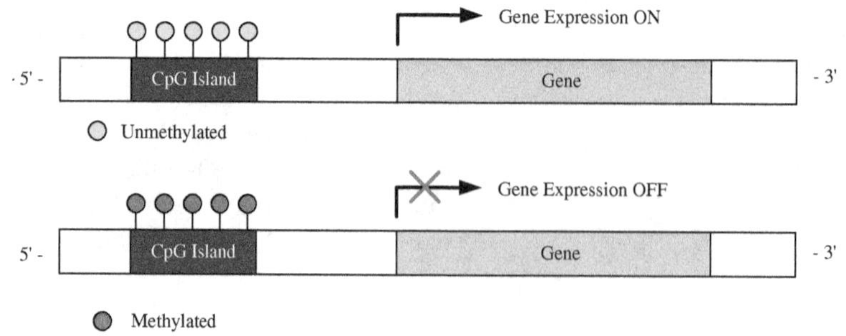

Figure 1 Difference between mythelated and unmythelated CpG Island.

It is evident from above discussion that the CGI identification methods and more importantly the criteria used therein play a crucial role in identifying CGIs. As such, development of fast and efficient computational methods with highly reliable CGI identification criteria is a necessity. Statistically optimal null filters (SONF) have been proven for their ability to efficiently estimate short-duration signals embedded in noise [35]. In this article, we propose a new DSP algorithm for identification of CGIs using SONF which combines maximum signal-to-noise ratio and least squares optimization criteria to estimate the message signal, characterizing the CGI, embedded in noise. Normally, the CGI identification accuracy is a lot dependent on the Markov models used and sometimes produces contrasting results. Also, one of the main objectives of the article is to find a uniform yet effective alternative CGI identification measure replacing the current measure based on transition probabilities. In the proposed scheme, we have formulated a simple basis function to be used in SONF which characterizes the CGI. Our criterion is devoid of any ambiguities associated with the choice of transition probabilities used in some of the algorithms. The proposed scheme is tested on a large number of already annotated DNA sequences obtained from human chromosomes 21 and 22. It is shown that our scheme is simple to implement and yet able to identify CGIs reliably and efficiently.

The rest of the article is organized as follows: the following section briefly describes a few existing DSP-based algorithms for the identification of CGIs. In Section "Proposed scheme", the proposed SONF-based scheme for identifying CGIs in DNA sequences is explained. Results obtained from the proposed scheme are depicted as well as tabulated in Section "Results and discussion". Finally, "Conclusion" section concludes the article describing some of the significant features of the proposed scheme.

Related study

In this section, we give a brief review of some of the existing CGI identification methods as a preparatory groundwork for the method to be proposed in Section "Proposed scheme".

Markov chain approach

In this method, a DNA sequence of length N, represented as $X = \{x(n), x(n+1), \ldots, x(n+N-1)\}$ where each symbol $x(n) \in \{A, C, T, G\}$ is considered as a first-order Markov chain [27] due to its conditional independence property, i.e., the nucleotide occurring at the location $(n-1)$ does not offer any information over and above that at n to predict the nucleotide occurring at $(n+1)$. In a CpG island, the probability of transition from the nucleotide base C to the base G is higher in comparison with that in a non-CGI. Let the probability of transition from a nucleotide β to a nucleotide γ in a CGI and a non-CGI be denoted as $p^{+}_{\beta\gamma}$ and $p^{-}_{\beta\gamma}$ respectively. Tables 1 and 2 taken from [2] show the transition probabilities for CGI and non-CGI Markov models. These tables are derived from 48 putative CGIs in human DNA sequences. Each row in the tables contains transition probabilities from a specific nucleotide base to each of the four bases. These transition probabilities $p^{\pm}_{\beta\gamma}$ are calculated using

$$p^{\pm}_{\beta\gamma} = \frac{n^{\pm}_{\beta\gamma}}{\sum_{k\in\{A,T,G,C\}} n^{\pm}_{\beta k}} \tag{1}$$

where $n^{+}_{\beta\gamma}$ is the number of dinucleotides $\beta\gamma$ in a DNA sequence. Naturally, every row in the tables adds up to unity. As expected, in Table 1, which corresponds to the CGI Markov model, the probability that a C is followed by a G is very high as compared with that in Table 2.

The CGIs in the DNA sequence X are identified by analyzing the windowed sequence $X_n = \{x(n), x(n+1), \ldots, x(n+L-1)\}$ of length L, and those obtained by shifting the window by one position at a time. The probability of observing a windowed sequence assuming that it belongs to a CGI is given by

$$\begin{aligned} &P(X_n|\text{CGI}) \\ &= P(x(n)\ldots x(n+L-1)|x(n-1), \text{CGI model}) \\ &= \prod_{i=0}^{L-1} p^{+}_{x(n-1+i)x(n+i)} \end{aligned} \tag{2}$$

Similarly, the probability of observing this sequence assuming it belongs to a non-CpG island region is

$$\begin{aligned} &P(X_n|\text{non-CGI}) \\ &= P(x(n)\ldots x(n+L-1)|x(n-1), \text{non-CGI}) \\ &= \prod_{i=0}^{L-1} p^{+}_{x(n-1+i)x(n+i)} \end{aligned} \tag{3}$$

Table 1 Transition probabilities inside a CGI

$p^{+}_{\beta\gamma}$	A	C	G	T
A	0.180	0.274	0.426	0.120
C	0.171	0.368	0.274	0.188
G	0.161	0.339	0.375	0.125
T	0.079	0.355	0.384	0.182

Table 2 Transition probabilities inside a non-CGI

$p^{-}_{\beta\gamma}$	A	C	G	T
A	0.300	0.205	0.285	0.210
C	0.322	0.298	0.078	0.302
G	0.248	0.246	0.298	0.208
T	0.177	0.239	0.292	0.292

If the value of $P(X_n|\text{CGI}) > P(X_n|\text{non-CGI})$, then, it is concluded that the DNA sequence X_n belongs to a CGI. Otherwise, it is more likely to be a non-CGI island. Alternatively, by formulating a log-likelihood ratio, given by

$$S(n) = \frac{1}{L}\log\frac{P(X_n|\text{CGI})}{P(X_n|\text{non-CGI})} \tag{4}$$

If $S(n) > 0$, the given DNA sequence is more likely to belong to a CGI, and if $S(n) < 0$ the sequence probably belongs to a non-CGI region.

IIR low-pass filter approach

Yoon and Vaidyanathan [25] have noted that the log-likelihood ratio given in (4) can be expressed as:

$$\begin{aligned} S(n) &= \frac{1}{L}\log\prod_{n=0}^{L-1}\frac{p^{+}_{x(n-1)x(n)}}{p^{-}_{x(n-1)x(n)}} \\ &= \frac{1}{L}\sum_{i=0}^{L-1} y(n+i) \\ &= y(n) * h_{ave}(n) \end{aligned} \tag{5}$$

where $y(n)$ is a sequence representing the log-likelihood ratio of a single transition given by

$$y(n) = \log\left(\frac{p^{+}_{x(n-1)x(n)}}{p^{-}_{x(n-1)x(n)}}\right) \tag{6}$$

and, $h_{ave}(n)$ is a simple averaging filter defined as

$$h_{ave}(n) = \begin{cases} 1/L, & \text{for } -L+1 \le n \le 0 \\ 0, & \text{otherwise.} \end{cases} \tag{7}$$

Then, they proposed using a bank of M filters each having different bandwidth, instead of using simply one low-pass filter $h_{\text{ave}}(n)$. Specifically, the filter used in the kth ($k = 0, \ldots, M-1$) channel has a transfer function given by

$$H_k(z) = \frac{1-\alpha_k}{1-\alpha_k z^{-1}} \tag{8}$$

where $0 < \alpha_0 < \alpha_1 < \cdots < \alpha_{M-1} < 1$. Since impulse response of a filter in the bank is $h_{\text{ave}}(k) = (1-\alpha_k)\alpha_k^k u(n)$ more recent inputs are given larger weights than the past ones in the averaging process of $y(n)$. The filter bank consists of 40 channels ($M = 40$), and the filter parameter α_k is chosen from 0.95 to 0.99 with an increment of 0.001. The log-likelihood ratio obtained from the output of the kth channel is given by

$$S_k(n) = y(n) * h_k(n) \tag{9}$$

The values of $S_k(n)$ obtained for all k and n are then used to obtain a two-level contour plot. The bands corresponding to $S_k(n) > 0$ determine the locations of CGIs.

In this method, the use of filter bank increases the computational overhead considerably. For fair comparison, instead of a bank on M filters, we have used one pole filter with optimized parameter $\alpha = 0.99$ to compare with other methods (this reduces the number of computations considerably).

Multinomial statistical model

This method by Rushdi and Tuqan [26] differs from the previous method by the way the transition tables are obtained and the type of digital filter used to calculate the log-likelihood ratio. Instead of using (1) to obtain the transition probability tables, they are generated by comparing the frequency of each dinucleotide with the one expected under a multinomial model [34]. Transition probabilities $p^{\pm}_{\beta\gamma}$ for the windowed sequence X_n are calculated using

$$p^{\pm}_{\beta\gamma} = \frac{c^{\pm}_{\beta\gamma}}{\sum\limits_{k\in\{A,T,G,C\}} c^{\pm}_{\beta k}} \tag{10}$$

where

$$c^{\pm}_{\beta\gamma} = \frac{\mathit{frequency}^{\pm}_{\beta\gamma}(n)}{(\mathit{frequency}^{\pm}_{\beta}(n))(\mathit{frequency}^{\pm}_{\gamma}(n))} \tag{11}$$

This method uses a FIR digital filter with variable coefficients generated by Blackman window to calculate the log-likelihood ratio $S(n)$ given in (4). The locations with $S(n)$ greater than zero are the probable locations of CGIs.

All of the above-mentioned methods rely on the transition probability tables to calculate log-likelihood ratio used to identify CGIs. The methods [25,26] specifically vary by the way $y(n)$, obtained from the respective transition tables, are averaged. It is shown later in Section "Results and discussion" that the choice of the transition tables may produces contrasting results. Hence, a more reliable and efficient scheme that is devoid of these transition tables is necessary for identifying CGIs.

Proposed scheme

In this study, we adopt the SONF approach, proposed in [35], to efficiently identify CGIs in DNA sequences. SONF is used for estimation of short duration signal, $S_n = \{s(m)\}$, embedded in noise $R_n = \{r(m)\}$ by combining maximum signal-to-noise ratio and least squares optimization criteria. The implementation of the twofold optimization in SONF is shown in Figure 2, where an instantaneous matched filter (IMF) is first used to detect the presence of a short duration signal embedded in noise by maximizing the signal-to-noise ratio over variable-time observation interval m. The IMF output, I_n, is then scaled by a locally generated function Λ_n, by least squares (LS) optimization procedure, to obtain the signal Y_n, an estimate of S_n. It has been shown that the SONF is equivalent to a Kalman filter with a much simpler implementation [35]. Also, SONF has the ability to track rapidly changing signals leading to more practical processing of short-duration signals [36,37]. Therefore, the proposed scheme is expected to perform better in situations even if the CGIs are of very short length of the order of 200 bp.

To be able to apply SONF approach to identify CGIs, the DNA sequence X, of length N, is first mapped to an appropriate binary numerical sequence $X_{CG} = \{x_{CG}(n)\}$. A sliding window of length L is used to evaluate if each of the windowed sequences, $X_n = \{x_{CG}(m)\}$, where $n = 1, 2, \ldots, N-L+1$ and $m = n, n+1, \ldots, n+L-1$, belong to a CGI or not. Each of the windowed sequence X_n can be expressed as

$$X_n = S_n + R_n \tag{12}$$

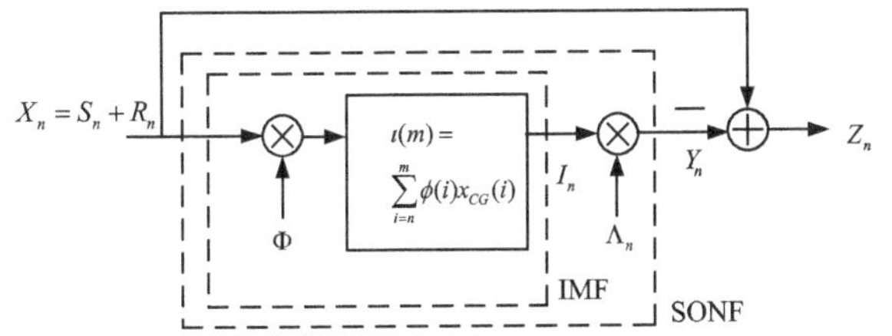

Figure 2 Statistically optimal null filter.

where $S_n = \{s(m)\}$ is a message signal corresponding to a CGI and $R_n = \{r(m)\}$ is a residual signal. S_n and R_n are each of length L. Let $\Phi = \{\phi(m)\}$ be a fixed binary basis sequence of length L having some characteristic property of CGI.

Now, the message signal corresponding to a CGI can be expressed as $S_n = V_n\Phi$, where $V_n = \{v(m)\}$ and Φ are sequences each of length L. The sequence $V_n\Phi$ is obtained by multiplying the corresponding elements of V_n and Φ. The sequence V_n is determined by minimizing R_n in least square sense. Let the message signal be denoted as $S_n = \{s(m)\}$. The objective of the proposed method is to choose the basis sequence such that V_n resulting from the optimization process has some discriminating feature of indicating whether the associated sequence X_n belongs to a CGI. The following subsections explain in detail the steps involved in identification of CGIs in a DNA sequence using SONF.

Numerical mapping of DNA sequences

As DNA sequences are alphabetical in nature, they need to be mapped to numerical sequences in order to employ the DSP techniques for DNA sequence analysis. There are several mapping techniques reported in the literature. One of the earliest and a popular mapping is that of Voss's binary indicator sequences [38]. A DNA sequence X can be mapped to a set of four digital signals by forming four binary indicator sequences, namely, X_A, X_T, X_G, and X_C. In each of these binary indicator sequences, '1' represents the presence and '0' absence of the corresponding bases A, T, G, and C in X. For instance, considering a DNA sequence $X = \{ATCCGAAGTATAACGAA\}$, the binary indicator sequence corresponding to G, i.e., X_G can be expressed as $X_G = \{00001001000000100\}$. Indicator sequences for the remaining three nucleotides can be represented in a similar fashion.

The problem of CGI identification deals with G and C content in a DNA sequence. Hence, we define a new indicator sequence $X_{CG} = \{x_{CG}(n)\}$, which indicates the presence of the nucleotides C and G in the DNA sequence. For example, the binary indicator sequence X_{CG} of the DNA sequence above is $X_{CG} = \{00111001000001100\}$.

Choosing the basis sequence

In this study, we have noticed that the dinucleotides CC, CG, GC, and GG occur more frequently in a CGI as compared to a non-CGI. For this study, we have calculated the occurrence of these four dinucleotides in the sequence L44140 taken from the chromosome X of *Homo sapiens*. The sequence L44140 is of length 219447 bp and has 17 CGIs whose locations are obtained from [39]. Figure 3 depicts the relative occurrence of the above four dinucleotides as compared to the remaining dinucleotides (AA, AC, AG, AT, CA, CT, GA, GT, TC, TG, TT, and TA)

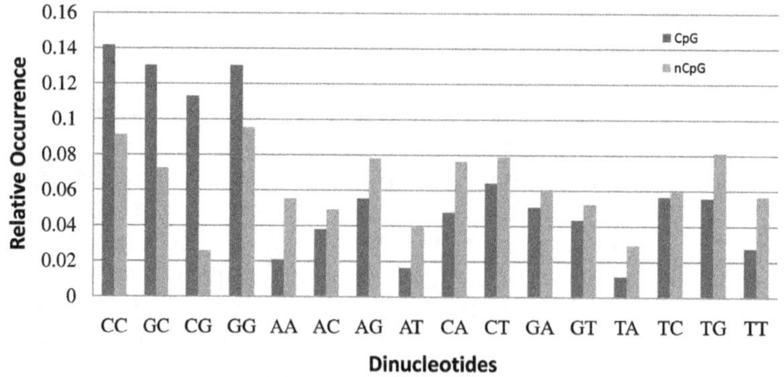

Figure 3 Comparison of relative occurrence of dinucleotides in CGIs and non-CGIs of L44140.

in CGIs and non-CGIs of L44140. Here, the relative occurrence of a particular dinucleotide is equal to the number of times that dinucleotide occurs in the sequence divided by the sequence length. It is evident that the dinucleotides CC, CG, GC, and GG occur more frequently in CGIs whereas the other dinucleotides occur more frequently in non-CGIs. This observation can also be inferred from the transition probability tables (Tables 1 and 2) as the values of $p^{+}_{\beta\gamma}$ are greater than $p^{-}_{\beta\gamma}$, where β and γ are either G or C. In Figure 3, the darker bars corresponding to the dinucleotides CC, CG, GC, and GG are taller in CGIs, whereas the darker bars corresponding to the other dinucleotides are shorter. Hence, instead of just considering the difference in relative occurrence of CG, it is more productive to consider the relative occurrence of the dinucleotides CC, CG, GC, and GG to distinguish between a CGI and a non-CGI.

Moreover, we have studied the difference in gap sizes between the dinucleotides CC, CG, GC, and GG in CGIs and non-CGIs of L44140. The shortest possible gap is of size 0 when the dinucleotides are adjacent to each other. Figure 4 shows the relative occurrence of gaps of various sizes in a CGI and a non-CGI. Here, relative occurrence of a particular gap size is equal to the number of times that gap size occurs in the sequence divided by the sequence length. Obviously, the gap of size 0 occurs more frequently in a CGI as compared to that of a non-CGI. And, it is found that the gap size in a non-CGI can go up to 40 where as in CGIs the maximum gap size was found to be 19. It can also be seen that the gaps of sizes 0, 1, and 2 occur more frequently in a CGI and the gap sizes of 3 and greater occur more frequently in a non-CGI. A gap of size 2 is the largest gap which can distinguish between a CGI and a non-CGI.

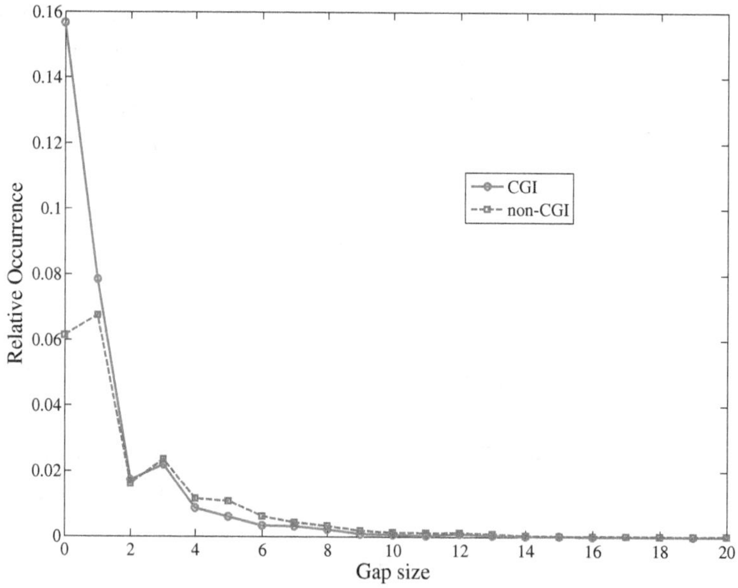

Figure 4 Relative occurrence of various gap sizes in CGIs and non-CGIs of L44140.

Based on the above observations, the basis sequence which characterizes a CGI can be formulated as $\Phi = \{1100110011\ldots001100\}$. The 1's in Φ represent either the nucleotide C or G. The 1's always appear in pairs where each pair representing one of the dinucleotide CC, CG, GC, or GG. The 0's in Φ form the gap between the dinucleotides. A gap size of 2 is chosen between the dinucleotides. This choice of Φ is also satisfies the basic criteria of a CGI, i.e., at least 50% of the nucleotide content in a CGI is due to C and G.

Now, in order to obtain the length of Φ (window size), we have analyzed CGIs and non-CGIs of different lengths for the relative occurrence of various gap sizes. Figure 5 shows the plot of Δ *versus* window size for various gap sizes. Here, Δ is the difference of relative occurrence of a particular gap in a CGI and a non-CGI for a fixed window length. It can be seen that Δ is maximum for gap size 0. As the window size increases Δ also increases before it reaches a steady value. Δ is negative for gap sizes of 3 and greater signifying that the gap sizes of 3 and higher are more probable in non-CGIs compared to CGIs. For the gap size 2, Δ stabilizes for window sizes greater than 200. Larger the window size, larger the number of computations, and hence in the proposed method we have used the length of Φ (window size) to be equal to 200.

IMF

The objective of IMF, which is the first stage of SONF shown in Figure 2, is to detect the presence of the waveform Φ in the input sequence X_n. IMF is an improvement over a matched filter, the difference being, in IMF optimal SNR is repeatedly calculated at every sample m, over an observation interval $m \in [n, n+L-1]$. IMF takes X_n and Φ as inputs and produces an output sequence $I_n = \{\iota(m)\}$ where

$$\iota(m) = \sum_{i=n}^{m} x_{CG}(i)\phi(i) \tag{13}$$

for $m = n, n+1, \ldots, n+L-1$. It can be seen that at each sample m, $\iota(m)$ is calculated over a varying interval $i \in [n, m]$. Note that, assuming $\iota(n-1) = 0$, $\iota(m)$ can also be calculated using the recursive relation given by

$$\iota(m) = \iota(m-1) + x_{CG}(m)\phi(m). \tag{14}$$

The output $\iota(m)$ leads to an optimal detection of Φ at each sample m, and can be expressed as

$$\iota(m) = v(m)c(m) + r_0'(m) \tag{15}$$

where $r_0'(m)$ is the residual signal in IMF output, and $c(m)$ is given by

$$c(m) = \sum_{i=n}^{m} \phi^2(i). \tag{16}$$

The $v(m) \in V_n$ in (15) is an unknown gain.

Least square optimization of the IMF output

The objective of the second stage in SONF is to determine a sequence $\Lambda = \{\lambda(m)\}$, which when used to scale the IMF output I_n, produces the SONF output, Y_n, such that $Y_n \to V_n\Phi$. Here, Y_n is an element wise product of V_n and Φ. Y_n is an estimate of S_n, which is the message signal corresponding to CGI.

Let us consider the suboptimal case in which a sample of the IMF output $\iota(m)$ in (15), when scaled by $\lambda(m) = \phi(m)/c(m)$, generates

$$\begin{aligned} y(m) &= v(m)c(m) + r_0' \frac{\phi(m)}{c(m)} \\ &= v(m)\phi(m) + r_0(m) \\ &= s(m) + r_0(m) \end{aligned} \tag{17}$$

where $y(m)$ is an element of the SONF output, Y_n. As we desire optimal null filtering, i.e., $y(m) = s(m)$, the residual element, $r_0(m)$, needs to be entirely eliminated.

Before determining the optimal Λ_n, corresponding to ideal null filtering, we define the sequence $Z_n = \{z(m)\}$ such that,

$$\begin{aligned} z(m) &= x_{CG}(m) - y(m) \\ &= s(m) + r(m) - \lambda(m)\iota(m) \end{aligned} \tag{18}$$

Ideally, $y(m) = s(m)$ and from (18), $z_{\text{ideal}}(m) = r(m)$. Now, the optimal $\Lambda_n = \{\lambda_{\text{opt}}(m)\}$ is determined by minimizing the mean square error, $E[e_\lambda^2(m)]$, with respect to $\lambda(m)$ where

$$e_\lambda(m) = z_{\text{ideal}}(m) - z(m). \tag{19}$$

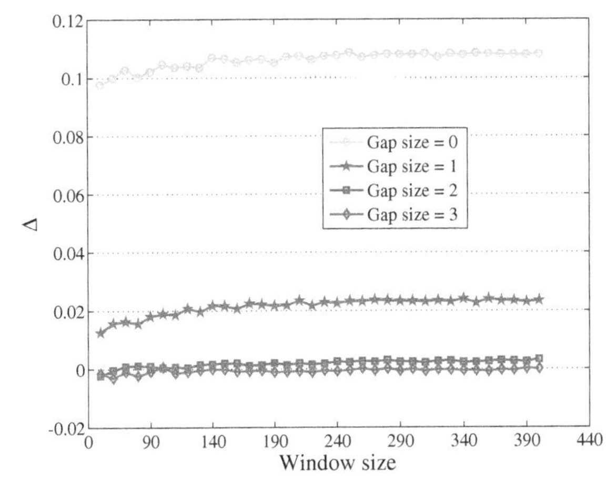

Figure 5 Difference of relative occurrence of a particular gap in a CGI and a non-CGI for different window lengths.

The optimal post IMF scaling sequence $\lambda_{\text{opt}}(m)$ obtained by carrying out the above mean square minimization is [35]

$$\lambda_{\text{opt}}(m) = \frac{\phi(m)}{c(m) + 1/\text{SNR}} \tag{20}$$

where SNR is the input signal-to-noise ratio (considering $r(m)$ to be noise).

In order to implement SONF, the value of the input SNR should be known. To circumvent this problem, a sub-optimal case, as shown in (17), is assumed considering $c(m) >> 1/\text{SNR}$, leading to

$$\lambda_{\text{subopt}}(m) \rightarrow \frac{\phi(m)}{c(m)} \tag{21}$$

It can be shown that as m increases, $\lambda_{\text{subopt}}(m) \rightarrow \lambda_{\text{opt}}(m)$ because the second term in the equation

$$\frac{\lambda_{\text{subopt}}(m)}{\lambda_{\text{opt}}(m)} = 1 + \frac{1}{(SNR)c(m)} \tag{22}$$

approaches zero (as the value of $c(m)$ progressively increases with m). So, the value of initial SNR in (20) will influence only the starting few samples in Y_n.

The SONF can easily be implemented recursively using the following equations [35]

$$\begin{aligned} \iota(m) &= \iota(m-1) + x_{CG}(m)\phi(m) \\ P(m) &= P(m-1) - \frac{P(m-1)\phi(m)\phi(m)P(m-1)}{1+\phi(m)P(m-1)\phi(m)} \\ \lambda(m) &= P(m)\phi(m) \\ y(m) &= \iota(m)\lambda(m) \end{aligned} \tag{23}$$

In this case of DNA analysis, one may choose the initial value of the gain $P(0)$ to be 1 and $\iota(0) = \iota(1)$.

The proposed SONF-based CGI identification algorithm for a DNA sequence of length N can now be summarized as follows:

Initialization: Set the base location index $n = 0$.

- **Step 1:** Apply a rectangular window of length $L = 200$ starting at the base location n of the DNA sequence X to obtain the windowed sequence X_n.
- **Step 2:** Obtain the binary indicator sequence X_{CG} for the windowed sequence, X_n, from Step 1.
- **Step 3:** X_{CG} from Step 2, along with the binary basis sequence Φ, form the inputs to SONF. The corresponding SONF output sequence, Y_n, is evaluated using the recursive relations given in (23), by assuming $P(0) = 1$ and $\iota(0) = \iota(1)$.
- **Step 4:** Compute the SNR power gain $G(X_n)$, which is the ratio of the variance of the SONF output, Y_n, to the variance of the corresponding input X_n.
- **Step 5:** Increment the value of n by 1, i.e., $n = n + 1$. If $n \leq (N - L)$ go to Step 1, else go to Step 7.
- **Step 6:** Plot $G(X_n)$ as a function of $n + L$ and get its upper envelope. The peaks in the resulting plot which are above the threshold, η, indicate the locations of CGIs identified in X.
- **Step 7:** Exit the algorithm.

Figure 6 shows the SONF implementation for better understanding of the proposed approach. Figure 6a,b shows an example of a CGI and a non-CGI with 80 bp. Naturally, in Figure 6a there are greater number of ones. Figure 6c,d shows the IMF output for a CGI and a non-CGI, respectively. It can be seen that the IMF output corresponding to a CGI progressively increases to a greater value of 35 as compared to 6 of that of a non-CGI. Figure 6e,f is the scaling functions for a CGI and a non-CGI, respectively. They are obtained using the relation $\lambda(m) = P(m)\phi(m)$ in (23). Finally, Figure 6g,h shows the estimated CGI characteristic in a CGI and a non-CGI, respectively. The SONF output corresponding to a CGI has greater amplitude as compared with that of a non-CGI.

Prediction measures

The identification of CGIs can have four possible outcomes; true positive (TP), true negative (TN), false positive (FP), or false negative (FN) as shown in Figure 7. Two basic measures of determining the accuracy of prediction are sensitivity (Sn) and specificity (Sp) [40]. Sensitivity, given by

$$Sn = \frac{TP}{TP + FN} \tag{24}$$

and is defined as the proportion of CGIs that have been predicted correctly. Whereas, specificity given by

$$Sp = \frac{TP}{TP + FP} \tag{25}$$

is defined as the proportion of the predicted CGIs that are real. Sensitivity and specificity can take on values from 0 to 1. For a perfect prediction, Sn = 1 and Sp = 1. Neither sensitivity nor specificity alone can provide a good measure of the global accuracy, because high sensitivity can be achieved with little specificity and vice versa. A measure that combines sensitivity and specificity values is called the correlation coefficient (CC) and is given by

$$\text{CC} = \frac{(TP \times TN) - (FN \times FP)}{\sqrt{(TP+FN)(TN+FP)(TP+FP)(TN+FN)}} \tag{26}$$

The value of CC ranges from -1 to 1, where a value of 1 corresponds to a perfect prediction; a value of -1 indicates that every CGI has been predicted as non-CGI, and vice versa.

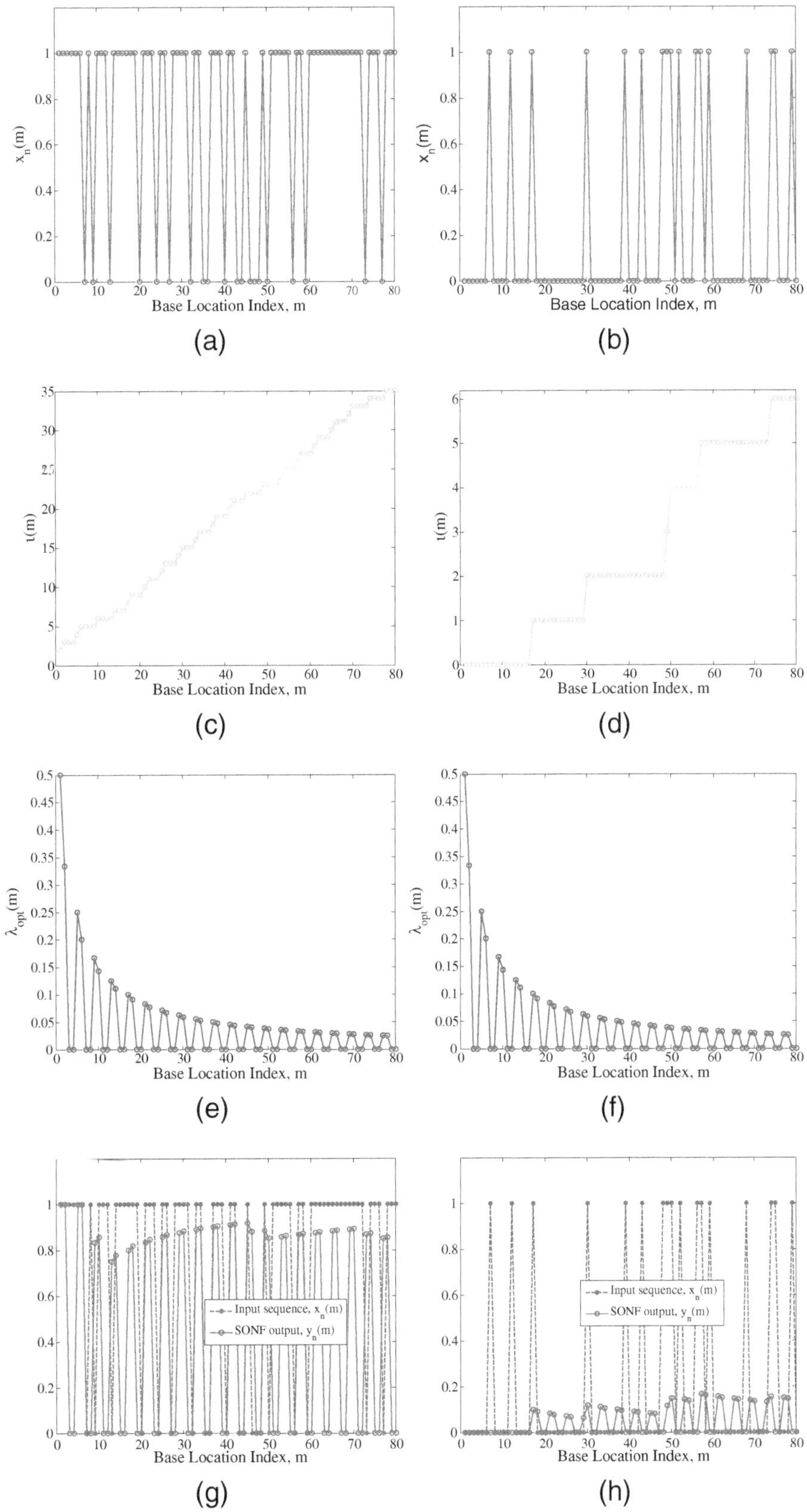

Figure 6 SONF implementation: (a) An example of a CGI; **(b)** An example of a non-CGI; **(c)** IMF output for CGI; **(d)** IMF output for non-CGI; **(e)** Scaling function for CGI; **(f)** Scaling function for non-CGI; **(g)** SONF output for CGI; and, **(h)** SONF output for non-CGI.

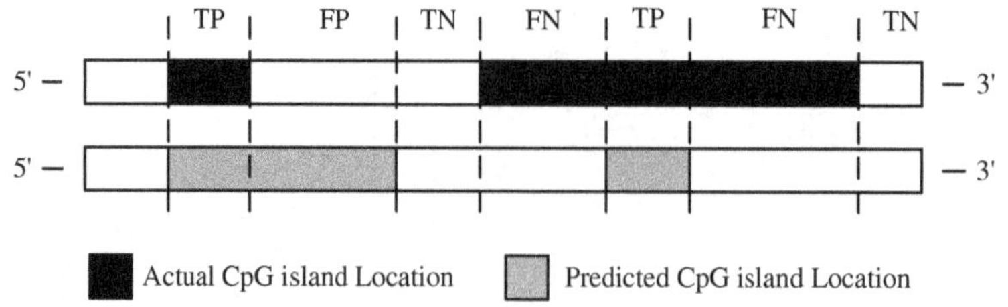

Figure 7 Four possible outcomes of CGI prediction.

Another measure, called the performance accuracy (Acc), used in our analysis is given by

$$\text{Acc} = \frac{TP + TN}{TP + FP + TN + FN} \tag{27}$$

In this article, we have evaluated the performance of different CGI identification methods at the nucleotide level. For example, the value of TP is obtained by adding all the nucleotides predicted to to true positive, and the other outcomes are calculated in the similar manner. At the CGI level, even if one nucleotide (or a threshold of a minimum number of nucleotides) corresponding to a CGI is predicted to be true positive the entire CGI is assumed to be predicted correctly.

Results and discussion

The proposed CGI prediction scheme is tested on several genomic sequences of varying lengths taken from the human chromosomes 21 and 22. More precisely, we have used the three contigs, NT_113952.1, NT_113954.1, and NT_113958.2 from chromosome 21, and the contig NT_028395.3 from chromosome 22 for our analysis. All the sequence data considered for this study are obtained from the GenBank Database [39]. The performance of the proposed scheme is compared with the other popular DSP-based approaches such as Markov chain [2], IIR low-pass filters [25], and multinomial model [26].

First, a DNA sequence from human chromosome X with the GenBank accession number of L44140 is analyzed for illustrative purpose. The sequence is of length 219447 bp and is already annotated, i.e., the locations of its CGIs are already known and can be obtained from [39]. The sequence L44140 is also used to obtain the values of threshold, η, used by the DSP-based methods being compared in this article.

Figure 8 shows the comparative performance of CGI prediction by the above-mentioned four approaches. Figure 8a shows the performance of Markov chain approach, where log-likelihood ratio $S(n)$ is plotted against base index of the sequence. The transition probability tables given in Tables 1 and 2 are used to calculate $S(n)$. All the base locations, n, with $S(n) > 0$ imply that they are very likely to be a part of a CGI. A window length of 200 bp is considered for the method. Markov chain method is able to detect most of the CGIs in the DNA sequence and it can be seen that the CGIs and non-CGIs can reasonably be differentiated by looking at the sign of $S(n)$. However, one of the major drawbacks of this method is the presence of a lot of false positives that falsely categorize non-CGIs into CGIs.

Figure 8b shows the performance of IIR low-pass filter approach where the log-likelihood ratio, $S(n)$, is plotted against base index of the sequence, n. The transition probability tables given in [25] are used to calculate $S(n)$. For fair comparison, instead of a bank on M filters, we have used one pole filter with optimized parameter $\alpha = 0.99$ for this method. All the base locations, n, with $S(n) > 0$ imply that they are very likely to be a part of a CGI. A window length of 200 bp is considered for the method. Similar to the Markov chain method, this method also produces a lot of false positives affecting the prediction accuracy.

Figure 8c shows the prediction of CGIs using the multinomial model in [26]. An underlying multinomial statistical model is employed to estimate the Markov chain model parameters that result in the transition probability tables given in [26]. A Blackman window of length 100 bp is employed for calculating the filtered log-likelihood ratio. The Blackman window gives larger weights for central samples of the window, thus reducing the edge effects. Windows with the positive filtered log-likelihood ratio are considered to be a part of a CGI. This method shows considerably high false positives making the CGI prediction unreliable.

Figure 8d shows performance of the proposed SONF scheme in predicting the CGIs. Unlike the above-mentioned methods, our scheme utilizes the binary basis sequence, Φ, instead of the probability transition tables. The proposed scheme first maximizes SNR of the output at each time instant using IMF, then it further enhances the estimated signal using least-square optimization criterion, to estimate the presence of Φ in the input windowed DNA sequence. A window size of 200 is used for the proposed method. Effectiveness of the proposed scheme is clearly visible in Figure 8d, which depict more contrasting peaks as compared to the other three approaches. These contrasting peaks make the identification

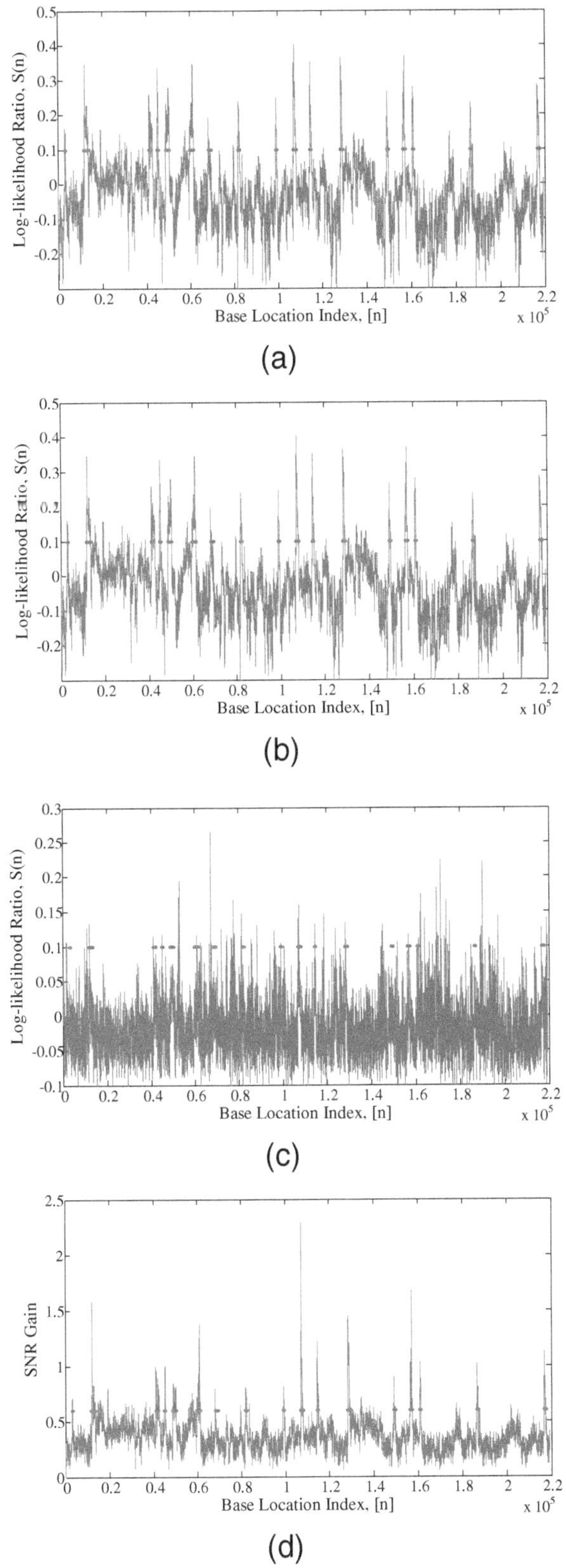

Figure 8 CGI prediction in the DNA sequence L44140 using **(a)** Markov chain method; **(b)** IIR Filter method; **(c)** Multinomial model; **(d)** SONF scheme.

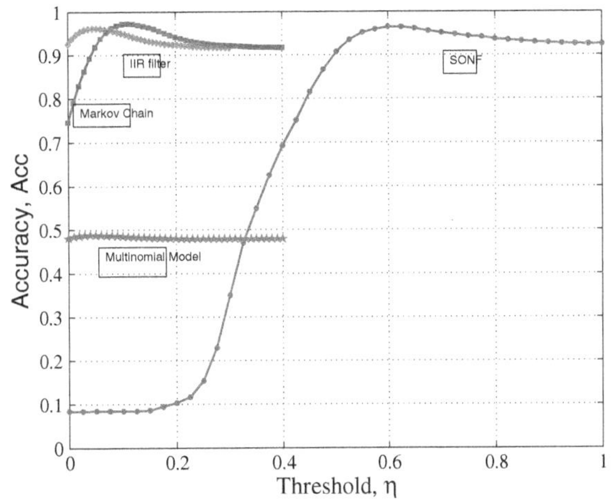

Figure 9 Relation between the performance Acc and threshold.

process comparatively easier resulting in less number of false positives.

It can be seen from Figure 8 that the default threshold on $\eta = 0$ produces a lot of false positives for the methods using transition probability tables. The optimal threshold values for the methods is obtained by calculating the prediction Acc for varying thresholds for each method (Figure 9). The optimal values of thresholds obtained for the Markov chain method, IIR filter method, and the proposed SONF approach are 0.1, 0.05, and 0.6, respectively. The actual locations of the CGIs, obtained from NCBI website, present in the sequence L44140 are represented by red horizontal spots in Figure 8. Figure 10 is receiver operating characteristic (ROC) curves plotted for the four methods. It can be seen that the proposed approach has better overall performance for the sequence L44140 with the area under the curve 0.7460. The Markov chain method is next with the area under the ROC curve

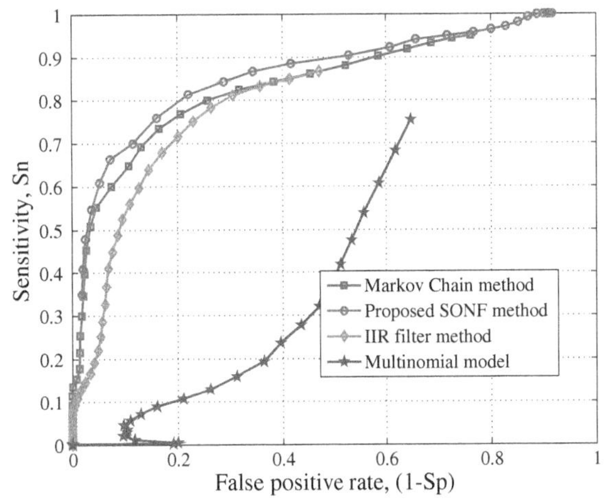

Figure 10 ROC curves obtained for the sequence L44140.

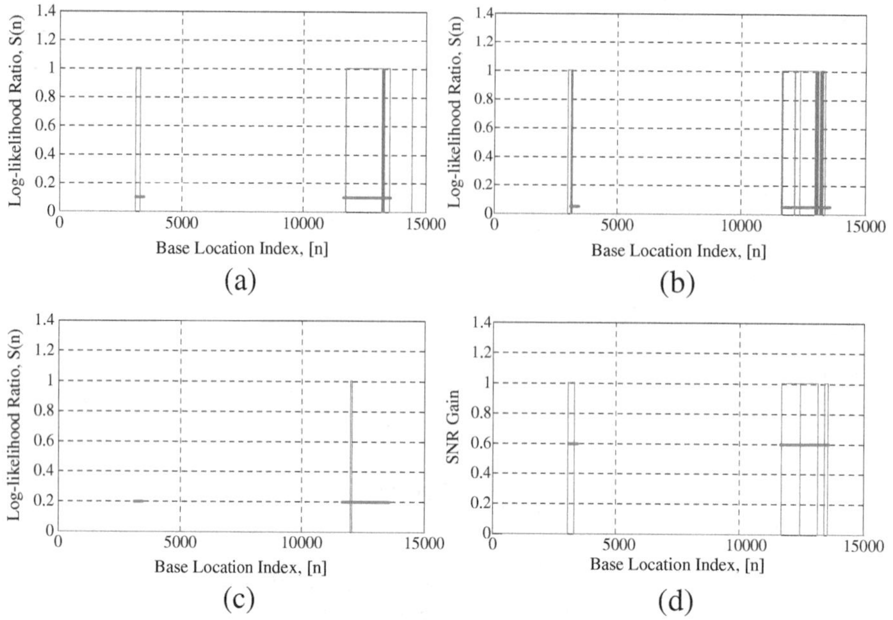

Figure 11 CGI prediction in the first 15000 bps of L44140 using (a) Markov chain method; (b) IIR filter method; (c) multinomial model; (d) SONF scheme. Binary decision based on respective threshold is plotted against the base location index.

0.6072. The area under the curve for IIR filter method is 0.3106. It can be seen that the multinomial model method has the least area under the ROC curve. The dismal performance of the multinomial model does not indicate anything about the method in itself but merely implies that the transition probability tables used may not be appropriate for the example considered.

We have evaluated the time complexity of the proposed method using the *tic-toc* function in MATLAB. Taking the necessary precautions (such as all applications except

Table 3 Comparison of different methods for identification of CGIs

Contig.	Performace	Methods				
		Markov Chain	IIR Filter	Multinomial model	CpGCluster	SONF
NT_113952.1	Sn	0.8466	0.8656	0.4524	0.5046	**0.8677**
Length = 184355	Sp	0.8728	0.8320	0.2833	0.9995	0.4457
	CC	0.8621	0.8180	0.3609	0.6941	0.6192
	Acc	0.9955	0.9848	0.4948	0.9778	0.9878
NT_113954.1	Sn	0.3285	0.2226	0.0055	0.2986	**0.5420**
Length = 129889	Sp	0.3082	0.2585	0.0021	0.9946	0.2094
	CC	0.3152	0.2369	0.0040	0.4381	0.4382
	Acc	0.9940	0.9940	0.4989	0.9690	0.9894
NT_113958.2	Sn	0.4555	0.3561	0.2938	0.2716	**0.8852**
Length = 209483	Sp	0.4652	0.4439	0.0202	0.9994	0.2880
	CC	0.4527	0.3899	0.0119	0.4996	0.4954
	Acc	0.9849	0.9845	0.4960	0.9532	0.9705
NT_028395.3	Sn	0.5440	0.4200	0.0000	0.4489	**0.8789**
Length = 647850	Sp	0.8233	0.7590	0.0000	0.9947	0.4534
	CC	0.6667	0.5616	-0.0116	0.9753	0.6267
	Acc	0.9945	0.9932	0.8710	0.9532	0.9887

MATLAB were closed, a fresh session of MATLAB was started for each task, and MATLAB was warmed up with the code, i.e., the first run of the code was ignored), the CPU time for processing a fixed length of sequence, the Markov chain method was found to be the least followed by SONF, IIR and multinomial approaches with an additional CPU time of 1.29%, 1.78%, and 1.82%, respectively. This difference is not substantial considering today's computing resources.

Figure 11 shows the performance of the four methods for the prediction of CGIs in the first 15000 bps of L44140. The red horizontal lines are the actual locations of CGIs. The blue binary decision curve depicts the locations of the predicted CGI by the methods. As can be seen from Figure 11c, the multinomial-based approach fails to detect the CGI located between base pairs 3095 and 3426 as opposed to other three methods implying that the probability transition parameters used for the CGI identification play a crucial role. Hence, it is important to have a CGI identification characteristic which is devoid of any ambiguity with the choice of different probability transition tables available. The binary basis sequence Φ in the proposed scheme successfully identifies the CGIs and can be reliably used as CPG identification characteristic.

Table 3 presents the summary of performance measures Sn, Sp, CC, and Acc obtained for the analysis of four contigs NT_113952.1, NT_113954.1, NT_113958.2, and NT_028395.3. The performance of the proposed scheme is also compared with that of CpGCluster [23], which uses the distance between CpG dinucleotides (and not the transition probability tables) for identifying CGIs. The proposed approach has the highest values of Sn for all the contigs (shown in bold) and has the highest values of CC for the contigs NT_113954.1 and NT_113958.2. The performance accuracy is also quiet high, consistently above 97% which is a good sign. This shows that the proposed method is reliable and the proposed binary basis sequence Φ is an alternative CGI identification characteristic. The multinomial method did not identify any of the CGIs in the contig NT_028395.3 and hence its Sn and Sp values are zero. The corresponding Acc value is high because the method predicting most of the true negatives correctly. The contig NT_028395.3 has short CGIs of the order of 200 bps and the proposed approach with better sensitivity is capable of identifying them.

Conclusion

In this article, a new DSP-based technique using SONFs is proposed for the prediction of CGIs in DNA sequences. A novel CPG identification characteristic is presented in the form of a binary basis sequence which is shown to identify CGIs reliably. It has also been shown that the performance of the existing methods which use discriminating transition probability tables for CGIs/non-CGIs is not consistent. The prediction accuracy of these methods are highly dependent on the training data used to obtain the transition probabilities of CGIs and non-CGIs. The inability of finding a unique CGI identification characteristic has resulted in failure in predicting many of the CGIs. This article makes an attempt to present a unique CGI identification characteristic which does not require any training. Furthermore, the ability of SONF to track short duration signals is exploited in identifying the CGIs in DNA sequences. SONF combines maximum signal-to-noise ratio and least squares optimization criteria to estimate the CGI identification characteristic in the DNA sequence. The performance of the proposed technique is tested on four randomly chosen contigs in chromosomes 21 and 22 of human beings. The simulation results comparing the performance of the proposed technique with the other three DSP-based CGI prediction techniques have shown that the proposed approach enjoys superior prediction accuracy in terms of sensitivity. The overall predicting accuracy of the proposed approach is also consistently above 97% and is comparable to that of the Markov chain method making it a reliable method.

Competing interests

The authors declare that they have no competing interests.

Acknowledgements

This study was supported in parts by the Natural Sciences and Engineering Research Council (NSERC) of Canada and in part by the Regroupement Strategic en Microelectronique du Quebec (ReSMiQ).

Author details

[1]Department of Electrical and Computer Engineering, Concordia University, 1455 de Maisonneuve Blvd. West Montreal, QC H3G1M8, Canada.
[2]Department of Electrical Engineering and Computer Science, University of Toledo, MS 308, 2801 W. Bancroft St., Toledo, OH 43606, USA.

References

1. H Lodish, A Berk, S Zipursky, P Matsudaira, D Baltimore, J Darnell, *Molecular Cell biology*. (Scientific American, New York,1995)
2. R Durbin, S Eddy, A Krogh, G Mitchison, *Biological sequence analysis*. (Cambridge University Press, Cambridge,1998)
3. F Antequera, A Bird, Number of CpG islands and genes in human and mouse. Proc. Natl Acad. Sci. USA. **90**(24), 11995–11999 (1993)
4. F Antequera, A Bird, CpG islands as genomic footprints of promoters that are associated with replication origins. Curr. Biol. **9**, 661–667 (1999)
5. I Ioshikhes, M Zhang, Large-scale human promoter mapping using CpG islands. Nat. Genet. **26**, 61–63 (2000)
6. F Antequera, Structure, function, evolution of CpG island promoters. Cell. Mol. Life Sci. **60**(8), 1647–1658 (2003)
7. S Saxonov, P Berg, D Brutlag, A genome-wide analysis of CpG dinucleotides in the human genome distinguishes two distinct classes of promoters. Proc. Natl Acad. Sci. USA. **103**(5), 1412–1417 (2006)
8. F Larsen, G Gundersen, R Lopez, H Prydz, CpG islands as gene markers in the human genome. Genomics (San Diego, CA). **13**(4), 1095–1107 (1992)
9. Y Wang, F Leung, An evaluation of new criteria for CpG islands in the human genome as gene markers. Bioinformatics. **20**(7), 1170 (2004)
10. A Bird, DNA methylation patterns and epigenetic memory. Genes Dev. **16**, 6–21 (2002)

11. J Herman, S Baylin, Gene silencing in cancer in association with promoter hypermethylation. New Engl. J. Med. **349**(21), 2042 (2003)
12. J Issa, CpG island methylator phenotype in cancer. Nat. Rev. Cancer. **4**(12), 988–993 (2004)
13. R Illingworth, A Kerr, D DeSousa, H Jorgensen, P Ellis, J Stalker, D Jackson, C Clee, R Plumb, J Rogers, A novel CpG island set identifies tissue-specific methylation at developmental gene loci. PLoS Biol. **6**, e22 (2008)
14. L Heisler, D Torti, P Boutros, J Watson, C Chan, N Winegarden, M Takahashi, P Yau, T Huang, P Farnham, CpG Island microarray probe sequences derived from a physical library are representative of CpG Islands annotated on the human genome. Nucleic Acids Res. **33**(9), 2952 (2005)
15. M Gardiner-Garden, M Frommer, CpG islands in vertebrate genomes. J. Mol. Biol. **196**(2), 261 (1987)
16. E Rouchka, R Mazzarella, David J States, Computational detection of CpG islands in DNA, Report: WUCS-97-39 (1997)
17. P Rice, I Longden, A Bleasby, EMBOSS: the European molecular biology open software suite. Trends Genetics. **16**(6), 276–277 (2000)
18. L Ponger, D Mouchiroud, CpGProD: identifying CpG islands associated with transcription start sites in large genomic mammalian sequences. Bioinformatics. **18**(4), 631 (2002)
19. N Dasgupta, S Lin, L Carin, Sequential modeling for identifying CpG island locations in human genome. IEEE Signal Process. Lett. **9**(12), 407–409 (2002)
20. P Luque-Escamilla, J Martínez-Aroza, J Oliver, J Gómez-Lopera, R Román-Roldán, Compositional searching of CpG islands in the human genome. Phys. Rev. E. **71**(6), 61925 (2005)
21. C Bock, J Walter, M Paulsen, T Lengauer, CpG island mapping by epigenome prediction. PLoS Comput. Biol. **3**(6), e110 (2007)
22. Y Sujuan, A Asaithambi, Y Liu, CpGIF: an algorithm for the identification of CpG islands. Bioinformation. **2**(8), 335–338 (2008)
23. M Hackenberg, C Previti, P Luque-Escamilla, P Carpena, J Martínez-Aroza, J Oliver, CpGcluster: a distance-based algorithm for CpG-island detection. BMC Bioinform. **7**, 446 (2006)
24. D Takai, P Jones, Comprehensive analysis of CpG islands in human chromosomes 21 and 22. Proc. Natl Acad. Sci. **99**(6), 3740–3745 (2002)
25. B Yoon, P Vaidyanathan, in *Proceedings of 11 th Digital Signal Processing Workshop*. Identification of CpG islands using a bank of IIR lowpass filters, Taos Ski Valley, New Mexico, Aug. 2004), pp. 315–319
26. A Rushdi, J Tuqan, in *Digital Signal Processing Workshop, 12th-Signal Processing Education Workshop, 4th*. A new DSP-based measure for CpG islands detection, IEEE , Teton National Park, Wyoming, 2006), pp. 561–565
27. L Rabiner, A tutorial on hidden Markov models and selected applications in speech recognition. Proc. IEEE. **77**(2), 257–286 (1989)
28. K Won, A Prugel-Bennett, A Krogh, Evolving the structure of hidden Markov models. IEEE Trans. Evol. Comput. **10**, 39–49 (2006)
29. D Anastassiou, Genomic signal processing. IEEE Signal Process. Mag. **18**(4), 8–20 (2001)
30. P Vaidyanathan, B Yoon, The role of signal-processing concepts in genomics and proteomics. J. Franklin Inst. **341**(1–2), 111–135 (2004)
31. P Ramachandran, A Antoniou, Identification of hot-spot locations in proteins using digital filters. IEEE J. Sel. Topics Signal Process. **2**(3), 378–389 (2008)
32. K Rao, M Swamy, Analysis of genomics and proteomics using DSP techniques. IEEE Trans. Circuits Syst. 1: Regular Papers. **55**, 358 (2008)
33. N Song, H Yan, Short exon detection in DNA sequences based on multifeature spectral analysis. EURASIP J. Adv. Signal Process. **2011**, 2 (2011)
34. B Liu, *Statistical Genomics: Linkage, Mapping, and QTL Analysis*. (CRC Press, Boca Raton,1998)
35. R Agarwal, E Plotkin, M Swamy, Statistically optimal null filter based on instantaneous matched processing. Circuits Syst. Signal Process. **20**, 37–61 (2001)
36. R Kakumani, V Devabhaktuni, M Ahmad, in *IEEE International Symposium on Circuits and Systems*. Prediction of protein-coding regions in DNA sequences using a model-based approach, Seattle, 2008), pp. 1918–1921
37. R Yadav, R Agarwal, M Swamy, in *Engineering in Medicine and Biology Society, 2009. EMBC 2009. Annual International Conference of the IEEE*. A new improved model-based seizure detection using statistically optimal null filter, Minneapolis, Minnesota, 2009), pp. 1318–1322
38. R Voss, Evolution of long-range fractal correlations and 1/f noise in DNA base sequences. Phys. Rev. Lett. **68**(25), 3805–3808 (1992)
39. National Centre for Biotechnology Information. http://www.ncbi.nlm.nih.gov
40. M Burset, R Guigo, Evaluation of gene structure prediction programs. Genomics. **34**(3), 353–367 (1996)

3

Gene regulatory network inference by point-based Gaussian approximation filters incorporating the prior information

Bin Jia[1] and Xiaodong Wang[2*]

Abstract

The extended Kalman filter (EKF) has been applied to inferring gene regulatory networks. However, it is well known that the EKF becomes less accurate when the system exhibits high nonlinearity. In addition, certain prior information about the gene regulatory network exists in practice, and no systematic approach has been developed to incorporate such prior information into the Kalman-type filter for inferring the structure of the gene regulatory network. In this paper, an inference framework based on point-based Gaussian approximation filters that can exploit the prior information is developed to solve the gene regulatory network inference problem. Different point-based Gaussian approximation filters, including the unscented Kalman filter (UKF), the third-degree cubature Kalman filter (CKF_3), and the fifth-degree cubature Kalman filter (CKF_5) are employed. Several types of network prior information, including the existing network structure information, sparsity assumption, and the range constraint of parameters, are considered, and the corresponding filters incorporating the prior information are developed. Experiments on a synthetic network of eight genes and the yeast protein synthesis network of five genes are carried out to demonstrate the performance of the proposed framework. The results show that the proposed methods provide more accurate inference results than existing methods, such as the EKF and the traditional UKF.

Keywords: Gene regulatory network; Point-based Gaussian approximation filters; Network prior information; Sparsity; Iterative thresholding

1 Introduction

Inferring gene regulatory network (GRN) has become one of the most important missions in system biology. Genome-wide expression data is widely used due to the development of several high-throughput experimental technologies. The gene regulatory network can be inferred from a number of gene expression samples taken over a period of time. Modeling of GRN is required before its structure can be inferred. Common dynamical modeling methods of GRN include Bayesian networks [1], Boolean networks [2], ordinary differential equations [3], state-space models [4,5], and so on. Various approaches based on different models have been used to infer the network from observed gene expression data, such as the Markov Chain Monte Carlo (MCMC) methods for the dynamic Bayesian network model [6] and the ordinary differential equation model [7], as well as the Kalman filtering methods for the state-space model [4,8] and the ordinary differential equation model [3]. Some survey papers can be found in [9-12].

Due to the 'stochastic' nature of the gene expression, the Kalman filtering approach based on the state-space model is one of the most competitive methods for inferring the GRN. The Kalman filter is optimal for linear Gaussian systems. However, the GRN is generally highly nonlinear. Hence, advanced filtering methods for nonlinear dynamic systems should be considered. The extended Kalman filter (EKF) is probably the most widely used nonlinear filter which uses the first-order Taylor series expansion to linearize the nonlinear model. However, the accuracy of the EKF is low when the system is highly nonlinear or contains large uncertainty. The point-based

*Correspondence: wangx@ee.columbia.edu
[2]Department of Electrical Engineering, Columbia University, New York, NY 10027, USA
Full list of author information is available at the end of the article

Gaussian approximation filters have been recently proposed to improve the performance of the EKF, which employ various quadrature rules to compute the integrals involved in the exact Bayesian estimation. Many filters fall into this category, such as the unscented Kalman filter (UKF) [13], the Gauss-Hermite quadrature filter [14], the cubature Kalman filter (CKF) [15], and the sparse-grid quadrature filter [16]. Besides the point-based Gaussian approximation filters, the particle filter has drawn much attention recently [17]. The particle filter uses random particles with weights to represent the probability density function (pdf) in the Bayesian estimation and provides better estimation result than the EKF. The main problem of the particle filter is that the computational complexity is high, and therefore, it is hard to use for high-dimensional problems, such as the problem considered in this paper.

The EKF and the particle filter have been used for the inference of GRN [4,8,18]. In this paper, we consider the point-based Gaussian approximation filters. Our main objective is to provide a framework of incorporating network prior information into the filters. For example, some gene regulations may be known [19] from literature and the inference accuracy of GRN can be improved by incorporating the known regulations of the GRN [20]. Integration of the prior knowledge or constraints with the GRN inference algorithm has been introduced to improve the inference result. The DNA motif sequence in gene promoter regions is incorporated in [21] while modeling of transcription factor interactions is incorporated in [22]. As mentioned in [20], experimentally determined physical interactions can be obtained. In addition, the sparsity constraint is frequently used in the inference of the GRN. To the best of the authors' knowledge, the most related work in incorporating the prior information in Bayesian filters is [8]. In that work, rather than directly getting the inference results from the filter, an optimization method is used. In particular, a cost function is used in which the sparsity constraint is enforced. However, the cost function in [8] does not consider the uncertainty of the state in the filtering. That cost function in fact is not coupled well with the filtering algorithm. In addition, it did not consider other kinds of prior information. In this paper, we propose a new framework that incorporates the prior information effectively in the filtering algorithm by solving a constrained optimization problem. Efficient recursive algorithms are provided to solve the associated optimization problem.

The remainder of this paper is organized as follows. In Section 2, the modeling of gene regulatory network is introduced. The point-based Gaussian approximation filters are briefly introduced in Section 3. The proposed new filtering framework is described in Section 4. In Section 5, experimental results are provided. Finally, concluding remarks are given in Section 6.

2 State-space modeling of gene regulatory network

The GRN can be described by a graph in which genes are viewed as nodes and edges depict causal relations between genes. The structure of GRN reveals the mechanisms of biological cells. Analyzing the structure of GRN will pave the way for curing various diseases [23]. The learning of GRN has drawn much attention recently due to the availability the microarray data. By analyzing collected gene expression levels over a period of time, one can identify various regulatory relations between different genes. To facilitate the analysis of the GRN, modeling of GRN is required. Different models can be used, such as Bayesian networks [1], Boolean networks [2], ordinary differential equation [3], and state-space model [4,5]. The state-space model has been widely used because it incorporates noise and can make use of computationally efficient filtering algorithms [5]. Thus, we also use the state-space modeling of GRN in this paper.

Under the discrete-time state-space modeling of the gene regulatory networks, the network evolution from time k to time $k-1$ can be described by

$$\boldsymbol{x}_k = \boldsymbol{f}(\boldsymbol{x}_{k-1}) + \boldsymbol{v}_k, \tag{1}$$

where $\boldsymbol{x}_k = [x_{1,k}, \ldots, x_{n,k}]^T$ is the state vector and $x_{i,k}$ denotes the gene expression level of the i-th gene at time k. $\boldsymbol{f}$ is a nonlinear function that characterizes the regulatory relationship among the genes. $\boldsymbol{v}_k$ is the state noise and it is assumed to follow a Gaussian distribution with mean $\boldsymbol{0}$ and covariance matrix $\boldsymbol{Q}_k$, i.e., $\boldsymbol{v}_k \sim \mathcal{N}(\boldsymbol{0}, \boldsymbol{Q}_k)$.

Following [8], we use the following nonlinear function in the state Equation (1):

$$\boldsymbol{f}(\boldsymbol{x}) = \boldsymbol{A}\boldsymbol{g}(\boldsymbol{x}), \tag{2}$$

with

$$\boldsymbol{g}(\boldsymbol{x}) = \begin{bmatrix} g_1(x_1) \\ \vdots \\ g_n(x_n) \end{bmatrix} \tag{3}$$

and

$$g_i(x) = \frac{1}{1 + e^{-\mu_i x}}. \tag{4}$$

In (2), $\boldsymbol{A}$ is the regulatory coefficient matrix with a_{ij} denoting the regulation coefficient from gene j to gene i. Note that a positive coefficient a_{ij} indicates that gene j activates gene i and a negative a_{ij} indicates that gene j represses gene i. In (4), μ_i is a parameter. Note that $\boldsymbol{A}$ and μ_i are unknown parameters. The discrete-time nonlinear stochastic dynamic system [24] shown in Eqs. (1)-(3) have been successfully used to describe the GRN [4,8]. Equation (4) is also called Sigmoid function which is frequently used since it is consistent with the fact that all concentrations get saturated at some point in time [25].

The Sigmoid function has been used in modeling GRN to verify various methods, such as artificial neural network [26], simulated annealing and clustering algorithm [27], extended Kalman filter [4], particle filter [8], and Genetic programming and Kalman filtering [25].

For the measurement model, we consider the following general nonlinear observation equation

$$\boldsymbol{y}_k = \boldsymbol{h}(\boldsymbol{x}_k) + \boldsymbol{n}_k, \tag{5}$$

where $\boldsymbol{h}(\cdot)$ is some nonlinear function, $\boldsymbol{n}_k$ is the measurement noise, which is assumed to follow the Gaussian distribution with mean $\mathbf{0}$ and covariance matrix $\boldsymbol{R}_k$, i.e., $\boldsymbol{n}_k \sim \mathcal{N}(\mathbf{0}, \boldsymbol{R}_k)$. For example, if the noise corrupted expression levels are observed, then $\boldsymbol{h}(\boldsymbol{x}) = \boldsymbol{x}$.

3 Network inference using point-based Gaussian approximation filters

3.1 Gaussian approximation filters

In this section, the framework of point-based Gaussian approximation filters for the state-space dynamic model is briefly reviewed. We consider the state-space model consisting of the state Equation (1) and the measurement Equation (5). We denote $\boldsymbol{y}^k \triangleq [\boldsymbol{y}_1, \ldots, \boldsymbol{y}_k]$.

The optimal Bayesian filter is composed of two steps: prediction and filtering. Specifically, given the prior pdf $p(\boldsymbol{x}_{k-1}|\boldsymbol{y}^{k-1})$ at time $k-1$, the predicted conditional pdf $p(\boldsymbol{x}_k|\boldsymbol{y}^{k-1})$ is given by

$$p(\boldsymbol{x}_k|\boldsymbol{y}^{k-1}) = \int p(\boldsymbol{x}_k|\boldsymbol{x}_{k-1})p(\boldsymbol{x}_{k-1}|\boldsymbol{y}^{k-1})\mathrm{d}\boldsymbol{x}_{k-1}. \tag{6}$$

After the measurement at time k becomes available, the filtered pdf is given by

$$p(\boldsymbol{x}_k|\boldsymbol{y}^k) = \frac{p(\boldsymbol{y}_k|\boldsymbol{x}_k)p(\boldsymbol{x}_k|\boldsymbol{y}^{k-1})}{\int p(\boldsymbol{y}_k|\boldsymbol{x}_k)p(\boldsymbol{x}_k|\boldsymbol{y}^{k-1})\mathrm{d}\boldsymbol{x}_k}. \tag{7}$$

The pdf recursions in (6) and (7) are in general computationally intractable unless the system is linear and Gaussian. The Gaussian approximation filters approximate (6) and (7) by invoking Gaussian assumptions. Specifically, the first assumption is that given $\boldsymbol{y}^{k-1}$, $\boldsymbol{x}_{k-1}$ has a Gaussian distribution, i.e., $\boldsymbol{x}_{k-1}|\boldsymbol{y}^{k-1} \sim \mathcal{N}(\hat{\boldsymbol{x}}_{k-1|k-1}, \boldsymbol{P}_{k-1|k-1})$. The second assumption is that $(\boldsymbol{x}_k, \boldsymbol{y}_k)$ are jointly Gaussian given $\boldsymbol{y}^{k-1}$.

It then follows from the second assumption that given $\boldsymbol{y}^{k-1}$, $\boldsymbol{x}_k$ has a Gaussian distribution, i.e., $\boldsymbol{x}_k|\boldsymbol{y}^{k-1} \sim \mathcal{N}(\hat{\boldsymbol{x}}_{k|k-1}, \boldsymbol{P}_{k|k-1})$. Using (1) and the first assumption, we have the predicted mean $\hat{\boldsymbol{x}}_{k|k-1}$ and covariance $\boldsymbol{P}_{k|k-1}$ given respectively by

$$\begin{aligned}\hat{\boldsymbol{x}}_{k|k-1} &\triangleq \mathbb{E}\{\boldsymbol{x}_k|\boldsymbol{y}^{k-1}\} = \mathbb{E}_{\boldsymbol{x}_{k-1}|\boldsymbol{y}^{k-1}}\left\{\boldsymbol{f}(\boldsymbol{x}_{k-1})\right\} \\ &= \int \boldsymbol{f}(\boldsymbol{x})\phi(\boldsymbol{x};\, \hat{\boldsymbol{x}}_{k-1|k-1}, \boldsymbol{P}_{k-1|k-1})\mathrm{d}\boldsymbol{x}, \end{aligned}\tag{8}$$

and

$$\begin{aligned}\boldsymbol{P}_{k|k-1} &\triangleq \mathrm{Cov}\{\boldsymbol{x}_k|\boldsymbol{y}^{k-1}\} \\ &= \mathbb{E}_{\boldsymbol{x}_{k-1}|\boldsymbol{y}^{k-1}}\Big\{(\boldsymbol{f}(\boldsymbol{x}_{k-1}) - \hat{\boldsymbol{x}}_{k|k-1}) \\ &\quad \times (\boldsymbol{f}(\boldsymbol{x}_{k-1}) - \hat{\boldsymbol{x}}_{k|k-1})^T\Big\} + \boldsymbol{Q}_{k-1} \\ &= \int (\boldsymbol{f}(\boldsymbol{x}) - \hat{\boldsymbol{x}}_{k|k-1}) \\ &\quad \times (\boldsymbol{f}(\boldsymbol{x}) - \hat{\boldsymbol{x}}_{k|k-1})^T \phi\left(\boldsymbol{x};\, \hat{\boldsymbol{x}}_{k-1|k-1},\right. \\ &\quad \left.\boldsymbol{P}_{k-1|k-1}\right)\mathrm{d}\boldsymbol{x} + \boldsymbol{Q}_{k-1}, \end{aligned}\tag{9}$$

where $\phi\left(\boldsymbol{x};\, \hat{\boldsymbol{x}}, \boldsymbol{P}\right)$ denotes the multivariate Gaussian pdf with mean $\hat{\boldsymbol{x}}$ and covariance $\boldsymbol{P}$.

Then, following the second assumption, given $\boldsymbol{y}^k = [\boldsymbol{y}^{k-1}, \boldsymbol{y}_k]$, $\boldsymbol{x}_k$ is Gaussian distributed, i.e., $\boldsymbol{x}_k|\boldsymbol{y}^k \sim \mathcal{N}(\hat{\boldsymbol{x}}_{k|k}, \boldsymbol{P}_{k|k})$. Using the conditional property of the multivariate Gaussian distribution, the filtered mean $\hat{\boldsymbol{x}}_{k|k}$ and covariance $\boldsymbol{P}_{k|k}$ are given respectively by

$$\begin{aligned}\hat{\boldsymbol{x}}_{k|k} &\triangleq \mathbb{E}\{\boldsymbol{x}_k|\boldsymbol{y}_k, \boldsymbol{y}^{k-1}\} \\ &= \hat{\boldsymbol{x}}_{k|k-1} + \boldsymbol{L}_k(\boldsymbol{y}_k - \hat{\boldsymbol{y}}_{k|k-1}) \end{aligned}\tag{10}$$

$$\begin{aligned}\text{and}\quad \boldsymbol{P}_{k|k} &\triangleq \mathrm{Cov}\{\boldsymbol{x}_k|\boldsymbol{y}_k, \boldsymbol{y}^{k-1}\} \\ &= \boldsymbol{P}_{k|k-1} - \boldsymbol{L}_k\boldsymbol{P}_k^{xy}, \end{aligned}\tag{11}$$

with

$$\begin{aligned}\hat{\boldsymbol{y}}_{k|k-1} &= \mathbb{E}_{\boldsymbol{x}_k|\boldsymbol{y}^{k-1}}\left\{\boldsymbol{h}(\boldsymbol{x}_k)\right\} \\ &= \int \boldsymbol{h}(\boldsymbol{x})\phi\left(\boldsymbol{x};\, \hat{\boldsymbol{x}}_{k|k-1}, \boldsymbol{P}_{k|k-1}\right)\mathrm{d}\boldsymbol{x}, \end{aligned}\tag{12}$$

$$\boldsymbol{L}_k = \boldsymbol{P}_k^{xy}(\boldsymbol{R}_k + \boldsymbol{P}_k^{yy})^{-1}, \tag{13}$$

$$\begin{aligned}\boldsymbol{P}_k^{xy} &= \mathbb{E}_{\boldsymbol{x}_k|\boldsymbol{y}^{k-1}}\left\{(\boldsymbol{x} - \hat{\boldsymbol{x}}_{k|k-1})(\boldsymbol{h}(\boldsymbol{x}) - \hat{\boldsymbol{y}}_{k|k-1})^T\right\} \\ &= \int (\boldsymbol{x} - \hat{\boldsymbol{x}}_{k|k-1})(\boldsymbol{h}(\boldsymbol{x}) - \hat{\boldsymbol{y}}_{k|k-1})^T \\ &\quad \phi\left(\boldsymbol{x};\, \hat{\boldsymbol{x}}_{k|k-1}, \boldsymbol{P}_{k|k-1}\right)\mathrm{d}\boldsymbol{x}, \end{aligned}\tag{14}$$

$$\begin{aligned}\boldsymbol{P}_k^{yy} &= \mathbb{E}_{\boldsymbol{x}_k|\boldsymbol{y}^{k-1}}\left\{(\boldsymbol{h}(\boldsymbol{x}) - \hat{\boldsymbol{y}}_{k|k-1})(\boldsymbol{h}(\boldsymbol{x}) - \hat{\boldsymbol{y}}_{k|k-1})^T\right\} \\ &= \int \left(\boldsymbol{h}(\boldsymbol{x}) - \hat{\boldsymbol{y}}_{k|k-1}\right)\left(\boldsymbol{h}(\boldsymbol{x}) - \hat{\boldsymbol{y}}_{k|k-1}\right)^T \\ &\quad \phi\left(\boldsymbol{x};\, \hat{\boldsymbol{x}}_{k|k-1}, \boldsymbol{P}_{k|k-1}\right)\mathrm{d}\boldsymbol{x}. \end{aligned}\tag{15}$$

3.2 Point-based Gaussian approximation filters

The integrals in (8), (9), (12), (14) and (15) are Gaussian type that can be efficiently approximated by various quadrature methods. Specifically, if a set of weighted points $\left\{(\boldsymbol{\gamma}_i, w_i), i = 1, \ldots, N\right\}$ can be used to approximate the integral

$$\int \boldsymbol{h}(\boldsymbol{x})\,\phi\left(\boldsymbol{x}; \mathbf{0}, \boldsymbol{I}\right)\mathrm{d}\boldsymbol{x} \approx \sum_{i=1}^{N} w_i\boldsymbol{h}(\boldsymbol{\gamma}_i), \tag{16}$$

then the general Gaussian-type integral can be approximated by

$$\int h(x)\phi\left(x;\hat{x},P\right)\mathrm{d}x \approx \sum_{i=1}^{N} w_i h(S\gamma_i+\hat{x}), \tag{17}$$

where $P = SS^T$ and S can be obtained by Cholesky decomposition or singular value decomposition (SVD).

Using (17), we can then approximate (8) and (9) as follows:

$$\hat{x}_{k|k-1} \approx \sum_{i=1}^{N} w_i f\left(\xi_{k-1,i}\right) \tag{18}$$

and

$$P_{k|k-1} \approx \sum_{i=1}^{N} w_i f\left(\xi_{k-1,i}-\hat{x}_{k|k-1}\right) \times \left(\xi_{k-1,i}-\hat{x}_{k|k-1}\right)^T + Q_{k-1}, \tag{19}$$

where $\xi_{k-1,i}$ is the transformed quadrature point obtained from the covariance decomposition, i.e.,

$$P_{k-1|k-1} = S_{k-1}S_{k-1}^T, \tag{20}$$

$$\xi_{k-1,i} = S_{k-1}\gamma_i + \hat{x}_{k-1|k-1}. \tag{21}$$

Similarly, we can approximate (12), (14) and (15) as follows:

$$\hat{y}_{k|k-1} = \sum_{i=1}^{N} w_i h\left(\tilde{\xi}_{k,i}\right), \tag{22}$$

$$P_k^{xy} = \sum_{i=1}^{N} w_i\left(\tilde{\xi}_{k,i}-\hat{x}_{k|k-1}\right)\left(h(\tilde{\xi}_{k,i})-\hat{y}_{k|k-1}\right)^T, \tag{23}$$

$$P_k^{yy} = \sum_{i=1}^{N} w_i\left(h(\tilde{\xi}_{k,i})-\hat{y}_{k|k-1}\right)\left(h(\tilde{\xi}_{k,i})-\hat{y}_{k|k-1}\right)^T, \tag{24}$$

where $\tilde{\xi}_{k,i}$ is the transformed point obtained from the decomposition of the predicted covariance, i.e.,

$$P_{k|k-1} = \tilde{S}_k\tilde{S}_k^T, \tag{25}$$

$$\tilde{\xi}_{k,i} = \tilde{S}_k\gamma_i + \hat{x}_{k|k-1}. \tag{26}$$

Various numerical rules can be used to form the approximation in (16), which lead to different Gaussian approximation filters. In particular, the unscented transformation, the Gauss-Hermite quadrature rule, and the sparse-grid quadrature rules are used in the unscented Kalman filter (UKF), the Gauss-Hermite quadrature Kalman filter (GHQF), and the sparse-grid quadrature filter (SGQF), respectively.

Recently, the fifth-degree quadrature filter has been proposed and shown to be more accurate than the third-degree quadrature filters, such as the UKF and the third-degree cubature Kalman filter (CKF_3), when the system is highly nonlinear or contains large uncertainty [16]. In this paper, we consider the UKF, CKF_3, and the fifth-degree cubature Kalman filter (CKF_5). Other filters such as the central difference filter [14] and divided difference filter [28] can also be used. The CKF_5 is based on Mysovskikh's method which uses fewer point than the fifth-degree quadrature filter in [16]. In the following, different numerical rules used in (16) are briefly summarized.

3.2.1 Unscented transform

In the unscented Kalman filter (UKF), we have $N = 2n+1$ where n is the dimension of x. The quadrature points and the corresponding weights are given respectively by

$$\gamma_i = \begin{cases} 0, & i=1, \\ \sqrt{(n+\kappa)}e_{i-1}, & i=2,\cdots,n+1, \\ -\sqrt{(n+\kappa)}e_{i-n-1}, & i=n+2,\cdots,2n+1, \end{cases} \tag{27}$$

and

$$w_i = \begin{cases} \dfrac{\kappa}{n+\kappa}, & i=1, \\ \dfrac{1}{2(n+\kappa)}, & i=2,\cdots,2n+1, \end{cases} \tag{28}$$

where κ is a tunable parameter, and e_i is the i-th n-dimensional unit vector in which the i-th element is 1 and other elements are 0.

3.2.2 Cubature rules

The left-hand side of (16) can be rewritten as

$$\int h(x)\,\phi\left(x;0,I\right)\mathrm{d}x = \frac{1}{\pi^{n/2}}\int h\left(\sqrt{2}x\right)\exp\left(-x^Tx\right)\mathrm{d}x. \tag{29}$$

Consider the integral

$$I\left(h\right) = \int h(x)\exp\left(-x^Tx\right)\mathrm{d}x. \tag{30}$$

By letting $x = rs$ with $s^Ts = 1$ and $r = \sqrt{x^Tx}$, $I(h)$ can be rewritten in the spherical-radial coordinate system as

$$I\left(h\right) = \int_0^\infty\int_{U_n} h(rs)r^{n-1}\exp\left(-r^2\right)\mathrm{d}\sigma\left(s\right)\mathrm{d}r, \tag{31}$$

where $U_n = \{s \in R^n : \|s\| = 1\}$, and $\sigma\left(\cdot\right)$ is the spherical surface measure or the area element on U_n.

Note that (31) contains two types of integrals: the radial integral $\int_0^\infty h_r\left(r\right)r^{n-1}\exp\left(-r^2\right)\mathrm{d}r$ and the spherical integral $\int_{U_n} h_s(s)\mathrm{d}\sigma(s)$.

If the radial rule can be approximated by

$$\int_0^\infty h_r(r)r^{n-1}\exp\left(-r^2\right)\mathrm{d}r \approx \sum_{i=1}^{N_r} w_{r,i}h_r(r_i), \tag{32}$$

and the spherical integral can be approximated by

$$\int_{U_n} h_s(s)\mathrm{d}\sigma(s) \approx \sum_{j=1}^{N_s} w_{s,j}h_s(s_j), \tag{33}$$

then (31) can be approximated by

$$I(\boldsymbol{h}) \approx \sum_{i=1}^{N_r} \sum_{j=1}^{N_s} w_{r,i} w_{s,j} \boldsymbol{h}(r_i \boldsymbol{s}_j). \tag{34}$$

A third-degree cubature rule to approximate (29) is obtained by using the third-degree spherical rule and radial rule [15]:

$$\int \boldsymbol{h}(\boldsymbol{x}) \phi\left(\boldsymbol{x}; \boldsymbol{0}, \boldsymbol{I}\right) \mathrm{d}\boldsymbol{x} \approx \frac{1}{2n} \sum_{i=1}^{n} \left[\boldsymbol{h}\left(\sqrt{n} \boldsymbol{e}_i\right) + \boldsymbol{h}\left(-\sqrt{n} \boldsymbol{e}_i\right)\right]. \tag{35}$$

Remark: The third-degree cubature rule is identical to the unscented transformation with $\kappa = 0$.

To construct the fifth-degree cubature rule, the Mysovskikh's method [29] and the moment matching method [16] are used to provide the fifth-degree spherical rule and radial rule, respectively. The final fifth-degree cubature rule is given by

$$\begin{aligned} \int \boldsymbol{h}(\boldsymbol{x}) \phi\left(\boldsymbol{x}; \boldsymbol{0}, \boldsymbol{I}\right) \mathrm{d}\boldsymbol{x} \approx & \frac{2}{n+2} \boldsymbol{h}(\boldsymbol{0}) + \\ & + \frac{n^2(7-n)}{2(n+1)^2(n+2)^2} \sum_{i=1}^{n+1} \left[\boldsymbol{h}\left(\sqrt{n+2}\boldsymbol{s}_1^{(i)}\right)\right. \\ & \left. + \boldsymbol{h}\left(-\sqrt{n+2}\boldsymbol{s}_1^{(i)}\right)\right] \\ & + \frac{2(n-1)^2}{(n+1)^2(n+2)^2} \sum_{i=1}^{n(n+1)/2} \left[\boldsymbol{h}\left(\sqrt{n+2}\boldsymbol{s}_2^{(i)}\right)\right. \\ & \left. + \boldsymbol{h}\left(-\sqrt{n+2}\boldsymbol{s}_2^{(i)}\right)\right], \end{aligned} \tag{36}$$

where the point $\boldsymbol{s}_1^{(i)}$ is given by

$$\boldsymbol{s}_1^{(i)} = \left[p_1^{(i)}, p_2^{(i)}, \cdots, p_n^{(i)}\right], \qquad i = 1, 2, \cdots, n+1, \tag{37}$$

with

$$p_j^{(i)} = \begin{cases} -\sqrt{\dfrac{n+1}{n(n-j+2)(n-j+1)}}, & j < i, \\ \sqrt{\dfrac{(n+1)(n-i+1)}{n(n-i+2)}}, & j = i, \\ 0, & j > i. \end{cases} \tag{38}$$

Moreover, the set of points $\{\boldsymbol{s}_2^{(i)}\}$ is given by

$$\left\{\boldsymbol{s}_2^{(i)}\right\} = \left\{\sqrt{\frac{n}{2(n-1)}} \left(\boldsymbol{s}_1^{(k)} + \boldsymbol{s}_1^{(l)}\right) : k < l,\ k, l = 1, 2, \cdots, n+1\right\}. \tag{39}$$

3.3 Augmented state-space model for network inference

In the state-space model for gene regulatory networks described in Section 3.2, the underlying network structure is characterized by the $n \times n$ regulatory coefficient matrix $\boldsymbol{A}$ in (2) and the parameters $\boldsymbol{\mu} = [\mu_1, \ldots, \mu_n]$ in (4). The problem of network inference then becomes to estimate $\boldsymbol{A}$ and $\boldsymbol{\mu}$. To do that, we incorporate the unknown parameters $\boldsymbol{A}$ and $\boldsymbol{\mu}$ into the state vector to obtain an augmented state-space model, and then apply the point-based Gaussian approximation filters to estimate the space vector and thereby obtaining the estimates of $\boldsymbol{A}$ and $\boldsymbol{\mu}$.

Specifically, we denote $\boldsymbol{\theta} = [a_{11}, a_{12}, \cdots, a_{1n}, \cdots, a_{nn}, \mu_1, \cdots, \mu_n]^T$ and the augmented state vector $\bar{\boldsymbol{x}}_k = \left[\boldsymbol{x}_k^T, \boldsymbol{\theta}^T\right]^T$. Then, the augmented state equation can be written as

$$\bar{\boldsymbol{x}}_k = \bar{\boldsymbol{f}}(\bar{\boldsymbol{x}}_{k-1}) + \bar{\boldsymbol{v}}_k = \begin{bmatrix} \boldsymbol{A}_{k-1} \boldsymbol{g}_{k-1}(\boldsymbol{x}_{k-1}) \\ \boldsymbol{\theta}_{k-1} \end{bmatrix} + \begin{bmatrix} \boldsymbol{v}_{k-1} \\ \boldsymbol{0} \end{bmatrix}. \tag{40}$$

Note that $\boldsymbol{A}_{k-1}$ and $\boldsymbol{g}_{k-1}$ can be obtained from $\boldsymbol{\theta}_{k-1}$, and $\bar{\boldsymbol{v}}_k \sim \mathcal{N}(\boldsymbol{0}, \bar{\boldsymbol{Q}}_k)$ with $\bar{\boldsymbol{Q}}_k = \mathrm{diag}\left(\left[\boldsymbol{Q}_k \quad \boldsymbol{O}_{n^2+n}\right]\right)$, where $\boldsymbol{O}_m$ denotes an $m \times m$ all-zero matrix.

In the remainder of this paper, we assume that the noisy gene expression levels are observed. Therefore, the augmented measurement equation becomes

$$\boldsymbol{y}_k = \boldsymbol{h}(\bar{\boldsymbol{x}}_k) + \boldsymbol{n}_k = \boldsymbol{B}\bar{\boldsymbol{x}}_k + \boldsymbol{n}_k, \tag{41}$$

where $\boldsymbol{B} = [\boldsymbol{I}_n, \boldsymbol{O}_{n \times (n^2+n)}]$, $\boldsymbol{O}_{n \times (n^2+n)}$ denotes an $n \times (n^2+n)$ all zeros matrix.

The point-based Gaussian approximation filters can then be used to obtain the estimate of the augmented state, $\hat{\bar{\boldsymbol{x}}}_k$, from which the estimates of the unknown network parameters, i.e., $\hat{\boldsymbol{A}}$ and $\hat{\boldsymbol{\mu}}$ can then be obtained.

Note that since the measurement Equation (41) is linear, the filtering Equations (10, 11) become

$$\hat{\bar{\boldsymbol{x}}}_{k|k} = \hat{\bar{\boldsymbol{x}}}_{k|k-1} + \boldsymbol{L}_k(\boldsymbol{y}_k - \boldsymbol{B}\hat{\bar{\boldsymbol{x}}}_{k|k-1}), \tag{42}$$

$$\text{and } \boldsymbol{P}_{k|k} = \boldsymbol{P}_{k|k-1} - \boldsymbol{L}_k \boldsymbol{B} \boldsymbol{P}_{k|k-1}, \tag{43}$$

$$\text{with } \boldsymbol{L}_k = \boldsymbol{P}_{k|k-1}\boldsymbol{B}^T(\boldsymbol{R}_k + \boldsymbol{B}\boldsymbol{P}_{k|k-1}\boldsymbol{B}^T)^{-1}, \tag{44}$$

which are the same as the filtering updates for Kalman filters.

4 Incorporating prior information

In practice, some prior knowledge on the underlying GRN is typically available. In this section, we outline approaches to incorporating such prior knowledge into the point-based Gaussian approximation filters for network inference. In particular, we consider two types of prior information, namely, sparsity constraints and range constraints on the network. For networks with sparsity constraints, we incorporate an iterative thresholding procedure into the Gaussian approximation filters.

And to accommodate range constraints, we employ PDF-truncated Gaussian approximation filters.

4.1 Optimization-based approach for sparsity constraints

4.1.1 The optimization formulations

Note that under the Gaussian assumption, the state estimation $\hat{\bar{x}}_{k|k}$ of the Kalman filter is equivalently given by the solution to the following optimization problem [30,31]

$$\hat{\bar{x}}_{k|k} = \arg\min_{\bar{x}} J(\bar{x}), \tag{45}$$

$$\text{with } J(\bar{x}) \triangleq \left(y_k - h(\bar{x})\right)^T R_k^{-1} \left(y_k - h(\bar{x})\right) + \left(\bar{x} - \hat{\bar{x}}_{k|k-1}\right)^T P_{k|k-1}^{-1} \left(\bar{x} - \hat{\bar{x}}_{k|k-1}\right). \tag{46}$$

To incorporate the prior information of the GRN, (46) is modified as

$$\tilde{J}(\bar{x}) = J(\bar{x}) + \lambda J_p(\bar{x}), \tag{47}$$

where $J_p(\bar{x})$ is a penalty function associated with the prior information and λ is a tunable parameter that regulates the tightness of the penalty.

For example, in gene regulatory networks, each gene only interacts with a few genes [20]. To capture such a sparsity constraint, a Laplace prior distribution can be used for the connection coefficient matrix A, i.e.,

$$p(A) = (\lambda/2)^{n^2} \exp\left(-\lambda \sum_{i=1}^{n}\sum_{j=1}^{n} |a_{ij}|\right). \tag{48}$$

Therefore, in this case, $J_p(\bar{x}) = -\log p(A) = c_1\|A\|_1 + c_2$ where c_1 and c_2 are constants. And, (47) can be rewritten as

$$\tilde{J}(\bar{x}) = J(\bar{x}) + \lambda\|A\|_1. \tag{49}$$

Note that (49) can also be interpreted as the result of applying the least squares shrinkage selection operator (LASSO) to (47). The LASSO adds an L_1-norm constraint to the GRN so that the regulatory coefficient matrix A tends to be sparse with many zero elements.

As another example, if some known regulatory relationship exists, then it should be taken into account to improve the estimation accuracy. Specifically, define an $n \times n$ indicator matrix $E = [e_{i,j}]$ where $e_{ij} = 1$ indicates that there is a lack of regulation from gene j to gene i. Then, similar to the use of LASSO, a penalty on a_{ij} should incur if $e_{ij} = 1$. Thus, (47) can be rewritten as

$$\tilde{J}(\bar{x}) = J(\bar{x}) + \lambda\|E \circ A\|_1. \tag{50}$$

Note that as in [20], here we do not force $a_{ij} = 0$ corresponding to $e_{ij} = 1$ but rather use an L_1-norm penalty. The advantage of such an approach is that it allows the algorithm to pick different structures but more likely to pick the edges without penalties. '$\circ$' denotes the entry-wise product operation of two matrices.

4.1.2 Iterative thresholding algorithm

Solving the optimization problems in (49) and (50) is not straightforward since $|a|$ is non-differentiable at $a = 0$. In the following, an efficient solver called the iterative thresholding algorithm is introduced.

For convenience, we consider a general optimization problem of the form

$$\arg\min_{\bar{x}} J(\bar{x}) = L(\bar{x}) + \|\boldsymbol{\lambda} \circ \bar{x}\|_1, \tag{51}$$

where $\boldsymbol{\lambda} = [\lambda_1, \lambda_2, \cdots, \lambda_{n^2+2n}]^T$ and $L(\bar{x})$ is a smooth function. Note that if $\boldsymbol{\lambda} = [\mathbf{0}_{1\times n}, \lambda \times \mathbf{1}_{1\times n^2}, \mathbf{0}_{1\times n}]^T$, then (51) becomes (49); and if $\boldsymbol{\lambda} = [\mathbf{0}_{1\times n}, \lambda \times \underline{\hat{\theta}}, \mathbf{0}_{1\times n}]^T$, then (51) becomes (50). Note that $\underline{\hat{\theta}} = [e_{11}, e_{12}, \cdots, e_{1n}, \cdots, e_{nn}]^T$.

The solution to (51) can be iteratively obtained by solving a sequence of optimization problems. As in Newton's method, the Taylor series expansion of $L(\bar{x})$ around the solution $\bar{x}^t$ at the t-th iteration is given by

$$L(\bar{x}^t + \Delta\bar{x}) \cong L(\bar{x}^t) + \Delta\bar{x}^T \nabla L(\bar{x}^t) + \frac{\alpha_t}{2}\|\Delta\bar{x}\|_2^2, \tag{52}$$

where ∇L is the gradient of L and α_t is such that $\alpha_t I$ mimics the Hessian $\nabla^2 L$. Then, $\bar{x}^{t+1}$ is given by [32]

$$\bar{x}^{t+1} = \arg\min_{z} (z - \bar{x}^t)^T \nabla L(\bar{x}^t) + \frac{\alpha_t}{2}\|z - \bar{x}^t\|_2^2 + \|\boldsymbol{\lambda} \circ z\|_1. \tag{53}$$

The equivalent form of (53) is given by [32]

$$\bar{x}^{t+1} = \arg\min_{z} \frac{1}{2}\|z - u^t\|_2^2 + \frac{1}{\alpha_t}\|\boldsymbol{\lambda} \circ z\|_1, \tag{54}$$

$$\text{with } u^t = \bar{x}^t - \frac{1}{\alpha_t}\nabla L(\bar{x}^t), \tag{55}$$

$$\alpha_t \approx \frac{(s^t)^T r^t}{\|s^t\|^2}, \tag{56}$$

$$s^t = \bar{x}^t - \bar{x}^{t-1}, \tag{57}$$

$$r^t = \nabla L(\bar{x}^t) - \nabla L(\bar{x}^{t-1}). \tag{58}$$

The solution to (54) is given by [32] $\bar{x}^{t+1} = \eta^S(u^t, \frac{\boldsymbol{\lambda}}{\alpha_t})$, where

$$\eta^S(u, a) = \mathrm{sign}(u)\max\{|u| - a, \mathbf{0}\} \tag{59}$$

is the soft thresholding function with $\mathrm{sign}(u)$ and $\max\{|u| - a, \mathbf{0}\}$ being component-wise operators.

Finally, the iterative procedure for solving (51) is given by

$$\bar{x}^{t+1} = \mathrm{sign}\left(\bar{x}^t - \frac{1}{\alpha_t}\nabla L(\bar{x}^t)\right) \max\left\{\left|\bar{x}^t - \frac{1}{\alpha_t}\nabla L(\bar{x}^t)\right| - \frac{\boldsymbol{\lambda}}{\alpha_t}, \mathbf{0}\right\}. \tag{60}$$

And the iteration stops when the following condition is met

$$\frac{|J(\bar{x}^t) - J(\bar{x}^{t-1})|}{|J(\bar{x}^{t-1})|} \leq \epsilon, \tag{61}$$

where ϵ is a given small number.

4.2 PDF truncation method for range constraints

If the range constraints on the regulatory coefficients are available, the inference accuracy can be improved by enforcing the constraints in the Gaussian approximation filters.

In particular, assume that we impose the following range constraints on the state vector $\bar{x}$

$$c \leq \bar{x} \leq d. \tag{62}$$

The PDF truncation method [31] can be employed to incorporate the above range constraint into the Gaussian approximation filters, by converting the updated mean $\hat{\bar{x}}_{k|k}$ and covariance $P_{k|k}$ to the pseudo mean $\hat{\bar{x}}^t_{k|k}$ and covariance $P^t_{k|k}$ which are then used in the next prediction and filtering steps.

We next briefly outline the PDF truncation procedure. We use $\hat{\bar{x}}^t_{k|k,i}$ and $P^t_{k|k,i}$ to denote the mean and covariance after the first i constraints have been enforced. Initially, we set $\hat{\bar{x}}^t_{k|k,0} = \hat{\bar{x}}_{k|k}$ and $P^t_{k|k,0} = P_{k|k}$. Consider the following transformation

$$z_{k,i} = \mathcal{G}_i \mathcal{D}_i^{-1/2} \mathcal{S}_i^T (\bar{x}_k - \hat{\bar{x}}^t_{k|k,i}) \tag{63}$$

where $\mathcal{S}_i$ and $\mathcal{D}_i$ are obtained from the Jordan canonical decomposition $\mathcal{S}_i \mathcal{D}_i \mathcal{S}_i^T = P^t_{k|k,i}$ and $\mathcal{G}_i$ is obtained by using the Gram-Schmidt orthogonalization and it satisfies [33]

$$\mathcal{G}_i \mathcal{D}_i^{1/2} \mathcal{S}_i^T e_i = \left[\left(e_i^T P^t_{k|k,i} e_i \right)^{1/2}, 0, \cdots, 0 \right]. \tag{64}$$

Then, the upper bound $e_i^T \bar{x} \leq d_i$ is transformed to [33]

$$[1, 0, \cdots, 0]\, z_{k,i} \leq \frac{d_i - e_i^T \hat{\bar{x}}^t_{k|k,i}}{(e_i^T P^t_{k|k,i} e_i)^{1/2}} \triangleq \tilde{d}_i. \tag{65}$$

Similarly, the lower bound $e_i^T \bar{x} \geq c_i$ is transformed to

$$[1, 0, \cdots, 0]\, z_{k,i} \geq \frac{c_i - e_i^T \hat{\bar{x}}^t_{k|k,i}}{(e_i^T P^t_{k|k,i} e_i)^{1/2}} \triangleq \tilde{c}_i. \tag{66}$$

The constraint requires that the first element of $z_{k,i}$ lies between $\tilde{c}_i$ and $\tilde{d}_i$. Hence, only the truncated PDF of the first element of $z_{k,i}$ is considered and it is given by [33]

$$f(z) = \alpha_i \exp(-z^2/2), \tag{67}$$

$$\text{with } \alpha_i = \frac{\sqrt{2}}{\sqrt{\pi}[\text{erf}(\tilde{d}_i/\sqrt{2}) - \text{erf}(\tilde{c}_i/\sqrt{2})]}. \tag{68}$$

Then, the mean and variance of the first element of $z_{k,i}$ after imposing the i-th constraint are given respectively by

$$\mu_i = \int_{\tilde{c}_i}^{\tilde{d}_i} z f(z) \mathrm{d}z = \alpha_i \left[\exp(-\tilde{c}_i^2/2) - \exp(-\tilde{d}_i^2/2) \right], \tag{69}$$

$$\begin{aligned} \sigma_i^2 &= \int_{\tilde{c}_i}^{\tilde{d}_i} (z - \mu_i)^2 f(z) \mathrm{d}z \\ &= \alpha_i \left[\exp(-\tilde{c}_i^2/2)(\tilde{c}_i - 2\mu_i) \right. \\ &\quad \left. - \exp(-\tilde{d}_i^2/2)(\tilde{d}_i - 2\mu_i) \right] + \mu_i^2 + 1. \end{aligned} \tag{70}$$

Thus, the mean and covariance of the transformed state vector after imposing the i-th constraint are given respectively by

$$\bar{z}_{k,i} = [\mu_i, 0, \cdots, 0]^T, \tag{71}$$

$$Q_{k,i} = \text{diag}([\sigma_i^2, 1, \cdots, 1]). \tag{72}$$

By taking the inverse transform of (63), we then get

$$\hat{\bar{x}}^t_{k|k,i+1} = \mathcal{S}_i \mathcal{D}_i^{1/2} \mathcal{G}_i^T \bar{z}_{k,i} + \hat{\bar{x}}^t_{k|k,i}, \tag{73}$$

$$P^t_{k|k,i+1} = \mathcal{S}_i \mathcal{D}_i^{1/2} \mathcal{G}_i^T Q_{k,i} \mathcal{G}_i \mathcal{D}_i^{1/2} \mathcal{S}_i^T. \tag{74}$$

After imposing all n constraints, the final constrained state estimate and covariance at time k are given respectively by $\hat{\bar{x}}^t_{k|k} \triangleq \hat{\bar{x}}^t_{k|k,n}$ and $P^t_{k|k} \triangleq P^t_{k|k,n}$.

5 Numerical results

5.1 Synthetic network

In this section, a synthetic network that contains eight genes is used to test the performance of the EKF, the

Table 1 Comparison of UKF with different κ

	True positive rate			False positive rate			Positive predictive rate		
Filters	Min	Max	Avg	Min	Max	Avg	Min	Max	Avg
UKF($\kappa = -5$)	0.7576	0.9355	0.8472	0.5000	0.7647	0.5955	0.5094	0.6279	0.5824
UKF($\kappa = -2$)	0.7576	0.9355	0.8406	0.5161	0.7647	0.5933	0.5094	0.6279	0.5825
UKF($\kappa = 0$)	0.7576	0.9375	0.8426	0.5161	0.7647	0.5918	0.5094	0.6364	0.5840
UKF($\kappa = 2$)	0.7576	0.9375	0.8407	0.5152	0.7353	0.5895	0.5098	0.6279	0.5841
UKF($\kappa = 5$)	0.7576	0.9063	0.8394	0.5161	0.7353	0.5933	0.5192	0.6279	0.5821

Table 2 Comparison of different filters

	True positives #			False positives #			True negatives #			False negatives #		
Filters	Min	Max	Avg	Min	Max	Avg	Min	Max	Avg	Min	Max	Avg
EKF	2	17	10.60	23	44	36.4	2	15	7.08	2	24	9.92
UKF	25	29	26.80	16	26	19.28	8	16	13.06	2	8	4.86
CKF_3	25	30	26.74	16	26	19.10	8	15	13.14	2	8	5.02
CKF_5	25	29	26.64	16	26	19.24	8	16	13.08	1	8	5.04

	True positive rate			False positive rate			Positive predictive rate		
Filters	Min	Max	Avg	Min	Max	Avg	Min	Max	Avg
EKF	0.0769	0.8667	0.5224	0.6053	0.9545	0.8358	0.0800	0.3208	0.2231
UKF	0.7576	0.9355	0.8472	0.5	0.7576	0.5955	0.5094	0.6279	0.5824
CKF_3	0.7576	0.9375	0.8426	0.5161	0.7647	0.5918	0.5094	0.6364	0.5840
CKF_5	0.7576	0.9667	0.8417	0.5000	0.7647	0.5946	0.5094	0.6279	0.5814

Table 3 Inferred results of the conventional filter and filters incorporating the prior information

	True positives #			False positives #			True negatives #			False negatives #		
Filters	**Min**	**Max**	**Avg**	**Min**	**Max**	**Avg**	**Min**	**Max**	**Avg**	**Min**	**Max**	**Avg**
UKF	25	29	26.80	16	26	19.28	8	16	13.06	2	8	4.86
UKF_{p1}	25	29	27.34	14	19	16.52	13	18	15.72	2	8	4.42
UKF_{p2}	23	26	24.16	13	16	13.86	16	18	17.20	7	10	8.78
UKF_{p3}	25	29	26.70	12	24	17.50	9	19	14.50	3	8	5.30

	True positive rate			False positive rate			Positive predictive rate		
Filters	**Min**	**Max**	**Avg**	**Min**	**Max**	**Avg**	**Min**	**Max**	**Avg**
UKF	0.7576	0.9355	0.8472	0.5	0.7647	0.5955	0.5094	0.6279	0.5824
UKF_{p1}	0.7576	0.9355	0.8614	0.4375	0.5935	0.5121	0.5778	0.6744	0.6239
UKF_{p2}	0.6970	0.7879	0.7335	0.4194	0.5000	0.4462	0.5897	0.6667	0.6355
UKF_{p3}	0.7576	0.9063	0.8348	0.3871	0.7273	0.5463	0.5294	0.6923	0.6049

Table 4 Comparison of UKF_{p1} using different λ

	True positive rate			False positive rate			Positive predictive rate		
Filters	Min	Max	Avg	Min	Max	Avg	Min	Max	Avg
UKF_{p1} ($\lambda = 0.1$)	0.7576	0.9355	0.8484	0.5000	0.7647	0.5900	0.5094	0.6279	0.5850
UKF_{p1} ($\lambda = 0.5$)	0.7576	0.9677	0.8535	0.4688	0.7647	0.5696	0.5094	0.6512	0.5948
UKF_{p1} ($\lambda = 1$)	0.7576	0.9355	0.8614	0.4375	0.5935	0.5121	0.5778	0.6744	0.6239
UKF_{p1} ($\lambda = 5$)	0.7500	0.9355	0.8439	0.3548	0.5455	0.4672	0.5814	0.7105	0.6456
UKF_{p1} ($\lambda = 10$)	0.7273	0.9063	0.8217	0.3226	0.4848	0.4156	0.6190	0.7368	0.6695

UKF, the CKF_3, the CKF_5, and their corresponding filters incorporating the prior information. Forty data points are collected to infer the structure of the network. The system noise and measurement noise are assumed to be Gaussian distributed with means $\mathbf{0}$ and covariances $\bar{\boldsymbol{Q}}_k = \text{diag}\big([0.01\boldsymbol{I}_8 \quad \boldsymbol{O}_{72}]\big)$ and $\boldsymbol{R}_k = 0.01\boldsymbol{I}_8$, respectively. The connection coefficient matrix is given by

$$\boldsymbol{A} = \begin{pmatrix} 0 & 0 & 0 & 0 & 0 & 0 & 2.4 & 3.2 \\ 0 & 0 & 0 & 4.1 & 0 & -2.4 & 0 & 4.1 \\ -5.0 & 2.1 & -1.5 & 0 & 4.5 & 0 & 2.1 & 0 \\ 0 & 1.3 & 2.5 & -3.7 & 1.8 & 0 & 0 & -3.1 \\ 0 & 0 & 0 & -2.6 & -3.2 & 0 & -1 & 4 \\ -1.5 & -1.8 & 0 & 3.4 & 1.4 & 1.1 & 0 & 1.7 \\ -1.8 & 0 & 0 & -3 & 1.1 & 2.4 & 0 & 0 \\ -1.3 & 0 & -1 & 0 & 2.1 & 0 & 0 & 2.2 \end{pmatrix} \tag{75}$$

and $\mu_i = 2$, $i = 1, \cdots, 8$. For the filter, each coefficient in $\hat{\boldsymbol{A}}$ is initialized from a Gaussian distribution with mean 0 and variance 0.2. Moreover, the coefficient μ_i is initialized from a Gaussian distribution with mean 1.5 and variance 0.2. The system state is initialized using the first measurement.

The metric used to evaluate the inferred GRN is the true positive rate (TPR), the false positive rate (FPR), and the positive predictive value (PPV). They are given by [34]

$$\text{TPR} = \frac{\text{TP\#}}{\text{TP\#} + \text{FN\#}}, \tag{76}$$

$$\text{FPR} = \frac{\text{FP\#}}{\text{FP\#} + \text{TN\#}}, \tag{77}$$

$$\text{PPV} = \frac{\text{TP\#}}{\text{TP\#} + \text{FP\#}}, \tag{78}$$

where the number of true positives (TP#) denotes the number of links correctly predicted by the inference algorithm; the number of false positives (FP#) denotes the number of incorrectly predicted links; the number of true negatives (TN#) denotes the number of correctly predicted nonlinks; and the number of false negatives (FN#) denotes the number of missed links by the inference algorithm [8].

5.1.1 Comparison of the EKF with point-based Gaussian approximation filters

The UKF with different parameter κ is tested. The simulation results based on 50 Monte Carlo runs are shown in Table 1. It can be seen that UKFs with $\kappa = 0, 2, 5$ have slight better performance than UKFs with $\kappa = -5, -2$. One possible reason is that the weights of all sigma points used in the UKF are all positive when $\kappa \geq 0$. In general, all positive weights will guarantee better stability of the filtering algorithm. However, it should be emphasized that, in this specific example, there is no big difference between UKFs with different κ. In addition, the objective of this paper was to investigate the proposed filter incorporating the prior information. Hence, the UKF is used to denote UKF with $\kappa = 3 - n$ and compare with the filters incorporating the prior information.

The inference results of the EKF, the UKF, the CKF_3, and the CKF_5 are summarized in Table 2, all results are based on 50 Monte Carlo runs. It can be seen that all point-based Gaussian approximation filters have better performance than the EKF since the average(avg) FPR is lower and the average TPR and precision are higher than that of the EKF. Although the CKFs exhibit slightly better

Table 5 Effect of strength of the links using different λ

	True positive rate			False positive rate			Positive predictive rate		
Filters	Min	Max	Avg	Min	Max	Avg	Min	Max	Avg
$UKF_{\bar{p}1}$ ($\lambda = 0.1$)	0.7576	0.9677	0.8484	0.4688	0.7647	0.5713	0.5094	0.6512	0.5929
$UKF_{\bar{p}1}$ ($\lambda = 0.5$)	0.7576	0.9333	0.8468	0.4516	0.7059	0.5422	0.5385	0.6512	0.6057
$UKF_{\bar{p}1}$ ($\lambda = 1$)	0.7500	0.9032	0.8221	0.3750	0.5758	0.4953	0.5814	0.6842	0.6257
$UKF_{\bar{p}1}$ ($\lambda = 5$)	0.7273	0.8750	0.8220	0.3548	0.5000	0.4169	0.6098	0.7179	0.6684
$UKF_{\bar{p}1}$ ($\lambda = 10$)	0.7500	0.8750	0.8214	0.3226	0.5000	0.4143	0.6098	0.7368	0.6696

Table 6 Effect of false prior information using different λ

	True positive rate			False positive rate			Positive predictive rate		
Filters	Min	Max	Avg	Min	Max	Avg	Min	Max	Avg
$UKF_{\bar{p}1}(\lambda = 0.1)$	0.7576	0.9667	0.8491	0.5000	0.7647	0.5933	0.5094	0.6279	0.5835
$UKF_{\bar{p}1}(\lambda = 0.5)$	0.7576	0.9355	0.8535	0.4839	0.7647	0.5962	0.5094	0.6279	0.5836
$UKF_{\bar{p}1}(\lambda = 1)$	0.7576	0.9333	0.8572	0.4839	0.7059	0.6001	0.5200	0.6279	0.5830
$UKF_{\bar{p}1}(\lambda = 5)$	0.6970	0.8125	0.7546	0.4194	0.5938	0.5000	0.5682	0.6486	0.6062
$UKF_{\bar{p}1}(\lambda = 10)$	0.5758	0.7576	0.6810	0.3226	0.5000	0.4066	0.5676	0.7059	0.6369

filtering performance than the UKF in some runs, they are comparable in terms of TPR, FPR, and PPV.

Based on the above tests, in the rest of the paper, only the UKF is used.

5.1.2 *Comparison of the UKF and the UKF incorporating the prior information*

As mentioned above, the UKF is used as a typical filter to compare the performance with and without the prior information.

Incorporating existing network information The following prior existing network information is assumed to be known: 1) gene1, gene5, and gene7 have little possibility to regulate gene2; 2) gene2, gene3, gene8 have little possibility to regulate gene7. Hence, the indicator matrix in (50) is given by

$$E = \begin{pmatrix} 0&0&0&0&0&0&0&0 \\ 1&0&0&0&1&0&1&0 \\ 0&0&0&0&0&0&0&0 \\ 0&0&0&0&0&0&0&0 \\ 0&0&0&0&0&0&0&0 \\ 0&0&0&0&0&0&0&0 \\ 0&1&1&0&0&0&0&1 \\ 0&0&0&0&0&0&0&0 \end{pmatrix}. \tag{79}$$

The comparison of the UKF and the UKF incorporating the existing network information (denoted by UKF_{p1}) with $\lambda = 2$ is shown in Table 3. It can be seen that the

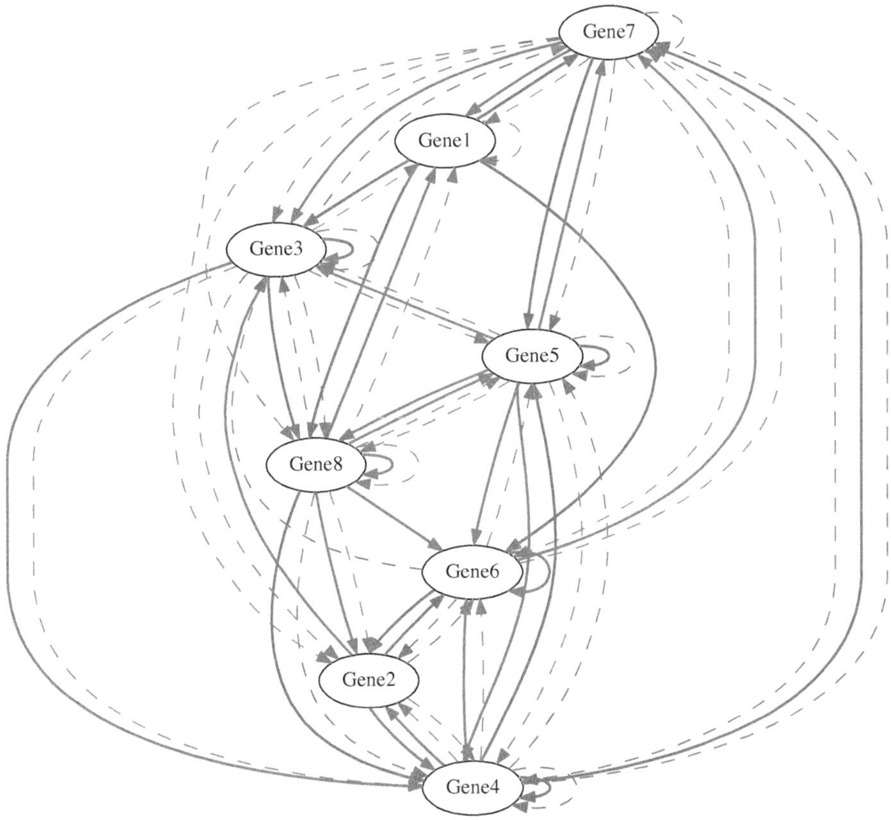

Figure 1 Inferred regulations of UKF_{p2} and true regulations.

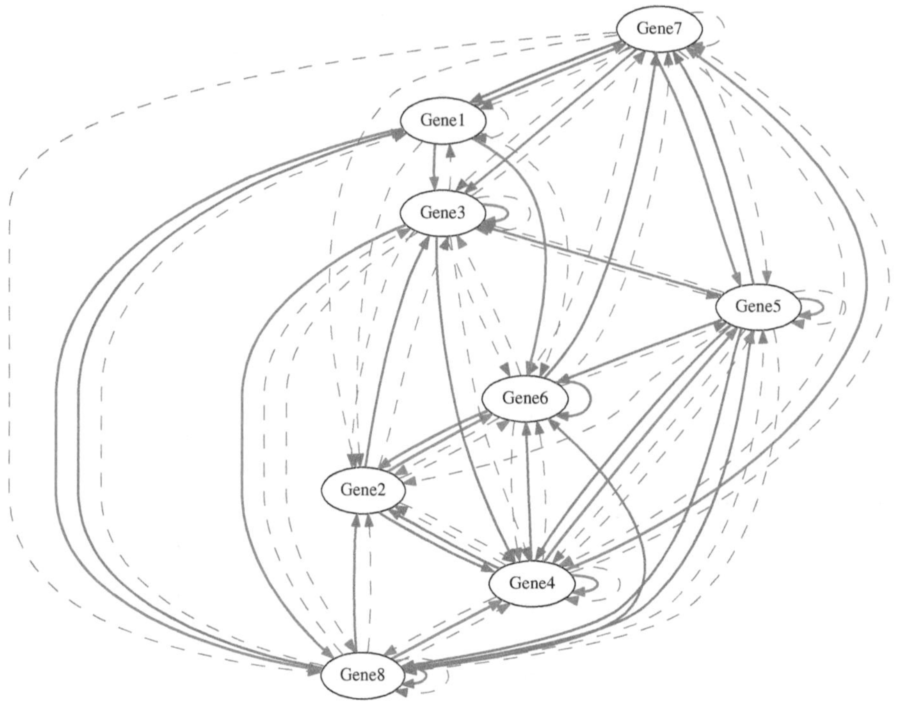

Figure 2 Inferred regulations of UKF and true regulations.

average TP# and TN# of the UKF_{p1} are both higher than those of the UKF. In addition, the average FP# and FN# of the UKF_{p1} are lower than those of the UKF. Hence, the UKF_{p1} predicts more correct links and nonlinks than the UKF. Moreover, the UKF_{p1} produces less incorrect links and missed links than the UKF. The average TPR and the precision of the UKF_{p1} are higher than those of the UKF. In addition, the average FPR of the UKF_{p1} is lower than that of the UKF. Hence, by using the existing network information, the inference accuracy can be improved.

The performance of UKF_{p1} with different λ is shown in Table 4. It is seen that the performance of UKF_{p1} and UKF is close when λ is small since only small regulation is imposed on the solution. When λ is large, the difference between the UKF_{p1} and UKF is large. In particular, the UKF_{p1} provides sparser solution than the UKF when λ is large. It can be seen from Table 4, the average FPR of UKF_{p1} decreases with the increasing of λ. The average TPR of UKF_{p1}, however, does not increase monotonically with the increasing of λ. The average PPR of UKF_{p1} increases with the increasing of λ. Hence, roughly speaking, the UKF_{p1} is better than the UKF when large λ is used.

To consider the strength of the links, rather than setting it to 1, e_{ij} (in the indicator matrix $\boldsymbol{E}$) is set to different values. Large e_{ij} is used if the strength of the link from gene j to gene i is strong. For convenience, the UKF considering the strength of links is denoted as $UKF_{\hat{p}1}$. To compare the performance of $UKF_{\hat{p}1}$ with UKF_{p1}, for $UKF_{\hat{p}1}$, the values of the second row in Equation (79) is multiplied by 5. The performance of $UKF_{\hat{p}1}$ using different λ is given in Table 5. It can be seen from Tables 4 and 5 that the performance of $UKF_{\hat{p}1}$ and UKF_{p1} is close when λ is small, e.g., $\lambda = 0.1$. In addition, the average TPR and FPR of $UKF_{\hat{p}1}$ is smaller

Table 7 Comparison of UKF_{p2} using different λ

	True positive rate			False positive rate			Positive predictive rate		
Filters	Min	Max	Avg	Min	Max	Avg	Min	Max	Avg
UKF_{p2} ($\lambda = 0.1$)	0.7576	0.9355	0.8304	0.4839	0.6970	0.5699	0.5306	0.6512	0.5914
UKF_{p2} ($\lambda = 0.5$)	0.6970	0.8710	0.7750	0.4194	0.5758	0.4902	0.5682	0.6585	0.6198
UKF_{p2} ($\lambda = 1$)	0.6970	0.7879	0.7335	0.4194	0.5000	0.4462	0.5897	0.6667	0.6355
UKF_{p2} ($\lambda = 5$)	0.4545	0.6667	0.5501	0.3226	0.4516	0.3791	0.5714	0.6471	0.6064
UKF_{p2} ($\lambda = 10$)	0.4545	0.5455	0.4800	0.2903	0.3871	0.3523	0.5556	0.6538	0.5920

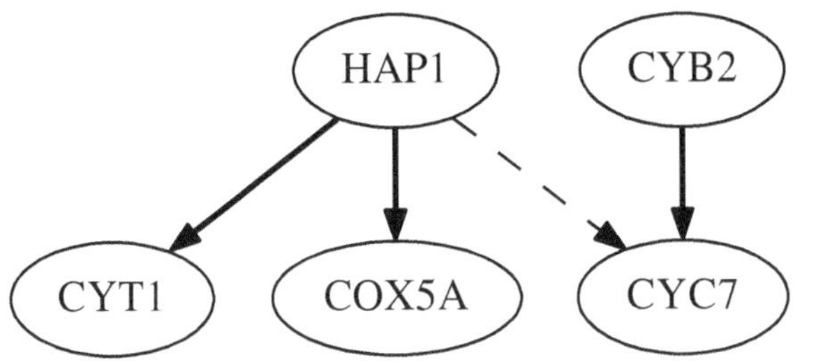

Figure 3 Pathway model of the five genes in yeast protein synthesis network.

than that of UKF_{p1} for all tested λ except for $\lambda = 0.1$. Hence, PPR is used to evaluate the performance of $\text{UKF}_{\hat{p}1}$ and UKF_{p1}. Although the average PPR of $\text{UKF}_{\hat{p}1}$ and UKF_{p1} is close when the λ is large, e.g., $\lambda = 10$, the average PPR of $\text{UKF}_{\hat{p}1}$ is consistently higher than that of UKF_{p1}. The results indicate that the inference accuracy of $\text{UKF}_{\hat{p}1}$ and UKF_{p1} are close when λ is very small or very large. The inference accuracy of $\text{UKF}_{\hat{p}1}$ outperforms UKF_{p1} when the appropriate strength of the link and parameter λ are used.

To consider the effect of false prior knowledge, the second row of the indicator matrix in Equation (79) is changed to $[0, 1, 1, 1, 0, 1, 0, 1]$, which conflicts with the truth. For convenience, we use $\text{UKF}_{\bar{p}1}$ to denote the UKF incorporating this false prior knowledge. In Table 6, the performance of $\text{UKF}_{\bar{p}1}$ with different λ is shown. It can be seen from Tables 4 and 6 that the average TPR of $\text{UKF}_{\bar{p}1}$ is smaller than that of UKF_{p1} when λ is small, e.g., $\lambda = 0.1, 0.5$. In addition, the average FPR of $\text{UKF}_{\bar{p}1}$ is larger than that of UKF_{p1} when λ is large, e.g., $\lambda = 5, 10$. Moreover, although the average PPR of $\text{UKF}_{\bar{p}1}$ is close to that of UKF_{p1} when λ is small, the average PPR of $\text{UKF}_{\bar{p}1}$ is consistently lower than that of UKF_{p1}. Hence, as expected, the results indicate that the false prior knowledge will lead to worse inference result.

Incorporating LASSO The problem setup is the same as before except that the LASSO rather than the existing network information is used. The UKF incorporating LASSO is denoted as UKF_{p2}.

As shown in Table 3, the average TP# and FP# of UKF_{p2} are lower than those of UKF and the average TN# and FN# of UKF_{p2} are higher than those of UKF. Hence, UKF_{p2} produces less links, including correct and incorrect ones.

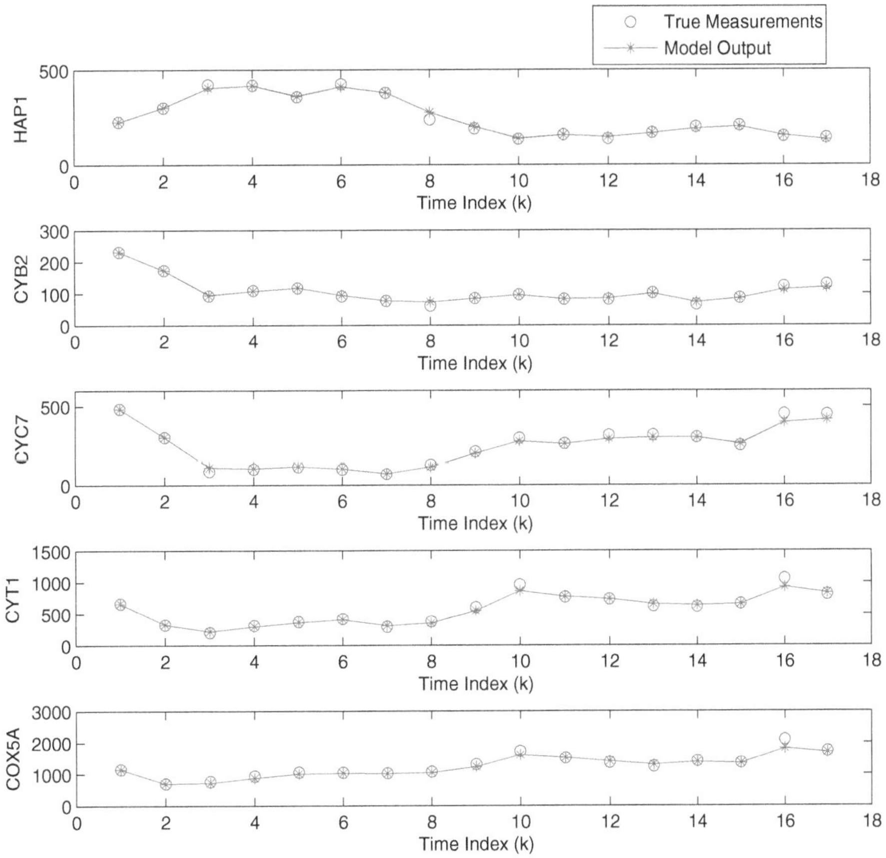

Figure 4 True gene expression and model output.

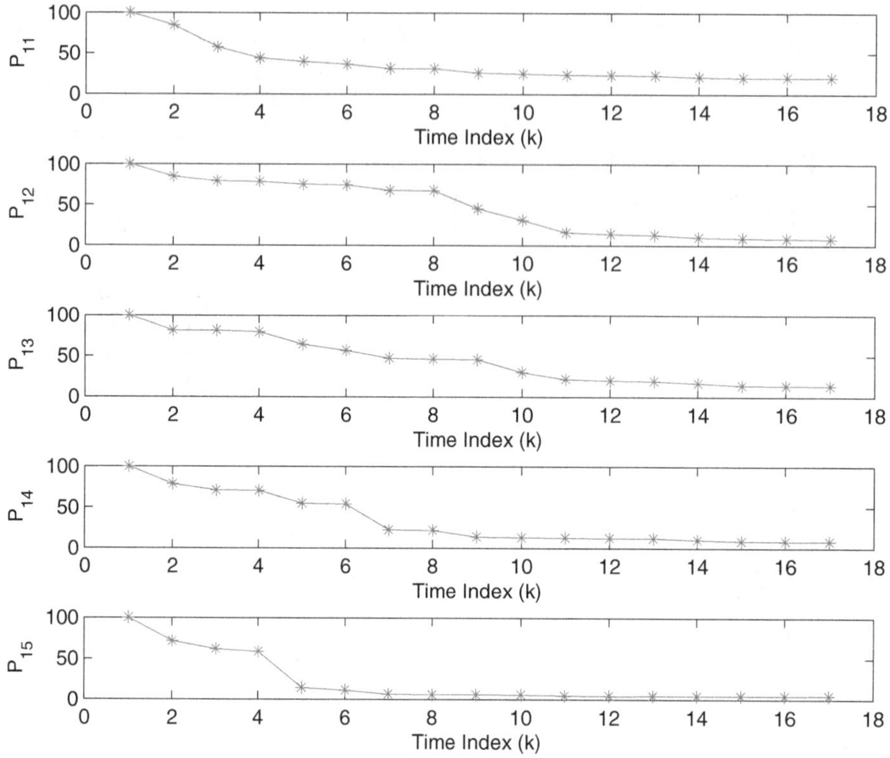

Figure 5 Variance of regulatory coefficients.

In addition, UKF_{p2} produces more nonlinks and missed links. It is consistent with the fact that the LASSO tends to provide a sparse solution. It can be seen from Table 3 that the average FPR of UKF_{p2} is lower than that of UKF and the average precision of UKF_{p2} is higher than that of UKF. Hence, by incorporating LASSO, the inference accuracy is improved.

A representative inference result of UKF_{p2} and the true regulations are shown in Figure 1. For comparison, the inference result of UKF and the true regulations are shown in Figure 2. By comparing Figure 2 and Figure 1, it can be seen that UKF falsely predicts the nonlinks from gene1 to gene2, from gene3 to gene6, from gene4 to gene8, from gene5 to gene2, and from gene6 to gene4 while UKF_{p2} does not.

The performance UKF_{p2} with different λ is shown in Table 7. It is seen that the performance of UKF_{p2} and UKF is close when λ is small since only small regulation is imposed on the solution. When λ is large, the difference between UKF_{p2} and UKF is large. The average TPR and FPR of UKF_{p2} decrease with the increasing of the λ. The average PPR does not increase monotonicallly with the increasing of λ. Generally speaking, for different λ, UKF_{p2} is more sensitive than that of UKF_{p1}. Although the performance of UKF_{p2} depends on λ, the average PPR of UKF_{p2} is consistently higher than that of UKF. Hence, roughly speaking, UKF_{p2} has better performance than UKF.

Incorporating the range constraint The existing network information can be used to provide the rough range constraint of $\bar{x}$. A tight constraint is forced on the regulation coefficient a_{ij} when there is a small regulation possibility from gene$j$ to gene$i$ and a loose constraint is forced on the regulation coefficient with no prior information.

Table 8 Inferred results of the UKF and UKF_{p2}

Filters	True positives #	False positives #	True negatives #	False negatives #
UKF	1	7	14	3
UKF_{p2}	2	3	18	2
Filters	**TPR**		**FPR**	**Precision**
UKF	0.25		0.3333	0.1250
UKF_{p2}	0.5000		0.1429	0.4000

In the simulation, for the coefficients corresponding to the zero elements in (79), the lower bound and the upper bound are set as -10 and 10, respectively. For the coefficients corresponding to the nonzero elements in (79), the lower bound and the upper bound are set as -0.1 and 0.1, respectively. The UKF incorporating the range constraint is denoted as UKF_{p3}. As shown in Table 3, the average FPR of UKF_{p3} is lower than that of UKF and the average precision of UKF_{p3} is higher than that of UKF.

5.2 Yeast protein synthesis network

In this section, time-series gene expression data of the yeast protein synthesis network is used. Five genes (HAP1, CYB2, CYC7,CYT1, and COX5A) of the yeast protein synthesis network are considered and 17 data points which can be found in [35] are collected. The regulation relationship between them has been revealed by the biological experiment and shown in Figure 3. The dashed arrow in Figure 3 denotes 'repression' and the solid arrow denotes 'activation.'

The GRN is inferred by the UKF and UKF_{p2}. The predicted gene expressions using parameters estimated by UKF_{p2} and the true measured gene expressions are shown in Figure 4. It can be seen that the model output fits the measured data well. The variances of the regulatory coefficients of HAP1 ($P_{1i}(1 \leq i \leq 5)$) are shown in Figure 5. It can be seen that the filter converges since the variance P_{1i} approaches zero. The results for other regulatory coefficients are similar and not shown here. The evaluation of the inferred GRN by UKF and UKF_{p2} is shown in Table 8.

By incorporating the sparsity constraint, UKF_{p2} provides much better inference results than UKF. As shown in Table 8, the TP# and TN# of UKF_{p2} are higher than those of UKF and the FP# and FN# are lower than those of UKF. In addition, it can be seen from Table 8, the FPR of UKF_{p2} is lower than that of UKF and the TPR and the precision of UKF_{p2} is higher than that of UKF.

6 Conclusions

In this paper, we have proposed a framework of employing the point-based Gaussian approximation filters which incorporates the prior knowledge to infer the gene regulatory network (GRN) based on the gene expression data. The performance of the proposed framework is tested by a synthetic network and the yeast protein synthesis network. Numerical results show that the inference accuracy of the GRN by the proposed point-based Gaussian approximation filter incorporating the prior information is higher than using the traditional filters without incorporating prior knowledge. The proposed method works for small- and medium-size GRNs due to the computational complexity considerations. It remains a future research topic how to adapt the proposed inference framework to handle large GRNs at reasonable computational complexity.

Competing interests

All authors declare that they have no competing interests.

Author details

[1]Intelligent Fusion Technology, Germantown, MD 20876, USA. [2]Department of Electrical Engineering, Columbia University, New York, NY 10027, USA.

References

1. M Zou, SD Conzen, A new dynamic Bayesian network (dbn) approach for identifying gene regulatory networks from time course microarray data. Bioinformatics **21**(1), 71–79 (2005)
2. X Zhou, X Wang, R Pal, I Ivanov, M Bittner, ER Dougherty, A Bayesian connectivity-based approach to constructing probabilistic gene regulatory networks. Bioinformatics **20**(17), 2918–2927 (2004)
3. M Quach, N Brunel, F d'Alché Buc, Estimating parameters and hidden variables in non-linear state-space models based on odes for biological networks inference. Bioinformatics **23**(23), 3209–3216 (2007)
4. Z Wang, X Liu, Y Liu, J Liang, V Vinciotti, An extended Kalman filtering approach to modeling nonlinear dynamic gene regulatory networks via short gene expression time series. Comput. Biol. Bioinformatics, IEEE/ACM Trans. **6**(3), 410–419 (2009)
5. X Wu, P Li, N Wang, P Gong, EJ Perkins, Y Deng, C Zhang, State space model with hidden variables for reconstruction of gene regulatory networks. BMC Syst Biol. **5**(Suppl 3), S3 (2011)
6. AV Werhli, D Husmeier, Reconstructing gene regulatory networks with Bayesian networks by combining expression data with multiple sources of prior knowledge. Stat. Appl. Genet. Mol. Biol. **6**, Article 15 (2007)
7. J Mazur, D Ritter, G Reinelt, L Kaderali, Reconstructing nonlinear dynamic models of gene regulation using stochastic sampling. BMC Bioinformatics **10**, 448 (2009)
8. A Noor, E Serpedin, M Nounou, H Nounou, Inferring gene regulatory networks via nonlinear state-space models and exploiting sparsity. Comput. Biol. Bioinformatics, IEEE/ACM Trans. **9**(4), 1203–1211 (2012)
9. M Hecker, S Lambeck, S Toepfer, E van Someren, R Guthke, Gene regulatory network inference: Data integration in dynamic models - a review. Biosystems **96**(1), 86–103 (2009)
10. F Markowetz, R Spang, Inferring cellular networks - a review. BMC Bioinformatics **8**(Suppl 6), S5 (2007)
11. Y Huang, I Tienda-Luna, Y Wang, Reverse engineering gene regulatory networks. Signal Process. Mag., IEEE **26**(1), 76–97 (2009)
12. H de Jong, Modeling and simulation of genetic regulatory systems: a literature review. J. Comput. Biol. **9**, 67–103 (2002)
13. SJ Julier, JK Uhlmann, Unscented filtering and nonlinear estimation. Proc. IEEE **92**(3), 401–422 (2004)
14. K Ito, K Xiong, Gaussian filters for nonlinear filtering problems. Automatic Control, IEEE Trans. **45**(5), 910–927 (2000)
15. I Arasaratnam, S Haykin, Cubature kalman filters. Automatic Control, IEEE Trans. **54**(6), 1254–1269 (2009)
16. B Jia, M Xin, Y Cheng, Sparse-grid quadrature nonlinear filtering. Automatica **48**(2), 327–341 (2012)
17. M Arulampalam, S Maskell, N Gordon, T Clapp, A tutorial on particle filters for online nonlinear/non-Gaussian Bayesian tracking. Signal Process., IEEE Trans. **50**(2), 174–188 (2002)
18. X Shen, H Vikalo, Inferring parameters of gene regulatory networks via particle filtering. EURASIP J. Adv. Signal Process. **2010**, 204612 (2010)
19. E Steele, A Tucker, PA 't Hoen, M Schuemie, Literature-based priors for gene regulatory networks. Bioinformatics **25**(14), 1768–1774 (2009)
20. S Christley, Q Nie, X Xie, Incorporating existing network information into gene network inference. PLoS ONE **4**(8), e6799 (2009)
21. Y Tamada, S Kim, H Bannai, S Imoto, K Tashiro, S Kuhara, S Miyano, Estimating gene networks from gene expression data by combining

Bayesian network model with promoter element detection. Bioinformatics **19**(suppl 2), 227–236 (2003)
22. H Li, M Zhan, Unraveling transcriptional regulatory programs by integrative analysis of microarray and transcription factor binding data. Bioinformatics **24**(17), 1874–1880 (2008)
23. N Bouaynaya, R Shterenberg, D Schonfeld, Methods for optimal intervention in gene regulatory networks [applications corner]. Signal Process. Mag., IEEE **29**(1), 158–163 (2012)
24. L Chen, K Aihara, Chaos and asymptotical stability in discrete-time neural networks. Physica D: Nonlinear Phenomena **104**(3), 286–325 (1997)
25. L Qian, H Wang, ER Dougherty, Inference of noisy nonlinear differential equation models for gene regulatory networks using genetic programming and Kalman filtering. Signal Process., IEEE Trans. **56**(7), 3327–3339 (2008)
26. J Vohradsky, Neural model of the genetic network. J. Biol. Chem. **276**(39), 36168–36173 (2001)
27. E Mjolsness, T Mann, R Castano, B Wold, From coexpression to coregulation: an approach to inferring transcriptional regulation among gene classes from large-scale expression data. in *Advances in Neural Information Processing Systems* **12**, 928–934 (1999)
28. M Nørgaard, NK Poulsen, O Ravn, New developments in state estimation for nonlinear systems. Automatica **36**(11), 1627–1638 (2000)
29. IP Mysovskikh, *The Approximation of Multiple Integrals by Using Interpolatory Cubature Formulae in Quantitative Approximation*, ed. by R DeVore, K Scherer (Academic Press, New York, 1980)
30. AH Jazwinski, *Stochastic Processes and Filtering Theory* (Academic Press Inc., Waltham, MA, 2007)
31. BO Teixeira, LA Tôrres, LA Aguirre, DS Bernstein, On unscented Kalman filtering with state interval constraints. J. Process Control **20**(1), 45–57 (2010)
32. S Wright, R Nowak, M Figueiredo, Sparse reconstruction by separable approximation. Signal Process., IEEE Trans. **57**(7), 2479–2493 (2009)
33. D Simon, DL Simon, Constrained Kalman filtering via density function truncation for turbofan engine health estimation. Int. J. Syst. Sci. **41**(2), 159–171 (2010)
34. F Emmert-Strib, M Dehmer, *Analysis of Microarray Data* (Wiley-Blackwell, Hoboken, NJ, 2008)
35. H Wang, L Qian, E Dougherty, Inference of gene regulatory networks using s-system: a unified approach. Syst. Biol., IET **4**(2), 145–156 (2010)

4

Phase computations and phase models for discrete molecular oscillators

Onder Suvak* and Alper Demir

Abstract

Background: Biochemical oscillators perform crucial functions in cells, e.g., they set up circadian clocks. The dynamical behavior of oscillators is best described and analyzed in terms of the scalar quantity, *phase*. A rigorous and useful definition for phase is based on the so-called *isochrons* of oscillators. Phase computation techniques for continuous oscillators that are based on isochrons have been used for characterizing the behavior of various types of oscillators under the influence of perturbations such as noise.

Results: In this article, we extend the applicability of these phase computation methods to biochemical oscillators as discrete molecular systems, upon the information obtained from a continuous-state approximation of such oscillators. In particular, we describe techniques for computing the instantaneous phase of discrete, molecular oscillators for stochastic simulation algorithm generated sample paths. We comment on the accuracies and derive certain measures for assessing the feasibilities of the proposed phase computation methods. Phase computation experiments on the sample paths of well-known biological oscillators validate our analyses.

Conclusions: The impact of noise that arises from the discrete and random nature of the mechanisms that make up molecular oscillators can be characterized based on the phase computation techniques proposed in this article. The concept of isochrons is the natural choice upon which the phase notion of oscillators can be founded. The isochron-theoretic phase computation methods that we propose can be applied to discrete molecular oscillators of any dimension, provided that the oscillatory behavior observed in discrete-state does not vanish in a continuous-state approximation. Analysis of the full versatility of phase noise phenomena in molecular oscillators will be possible if a proper phase model theory is developed, without resorting to such approximations.

Keywords: discrete molecular oscillators, oscillator phase, noise, phase noise, numerical methods, Monte Carlo methods, Stochastic Simulation Algorithm (SSA), isochrons, phase equations, phase computation schemes, phase models

1. Introduction

1.1 Oscillators in biological and electronic systems

Oscillatory behavior is encountered in many types of systems including electronic, optical, mechanical, biological, chemical, financial, social and climatological systems. Carefully designed oscillators are intentionally introduced into many engineered systems to provide essential functionality for system operation. In electronic systems, oscillators are used to generate clock signals that are needed in the synchronization of operations in digital circuits and sampled-data systems. The periodic signal generated by an electronic oscillator or monochromatic light from a laser is used as a carrier and for frequency translation of signals in wireless and optical communication systems. Oscillatory behavior in biological systems is seen in population dynamics models (prey-predator systems), in neural systems [1], in the motor system, and in circadian rhythms [2]. Intracellular and intercellular oscillators of various types perform crucial functions in biological systems. Due to their essentialness, and intricate and interesting dynamic behavior, biological oscillations have been a research focus for decades. Genetic oscillators that are responsible for setting up the circadian rhythms have received particular attention [3]. Circadian rhythms are crucial for the survival of many species, and there are many

* Correspondence: osuvak@ku.edu.tr
Department of Electrical and Electronics Engineering, College of Engineering, Koç University Rumeli Feneri Yolu 34450 Sariyer Istanbul, Turkey

health problems associated with the disturbance of these clocks in humans [4,5]. For instance, working night shifts has been recently listed as a probable cause of cancer by the World Health Organization [6-8]. A milestone in synthetic biology is the work in [9] reporting on a genetic regulatory network called the repressilator, essentially a synthetic genetic oscillator.

Oscillators in electronic and telecommunication systems are adversely affected by the presence of undesired disturbances in the system. Various types of disturbances such as noise affect the spectral and timing properties of the ideally periodic signals generated by oscillators, resulting in power spreading in the spectrum and jitter and phase drift in the time domain [10]. Unlike other systems which contain an implicit or explicit time reference, autonomously oscillating systems respond to noise in a peculiar and somewhat nonintuitive manner. Understanding the behavior of oscillators used in electronic systems in the presence of disturbances and noise has been a preoccupation for researchers for many decades [11]. The behavior of biological oscillators under various types of disturbances has also been the focus of a good deal of research work in the second half of the 20th century [1,2,12,13].

1.2 Phase models for oscillators

The dynamical behavior of oscillators is best described and analyzed in terms of the scalar quantity, *phase*. Of the pertaining notions in the literature, the most straightforward phase definition is obtained when a planar oscillator is expressed in polar coordinates, with amplitude and polar angle as the state variables. The usefulness of the polar angle as phase does not generalize to higher dimensional oscillators. In the general case, it is our conviction that the most rigorous and precise definition of phase is the one that is based on the so-called *isochrons* (formed from in-phase points in the state-space) of an oscillator [1,2,14,15]. The notion of isochrons was first proposed by Winfree [2,14] in 1974. It was later revealed that isochrons are intimately related to the notion of asymptotic phase in the theory of differential equations [16,17]. The isochron theoretic phase of a free-running, noiseless oscillator is simply time itself. Such an unperturbed oscillator serves as a perfect time keeper if it is in the process of converging to a limit cycle, even when it has not yet settled to a periodic steady-state solution. Perturbations make the actual phase deviate from time, due to the degrading impact of disturbances on the time keeping ability.

Phase is a quantity that compactly describes the dynamical behavior of an oscillator. One is then interested in computing the phase of a perturbed oscillator. If this can be done in a semi or fully analytical manner for a practical oscillator, one can draw conclusions and obtain useful characterizations in assessing the time keeping performance. Indeed, we observe in the literature that, in various disciplines, researchers have derived *phase equations* that compactly describe the dynamics of weakly perturbed oscillators [1,11]. It appears that a phase equation for oscillators has first been derived by Malkin [18] in his work on the reduction of weakly perturbed oscillators to their phase models [1], and the same equation has been subsequently reinvented by various other researchers in several disciplines [2,11,19]. This phase equation has been used in mathematical biology to study circadian rhythms and coupled oscillators in the models of neurological systems [1,2,20], and in electronics for the analysis of phase noise and timing jitter in oscillators [11,21]. Phase equations have great utility in performing (semi) analytical phase computations. However, simpler and more accurate schemes for numerical phase computations have been recently proposed [15,22]. In some applications, merely a technique for computing the instantaneous phase of an oscillator for a given perturbation is needed. In this case, not only the machinery of phase equations is not necessary but also one can perform *more accurate* phase computations in a much simpler and straightforward manner.

1.3 Phase computations for discrete oscillators

We have proposed in [15] a numerical method for the computation of quadratic approximations for the isochrons of oscillators. In [22], we have reviewed the derivation of the first-order phase equation (which is based on the linear approximations for isochrons [1,2,20]), with a formulation based on the isochron-theoretic oscillator phase. On top of this, in [22] we have also made use of again the quadratic isochron approximations of [15] to derive a novel second-order phase equation that is more accurate than the first-order. However, the phase equations [22] and phase computation schemes [15] discussed above are founded on continuous oscillators described by differential equations. Therefore, these models and techniques do not directly apply to the analysis of molecular oscillators with discrete-space models. In this article, we present a methodology, enabling the application of these continuous phase models [22] and the phase computation schemes [15] on biological oscillators modeled in a discrete manner at the molecular level. Our preliminary results recently appeared in a workshop presentation [23]. This article details and expands on our contributions over this methodology.

We now summarize the workflow followed in the methodology and also give an outline of the article. Section 2 provides background information describing how the discrete model of the oscillator is transformed into a continuous, differential equation model through a limiting process based on the assumption that the concentration of molecular species in the model of the oscillator are large so that discrete effects are negligible [24-30]. It should be particularly noted that the reaction events in an SSA sample path (as generated by Gillespie's Stochastic Simulation Algorithm (SSA) [25]) are the most crucial ingredients in translating the continuous-state formalism on oscillator phase for use on molecular oscillators.

Section 3 actually describes our major contribution, i. e., how discrete-state oscillator phase computation is accomplished using the paradigms of phase equations and phase computation schemes. Using the phase modeling techniques mentioned above, a continuous phase model (depending on the model developed in Section 2) is constructed and discretized. The noise sources in this discretized phase model are represented as a cumulation of the events occurring in the discrete model of the oscillator. This two-way continuous-discrete transformation mechanism enables us to perform phase computations for discrete, molecular oscillators based on the continuous phase model theory [22]. Moreover, the fact that the noise sources in the phase computation are synthesized from the same events in the SSA sample path makes one-to-one comparisons with full SSA [25] based simulations possible. The phase model constructed as such from the continuous-limit model of the oscillator is accurate when a large number of molecules exist for every species. However, in many biological molecular oscillators, the number of molecules can be quite small. Large deviations from the continuous limit for such oscillators cause computations via continuous first-order phase models based on linear isochron approximations to become inaccurate. This was the observation that prompted our work on the quadratic (as opposed to linear) approximation theory and computational techniques for the isochrons of oscillators [15,22]. With phase computation schemes based on quadratic isochron approximations [15], deviations from the continuous-deterministic limit are much better captured and more accurate phase computations for discrete oscillators even with few molecules can be performed.

In Section 4, we provide a brief literature review of the approaches taken in the phase noise analysis of oscillators. Several seminal articles in the literature [11,31-36] are categorized according to three classification schemes in particular: the nature of the oscillator model used, the nature of the analysis method, and the phase definition adopted. We also classify in Section 4 the approach proposed in this article within the same framework.

Section 5 provides performance results for the proposed phase computation methods running on intricate molecular oscillators. The results are as expected, i.e., phase equations are quite accurate and fast for oscillators in a larger volume with big molecule numbers for the species, but they lose accuracy when a smaller volume is considered and noise effects become pronounced. Phase computation schemes are always very accurate, even in smaller volumes, but they are not as fast as the equations. Several crucial points in the theory underlying the methods are also emphasized in the discussion throughout this section. Section 6 concludes the article and suggests some future research directions.

The next three sections constitute the detailed explanation of the proposed methods. Sections 7 and 8 are expanded versions of Sections 2 and 3, respectively, with hints and references to derivations. Section 9 explains how and where molecular oscillator models can be obtained to test the proposed algorithms, which types of information are obtained from the models in preparation for oscillator phase analysis, numerical implementation details for the proposed phase computation methods, and in this section are also derived the computational complexities for these methods.

2 Modeling and simulation of discrete molecular oscillators

Biochemical models for molecular oscillators are generally specified as a set of molecular species participating in a number of reactions with predefined propensities. These models based on a stochastic chemical kinetics formalism capture the inherent stochastic and noisy behavior arising from the discrete and random nature of molecules and reactions. The (instantaneous) number of each molecular species, i.e., reactant, constitutes the state of the model. The time-dependent state probabilities for the system are described precisely with the Chemical Master Equation (CME) [28]. The generic form of the CME is as in

$$\frac{d\,\mathbb{P}(\mathbf{x},t)}{dt} = \sum_{j=1}^{M} \left[a_j(\mathbf{x}-\mathbf{s}_j)\,\mathbb{P}\,(\mathbf{x}-\mathbf{s}_j,t) - a_j(\mathbf{x})\,\mathbb{P}\,(\mathbf{x},t)\right] \tag{1}$$

Above in (1), $\mathbf{x}$ represents the state of a molecular oscillator. The solution of this equation yields $\mathbb{P}(\mathbf{x},t)$, i.e., the probability that the oscillator is visiting a certain state $\mathbf{x}$ at time t. Also, in (1), $a_j(\mathbf{x})$ is called the *propensity* of the j th reaction (note that we have M possible reactions), while the oscillator is again visiting the state $\mathbf{x}$. This propensity function facilitates the quantification of how much of a probability we have of reaction j occuring in the next infinitesimal time. The constant vector $\mathbf{s}_j$ defines the changes in the numbers of molecules for the species constituting the oscillatory system, when reaction j occurs. The CME corresponds to a continuous-time Markov chain. Due to the exponential number of state configurations for the system, CME is generally very hard to construct and solve. Therefore, one prefers to generate sample paths for the system using Gillespie's SSA [25], whose ensemble obeys the probability law dictated by the CME.

Continuous state-space models for molecular oscillators that serve as approximations to the discrete model described above are also used. Based on the CME and employing certain assumptions and approximations, one may derive a continuous state-space model as a system of stochastic differential equations, known as the Chemical Langevin Equations (CLEs). A CLE is of the generic form in

$$\frac{\mathrm{d}\,\mathbf{X}(t)}{\mathrm{d}t} = \mathbf{S}\;\mathbf{a}(\mathbf{X}(t)) + \mathbf{S}\mathbb{D}\left(\left[\sqrt{\mathbf{a}(\mathbf{X}(t))}\right]\right)\xi(t) \tag{2}$$

Above in (2), $\mathbf{X}(t)$ is the state of the oscillator, i.e., the solution of the SDE for a particular realization. Vectors $\mathbf{s}_j$ defined above are stacked side by side for all of the M reactions to compose the stoichiometric matrix $\mathbf{S}$ in (2). Note also that $\mathbb{D}\left(\left[\sqrt{\mathbf{a}(\mathbf{X}(t))}\right]\right)$ is a square diagonal matrix with its diagonal entries given by $\sqrt{a_j(\mathbf{X}(t))}$ for $j = 1, ..., M$, with $\mathbf{a}(\mathbf{X}(t))$ the vector of propensity functions. The vector $\xi(t)$ is composed of independent zero-mean Gaussian random variables with variance one. The deterministic limit of the CLEs is in turn called the Reaction Rate Equations (RREs). The generic form of an RRE is as in

$$\frac{\mathrm{d}\,\mathbf{X}(t)}{\mathrm{d}t} = \sum_{j=1}^{M} \mathbf{s}_j\, a_j(\mathbf{X}(t)) = \mathbf{S}\;\mathbf{a}(\mathbf{X}(t)) \tag{3}$$

which is mathematically obtained by crossing out the second term on the right-hand side of (2). The RRE model for an oscillator has a solution that is perfectly periodic without noisy fluctuations. On the other hand, the solution of the CLEs produces oscillatory sample paths with fluctuations around the periodic orbit on top of the deterministic solution of the RREs [28].

The reader is referred to Figure 1, in which a summary of the models (along with their respective natures) for molecular oscillators and the algorithms used to solve these models are provided. The instantaneous phase computations we describe in this article are performed on the sample paths generated by SSA simulations based on a fully discrete model of the oscillator. However, the isochron characterization (computation of linear and quadratic isochron approximations) for the oscillator is based on the continuous-space RRE and CLE model, as we describe in the next section.

3 Phase computations based on Langevin models

In performing phase characterizations, we compute sample paths for the instantaneous phase $\hat{t}$ (in units of time) of a molecular oscillator. In the absence of noise and disturbances, i.e., for an unperturbed oscillator, the phase $\hat{t}$ is always exactly equal to time t itself, even if the oscillator is not at periodic steady-state. Perturbations and noise result in deviations in the phase $\hat{t}$ and cause it to be different from time t [1,2,11,15,22]. The perpetual effect of noise and disturbances causes this deviation in the phase $\hat{t}$ to accumulate. Our goal is to compute the instantaneous phase $\hat{t}$ that corresponds to an SSA generated sample path for a molecular oscillator. A pictorial description of this phase computation problem for oscillators is given in Figure 2.

We assume that the deterministic RREs for a molecular oscillator have a stable periodic solution $\mathbf{x}_s(t)$ that represents a periodic orbit or limit cycle. An isochron of an oscillator associated with the limit cycle $\mathbf{x}_s(t)$ is a set of points (in the state-space) that have the same phase. For an oscillator with N state variables, each isochron is an N-1*-dimensional hypersurface*. The union of isochrons covers the neighborhood of its periodic orbit [1,14]. See Figure 3 for the limit cycle and isochrons of a simple polar oscillator. Isochrons form the basis for a rigorous phase definition and phase computations for oscillators [22]. Another crucial quantity in devising phase computation schemes, in addition to isochrons, is the orbital deviation, i.e., the instantaneous difference between the noisy oscillator state and the in-phase point on the limit cycle (by definition, the two points are on the same isochron) [22].

The perturbation projection vector (PPV) $\mathbf{v}(t)$ is defined as the *gradient* of the *phase* $\hat{t}$ of an oscillator [22] on the limit cycle represented by $\mathbf{x}_s(t)$. The PPV, which is equivalent to the infinitesimal *phase response curves (PRCs)* [1], is instrumental in forming linear approximations for the isochrons of an oscillator. The matrix $\mathbf{H}(t)$ is defined as the *Hessian* of the phase $\hat{t}$ (and the Jacobian of the PPV) [22] on the limit cycle. The phase Hessian $\mathbf{H}(t)$ is useful in forming quadratic approximations for the isochrons of an oscillator. The PPV $\mathbf{v}(t)$ and the Hessian $\mathbf{H}(t)$ can be computed using the techniques described in [15].

Phase equations (differential equations for the phase $\hat{t}$) can be derived based on the CLE model of an oscillator. Phase equations come in various flavors, depending on whether a linear or quadratic approximation is used for the isochrons and the orbital deviation [22]. The acclaimed phase equation, used in multiple disciplines [1,2,11], of the form

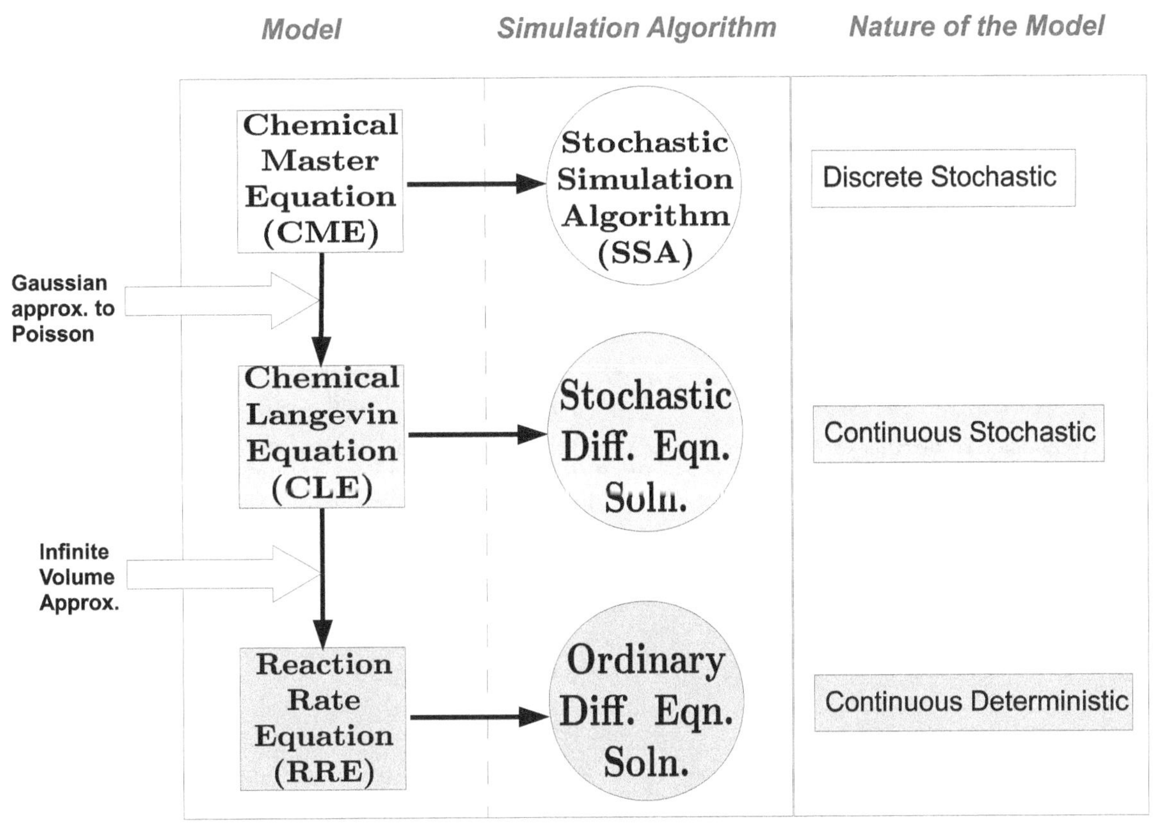

Figure 1 Summary of molecular models and corresponding algorithms. The models, their natures, and the simulation algorithms for these models are given. CME (of discrete stochastic nature) dictates the probability evolution of the ensemble of the sample paths generated by the SSA algorithm. Applying to the CME the τ-leap criterion and Gaussian approximation to Poisson random variables, CLE (continuous stochastic) is derived. CLE sample paths are obtained via appropriate SDE Solutions. The infinite volume approximation acting on the CLE leads us to the RRE (continuous deterministic), whose solutions we get through algorithms for ODEs.

$$\frac{d\hat{t}}{dt} = 1 + \mathbf{v}^T(\hat{t})\mathbf{b}(\mathbf{x}_s(\hat{t}), t) \tag{4}$$

is based on linear isochron approximations and a linear differential equation for the orbital deviation (not shown here). Above, **b** is the noise excitation which is synthesized as a cumulation of the events that occur in the discrete, molecular level model of the oscillator. We call the model of (4) PhEqnLL (the first L for the isochron and the second one for the orbital deviation approximation, the natures of both of which are linear). We also have PhEqnQQ (quadratic approximations for both isochrons and orbital deviation) and PhEqnQL (quadratic approximations for isochrons and linear approximations for orbital deviation) [22]. See Figure 4 for a high-level representation of the phase computations methodology using phase equations.

With the phase equations based on linear and quadratic isochron approximations, we can compute the phase of an oscillator without having to run SSA simulations based on its discrete, molecular model (unless a one-to-one comparison between the results of phase computations based on phase equations and SSA simulations is required). On the other hand, more accurate phase computations can be attained if they are based on, i.e., use information, from SSA simulations. In this scheme, we run an SSA simulation based on the discrete, molecular model of the oscillator. For points (in the state-space) on the sample path generated by the SSA simulation, we compute a corresponding phase by essentially determining the isochron on which the point in question lies. Here, one can either employ no approximations (PhCompBF) for the isochrons or perform phase computations based on linear (PhCompLin) or quadratic

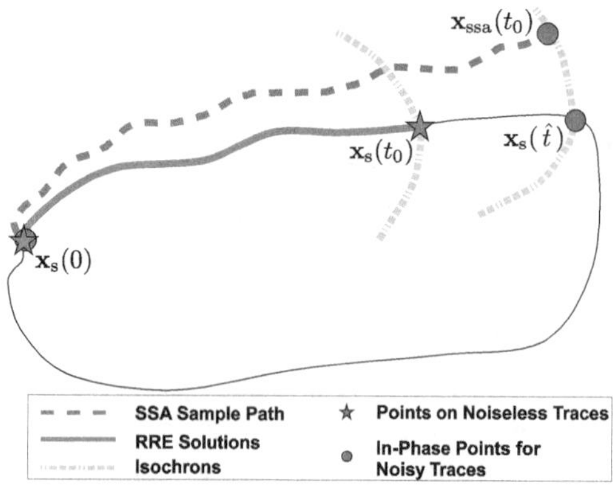

Figure 2 Phase computation problem for oscillators. The two trajectories $\mathbf{x}_s(t)$, the periodic solution of the RRE, and $\mathbf{x}_{ssa}(t)$, a sample path, start at the same point on the limit cycle, but at $t = t_0$ they end up at different points and possibly on different isochrons. The point $\mathbf{x}_{ssa}(t_0)$ has registered a phase shift with respect to $\mathbf{x}_s(t_0)$. According to isochron theory, there is a point $\mathbf{x}_s(\hat{t})$ that is on the same isochron as $\mathbf{x}_{ssa}(t_0)$, therefore the two points are in-phase. The time argument $\hat{t}$ of the point $\mathbf{x}_s(\hat{t})$ is the instantaneous phase value of $\mathbf{x}_{ssa}(t_0)$. Phase computation methods aim to calculate this value $\hat{t}$.

(PhCompQuad) isochron approximations. Brute-force phase computations without isochron approximations (PhCompBF) are computationally costly [15,22]. See Figure 5 for a pictorial description of PhCompBF. Phase computations based on isochron approximations and SSA simulations proceeds as follows: Let $\mathbf{x}_{ssa}(t)$ be the

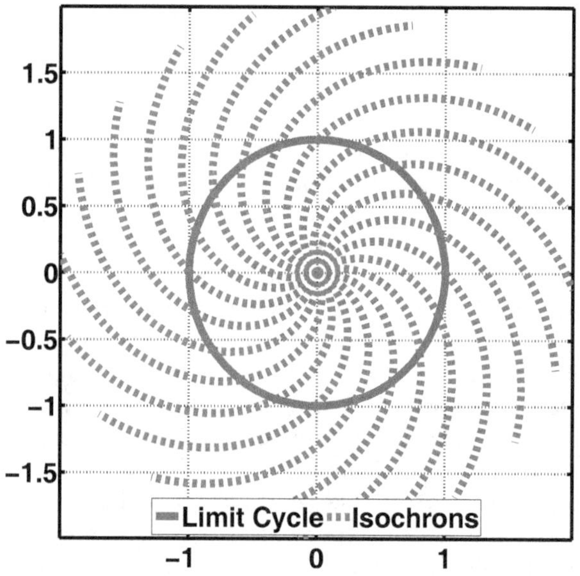

Figure 3 Limit cycle and isochrons of a polar oscillator (figure from [15]). For this oscillator, the isochrons are analytically calculable. Note that each isochron crosses the limit cycle exactly at a single point.

sample path for the state vector of the oscillator that is being computed with SSA. We solve

$$\mathbf{v}^T(\hat{t})\left[\mathbf{x}_{ssa}(t) - \mathbf{x}_s(\hat{t})\right] = 0 \tag{5}$$

based on linear isochron approximations (PhCompLin)–or a similar equation that also involves the phase Hessian $\mathbf{H}(t)$ based on quadratic isochron approximations (PhCompQuad)–for the phase $\hat{t}$ that corresponds to $\mathbf{x}_{ssa}(t)$. Figure 6 provides a description for PhCompLin. The above computation needs to be repeated for every time point t of interest. Above, for $\mathbf{x}_{ssa}(t)$, we essentially determine the isochron (in fact, a linear or quadratic approximation for it) that passes through both the point $\mathbf{x}_s(\hat{t})$ on the limit cycle and $\mathbf{x}_{ssa}(t)$. The phase of $\mathbf{x}_s(\hat{t})$, i.e., $\hat{t}$, is then the phase of $\mathbf{x}_{ssa}(t)$ as well since they reside on the same isochron. We should note here that, even though $\mathbf{x}_{ssa}(t)$ above is computed with an SSA simulation based on the discrete model of the oscillator, the steady-state periodic solution $\mathbf{x}_s(\hat{t})$, the phase gradient $\mathbf{v}(\hat{t})$ and the Hessian $\mathbf{H}(\hat{t})$ (i.e., all of the information that is used in constructing the isochron approximations) are computed based on the continuous, RRE model of the oscillator. See Figure 7 for the high-level representation of the phase computations methodology using phase computation schemes. The phase computation schemes we describe here can be regarded as *hybrid* techniques that are based both on the continuous, RRE and also the discrete, molecular model of the oscillator. On the other hand, the phase computations based on phase equations are completely founded upon the continuous, RRE and CLE models of the oscillator.

In summary, we point out the acronyms and some properties of the proposed phase computation methods for convenience. The phase equations are PhEqnLL, PhEqnQL, and PhEqnQQ. The phase computation schemes are PhCompBF (the most accurate but computationally expensive method), PhCompLin, and PhCompQuad. The schemes employ no approximations in orbital deviation, therefore they are expected to be more accurate with respect to the equations. The equations, on the other hand, have low computational complexity and can generate results very fast. We also show in this article that there is a trade-off between accuracy and computational complexity for these methods.

4 Related work

A classification scheme for categorizing previous work, pertaining to the phase noise analysis of biochemical oscillators, can be described as follows.

First, we note that there are basically two types of models for inherently noisy biochemical oscillators, i.e., discrete and continuous-state. CME describes the

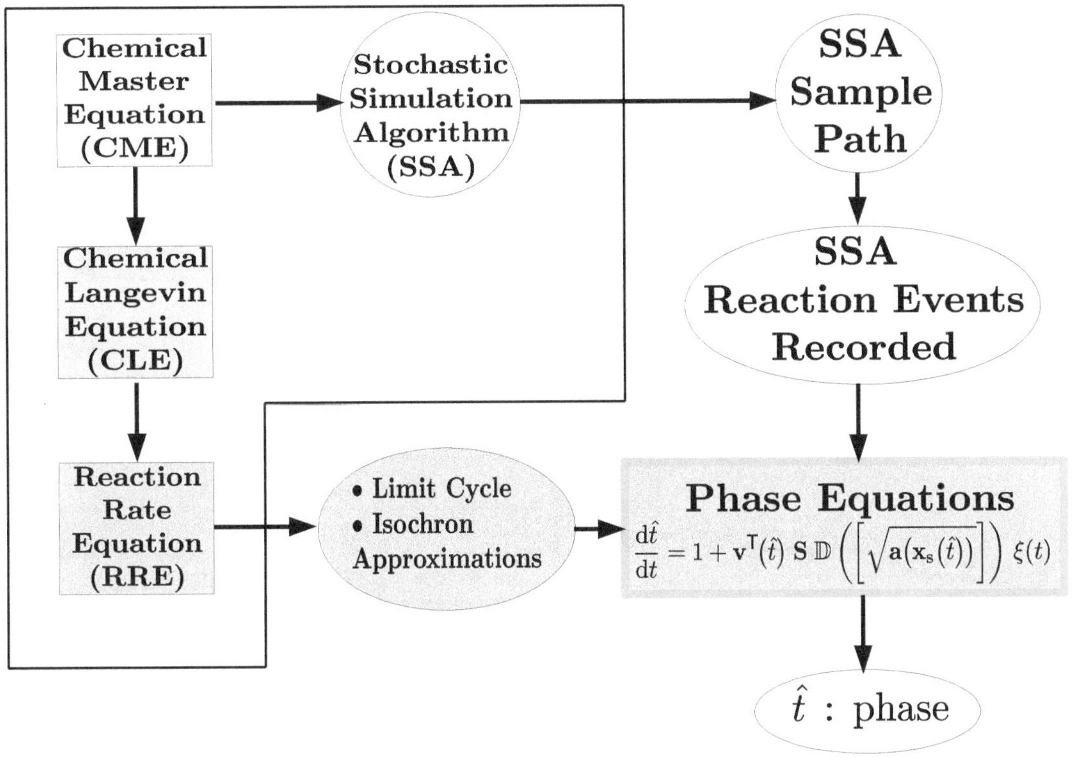

Figure 4 Phase computations through phase equations methodology. The events in the SSA-generated sample path are recorded. From the RRE, the limit cycle and isochron approximation information is computed. Phase equations make use of these two pieces of information to compute the instantaneous phase corresponding to each point in the sample path. The first-order phase equation as adapted to this methodology is given in the figure.

probabilistic evolution of the states of an oscillator, and it is referred to as the most accurate characterization for discrete molecular oscillators. Through approximations, one derives from CME the CLE, a continuous-state noisy model. CLE can be used to extract crucial information about the continuous-state system that is an approximate representation of its discrete-state ancestor. We note here that, in oscillator phase noise analyses, mostly the continuous-state model has been utilized [11,31-36].

Second, the nature of the phase noise analyses conducted can be considered in two categories, i.e., semi-analytical techniques and sample path-based approaches. Semi-analytical techniques have been developed, in particular, for the stochastic characterization of phase diffusion in oscillators [11,31-36]. In biology, CLE has been used as a tool in illustrating and quantifying the phase diffusion phenomena [31-34,36]. Characterization and computations pertaining to phase diffusion in electronic oscillators were carried out through a stochastic phase equation and the probabilistic evolution of its solutions [11], noting that the phase equation used was derived from an SDE (a Stochastic Differential Equation describing a noisy electronic oscillator) that corresponds to the CLE for biochemical oscillators. In all, these semi-analytical techniques are based on the continuous-state model of an oscillator. Regarding sample path-based approaches, one may recall that, in discrete state, SSA is used to generate sample paths, whose ensemble obeys the CME. In continuous state, CLE can in turn be used to generate sample paths. A recent study [35] illustrates derivations of the crucial findings presented in [11,33,34] and adopts an approach for phase diffusion constant computation, based on the transient phase computation of CLE-generated sample paths in an ensemble.

Third, oscillator phase can be defined via two different methods. There are the Hilbert transform-based and the isochron-based definitions. The phase computation based on the Hilbert transform [37] takes the evolution of a single state variable within a sample

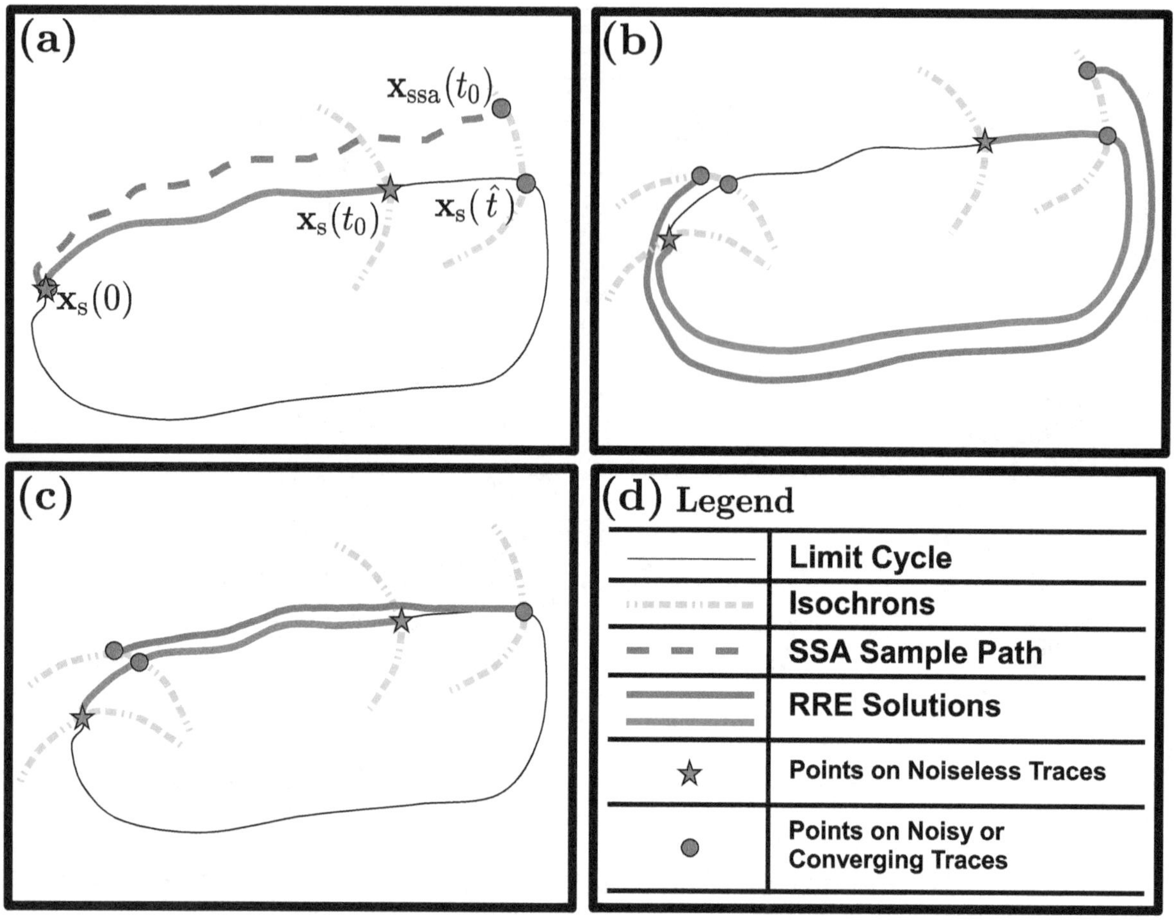

Figure 5 Brute-force phase computation scheme (PhCompBF). (**a**) An SSA sample path and a noiseless RRE solution (running in parallel) end up at different isochrons at t_0. (**b**) The last timepoints in the two simulations for part (**a**) are separately fed as initial conditions to the RRE in order to generate the two separate traces shown in this subfigure. The RRE solution that was already on the periodic orbit continues tracing it, and the off-orbit solution in turn approaches the limit cycle. (**c**) The off-orbit solution finally becomes periodic and the phase shift between the two RRE solutions can be found, switching to the plots in the time domain and applying appropriate algorithms to compute the phase shift. (**d**) Legend for the traces in the subplots.

path to compute the phases of all time points in the whole sample path. The Hilbert transform-based phase computation technique can be used to compute the phase of any oscillatory waveform, without any information as to where this waveform came from. The oscillatory waveform could belong to one of the state variables of an oscillator generated with a simulation. This method has been utilized in [31,35] for phase computations of sample paths. The isochron-theoretic phase (recall that an isochron portrait belongs to a limit cycle of the deterministic RRE) makes use of all of the state variables and equations for an oscillator. The isochron-based phase definition assigns a phase value to the points in the state space of the oscillator, making phase a property of the whole oscillator, not a property of just a certain state variable or a waveform obtained with a simulation of the oscillator [15,22]. Note that even though there appears to be empirical evidence [31,35] that there is a correspondence between the Hilbert transform-based and isochron-based phase definitions, a precise connection has not been worked out in the literature.

The hybrid phase computation techniques proposed in this article apply to discrete-state models and particularly the SSA generated sample paths of these models, based on the isochron-theoretic oscillator phase definition. Our approach is hybrid because isochrons are obtained based on the continuous model but the phase traces are computed for the sample paths generated by an SSA simulation that is based on the discrete model for an oscillator. This hybrid approach targets moderately noisy oscillators, within a container of not too

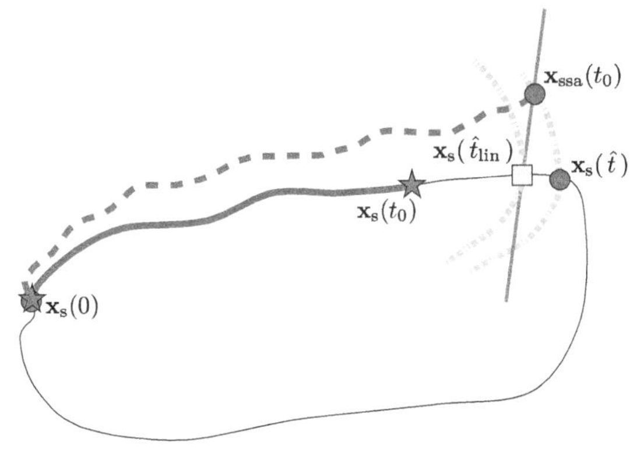

Figure 6 Phase computation scheme depending on linear isochron approximations. An isochron whose linear approximation passes through the point $\mathbf{x}_{ssa}(t_0)$ is found. The point where this hyperplane crosses the limit cycle is $\mathbf{x}_s(\hat{t}_{lin})$, with $\hat{t}_{lin}$ the solution of this phase computation scheme. The difference between the exact solution $\hat{t}$ and the approximate solution $\hat{t}_{lin}$ is reduced if the isochrons are close to being linear.

large or small volume, consequently with not too high or low molecule numbers for the species in the system, respectively.

5 Results and discussion

We now present results obtained with the proposed methods for oscillator phase computations on several intricate molecular oscillators. Accuracy demonstrations and computational speed-up figures will be given with respect to PhCompBF, the brute-force scheme, which we accept as the golden reference for oscillator phase computations, since this method does not employ any approximations in either isochrons or orbital deviations. Section 5.1 below, in which we analyze the brusselator, contains details pertaining to the general flow of the phase computations and the preparatory procedures for all the methods. Sections 5.2 and 5.3 are brief sections illustrating the performance of the methods for oscillators called the oregonator and the repressilator, respectively. All simulations were run on a computer with an Intel i7 processor at 3.07 GHz and accommodating 6 GB of memory.

5.1 Brusselator

The Brusselator is a theoretical model for a type of autocatalytic reaction. The Brusselator actually describes a type of chemical clock, and the Belousov-Zhabotinsky (BZ in short) reaction is a typical example [38]. The model below in (6) has been largely adapted from [39], which is based on [38].

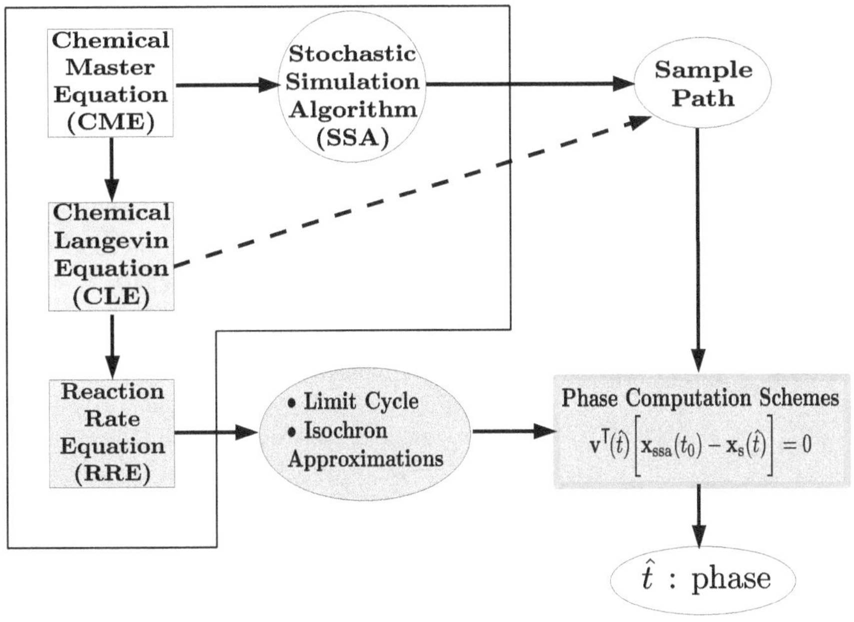

Figure 7 Phase computation schemes methodology. An SSA-generated sample path (alternatively one that is generated through the CLE) and the limit cycle and isochron approximation information are fed to the phase computation schemes, which compute the instantaneous phase corresponding to each point in the sample path. The algebraic equation for the scheme depending on linear isochron approximations is given as an example.

$$
\begin{aligned}
A &\xrightarrow{k_1} X \\
B + X &\xrightarrow{k_2} R + Y \\
Y + 2X &\xrightarrow{k_3} 3X \\
X &\xrightarrow{k_4} S
\end{aligned} \tag{6}
$$

Parameter values in (6) are: $k_1 = 0.025\ s^{-1}$, $k_2 = 1\ s^{-1}$ mL, $k_3 = 1\ s^{-1}\ (mL)^2$, and $k_4 = 0.01\ s^{-1}$. Volume is set to 250 mL. Molecule numbers of A, B, R, and S are held, constant.

Several models and quantities must be derived from the reactions in (6) before moving onto phase analysis. The stoichiometric matrix in this case reads

$$
\mathbf{S} = \begin{bmatrix} 1 & -1 & 1 & -1 \\ 0 & 1 & -1 & 0 \end{bmatrix} \tag{7}
$$

where the first row is for the species X and the second is for Y. The columns each denote the changes in molecule numbers as a reaction takes place, e.g., column one is for the first reaction in (6). Let us also call X the random process denoting the instantaneous molecule number for the species X, similarly Y is for Y in the same fashion. Then, the random process vector $\mathbf{X} = [X\ Y]^T$ concatenates these numbers for convenience. The propensity functions for the reactions can be written as

$$
\begin{aligned}
a_1(\mathbf{X}) &= k_1 A \\
a_2(\mathbf{X}) &= \frac{k_2 B\, X}{\Omega} \\
a_3(\mathbf{X}) &= \frac{k_3 Y\, X(X-1)}{\Omega^2} \\
a_4(\mathbf{X}) &= k_4 X
\end{aligned} \tag{8}
$$

where Ω denotes the volume parameter. Using (8), the CME for the Brusselator can be derived in line with (1) as

$$
\begin{aligned}
\frac{d\,\mathbb{P}(X,Y;t)}{dt} = &-\left[k_1 A + \frac{k_2 B\, X}{\Omega} + \frac{k_3 Y\, X\,(X-1)}{\Omega^2} + k_4 X\right] \mathbb{P}\,(X,Y;t) \\
&+ k_1\, A\, \mathbb{P}\,(X-1,\ Y;t) \\
&+ \frac{k_2 B\,(X+1)}{\Omega}\, \mathbb{P}\,(X+1,\ Y-1;t) \\
&+ \frac{k_3 (Y+1)\,(X-1)\,(X-2)}{\Omega^2} \\
&\mathbb{P}(X-1,\ Y+1;t) \\
&+ k_4 (X+1)\, \mathbb{P}\,(X+1,Y;t)
\end{aligned} \tag{9}
$$

Now it is possible to derive the CLE as in (2)

$$
\begin{aligned}
\frac{dX}{dt} = &\left[k_1 A - \frac{k_2 B\, X}{\Omega} + \frac{k_3 Y\, X(X-1)}{\Omega^2} - k_4 X\right] \\
&+ \sqrt{k_1 A}\,\xi_1(t) - \sqrt{\frac{k_2\, B\, X}{\Omega}}\,\xi_2(t) \\
&+ \sqrt{\frac{k_3\, Y\, X(X-1)}{\Omega^2}}\,\xi_3(t) \\
&- \sqrt{k_4 X}\,\xi_4(t)\Big] \\
\frac{dY}{dt} = &\left[\frac{k_2 B\, X}{\Omega} - \frac{k_3 Y\, X(X-1)}{\Omega^2}\right] \\
&+ \left[\sqrt{\frac{k_2 B\, X}{\Omega}}\,\xi_2(t) - \sqrt{\frac{k_3 Y\, X(X-1)}{\Omega^2}}\,\xi_3(t)\right]
\end{aligned} \tag{10}
$$

It is easy to extract from (10) the RRE in (3) as

$$
\begin{aligned}
\frac{dX}{dt} &= \left[k_1 A - \frac{k_2\, B\, X}{\Omega} + \frac{k_3 Y\, X(X-1)}{\Omega^2} - k_4 X\right] \\
\frac{dY}{dt} &= \left[\frac{k_2\, B\, X}{\Omega} - \frac{k_3\, Y\, X(X-1)}{\Omega^2}\right]
\end{aligned} \tag{11}
$$

Note that in deriving (10) and (11) from (9), the variables X and Y (which represent molecule numbers, not concentrations, of the species X and Y, respectively) have become continuous instead of remaining discrete. In preparation for phase analysis, some computational quantities have to be derived from (11).

The phase analysis of a continuous oscillator (modeled by nonlinear systems of ODEs such as an RRE) depends on linearizations around the steady-state periodic waveform $\mathbf{x}_s(t)$ solving the RRE. The periodic solution $\mathbf{x}_s(t)$ for the Brusselator in (6) is given in Figure 8. This function has been computed for a whole period (with the actual approximate value for the period $T = 1000$ s) through the shooting method [40]. The species A, B, R, and S, with their molecule numbers constant, should be excluded from the machinery of the shooting method for it to work.

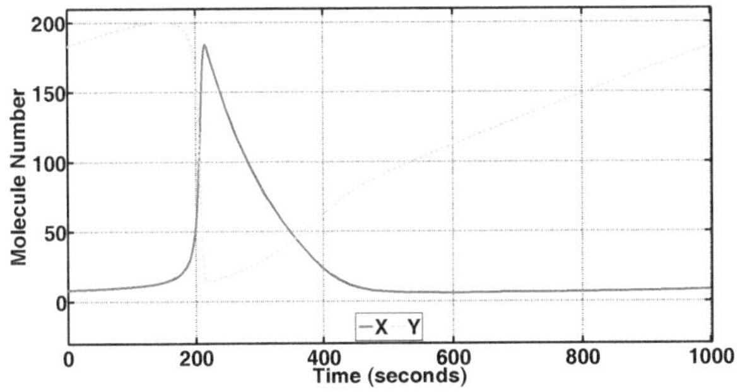

Figure 8 The periodic solution $\mathbf{x}_s(t)$ for the Brusselator. The periodic solution (consisting of the changes in the molecule numbers for the species X and Y) of the RRE (the continuous deterministic model) for the Brusselator. This periodic solution vector function is called $\mathbf{x}_s(t)$. Note that the oscillating molecular system has discrete states, i.e., it has discrete numbers for the molecule numbers for each species. However, through the continuous-state limit, we have derived the RRE and CLE, which are continuous, from the original oscillator model. Therefore, entries of the periodic solution $\mathbf{x}_s(t)$ in this figure are continuous valued. Also, in the transformation from the discrete model to the continuous one, we have chosen to stick with molecule numbers for species rather than switching to concentrations, because we would like to plot on top of each other, compare, and use in computational analysis the SSA sample paths obtained from the discrete model and sample paths and deterministic solutions obtained from the continuous models.

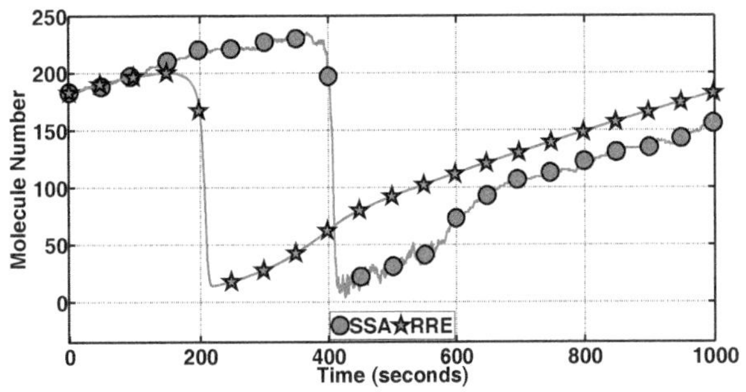

Figure 9 An SSA-generated sample path as compared to the deterministic periodic solution for the Brusselator (showing changes in the molecule number for only the species Y). Changes in the molecule number for only species Y monitored. The noisy sample path is compared to the noiseless RRE solution. The noise has an adverse effect such that it has apparently caused the oscillator to lag behind the deterministic solution. A quantitative measure of this phase shift on a point by point basis (for all points) in the sample path is to be obtained by the phase computation methods proposed in this article.

In fact, $\mathbf{x}_s(t)$ computation is enough preparation for running the brute-force scheme PhCompBF as will be demonstrated next. Recalling that we aim to solve for the possibly constantly changing phase along individual SSA-generated sample paths, we run the SSA algorithm to generate the sample path given in Figure 9. In this plot, the SSA simulation result and the unperturbed $\mathbf{x}_s(t)$ have been plotted on top of each other, for only species Y, for illustration purposes. It must be noted that both $\mathbf{x}_s(t)$ and the SSA sample path start initially at the same state on the limit cycle, therefore the star and the circle are on top of each other at $t = 0$ s. Due to isochron-theoretic oscillator phase theory, the initial relative phase, or the initial phase shift of the SSA sample path with respect to $\mathbf{x}_s(t)$, is zero.

In Figure 9, we would like to solve eventually for the time-evolving relative phase shift of the SSA sample path, for now with PhCompBF. This means solving for the phase shift for the visited states in the sample path, denoted by circles in the figure, and preferably for all the states in between the circles along the path as well. PhCompBF requires running a particular type of simulation for computing the relative phase shift of each visited state. We will demonstrate the method shortly, but let us comment on how much information can be gained by inspecting only the plot in Figure 9. The SSA simulation suggests that the system continually introduces noise, so that everything about the system appears noisy, the phase, the amplitude, etc. Phase is a particular quantity that helps quantify the effect of noise on an autonomously oscillating system. One may easily guess that the relative phase shift of the SSA sample path is always changing along the interval of simulation. It is not obvious at all how to compute this phase shift at particular points in time in Figure 9. Perhaps, one may argue that the sudden decrease that should take place at about $t = 200$ s for the unperturbed $\mathbf{x}_s(t)$, appears about 200s in time later for the SSA path. However, this is only an educated guess and an approximate value. Also, that the stars and circles appear very close to each other for example in between 600 and 1000s does not directly help invoke the isochron-theoretic phase theory to deduce that the phase shift along this interval is close to zero. Recalling that Figure 9 depicts only species Y, one has to inspect also the other species to arrive at such a conclusion. It is also needless to state as a reminder that for two states to have the same relative phase, having the two states equal to each other is a sufficient but not necessary condition, again due to isochron theory. In all, accurately what happens to the phase shift along the interval is still obscure. As a side note, one should also note that without the perfectly periodic $\mathbf{x}_s(t)$, it is awfully difficult to guess the period T, inspecting only a long SSA sample path. Relevant theory for noisy oscillators suggests that inspecting the zero-crossings of a whole ensemble of long and mildly noisy SSA sample paths yields information related to the period and phase diffusion constant of an oscillator, in a brute-force manner [11].

In order to demostrate PhCompBF, we have first plotted both the SSA sample path and the limit cycle (the closed curve traced over and over by $\mathbf{x}_s(t)$) in 2-D state space as in Figure 10. As stated earlier, the star and the circle are initially coincident. Then, as time progresses, $\mathbf{x}_s(t)$ just traces the limit cycle, but the SSA sample path $\mathbf{x}_{ssa}(t)$ runs berserk. At $t_0 = 600$ s, we have again indicated where the two traces end up. The SSA path at this time is off the limit cycle. Since we do not have exact isochron information, it is not possible to compute the phase $\hat{t}$ value that makes $\mathbf{x}_{ssa}(t_0 = 600\ \text{s})$ and $\mathbf{x}_s(\hat{t})$ in-phase, i.e., on the same isochron. If we could find this $\hat{t}$ value, then $\alpha(t_0 = 600\,\text{s}) = \hat{t} - 600$ would be the sought phase shift value.

The value of the phase shift α can, however, be computed through a possibly long, ideally infinitely long, simulation, in line with the theory of asymptotic phase (a theory on intimate terms with isochrons). The following is the essence of PhCompBF. One takes in Figure 10 the states $\mathbf{x}_{ssa}(t_0 = 600\ \text{s})$ (the circle on the SSA path) and $\mathbf{x}_s(t_0 = 600\ \text{s})$ (the star on the limit cycle) and feeds them as initial conditions to the RRE in (21) and then simulates both traces for some time. The result is the two traces in Figure 11. In this plot, again only the species Y is demonstrated. The circular marker (along with the corresponding star) has been put only at the beginning of the simulation in Figure 11 to note the fact that only the initial value belongs to the SSA sample path. After this initial time, both traces are parts of separate RRE solutions. Incorporation of these two new simulated traces into the plot of Figure 10 would be as follows (see Figure 12): The plot starting with the circle in Figure 11 (with both of the two states) would be a curve in the state space of Figure 10 starting from the circle off the limit cycle but gradually converging to it. Meanwhile, the plot starting from the star in Figure 11 would resume tracing the limit cycle in Figure 10 from again the star. Then, as shown in Figure 12, the two simulated

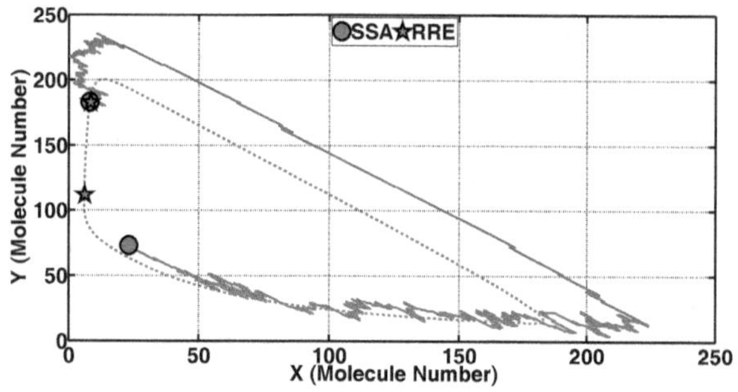

Figure 10 Limit cycle and SSA sample path shown on the state space for the Brusselator. Both trajectories start at the same point on the limit cycle. The star traces the limit cycle in clockwise direction, whereas the noisy sample path wanders around though remaining close to the periodic orbit. After some time has passed, the star (of the noiseless path) and the circle (of the noisy sample path) are found to be at different locations. The qualitative difference in terms of phase between these two points is explained by the concept of isochrons.

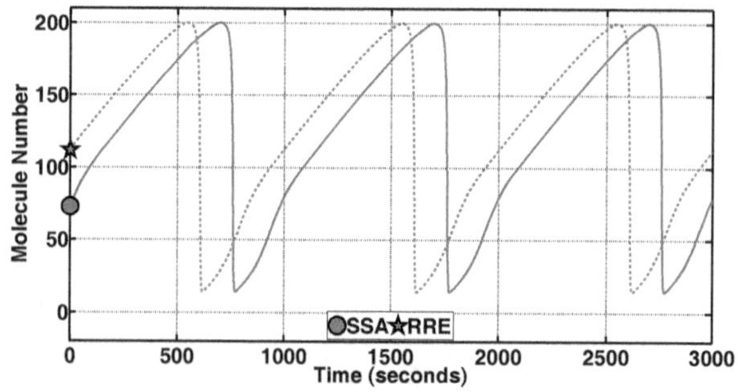

Figure 11 Mechanism of PhCompBF (the brute-force phase computation scheme) in time domain for the Brusselator (changes in the molecule number for the species Y are monitored). The star and the circle obtained at the end of the simulations (let us call this time t_0) in Figure 10 are fed as initial conditions to the RRE in (11), hence the star and the circle at the beginning of the traces in this figure. The waveforms in this figure monitor the same entry for these two different RRE solutions, i.e., the changes in the molecule number for the species Y are shown. The curve starting with the circle should come to be almost periodic in a matter of a few periods for this oscillator. Then the phase shift between the two waveforms can be computed. This phase shift belongs to the point identified by the circle in Figure 10 at the end of the simulation (we have called this time t_0). This phase shift has been obtained with respect to the star in Figure 10 at again the time t_0.

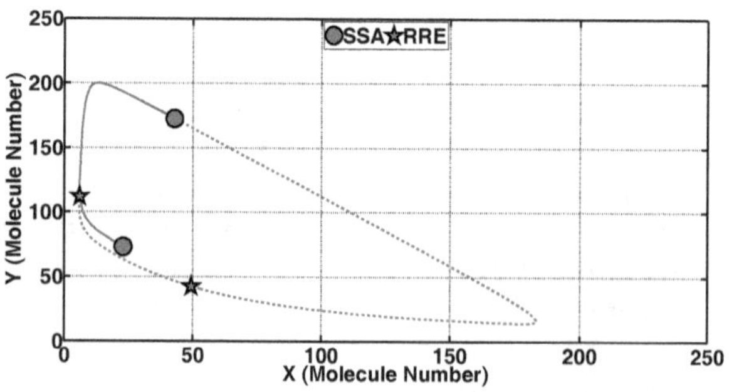

Figure 12 Mechanism of PhCompBF (the brute-force phase computation scheme) in state space for the Brusselator (changes in molecule numbers for both species are monitored). This is the state-space pictorial description of PhCompBF that corresponds to Figure 11. There are two RRE solutions in this figure. The final states of the solutions in Figure 10 are fed as initial conditions to the RRE in (11) for the Brusselator. The RRE solution, whose initial and final conditions are indicated by the circle, approaches the limit cycle and almost starts tracing it, traveling clockwise. The solution indicated by the star, which is actually leading in terms of phase that indicated by the circle, has already made the rightmost turn at the end of this simulation. The circle is way behind. The actual phase shift between the two solutions has to be computed as explained in Figure 11.

plots are observed to be tracing the limit cycle after simulating long enough in time, the star of the unperturbed path always leading the circle of the initially perturbed path (but notice that during the simulation for both traces in Figure 12 all perturbations or noise are removed). Observe in Figure 12 that the star has went ahead to make the rightmost turn on the limit cycle, travelling clockwise, whereas the circle is still way behind. However, all along this simulation of Figure 12, the instantaneous phase shift between the two traces has remained the same. As the simulation goes on along the limit cycle, the circle (originating from the SSA simulation) and the star (of the unperturbed $\mathbf{x}_s(t)$) would appear sometimes near, and sometimes far away from each other. This effect is due to particularly the varying velocity along the limit cycle, all determined by the dynamic properties of the RRE. The constant difference in time between the circle and star is the phase shift α (t_0 = 600 s) that we aim to compute. Notice that in the state space of Figures 10 and 12, time is only an implicit parameter. Therefore, we have to inspect plots of the type in Figure 11 to obtain the desired phase shift value.

For some oscillators (as determined by the dynamics of the RRE again), a state off the limit cycle converges fast to begin tracing quickly an almost periodic curve, as in the case in hand. Almost two periods are enough to deduce the phase shift between the two curves. After RRE simulations, the phase shift can be computed using Fourier transforms [15].

One question that may arise is why we are particularly using the traces belonging to the species Y to compute phase shifts in Figure 11. Indeed, it follows from the theory that phase is a scalar-valued property of the whole system, therefore investigating phase shifts over non-constant periodic molecule numbers for any species in a system would yield the same phase shift value. In this case, employing Y is only a matter of choice.

Notice that this brute-force scheme is carried out to compute the relative phase shift of the SSA sample path at only t_0 = 600 s. The phase shift for each state along the sample path can be computed one by one through the just outlined PhCompBF.

It has already been stated that PhCompBF is almost the golden reference for phase computations but also that the method is very time-consuming. It was for this reason that new methods depending on isochron and orbital deviation approximations were proposed. Particularly, two quantities are necessary for characterizing isochron approximations: the phase gradient $\mathbf{v}(t)$ and the phase Hessian $\mathbf{H}(t)$. These are depicted for the Brusselator respectively in Figures 13 and 14. Recall that $\mathbf{v}(t)$ is a vector function, but $\mathbf{H}(t)$ is a matrix function.

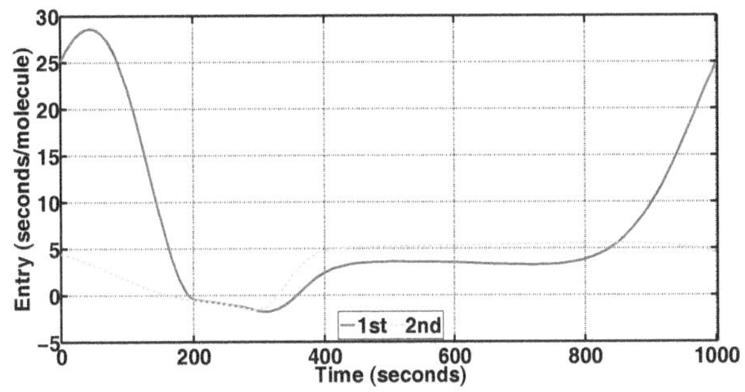

Figure 13 Phase gradient for the Brusselator. Entries of the phase gradient (a vector function) as periodic functions, computed through the algorithm described in [11]. The phase gradient is referred to as $\mathbf{v}(t)$ in this article.

Therefore, only the phase Hessian diagonals have been plotted in Figure 14.

Phase computation schemes are fairly easy to comprehend geometrically. Regarding for example the limit cycle depicted in Figure 10, there are both a hyperplane (accounting for the linear isochron approximation) and a quadric surface (for quadratic approximation) associated with each point on the limit cycle. Equations for these characterizations are given in (40) and (41), respectively. A phase computation scheme aims to solve for that point on the limit cycle whose linear or quadratic isochron approximation passes through a given point, for example the stated point denoted by the circle off the limit cycle in Figure 10, $\mathbf{x}_{ssa}(t_0$ = 600 s). Notice that PhCompBF is also a variant of these phase computation schemes, but in this case not the isochron approximations but the exact isochrons themselves associated with points on the limit cycle are used.

The geometrical interpretations of phase equations, on the other hand, are not easy to visualize. As stated in previous sections, phase equations are differential equations involving orbital deviation in addition to isochron

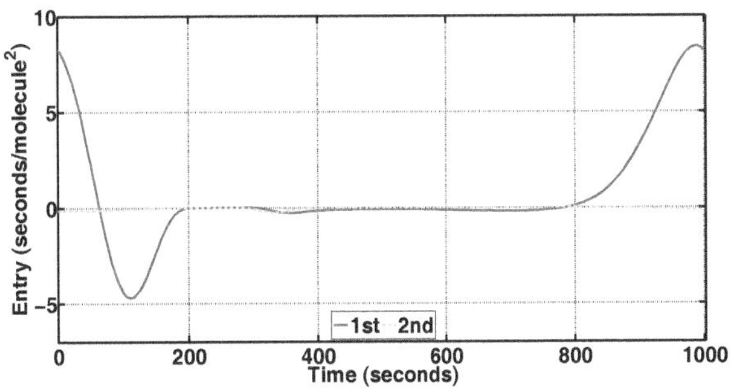

Figure 14 Phase Hessian diagonals for the Brusselator. Diagonal entries of the phase Hessian (a square matrix function) as periodic functions, computed through the algorithm described in [15]. The phase Hessian is referred to as $\mathbf{H}(t)$ in this article.

approximations. Phase computation schemes are expected to be more costly but then more accurate with respect to phase equations. Phase equations, as they are differential equations and need to be discretized, suffer from local truncation errors and global errors, whereas this is not the case for the schemes that are in the form of algebraic equations. An approximate phase computation scheme may deviate from the golden reference (PhCompBF result) at times (particularly if the noisy state is too far off the limit cycle), but the scheme (if carefully designed) does not suffer from the accumulation of truncation errors and its phase results are expected to be almost always very close to that of PhCompBF.

We now check the performance of the phase computation methods for this oscillator, on a sample path that lasts about 1000 s, with the period about the same as that. The results are depicted in Figure 15. PhCompBF takes about 138 min. Speed-up of the methods on this duration are as follows: PhCompLin (the scheme depending on linear isochron approximations) 56x, PhEqnLL (the phase equation that employs linear isochron approximations and a linear differential equation model for orbital deviations) 8583x, and PhEqnQL (the phase equation with quadratic isochron and linear orbital deviation approximations) 2257x. The phase equations are most of the time sharing a common accuracy level, not disregarding the apparent attempt of PhEqnQL to come closer to PhCompBF around 400-600 s. PhCompLin is slower than the equations but almost as accurate as can be.

5.2 Oregonator

In this section, we present phase computation results for a well-known and studied biochemical oscillator, the oregonator [38]. This realistic oscillator accurately models the Belousov-Zhabotinsky reaction, an autocatalytic reaction that serves as a classical example of non-equilibrium thermodynamics. The molecular reactions model, adapted mostly from [39], is given as follows. Names of the reactants have been simplified for convenience.

$$\begin{aligned} A + Y &\xrightarrow{k_1} X + R \\ X + Y &\xrightarrow{k_2} 2R \\ A + X &\xrightarrow{k_3} 2X + 2Z \\ 2X &\xrightarrow{k_4} A + R \\ 2B + 2Z &\xrightarrow{k_5} Y \end{aligned} \tag{12}$$

In (12), the propensity functions, employing also the volume of the container, can easily be derived. Parameter values are: $k_1 = 0.005\ s^{-1}\ mL$, $k_2 = k_3 = k_4 = 1\ s^{-1}\ mL$, and $k_5 = 1.25 \times 10^{-4}\ s^{-1}\ (mL)^3$. Molecule numbers for the reactants A, B, and R are held constant. For this model, the volume initially is set to 12,000 mL. In this case, noise will not have considerable effect on a sample path. Then, we set the volume to 3,200 mL in order to obtain a moderately noisy oscillator. Later on, we will, halve the value of the volume parameter, resulting in a very noisy oscillator, and the performance of the phase computation methods will be demonstrated for this latter case as well.

With the volume as 12,000 mL, the performance of the phase computation methods on a particular sample path of length 4×10^4 s (the period is about 4.43×10^4 s) is depicted in Figure 16. PhCompBF simulation takes 502 minutes, with two periods of RRE computations before setting out to compute the phase shift values. There are a total of 8114 timepoints on the sample path. As the volume is decreased, the number of timepoints per unit time will reduce. The speed-up of the methods over PhCompBF are: PhCompLin (on linear isochron approximations) 70x, PhEqnLL (on linear isochron and linear orbital deviation approximations) 10733x, PhCompQuad (on quadratic isochron approximations) 46x, and PhEqnQL (on quadratic isochron and linear orbital deviation approximations) 2791x. It is observed that all the methods for a good part of the sample path stick to the PhCompBF result. However, towards the end the phase equations (with PhEqnQL a little more accurate compared to PhEqnLL) begin accumulating global errors, Otherwise, they are exquisitely fast all the time and accurate at the beginning until they start deviating from the golden reference. The phase computation schemes are not as fast as the equations, but they are always accurate in this simulation.

We have also tested the phase computation methods on a sample path, with the volume set to 3,200 mL. Figure 17 illustrates the results. The simulation interval length (5×10^4 s) is a little more than the period (about 4.37×10^4 s). The simulation for PhCompBF took 242 minutes, and there are 2981 timepoints in total. The observed speed-ups were: PhCompLin 70x, PhEqnLL 13971x, PhCompQuad 51x, and PhEqnQL 3203x. It is observed that the phase equations are really fast, keeping track of the exact phase though not very closely, whereas the computation schemes, though not as fast, are almost a perfect match for the exact phase in terms of accuracy.

We then set volume to 1,600 mL, resulting in a noisier oscillator. We expect the phase equations results to deviate much more from the exact one, and the computation schemes to still do well. Again for a sample path (of length 5×10^4 s with the period 4.3×10^4 s), the PhCompBF simulation now takes 76 min. There are 1033 timepoints. Speed-ups with the methods are: 12637x (PhEqnLL), 74x (PhCompLin), and 44x (PhCompQuad). PhEqnQL apparently suffers from numerical problems

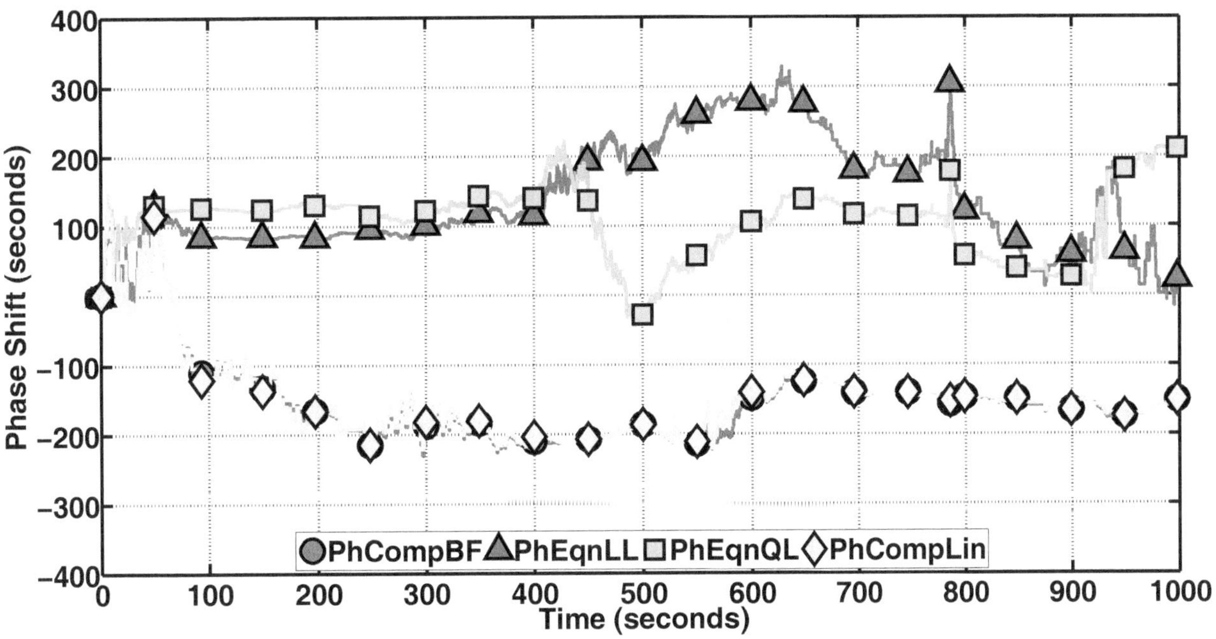

Figure 15 Phase computation methods on the Brusselator. The approximate schemes are almost a perfect match for the golden reference PhCompBF. The equations are very fast as indicated by the speed-up figures given in the text. Results of the phase equations are quite close to each other. In the interval 400-600 s, PhEqnQL comes closer to the true value. The following observations and facts are iterated for this first figure of the results. For convenience, these comments are not going to be repeated for every figure that follows. Note that the phase equations are in reality differential equations, solving one by one for the instantaneous phase of points in an oscillator sample path. Therefore, due to the approximations involved in their design and, furthermore, due to the imperfect discretizations (of the differential equations that they are represented by) for their numerical solutions, the phase equations are doomed to suffer from accumulating truncation errors. This is why, in many results figures for the oscillators in this article, we observe the results of phase equations tending to deviate from the golden reference PhCompBF as time progresses. However, computational complexity-wise the phase equations are indeed very fast. This makes the phase equations a feasible and accurate choice for the phase computations of less noisy oscillators, possibly with a dense grid of timepoints in an SSA sample path and high molecule numbers for every species in the system (especially in a container of large volume), deviating not much from their limit cycles. The phase computation schemes, on the other hand, do not employ as many approximations as the phase equations do in their design. Furthermore, these schemes are in the form of algebraic equations, again solving one by one for the instantaneous phase of points in an oscillator sample path. Therefore, the schemes, for their numerical solution, do not involve time discretizations as the phase equations do. This means that the schemes do not suffer from truncation error accumulation. The schemes are subject to errors originating from the approximations committed in their theoretical development, and once again, these approximations are not on the same scale as those employed in the derivation of phase equations, i.e., the schemes are much more accurate than the equations. However, the numerical procedures associated with the schemes render them more costly in computational complexity with respect to the equations. Therefore, one may rightfully contend that the phase computation schemes are tailored to fit phase computations for moderately noisy oscillators in small volume, with low molecule numbers for each species and possibly a sparse grid of timepoints in an SSA sample path.

for such a noisy oscillator, and the result for this method is not included. In Figure 18, we observe in line with our expectations that although PhEqnLL is again very fast, the result it produces is almost unacceptably inaccurate, whereas both the computation schemes maintain their relative speed-ups (as compared to the less noisy version) along with their accuracies.

5.3 Repressilator

The Repressilator is a synthetic genetic regulatory network, designed from scratch and implemented in *Escherichia coli* using standard molecular biology methods [9]. Its development is a milestone in synthetic biology. We have obtained the model as an SBML file in XML format [41-43]. We have used the libSBML [44] and SBMLToolbox [45] libraries to interpret the model and incorporate it to our own manipulation and simulation toolbox for phase computations. The period of the continuous oscillator obtained from the model is about 2.57 h. A sample path running for about 3 h was generated, and the phase methods were applied. The results are in Figure 19. PhCompBF (the brute-force scheme) takes about 76 min. Speed-ups obtained with the methods are: PhCompLin (on linear isochron approximations) 58x, PhEqnLL (on linear isochron and linear orbital deviation approximations) 7601x, and PhEqnQL (on quadratic isochron and linear orbital deviation approximations) 1994x. It appears in Figure 19 that

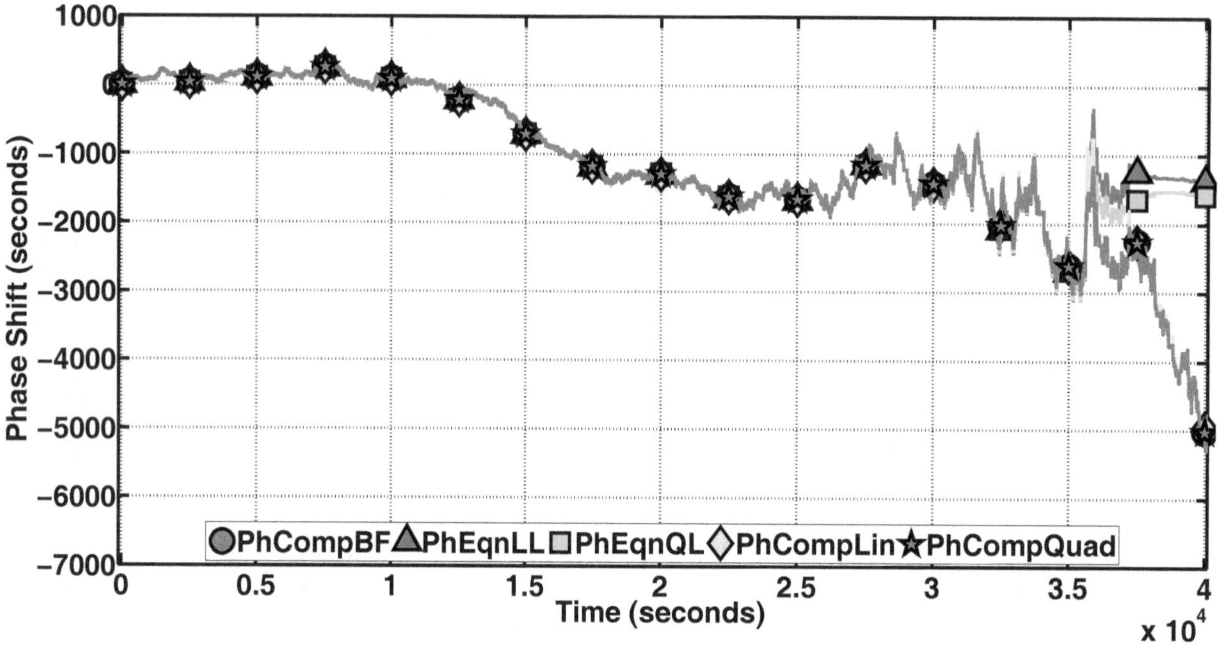

Figure 16 Phase computation methods on the Oregonator. (volume = 12, 000 mL). In a large volume, the system is not expected to be very noisy. The phase is closer to ideal. Therefore, all phase computation methods are quite accurate, but the phase equations have started to accumulate global errors towards the end of the simulation, as they are differential equations.

PhEqnLL towards the end of the simulation has started to accumulate a global error. PhEqnQL looks a little more accurate. Again PhCompLin is, excepting a few minor intervals, the most accurate.

6 Conclusions and future work

The phase computation methods described in this article basically target three classes of discrete molecular oscillators. First, the continuous phase models, based on

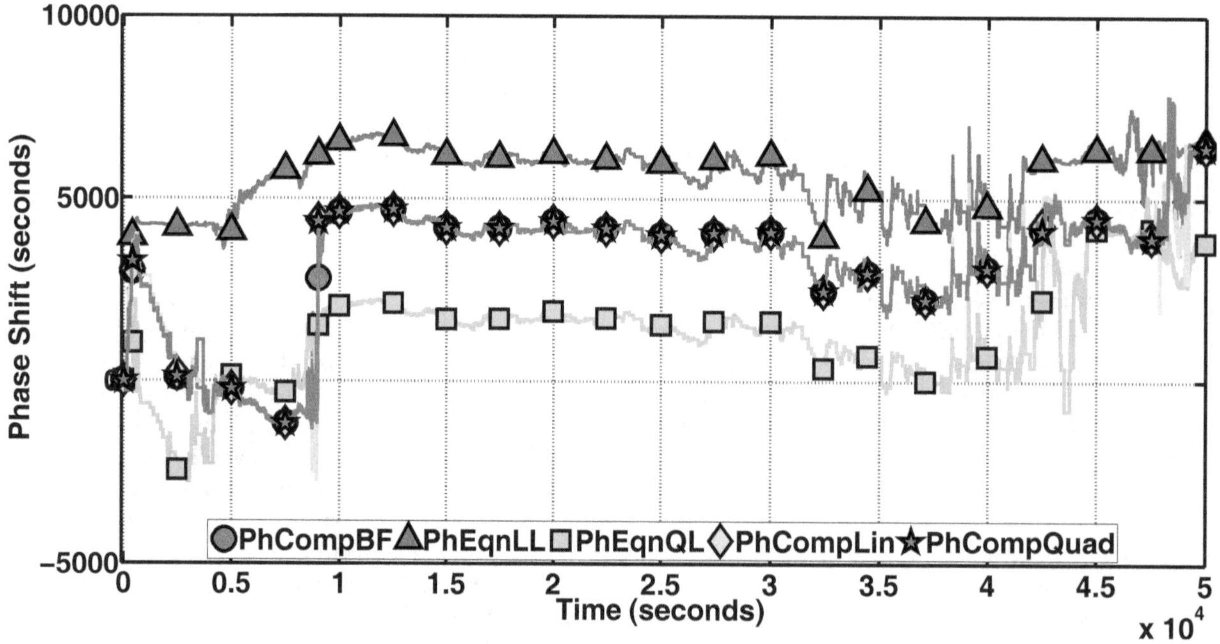

Figure 17 Phase computation methods on the Oregonator. (volume = 3, 200 mL). In a smaller volume, the system is noisier. Phase equation results deviate in accuracy. PhEqnQL is a little more accurate. The schemes retain their accuracies.

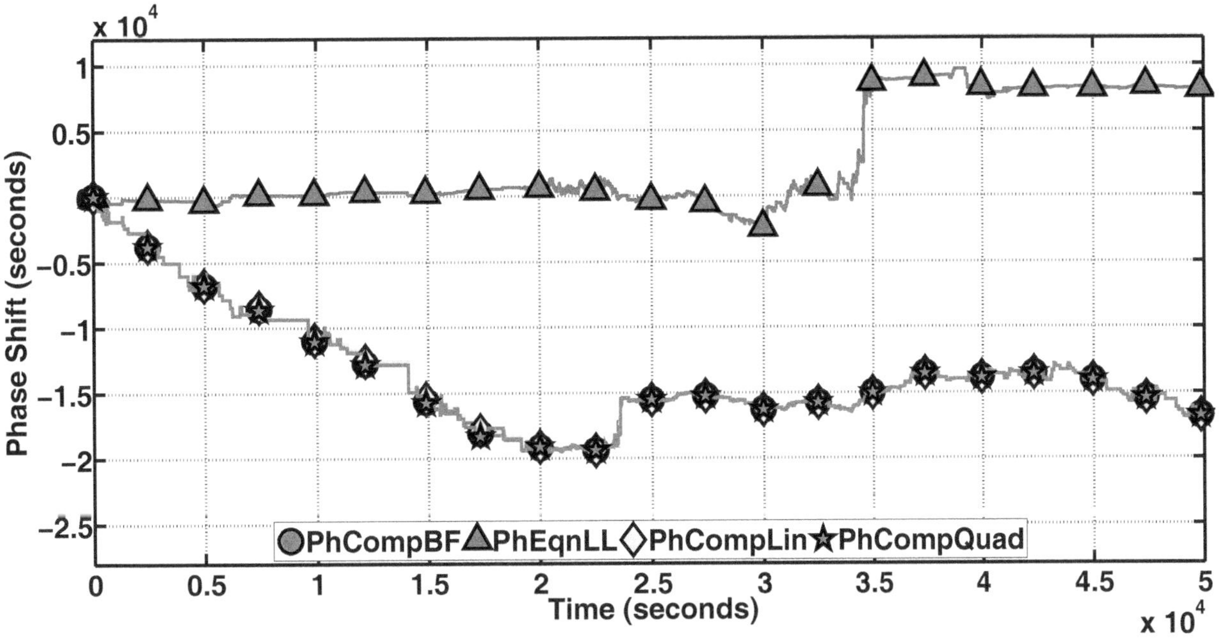

Figure 18 Phase computation methods on the Oregonator. (volume = 1, 600 mL). In an even smaller volume, the system is very noisy. PhEqnLL computes the phase shift result very fast, but this result is unacceptably inaccurate. The schemes are still accurate.

the information obtained from the oscillator model in the continuous-state limit (i.e., basically the limit cycle and isochron approximations), are acceptably accurate for discrete molecular oscillators with a large number of molecules for each species, in a big volume. Indeed, we have shown in this article that the phase equations serve this purpose well. Second, for oscillators with very few molecules for each species in a small volume, a new phase concept needs to be developed, without resorting to continuous limit approximations. This one is as yet

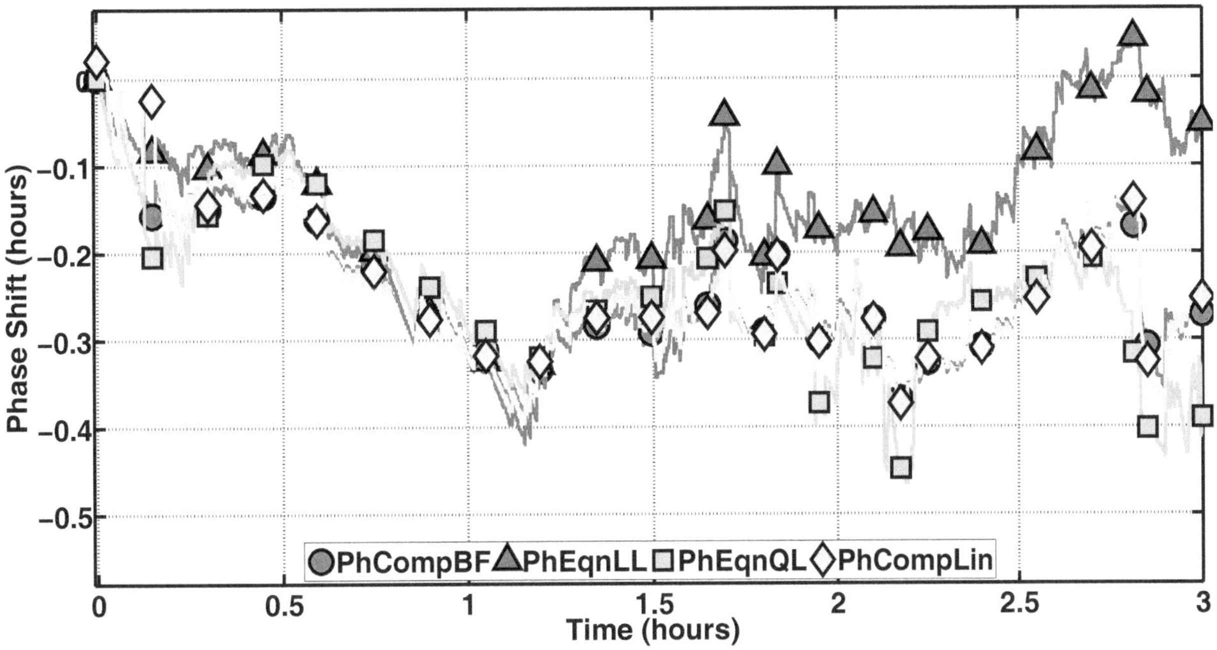

Figure 19 Phase computation methods on the Repressilator. PhEqnQL is more accurate than PhEqnLL, but the scheme PhCompLin is the most accurate.

an unsolved problem. Third, there are systems in between the two classes just stated, with moderate number of molecules, for which the continuous phase concept is still useful but requires a hybrid approach with combined use of both discrete and continuous models for acceptable accuracy (note that the phase computation schemes are tailored to concretize this hybrid approach), and this is where the contribution of this article should be placed.

As yet, the described methods benefit extensively from continuous state-space approxi-mations derived from the molecular descriptions of such oscillators, and the assumed most accurate brute-force scheme shares this aspect. A future direction furthering this study can be described as follows, in line with the necessity of handling the second class of oscillators stated above. A proper phase model theory (not relying on continuous limit approximations) for discrete-space oscillators modeled with Markov chains needs to be developed. We believe that such a discrete phase model theory can be developed based on *cycle representations* for Markov chains [46-48]. We made progress also on this problem. We have developed a theory that precisely characterizes the phase noise of a single cycle in a continuous-time Markov chain. We were able to show that the phase noise theory we have developed for a single cycle in fact reduces to the previously developed continuous-space phase noise theory in the limit. We are currently working on extending this discrete phase noise theory to many cycles, i.e., to a *cycle decomposition* of a continuous-time Markov chain.

7 Methods - Modeling and simulation of discrete molecular oscillators

In this section we review, after giving preliminary information (Section 7.1), some crucial paradigms in the modeling of discrete molecular oscillators: a model that is the complete probabilistic characterization of a discrete system, known as the CME (Section 7.2), a continuous deterministic approximation to the CME in the form of the Reaction Rate Equation (Section 7.3), and the steps that let us proceed to a continuous stochastic model, the Chemical Langevin Equation, from again the CME (Section 7.4). Also a descriptive review of the SSA algorithm of Gillespie [25] for the simulation of molecular models is provided in Section 7.5.

7.1 Preliminaries

We first describe a mathematical model for an autonomous, discrete molecular oscillator based on a stochastic chemical kinetics formalism [24-28,30]. We consider N molecular species denoted by $S_1, S_2, \ldots, S_N$. Let $\mathbf{X}$ be the stochastic vector $[X_1, X_2, \ldots, X_N]^T$ where X_i is the number of molecules of species S_i in the reaction chamber (i.e., a cell). The M reactions taking place among these molecular species are denoted by $R_1, R_2, \ldots, R_M$. Let a_j $(\mathbf{X})$ denote the *propensity* [25,27] of reaction j, i.e., the probability that one R_j reaction will occur somewhere in the system in the next infinitesimal time interval $[t, t + dt)$ is given by $a_j(\mathbf{X})\, dt$, i.e.,

$$\mathbb{P}(R_j \text{ occurs in}[t, t + dt)) = a_j(\mathbf{X})dt \tag{13}$$

Let s_{ji} denote the change in the number of molecules of species S_i as a result of one R_j reaction. We define the stoichiometry vector $\mathbf{s}_j$

$$\mathbf{s}_j = [s_{j1}, s_{j2}, \ldots, s_{jN}]^T \tag{14}$$

for reaction R_j, and the $N \times M$ stochiometry matrix [27]

$$\mathbf{S} = [\mathbf{s}_1, \mathbf{s}_2, \ldots, \mathbf{s}_M] \tag{15}$$

7.2 Chemical master equation

The following derivation follows closely that outlined in [27]. Let us take a note of the events $\mathbf{X}(t + dt) = \mathbf{x}$, $\mathbf{X}(t) = \mathbf{x} - \mathbf{s}_j$ and $\mathbf{X}(t) = \mathbf{x}$, where dt is an infinitesimal time element. Through several manipulations making use of these events and taking the limit as $dt \to 0$ [27], we obtain

$$\frac{d\,\mathbb{P}(\mathbf{x}, t)}{dt} = \sum_{j=1}^{M} [a_j(\mathbf{x} - \mathbf{s}_j)\,\mathbb{P}(\mathbf{x} - \mathbf{s}_j, t) - a_j(\mathbf{x})\,\mathbb{P}(\mathbf{x}, t)] \tag{16}$$

where $\mathbb{P}(\mathbf{x}, t)$ denotes the probability that the system is at state $\mathbf{x}$ at time t. The above is known as the CME [27-30]. If we enumerate all the (discrete) state configurations $\mathbf{X}$ can be in as $C_1, C_2, \ldots, C_{ns}$ and define,

$$p_i(t) = \mathbb{P}(\mathbf{x} = C_i, t) \tag{17}$$

$$\mathbf{p}(t) = [p_1(t), p_2(t), \ldots, p_{ns}(t)]^T \tag{18}$$

then, the CME in (16) can be written as

$$\frac{d\,\mathbf{p}(t)}{dt} = \mathbf{Q}\,\mathbf{p}(t) \tag{19}$$

where $\mathbf{Q}$ is a constant square matrix with dimension $ns \times ns$, known as the *transition rate matrix* [28,29]. The above is a linear system of homogeneous ODEs, but the number of state configurations ns is possibly huge. It is usually not practically feasible to construct and solve (19). CME in (16) and (19) above corresponds to a homogeneous, continuous-time Markov chain model [28-30]. The state transitions of this Markov chain are highly structured and compactly described by the list of the reactions as in the CME. The CME provides the ultimate probabilistic characterization for a discrete molecular oscillator. It was shown that the solution of the CME converges to a unique stationary distribution. For a discrete molecular oscillator with a limit cycle, this stationary probability distribution takes the form of a "probability crater" for a planar system with two species [47].

7.3 From the stochastic CME to the deterministic rate equations

If we multiply both sides of CME in (16) with $\mathbf{x}$ and sum over all $\mathbf{x}$, we obtain, as shown especially in [24,27],

$$\frac{\mathrm{d}\mathbb{E}[\mathbf{X}(t)]}{\mathrm{d}t} = \sum_{j=1}^{M} \mathbf{s}_j \, \mathbb{E}[a_j(\mathbf{X}(t))] \tag{20}$$

We note here that $\mathbb{E}\,[a_j(\mathbf{X}(t))] \neq a_j(\mathbb{E}\,[\mathbf{X}(t)])$ unless $a_j(\mathbf{x})$ is a linear function of $\mathbf{x}$. Thus, in general, (20) can not be solved for $\mathbb{E}\,[(\mathbf{X}(t)]$ since the term $a_j\left(\mathbb{E}\,[(\mathbf{X}(t)]\right)$ involves higher-order moments of $\mathbf{X}(t)$ [27]. However, if we assume that the fluctuations of $\mathbf{X}(t)$ around its mean $\mathbb{E}\,[(\mathbf{X}(t)]$ is negligible and thus can perform a crude moment closure scheme, i.e., if $\mathbb{E}\,[(\mathbf{X}(t)] = X(t)$, then (20) simplifies to

$$\frac{\mathrm{d}\mathbf{X}(t)}{\mathrm{d}t} = \sum_{j=1}^{M} \mathbf{s}_j \, a_j(\mathbf{X}(t)) = \mathbf{S}\,\mathbf{a}(\mathbf{X}(t)) \tag{21}$$

where $\mathbf{S}$ is the stoichiometry matrix defined in (15) and

$$\mathrm{a}(\mathbf{X}(t)) = [a_1(\mathbf{X}(t)),\ a_2(\mathbf{X}(t)),\ \ldots,\ a_M(\mathbf{X}(t))]^{\top} \tag{22}$$

is an $M \times 1$ column vector of reaction propensities evaluated at $\mathbf{X}(t)$. The above system of deterministic ODEs in (21) is known as the RRE [24,27].

7.4 From CME to Langevin model

The derivations in this section have been particularly borrowed from [26]. If we assume that the reaction propensities $a_j(\mathbf{X}(t))$ for $j = 1, \ldots, M$ are constant in $[t, t + \mathrm{d}t)$ (known as the *leap condition*) [26,27], then the number of the times reactions fire in $[t, t + \tau)$ are independent Poisson random variables [26-30] with mean and variance equal to $a_j(\mathbf{x}(t))\ \tau$, denoted by $\mathcal{P}_j(a_j(\mathbf{x}(t))\tau)$ for $j = 1, \ldots, M$. Hence, we can write,

$$\mathbf{X}(t+\tau) = \mathbf{X}(t) + \sum_{j=1}^{M} \mathcal{P}_j(a_j(\mathbf{X}(t))\tau)\mathbf{s}_j \tag{23}$$

If we further assume that $a_j(\mathbf{x}(t))\ \tau \gg 1$, then $\mathcal{P}_j(a_j(\mathbf{x}(t))\tau)$ can be approximated with Gaussian random variables:

$$\mathcal{P}_j(a_j(\mathbf{x}(t))\tau) \approx a_j(\mathbf{x}(t))\tau + \sqrt{a_j(\mathbf{x}(t))\tau}\ \mathcal{N}_j(0,1) \tag{24}$$

where $\mathcal{N}_j(0,1)$ for $j = 1, \ldots, M$ are independent Gaussian random variables with zero mean and unity variance [26-30]. Incorporating (24) into (23), we recognize the (forward) Euler discretization of the following *stochastic differential equation* (SDE), known as a *Langevin equation* [26-28,30]:

$$\frac{\mathrm{d}\,\mathbf{X}(t)}{\mathrm{d}t} = \mathbf{S}\,\mathbf{a}(\mathbf{X}(t)) + \mathbf{S}\mathbb{D}\left(\left[\sqrt{\mathbf{a}(\mathbf{X}(t))}\right]\right)\xi(t) \tag{25}$$

where $\xi(t)$ denotes an $M \times 1$ vector of independent white stationary Gaussian processes with unity (two-sided) spectral density, and

$$\mathbb{D}\left(\left[\sqrt{a(\mathbf{X}(t))}\right]\right) = \begin{bmatrix} \sqrt{a_1(\mathbf{X}(t))} & 0 & \cdots & \cdots & 0 \\ 0 & \sqrt{a_2(\mathbf{X}(t))} & 0 & \cdots & 0 \\ \vdots & 0 & \ddots & \ddots & \vdots \\ \vdots & \vdots & \ddots & \ddots & 0 \\ 0 & 0 & \cdots & 0 & \sqrt{a_M(\mathbf{X}(t))} \end{bmatrix} \tag{26}$$

denotes the diagonal $M \times M$ matrix function shown in (25). We note here that if the stochastic, fluctuation term (known as the *diffusion* term) above is omitted, we obtain the RREs in (21). We note here that, with the Langevin model, the stochastic fluctuations in the oscillator are captured by the second term in the right hand side in (25). This term represents an *additive* noise in the model. By zeroing this additive noise term, we are able to obtain the mean, deterministic dynamics of the oscillator as the solution of the RREs in (21). On the other hand, in the discrete, Markov chain model of the oscillator, the mean, deterministic behavior of the system and the stochastic fluctuations are not separable from each other [26-28,30].

7.5 Stochastic simulation algorithm (SSA)

Even though the CME in (16) and (19) provides the ultimate probabilistic characterization for a discrete molecular oscillator, its solution is most often not practical due to the huge number of possible state configurations. As a result, one most often performs a stochastic simulation of the continuous-time Markov chain that models the oscillator and generates a sample path or a realization for the state vector $\mathbf{X}(t)$ as a function of time t. This kind of a simulation can be performed with a technique called the SSA, proposed in Gillespie's seminal work [25]. In the original SSA algorithm [25], the computational cost per reaction event (due to the generation of a random variable from a dynamic discrete probability distribution) is $\mathcal{O}(M)$ in the number of reactions M.

The cost per reaction event can be reduced to $\mathcal{O}(\log M)$ by using a binary tree for random selection of reactions [49], and to $\mathcal{O}(1)$ under certain conditions [50]. One also has to consider the fact that the time gap between reactions tends to shrink as the number of reactions M, the number of species N, and the number of molecules of every species increases. This means that the total computational cost of SSA for a given time period increases as a result [24]. On the other hand, if the numbers of molecules of all of the species are very large, discrete stochastic simulation of a discrete molecular oscillator in the sense of SSA may be unnecessary [24,27]. In this case, the fluctuations around the deterministic limit cycle will be small, and the continuous Langevin model in (25) may be adequate. As the number of molecules increase, the reaction propensities $a_j(\mathbf{X}(t))$ become larger, and the fluctuation term in the Langevin model in (25) become less and less pronounced in comparison with the drift term, since the magnitude of the drift term is proportional to the reaction propensities whereas the fluctuation term is proportional to their square root [26-28].

Molecular models, their nature (as discrete or continuous, and as stochastic or deterministic), and the algorithms to solve these models are summarized in Figure 1. The approximation that leads us from the discrete stochastic CME to the continuous stochastic CLE is the Gaussian approximation to Poisson random variables and accordingly the τ-leap approximation. Similarly, infinite volume approximation takes us from the CLE to the continuous deterministic RRE. Sample paths in line with the CME can be generated through SSA. CLE is a type of stochastic differential equation, so it can be solved via appropriate algorithms. Solution of the RRE requires algorithms designed for ordinary differential equations (ODEs) [26-28].

8 Methods - Phase computations based on Langevin models

There exists a well developed theory and numerical techniques for phase characterizations of oscillators with continuous-space models based on differential and stochastic differential equations [15,22]. As described in Sections 7.3 and 7.4, continuous models in the form of differential and stochastic differential equations can be constructed in a straightforward manner for discrete molecular oscillators. Thus, one can in principle apply the previously developed phase models and computation techniques [15,22] to these continuous models.

The outline of this section is as follows: After presenting the preliminaries (Section 8.1), the phase computation problem is introduced (Section 8.2). The methods in Section 8.3 (phase models in the form of ODEs) and in Section 8.4 (phase computation schemes that involve the numerical solution of certain algebraic equations) are designed to numerically solve the phase computation problem of Section 8.2.

8.1 Preliminaries

For a molecular oscillator, we assume that the deterministic RREs in (21) have a stable periodic solution $\mathbf{x}_s(t)$ (with period T) that represents a periodic orbit or limit cycle.

An isochron of an oscillator associated with the limit cycle $\mathbf{x}_s(t)$ is a set of points that have the same phase. For an N-dimensional oscillator, each isochron is an N-1-*dimensional hypersurface*. The union of isochrons covers the neighborhood of its periodic orbit [1,14]. Isochrons form the basis for phase definition and phase computations for oscillators [22]. In Figure 3, the limit cycle and the isochron portrait of a simple polar oscillator are shown [2,15].

Expanding (21) to first-order (linearization) around $\mathbf{x}_s(t)$, with

$$\mathbf{G}(t) = \mathbf{G}(\mathbf{x}_s(t)) = \left.\frac{\partial \mathbf{S}\,\mathbf{a}(\mathbf{x})}{\partial \mathbf{x}}\right|_{\mathbf{x}=\mathbf{x}_s(t)} \tag{27}$$

yields

$$\frac{d\mathbf{y}}{dt} = \mathbf{G}(t)\mathbf{y} \tag{28}$$

(28) is a linear periodically time-varying (LPTV) system. The adjoint form of (28) is given by

$$\frac{d}{dt}\mathbf{z} = -\mathbf{G}^{\mathrm{T}}(t)\,\mathbf{z} \tag{29}$$

The PPV $\mathbf{v}(t)$ is defined as the T-periodic solution of the adjoint LPTV equation in (29), which satisfies the following *normalization condition*

$$\mathbf{v}^{\mathrm{T}}(t)\frac{d\,\mathbf{x}_s(t)}{dt} = \mathbf{u}^{\mathrm{T}}(t)\frac{d\,\mathbf{u}(t)}{dt} = 1 \tag{30}$$

where $\mathbf{u}(t) = d\mathbf{x}_s(t)/dt$. The entries of the PPV are the infinitesimal PRCs [1]. The PPV is instrumental in forming linear approximations for the isochrons of an oscillator and in fact is the *gradient* of the *phase* of an oscillator [22] on the limit cycle represented by $\mathbf{x}_s(t)$.

We next define the matrix $\mathbf{H}(t)$ as the Jacobian of the PPV as follows

$$\mathbf{H}(t) = \mathbf{H}(\mathbf{x}_s(t)) = \frac{\partial \mathbf{v}(\mathbf{x}_s(t))}{\partial \mathbf{x}_s(t)} = \left.\frac{\partial \mathbf{v}(\mathbf{x})}{\partial \mathbf{x}}\right|_{\mathbf{x}=\mathbf{x}_s(t)} \tag{31}$$

taking into note that actually both $\mathbf{v}(t) = \mathbf{v}(\mathbf{x}_s(t))$ and $\mathbf{H}(t) = \mathbf{H}(\mathbf{x}_s(t))$ are functions of the periodic solution $\mathbf{x}_s(t)$. The function $\mathbf{H}(t)$ is in fact the *Hessian* of the phase of an oscillator [22] on the limit cycle represented by $\mathbf{x}_s$

(t). This matrix function is useful in forming quadratic approximations for the isochrons of an oscillator.

8.2 Phase computation problem

The phase computation problem for oscillators can be stated as follows. It is observed in Figure 2 that assuming an SSA sample path and the periodic RRE solution start at the same point on the limit cycle (note that the two are in-phase initially), the two trajectories may end up on different isochrons instantaneously at $t = t_0$ (i.e., the two traces at this instant are out of phase). However, according to the properties of isochrons, there is always a point on the limit cycle that is in-phase with a particular point near the limit cycle. Therefore, the existence of $\mathbf{x}_s(\hat{t})$ in-phase with the instantaneous point $\mathbf{x}_{ssa}(t_0)$ is guaranteed. We call then the time argument $\hat{t}$ of $\mathbf{x}_s(\hat{t})$ the instantaneous *phase* of $\mathbf{x}_{ssa}(t_0)$ [1,2,14,22]. All methods described below in this section are designed to numerically compute this phase value.

8.3 Phase equations based on Langevin models

In this section, oscillator phase models in the form of ODEs are described. In [22], we have reviewed the first order phase equation based on linear isochron approximations, and we have also developed novel and more accurate second order phase equations depending on quadratic approximations for isochrons. We will, furthermore in this section, explain how to apply these models to discrete oscillator phase computation.

8.3.1 First-order phase equation based on linear isochron approximations

The first-order phase equation based on linear isochron approximations can be derived from the continuous Langevin model in (25) using the theory and numerical techniques described in [15,22], which takes the form

$$\frac{d\hat{t}}{dt} = 1 + \mathbf{v}^T(\hat{t})\mathbf{S}\,\mathbb{D}\left(\left[\sqrt{\mathbf{a}(\mathbf{x}_s(\hat{t}))}\right]\right)\xi(t), \quad \hat{t}(0) = 0, \quad (32)$$

where $\hat{t}$ represents the total phase of the oscillator (in units of time) and $\mathbf{v}(t)$ is the PPV discussed above. The value $\mathbf{x}_s(\hat{t})$, the periodic solution $\mathbf{x}_s(t)$ evaluated at the perturbed phase $\hat{t}$, represents possibly a good approximation for the solution of the Langevin equation in (25) provided that the perturbed oscillator does not wander off too far away from the deterministic limit cycle represented by $\mathbf{x}_s(t)$.

The phase $\hat{t}$ defined above and the phase equation in (32), capture the deviations (from the periodic steady-state) of the perturbed oscillator only along the limit cycle, i.e., phase deviations. A perturbed oscillator also exhibits orbital deviations away from its deterministic limit cycle. Moreover, for a discrete, molecular oscillator, the deterministic periodic solution $\mathbf{x}_s(t)$ is merely the solution of its continuous and deterministic limit when the number of molecules are assumed to be very large. As such, the solution of a discrete molecular oscillator may exhibit large fluctuations around this continuous and deterministic limit. Thus, $\mathbf{x}_s(\hat{t})$ may not serve as a good approximation in such a case. In order to truly assess the quality of $\mathbf{x}_s(\hat{t})$ as an approximation in a meaningful manner, we need to compare it with a sample path solution of the discrete, Markov chain model that can be generated with an SSA simulation. However, a one-to-one comparison of $\mathbf{x}_s(\hat{t})$ based on the solution of the phase equation in (32) and a sample path obtained with an SSA simulation is not straightforward. In solving (32), one would normally generate sample paths for the independent white stationary Gaussian processes denoted by $\xi(t)$. In an SSA simulation, sample paths are generated as described in Section 7.5. If done so, a one-to-one comparison between a sample path from an SSA simulation and $\mathbf{x}_s(\hat{t})$ would not make sense. In order to make this sample path based comparison meaningful, we use the same discrete random events that are generated in an SSA simulation in order to synthesize the sample paths for the independent white stationary Gaussian processes $\xi(t)$ in the numerical simulation of (25). More precisely, we proceed as follows. We numerically compute the solution of (32) in parallel and synchronous with an SSA simulation. We discretize the SDE in (32) using time steps that are dictated by the reaction occurrence times in the SSA simulation. Assuming that the last reaction has just occurred at time t, the next reaction will occur at time $t + \tau$ and it will be the jth reaction, we form the update equation for $\hat{t}$ as follows

$$\hat{t}(t+\tau) = \hat{t}(t) + \tau + \mathbf{v}^T(\hat{t}(t))\mathbf{S}\left[\mathbf{e}_j - \mathbf{a}(\mathbf{x}_s(\hat{t}(t)))\tau\right] \quad (33)$$

where $\mathbf{e}_j$ is the $M \times 1$ unit vector with the jth entry set to 1 and the rest of the entries set to 0, and

$$\mathbf{a}(\mathbf{x}_s(\hat{t})) = \left[a_1(\mathbf{x}_s(\hat{t})), a_2(\mathbf{x}_s(\hat{t})), \ldots, a_M(\mathbf{x}_s(\hat{t}))\right]^T \quad (34)$$

is an $M \times 1$ column vector of reaction propensities evaluated at $\mathbf{x}_s(\hat{t})$. The form of the update rule above in (33) can be deduced by examining (24) where we have approximated a Poisson random variable with a Gaussian one. With (33) above, the sample paths for the white Gaussian processes $\xi(t)$ in (25) (and hence the Wiener processes as their integral) are being generated as a cumulation of the individual events, i.e., reactions, that occur in the SSA simulation of the oscillator at a discrete, molecular level. In the update rule (33), we subtract $\mathbf{a}(\mathbf{x}_s(\hat{t}(t)))\,\tau$ from $\mathbf{e}_j$ that represents an individual reaction event in order to make the synthesized $\xi_j(t)$ zero mean. The mean, deterministic behavior of the oscillator is captured by the first drift term on the right hand side of (25) which is used in the computation of the periodic steady-state solution $\mathbf{x}_s(t)$ and the PPV $\mathbf{v}(t)$. Thus, the mean behavior is already captured, and that is why, it needs to be subtracted in (33). We can now compare $\mathbf{x}_s(\hat{t})$ and the SSA generated sample path in a one-to-one manner in order to assess the quality of $\mathbf{x}_s(\hat{t})$. We should note here that the SSA simulation that is run in parallel and synchronous with the solution of the phase equation in (32) is necessary only for a meaningful sample path based comparison. One would normally not run an SSA simulation but simply generate sample paths for the Gaussian processes $\xi(t)$ and numerically solve (32) with an appropriate technique and generate a sample path for the phase $\hat{t}$. In this case, we would not be synthesizing $\xi(t)$ as a cumulation of reaction events from SSA, but instead directly as white Gaussian processes.

Figure 4 summarizes the phase equations (as opposed to the phase computation schemes, to be introduced later) approach for oscillator phase computations. An SSA sample path is generated. Then, the reaction events in the SSA sample path are recorded. This information, along with limit cycle and isochron approximations computed from the RRE, are fed into phase equations (the first-order phase equation in (32) has been given as an example in Figure 4), which in turn yield the phase $\hat{t}$. A high-level pseudocode description of phase computations using the first order phase equation is given in Algorithm 1.

In (33), we evaluate the reaction propensities at $\mathbf{x}_s(\hat{t})$, on the solution of the system projected onto the limit cycle represented by $\mathbf{x}_s(t)$. However, the oscillator also experiences orbital fluctuations and rarely stays on its limit cycle. Based on linear isochron approximations, we can in fact compute an approximation for the orbital fluctuations as well by solving the following equation [22]

$$\frac{d\,\mathbf{Y}(t)}{dt} = \mathbf{G}(\hat{t})\,\mathbf{Y}(t) + \mathbf{S}\,\mathbb{D}\left(\left[\sqrt{\mathbf{a}(\mathbf{x}_s(\hat{t}))}\right]\right)\xi(t) - \left[\mathbf{v}^T(t)\,\mathbf{S}\,\mathbb{D}\left(\left[\sqrt{\mathbf{a}(\mathbf{x}_s(\hat{t}))}\right]\right)\xi(t)\right]\mathbf{u}(\hat{t}) \qquad (35)$$

With the orbital fluctuation computed by solving the above linear system of differential equations, we can form a better approximation for the solution of the oscillator:

$$\mathbf{X}(t) \approx \mathbf{x}_s(\hat{t}) + \mathbf{Y}(t) \qquad (36)$$

Then, one can evaluate the reaction propensities at $\mathbf{x}_s(\hat{t}) + \mathbf{Y}(t)$ instead of $\mathbf{x}_s(\hat{t})$, in (32), (33) and (35), in order to improve the accuracy of phase computations. One can further improve accuracy, by replacing $\mathbf{G}(\hat{t})$ in (35) with

$$\mathbf{G}(\mathbf{x}_s(\hat{t}) + \mathbf{Y}(t)) = \left.\frac{\partial \mathbf{S}\,\mathbf{a}(\mathbf{x})}{\partial \mathbf{x}}\right|_{\mathbf{x}=\mathbf{x}_s(\hat{t})+\mathbf{Y}(t)} \qquad (37)$$

marking also that the matrix $\mathbf{G}$ is indeed a function of explicitly the state variables. Still, the equations in (32) and (35) are both based on linear isochron approximations. Phase and orbital deviation equations based on quadratic approximations for isochrons will provide even better accuracy, which we discuss next.

8.3.2 Second-order phase equation based on quadratic isochron approximations

The second-order phase equation based on quadratic isochron approximations can be derived from the continuous Langevin model in (25) using the theory and numerical techniques described in [15,22], which takes the form

$$\frac{d\hat{t}}{dt} = 1 + [\mathbf{v}(\hat{t}) + \mathbf{H}(\hat{t})\,\mathbf{Y}(t)]^T\,\mathbf{S}\,\mathbb{D}\left(\left[\sqrt{\mathbf{a}(\mathbf{X}(t))}\right]\right)\xi(t) \qquad (38)$$
$$\hat{t}(0) = 0,$$

with

$$\frac{d\mathbf{Y}(t)}{dt} = \mathbf{G}(\hat{t})\,\mathbf{Y}(t) + \frac{1}{2}\left.\frac{\partial \mathbf{C}(\mathbf{x})}{\partial \mathbf{x}}\right|_{\mathbf{x}=\mathbf{x}_s(t)}(\mathbf{Y}(t)\otimes\mathbf{Y}(t)) + \mathbf{S}\,\mathbb{D}\left(\left[\sqrt{\mathbf{a}(\mathbf{X}(t))}\right]\right)\xi(t) - \left\{\left[\mathbf{v}(\hat{t}) + \mathbf{H}(\hat{t})\mathbf{Y}(t)\right]^T\mathbf{S}\,\mathbb{D}\left(\left[\sqrt{\mathbf{a}(\mathbf{X}(t))}\right]\right)\xi(t)\right\}[\mathbf{u}(\hat{t}) + \mathbf{G}(\hat{t})\mathbf{Y}(t)] \qquad (39)$$

where $\mathbf{X}(t) = \mathbf{x}_s(\hat{t}) + \mathbf{Y}(t)$, $\left.\frac{\partial \mathbf{G}(\mathbf{x})}{\partial \mathbf{x}}\right|_{\mathbf{x}=\mathbf{x}_s(t)}$ represents an $N \times N^2$, matrix, and $\otimes$ denotes the, Kronecker product making $\mathbf{Y}(t) \otimes \mathbf{Y}(t)$ an $N^2 \times 1$ vector.

With quadratic approximations for the isochrons of the oscillator, the phase computations based on (38) and (39) will be more accurate. We can assess the accuracy of the results obtained with these equations again by numerically solving them in synchronous fashion with an SSA simulation while synthesizing the white Gaussian processes $\xi(t)$ as a cumulation of the reaction events in SSA, as described in Section 8.3.1.

8.4 Phase computation schemes based on Langevin models and SSA simulations

With the phase equations based on linear and quadratic isochron approximations described in Section 8.3, we can compute the phase of an oscillator without having to run SSA simulations based on its discrete, molecular model. We note here again that the SSA simulations described in (32) were necessary only when a one-to-one comparison between the results of phase computations based on phase equations and SSA simulations was required. On the other hand, more accurate phase computations can be attained if they are based on, i.e., use information, from SSA simulations. In this hybrid scheme, we run an SSA simulation based on the discrete, molecular model of the oscillator. For points (in the state-space) on the sample path generated by the SSA simulation, we compute a corresponding phase by essentially determining the isochron on which the point in question lies. Here, one can either employ no approximations for the isochrons or perform phase computations based on linear or quadratic isochron approximations. In [15], we have established the theory for these types of approximate phase computation schemes based on linear and quadratic isochron approximations.

The brute-force phase computations without isochron approximations, which we call Ph-CompBF in short, aims to compute the phase difference between two individual given points, based on the isochron-theoretic phase definition with respect to the periodic solution $\mathbf{x}_s(t)$ tracing the limit cycle. This method is computationally costly [15,22], as the following explanation based on Figure 5 will reveal. An SSA sample path is computed and the instantanous phase of $\mathbf{x}_{ssa}(t_0)$ is desired to be found. Note that t_0 is a particular value in time. For this purpose, in the transition from Figure 5a to 5b, all noise is switched off and RRE solutions (trajectories in state space) starting from $\mathbf{x}_s(t_0)$ (star on the limit cycle) and $\mathbf{x}_{ssa}(t_0)$ (circle off the limit cycle) in Figure 5a are computed. We can compute the phase shift between these two traces only when the off-cycle solution converges as in Figure 5c, that is we will have to integrate RRE for this solution until it becomes approximately periodic in the time domain. In this plot, the illustration has been prepared such that the convergence to the limit cycle takes one period or so, but this may not always be the case. Indeed, ideally this process takes infinite time. This is why the brute-force method is costly. Eventually, the phase shift between the two trajectories can be computed and added to instantaneous time t_0, to compute the phase $\hat{t}$ [15,22].

The phase computation based on isochron approximations and SSA simulations proceeds as follows: Let $\mathbf{x}_{ssa}(t)$ be the sample path for the state vector of the oscillator that is being computed with SSA. We either solve

$$\mathbf{v}^T(\hat{t})\left[\mathbf{x}_{ssa}(t) - \mathbf{x}_s(\hat{t})\right] = 0 \tag{40}$$

based on linear isochron approximations or

$$\mathbf{v}^T(\hat{t})\left[\mathbf{x}_{ssa}(t) - \mathbf{x}_s(\hat{t})\right] + \frac{1}{2}\left[\mathbf{x}_{ssa}(t) - \mathbf{x}_s(\hat{t})\right]^T \mathbf{H}(\hat{t})\left[\mathbf{x}_{ssa}(t) - \mathbf{x}_s(\hat{t})\right] = 0 \tag{41}$$

based on quadratic isochron approximations for the phase $\hat{t}$ that corresponds to $\mathbf{x}_{ssa}(t)$ [15,22]. The above computation needs to be repeated for every time point t of interest. Above, for $\mathbf{x}_{ssa}(t)$, we essentially determine the isochron (in fact, a linear or quadratic approximation for it) that passes through both the point $\mathbf{x}_s(\hat{t})$ on the limit cycle and $\mathbf{x}_{ssa}(t)$. The phase of $\mathbf{x}_s(\hat{t})$, i.e., $\hat{t}$, is then the phase of $\mathbf{x}_{ssa}(t)$ as well since they reside on the same isochron. An illustration of the scheme founded upon linear isochron approximations is given in Figure 6. In this plot, we are looking for an isochron whose linear approximation goes through $\mathbf{x}_{ssa}(t_0)$, and this is the isochron of the point $\mathbf{x}_s(\hat{t}_{lin})$. Notice that the linear approximation (the straight line in Figure 6) is tangent to the isochron of $\mathbf{x}_s(\hat{t}_{lin})$ at exactly $\mathbf{x}_s(\hat{t}_{lin})$. The value $\hat{t}_{lin}$ then is the phase computed by this scheme. Notice that there is some difference between the exact solution $\hat{t}$ and the approximate $\hat{t}_{lin}$. This difference is certain to shrink if the isochrones are locally closer to being linear. For more accurate but still approximate solutions, the quadratic scheme can be used [15,22].

We should note here that, even though $\mathbf{x}_{ssa}(t)$ above is computed with an SSA simulation based on the discrete model of the oscillator, the steady-state periodic solution $\mathbf{x}_s(\hat{t})$, the phase gradient $\mathbf{v}(\hat{t})$ and the Hessian $\mathbf{H}(\hat{t})$ (i.e., all of the information that is used in constructing the isochron approximations) are computed based on the continuous, RRE model of the oscillator [15,22]. The phase computation schemes we describe here can be regarded as *hybrid* techniques that are based both on the continuous, RRE and the discrete, molecular model of the oscillator. On the other hand, the phase computation schemes discussed in Section 8.3 based on phase equations are completely based on the continuous, RRE and Langevin models of the oscillator. Figure 7 explains the ingredients that the phase computation schemes utilize. An SSA sample path is generated (note that alternatively a sample path may be generated through the CLE). From the RRE model, limit cycle information ($\mathbf{x}_s(t)$) and isochron approximations ($\mathbf{v}(t)$ and $\mathbf{H}(t)$) are computed. All this information is fed into the phase computation schemes (in Figure 7 we have given the expression for the scheme utilizing linear approximations for convenience, as this is the method likely to be preferred due to its lower complexity despite its inferior accuracy as compared to the quadratic scheme) and then finally the phase $\hat{t}$ is found. A high level pseudocode of phase computations using the scheme depending on linear isochron approximations is given in Algorithm 2.

9 Methods - Oscillator models, numerical methods, and implementation notes

This section briefly describes where suitable oscillator models can be found particularly on the internet and how these models can be modified when possible (Section 9.1), how the obtained ODE models can be handled computationally (Section 9.2), a description of the numerical methods used in the simulations (Section 9.3), and the computational costs that they incur (Section 9.4).

9.1 Biochemical oscillator models

Oscillator models for analysis can be found from multiple resources on the web. Models generally come in two separate forms, described briefly as follows.

Models of the first type are translated directly from actual biochemical reactions. Propensities of the reactions are functions of a reaction rate parameter and appropriate algebraic expressions of molecule numbers associated with the reacting species. As such, the propensities are always positive. Moreover, the volume parameter (associated with the container or the cell accommodating the species) can easily be incorporated into the propensity functions. Volume of the cell implies the level of noisiness in the sample path simulations, i.e., basically, the more voluminous a cell, the more the number of each reacting species, and then the closer the sample path solution to the ensemble average. Therefore, one may rightfully declare that every different value for the volume parameter defines a new oscillator to be analyzed, although the mechanism of the reactions and the pattern for the propensities remain the same for a pre-determined setting.

Models of the second type are provided directly as ODE models. In some cases, the propensity functions are difficult to handle, and it is not obvious how the crucial volume parameter can be incorporated into the equations. Then, it happens that analysis of these oscillators is a little restricted, not having the capability to adjust the level of noisiness in a correct and reliable manner. However, in all, the simulations can be carried out for the value of the volume implied by the ODE model.

As to where oscillator models can be found on the web, there are multiple alternatives. http://www.xmds.org/[39] is the website for a simulator, in which particularly models from [38] have been modified in appropriate form to be analyzed. We have benefitted extensively from the models we have obtained from these references, as most of them are models of the first type described above. One of the other alternatives is obtaining ODE models (models of the second type stated above) from online repositories such as [41-43] and manipulate them via appropriate software toolboxes [44,45].

9.2 Information computed from the ODE model and SSA

Oscillator models are approximated by ODEs in the deterministic sense, through procedures already explained in the previous sections. Our purpose before handling a sample path generated by SSA is to have available in hand some crucial computational quantities that will help compute the phase along the sample path. All these crucial quantities will be computed using the ODE model. A shooting type of formulation [40] is preferred to obtain the periodic solution, more particularly a number of discrete timepoints for $\mathbf{x}_s(t)$ along a single period. The shooting method solves this boundary value problem efficiently even for large systems of ODEs [40]. A further key benefit is that by-products of the shooting method can be utilized in solving for $\mathbf{v}(t)$, namely the PPV or the phase gradient [11]. On top of $\mathbf{x}_s(t)$ and $\mathbf{v}(t)$ and using again the by-products of these computations, $\mathbf{H}(t)$, the phase Hessian, can be obtained through the algorithm proposed in [15]. Now, SSA simulations for the sample paths of the noisy molecular oscillator can be performed [25], and these sample paths are analyzed in terms of phase with the following numerical methods. It should be recalled, however, that during the SSA simulation, also pieces of information have to be stored at each reaction event, conveying which reaction was chosen randomly to be simulated and what were the propensity function values at that particular instant.

9.3 Phase simulations

In this section, we provide details concerning the numerical aspects of the proposed phase computation methods.

The brute-force scheme (PhCompBF) (described in Section 8.4) is basically run for all of the timepoints in an SSA-generated sample path, and it is very costly in terms of computation. If $\mathbf{x}_{ssa}(t_0)$ is a timepoint in the sample path (naturally at where a state change takes place) the RRE is integrated with this initial condition at $t = 0$ for a long time so that this deterministic solution settles to the limit cycle in continuous time. The solution of the RRE with the initial condition $\mathbf{x}_s(t_0)$ at t=0 can be readily computed, this is a shifted version of the periodic solution $\mathbf{x}_s(t)$ that is available. If the phase shift between the two solutions is computed, this shift is the phase shift of the sample path $\mathbf{x}_{ssa}$ at $t = t_0$ [15]. Since one generally does not know the phase value at the very first timepoint of an SSA sample path, the brute-force scheme is mandatory in computing this phase value and providing the initial condition, on which all of the other approximate phase computation schemes and equations can operate.

The approximate phase computation schemes [15] (again described in Section 8.4) consist of solving the algebraic equation in (40) or (41), depending on whether linear or quadratic approximations are respectively preferred to be used, and they are also run for all points in the SSA sample path (see Algorithm 2 for the pseudocode of phase computations utilizing the scheme founded upon the linear isochron approximations). Benefitting from the scalar nature of these equations, the bisection method is used extensively in their numerical solution. Details and subtleties involved with these schemes (of considerably less computational load compared to PhCompBF) are provided in [15].

Phase equations [22], described in Section 8.3 are in this context stochastic differential equations, operating on the recorded reaction events of an SSA sample path. The specific discretization scheme applied to the first order phase equation is explained in detail in Section 8.3.1 (see Algorithm 1 for the pseudocode of phase computations with this first order equation). This discretization scheme can be easily extended to the second order phase equation of Section 8.3.2.

We will denote each method analyzed and used in generating results by some abbreviations, for ease of reference. The brute-force scheme explained above is denoted by Ph-CompBF, the scheme depending on linear isochron approximations (summarized by (40)) by PhCompLin, and that depending on quadratic in (41) by PhCompQuad. The first order phase equation of (32) is denoted by PhEqnLL (the first L for linear isochron approximations and the second L for linear orbital deviation approximations). The second order phase equation of (38) and (39) is denoted by PhEqnQQ (Q for both type of approximations, isochron and orbital deviation). We prefer to use instead of PhEqnQQ a simpler, but numerically more reliable, version of the second order equation. This simpler version is described by the equations (38) and (35). Equation (35) is the orbital deviation equation belonging to the first order phase equation theory. In turn, we denote this simpler model by PhEqnQL [22].

9.4 Analysis of computational complexities

In this section, we analyze the computational costs of phase computation schemes and phase equations. Let us denote by N the number of states in an oscillator, M the number of reactions, K the number of timepoints along a single period, L the number of total timepoints along the interval where a phase computation method is run.

Preliminary statements on computational complexities are as follows. We assume as well-known complexities that $\mathbf{x}_s(t)$, $\mathbf{G}(t)$ (assumed to be sparse), $\mathbf{u}(t)$ and $\mathbf{v}(t)$ are computable along a single period in $\mathcal{O}(N\,K)$ time. The computation of $\mathbf{H}(t)$ (which is usually not sparse) upon the stated quantities takes $\mathcal{O}(N^3\,K)$ time [15]. We assume that if a matrix is sparse, then matrix vector multiplications and solving a linear system of equations involving this matrix can be done in linear time.

For PhCompBF (see Section 8.4 and Figure 5 for explanations), in order to compute the phase of a point $\mathbf{x}_{ssa}(t_0)$, we have to integrate the RRE with initial condition $\mathbf{x}_{ssa}(t_0)$ for an ideally infinite number, namely n_{per}, of periods, so that the states vector can be assumed more or less to be tracing the limit cycle. If FFT (fast Fourier transform) properties are used to compute the phase shift between periodic waveforms, the overall complexity of PhCompBF can be shown to amount to $\mathcal{O}(n_{per}K\;N\;L + L\;K\log_2 K)$ [22].

The approximate phase computation schemes consist of solving the algebraic equations in (40) or (41) (depending on whether the linear or quadratic scheme is preferred). The bisections method is used to solve these equations. In order to compute the phase value of a particular timepoint, an interval has to be formed. In forming such an interval, we start with an interval, of length d_{min} and centered around the phase value of the previous timepoint, and double this length value until the interval is certain to contain the phase solution. The allowed maximum interval length is denoted by d_{max}. Then, the bisections scheme starts to chop down the interval until a tolerance value d_{tol} for the interval length is reached. See Algorithm 2 for the pseudocode of phase computations using PhCompLin (the scheme depending on linear isochron approximations), based on this explanation. More explanations on the flow of PhCompLin are given in Section 8.4 and Figure 6. The PhCompLin computational complexity can be shown to be

$$\mathcal{O}\left(N\;L\log_2\left\lceil\frac{d_{max}^2}{d_{tol}d_{min}}\right\rceil\right) \tag{42}$$

and PhCompQuad (which depends on quadratic isochron approximations) complexity is

$$\mathcal{O}\left(N^2\;L\log_2\left\lceil\frac{d_{max}^2}{d_{tol}d_{min}}\right\rceil\right) \tag{43}$$

based on the explanations above.

The computational complexity expressions for all of the phase computation schemes are summarized in Table 1.

Phase equation solution complexities depend (in extreme conditions) mainly on the stoichiometric matrix $\mathbf{S}$ being sparse (few nonzero entries per row) or totally dense. Note that in realistic problems $\mathbf{S}$ is observed to be usually sparse. These stated respective conditions lead us to come up with best and worst case complexities.

Table 1 Computational complexities for the phase computation schemes

Scheme	Computational complexity
PhCompBF	$\mathcal{O}(n_{\text{per}}K\ N\ L + L\ K\log_2 K)$
PhCompLin	$\mathcal{O}\left(N\ L\log_2\left\lceil\frac{d^2_{\max}}{d_{\text{tol}}d_{\min}}\right\rceil\right)$
PhCompQuad	$\mathcal{O}\left(N^2\ L\ \log_2\left\lceil\frac{d^2_{\max}}{d_{\text{tol}}d_{\min}}\right\rceil\right)$

In order of increasing computational complexity, the schemes are PhCompLin (on linear isochron approximations), PhCompQuad (on quadratic isochron approximations), and PhCompBF (with no approximations). We denote by N the number of states in an oscillator, K the number of timepoints along a single period, and L the number of total timepoints along the interval where a phase computation method is run. We have n_{per} as the number of periods that we simulate the RRE with the initial condition that is off the orbit, so that this solution of the RRE can be expected in practice to settle into periodicity, and the phase value associated with the stated initial condition can be computed (note that this is the essence of PhCompBF). The values $d_{\max}$ and $d_{\min}$ are respectively the maximum and minimum lengths of the interval in which a solution for phase is sought. The value d_{tol} denotes a tolerance.

As such, PhEqnLL (the equation employing linear isochron and linear orbital deviation approximations) complexity in the best and worse case can be shown to be $\mathcal{O}(M\ L + N\ L)$ and $\mathcal{O}(N\ M\ L)$, respectively. PhEqnQL (with quadratic isochron and linear orbital deviation approximations) complexities are $\mathcal{O}(N^2\ L +\ M\ L)$ (best case) and $\mathcal{O}(N^2\ L +\ N\ M\ L)$ (worst case). Complexities for the phase equations are summarized in Table 2. For a pseudocode of phase computations using PhEqnLL, see the explanation in Section 8.3.1 and Algorithm 1 based on this account.

The essence of the above analyses is that there is a trade-off between accuracy and computational complexity [22]. For mildly noisy oscillators, the phase equations should remain somewhat close to the results of the golden reference PhCompBF and the other approximate phase computation schemes, which imitate PhCompBF very successfully with much less computation times. For more noisy oscillators, we should expect the phase computation schemes to do still well, although the phase equations will compute some inaccurate results very fast. PhCompBF is always very slow [22].

Table 2 Computational complexities for the phase equations

Equation	Complexity (best)	Complexity (worst)
PhEqnLL	$\mathcal{O}(M\ L + N\ L)$	$\mathcal{O}(N\ M\ L)$
PhEqnQL	$\mathcal{O}(N^2\ L +\ M\ L)$	$\mathcal{O}(N^2\ L +\ N\ M\ L)$

We provide the best and worst case computational complexities for the phase equations, PhEqnLL (on linear isochron and linear orbital deviation approximations) and PhEqnQL (on quadratic isochron and linear orbital deviation approximations), according as the stoichiometric matrix S is sparse (few entries per row) or fully dense. Note that the computational load the equations entail are much less than those of the phase computation schemes. We denote by N the number of states in an oscillator, M the number of possible reactions that can occur, K the number of timepoints along a single period, and L the number of total timepoints along the interval where a phase computation method is run.

Algorithm 1 - PhEqnLL pseudocode

input : oscModel and ssaPath
output: phase and phaseShift of points in ssaPath
//compute limit cycle [40]
1 $\mathbf{x}_s(t)$ = computeLimitCycle (oscModel);
//compute linear isochron approximations along a single period [11]
2 $\mathbf{v}(t)$ = computePhaseGradient (oscModel);
//obtain SSA path data
3 pts = pts in ssaPath;
//compute phase
4 **for** $i \leftarrow 1$ **to** size(pts in ssaPath) **do**
//for the first timepoint, use the brute-force scheme PhCompBF
//refer to Section 8.4 and Figure 5 for explanations
//refer to Section 9.4 for computational complexity
5 **if** *i is equal to 1* **then**
//tValue of pts(i) : the time at which pts(i) occurs
//value of pts(i) : state vector for the oscillator at tValue of pts(i)
6 phaseShift(i) = PhCompBF(oscModel, $\mathbf{x}_s(t)$, tValue *of* pts(i), value *of* pts(i));
7 phase(i) = [tValue of pts(i)] + phaseShift(i);
8 end
//for the other timepoints, use the first order phase equation
//PhEqnLL update rule is given in (33) of Section 8.3.1
//more implementation details and computational complexity in Section 9.4
//stoichiometric matrix (**S**) and propensity function (a(**X**))
//information are embedded in oscModel
9 **if** *i is not equal to 1* **then**
10 tau = [tValue of pts(i)] - [tValue of pts($i-1$)];
//Now apply the update rule in (33)
//reactionNo of pts(i) : number of the reaction occuring at tValue of pts(i)
//$\mathbf{e}_j$ is an M-sized vector with its j th entry one
11 phase(i) =
phase($i-1$) + tau + $\mathbf{v}^{\mathrm{T}}$(phase($i-1$)) **S** [$\mathbf{e}_{\text{reactionNo of pts}(i)}$ - $\mathbf{a}(\mathbf{x}_s(\text{phase}(i-1)))$ tau];
12 phaseShift (i)=phase(i)-[tValue of pts(i)];
13 end
14 end

Algorithm 1: PhEqnLL pseudocode

Extended caption for Algorithm 1: Lines 1-2 compute the limit cycle and the phase gradient. In lines 4-14, the phase computation is described. Lines 5-8 describe the use of the brute-force scheme PhCompBF for the phase computation of the first timepoint. In lines 9- 13, the phase computation of the other timepoints is accomplished via PhEqnLL (the phase equation founded upon the linear isochron and the linear orbital deviation approximations).

Algorithm 2 - PhCompLin pseudocode

input : oscModel and ssaPath

output: phase and phaseShift of points in ssaPath

//compute limit cycle [40] and linear isochron approximations [11]

1 $\mathbf{x}_s(t)$ = computeLimitCycle (oscModel); $\mathbf{v}(t)$ = computePhaseGradient (oscModel);

//obtain SSA path data

2 pts = pts in ssaPath;

//compute phase

3 **for** $i \leftarrow 1$ **to** size(pts in ssaPath) **do**

//for the first timepoint, use the brute-force scheme PhCompBF

4 **if** *i is equal to 1* **then**

5 phaseShift(i) = PhCompBF(oscModel, $\mathbf{x}_s(t)$, tValue *of* pts(i), value *of* pts(i));

6 phase(i) = [tValue of pts(i)] + phaseShift(i);

7 end

//for the other timepoints, use PhCompLin, see (40) of Section 8.4

//pictorial description in Figure 6

//algorithm description and computational complexity in Section 9.4

8 **if** *i is not equal to 1* **then**

//phase(i-1) used as the midpoint of the interval

9 $d = d_{\min}/2$; interval = [phase(i-1) - d, phase(i-1) + d];

10 **while** length(interval) < $d_{\max}/2$ **do**

//Check if the solution $\hat{t}$ to the following equality (40) is in interval

$//\mathbf{v}^{\mathrm{T}}(\hat{t})\left[[\text{value of pts}(i)] - \mathbf{x}_s(\hat{t})\right] = 0$

11 **if** *solution is in* interval **then** break;

12 $d = 2^* d$; interval = [phase(i-1) - d, phase(i-1) + d];

13 end

//use bisection method to compute the solution to (40)

14 phase(i) = BisectionMethod(oscModel, $\mathbf{x}_s(t)$, $\mathbf{v}(t)$, interval, value *of* pts(i));

15 phaseShift(i) = phase(i) - [tValue of pts(i)];

16 end

17 end

Algorithm 2: PhCompLin pseudocode

Extended caption for Algorithm 2: Line 1 computes the limit cycle and the phase gradient. In lines 3-17, the phase computation is described. Lines 4-7 describe the use of the brute-force scheme PhCompBF for the phase computation of the first timepoint. In lines 8-16, the phase computation of the other timepoints is accomplished via PhCompLin (the phase computation scheme founded upon the linear approximations for isochrons).

Abbreviations

SSA: Stochastic Simulation Algorithm; CME: Chemical Master Equation; CLE: Chemical Langevin Equation; RRE: Reaction Rate Equation; SDE: Stochastic Differential Equation; ODE: Ordinary Differential Equation; PhCompBF: brute-force phase computation scheme; PhCompLin: phase computation scheme depending on linear approximations for isochrons; PhCompQuad: phase computation scheme depending on quadratic approximations for isochrons; PhEqnLL: phase equation depending on linear approximations for isochrons and linear approximations for orbital deviation; PhEqnQL: phase equation depending on quadratic approximations for isochrons and linear approximations for orbital deviation; PhEqnQQ: phase equation depending on quadratic approximations for isochrons and quadratic approximations for orbital deviation.

Acknowledgements

This work was supported by the Scientific and Technological Research Council of Turkey (TUBITAK).

Competing interests

The authors declare that they have no competing interests.

References

1. EM Izhikevich, Dynamical Systems in Neuroscience: The Geometry of Excitability and Bursting, (MIT Press, Cambridge, 2007)
2. AT Winfree, The Geometry of Biological Time, (Springer, New York, 2001)
3. A Goldbeter, Biochemical Oscillations and Cellular Rythms, (Cambridge University Press, Cambridge, 1996)
4. L Fu, CC Lee, The circadian clock: pacemaker and tumour suppressor. Nat Rev Cancer. **3**, 350–361 (2003). doi:10.1038/nrc1072
5. L Fu, H Pelicano, J Liu, P Huang, C Lee, The circadian gene Period2 plays an important role in tumor suppression and DNA damage response in vivo. Cell. **111**, 41–50 (2002). doi:10.1016/S0092-8674(02)00961-3
6. S Davis, DK Mirick, Circadian disruption, shift work and the risk of cancer: a summary of the evidence and studies in Seattle. Cancer Causes Control. **17**, 539–545 (2006). doi:10.1007/s10552-005-9010-9
7. ES Schernhammer, F Laden, FE Speizer, WC Willett, DJ Hunter, I Kawachi, CS Fuchs, GA Colditz, Night-shift work and risk of colorectal cancer in the nurses' health study. J Natl Cancer Inst. **95**, 825–828 (2003). doi:10.1093/jnci/95.11.825
8. K Straif, R Baan, Y Grosse, BE Secretan, FE Ghissassi, V Bouvard, A Altieri, L Benbrahim-Tallaa, V Cogliano, Carcinogenicity of shift-work, painting, and fire-fighting. Lancet Oncol. **12**(8), 1065–1066 (2007)
9. MB Elowitz, S Leibler, A synthetic oscillatory network of transcriptional regulators. Nature. **403**(6767), 335–338 (2000). doi:10.1038/35002125
10. A Demir, A Sangiovanni-Vincentelli, Analysis and Simulation of Noise in Nonlinear Electronic Circuits and Systems, (Kluwer Academic Publishers, Boston, 1998)
11. A Demir, A Mehrotra, J Roychowdhury, Phase noise in oscillators: A unifying theory and numerical methods for characterisation. IEEE Trans Circ Syst I Fund Theory Appl. **47**(5), 655–674 (2000). doi:10.1109/81.847872
12. JMG Vilar, HY Kueh, N Barkai, S Leibler, Mechanisms of noise-resistance in genetic oscillators. Proc Natl Acad Sci USA. **99**(9), 5988–5992 (2002). doi:10.1073/pnas.092133899
13. A Goldbeter, Computational approaches to cellular rhythms. Nature. **420**(6912), 238–245 (2002). doi:10.1038/nature01259
14. K Josic, ET Shea-Brown, J Moehlis, Isochron. Scholarpedia. **1**(8), 1361 (2006). doi:10.4249/scholarpedia.1361
15. O Suvak, A Demir, Quadratic approximations for the isochrons of oscillators: a general theory, advanced numerical methods and accurate phase

computations. IEEE Trans Comput Aided Design Integr Circ Syst. **29**(8), 1215–1228 (2010)
16. M Farkas, Periodic Motions, (Springer-Verlag, New York, 1994)
17. A Demir, Fully nonlinear oscillator noise analysis: an oscillator with no asymptotic phase. Int J Circ Theory and Appl. **35**, 175–203 (2007). doi:10.1002/cta.387
18. IG Malkin, Methods of Poincare and Liapunov in Theory Of Non-Linear Oscillations, (Gostexizdat, Moscow, 1949)
19. Y Kuramato, Chemical Oscillations, Waves, and Turbulence, (Springer-Verlag, New York, 1984)
20. E Brown, J Moehlis, P Holmes, On the phase reduction and response dynamics of neural oscillator populations. Neural Comput. **16**(4), 673–715 (2004). doi:10.1162/089976604322860668
21. FX Kaertner, Analysis of white and $f^{-\alpha}$ noise in oscillators. Int J Circ Theory Appl. **18**, 485–519 (1990). doi:10.1002/cta.4490180505
22. O Suvak, A Demir, On phase models for oscillators. IEEE Trans Comput Aided Design Integr Circ Syst. **30**(7), 972–985 (2011)
23. O Suvak, A Demir, Phase models and computations for molecular oscillators, in *Proc 8th Internat. Workshop on Computational Systems Biology (WCSB 2011)*, (ETH Zurich, Switzerland, 6–8 June 2011), pp. 173–176
24. DT Gillespie, Stochastic simulation of chemical kinetics. Ann Rev Phys Chem. **58**, 35–55 (2007). doi:10.1146/annurev.physchem.58.032806.104637
25. DT Gillespie, Exact stochastic simulation of coupled chemical reactions. J Phys Chem. **81**(25), 2340–2361 (1977). doi:10.1021/j100540a008
26. DT Gillespie, The chemical Langevin equation. J Chem Phys. **113**(1), 297–306 (2000). doi:10.1063/1.481811
27. DJ Higham, Modeling and simulating chemical reactions. SIAM Rev. **50**(2), 347–368 (2008). doi:10.1137/060666457
28. NG van Kampen, Stochastic Processes in Physics and Chemistry, (North-Holland, Amsterdam, 1992)
29. CW Gardiner, Handbook of Stochastic Methods for Physics, Chemistry and the Natural Sciences, (Springer-Verlag, Berlin, 1983)
30. DJ Wilkinson, Stochastic Modelling for System Biology, 1st edn. (CRC Press, New York, 2006)
31. M Amdaoud, M Vallade, C Weiss-Schaber, I Mihalcescu, Cyanobacterial clock, a stable phase oscillator with negligible intercellular coupling. Proc Natl Acad Sci USA. **104**, 7051–7056 (2007). doi:10.1073/pnas.0609315104
32. LG Morelli, F Julicher, Precision of genetic oscillators and clocks. Phys Rev Lett. **98**(22), 228101 (2007)
33. W Vance, J Ross, Fluctuations near limit cycles in chemical reaction systems. J Chem Phys. **105**, 479–487 (1996). doi:10.1063/1.471901
34. P Gaspard, The correlation time of mesoscopic chemical clocks. J Chem Phys. **117**, 8905–8916 (2002). doi:10.1063/1.1513461
35. H Koeppl, M Hafner, A Ganguly, A Mehrotra, Deterministic characterization of phase noise in biomolecular oscillators. Phys Biol. **8**(5), 055008 (2011). doi:10.1088/1478-3975/8/5/055008
36. T Tomita, T Ohta, H Tomita, Irreversible circulation and orbital revolution. Prog Theory Phys. **52**, 1744–1765 (1974). doi:10.1143/PTP.52.1744
37. D Gabor, Theory of communication. J IEE Lond. **93**, 429–457 (1946)
38. WH Cropper, Mathematica Computer Programs for Physical Chemistry, (Springer-Verlag, New York, 1998)
39. eXtensible Multi-Dimensional Simulator, http://www.xmds.org/
40. K Kundert, JK White, A Sangiovanni-Vincentelli, Steady-State Methods for Simulating Analog and Microwave Circuits, (Kluwer, Norwell, 1990)
41. Cellerator Model Repository, http://www.cellerator.info/nb.html
42. Cellular Models, http://www.cds.caltech.edu/hsauro/models.htm
43. Website E-Cellhttp://www.e-cell.org/ecell/
44. BJ Bornstein, SM Keating, A Jouraku, M Hucka, LibSBML: an API library for SBML. Bioinformatics. **24**(6), 880–881 (2008). doi:10.1093/bioinformatics/btn051
45. SM Keating, BJ Bornstein, A Finney, M Hucka, SBMLToolbox: an SBML toolbox for MAT-LAB users. Bioinformatics. **22**(10), 1275–1277 (2006). doi:10.1093/bioinformatics/btl111
46. SL Kalpazidou, Cycle Representations of Markov Processes, (Springer-Verlag, Berlin, 2006)
47. R Feistel, W Ebeling, Deterministic and stochastic theory of sustained oscillations in autocatalytic reaction systems. Phys A Stat Theor Phys. **93**(1-2), 114–137 (1978). doi:10.1016/0378-4371(78)90213-3
48. TL Hill, Free Energy Transduction and Biochemical Cycle Kinetics, (Springer-Verlag, New York, 1989)
49. MA Gibson, J Bruck, Exact stochastic simulation of chemical systems with many species and many channels. J Phys Chem A. **104**, 1876–1889 (2000). doi:10.1021/jp993732q
50. A Slepoy, AP Thompson, SJ Plimpton, A constant-time kinetic Monte Carlo algorithm for simulation of large biochemical reaction networks. J Chem Phys. **128**, 205101 (2008)

5

Template-based intervention in Boolean network models of biological systems

Michael P Verdicchio[1] and Seungchan Kim[2*]

Abstract

Motivation: A grand challenge in the modeling of biological systems is the identification of key variables which can act as targets for intervention. Boolean networks are among the simplest of models, yet they have been shown to adequately model many of the complex dynamics of biological systems. In our recent work, we utilized a logic minimization approach to identify quality single variable targets for intervention from the state space of a Boolean network. However, as the number of variables in a network increases, the more likely it is that a successful intervention strategy will require multiple variables. Thus, for larger networks, such an approach is required in order to identify more complex intervention strategies while working within the limited view of the network's state space. Specifically, we address three primary challenges for the large network arena: the first challenge is how to consider many subsets of variables, the second is to design clear methods and measures to identify the best targets for intervention in a systematic way, and the third is to work with an intractable state space through sampling.

Results: We introduce a multiple variable intervention target called a template and show through simulation studies of random networks that these templates are able to identify top intervention targets in increasingly large Boolean networks. We first show that, when other methods show drastic loss in performance, template methods show no significant performance loss between fully explored and partially sampled Boolean state spaces. We also show that, when other methods show a complete inability to produce viable intervention targets in sampled Boolean state spaces, template methods maintain significantly consistent success rates even as state space sizes increase exponentially with larger networks. Finally, we show the utility of the template approach on a real-world Boolean network modeling T-LGL leukemia.

Conclusions: Overall, these results demonstrate how template-based approaches now effectively take over for our previous single variable approaches and produce quality intervention targets in larger networks requiring sampled state spaces.

Keywords: Boolean networks; Attractors; Logic minimization; Intervention; Leukemia

Introduction

Motivation

The very nature of medicine is to know when and how to intervene in order to shift the steady behavior of a system to a more desirable state [1]. Ideally, such interventions would be as minimally damaging as possible; however, we know that especially with diseases such as cancer, interventions like chemotherapy are anything but minimal. In the path towards personalized medicine and individualized treatments with minimal collateral damage, designing and studying interventions that take advantage of our system-level understanding and available data is and will remain of paramount importance, as working with computational models allows us to perform tests, execute simulations, and make predictions in inexpensive ways that require no human subjects [2].

Biological systems are complex in many dimensions as endless transportation and communication networks all function simultaneously [3]. Despite its simplicity, the Boolean network model has proven to be quite viable at approximating certain aspects of biological processes [1]. For example, it has been used to simulate the yeast

*Correspondence: skim@tgen.org
[2]Integrated Cancer Genomics Division, Translational Genomics Research Institute, Phoenix, AZ 85004, USA
Full list of author information is available at the end of the article

cell cycle [4], which we looked at closely in our work [5]. It has also been used to simulate the expression pattern of segment polarity genes in *Drosophila melanogaster* [6], as well as the vocal communication system of the songbird brain [7,8]. Since Kauffman's seminal work [9], there have been countless variations and extensions of the use of Boolean networks for modeling biological systems, and various inference procedures have been proposed for them [10-12].

An intervention, in the context of a Boolean network, is defined as a modification (set/reset) to one or more variables in an attractor state of a source basin with the intention that network rules will transition to any state in a given goal basin (thus eventually reaching the attractor of the goal basin). In our recent work [5], we employed a logic reduction algorithm to reduce the Boolean states comprising the basins of attraction to minimal representations, and from those minimizations, we identified high-quality intervention targets comprised of single variables. However, as the number of variables in a biological network increases, the more likely it is that a successful intervention target will require the combined efforts of multiple variables. Thus, for larger networks, a new approach is required beyond our previous work in order to identify coherent, multi-valued intervention targets while working in with the limited view of the network's state space.

Related work

In this section, we detail pioneering efforts in the Boolean network field, especially in its application to biology, and we describe other attempts to identify key variables in networks while dealing with increasingly large state spaces. In the end, we find a remaining need for the results presented in this study.

Within the world of *in silico* modeling and intervention studies, significant groundwork has been laid. Boolean networks allow modeling at the most simplified extreme of the spectrum due to their coarse discretization of values to 0 and 1 and their simplified, rule-based update mechanism, yet have still been shown to adequately model complex behaviors seen in the biological system. In the next section, we give formal descriptions of Boolean networks and the basin of attraction field they generate. Over 30 years after Kauffman's seminal work [9], Shmulevich et al. [13] pioneered work on a stochastic extension to the model called probabilistic Boolean networks (PBNs), which share the rule-based nature of Boolean networks but also handle uncertainty well. Within this extended framework of PBNs, studies were performed by Datta et al. [14,15], which focused on external system control; studies by Pal et al. [16] and Choudhary et al. [17] explored intervention in PBNs to avoid undesirable states. Our previous work [18] mapped the biological intervention planning problem to a finite horizon partially observable Markov decision process (POMDP). While this formulation generates high-quality sequentially administered intervention plans, it takes as input a set of variables upon which to intervene and is not designed to elucidate the intervention targets themselves.

One major challenge in using Boolean networks is the exponential growth of the basin of attraction field, or state transition diagram (described below), with the linear growth of the number of variables, prompting others to work in the Boolean framework itself to achieve some kind of improvement. The approach of Richardson [19] attempted to shrink the size of the state space through the careful removal of 'frozen nodes' and network leaf nodes. The smaller state space then lent itself more readily to the discovery of attractors and basins by sampling methods. Dubrova et al. [20] explored properties of random Boolean networks, particularly their robustness in the face of topological changes and the removal of 'redundant vertices', thus shrinking the state space. Saadatpour et al. [21] build on the work of Naldi et al. [22] with a method of network simplification which eliminates stabilized nodes and mediator nodes, which can reduce networks to just a handful of significant variables. In fact, we apply their strategy later in this work to slightly reduce a network from 60 to 43 variables. All of these methods are effective at reducing network representations to facilitate powerful analysis approaches designed for more compact networks, despite the inherent risk of eliminating important variables in the reduction process. An improvement to these methods, however, would allow analysis on larger networks, and thus reduce the risk of deleting key variables by eliminating the need to oversimplify the networks. In this paper, we propose such an approach.

Wuensche [3] and others also have studied the basins of attraction in Boolean network models of genomic regulation, specifically the relationship of their structures to the stability of attractors (cell types) in the face of perturbations. However, because of the size complexity of basins of attraction, they are often neglected in analysis in favor of the attractor states. As a basin of attraction is a collection of states leading into a corresponding attractor, i.e., phenotype, careful analysis of these basins could reveal interesting biological characteristics that determine cell fate. This is precisely the avenue we pursue in this work.

Willadsen and Wiles [23] form a compact representation of Boolean network state space by creating what they call *schemas*. Using a ternary representation with ones, zeros, and wildcards similar to the don't-cares of logic minimization, they are able to create an abstract representation of Boolean network basins of attraction, which they use to quantify dynamics and robustness. These schemas provide the authors with a convenient way of representing groups of related, neighboring states as they compute a state space robustness metric called *structural coherency*. While powerful in exploring relationships between state space structure and robustness in random Boolean networks of up to a couple dozen variables, the approach is not intended to identify standout variables that can function as intervention targets.

Boolean network framework

A Boolean network $\mathbf{B}(V, \mathbf{f})$ is made of a set of binary nodes $V = \{x_1, x_2, \cdots, x_n\}$ and a set of functions $\mathbf{f} = \{f_1, f_2, \cdots, f_n\}$. The binary value of variable $x_i \in V$ at time $(t+1)$ is determined by other variables $x_{j_1(i)}, x_{j_2(i)}, \ldots, x_{j_{k_i}(i)}$ at time (t) by means of a Boolean function $f_i \in \mathbf{f}$. That is, there are k_i variables assigned to x_i, and the mapping j_k: $\{1, \cdots, n\} \rightarrow \{1, \cdots, n\}, k = 1, \cdots, k_i$ determines the 'wiring' of variable x_i. Thus, k_i is called the *connectivity* of x_i, which is to say the number of inputs to its particular Boolean function. The values of the variables at time $(t+1)$ are always a function of the values of the k_i respective input variables at time t. Formally,

$$x_i(t+1) = f_i(x_{j_1(i)}(t), x_{j_2(i)}(t), \ldots, x_{j_{k_i}(i)}(t)) \quad (1)$$

State transition diagram

The state of a Boolean network at time t refers to the state vector for all variables, $\mathbf{x}(t) = (x_1(t), x_2(t), \ldots, x_n(t))$, where a specific state can be expressed as an n-dimensional binary vector. The state space of the network is $\{0,1\}^n = \{00\cdots0, 00\cdots1, \ldots, 11\cdots1\}$, whose size is 2^n. Letting $\mathbf{x}(t)$ take on the value of each of the possible 2^n states and obtaining the next states $\mathbf{x}(t+1)$ gives a set of 2^n one-step transitions that completely characterize the dynamics of the system. Let this set of all states be called S, such that $S = \{\mathbf{x}_1, \mathbf{x}_2, \cdots, \mathbf{x}_{2^n}\}$, and let the set of all transitions between the states of S be called E. The state transition diagram $\mathbf{G}(S, E)$ for a Boolean network $\mathbf{B}(V, \mathbf{f})$ with n nodes is a directed graph where $|S| = |E| = 2^n$. Each of the vertices $\mathbf{x} \in S$ represents one possible configuration of $x_1, x_2, \ldots, x_n$ and each of the directed edges represents one of the one-step transitions between two states as we synchronously apply Boolean functions to all variables. We choose the synchronous approach [9,24] over the asynchronous option [25,26] for its determinism and its origins in relating attractors to biological cell types[a]. The state transition diagram is also called the *basin of attraction field* and more simply as the *state space* of a network. An illustration of Boolean network topology and the state space generated by its functions can be seen in Figure 1 and Table 1.

Attractors and basins

In the absence of interventions or perturbations, beginning in any initial state, repeated application of transition functions will bring the network to a finite set of states and cycle among them forever in fixed sequence. This set of states is known as an *attractor*, denoted A_i. The complete set of states from which a network will eventually reach A_i is known as the *basin of attraction* for A_i, denoted B_i. Formally, the states of basin B_i are precisely those that, given $w \leq 2^n$ applications of Boolean functions to an evolving state, end up in attractor A_i: $B_i = \{\mathbf{x} \mid f^{(w)}(\mathbf{x}) \in A_i\}, i, w \leq 2^n$. The basins of attraction correspond precisely to the *weakly connected components* of the state transition diagram (i.e., a directed subgraph such that every pair of vertices u and v is connected either by a directed path from u to v or a directed path from v to u), and the attractors correspond precisely to the *strongly connected components* of the state transition diagram (i.e., a subgraph such that every pair of vertices u and v is connected by a directed path both from u to v and also from v to u).

An individual basin B_i and its attractor A_i can be described in terms of the collection of states comprising

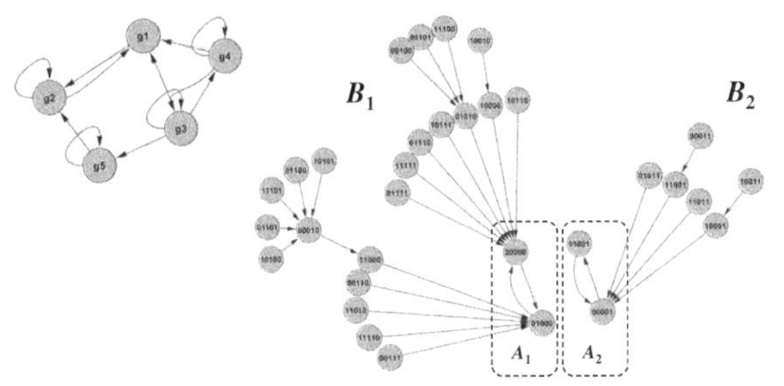

Figure 1 Five-variable example Boolean network and state transitions. On the left is the network topology and Boolean function inputs for each variable. Boolean functions for each variable are shown in Table 1. On the right are the 32 states comprising the state transition diagram partitioned into two attractor basins.

Table 1 Boolean functions for 5-variable example network

$x_{j_1}, x_{j_2}, \ldots, x_{j_{k_i}}$	f_1	f_2	f_3	f_4	f_5
00/000	0	1	0	0	0
01/001	1	1	0	0	1
10/010	0	0	0	1	0
11/011	0	0	0	0	0
100	0	0	-	-	-
101	0	0	-	-	-
110	0	1	-	-	-
111	0	0	-	-	-
j_1	2	1	3	3	3
j_2	3	2	4	4	5
j_3	4	5	-	-	-

In the table are Boolean functions for each of the five variables in Figure 1. Input variables are shown at the bottom and output values are shown for each binary combination of inputs.

them, $A_i \subseteq B_i \subseteq S = \{\mathbf{x}_1, \mathbf{x}_2, \cdots, \mathbf{x}_{2^n}\}$. Let the size of each attractor $\|A_i\| = p_i$, where p_i is the period, or length of the attractor cycle. An attractor with $p = 1$ is called a point, or singleton attractor, and an attractor with $p > 1$ is called a cyclic attractor (with cycle length equal to p). If $\mathbf{x}_i$ is a state in A_i, we can describe the next state of a point attractor as $\mathbf{x}_i(t + 1) = \mathbf{x}_i(t)$, and the behavior of a cyclic attractor as $\mathbf{x}_i(t+p) = \mathbf{x}_i(t)$. Boolean networks may have anywhere from one cyclic attractor comprised of 2^n states to 2^n point attractors, although most commonly a network will have just a handful of singleton or short-cycle attractors.

All attractors are subsets of their basins (i.e., $A_i \subseteq B_i, \forall_i$), all basins (and concordantly all attractors also) are mutually exclusive (i.e. $B_i \bigcap B_j = \emptyset, \forall_{i \neq j}$), and the complete state space is comprised entirely of all basins (i.e., $\bigcup_i B_i = S$). For referencing specific basins and attractors, the set of all basins is denoted $\mathbf{B} = \{B_1, B_2, \cdots, B_L\}$, and the set of all corresponding attractors is denoted $\mathbf{A} = \{A_1, A_2, \cdots, A_L\} \subseteq S, 1 \leq L \leq 2^n$.

Previous work

Here, we briefly describe pertinent points of our previous work [5] upon which the current methods and results build.

Logic minimization

Logic minimization (or reduction) is a classic problem from digital circuit design employed to reduce the number of actual logic gates needed to implement a given function [27]. With careful logic minimization, one can reduce the number of gates required and thus include more functionality on a single chip. Minimization identifies variables which have no influence on the outcome of a function and marks them appropriately as a *don't-care*. As a simple example, we take the Boolean function: $(A \wedge B) \vee (\neg A \wedge B)$ (two signals, four gates). Since the role of A changes while B remains *ON* with the same output, it is clear to see that the only influencing variable is B, which can be given with just that signal itself (0 gates).

We employ the Espresso tool [28], which is a heuristic logic minimizer designed to efficiently reduce logic complexity even for large problems. We supply as input the set of states in a particular basin of attraction B_i (the complete state space is comprised entirely of all basins (i.e., $\bigcup_i B_i = S$)); this input comprises the *ON-cover* (or truth table) in disjunctive normal form (DNF) for a Boolean function whose output is *ON* for the states of B_i ($\{\mathbf{x}_{i_1} \vee \mathbf{x}_{i_2} \vee \cdots \vee \mathbf{x}_{i_M}\} \mapsto ON$) and whose output is *OFF* for the states of $S \setminus B_i$. Espresso analyzes this cover and returns a minimal (though not necessarily unique) DNF set comprised of one or more terms, denoted $T_i = \{\mathbf{t}_{i_1}, \mathbf{t}_{i_2}, \cdots, \mathbf{t}_{i_N}\}$, where $N \leq M$. These $\mathbf{t}_i$ have some variables set to *ON* (denoted 1), some set to *OFF* (denoted 0), and some set as *don't-care* (denoted '-'). The presence of these don't-care variables in some terms is what allows the reduction.

For a reasonable number of variables, enumerating all 2^n states in the state transition diagram is not an issue. By starting at each state and evolving the network forward, each attractor and its basin can be enumerated. Exhaustive enumeration is the best possible situation for logic minimization because with more states, more common values can be identified and summarized in the reduction. In contrast, a partial enumeration obtained by a sampling approach greatly hinders the reduction step and results in many remaining terms with fewer don't-cares. Enumerating the full state transition diagram runs in time exponential in n, specifically $O(2^n)$, due to computing the next state for each of the 2^n states.

Single-variable intervention targets

We next review measures first introduced in our initial work [5] for finding single variable intervention targets. The first measure describes how frequently a variable v is required to be *ON* or *OFF* across different terms, called *Popularity* ($p(v) = x/y$), where x represents the number of times v is set in a term T_i and y represents the total number of terms in T_i. Next, we identify terms which are powerful due to the combinatorial effect of their few set variables over the remaining unset variables. *Term power* is defined as ($P_T(\mathbf{t}) = 1 - a/n$), where a is the number of variables set in a term ($\mathbf{t}$) and n is the number of variables in the network. One can also consider variables which preside over powerful terms to make excellent candidates for intervention targets. *Variable power* is defined as the average term power over the terms in which a variable v is explicitly configured, where b is the number of terms where v is set and y is the total number of terms in T_i, namely, $P_V(v) = [\sum_{i=1}^{y} P_T(\mathbf{t_i}) | (v \textit{ is set in } \mathbf{t_i})] / b$.

We have found that for networks of a size manageable enough to exhaustively enumerate the state space, popularity and variable power can be used to identify key variables which make excellent candidate intervention targets. As described in the Additional files, we have performed a simulation experiment to identify the best single-variable measures between popularity, power, and related measures described in our previous work [5] [See Additional file 1]. We found in a simulation study over thousands of random networks with between 7 and 16 variables, that popularity, power, and their combination in the form of an harmonic mean[b] showed the most statistically significant differences in intervention success rates of all 14 methods compared. Included in the comparison were Boolean network measures as well as graph theoretic measures.

Unfortunately, however, larger networks present some problems for these measures and require a different approach. The problems in larger networks manifest because popularity and power depend heavily upon the reducibility of the basin of attraction field by logic minimization. In larger networks, where we are forced to explore the basin of attraction field by sampling, the reducibility of the state space is greatly hindered and our single-variable measures are rendered unusable.

In this work, we contribute a multiple variable intervention target called a template and show how, even in large networks with sampled state spaces, that they are still able to identify powerful targets for intervention. Thus, we see the template approach effectively taking over for the former single-variable measures, especially in larger networks. Finally, we contribute an example templates application to a T-LGL leukemia network and analyze the implications of our approach on this real world scenario.

Methods

As the number of variables in a biological interaction network increases, the more likely it is that a successful intervention will require multiple variables. In fact, in our work in AI planning [18], we found that a planned sequence of interventions was an effective way to transition to a desired steady state. Our previous measures of popularity and power are capable of identifying multiple high-value intervention targets separately in smaller networks. In this section, we will introduce intervention templates to take into account the multivariate effects of gene regulation and propose an approach to address larger networks. We will be faced with several challenges such as: (1) how to consider many subsets of variables in each basin of attraction, (2) to design clear methods and measures to identify the best template-based intervention targets in a systematic way, and (3) to work with an intractable state space through sampling to cope with larger networks. We end by outlining a robust simulation study designed to illustrate achievement in these three areas.

Template-based intervention targets

Let the term *template* indicate a subset of variables (ordering not important) in a specific 0/1 (*OFF*/*ON*) configuration. Let the term *k-template* refer to a template with k variables; call the maximum value of k being considered K. Thus, for n variables there exist $\sum_{k=1}^{K} 2^k \binom{n}{k}$ templates. This follows from $\binom{n}{k}$ ways of selecting k unique sets of variables from n total, 2^k binary value combinations for each of those sets, and K values of k.

Since a template is a subset of n network variables assigned to a specific Boolean configuration, each template with k variables covers 2^{n-k} other states. The smallest extreme is a template with $k = 1$, or a 1-template, which is a single-variable assigned to *ON* or *OFF*. The largest extreme would be a template with $k = n$ — i.e., a single state in the state space. Such a template would cover no additional states, would not provide any further insights, and would be trivial to count. In practice, k is typically small, in the range 1 to 5 depending on n. Because there are $(2^k)\binom{n}{k}$ templates for every k, counting (and studying) quickly becomes intractable. However, this is not typically an issue when seeking to identify intervention targets in biological networks since the difficulty of intervening increases with the number of variables required in the actual intervention.

Our combinatorial analysis involves counting the occurrence of each template remaining in the minimized DNF terms (T_i) of the original basins of attraction, (B_i), and is described in Algorithm 1. Due to properties of the binomial coefficient [29], the algorithm executes with a runtime exponential on n and the size of the templates[c].

Algorithm 1: Template Analysis in Attractor Basins

foreach *Basin* B_i : **B** **do**
  for $k = 1 : K$ **do**
    foreach *Template* **template**$_{j,i}$ *for* $j = 1 : 2^k\binom{n}{k}$ **do**
      foreach *Term* $\mathbf{t}_l : T_i$ **do**
        if *Template* **template**$_{j,i}$ *is found in* $\mathbf{t}_l$ **then**
          increment count(**template**$_{j,i}$) for k

Template-based scores for intervention target selection

With the vast number of templates, we require ways to identify the important, top templates most likely to make the best intervention targets. After counting the occurrence of all templates in all basins, we begin by analyzing the most frequently counted templates as potential top intervention targets. Since logic minimization can greatly reduce the representation of the attractor basins (and thus the overall template counts), we provide a second measure to identify top templates with frequencies diminished by the logic minimization step.

While we apply our measures to templates of all considered sizes, there is not an explicit penalty applied to larger templates. This decision is motivated by the fact that all interventions must be interpreted and evaluated in context, since it may be that a 'larger' intervention could involve easier-to-target genes and/or be less invasive than a smaller intervention, or that a seemingly ideal smaller intervention may not be biologically or medically possible. Thus, we report the best templates over several smaller sizes and leave the translation from mathematically best targets to medically best targets to domain experts who, we hope, would prefer the least invasive options.

Template frequency (F): the most frequently counted templates in a particular basin are the first place to look for templates likely to make top intervention targets. By examining the set of terms T_i (reduced states with some don't-care variables) of a basin B_i, we can, for each of the $j = 1$: $(2^k)\binom{n}{k}$ templates, count how many times that template appears in the terms of T_i. Formally, $F_{j,i}$ is the final count of occurrences of template$_{j,i}$ in the set of terms T_i (corresponding to basin B_i). The maximum value of $F_{j,i}$ is 2^{n-k} (i.e., the total number of Boolean states covered when the k variables of the template are fixed and none of the remaining $n-k$ variables have been eliminated by logic minimization), though in practice, the value of $F_{j,i}$ is much lower, especially when state spaces are exhaustively enumerated and then greatly reduced by logic minimization. We can rank templates by $F_{j,i}$ to find top template candidates.

Template basin distribution percentage (D): just because a k-template is the most frequently counted template in a particular basin does not necessarily mean that it is the most significant. Sometimes, especially when logic minimization is able to significantly reduce the number of states in a basin to a much smaller set of terms, the frequencies of important templates will be diminished due to the introduction of many don't-care values. Thus, we need a way to identify these high-value templates despite their lower frequencies of occurrence. To do this, we consider the distribution of a particular template across all basins, or in other words, the affinity of a template to a particular basin. Since templates can and often do appear in terms of multiple basins, we will calculate the ratio of occurrence in each basin and of the total number of occurrences. Formally,

$$D_{j,i} = \frac{F_{j,i}}{\sum_{m=1}^{L} F_{j,m}}, \tag{2}$$

where L is the total number of basins, j is the template number, and i is the basin number. Like frequency, for each basin, we can rank the templates by this ratio to find top template candidates.

These template measures provide two ways to identify a subset of templates warranting further investigation. By analyzing templates among the highest values of $F_{j,i}$, we will identify variables occurring together in a particular basin most often. By analyzing templates among the highest values of $D_{j,i}$, we will identify variables that may not be the most frequent but retain the most affiliation with a particular basin even after logic minimization.

Intervention targets

For each basin of attraction, full or partial, we can compute the best intervention targets using the following 11 methods. The first three methods comprise the best of the previous small network measures, namely, popularity, power, and their harmonic mean (abbreviated POP, POW, and HPP). The next four are the top templates of sizes 1, 2, 3, and 4 computed according to D (abbreviated K1TBDP, K2TBDP, K3TBDP, K4TBDP). The final four are the top templates of sizes 1, 2, 3, and 4 computed according to F (abbreviated K1FREQ, K2FREQ, K3FREQ, K4FREQ). For the simulation study described later in this section, we compare the single best template identified by each of these 11 methods. For our application to T-LGL leukemia, we examine the sets of top templates identified by K1FREQ, K2FREQ, and K3FREQ.

Illustration

Let us consider for now the *unreduced* state space of the five-variable example network shown in Figure 1 and observe how to identify templates and how those with high F and D values can be used as interventions. The states from the diagram are collected and listed in Figure 2 (left). We will count a few specific templates visually from the complete set (on the left), but later on in practice, we will count templates from the set reduced by logic minimization (on the right). We can quickly see from the dramatic reduction (Figure 2 (right)) that g_3 and g_5 are the key players in the network and that they display contrasting behavior between the two basins. As such, let us examine only 1- and 2-templates involving g_3 and g_5 and observe their frequency and template basin distribution patterns. We begin with $k = 1$, and follow its discussion with $k = 2$.

We will first consider the four 1-templates involving g_3 and g_5 and look for any disproportionate patterns among the two basins. By inspection of the states of B_1, we can quickly see that each of the 16 occurrences of $g_3 = 1$ and of $g_5 = 0$ are counted there and that these are the only 1-templates with a maximal count of 16 in either basin.

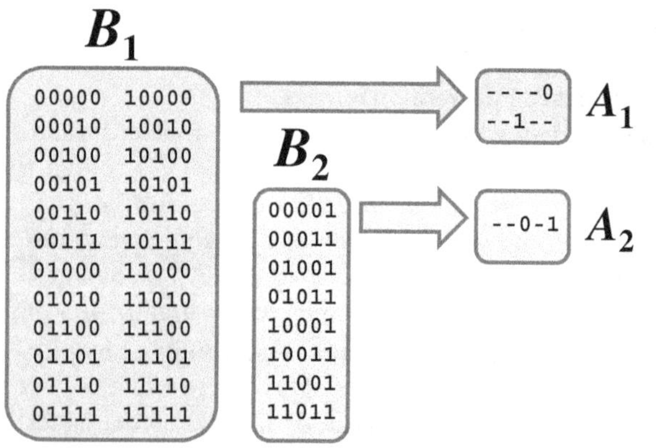

Figure 2 Example of Boolean network basin state minimizations. On the left are two boxes containing each state in the two basins shown on the right of Figure 1. On the right are the terms produced from applying logic minimization to each basin. The larger basin is reduced to two terms with one value each (OR relationship between the variables) and the smaller basin is reduced to one term with two variables set (AND relationship between the variables).

These counts are contrasted in B_2 where we find the 1-templates for $g_3 = 0$ and $g_5 = 1$ (opposite configuration) counted the maximum of eight times (since there are only eight states in the basin). With no logic reduction in this example, these F values produce proportional D values that elevate $g_3 = 1$ and $g_5 = 0$ for B_1 and $g_3 = 0$ and $g_5 = 1$ for B_2.

There are 40 countable 2-templates (2^2 combinations of $\binom{5}{2} = 10$ templates) with a maximum frequency of 8 for each template. We next consider just the 2-templates involving g_3 and g_5. B_2 counts just one of the 40 total 2-templates the maximum of eight times - precisely the template remaining after logic reduction: $g_3 = 0$ and $g_5 = 1$. B_1 counts 15 of the 40 total 2-templates eight times, 12 of them six times, 12 of them four times, and 1 of them zero times, but counts none exclusively. Of the 15 templates counted the maximum of eight times in B_1, all templates for g_3 and g_5 complementary to those counted in B_2 are among them.

With the increased value of k, we observe more dramatic template basin distributions and now reveal a template with complete affinity for B_2, which we did not see for $k = 1$. We now find all eight 2-template occurrences of $g_3 = 1$ and $g_5 = 0$ simultaneously and exclusively in B_2 (100%), and this is corroborated by the logic minimization of B_2 which left us one single term with the same variables remaining in the same values we now find. Thus, we observe that the templates with the highest F and/or D values correspond to the variables shown to exhibit the most network influence by logic minimization. Concordantly, while a single-variable intervention is able to transition to A_1 from any starting state in the network, we observe that a transition to A_2 from anywhere in the network requires the multi-variable intervention revealed by our highest frequency template for B_2. Since single-variable measures based on the results of logic minimization produced good targets in our previous work, we are motivated to further investigate the intervention viability of templates given their correlation with logic minimization results.

Sampling large state spaces

As the size of the network grows, exhaustive enumeration of the state space (size 2^n) quickly becomes intractable and a sampling approach is required. While Wuenche's method of directly computing pre-images [30] allows exhaustive state space enumeration for up to 31 variables with the DDLab software [31] (and even > 31 for single attractor basins), our implementation of state space enumeration begins to suffer performance degradations after 22 variables. Because we are interested in networks well beyond 31 variables, we transition to a sampling strategy whereby we randomly and uniformly sample a number of initial starting states from the state space range $[1 : 2^n]$. From each starting state, the network is then run forward to the corresponding attractor, collecting any states visited along the *transient* path. Attractors are noted and all corresponding states are collected into a partial basin, and it is from these partial basins that we identify our intervention targets. This approach will sometimes miss attractors with very small basins leading to them, but it certainly finds the largest ones, and for a large number of samples, gives us a significant set of member states to analyze. We can also approximate the percentage of the total state space occupied by each basin based on the percentage of total samples associated with it. It should be carefully noted that when sampling, the identified partial basins are themselves proper subsets of the complete basins. In other words, the sampling approach creates no incorrect assignments of basin states to attractors. With exhaustive enumeration, we complete the state space exploration and acquire all states in each basin. Thus, both sampling and exhaustive enumeration provide correct basin states, just with sampling being an incomplete picture and exhaustive being a complete picture.

Evaluating intervention success

Abstractly, an intervention should shift the steady behavior of a system to a different (usually more desirable) state. In the context of the Boolean network formalism, this is represented by shifting the steady behavior of the system, represented by an attractor state or cycle, into a different basin of attraction. Specifically, our intervention goal is to identify minimally sized templates that reliably transition the network from undesirable attractors to desirable attractors. Depending on the patient and the biology of the identified template variables, this could mean preferring smaller templates (possibly less invasive) with a lower chance of success or choosing slightly larger templates (possibly more complex) with a higher chance of success. A successful intervention needs only to shift the state from a starting attractor state into any state in the basin of the goal attractor, as the network dynamics will then naturally bring the state to the attractor itself.

With the top intervention template candidates determined by F and D for each basin, we estimate intervention success rates by attempting interventions to each basin as a goal destination, starting from attractor states from each outside basin, recording each attempt as a success or failure. Across many Boolean networks, we will find a range of the number of attractor basins, from one or two to dozens, and within those basins, attractor cycles of various periods, from 1 to 5 to 100 or more. In estimating intervention success, we should not let abnormally large attractor cycles bias the results by providing too many of the intervention starting states. For example, if we have a network with a point attractor in one basin and an attractor cycle of 50 states in the second basin, our intervention success estimates would be based on an unfair distribution of starting states. In practice, if an attractor cycle is longer than ten states, we randomly sample ten attractor states for that basin upon which to apply candidate interventions. If it is less than ten, we use them all.

In our simulation study (described next), we must compare the performance of top intervention methods across various network sizes and between the methods themselves. As we will be comparing pairs of success proportions for independent interventions, which qualify as Bernoulli trials under the binomial model, we will use a two-proportion Z-test with the null hypothesis of having equal success proportions [32].

Simulation study

Our two main challenges with the template approach involve performance as we transition from fully enumerated state spaces to sampled state spaces and also performance as we increase the size of the networks. To address these concerns, we design a simulation study over hundreds of randomly generated Boolean networks within which we compare performance of the former single-variable measures and the new template-based approach.

In-silico network models

In order to test interventions over an adequate range of network sizes, we create multiple random networks with 10, 12, 18, 20, 25, and 40 variables each, for a total of 200 networks. In each network, we randomly generate Boolean update rules, which creates random network connectivity as we randomly choose k_i inputs for each variable x_i. In order to create biologically inspired networks, we adopt the per-variable connectivity distribution from Albert and Othmer [6] used originally for a *D. melanogaster* network, shown in Table 2. Once the inputs are chosen for each variable, random Boolean functions are formed by generating random and independent zeros or ones for each binary input combination. Thus, all $2^{2^{k_i}}$ Boolean functions are possible in our random networks.

Table 2 Connectivity distribution for random networks

Number of inputs	Probability
1	0.101
2	0.233
3	0.267
4	0.183
5	0.083
6	0.083
7	0.050

In the table, we see the probability of assigning various numbers of inputs to random Boolean functions.

Once network connectivity and rules are determined, the basin of attraction fields must be generated in full or in part. For the networks of size 10, 12, and 18, we use half the networks for exhaustive enumeration of the basins of attraction, and for the other half of networks, we enumerated partial basins through sampling. For networks of size 20, 25, and 40, only sampled state spaces were used.

Performing interventions

An intervention is defined as a modification (set/reset) to one or more variables in an attractor state of a source basin with the intention that network rules will transition to any state in a given goal basin (thus eventually reaching the attractor of the goal basin). For the simulation study, we do not attempt interventions where the goal and source basins are the same, since these are more likely to succeed and would inflate our results. Likewise, we do not attempt interventions to goal basins estimated to occupy less than 15% of the total state space since reaching these very rare basins is the most difficult and has little biological relevance. Our 200 original random networks, through their various numbers of attractor basins and attractor cycle lengths, produced 4,223 individual intervention attempts, each applied separately with all 11 methods.

Results

Next, we present the results of the simulation study described in the Methods section, which reveals the ability of template-based interventions to maintain performance between exhaustive and sampled state spaces and also in increasingly large random networks with sampled state spaces. We then provide a demonstration of the approach on a real-world network modeling T-LGL leukemia, originally hand-created by domain experts.

Simulation study for template methods

In order to demonstrate the robustness of template-based interventions, we present the results of the simulation study described in the 'Methods' section. The study addresses two main questions: (1) what effect does the change to sampled Boolean network state spaces have on the performance of template-based interventions? and (2) what effect does increasing network size have on the performance of template-based interventions? To address these questions, we analyze hundreds of randomly generated Boolean networks for which we compare performance of single-variable measures and the variations of the new template-based approach.

The effect of sampling on template interventions

To address the challenge of whether or not template-based approaches remain robust as we transition from a fully enumerated state space to a sampled one, we compare the performance of each measure between full and sampled versions of the 10, 12, and 18 variable networks. Since these networks are small enough to exhaustively enumerate the full state space, the comparison will provide a full assessment of any performance degradation due to sampling. For each network size, we compare the proportions of successful interventions of each type between exhaustive and sampled networks. Interventions that show a significant change in proportion between exhaustive and sampled state spaces will be noted. Success rates can be seen in Figure 3 (with Figure 3 significance values in Table 3), for which we note the following observations:

In the networks with 10 variables, 9 of 11 methods showed a decrease in performance from exhaustive to sampled, with 6 of those being statistically significant changes. Interestingly, 2 of the 11 methods showed an increase in performance, with one of those being statistically significant at the 0.05 alpha level; both of those cases involved frequency based templates. While showing decreases in performance between exhaustive and sampling with each template size, template basin distribution percentage templates registered among the highest success proportions overall, indicating that they might be a suitable replacement for single-variable methods in exhaustive cases if the computational cost of templates can be afforded.

In the networks with 12 variables, all four template sizes for frequency-based templates showed an increase in performance in the sampled cases, with all four differences in proportions being statistically significant. All seven other methods showed visible decreases in performance, with two of them being considered statistically significant. Again, template basin distribution percentage templates had among the best performances in the exhaustive cases.

In the networks with 18 variables, we see the clear resistance of frequency-based template approaches to the side effects of sampled state spaces. With one statistically significant increase in performance and no significant decreases, frequency-based templates overwhelmingly dominate performance in sampled cases while all other methods drastically decrease.

It is very interesting to observe any increase in performance between a fully enumerated space and a sampled space. In our case, we observe this behavior because, in the sampled condition, the intervention targets are computed from a larger amount of terms. This is due to the fact that the logic minimization ability is highest when every state is known beforehand and it is hindered greatly by not knowing all basin states ahead of time. Only the templates (especially the larger ones) benefit from this situation - single-variable measures like popularity and power suffer when there are *fewer* don't-cares in the terms, and some template measures suffer when there are *too many* don't-cares (i.e., exhaustive case). Thus, while drastic logic minimization on exhaustive state spaces allows popularity and power to quickly reveal decent targets, a less effective logic minimization leaving many more terms behind after reduction benefits the template approach by providing more information from which to identify the best templates while still eliminating the least important variables. In some cases, this benefit outweighs the benefit of a full logic minimization.

While we expected to avoid recording, for template approaches, significant success proportion decreases for sampled network state spaces, we not only failed to detect that trend altogether in frequency-based templates but also in many cases detected significant increases. We also began to see the template basin distribution percentage templates as most ideally suited to smaller networks in exhaustive cases, perhaps as a more thorough alternative to the former single-variable measures. From these data, we conclude that frequency-based template methods are much more robust in sampled state spaces than their single-variable counterparts. The next step is to observe if this trend continues with increasing network size.

The effect of increasing network size on template interventions

Satisfied that template measures remain robust in networks with sampled state spaces, we now investigate

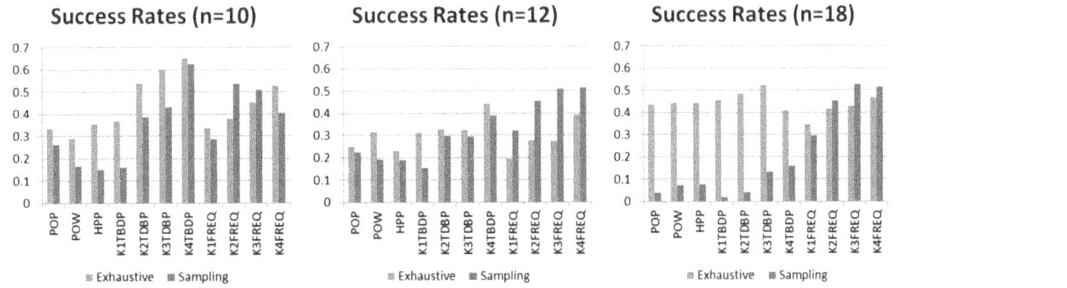

Figure 3 Success rates between exhaustive and sampled state spaces. For three network sizes, we see proportions of successful interventions across single-variable and template-based approaches. The first three sets of bars in each subfigure are the single-variable measures of popularity, power, and their harmonic mean. The latter eight are the two template approaches of *D* and *F* across four template sizes. *P* values reflecting proportion differences can be found in Table 3.

Table 3 *P* values for two-proportion *Z*-tests

	10E/10S	12E/12S	18E/18S
POP	0.0920	0.4619	0.0000
POW	0.0013	0.0003	0.0000
HPP	0.0000	0.2030	0.0000
K1TBDP	0.0000	0.0000	0.0000
K2TDBP	0.0007	0.4421	0.0000
K3TDBP	0.0002	0.4391	0.0000
K4TBDP	0.5424	0.1385	0.0000
K1FREQ	0.2197	0.0002	0.2038
K2FREQ	0.0004	0.0000	0.3964
K3FREQ	0.2015	0.0000	0.0192
K4FREQ	0.0062	0.0014	0.2310

In the table, we see the *P* values for two-proportion *Z*-tests across 11 intervention targets between exhaustively enumerated (E) and sampled (S) networks with 10, 12, and 18 variables. For *P* values below the $\alpha = 0.05$ significance level, we reject the null hypothesis and conclude that there exists a statistically significant difference in success proportions between the exhaustive and the sampled state space cases. These differences can be inspected visually in Figure 3.

larger random networks. It is expected that any measure or technique will decrease in performance as the size and/or complexity of the network increases. However, with the knowledge that the single-variable measures fail completely with sampled state spaces even for small networks, we need to be assured that template performance remains robust. We generate further random networks with 20, 25, and 40 variables, which produce state space sizes of 2^{20}, 2^{25}, and 2^{40}. We sample these enormous state spaces with about 1% or less coverage in initial states and estimate the intervention success of the top scoring intervention targets from our 11 methods (3 classic single variable, 4 sizes of *D* templates, and 4 sizes of *F* templates). For the 40-variable network, we do not include size-4 templates for computational considerations of the simulation. In Figure 4A, we show the performance of template basin distribution (*D*)-based templates at template sizes of 1 to 4 and the single-variable measures of variable popularity (POP), variable power (POW), and the harmonic mean of the two measures (HPP). In Figure 4B, we show the performance of frequency (*F*)-based templates of sizes 1 to 4 against the same single-variable methods. Both subfigures show performance over networks of size 10, 12, 18, 20, 25, and 40, all with sampled basins of attraction. Error bars shown reflect the 95% binomial confidence intervals.

In Figure 4A, we observe that template basin distribution percentage templates do not consistently show significant differences in success proportions with POP, POW, or HPP. We do note that K3TDBP and K4TBDP do show significant performance over POP, POW, and/or HPP in all networks up to 25 variables, but they are significantly outperformed by their frequency-based counterparts in Figure 4B. In Figure 4B, we observe that the only time a frequency-based template does not show a significant difference in proportion is in the 10-variable network for the template with only one variable (the most extreme case); though in practice, we would not apply template analysis on such small networks. A complete separation of 95% confidence intervals surely indicates a significant separation in success proportions [33], but to further reinforce these observations and to reveal any significant differences in proportions not obvious from confidence intervals, we computed two proportion *Z*-tests for independence for each pair of methods for each network size. These pairwise matrices of *P* values revealed even stronger conclusions than the graphs in Figure 4A,B, further confirming the statistically significant differences beyond what is obvious by visual inspection of the error bars. As they do not reveal any critical trends not visible in Figure 4A or B, we reserve these *P* value matrices for the Additional files [See Additional file 2].

Summary of simulation study

Over all network sizes between *F*-based and *D*-based templates, it is clear that *F*-based (frequency) templates not only maintain performance between exhaustive and sampled networks but also provide consistent success rates with increasing network sizes despite the exponential explosion of state space sizes. We were also interested to observe that in some cases, the inhibited reducibility of sampled state spaces actually contributed additional information to the computation of the larger template targets - in some cases actually improving their performance in sampled networks over their performance in maximally reduced state spaces. Template basin distribution percentage-based templates are sometimes useful in smaller networks and are the most effective in smaller, exhaustive networks as a more thorough alternative to the simpler, single-variable measures of POP, POW, and HPP, albeit at an increased computational cost.

Application to T-LGL leukemia network

In our previous work [5], we identified useful intervention targets using the single-variable measures in real-world networks for melanoma, the yeast cell cycle, and for human aging. Because we saw in our simulation study that no significant new information is revealed by template approaches in exhaustive state spaces, we do not apply our template approaches to those previously explored networks here. Instead, because of the robustness of the templates approach for large networks with sampled state spaces, we make application to a 43-variable network for large granular lymphocytic (T-LGL) leukemia where the single-variable measures have no usefulness.

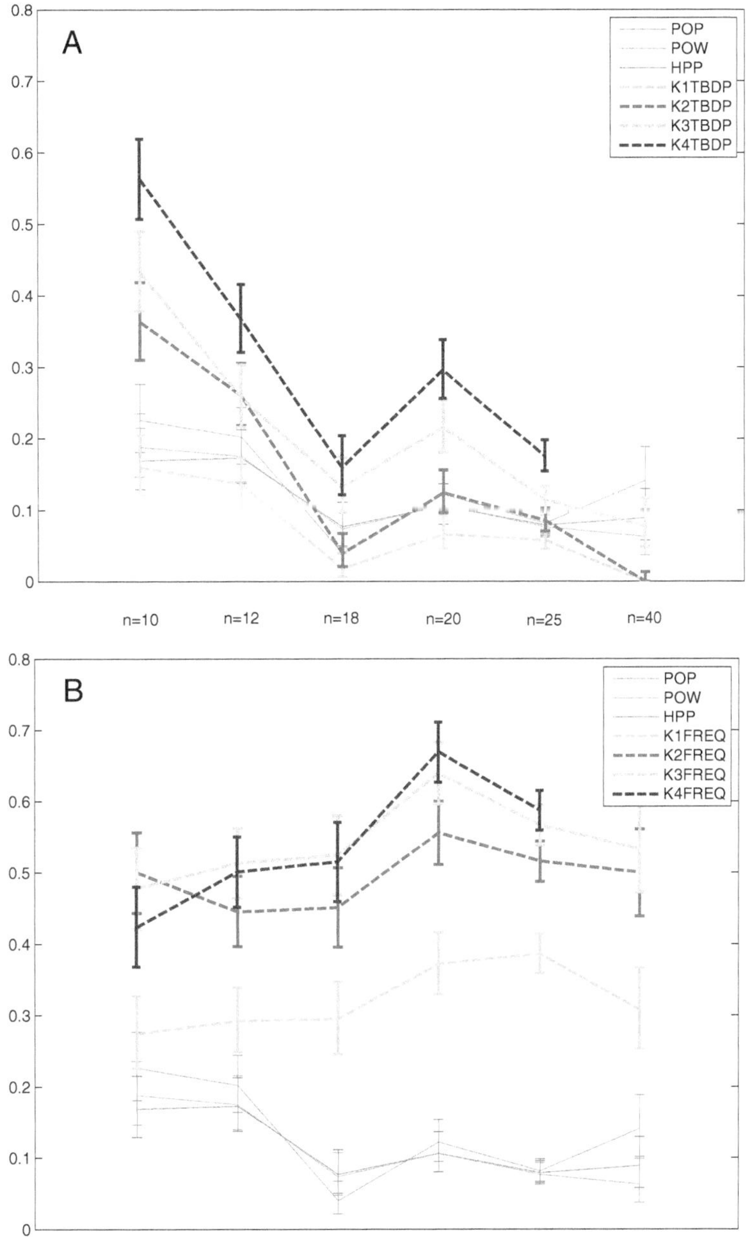

Figure 4 Success rates for *D* and *F* templates. (A) We see the proportions of successful intervention attempts for *D*-based templates of four sizes across six different network sizes. **(B)** We see the same for *F*-based templates. Both subfigures include the performance of the single-variable approaches for comparison. While *D*-based templates perform reasonably well in the smallest network sizes, it is clear that only the *F*-based templates show consistent and significant performance across all network sizes. Note that 4-variable templates are not included on the 40-variable network for computational reasons.

Zhang et al. [34] have methodically constructed a model of the blood cancer T cell large granular lymphocyte (T-LGL) leukemia from hundreds of literature sources. The original study, as well as others based on variations of this large network [21], have searched for therapeutic targets and have even validated some experimentally. However, these predictions required expert-level topological reduction and simplification of the network in various ways. But because of the validated findings, this network makes an ideal situation in which to apply our approach, which is purely computational and requires no expert-level knowledge of the disease system. If our results on the larger, less simplified network are reasonable, our approach will be shown useful and applicable on large networks for which we may not have expert-level knowledge and/or the ability to systematically simplify.

Network construction

The original network [34] created from the literature contained 128 nodes and 287 edges but was simplified by the authors through software and manual adjustments to 60 nodes and 142 regulatory edges. After collaborating with a principle author from [34], we performed further reductions on the network according to techniques described in related work involving this same network [21,35]. The goal of further reduction was to remove nodes which mask the dynamic behavior of the network variables (i.e., the overarching influence of the apoptosis node as well as control nodes); since steady-state analysis will be performed over many randomly generated states, control variables are not necessary since variables they control will be forced to take on different values through random starting state assignment. After the simplifications described in the Additional files, we obtain the 43-variable version shown in Figure 5 [See Additional file 3]. A list of the Boolean functions is also given in the supplements [See Additional file 3].

Network and state space properties

With 50,000 randomly and uniformly sampled initial states, the partial basin of attraction field was enumerated, resulting in five basins of attraction, four of which comprise greater than 99% of the state space (estimated), and will thus be the focus of the analysis. These four basins are summarized in Table 4. In other sampling, runs up to seven attractors were identified, but these additional two, when discovered, were estimated to occupy thousandths, if not tens of thousandths of 1% percent of the state space and would be discarded for analysis along with the fifth basin. Due to the massive size of the full state space (2^{43}, over 8 trillion states), 50,000 initial sampled states was chosen first due to it being large enough to proportionally reveal all major basins and, second, because choosing more samples, such as 100,000 or 200,000, would only marginally increase the coverage of the full state space.

We have categorized the four basins to either healthy (i.e., normal apoptosis function) or T-LGL (i.e., cancer state) based on the values of certain key variables in the steady attractor states/cycles. In the original 60-variable network, the presence of control nodes, including one for apoptosis, simplified classification of attractor states. Since the apoptosis node was wired to nearly every other node for purposes of the original study [34], its behavior dominated the dynamics of the entire network. Since we have stripped the network of the apoptosis node, as well as other control nodes, we must interpret the attractor states based on other criteria. These criteria involve precisely the series of input regulatory nodes controlling the former

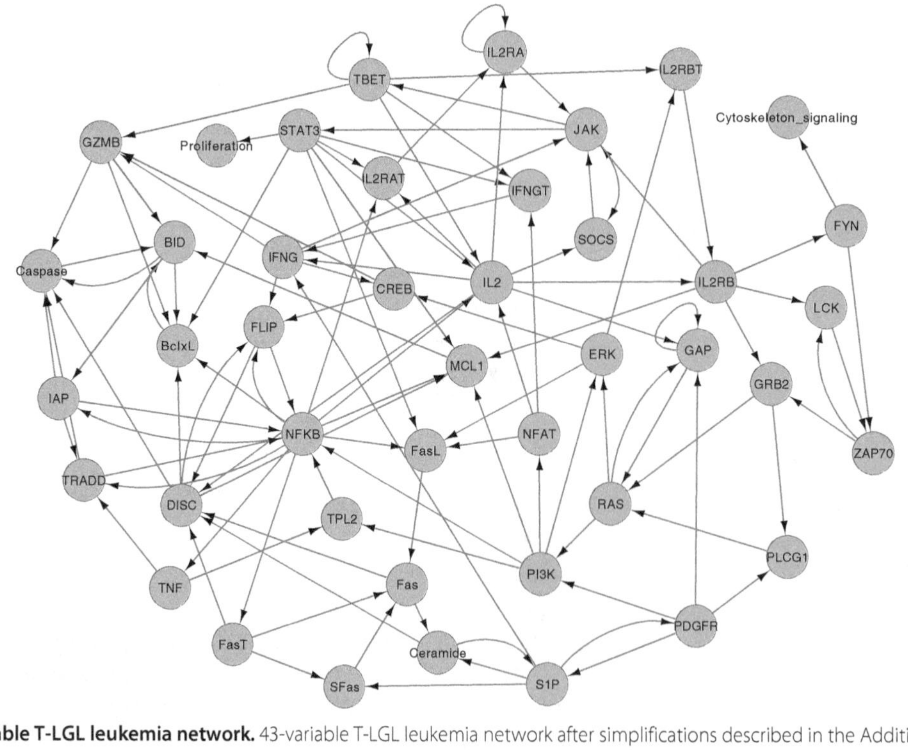

Figure 5 43-variable T-LGL leukemia network. 43-variable T-LGL leukemia network after simplifications described in the Additional files [See Additional file 3].

Table 4 Summary of four attractor basins for the 43-variable leukemia network

	Basin number	Attractor period (P)	Number of states	Estimated % coverage	Attractor type
	1	4	58713	40.88	Healthy
50,000 Sampled + 93,618	2	1	57359	39.94	T-LGL
Transient = 143,618 Total states	3	1	17099	11.91	T-LGL
	4	4	10441	7.27	Healthy

We observe the attractor length, numbers of states identified, and the estimated state space coverage for each basin. Attractor type classification criteria are described in the text.

apoptosis node. Nodes found in identical steady states across all four attractors were not considered, but several variables, namely FasT, Fas, Ceramide, and FLIP, were used in their boolean functions to effectively determine whether or not an apoptosis node would have been active or inactive in the attractor. Full attractor states are given in Additional file 3. Here, we have four attractor basins, with two classified as healthy and two as T-LGL. Among the two in each category, one exhibited stronger, more consistent behavior. Specifically, Basin 1, as the largest basin in the space, was classified as healthy but had oscillatory values for DISC and FLIP, direct influences on apoptosis. Basin 4, on the other hand, had consistent behavior for both DISC and FLIP despite the cyclic nature of the attractor. Thus, due to the small size of Basin 4 and its pure behavior even with a cyclic attractor, it is considered the healthiest attractor. For complimentary reasons, Basin 2 is the larger and thus more general T-LGL attractor, and Basin 3 is the smaller, more precise T-LGL attractor. A total of 11 attractor states were identified: a cycle of 4 states in Basins 1 and 4, and singleton attractor states in Basins 2, 3, and 5, the latter of which was not considered as a goal state.

Templates analysis

Next, we identify key variables from k-templates for $k = 1, 2$, and 3. The 43 network variables give 86 1-templates, 3,612 2-templates, and 98,728 3-templates to count across the minimized terms in our four basins. We stop with $k = 3$ since $k = 4$ provides nearly 2 million 4-templates to count, but only across less than 120,000 terms. Future work intends to parallelize and split up the computational burden of the sequential counting algorithm and offer conditions under which we can test the efficacy of counting orders of magnitude more templates across relatively few terms.

After counting k-templates for $k = 1, 2$, and 3, we estimated the intervention success rate for the 30 most frequent templates (highest values for $F_{j,i}$) in each size and for each basin. Full listings of these templates can be found in Additional file 3, but a listing of interesting templates is found here in Table 5. To estimate a success rate, we apply each top template intervention to all 11 attractor states across all basins in the T-LGL network and compute the distribution of basins reached. If a template causes a significant number of these attractor states to jump to (or remain in) a desired basin, such a template is of great interest. In general, we expect an attractor state to remain robust to perturbation but expect the larger templates to have the best chance at changing the steady state of the system. Since Basins 1 and 4 each contain a four-cycle of attractor states, we expect at least 4 of the 11 destination states (36%) to remain in those basins (due to the expectation of robustness mentioned). Likewise, the remaining basins each have a single attractor state each and we expect 1 of the 11 destination states (9%) to remain in these basins. Of the top 30 templates for each k and each basin, we indeed saw these expected distributions of goal states very frequently. Numbers above and beyond these expectations warrant closer inspection, which we provide for the most interesting templates listed in Table 5.

While the simulation study was clear that intervening with a template of high frequency was sufficient to best comparable methods, before continuing, we provide a comparison demonstrating that more successful templates and fewer powerless templates are found among the

Table 5 Notable leukemia network templates

Basin	Rank	Variables	Values	$F_{j,i}$	Success
1	18	Ceramide PDGFR S1P	0 1 0	22,936	0.73[a]
2	27	PDGFR S1P TBET	0 0 1	28,057	1.00
3	1	Ceramide PDGFR S1P	0 1 1	14,404	1.00
4	6	TBET	0	6,404	0.73

[a]Remaining 27% of interventions lead Basin 4 (also healthy). Listed in the table is a selection of interesting templates from the analysis of the leukemia network. Complete lists of the top frequency templates for each basin and each template size can be found in Additional file 3.

most frequently counted. To do this, we compute success rates for 3-templates in three categories: the 1,000 most frequent, 1,000 random, and the 1,000 least frequent templates. These rates are shown in Table 6 and, as expected, we see with statistical confidence that the top 1,000 most frequent templates have higher proportions of success than the other groups.

Top templates for healthy and T-LGL attractors

We discuss two templates with high success rates leading to healthy attractor states followed by two templates with high rates of leading to T-LGL states. Lastly, we observe the single template which best differentiates the healthy and T-LGL states.

The first healthy intervention template of interest is for Basin 1, where we find a 3-template (Ceramide, PDGFR, and S1P set 0/1/0, respectively) with a high frequency and the ability to guide 73% of intervention attempts into Basin 1. In fact, the 27% remaining attempts not leading to Basin 1 lead to Basin 4, which is the other attractor classified as 'healthy'. Thus, this template completely avoids the T-LGL basins. S1P is known to be 1 (*ON*) in a T-LGL state [36], and so it is biologically consistent to find it set to 0 (*OFF*) in the template.

The second healthy intervention template of interest is found in Basin 4 - the smallest classified basin considered in this study. In it, we find a powerful 1-template, TBET 0, which transitions 73% of intervention attempts to this very small basin covering only about 7% of the total state space. TBET is known to be 1 in T-LGL [34], so as a healthy basin, this setting is biologically consistent. Due to the small size of the basin, none of the top two or three templates were able to improve on this rate, and any that matched it included TBET 0 as part of the template. Any time a single variable can exert such a high degree of influence on a network, it is noteworthy.

The first T-LGL 'intervention' template is found in Basin 2. While it may seem contradictory to describe an 'intervention' which leads to a disease state, we nonetheless consider the power in the variable combination, perhaps as a trigger to avoid. In Basin 2, we quickly find the standout behavior of the three-template PDGFR/S1P/TBET, which is set 0/0/1, respectively. This template had a 100% intervention success rate, guiding network dynamics to Basin 2 upon every application. As in the previous template, we again see TBET; however, this time it is set 1, which is biologically consistent with the T-LGL state.

For Basin 3, which is also classified as a T-LGL attractor, we find another very powerful template, namely Ceramide, PDGFR, and S1P set 0/1/1, respectively. Not only does this template have a 100% intervention success rate but also each of its variable settings is known to be biologically consistent [36-38]. As the attractor state for Basin 3 is classified to be the stronger of the two T-LGL basins, and as Basin 3 is estimated to occupy only about 12% of the total state space, such a powerful template with perfect biological consistency is significant indeed.

Perhaps most interesting is the observation that this three-template in Basin 3 and the three-template for Basin 1 share the same three variables, with one going to 100% healthy attractors and the other going 100% to a T-LGL attractor. The templates have the same settings for Ceramide and PDGFR but differ in the setting for S1P, which is the biologically consistent setting across both basins. This reveals that, while Ceramide and PDFGR do not have biologically meaningful settings in Basin 1, for Basins 1 and 3, they still open the path, in terms of network dynamics, for the biologically consistent behavior of S1P to accurately and powerfully shift the network between healthy and T-LGL attractors. Thus, we conclude that, for this network, S1P is the key differentiator between healthy and T-LGL steady states, assisted by the combinatorial power of Ceramide and PDGFR.

Our work with the Leukemia network has produced some notable findings. First, we note that while all single-variable measures were unable to produce helpful intervention targets because of the 43 network variables, the template-based approaches did produce single and multi-variable intervention targets with observable separation in per-basin frequencies and in intervention success rates. Second, we observed that identifying the best template can benefit greatly from expert assignment of the basins of attraction to biological contexts (e.g., health vs. disease).

Finally, we saw that the biological significance of the results depends quite heavily on network rules. Basin 2 produced some biologically unexpected advice (i.e., S1P set to 0) within the templates, while the large, healthy

Table 6 Frequent templates are more successful than others

	Top 1,000	Random 1,000	*Z*-score	*P* value
Basin 1	4,493	4,293	2.753	0.00298
Basin 2	3,838	1,783	31.767	0.00000
Basin 3	2,534	1,073	26.605	0.00000
Basin 4	4,520	3,378	16.050	0.00000
	Top 1,000	**Bottom 1,000**	**Z-score**	***P* value**
Basin 1	4,493	1,979	37.196	0.00000
Basin 2	3,838	8	67.986	0.00000
Basin 3	2,534	1,000	28.166	0.00000
Basin 4	4,520	2,315	32.124	0.00000

Listed in the table are intervention success counts, *Z*-scores and *P* values for two-proportion *Z*-tests between the top 1,000 most frequent 3-templates and 1,000 random templates or the 1,000 least frequent templates. With 11 intervention starting states over 1,000 templates, each number of successes is out of 11,000 intervention attempts. In each case we find, with statistical confidence, the top frequency template group provides a higher proportion of successful interventions than the other groups.

Basin 1 and also the smaller T-LGL Basin 3 contained templates with immense power and great biological significance. This discrepancy can be attributed to many causes, including a network more focused on modeling the disease state (relatively rare) vs. the healthy state, which may be acceptable depending on the application. In our case, we saw two variables fixed between healthy and T-LGL interventions while the biologically consistent setting of the third variable, enabled by the combinatorial power of the first two, was able to dictate network fate.

Thus, while templates are capable of revealing novel biological insights, they may also reveal or confirm sensitivities in the network rule system that may or may not be desirable for a particular biological model. In the end, template-based analysis reveals the most powerful triggers for altering network dynamics into desired attractor basins strictly based upon the given Boolean rules. In our look into the T-LGL leukemia network, our templates were realized, and in most cases biologically reinforced, on a network with over 8 trillion states in the basin of attraction field based sampling only 50,000 initial states.

Conclusions

Our work thus far has clearly established a usefulness in analyzing basins of attraction in identifying intervention targets. Our use of logic minimization reduces the representation of basins of attraction, and the template measures stratify the terms, revealing not only the key players in the system but also how to manipulate them. Perhaps the most important aspect of our revealed intervention targets is the fact that they are both basin- and value-specific; in other words, we provide not just targets, but how exactly to intervene (value) and also a context in which the intervention is appropriate (basin).

With small network sizes (less than 20), it is likely that many variables will either be important in some way (known beforehand) or may even represent an amalgamation of multiple entities. Thus, intervention targets revealed may be true, but they may also be obvious depending on the study. This, along with the fact that the single-variable measures fail in larger networks requiring a sampled state space, motivated our work to expand our approach for larger networks with dozens of variables and more, allowing us to include variables which are less well known and that may not be obvious intervention targets. By introducing the template counting approach to supersede the small network popularity and power measures, we have made possible the identification of powerful intervention targets despite sampled state spaces.

We first demonstrated the maintained success proportions of frequency-based template interventions between exhaustively enumerated and sampled state spaces. Convinced that key information was preserved by the measures despite sampling, we next showed the consistent success proportions across networks of increasing sizes as other methods fell away in performance. These investigations into robustness convinced us that the template approach was sure to provide the critical information needed regarding intervention targets.

We have also demonstrated the efficacy of the approach on a larger T-LGL leukemia network crafted by domain experts. We note that when all single-variable measures were unable to produce helpful intervention targets, the template-based approaches did produce single and multi-variable intervention targets with high intervention success rates. In the end, the template-based analysis revealed the most powerful triggers for altering network dynamics into desired attractor basins, and these results were realized, and in many cases, biologically corroborated, on a network with over 8 trillion states in the basin of attraction field based sampling only 50,000 initial states

Despite the progress in sampling large state spaces, we will always be limited by the exponential growth of the state space with the number of variables. Fortunately as network sizes race into intractability, so too does the reliability of such networks, which is a direct influence on the quality of our results. In the end, our measures will always reveal the true triggers of network dynamics based on the given rules of the system. Thus, while they are capable of revealing novel biological insights, they may also reveal or confirm sensitivities in the network rule system that may or may not be desirable for a particular biological model. Since there are quality handmade networks with sizes into the dozens of variables, such as our T-LGL leukemia network, a Drosophila network from Albert et al. [6], and others, our leap to the 40 to 50 variable size level is significant. With improvements to algorithm implementation and with the incorporation of parallelization, we plan to improve the large networks approach in terms of speed and network size capability, ideally towards the 75 to 100 variable mark. At the same time, we also wish to incorporate the ability to prefer certain variables over others as template members if information regarding the downstream effects of intervention reveals possible redundancies. In addition, because interventions can and do alter the rule structure of the network, we wish to investigate the use of the PBN model, which is a stochastic extension of Boolean networks and is able to model such changes in biological context. In such cases, basins of attraction would need to be revised to reflect the new stochastic behavior, especially the steady-state distributions of PBNs, as these distributions reflect the long-run behavior of the network [13].

Endnotes

[a]We adhere to the traditional, synchronous update scheme due to its origins in relating attractors to biological cell types [9] and because its determinism is

exploited by our analysis approach. Some validly claim that real biological systems do not 'march in step' and that asynchronous update mechanisms are more appropriate [25,26]. Recent work [26,35] comparing asynchronous update approaches identified the general asynchronous (GA) method, wherein a random node is updated at each time step, as superior. However, because neither do real biological systems 'take turns' updating, because synchronous networks are able to be analyzed by our methods without the dramatic reduction seen with asynchronous network analysis, because the nondeterminism associated with asynchronous networks may invalidate Kauffman's hypothesis relating attractors to cell types, and because that synchronicity is still related to living systems [24], we work under the synchronous assumption even though there is no perfect answer.

[b]Harmonic mean (H) is one kind of average. For two numbers, x and y, $H = \frac{2xy}{x+y}$.

[c]Step 1 of this algorithm is a simple partitioning of the total iterations, and thus has a constant overhead. Step 2 of this algorithm is governed by the value K. In practice, K will be a small number and certainly much less than (and not dependent upon) n. Step 3 executes once for each unique template, namely, $2^K\binom{n}{K}$ times. It is known that the binomial coefficient $\binom{n}{k}$ is bounded above by $(n \times e/k)^k$ [29]. Step 4 executes once for each term, where the number of terms is at most 2^n (i.e., no logic minimization at all). Steps 5 and 6 are a constant time operation. Because all steps are nested, the runtime is a product, from which constants can be removed, bounded above by a constant factor of 2^n.

Additional files

Additional file 1: Single-variable measures performance. This supplement will show that variable popularity, variable power, and the harmonic mean of the two typically produce the most successful single variable intervention targets compared with other traditional network measures, including centralities, topological measures, etc.

Additional file 2: *P* value matrices for template simulation study. This supplement contains pairwise *P* value matrices for sampled networks in the simulation study for template interventions. These values support the information communicated in Figures 4A,B.

Additional file 3: T-LGL leukemia network. This supplement contains various additional information regarding the T-LGL Leukemia network. Specifically, this supplement will detail the steps and reasoning behind reducing the 60-variable T-LGL leukemia network down to 43 variables, the listing of Boolean network rules for the T-LGL leukemia network. These rules were translated directly into the Boolean functions governing the dynamics of the network, the Boolean states of the four main attractors with a description of their classification, and the listings of the 30 *F*-based templates for each of the four main basins of attraction with the highest intervention success estimates. The tables will also show the estimated chances of transitioning the network to each of the other three basins as well in order to illustrate how some intervention targets may be desirable for their ability to avoid undesirable basins in addition to their ability to find desirable ones.

Abbreviations

D or TBDP, template basin distribution percentage; *F* or FREQ, frequency (based template); HPP, harmonic mean of POP and POW; KxFREQ or KxTBDP, *F*- or *D*-based template with *x* variables (i.e., K1FREQ, K2TBDP, etc.); POP, variable popularity; POW, variable power.

Competing interests

The authors declare that they have no competing interests.

Authors' contributions

MV designed the methodology, carried out the experiments, analysis and applications, and drafted the manuscript. SK conceived of the logic minimization approach, helped design the simulation study, and directed manuscript revisions. Both authors read and approved the final manuscript.

Acknowledgments

The authors wish to thank Dr. Andy Wuensche and Dr. Dan Bryce for helpful discussions. MV was partially supported by a grant from The Citadel Foundation.

Author details

[1]Department of Mathematics and Computer Science, The Citadel, Charleston, SC 29409, USA. [2]Integrated Cancer Genomics Division, Translational Genomics Research Institute, Phoenix, AZ 85004, USA.

References

1. SA Kauffman, *The Origins of Order: Self-Organization and Selection in Evolution*, 1st edn. (Oxford University Press, 1993)
2. S Ekins, SA Wrighton, Application of in silico approaches to predicting drug-drug interactions. J. Pharmacol. Toxicol. Methods **45**, 65–69 (2001). http://dx.doi.org/10.1016/s1056-8719(01)00119-8
3. A Wuensche, Genomic regulation modeled as a network with basins of attraction, in *Pacific Symposium on Biocomputing*, vol. 3, (1998), pp. 89–102. http://view.ncbi.nlm.nih.gov/pubmed/9697174
4. F Li, T Long, Y Lu, Q Ouyang, C Tang, The yeast cell-cycle network is robustly designed. Proc. Natl. Acad. Sci. USA **101**(14), 4781–4786 (2004). [http://dx.doi.org/10.1073/pnas.0305937101]
5. M Verdicchio, S Kim, Identifying targets for intervention by analyzing basins of attraction. Pac. Symp. Biocomput, 350–361 (2011). http://view.ncbi.nlm.nih.gov/pubmed/21121062
6. R Albert, HG Othmer, The topology of the regulatory interactions predicts the expression pattern of the segment polarity genes in Drosophila melanogaster. J. Theor. Biol. **223**, 1–18 (2003). http://dx.doi.org/10.1016/S0022-5193(03)00035-3
7. J Yu, VA Smith, PP Wang, AJ Hartemink, ED Jarvis, Advances to Bayesian network inference for generating causal networks from observational biological data. Bioinformatics **20**(18), bth448–3603 (2004). http://dx.doi.org/10.1093/bioinformatics/bth448
8. VA Smith, ED Jarvis, AJ Hartemink, Evaluating functional network inference using simulations of complex biological systems. Bioinformatics **18**(suppl 1), S216—224 (2002). http://dx.doi.org/10.1093/bioinformatics/18.suppl_1.S216
9. S Kauffman, Metabolic stability and epigenesis in randomly constructed genetic nets. J. Theor. Biol. **22**(3), 437–467 (1969). http://dx.doi.org/10.1016/0022-5193(69)90015-0
10. T Akutsu, S Miyano, S Kuhara, Identification of genetic networks from a small number of gene expression patterns under the Boolean network model. Pac. Symp. Biocomput, 17–28 (1999). http://view.ncbi.nlm.nih.gov/pubmed/10380182
11. I Shmulevich, A Saarinen, Yli-O Harja, J Astola, ed. by W Zhang, I Shmulevich, Inference of genetic regulatory networks via best-fit extensions, in *Computational and Statistical Approaches to Genomics* (Kluwer Academic Publishers Boston, 2003), pp. 197–210. http://dx.doi.org/10.1007/0-306-47825-0_11
12. H Lähdesmäki, I Shmulevich, O Yli-Harja, On learning gene regulatory networks under the boolean network model. Mach. Learn. **52**, 147–167 (2003). http://dx.doi.org/10.1023/A:1023905711304

13. I Shmulevich, ER Dougherty, S Kim, W Zhang, Probabilistic Boolean networks: a rule-based uncertainty model for gene regulatory networks. Bioinformatics **18**(2), 261–274 (2002). http://dx.doi.org/10.1093/bioinformatics/18.2.261
14. A Datta, A Choudhary, ML Bittner, ER Dougherty, External control in Markovian genetic regulatory networks. Mach. Learn. **52**, 169–191 (2003). http://dx.doi.org/10.1023/A:1023909812213
15. A Datta, A Choudhary, ML Bittner, ER Dougherty, External control in Markovian genetic regulatory networks: the imperfect information case. Bioinformatics **20**(6), 924–930 (2004). http://dx.doi.org/10.1093/bioinformatics/bth008
16. R Pal, A Datta, ML Bittner, ER Dougherty, Intervention in context-sensitive probabilistic Boolean networks. Bioinformatics **21**(7), 1211–1218 (2005). http://dx.doi.org/10.1093/bioinformatics/bti131
17. A Choudhary, A Datta, ML Bittner, ER Dougherty, Intervention in a family of Boolean networks. Bioinformatics **22**(2), 226–232 (2006). http://dx.doi.org/10.1093/bioinformatics/bti765
18. D Bryce, M Verdicchio, S Kim, Planning interventions in biological networks. ACM Trans. on Intell. Syst. Technol. **1**(2), 11 (2010)
19. KA Richardson, Simplifying Boolean networks. Adv. Complex Syst. **8**(4), 365–382 (2005)
20. E Dubrova, M Teslenko, H Tenhunen, ed. by C Priami, F Dressler, O Akan, and A Ngom, A computational scheme based on random Boolean networks, in *Transactions on Computational Systems Biology X, Volume 5410 of Lecture Notes in Computer Science* (Springer Berlin, Heidelberg, 2008), pp. 41–58. dx.doi.org/10.1007/978-3-540-92273-5_3 [10.1007/978-3-540-92273-5_3]
21. A Saadatpour, RS Wang, A Liao, X Liu, TP Loughran, I Albert, R Albert, Dynamical and structural analysis of a T cell survival network identifies novel candidate therapeutic targets for large granular lymphocyte leukemia. PLoS Comput. Biol. **7**(11), e1002267+ (2011). http://dx.doi.org/10.1371/journal.pcbi.1002267
22. A Naldi, E Remy, D Thieffry, C Chaouiya, Dynamically consistent reduction of logical regulatory graphs. Theor. Comput. Sci. **412**(21), 2207–2218 (2011). http://www.sciencedirect.com/science/article/pii/S0304397510005839
23. K Willadsen, J Wiles, Robustness and state-space structure of Boolean gene regulatory models. J. Theor. Biol. **249**(4), 749–765 (2007). http://dx.doi.org/10.1016/j.jtbi.2007.09.004
24. C Gershenson, ed. by J Pollack, M Bedau, P Husbands, T Ikegami, and RA Watson, Updating schemes in random Boolean networks: do they really matter? in *Artificial Life IX, Proceedings of the Ninth International Conference on the Simulation and Synthesis of Living Systems* (MIT Press, 2004), pp. 238–243. http://arxiv.org/abs/nlin/0402006
25. R Thomas, Boolean formalization of genetic control circuits. J. Theor. Biol. **42**(3), 563–585 (1973). http://www.sciencedirect.com/science/article/pii/0022519373902476
26. I Harvey, T Bossomaier, Time out of joint: attractors in asynchronous random Boolean networks, in *Proceedings of the Fourth European Conference on Artificial Life (ECAL97)*, (1997), pp. 67–75. http://citeseerx.ist.psu.edu/viewdoc/summary?doi=10.1.1.48.6693
27. A Marcovitz, *Introduction to Logic Design*, 1st edn. (McGraw-Hill Science/Engineering/Math, New York, 2002). http://www.worldcat.org/isbn/0072951761
28. RL Rudell, AL Sangiovanni-Vincentelli, ESPRESSO-MV, Algorithms for multiple valued logic minimization, in *Proc. of the IEEE Custom Integrated Circuits Conference* (IEEE New York, 1985)
29. TH Cormen, CE Leiserson, RL Rivest, C Stein, *Introduction to Algorithms, Third Edition*, 3rd edn. (The MIT Press, 2009). http://portal.acm.org/citation.cfm?id=1614191
30. A Wuensche, *Exploring Discrete Dynamics.* (Luniver Press, 2011)
31. A Wuensche, ed. by M Komosinski, A Adamatzky, Discrete Dynamics Lab: tools for investigating cellular automata and discrete dynamical networks, chapter 8, in *Artificial Life Models in Software* (Springer London London, 2009), pp. 215–258. http://dx.doi.org/10.1007/978-1-84882-285-6_8
32. RB D'agostino, W Chase, A Belanger, The appropriateness of some common procedures for testing the equality of two independent binomial populations. Am. Stat. **42**(3), 198–202 (1988). http://dx.doi.org/10.1080/00031305.1988.10475563
33. A Knezevic, *Overlapping Confidence Intervals and Statistical Significance.* (Cornell Statistical Consulting Unit, Ithaca, 2008)
34. R Zhang, MV Shah, J Yang, SB Nyland, X Liu, JK Yun, R Albert, TP Loughran, Network model of survival signaling in large granular lymphocyte leukemia. Proc. Natl. Acad. Sci. **105**(42), 16308–16313 (2008). http://dx.doi.org/10.1073/pnas.0806447105
35. A Saadatpour, I Albert, R Albert, Attractor analysis of asynchronous Boolean models of signal transduction networks. J. Theor. Biol. **266**(4), 641–656 (2010). http://dx.doi.org/10.1016/j.jtbi.2010.07.022
36. RA Weinberg, *The Biology of Cancer HB*, 1st edn. (Garland Science, 2006). http://www.amazon.com/exec/obidos/redirect?tag=citeulike07-20&path=ASIN/0815340788
37. J Yang, X Liu, SB Nyland, R Zhang, LK Ryland, K Broeg, KTT Baab, NRR Jarbadan, R Irby, TP Loughran, Platelet-derived growth factor mediates survival of leukemic large granular lymphocytes via an autocrine regulatory pathway. Blood **115**, 51–60 (2010). http://dx.doi.org/10.1182/blood-2009-06-223719
38. T Lamy, JH Liu, TH Landowski, WS Dalton, TP Loughran, Dysregulation of CD95/CD95 ligand-apoptotic pathway in CD3(+) large granular lymphocyte leukemia. Blood. **92**(12), 4771–4777 (1998). http://view.ncbi.nlm.nih.gov/pubmed/9845544

Identification of thresholds for dichotomizing DNA methylation data

Yihua Liu[1], Yuan Ji[2] and Peng Qiu[1*]

Abstract

DNA methylation plays an important role in many biological processes by regulating gene expression. It is commonly accepted that turning on the DNA methylation leads to silencing of the expression of the corresponding genes. While methylation is often described as a binary on-off signal, it is typically measured using beta values derived from either microarray or sequencing technologies, which takes continuous values between 0 and 1. If we would like to interpret methylation in a binary fashion, appropriate thresholds are needed to dichotomize the continuous measurements. In this paper, we use data from The Cancer Genome Atlas project. For a total of 992 samples across five cancer types, both methylation and gene expression data are available. A bivariate extension of the StepMiner algorithm is used to identify thresholds for dichotomizing both methylation and expression data. Hypergeometric test is applied to identify CpG sites whose methylation status is significantly associated to silencing of the expression of their corresponding genes. The test is performed on either all five cancer types together or individual cancer types separately. We notice that the appropriate thresholds vary across different CpG sites. In addition, the negative association between methylation and expression is highly tissue specific.

Introduction

DNA methylation plays an important role in cancer through hypermethylation to turn off tumor suppressors and hypomethylation to activate oncogenes [1,2]. It is widely accepted that DNA methylation is associated with silencing of gene expression [3]. With data from high-throughput array and sequencing technologies, several studies have analyzed the relationship between methylation and gene expression [4-6].

When the relationship between methylation and gene expression is discussed, both are often described as binary signals (i.e., on-off, high-low) [7]. For example, for a gene whose expression can be controlled by the methylation of a CpG site in its promoter region: if the CpG site is methylated, the gene's expression is typically low; if the CpG site is unmethylated, the expression of the gene can be either high or low, depending on other controlling mechanisms. On the other hand, measurements of methylation and expression obtained using microarrays and sequencing technologies are in continuous values. If we want to interpret the relationship between methylation and gene expression data using the binary language, appropriate thresholds are needed to dichotomize the measurements.

To jointly analyze methylation and gene expression, an ideal dataset would be a large collection of samples for which both data types are available. The Cancer Genome Atlas (TCGA) project provides such data for a large number of cancer samples [8-11]. Moreover, the TCGA samples are derived from multiple cancer and tissue types. The diversity among the samples may enable us to see relationships that cannot be observed in individual tissue types.

In this paper, we downloaded DNA methylation and gene expression data in TCGA. Data for a total of 992 samples were available, covering five cancer types. We extended the StepMiner algorithm [12] to identify thresholds to dichotomize methylation and expression measurements. Hypergeometric test was used to identify CpG sites whose methylation is significantly associated to silencing of expression of their corresponding genes. We observed that appropriate thresholds are highly CpG site specific, and the methylation-expression association for many genes is tissue-type specific.

*Correspondence: pqiu@mdanderson.org
[1] Department of Bioinformatics and Computational Biology, University of Texas MD Anderson Cancer Center, Houston, TX 77030, USA
Full list of author information is available at the end of the article

Materials and methods

Methylation and expression data from TCGA

TCGA data portal (https://tcga-data.nci.nih.gov/tcga/tcgaDownload.jsp) provides three ways for accessing the data. Two of them, 'data matrix' and 'bulk download,' require investigators to manually select a subset of the data and then automatically collect relevant data files into a compressed .tar file for download. After that, additional effort is needed to parse and assemble the downloaded files into formats useful to programming environments such as Matlab or R. Since TCGA data keep growing and the manual selection can be tedious when multiple data types and disease types are considered, it is difficult to keep track of the manual selections and guarantee reproducibility. Therefore, we chose the third way, 'open-access http directory,' which contains links for all individual data files in TCGA (http://tcga-data.nci.nih.gov/tcgafiles/ftp_auth/distro_ftpusers/anonymous/tumor/). We created Matlab scripts to programmatically grab methylation and RNA-seq data files for each individual disease type, automatically parse them, and organize them into tab delimited spreadsheets for subsequent analysis. Our scripts for automatically downloading TCGA data are available at http://odin.mdacc.tmc.edu/~pqiu/software/DownloadTCGA/.

Genome-wide methylation measurements were generated using the Illumina Infinium Human DNA Methylation27 array platform (Illumina, Inc., San Diego, CA, USA), which interrogates the methylation status of 27,578 CpG sites in proximal promoter regions of 14,475 genes in the human genome. As of 12 February 2013, methylation data for 2,796 samples across 12 cancer types were available. We downloaded the TCGA level 3 preprocessed data, which are the ratio $M_i/(U_i + M_i)$ for each CpG site *i*. M_i represents the signal intensity of the methylated probe for CpG site *i*, and U_i is the signal intensity of the unmethylated probe. Therefore, the numerical range of the data is between 0 and 1. Zero (0) indicates unmethylated, whereas 1 indicates completely methylated. The data contain a small fraction of empty entries, because the corresponding probes either overlap with known single-nucleotide polymorphisms or other genomic variations, or their signal intensities are lower than the background.

TCGA uses several platforms to quantify gene expression, among which the Illumina GA II and HiSeq platforms profiled the largest number of samples. As of 12 February 2013, preprocessed RNA-seq data for 4,108 samples across 11 cancer types were available. The preprocessed data are the RPKM values for 20,532 genes in each sample. Roughly, the numerical range of the data is between 0 and 10^5. For each gene, we replaced the zero entries with the minimal non-zero value of this gene across all samples and transformed the data to log scale.

The total number of overlapping samples between the above methylation and expression data was 992. The overlap covered five different cancer types: breast cancer (BRCA, 313 samples), colon and rectal cancer (COAD/READ, 227 samples), kidney renal clear cell carcinoma (KIRC, 208 samples), squamous cell lung cancer (LUSC, 129 samples), and uterine corpus endometrioid carcinoma (UCEC, 115 samples). Our analysis was performed based on these 992 overlapping samples.

Extend StepMiner for dichotomizing methylation and expression data

StepMiner was originally developed to extract binary patterns in microarray gene expression data [13] and study the boolean implications between expression of pairs of genes [12]. StepMiner examines data in a univariate fashion. Given a random variable X with an unknown probability distribution and n independent observations of the random variable $x_{k,(k=1,2,...,n)}$, the algorithm first sorts the observations in ascending order $x_{(1)} \leq x_{(2)} \leq ... \leq x_{(n)}$. Then, the sorted data are fitted by a step function, $f(i) = \mu_1 I(i \leq t) + \mu_2 I(i > t)$, where $i = 1, 2, ..., n$ and $I(.)$ is an indicator function. Denote the mean of all observations as μ, the deviation of the fitted step function to sample mean as signal $= \sum_{i=1}^{n}(f(i) - \mu)^2$, and the fitting error as noise $= \sum_{i=1}^{n}(f(i) - x_{(i)})^2$. The goodness of fit can be defined by a signal-to-noise ratio (SNR), and the best fit parameters can be found by maximizing SNR $= \frac{\text{signal}}{\text{noise}}$. Operationally, the maximization problem can be solved by exhaustively enumerating all possible integer values for $1 \leq t < n$. For each possible value of t, calculating the ratio is straight forward because μ_1 is the mean of the first t observations in the sorted data and μ_2 is the mean of the remaining observations. Once the t^* that maximizes SNR is identified, the threshold for dichotomizing the observation can be defined as $\frac{1}{2}(x_{(t^*)} + x_{(t^*+1)})$. The maximum value of signal-to-noise ratio SNR(t^*) depends on the distribution of X. If X has an extreme bi-modal distribution and its probability density function is a sum of two delta functions, SNR(t^*) approaches positive infinity. If X follows a uniform distribution, SNR(t^*) equals to 3. If X follows a Gaussian distribution, SNR(t^*) is approximately 1.75, regardless of the values of mean and variance of the Gaussian. Two examples using real data are shown in Figure 1, illustrating how univariate StepMiner identifies thresholds for gene expression of ESR1, and cg20253551 which measures the methylation status of a CpG site of that gene.

As shown above, StepMiner is a univariate algorithm, which determines a threshold for each feature by its marginal distribution. Since we are interested in the relationship between the expression of a gene and its methylation, one natural idea is to extend the algorithm to

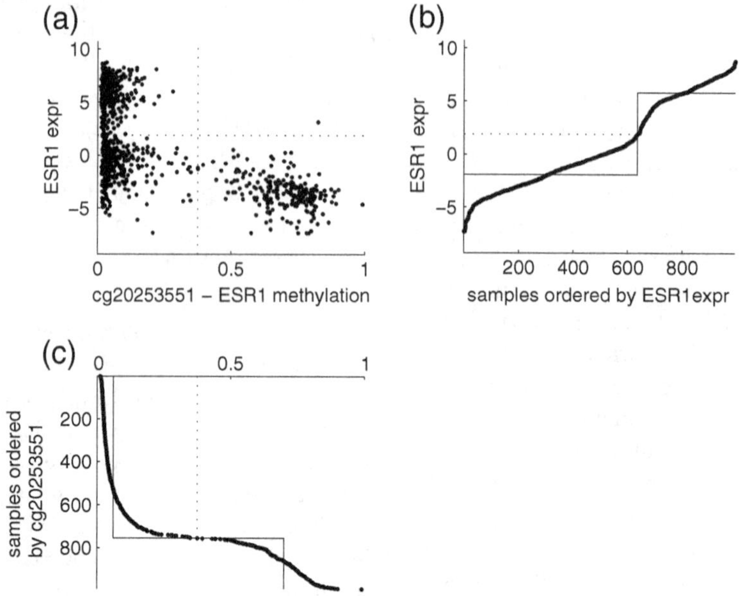

Figure 1 Two examples of univariate StepMiner. (**a**) Scatter plot of ESR1's gene expression and methylation (cg20253551). The dotted lines indicate thresholds identified by StepMiner. (**b**) Samples are ordered according to ESR1 expression, and a step function is fitted to the ordered expression data and identify a threshold to dichotomize expression. (**c**) A step function is fitted to the ordered methylation data and identify a threshold to binarize methylation.

a bivariate analysis and jointly consider two variables, which we call StepMiner2D. As shown in Figure 1b, the univariate StepMiner assigns each observation to a point, whose x-coordinate is the rank of this observation, and y-coordinate is the observed value itself. The collection of all observations forms a non-decreasing curve which is fitted by a step function. In order to extend the algorithm to bivariate, we define a non-decreasing surface and fit it with a bivariate step function. Given n observations of two random variable X and Y, $(x_k, y_k)_{,(k=1,2,\ldots,n)}$, we assign each observation (x_k, y_k) to a point in a three-dimensional (3D) space. The x-coordinate of the point is the rank of x_k with respect to all the observations for X; the y-coordinate of the point is the rank of y_k with respect to all the observations for Y; and the z-coordinate of the point is $x_k + y_k$. The collection of all points forms a surface, which is fitted by a bivariate step function with six parameters,

$$f(i,j) = \mu_{11} I(i \le t_x, j \le t_y) + \mu_{12} I(i > t_x, j \le t_y) + \mu_{21} I(i \le t_x, j > t_y) + \mu_{22} I(i > t_x, j > t_y), \quad (1)$$

where i and j both range from 1 to n.

To illustrate how to compute StepMiner2D, one example is shown in Figure 2 using the same data as the previous example. Scatter plot of ESR1's methylation and expression is shown in Figure 2a, along with the thresholds identified by StepMiner2D. To compute the thresholds, we first perform rank transformation. Assume x_k is the ith smallest among all observed value for X, and y_k is the jth smallest among all observed value for Y, the data point (x_k, y_k) is mapped to point (i,j). The rank transformed data are shown in Figure 2b. To form a non-decreasing surface sitting on top of the rank transformed data, a 'height' $z(i,j) = x_k + y_k$ is defined at point (i,j) to which the kth observation is mapped. For an (i,j) point to which no observation is mapped, we define $z(i,j) = \max_{u \le i, v \le j} z(u,v)$. Such a definition guarantees that the surface is non-decreasing, i.e., $z(i,j) \ge \max_{u \le i, v \le j} z(u,v)$. To ensure that X and Y contribute equally, the observations are normalized to zero-mean-unit-variance before defining z. Finally, denote $\mu = \frac{1}{n^2} \sum_{i,j=1}^{n} z(i,j)$, the parameter values of the best fit two-dimensional (2D) step function can be found by optimizing an SNR $= (\sum_{i,j=1}^{n} (f(i,j) - \mu)^2) / (\sum_{i,j=1}^{n} (f(i,j) - z(i,j))^2)$ in a similar exhaustive search fashion as the one-dimensional (1D) case. Computing z and optimizing SNR on a $n \times n$ grid can be time consuming when n is large. For computational efficiency, we approximate the surface on a 50×50 grid. In Figure 2c, the surface z is shown as a heatmap, where blue indicates small value and red indicates large value. Figure 2d shows the points (x_k, y_k, z_k) and the best fit

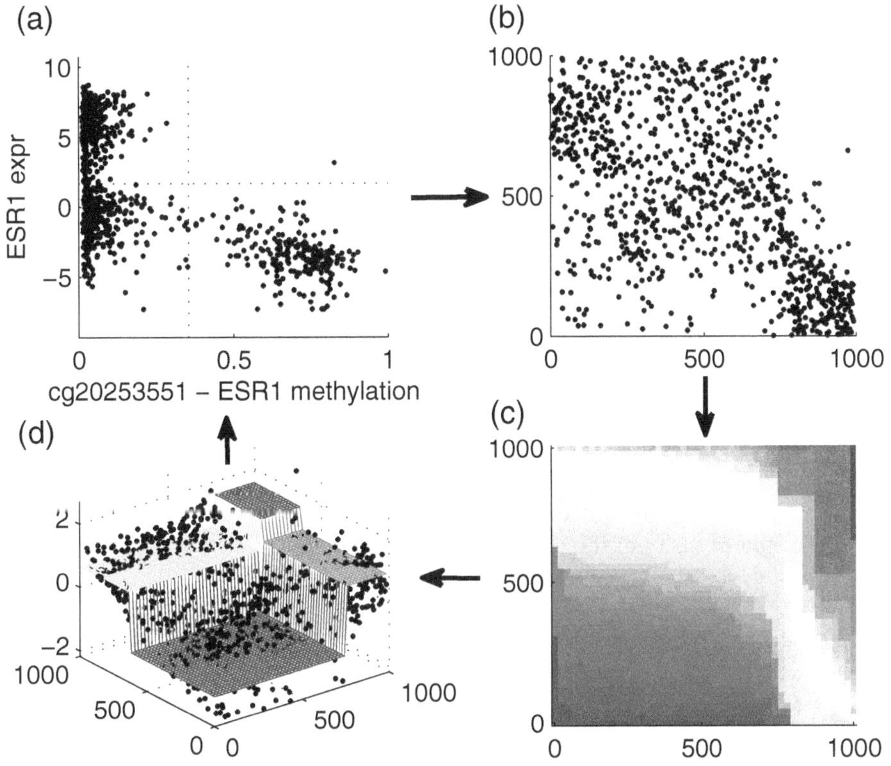

Figure 2 An example of StepMiner2D. (**a**) Scatter plot of ESR1's gene expression and methylation. The dotted lines indicate threshold identified by StepMiner2D. (**b**) Scatter plot of rank transformed data. (**c**) Heatmap showing a non-decreasing surface sitting on top of the rank transformed data. (**d**) Three-dimensional visualization of points on the non-decreasing surface and the best fit bivariate step function.

bivariate step function. The optimal SNR for this example is 5.17. Similar to the 1D case, the maximum value of SNR depends on the joint distribution of X and Y. If the joint probability density function is a sum of two or three delta functions, the optimal SNR approaches positive infinity. If X and Y are independent, the optimal SNR is 3 for uniform distribution and approximately 1.75 for Gaussian distribution.

Hypergeometric test for methylation controlled genes

The optimal SNR value in StepMiner2D measures the multi-modality of the joint distribution of X and Y, rather than the association between the two variables. For example, if X and Y independently follow two bi-modal distributions, although there is no association between the two variables, the optimal SNR can be large. Thus, SNR does not seem to be suitable for evaluating the association between methylation and expression. Here, we are interested in one particular kind of association, whether methylation of a CpG site leads to down-regulation of its corresponding gene expression. After dichotomizing methylation and expression data, the sufficient statistics become counts of points in the four quadrants in Figure 2a. The significance of methylation controlled gene can be intuitively explained as whether the observed count in the upper-right quadrant is significantly less than expected. Popular statistical tests for 2 × 2 contingency tables, such as Fisher exact and chi-square tests, are designed to evaluate the whether counts are significantly unbalanced but not toward a specific direction. We choose to use hypergeometric test. Let N denote the total number of samples; R is the total number of methylated samples (sum of points in the upper-right quadrant and the lower-right quadrant); U is the total number of samples with high gene expression (total number of points in the two upper quadrants). Condition on N, R, and U, if the methylation and expression are independent, the number of samples in the upper-right quadrant k follows a hypergeometric distribution $p(k) = \binom{U}{k}\binom{N-U}{R-k}/\binom{N}{R}$. To evaluate the significance of the observed count in the upper-right quadrant K, we can compute the probability of observing K or less points under the assumption that methylation and expression are independent p value $= \sum_{k=0}^{K} p(k)$. This is a hypergeometric test specifically for evaluating the significance of whether methylation turns off gene expression.

Results

Data preprocessing

We preprocessed the TCGA data by filtering out CpG sites with small variance or many missing data points and matching methylation and expression data according to genes. The methylation data we downloaded from TCGA were generated by the Methylation27 array platform, which provided the methylation status of 27,578 CpG sites in 14,475 genes across 992 cancer samples. We excluded CpG sites whose annotated genes are not present in the expression data. We also excluded CpG sites with more than 1% missing data and ones whose methylation beta value is smaller than 0.01 for more than 95% of the samples. After applying these filtering criteria, we obtained a total of 11,189 CpG sites annotated to 7,344 unique genes. For approximately half of the genes, only one CpG site is measured for each gene; data for two CpG sites are available for the majority of the other half; for a very small number of genes, measurements of multiple CpG sites are available. In the subsequent subsections, for the methylation data of each of the 11,189 CpG sites, we extracted the expression data of its corresponding gene and focused our bivariate analysis on features paired according to genes. Preprocessed data and the code for our analysis is available at http://odin.mdacc.tmc.edu/~pqiu/projects/MethExpr/ .

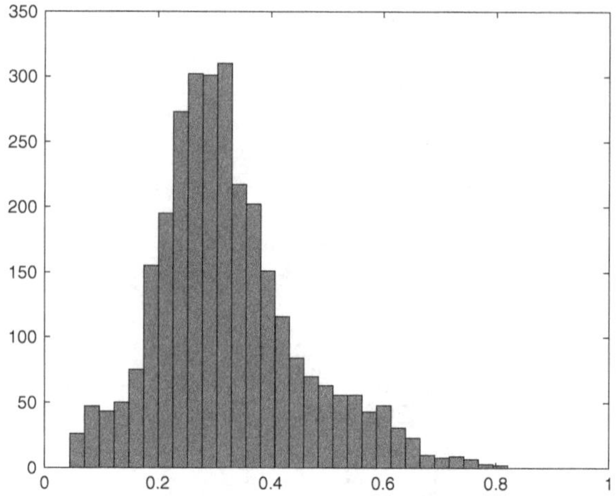

Figure 3 Histogram of thresholds for dichotomizing methylation data. For the 2,976 significant methylation-expression associations, StepMiner2D identified 2,976 thresholds for dichotomizing the methylation data. A histogram of those thresholds shows that the appropriate value for binarizing methylation varies for different methylation sites.

Identification of methylation on-off threshold

For each of the 11,189 methylation-expression pairs, we applied StepMiner2D to examine the data for all 992 samples together. Using such a pan-cancer analysis strategy, we identified thresholds to dichotomize the data. We performed hypergeometric test to examine whether methylation was significantly associated to the down-regulation of expression of its corresponding gene. We filtered out cases where the number of samples in the upper-right quadrant minus that in the lower-left quadrant was more than 10% of the total number of samples, which obviously did not support the concept of methylation turning off the expression. Using a p value threshold of 0.01 and Bonferroni correction, 2,976 pairs showed significant association, and the ESR1 example in Figures 1 and 2 was among the significant ones. Figure 3 shows a histogram of the identified methylation thresholds for the 2,976 significant associations, where we observed a wide-spread distribution. This result indicates that although the beta value quantification of methylation has a consistent numerical range of [0, 1] across different genes, the appropriate threshold for dichotomizing the beta values is highly CpG site specific.

The association between methylation and expression of ESR1 was significant when all 992 samples were examined together. However, when we examined individual cancer types separately, the methylation-expression association for ESR1 became insignificant. In Figure 4, the thresholds in all the plots are the same, and they were derived by considering all cancer types together. If we focus on breast cancer samples and ignore the rest, we see that almost all breast cancer samples are ESR1 unmethylated, and their ESR1 expression can be either high or low, which does not contradict with the concept that methylation turns off the expression. However, since very few breast cancer samples are methylated, we do not know whether methylated samples will have high ESR1 expression or low expression. Thus, we do not have strong evidence that ESR1 methylation turns off its expression in breast cancer samples, because we do not have enough points in the upper-right and lower-right quadrants. In this case, the lack of ESR1 methylated samples makes it impossible to prove the association between ESR1's methylation and expression in breast cancer. Similarly, for COAD/READ, although most samples exhibit high methylation and low expression, the association is also insignificant. Since ESR1 is seldom highly expressed in either methylated or unmethylated samples of COAD/READ, there is little evidence that the low expression of ESR1 in COAD/READ is caused by methylation or some other regulatory mechanisms. Similar observations can be made for other cancer types in Figure 4. In fact, if the StepMiner2D method is applied to individual cancer types separately, we will not be able to identify the appropriate thresholds for dichotomizing the methylation data. This observation illustrates the power of the pan-cancer analysis strategy that includes multiple cancer types. However, this also raises a question. Maybe the observed ESR1 methylation-expression association is simply a statistical property induced by tissue

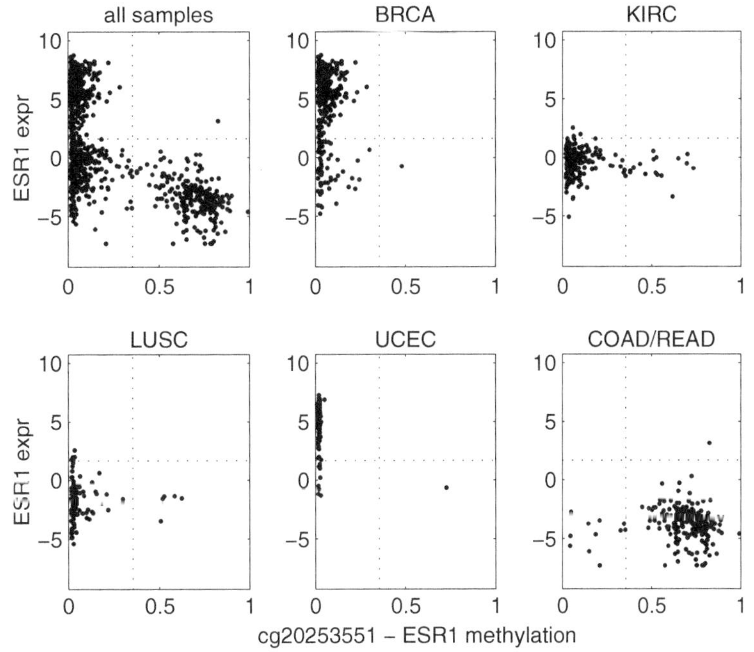

Figure 4 ESR1 methylation and expression. Scatter plots of methylation and expression data for ESR1 in all five cancer types together and individual cancer types separately. The dotted lines indicate the thresholds identified by StepMiner2D using all cancer types together. The association is significant when all cancer types are examined together but insignificant in individual cancer types.

differences, rather than an indication of a real mechanistic interaction. In the next subsection, we will discuss this issue further.

Tissue-specific association between methylation and expression

We evaluated the association between methylation and expression using samples in individual cancer types separately. Figure 5 shows the number of significant methylation-expression associations, when all cancer types were examined together and separately. One hundred eleven insignificant associations in pan-cancer analysis turned out to be significant in an individual cancer type. Among all the 2,976 significant associations in pan-cancer analysis, 2,072 were insignificant in all five individual cancer types, similar to the pattern shown in Figure 4. The majority of the remaining associations were significant in only one or two cancer types, indicating that the association between methylation and expression is highly tissue specific. For example, Figure 6 shows that the methylation of SOX8 is significantly associated to low SOX8 expression in breast cancer and kidney renal clear cell carcinoma but not in the other three cancer types. Such tissue-specific relationship echoes a previous result that hierarchical clustering of methylation data is able to separate tissue types and cancer subtypes [14,15]. Four genes showed significant methylation-expression association in all five individual cancer types, BST2, SLA2, GSTT1, and GSTM1. Figure 7 shows the data for BST2. We think that genes showing significant association in at least one individual cancer type are more likely to represent mechanistic methylation-expression interactions, compared to the ones that are only significant when all cancer types are considered.

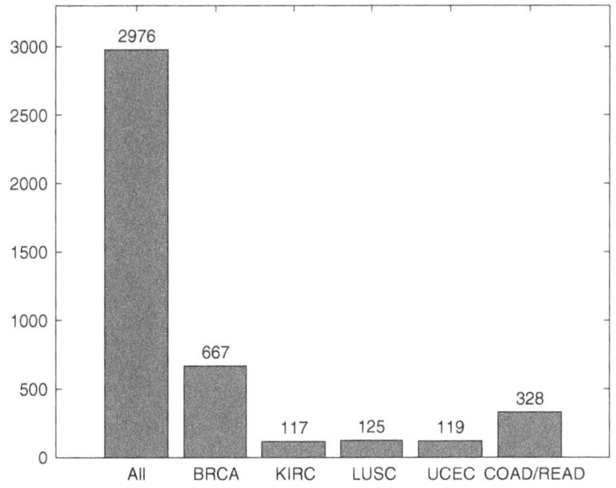

Figure 5 Methylation-expression association is tissue specific. The bar plot shows the number of significant associations when all cancer types are considered together and the numbers when individual cancer types are considered separately.

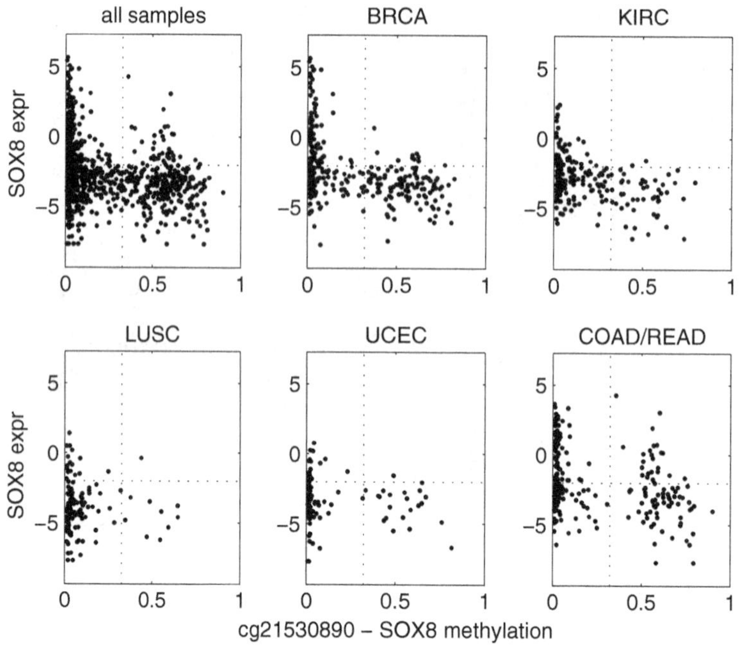

Figure 6 SOX8 methylation and expression. The methylation-expression association for SOX8 is significant in BRCA and KIRC but not in the other three cancer types.

Conclusions

We performed integrative analysis of methylation and gene expression data of five cancer types in TCGA. First, we pooled samples from all five cancer types together and applied StepMiner2D to identify thresholds for dichotomizing the methylation and expression data. In such a pan-cancer analysis strategy, the diversity and variation among samples allow us to observe positive and negative signals in sufficient number of samples and empower the method to identify the appropriate thresholds. Then,

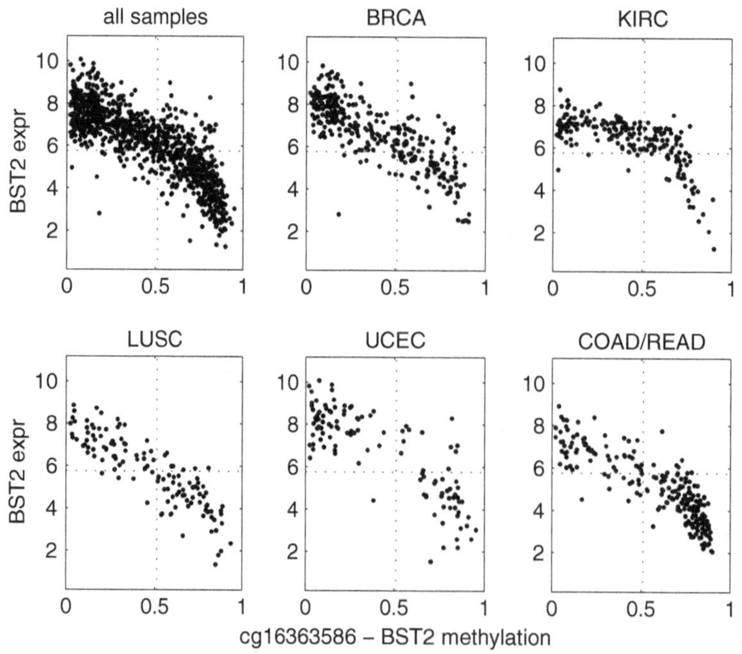

Figure 7 BST2 methylation and expression. The methylation-expression association for BST2 is significant in all five cancer types examined here.

we applied hypergeometric test to identify CpG sites whose methylation is significantly associated to silencing of the expression of their corresponding genes, either using all five cancer types together or using individual cancer types separately. When all five cancer types were examined together, 2,976 CpG sites showed significant negative association with gene expression. However, when samples in different cancer types were considered separately, a much smaller number of significant associations were observed in at least one cancer type. We speculate that the associations only significant in pan-cancer analysis are likely to be induced by tissue differences, whereas significant associations observed in individual cancer types are more likely to reflect regulatory relationships between methylation and gene expression. For future work, there are a few possible extensions. The methylation data used here are generated by the Illumina Methylation 27k platform. TCGA also generates methylation data using the Illumina Methylation 450k platform, which measures roughly 20 times more CpG sites. We plan to redo the analysis using the 450k methylation data, which will enable us to identify more associations between methylation and expression. Moreover, the proposed analysis strategy can also be applied to examine associations among measurements made by other modalities, such as microRNA expression, DNA copy number variation, protein expression, etc.

Competing interests

The authors declare that they have no competing interests.

Acknowledgements

The authors would like to acknowledge The Cancer Genome Atlas Research Network for providing the methylation and expression data used in this paper. This work was partially supported by TCGA Genome Data Analysis Center grant at the University of Texas MD Anderson Cancer Center (U24 CA143883 02 S1), as well as NIH grants (R01CA163481 and R01CA174385) from the National Cancer Institute.

Author details

[1]Department of Bioinformatics and Computational Biology, University of Texas MD Anderson Cancer Center, Houston, TX 77030, USA. [2]Center for Clinical and Research Informatics, NorthShore University HealthSystem, Chicago, IL 60201, USA.

References

1. E Ballestar, An introduction to epigenetics. Adv. Exp. Med. Biol. **711**, 1–11 (2011)
2. P Jones, S Baylin, The fundamental role of epigenetic events in cancer. Nat. Rev. Genet. **3**(6), 415–428 (2002)
3. P Laird, Principles and challenges of genomewide dna methylation analysis. Nat. Rev. Genet. **11**(3), 191–203 (2010)
4. M Li, C Balch, J Montgomery, M Jeong, J Chung, P Yan, T Huang, S Kim, K Nephew, Integrated analysis of DNA methylation and gene expression reveals specific signaling pathways associated with platinum resistance in ovarian cancer. BMC Med. Genomics. **2**, 34 (2009)
5. R Shaknovich, H Geng, N Johnson, L Tsikitas, L Cerchietti, J Greally, R Gascoyne, O Elemento, A Melnick, DNA methylation signatures define molecular subtypes of diffuse large B-cell lymphoma. Blood. **116**(20), e81–89 (2010)
6. M Widschwendter, G Jiang, C Woods, H Muller, H Fiegl, G Goebel, C Marth, E Muller-Holzner, A Zeimet, P Laird, M Ehrlich, DNA hypomethylation and ovarian cancer biology. Cancer Res. **64**(13), 4472–4480 (2004)
7. J Newell-Price, A Clark, P King, DNA methylation and silencing of gene expression. Trends Endocrinol. Metab. **11**(4), 142–148 (2000)
8. Cancer Genome Atlas Research Network, Integrated genomic analyses of ovarian carcinoma. Nature. **474**(7353), 609–615 (2011)
9. Cancer Genome Atlas Research Network, Comprehensive genomic characterization of squamous cell lung cancers. Nature. **487**(7417), 519–525 (2012)
10. Cancer Genome Atlas Research Network, Comprehensive molecular characterization of human colon and rectal cancer. Nature. **487**(7407), 330–333 (2012)
11. Cancer Genome Atlas Research Network, Comprehensive molecular portraits of human breast tumours. Nature. **490**(7418), 61–70 (2012)
12. D Sahoo, D Dill, A Gentles, R Tibshirani, S Plevritis, Boolean implication networks derived from large scale, whole genome microarray datasets. Genome Biol. **9**(10), R157 (2008)
13. D Sahoo, D Dill, R Tibshirani, S Plevritis, Extracting binary signals from microarray time-course data. Nucleic Acids Res. **35**(11), 3705–3712 (2007)
14. T Hinoue, D Weisenberger, C Lange, H Shen, H Byun, D Van Den Berg, S Malik, F Pan, H Noushmehr, C van Dijk, R Tollenaar, P Laird, Genome-scale analysis of aberrant dna methylation in colorectal cancer. Genome Res. **22**(2), 271–282 (2012)
15. P Qiu, L Zhang, Identification of markers associated with global changes in DNA methylation regulation in cancers. BMC Bioinformatics. **13** (Suppl 13), S7 (2012)

7

Harmonic analysis of Boolean networks: determinative power and perturbations

Reinhard Heckel[1*], Steffen Schober[2] and Martin Bossert[2]

Abstract

Consider a large Boolean network with a feed forward structure. Given a probability distribution on the inputs, can one find, possibly small, collections of input nodes that determine the states of most other nodes in the network? To answer this question, a notion that quantifies the *determinative power* of an input over the states of the nodes in the network is needed. We argue that the mutual information (MI) between a given subset of the inputs $\mathbf{X} = \{X_1, ..., X_n\}$ of some node *i* and its associated function $f_i(\mathbf{X})$ quantifies the determinative power of this set of inputs over node *i*. We compare the determinative power of a set of inputs to the sensitivity to perturbations to these inputs, and find that, maybe surprisingly, an input that has large sensitivity to perturbations does not necessarily have large determinative power. However, for *unate* functions, which play an important role in genetic regulatory networks, we find a direct relation between MI and sensitivity to perturbations. As an application of our results, we analyze the large-scale regulatory network of *Escherichia coli*. We identify the most determinative nodes and show that a small subset of those reduces the overall uncertainty of the network state significantly. Furthermore, the network is found to be tolerant to perturbations of its inputs.

1 Introduction

A Boolean network (BN) is a discrete dynamical system, which is, for example, used to study and model a variety of biochemical networks such as genetic regulatory networks. BNs have been introduced in the late 1960s by Kauffman [1,2] who proposed to study random BNs as models of gene regulatory networks. Kauffman investigated their dynamical behavior and a phenomena called self-organization. Aside from its original purpose, BNs were also used to model (small-scale) genetic regulatory networks; for example, in [3-5], it was demonstrated that BNs are capable of reproducing the underlying biological processes (i.e., the cell cycle) well. BNs are also used to model large-scale networks, such as the *Escherichia coli* regulatory network [6] which is analyzed in Section 6. This network is, in contrast to Kauffman's automata and the regulatory networks considered in [3-5], not an autonomous system, since the gene's states are determined by external factors.

In the literature addressing the analysis of BNs, it is common to consider measures that quantify the effect of perturbations. Whether a random BN operates in the so called ordered or disordered regime is determined by whether a single perturbation, i.e., flipping the state of a node, is expected to spread or die out eventually. Kauffman [2] argues that biological networks must operate at the border of the ordered and disordered regime; hence, they must be tolerant to perturbations to some extent.

In contrast to measures of perturbations, determinative power in BNs has not received much attention, even though there are several settings where such a notion is of interest. For example, given a feed forward network where the states of the nodes are controlled by the states of nodes in the input layer, we might ask whether a possibly small set of inputs suffices to determine most states, i.e., reduces the uncertainty about the network's states significantly. This can be addressed by quantifying the determinative power of the input nodes. For example, in the *E. coli* regulatory network, it turns out that a small set of metabolites and other inputs determine most genes that account for *E. coli*'s metabolism (see Section 6).

In this paper, we view the state of each node in the network as an independent random variable. This modeling

*Correspondence: heckel@nari.ee.ethz.ch
[1] Department of Information Technology and Electrical Engineering, ETH Zürich, Zürich, Switzerland
Full list of author information is available at the end of the article

assumption applies for networks with a tree-like topology, e.g., a feed forward network, and is often applied when studying the effect of perturbations. For this setting, determinative power of nodes and perturbation-related measures are properties of single functions; hence, the analysis of the BN reduces to the analysis of single functions. Our main tool for the theoretical results is Fourier analysis of Boolean functions. Fourier analytic techniques were first applied to BNs by Kesseli et al. [7,8]. In [7,8], results related to Derrida plots and convergence of trajectories in random BNs were derived. Ribeiro et al. [9] considered the pairwise mutual information in time series of random BNs, under a different setup that we use. Specifically, in [9], the functions are random; whereas here, the functions are deterministic, but the argument is random. Finally, note that part of this paper was presented at the 2012 International Workshop on Computational Systems Biology [10].

1.1 Contributions

Mutual information between a set of inputs to a node and the state of this node is a measure of the determinative power of this set of inputs, as mutual information quantifies mutual dependence of random variables. In order to understand the determinative power and mutual dependencies in Boolean networks, we systematically study the mutual information of sets of inputs and the state of a node. We relate mutual information to a measure of perturbations and prove that (maybe surprisingly) a set of inputs that is highly sensitive to perturbations might not necessarily have determinative power. Conversely, a set of inputs which has determinative power must be sensitive to perturbations. To prove those results, we show that the concentration of weight in the Fourier domain on certain sets of inputs characterizes a function in terms of tolerance to perturbations and determinative power of input nodes. Furthermore, we generalize a result by Xiao and Massey [11], which gives a necessary and sufficient condition of statistical independence of a set of inputs and a function's output in terms of the Fourier coefficients. This result can for instance be applied to decide for which classes of functions the algorithm presented in [12], which detects functional dependencies based on estimating mutual information, can succeed or fails. For *unate* functions, we show that any input and the function's output are statistically dependent and provide a direct relation between the mutual information and the influence of a variable. The class of unate functions is especially relevant for biological networks, as it includes all linear threshold functions and all nested canalizing functions, and describes functional dependencies in gene regulatory networks well [13]. As an application of the theoretical results in this paper, we show that mutual information can be used to identify the determinative nodes in the large-scale model of the control network of *E. coli*'s metabolism [6].

1.2 Outline

The paper is organized as follows. Boolean networks and Fourier analysis of Boolean functions are reviewed in Section 2. In Section 3, the influence and average sensitivity as measures of perturbations are reviewed, and their relation to the Fourier spectrum is discussed. In Section 4, we study the mutual information of sets of inputs and the function's output. Section 5 is devoted to unate functions. Section 6 contains an analysis of the large-scale *E. coli* regulatory network, using the tools and ideas developed in previous sections.

2 Preliminaries

We start with a short introduction to Boolean networks and Fourier analysis of Boolean functions, and introduce notation.

2.1 Boolean networks

A (synchronous) BN can be viewed as a collection of n nodes with memory. The state of a node i is described by a binary state $x_i(t) \in \{-1,+1\}$ at discrete time $t \in \mathbb{N}$. Choosing the alphabet to be $\{-1,+1\}$ rather than $\{0,1\}$ as more common in the literature on BNs will turn out to be advantageous later. However, both choices are equivalent. The state of the network at time t can be described by the vector $\mathbf{x}(t) = [x_1(t),...,x_n(t)] \in \{-1,+1\}^n$. The network dynamic is defined by

$$x_i(t+1) = f_i(\mathbf{x}(t)), \tag{1}$$

where $f_i\colon \{-1,+1\}^n \to \{-1,+1\}$ is the Boolean function associated with node i. At time $t = 0$, an initial state $\mathbf{x}(0) = \mathbf{x}_0$ is chosen. In general, not all arguments $x_1,...,x_n$ of a function $f_i(\mathbf{x})$ need to be *relevant*. The variable $x_j, j \in \{1,...,n\}$ is said to be relevant for f_i if there exists at least one $\mathbf{x} \in \{-1,+1\}^n$, such that changing x_j to $-x_j$ changes the function's value. In most of the BN models in biology, the functions depend on a small subset of their arguments only. Furthermore, not every state must have a function associated with it; states can also be external inputs to the network.

To study the determinative power and tolerance to perturbations, a probabilistic setup is needed. In our analysis, we assume that each state is an independent random variable X_i with distribution $P[X_i = x_i]$, $x_i \in \{-1,+1\}$. The assumption of independence holds for networks with tree-like topology, but is not feasible for networks with strong local dependencies and feedback loops. However, in many relevant settings, a BN has a tree-like topology, for instance the *E. coli* network analyzed in Section 6. For a network with few local dependencies, assuming independence will lead to a small modeling error. Major results concerning the analysis of BNs have been obtained under the assumptions as stated above, e.g., the annealed approximation [14], an important result on the spread of perturbations in random BNs. Several important results on random BNs, e.g., [14], let the network size n tend to infinity; hence, there are no local dependencies.

2.2 Notation

We use $[n]$ for the set $\{1, 2, ..., n\}$, and all sets are subsets of $[n]$. With $\sum_{S \subseteq A}(\cdot)$, we mean the sum over all sets S that are subsets of A. Throughout this paper, we use capital letters for random variables, e.g., X, and lower case letters for their realizations, e.g., x. Boldface letters denote vectors, e.g., $\mathbf{X}$ is a random vector, and $\mathbf{x}$ its realization. For a vector $\mathbf{x}$ and a set $A \subseteq [n]$, $\mathbf{x}_A$ denotes the subvector of $\mathbf{x}$ corresponding to the entries indexed by A.

2.3 Fourier analysis of Boolean functions

In the following, we give a short introduction to Fourier analysis of Boolean functions. Let $\mathbf{X} = (X_1, ..., X_n)$ be a binary, product distributed random vector, i.e., the entries of $\mathbf{X}$ are independent random variables $X_i, i \in [n]$ with distribution $\mathrm{P}[X_i = x_i], x_i \in \{-1, +1\}$. Throughout this paper, probabilities $\mathrm{P}[\cdot]$ and expectations $\mathbb{E}[\cdot]$ are with respect to the distribution of $\mathbf{X}$. We denote $p_i \triangleq \mathrm{P}[X_i = 1]$, the variance of X_i by $\mathrm{Var}(X_i)$, its standard deviation by $\sigma_i \triangleq \sqrt{\mathrm{Var}(X_i)}$ and finally $\mu_i \triangleq \mathbb{E}[X_i]$. The inner product of $f, g : \{-1, +1\}^n \to \{-1, +1\}$ with respect to the distribution of $\mathbf{X}$ is defined as

$$\langle f, g \rangle \triangleq \mathbb{E}[f(\mathbf{X})g(\mathbf{X})] = \sum_{\mathbf{x} \in \{-1,1\}^n} \mathrm{P}[\mathbf{X}=\mathbf{x}] f(\mathbf{x}) g(\mathbf{x}) \tag{2}$$

which induces the norm $\|f\| = \sqrt{\langle f, f \rangle}$. An orthonormal basis with respect to the distribution of $\mathbf{X}$ is

$$\Phi_S(\mathbf{x}) = \prod_{i \in S} \frac{x_i - \mu_i}{\sigma_i}, \quad S \subseteq [n] \setminus \emptyset$$

and

$$\Phi_S(\mathbf{x}) = 1, \quad S = \emptyset.$$

This basis was first proposed by Bahadur [15]. Thus, each Boolean function $f: \{-1, +1\}^n \to \{-1, +1\}$ can be uniquely expressed as

$$f(\mathbf{x}) = \sum_{S \subseteq [n]} \hat{f}(S) \Phi_S(\mathbf{x}), \tag{3}$$

where $\hat{f}(S) \triangleq \langle f, \Phi_S \rangle$ are the Fourier coefficients of f. Note that (3) is a representation of f as a multilinear polynomial. As an example, consider the AND2 function defined as $f_{\mathrm{AND2}}(\mathbf{x}) = 1$ if and only if $x_1 = x_2 = 1$, and let $p_1 = p_2 = 1/2$. According to (3)

$$f_{\mathrm{AND}}(\mathbf{x}) = -\frac{1}{2} + \frac{1}{2}x_1 + \frac{1}{2}x_2 + \frac{1}{2}x_1 x_2.$$

As a second example consider PARITY2, i.e., the XOR function, defined as $f_{\mathrm{PARITY2}}(\mathbf{x}) = 1$ if $x_1 = x_2 = 1$ or if $x_1 = x_2 = -1$, and $f_{\mathrm{PARITY2}}(\mathbf{x}) = -1$ for all other choices of $\mathbf{x}$. Written as a polynomial, $f_{\mathrm{PARITY2}}(\mathbf{x}) = x_1 x_2$. We conclude this section by listing properties of the basis functions which are used frequently throughout this paper.

Decomposition: Let $A \subseteq [n]$ and $S \subset A$, and denote $\bar{S} = A \setminus S$. Then,

$$\Phi_A(\mathbf{x}) = \Phi_S(\mathbf{x}) \Phi_{\bar{S}}(\mathbf{x}).$$

Orthonormality: For $A, B \subseteq [n]$,

$$\mathbb{E}[\Phi_A(\mathbf{X}) \Phi_B(\mathbf{X})] = \begin{cases} 1, \text{if} A = B \\ 0, \text{otherwise.} \end{cases}$$

Parseval's identity: For $f: \{-1, +1\}^n \to \{-1, +1\}$,

$$\mathbb{E}\left[f(\mathbf{X})^2\right] = \|f\|^2 = \sum_{S \subseteq [n]} \hat{f}(S)^2 = 1.$$

3 Influence and average sensitivity

Next, we discuss measures of perturbations and their relation to the Fourier spectrum. We start with a measure of the perturbation of a single input.

Definition 1 ([16]). Define the influence of variable i on the function f as

$$I_i(f) = \mathrm{P}\left[f(\mathbf{X}) \neq f(\mathbf{X} \oplus e_i)\right],$$

where $\mathbf{x} \oplus e_i$ is the vector obtained from $\mathbf{x}$ by flipping its ith entry.

By definition, the influence of variable i is the probability that perturbing, i.e., flipping, input i changes the function's output. Influence can be viewed as the capability of input i to change the output of f. In BNs, usually, the sum of all influences, i.e., the *average sensitivity* is studied.

Definition 2. The average sensitivity of f to the variables in the set A is defined as

$$I_A(f) = \sum_{i \in A} I_i(f).$$

The average sensitivity of f is defined as $\mathrm{as}(f) \triangleq I_{\{1,\ldots,n\}}(f)$.

$I_A(f)$ captures whether flipping an input chosen uniformly at random from A affects the function's output. Most commonly, all inputs are taken into account, i.e., the average sensitivity $\mathrm{as}(f)$ is studied. As an example, $\mathrm{as}(f_{\mathrm{PARITY2}}) = 2$ and $\mathrm{as}(f_{\mathrm{AND2}}) = 1$; hence, PARITY2 is more sensitive to single perturbations than AND2. Influence and average sensitivity have the following convenient expressions in terms of Fourier coefficients.

Proposition 1 (Lemma 4.1 of [17]). *For any Boolean function f,*

$$I_i(f) = \frac{1}{\sigma_i^2} \sum_{S \subseteq [n]:\, i \in S} \hat{f}(S)^2. \tag{4}$$

Proposition 2. *For any Boolean function f,*

$$I_A(f) = \sum_{S \subseteq [n]} \hat{f}(S)^2 \sum_{i \in S \cap A} \frac{1}{\sigma_i^2}. \tag{5}$$

Proposition 2 follows directly from Proposition 1 and the definition of $I_A(f)$. From (5), we see that $\mathrm{as}(f)$ is large if the Fourier weight is concentrated on the coefficients of high degree $d = |S|$, i.e., if $\sum_{S:\,|S| \geq d} \hat{f}(S)^2$ is large (i.e., close to one). For this case, Parseval's identity implies that the $\hat{f}(S)^2$ with $|S| < d$ must be small. Let's see an example: Suppose $p_1 = p_2 = p_3 = 1/2$ and consider the AND3 function, i.e., $f_{\mathrm{AND3}}(x_1, x_2, x_3) = 1$ if and only if $x_1 = x_2 = x_3 = 1$. f_{AND3} is tolerant to perturbations since $\mathrm{as}(f_{\mathrm{AND3}}) = 0.75$, and as Figure 1 shows, its spectrum is concentrated on the coefficients of low degree. In contrast for $f_{\mathrm{PARITY3}}(x_1, x_2, x_3) \triangleq x_1 x_2 x_3$, $\mathrm{as}(f_{\mathrm{PARITY}}) = 3$. Hence, PARITY3 is maximally sensitive to perturbations. Figure 1 shows that its spectrum is maximally concentrated on the coefficient of highest degree.

According to (5) $\mathrm{as}(f)$ is small only if the Fourier weight is concentrated on the coefficients of low degree. This is the case either if f is strongly biased (i.e., if $f(\mathbf{x}) = a$, for most inputs $\mathbf{x}$, where $a \in \{-1, 1\}$ is a constant) or if f depends on few variables only. This is in accordance with the results of Kauffman [1]; he found that a random BN operates in the ordered regime if the functions in the network depend on average on few variables.

We will state our result for measures of single perturbations. However, these results also apply to other noise models, specifically to the *noise sensitivity* of f. That is,

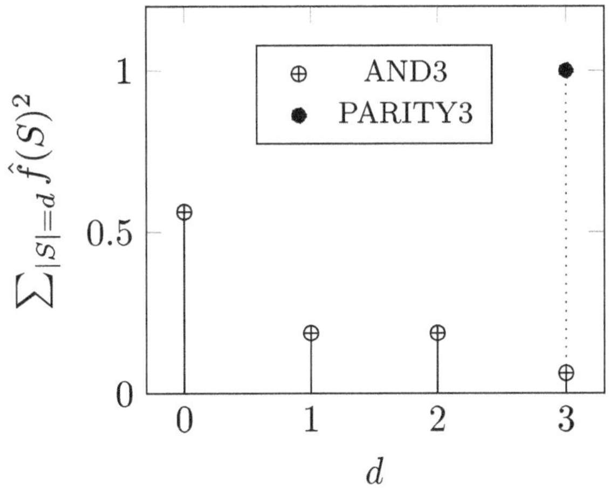

Figure 1 The Fourier spectrum of AND3 and PARITY3.

because the noise sensitivity of f is small if f is tolerant to single perturbations. The noise sensitivity of a Boolean function is defined as the probability that the function's output changes if each input is flipped independently with probability ϵ. For uniformly distributed $\mathbf{X}$, $\epsilon\, \mathrm{as}(f)$ is an upper bound for the noise sensitivity; for small values of ϵ, $\epsilon\, \mathrm{as}(f)$ approximates the noise sensitivity well. For the X_i being equally but possibly nonuniformly distributed and a slightly different noise model, it was found in [18] that $\epsilon\, \mathrm{as}(f)$ still upper bounds the noise sensitivity. This result was generalized to product distributed $\mathbf{X}$ in [19].

4 Mutual information and uncertainty

In this section, we study the determinative power of a subset of variables $\mathbf{X}_A$, where $\mathbf{X}_A$ consists of the entries of $\mathbf{X}$ corresponding to the indices in the set $A \subseteq [n]$, over the function's output $f(\mathbf{X})$. As a measure of determinative power, we take the mutual information $\mathrm{MI}(f(\mathbf{X}); \mathbf{X}_A)$ between $f(\mathbf{X})$ and $\mathbf{X}_A$, since $\mathrm{MI}(f(\mathbf{X}); \mathbf{X}_A)$ quantifies the statistical dependence between the random variable $\mathbf{X}_A$ and $f(\mathbf{X})$. Hence, this section is devoted to the study of $\mathrm{MI}(f(\mathbf{X}); \mathbf{X}_A)$.

Before giving a formal definition of mutual information, let us start with an example. Consider the PARITY2 function and let its inputs X_1, X_2 be uniformly distributed. Intuitively, if X_1 has determinative power, knowledge about X_1 should provide us with information about $f_{\mathrm{PARITY2}}(\mathbf{X})$. Suppose we know the value of X_1, say $X_1 = 1$. Since $f_{\mathrm{PARITY2}}(\mathbf{x}) = x_1 x_2$, we have with $\mathrm{P}[X_2 = 1] = 1/2$ that $\mathrm{P}\big[f_{\mathrm{PARITY2}}(\mathbf{X}) = 1\big] = \mathrm{P}\big[f_{\mathrm{PARITY2}} = 1 | X_1 = 1\big]$. Hence, knowledge of X_1 does not help to predict the value of $f_{\mathrm{PARITY2}}(\mathbf{X})$. Therefore, X_1 has no determinative power over $f_{\mathrm{PARITY2}}(\mathbf{X})$. We indeed have $\mathrm{MI}(f_{\mathrm{PARITY2}}(\mathbf{X}); X_1) = 0$.

We next define mutual information. Mutual information is the reduction of uncertainty of a random variable Y due to the knowledge of X; therefore, we need to define a measure of uncertainty first, which is entropy. As a reference for the following definitions, see [20].

Definition 3. The entropy $H(X)$ of a discrete random variable X with alphabet $\mathcal{X}$ is defined as

$$H(X) \triangleq -\sum_{x\in\mathcal{X}} \mathrm{P}[X = x] \log_2 \mathrm{P}[X = x] .$$

Definition 4. The conditional entropy $H(Y|X)$ of a pair of discrete and jointly distributed random variables (Y, X) is defined as

$$H(Y|X) \triangleq \sum_{x\in\mathcal{X}} \mathrm{P}[X = x]\, H(Y|X = x).$$

Definition 5. The mutual information $\mathrm{MI}(Y;X)$ is the reduction of uncertainty of the random variable Y due to the knowledge of X

$$\mathrm{MI}(Y;X) \triangleq H(Y) - H(Y|X).$$

For a binary random variable X with alphabet $\mathcal{X} = \{x_1, x_2\}$ and $p \triangleq \mathrm{P}[X = x_1]$, we have $H(X) = h(p)$, where $h(p)$ is the binary entropy function, defined as

$$h(p) \triangleq -p\log_2 p - (1-p)\log_2(1-p). \tag{6}$$

The properties of mutual information are what we intuitively expect from a measure of determinative power: If knowledge of X_i reduces the uncertainty of $f(\mathbf{X})$, then X_i determines the state of $f(\mathbf{X})$ to some extent, because then, knowledge about the state of X_i helps in predicting $f(\mathbf{X})$. Furthermore, we require from a measure of determinative power that not all variables can have large determinative power simultaneously. This is guaranteed for mutual information as

$$\sum_{i=1}^{n} \mathrm{MI}(f(\mathbf{X}); X_i) \leq \mathrm{MI}(f(\mathbf{X}); \mathbf{X}) \leq 1, \tag{7}$$

which follows from the chain rule of mutual information (as a reference, see [20]) and independence of the $X_i, i \in [n]$. Hence, if $\mathrm{MI}(f(\mathbf{X}); X_i)$ is large, i.e., close to 1, we can be sure that X_i has determinative power over $f(\mathbf{X})$ since (7) implies that $\mathrm{MI}(f(\mathbf{X}); X_j)$ for $j \neq i$ must be small then.

4.1 Mutual information and the Fourier spectrum

In order to study determinative power, its relation to measures of perturbations, and statistical dependencies, we start by characterizing the mutual information in terms of Fourier coefficients. Our results are based on the following novel characterization of entropy in terms of Fourier coefficients.

Theorem 1. *Let f be a Boolean function, let $\mathbf{X}$ be product distributed, and let $\mathbf{X}_A = \{X_i\colon i \in A\}$ be a fixed set of arguments, where $A \subseteq [n]$. Then,*

$$H(f(\mathbf{X})|\mathbf{X}_A) = \mathbb{E}\left[h\left(\frac{1}{2}\left(1 + \sum_{S\subseteq A}\hat{f}(S)\Phi_S(\mathbf{X}_A)\right)\right)\right],$$

where $h(\cdot)$ is the binary entropy function as defined in ().

Proof. See Appendix 2. For the special case of uniformly distributed $\mathbf{X}$, a proof appears in [21], in the context of designing S-boxes. □

Using the definition of mutual information, an immediate corollary of Theorem 1 is the following:

Corollary 1. *Let f be a Boolean function, $\mathbf{X}$ be product distributed, and $\mathbf{X}_A = \{X_i\colon i \in A\}$. Then,*

$$\mathrm{MI}(f(\mathbf{X}); \mathbf{X}_A) = h\left(1/2(1 + \hat{f}(\emptyset)\right) - \mathbb{E}\left[h\left(\frac{1}{2}\left(1 + \sum_{S\subseteq A}\hat{f}(S)\Phi_S(\mathbf{X}_A)\right)\right)\right]. \tag{8}$$

Theorem 1 (and Corollary 1) shows that the conditional entropy $H(f(\mathbf{X})|\mathbf{X}_A)$ and the mutual information $\mathrm{MI}(f(\mathbf{X}); \mathbf{X}_A)$ are functions of the coefficients $\{\hat{f}(S)\colon S \subseteq A\}$ only. This already hints at a fundamental difference to the average sensitivity, since the average sensitivity depends on the coefficients $\{\hat{f}(S)\colon |S \cap A| > 0\}$, according to (5).

We next discuss $\mathrm{MI}(f(\mathbf{X}); X_i)$ based on (8). First, note that $\mathrm{MI}(f(\mathbf{X}); X_i)$ has previously been studied under the notion *information gain* as a measure of 'goodness' for split variables in greedy tree learners [22] and also under the notion of *informativeness* to quantify voting power [23]. According to (8), the mutual information $\mathrm{MI}(f(\mathbf{X}); X_i)$ just depends on $\hat{f}(\{i\}), \hat{f}(\emptyset)$, and p_i. In contrast, the influence $I_i(f)$ is a function of the coefficients $\{\hat{f}(S)\colon S \in [n], i \in S\}$, according to (4). In Figure 2, we depict $\mathrm{MI}(f(\mathbf{X}); X_i)$ for $p_i = 0.3$ as a function of $\hat{f}(\{i\})$ and $\hat{f}(\emptyset)$.

It can be seen that $\mathrm{MI}(f(\mathbf{X}); X_i) = 0$, i.e., $f(\mathbf{X})$ and X_i are statistically independent if and only if $\hat{f}(\{i\}) = 0$. That can be formalized as follows: $\mathrm{MI}(f(\mathbf{X}); X_i)$ is convex in $\hat{f}(\{i\})$. This can be proven by taking the second derivative of (8) and observing that it is larger than zero for all pairs of values $(\hat{f}(\emptyset), \hat{f}(\{i\}))$ for which $\mathrm{MI}(f(\mathbf{X}); X_i)$ is defined. Next, from (8), we see that $\mathrm{MI}(f(\mathbf{X}); X_i) = 0$ if $\hat{f}(\{i\}) = 0$; hence, it follows that $\mathrm{MI}(f(\mathbf{X}); X_i) = 0$ if and only if $\hat{f}(\{i\}) = 0$, which proves the following result:

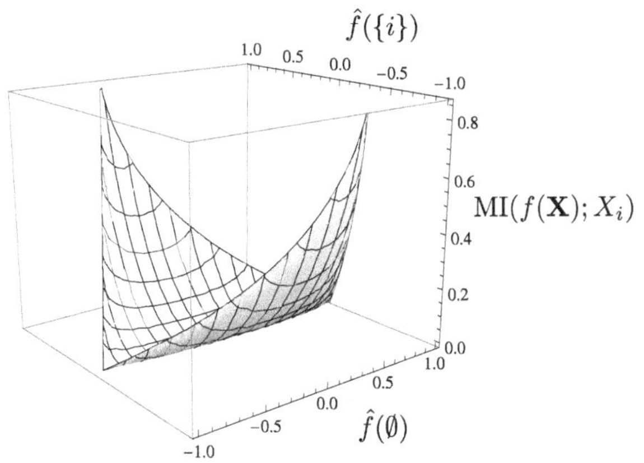

Figure 2 MI(f(X); X_i) as a function of $\hat{f}(\{i\})$ and $\hat{f}(\emptyset)$ for $p_i = 0.3$.

Corollary 2. *Let f be a Boolean function, and* **X** *be product distributed.* X_i *and* $f(\mathbf{X})$ *are statistically independent if and only if* $\hat{f}(\{i\}) = 0$.

Corollary 2 also follows immediately from a more general result, namely Theorem 5, which is presented later. Recall that for PARITY2, $\text{MI}(f_{\text{PARITY2}}(\mathbf{X}); X_1) = 0$ and $\hat{f}(\{1\}) = 0$; hence, Corollary 2 comes at no surprise.

From Figure 2, it can be seen that the larger $|\hat{f}(\{i\})|$, the larger $\text{MI}(f(\mathbf{X}); X_i)$ becomes. Formally, it follows from the convexity of $\text{MI}(f(\mathbf{X}); X_i)$ and Corollary 2 that $\text{MI}(f(\mathbf{X}); X_i)$ is increasing in $|\hat{f}(\{i\})|$. Hence, X_i has large determinative power, i.e., $\text{MI}(f(\mathbf{X}); X_i)$ is large, if and only if $|\hat{f}(\{i\})|$ is large (i.e., close to one). $|\hat{f}(\{i\})|$ is trivially maximized for the *dictatorship function,* i.e., for $f(\mathbf{x}) = x_i$, or its negation, i.e., $f(\mathbf{x}) = -x_i$. The output $f(\mathbf{X})$ of the dictatorship function is fully determined by x_i.

Next, let us consider the (trivial) case where $A = [n]$ and hence $\mathbf{X}_A = \mathbf{X}$. Then, $\text{MI}(f(\mathbf{X}); \mathbf{X}) = h(1/2(1 + \hat{f}(\emptyset))$. It follows that $\text{MI}(f(\mathbf{X}); \mathbf{X})$ is maximized for $\hat{f}(\emptyset) = 0$, i.e, $\text{P}[f(\mathbf{X}) = 1] = 1/2$, i.e., if the variance of $f(\mathbf{X})$ is 1. In general, the closer to zero $\hat{f}(\emptyset)$ is, the larger the mutual information between a function's output and all its inputs becomes. Let us finally relate the conditional entropy $H(f(\mathbf{X})|\mathbf{X}_A)$ to the concentration of the Fourier weight on the coefficients $\{S \colon S \subseteq A\}, A \subseteq [n]$.

Theorem 2. *Let f be a Boolean function, let* **X** *be product distributed, and let* $\mathbf{X}_A = \{X_i \colon i \in A\}$ *be a fixed set of arguments, where* $A \subseteq [n]$. *Then,*

$$\left(1 - \sum_{S \subseteq A} \hat{f}(S)^2\right)^{\frac{1}{\ln(4)}} \geq H(f(\mathbf{X})|\mathbf{X}_A) \geq 1 - \sum_{S \subseteq A} \hat{f}(S)^2.$$

Proof. See Appendix 3. □

Theorem 2 shows that $H(f(\mathbf{X})|\mathbf{X}_A)$ can be approximated with $1 - \sum_{S \subseteq A} \hat{f}(S)^2$. It further shows that $H(f(\mathbf{X})|\mathbf{X}_A)$ is small if the Fourier weight is concentrated on the variables in the set A, i.e., if $\sum_{S \subseteq A} \hat{f}(S)^2$ is close to one. In contrast, as mentioned previously, for $I_A(f)$, it is relevant whether the Fourier weight is concentrated on the coefficients with high degree.

4.2 Relation to measures of perturbation

Mutual information and average sensitivity are related as follows.

Theorem 3. *For any Boolean function f, for any product distributed* **X**,

$$I_A(f) \geq \min_{i \in A} \left(\frac{1}{\sigma_i^2}\right) \left(\text{MI}\left(f(\mathbf{X}); \mathbf{X}_A\right) - \Psi\left(\text{Var}\left(f(\mathbf{X})\right)\right)\right) \tag{9}$$

with

$$\Psi(x) \triangleq (x)^{1/\ln(4)} - x. \tag{10}$$

Proof. See Appendix 4. □

Note that the term $\Psi\left(\text{Var}\left(f(\mathbf{X})\right)\right)$ is close to zero. Specifically, for any $f(\mathbf{X})$ we have $0 \leq \Psi\left(\text{Var}\left(f(\mathbf{X})\right)\right) < 0.12$, and for settings of interest, $\Psi\left(\text{Var}\left(f(\mathbf{X})\right)\right)$ is very close to zero, as explained in more detail in the following. Theorem 3 shows that if $\text{MI}(f(\mathbf{X}); \mathbf{X}_A)$ if large (i.e., close to one), f must be sensitive to perturbations of the entries of $\mathbf{X}_A$. Moreover, if $I_A(f)$ is small (i.e., if f is tolerant to perturbations of the entries of $\mathbf{X}_A$), then $\text{MI}(f(\mathbf{X}); \mathbf{X}_A)$ must be small (i.e., the entries of $\mathbf{X}_A$ do not have determinative power). For the case that $A = [n]$, Theorem 3 states that the average sensitivity $\text{as}(f)$ is lower-bounded by $\text{MI}(f(\mathbf{X}); \mathbf{X})$ minus some small term.

We next discuss the special case that $A = \{i\}$. Theorem 3 evaluated for $A = \{i\}$ yields a lower bound on the influence of a variable in terms of the mutual information of that variable, namely

$$I_i(f) \geq \frac{1}{\sigma_i^2} \left(\text{MI}\left(f(\mathbf{X}); X_i\right) - \Psi\left(\text{Var}\left(f(\mathbf{X})\right)\right)\right). \tag{11}$$

Again, $\Psi\left(\text{Var}\left(f(\mathbf{X})\right)\right)$ is close to zero for settings of interest, as the following argument explains. Equation (11) will not be evaluated for small $\text{Var}\left(f(\mathbf{X})\right)$; since then, $f(\mathbf{X})$ is close to a constant function (i.e., close to $f(\mathbf{X}) = 1$ or $f(\mathbf{X}) = -1$), and $I_i(f)$ and $\text{MI}(f(\mathbf{X}); X_i)$ must both be small (i.e., close to zero) anyway. Hence, (11) is of interest when $\text{Var}\left(f(\mathbf{X})\right)$ is large, i.e., close to 1; for this case, the term $\Psi\left(\text{Var}\left(f(\mathbf{X})\right)\right)$ is small (e.g., for $\text{Var}\left(f(\mathbf{X})\right) > 0.8$, $\Psi\left(\text{Var}\left(f(\mathbf{X})\right) < 0.05\right)$. Observe that, according to (11), if

$\mathrm{MI}(f(\mathbf{X}); X_i)$ is large, then $I_i(f)$ is also large. That proves the intuitive idea that if an input determines $f(\mathbf{X})$ to some extent, this input must be sensitive to perturbations. Conversely, as mentioned previously, an input i can have large influence and still $\mathrm{MI}(f(\mathbf{X}); X_i) = 0$. E.g., for the PARITY2 function, we have $I_i(f) = 1$ and $\mathrm{MI}(f(\mathbf{X}); X_i) = 0$.

Interestingly, the influence also has an information theoretic interpretation. The following theorem generalizes Theorem 1 in [23].

Theorem 4. *For any Boolean function f, for any product distributed* **X**,

$$I_i(f) = \frac{H\big(f(\mathbf{X})|\mathbf{X}_{[n]\setminus\{i\}}\big)}{H(X_i)}.$$

Proof. See Appendix 5. For uniformly distributed **X**, a proof appears in [23]. □

Theorem 4 shows that the influence of a variable is a measure for the uncertainty of the function's output that remains if all variables except variable i are set.

4.3 Statistical independence of inputs to a Boolean function

Next, we characterize statistical independence of $f(\mathbf{X})$ and a set of its arguments $\mathbf{X}_A$ in terms of Fourier coefficients. This result generalizes a theorem derived by Xiao and Massey [11] from uniform to product distributed **X**.

Theorem 5. *Let $A \subseteq [n]$ be fixed, f be a Boolean function, and* **X** *be product distributed. Then, $f(\mathbf{X})$ and the inputs $\mathbf{X}_A = \{X_i : i \in A\}$ are statistically independent if and only if*

$$\hat{f}(S) = 0 \textit{ for all } S \subseteq A \setminus \emptyset.$$

Proof. See Appendix 6. For uniformly distributed **X**, i.e., $\mathrm{P}[X_i = 1] = 1/2$ for all $i \in [n]$, Theorem 5 has been derived by Xiao and Massey [11]. Note that the proof provided here is also conceptually different from the proof for the uniform case in [11], as it does not rely on the Xiao-Massey lemma. □

Theorem 5 shows that a function and small sets of its inputs are statistically independent if the spectrum is concentrated on the coefficients of high degree $d = |S|$. The most prominent example is the parity function of n variables, i.e., $f_{\mathrm{PARITYN}}(\mathbf{x}) = x_1 x_2 ... x_n$: For uniformly distributed **X**, each subset of $n-1$ or fewer arguments and $f_{\mathrm{PARITYN}}(\mathbf{X})$ are statistically independent. Conversely, if a function is concentrated on the coefficients of low degree $d = |S|$, which is the case for functions that are tolerant to perturbations, then small sets of inputs and the function's output are statistically dependent.

Theorem 5 also has an important implication for algorithms that detect functional dependencies in a BN based on estimating the mutual information from observations of the network's states, such as the algorithm presented in [12]. Theorem 5 characterizes the classes of functions for which such an algorithm may succeed and for which it will fail. Moreover, Theorem 5 shows that in a Boolean model of a genetic regulatory network, a functional dependency between a gene and a regulator cannot be detected based on statistical dependence of a regulator X_i and a gene's state $f_j(\mathbf{X})$, unless the regulatory functions are restricted to those for which $|\hat{f}(\{i\})| > 0$ holds for each relevant input i.

5 Unate functions

In this section, we discuss unate, i.e., locally monotone functions.

Definition 6. A Boolean function f is said to be unate in x_i if for each $\mathbf{x} = (x_1, ..., x_n) \in \{-1, +1\}^n$ and for some fixed $a_i \in \{-1, +1\}$, $f(x_1, ..., x_i = -a_i, ..., x_n) \leq f(x_1, ..., x_i = a_i, ..., x_n)$ holds. f is said to be unate if f is unate in each variable x_i, $i \in [n]$.

Each linear threshold function and nested canalizing function is unate. Moreover, most, if not all, regulatory interactions in a biological network are considered to be unate. That can be deduced from [13,24], and the basic argument is the following: If an element acts either as a repressor or an activator for some gene, but never as both (which is a reasonable assumption for regulatory interactions[13,24]), then the function determining the gene's state is unate by definition. For unate functions, the following property holds:

Proposition 3. *Let $f : \{-1, +1\}^n \to \{-1, +1\}$ be unate. Then,*

$$\hat{f}(\{i\}) = a_i \sigma_i I_i(f), \; \forall i \in [n], \tag{12}$$

where $a_i \in \{-1, +1\}$ is the parameter in Definition 6.

Proof. Goes along the same lines as the proof for monotone functions in Lemma 4.5 of [17]. □

Note that conversely, if (12) holds for each $x_i, i \in [n]$, f is not necessarily unate. Inserting (12) into (8) yields

$$\mathrm{MI}(f(\mathbf{X}); X_i) = h\left(\frac{1}{2}(1 + \hat{f}(\emptyset))\right) - \mathbb{E}\left[h\left(\frac{1}{2}\left(1 + \hat{f}(\emptyset) + a_i \sigma_i I_i(f) \frac{X_i - \mu_i}{\sigma_i}\right)\right)\right], \tag{13}$$

where the expectation in (13) is over X_i. Based on (13), the discussion from Section 4.1 on $\mathrm{MI}(f; X_i)$ applies by using $\hat{f}(\{i\})$ and $a_i \sigma_i I_i(f)$ synonymously. Hence, for unate functions, the mutual information $\mathrm{MI}(f; X_i)$ is increasing in the influence $|I_i(f)|$. Moreover, if f is unate, and x_i is a relevant variable, i.e., a variable on which the functions actually depend on, then $|\hat{f}(\{i\})| > 0$. From this fact and the same arguments as given in Section 4.1 follows:

Theorem 6. *Let* $f: \{-1,+1\}^n \to \{-1,+1\}$ *be unate. If and only if* x_i *is a relevant variable, then* $MI(f(\mathbf{X}); X_i) \neq 0$.

In a Boolean model of a biological regulatory network, this implies that if the functions in the network are unate, then a regulator and the target gene must be statistically dependent.

6 *E. coli* regulatory network

In [6], the authors presented a complex computational model of the *E. coli* transcriptional regulatory network that controls central parts of the *E. coli* metabolism. The network consists of 798 nodes and 1160 edges. Of the nodes, 636 represent genes and of the remaining 162 nodes, most (103) are external metabolites. The rest are stimuli, and others are state variables such as internal metabolites. The network has a layered feed-forward structure, i.e., no feedback loops exist. The elements in the first layer can be viewed as the inputs of the system, and the elements in the following seven layers are interacting genes that represent the internal state of the system. Our experiments revealed that all functions are unate; therefore, the properties derived in Section 5 apply. Note that all functions being unate is a special property of the network, since if functions are chosen uniformly at random, it is unlikely to sample a unate function, in particular if the number of inputs n is large.

6.1 Determinative nodes in the *E. coli* network

We first identify the input nodes that have large determinative power (we will define what that means in a network setting shortly) and then show that a small number thereof reduces the uncertainty of the network's state significantly. Specifically, we show that on average, the entropy of the node's states conditioned on a small set of determinative input nodes, is small.

To put this result into perspective, we perform the same experiment for random networks with the same and different topology as the *E. coli* network. We denote by $\mathbf{X} = \{X_1, ..., X_n\}, n = 145$ the set of inputs of the feed forward network and assume that the X_i are independent and uniformly distributed. The remaining variables are denoted by $\mathbf{Y} = \{Y_1, ..., Y_m\}, m = 653$ and are a function of the inputs and the network's states, i.e., $Y_i = f_i'(\mathbf{X}, \mathbf{Y})$. For our analysis, the distributions of the random variables $Y_1, ..., Y_m$ need to be computed, since some of those variables are arguments to other functions. This can be circumvented by defining a collapsed network, i.e., a network where each state of a node is given as a function of the input nodes only, i.e., $Y_i = f_i(\mathbf{X})$. The collapsed network is obtained by consecutively inserting functions into each other, until each function only depends on states of nodes in the input layer, i.e., on $\mathbf{X}$. The collapsed network reveals the dependencies of each node on the input variables. Interestingly, in the collapsed network, it is seen that the variables chol_xt>0, salicylate, 2ddglcn_xt>0, mnnh>0, altrh>0, and his-l_xt>0 (here, and in the following, we adopt the names from the original dataset), which appear to be inputs when considering the original *E. coli* network, turn out to be not. Consider, for example, the node salicylate. The only node dependent on salicylate is mara = ((NOT arca OR NOT fnr) OR oxyr OR salicylate). However, arca = (fnr AND NOT oxyr), and it is easily seen that mara simplifies to mara = 1.

Next, we identify the determinative nodes. As argued in Section 4, $\mathrm{MI}(f_i(\mathbf{X}); X_j)$ is a measure of the determinative power of X_j over $Y_i = f_i(\mathbf{X})$. This motivates the definition of the determinative power of input X_j over the states in the network as

$$D(j) \triangleq \sum_{i=1}^{m} \mathrm{MI}(f_i(\mathbf{X}); X_j).$$

Note that a small value of $D(j)$ implies that X_j alone does not have large determinative power over the network's states, but X_j may have large determinative power over the network states in conjunction with other variables. In principle $\sum_{i=1}^{m} \mathrm{MI}(f_i(\mathbf{X}); X_j, X_k)$ can be large for some $j, k \in [n]$, even though $D(j)$ and $D(k)$ are equal to zero. This is, however, not possible in the *E. coli* network since the functions are unate. Specifically, $\mathrm{MI}(f_i(\mathbf{X}); X_j, X_k) \neq 0$ implies that x_j or x_k are relevant variables, and according to Theorem 6, $\mathrm{MI}(f_i(\mathbf{X}); X_j) \neq 0$ or $\mathrm{MI}(f_i(\mathbf{X}); X_k) \neq 0$. We computed $D(j)$ for each input variable and found that $D(j)$ is large just for some inputs, such as o2_xt (37 bit), leu-l_xt (20.9 bit), glc-d_xt (19.3 bit), and glcn_xt>0 (17 bit), but is small for most other variables. Partly, this can be explained by the out-degree (i.e., the number of outgoing edges of a node) distribution of the input nodes. However, having a large out-degree does not necessarily result in large values of $D(j)$. In fact, in the *E. coli* network, glc-d_xt, glcn_xt>0, and o2_xt have 99, 93, and 73 outgoing edges, respectively. On the other hand, D(glc-d_xt) = 19.3 bit and D(glcn_xt>0) = 17 bit, whereas D(o2_xt) = 37 bit.

Denote τ as a permutation on $[n]$, such that $D(X_{\tau(1)}) \geq D(X_{\tau(2)}) \geq ... \geq D(X_{\tau(n)})$, i.e., τ orders the input nodes in descending order in their determinative power. We next consider $H(\mathbf{Y}|X_{\tau(1)}, ..., X_{\tau(l)})$ as a function of l to see whether knowledge of a small set of input nodes reduces the entropy of the overall network state significantly. $H(\mathbf{Y}|X_{\tau(1)},...,X_{\tau(l)})$ has an interesting interpretation which arises as a consequence of the so called asymptotic equipartition property [20] (as discussed in greater detail in [25]): Consider a sequence $\mathbf{y}_1,...,\mathbf{y}_k$ of k samples of the random variable $\mathbf{Y}$. For $\epsilon > 0$ and k sufficiently large, there exists a set $A_\epsilon^{(k)}$ of typical sequences $\mathbf{y}_1,...,\mathbf{y}_k$, such that

$$|A_\epsilon^{(k)}| \leq 2^{k(H(\mathbf{Y})+\epsilon)}$$

and

$$\mathrm{P}\left[\mathbf{Y} \in A_\epsilon^{(k)}\right] > 1 - \epsilon,$$

where $|A_\epsilon^{(k)}|$ denotes the cardinality of the set $A_\epsilon^{(k)}$. This shows that the sequences obtained as samples of $\mathbf{Y}$ are likely to fall in a set of size determined by the uncertainty of $\mathbf{Y}$. Since the output layer consists of 653 nodes, the network's state space has maximal size 2^{653}. Since $\mathbf{Y}$ is a function of $\mathbf{X}$, $H(\mathbf{Y}) \leq H(\mathbf{X}) = 145$bit, where for the last equality, we assume uniformly distributed inputs. Thus, without knowing the state of any input variable, the network's state is likely to be in a set of size roughly 2^{145}. Given the knowledge about the states $X_{\tau(1)},...,X_{\tau(l)}$, the state of the network is likely to be in a set of size roughly $2^{H(\mathbf{Y}|X_{\tau(1)},...,X_{\tau(l)})}$. For a large network, however, $H(\mathbf{Y}|X_{\tau(1)},...,X_{\tau(l)})$ is expensive to compute as by definition:

$$H(\mathbf{Y}|\mathbf{X}_A) = \sum_{\mathbf{x}_A} \mathrm{P}[\mathbf{X}_A = \mathbf{x}_A] \times \sum_{\mathbf{y}} \mathrm{P}\big[\mathbf{Y} = \mathbf{y}|\mathbf{X}_A = \mathbf{x}_A\big] \log_2 \mathrm{P}\big[\mathbf{Y} = \mathbf{y}|\mathbf{X}_A = \mathbf{x}_A\big]. \quad (14)$$

Hence, the number of terms in the sum is exponential in n and $|A|$. An estimate of (14) can be obtained by sampling uniformly at random over $\mathbf{x}_A$ and $\mathbf{y}$. Instead, we will consider the following upper bound which is computationally inexpensive to compute:

$$H(\mathbf{Y}|X_{\tau(1)},...,X_{\tau(l)}) \leq A(l)$$

with

$$A(l) \triangleq \sum_{i=1}^{m} H(Y_i|X_{\tau(1)},...,X_{\tau(l)}).$$

The bound above follows from the chain rule for entropy [20]. $H(Y_i|X_{\tau(1)},...,X_{\tau(l)})$ is computationally inexpensive to compute, since Y_i depends on few variables only (in the *E. coli* network, on $\leq$ 8). For the *E. coli* network, $A(l)$ is depicted in Figure 3 as a function of l. Figure 3 shows that knowledge of the states of the most determinative nodes reduces the uncertainty about the network's states significantly. In fact, the upper bound $A(l)$ is loose; hence, we even expect $H(\mathbf{Y}|X_{\tau(1)},...,X_{\tau(l)})$ to lie significantly below $A(l)$. Also, note that when $A(l)$ is small, $H(Y_i|X_{\tau(1)},...,X_{\tau(l)})$ must be small on average; hence, $\mathrm{P}\big[Y_i = 1|X_{\tau(1)},...,X_{\tau(l)}\big]$ is close to one or zero on average.

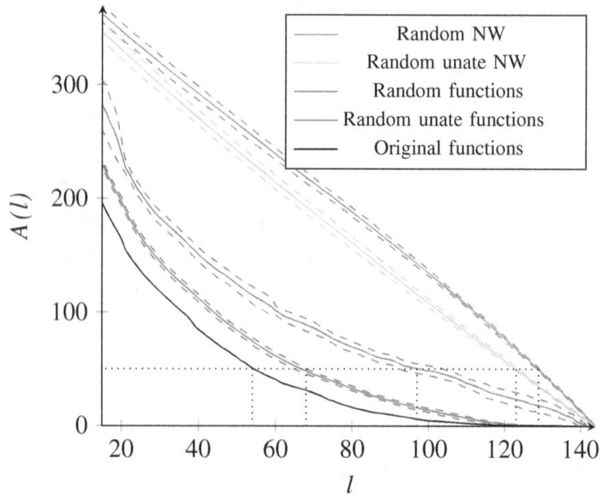

Figure 3 The upper bound $A(l)$ on $H(\mathbf{Y}|X_{\tau(1)},...,X_{\tau(l)})$ as a function of l for the *E. coli* network and random networks.

To put $A(l)$ for the *E. coli* network in Figure 3 into perspective, we compute $A(l)$ for random networks. First, we took the *E. coli* network and exchanged each function with one chosen uniformly at random from the set of all Boolean functions of corresponding degree. We also exchanged each function with one chosen uniformly at random from all unate functions. We performed the same experiment for the original *E. coli* network for 25 choices of random and random unate functions, respectively. The mean of $A(l)$, along with one standard deviation from the mean (dashed lines), is plotted in Figure 3 for random and random unate functions. It is seen that fewer inputs determine the output of the original *E. coli* network, compared to its random counterparts. For example, to obtain $A(l) = 50$, about twice as many inputs need to be known if the functions in the *E. coli* network are exchanged for functions chosen uniformly at random.

Next, we generated at random feed forward networks with $m = 653$ outputs and $n = 145$ inputs, each with out-degree 8, i.e., the average out-degree of the inputs in the collapsed *E. coli* network. Again, we computed $A(l)$ for 25 choices of random and random unate functions, respectively. The mean and one standard deviation from the mean are depicted in Figure 3. The results show that,

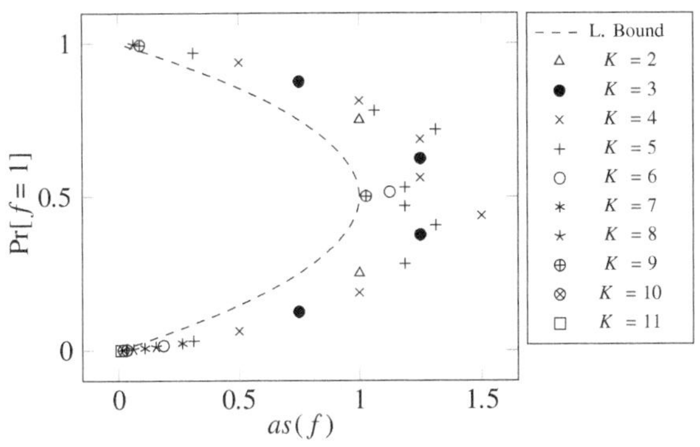

Figure 4 Average sensitivity in the *E. coli* network. Pairs of values $(\mathrm{as}(f), \Pr[f(\mathbf{X}) = 1])$ of each function in the *E. coli* network for different in-degrees K and uniformly distributed $\mathbf{X}$. Moreover, a lower bound on the average sensitivity $\mathrm{as}(f)$, i.e., Poincare's inequality, is plotted.

as expected, for a random feed forward network, there seems to be no small set of inputs that determines the outputs.

6.2 Tolerance to perturbations

Finally, we discuss the average sensitivity of individual functions in the *E. coli* network. In Section 3, we found that the average sensitivity is small if the Fourier spectrum is concentrated on the coefficients of low degree. This appears to be the case for functions that are highly biased and for functions that depend on few variables only. Figure 4 shows pairs of values $(\mathrm{as}(f), \Pr[f(\mathbf{X}) = 1])$ for each function in the *E. coli* network, again assuming that the X_i are independent and uniformly distributed. We can see from Figure 4 that the average sensitivity of all functions is close to the lower bound on the average sensitivity. Note that the functions with high in-degree K (i.e., number of relevant input variables), which could have average sensitivity up to K, also have small average sensitivity, because those functions are highly biased. We, therefore, can conclude that the functions have small average sensitivity either because they depend on few variables only or because they are highly biased. For other input distributions, i.e., other values of $p = \mathrm{P}[X_i = 1], \forall i \in [n]$, we obtained the same results.

7 Conclusion

In a Boolean network, tolerance to perturbations, determinative power, and statistical dependencies between nodes are properties of single functions in a probabilistic setting. Hence, we analyzed single functions with product distributed argument. We used Fourier analysis of Boolean functions to study the mutual information between a function $f(\mathbf{X})$ and a set of its inputs $\mathbf{X}_A$, as a measure of determinative power of $\mathbf{X}_A$ over $f(\mathbf{X})$. We related the mutual information to the Fourier spectrum and proved that the mutual information lower bounds the influence, a measure of perturbation. We also gave necessary and sufficient conditions for statistical independence of $f(\mathbf{X})$ and $\mathbf{X}_A$. For the class of unate functions, which are particularly interesting for biological networks, we found that mutual information and influence are directly related (not just via an inequality). We also found that $\mathrm{MI}(f(\mathbf{X}); X_i) > 0$ for each relevant input i, which, as an application, implies that in a unate regulatory network, a gene and its regulator must be statistically dependent. As an application of our results, we analyzed the large-scale regulatory network of *E. coli*. We identified the most determinative input nodes in the network and found that it is sufficient to know only a small subset of those in order to reduce the uncertainty of the overall network state significantly. This, in turn, reduces the size of the state space in which the network is likely to be found significantly.

A possible direction for future work is to provide an analysis similar to that of the *E. coli* regulatory network for other Boolean models of biological networks, and see if similar conclusions as in Section 6 can be reached. One of the main assumptions in our work is the independence among the input variables of the network. It would be interesting to provide methods that can be used beyond this setup. However, deriving such results is challenging because for dependent inputs, the basis functions $\Phi_S(\mathbf{x})$ do not factorize as in (3), and many results cited and derived in this paper make use of this particular form of the basis functions. In this paper, we focused on generic properties of information-processing networks that may help identify possible principles that underly biological networks. Assessing our findings from a biological perspective would be an interesting next step.

Appendices

Appendix 1

Lemma 1

For the proof of Theorems 1 and 5, we will need the following lemma:

Lemma 1. *Let f be a Boolean function, let $\mathbf{X}$ be product distributed, and let $A \subseteq [n]$ and some fixed $\mathbf{x_A} \in \{-1, +1\}^{|A|}$ be given. Then,*

$$\mathbb{E}[f(\mathbf{X})|\mathbf{X}_A = \mathbf{x}_A] = \sum_{S \subseteq A} \hat{f}(S)\Phi_S(\mathbf{x}_A). \tag{15}$$

Proof. Inserting the Fourier expansion of $f(\mathbf{X})$ given by (3) in the left-hand side of (15) and utilizing the linearity of conditional expectation yields

$$\mathbb{E}[f(\mathbf{X})|\mathbf{X}_A = \mathbf{x}_A] = \sum_{S \subseteq [n]} \hat{f}(S)\, \mathbb{E}[\, \Phi_S(\mathbf{X})|\mathbf{X}_A = \mathbf{x}_A] \,.$$

For $S \subseteq A$,

$$\mathbb{E}[\,\Phi_S(\mathbf{X})|\mathbf{X}_A = \mathbf{x}_A] = \Phi_S(\mathbf{x}_A).$$

Conversely, for $S \nsubseteq A$,

$$\mathbb{E}[\,\Phi_S(\mathbf{X})|\mathbf{X}_A = \mathbf{x}_A] = 0.$$

To see this, assume without loss of generality that $S = A \cup \{j\}$ and $j \notin A$. Using the decomposition property of the basis function as given in Section 2.3,

$$\mathbb{E}[\,\Phi_S(\mathbf{X})|\mathbf{X}_A = \mathbf{x}_A] = \mathbb{E}\left[\prod_{i\in S}\Phi_{\{i\}}(\mathbf{X})|\mathbf{X}_A = \mathbf{x}_A\right] = \prod_{i\in S}\mathbb{E}[\,\Phi_{\{i\}}(\mathbf{X})|\mathbf{X}_A = \mathbf{x}_A]$$

which is equal to zero as

$$\mathbb{E}[\,\Phi_{\{j\}}(\mathbf{X})|\mathbf{X}_A = \mathbf{x}_A] = \mathbb{E}[\,\Phi_{\{j\}}(\mathbf{X})] = 0.$$

□

Appendix 2

Proof of Theorem 1

First,

$$\mathrm{P}\big[f(\mathbf{X}) = 1|\mathbf{X}_A = \mathbf{x}_A\big] = \frac{1}{2}\left(1 + \mathbb{E}[f(\mathbf{X})|\mathbf{X}_A = \mathbf{x}_A]\right) = \underbrace{\frac{1}{2}\left(1 + \sum_{S\subseteq A}\hat{f}(S)\Phi_S(\mathbf{x}_A)\right)}_{q(\mathbf{x}_A)}, \tag{16}$$

where (16) follows from an application of Lemma 1. By definition of the conditional entropy,

$$\begin{aligned} H(f(\mathbf{X})|\mathbf{X}_A) &= \sum_{\mathbf{x}_A\in\{-1,1\}^{|A|}} \mathrm{P}[\mathbf{X}_A = \mathbf{x}_A]\,H(f(\mathbf{X})|\mathbf{X}_A = \mathbf{x}_A) \\ &= \sum_{\mathbf{x}_A\in\{-1,1\}^{|A|}} \mathrm{P}[\mathbf{X}_A = \mathbf{x}_A]\,h(\mathrm{P}\big[f(\mathbf{X}) = 1|\mathbf{X}_A = \mathbf{x}_A\big]) \\ &= \sum_{\mathbf{x}_A\in\{-1,1\}^{|A|}} \mathrm{P}[\mathbf{X}_A = \mathbf{x}_A]\,h(q(\mathbf{x}_A)) \qquad (17) \\ &= \mathbb{E}[\,h(q(\mathbf{X}_A))], \qquad (18) \end{aligned}$$

where $h(\cdot)$ is the binary entropy function as defined in (6). To obtain (17), we used (16). The expectation in (17) is with respect to the distribution of $\mathbf{X}_A$. Inserting $q(\mathbf{X}_A)$ as given by (16) in (18) concludes the proof.

Appendix 3

Proof of Theorem 2

First, note that with $q(\cdot)$ as defined in (16), we have

$$\begin{aligned} \mathbb{E}[\,4q(\mathbf{X}_A)(1 - q(\mathbf{X}_A))] &= \mathbb{E}\left[1 - \left(\sum_{S\subseteq A}\hat{f}(S)\Phi_S(\mathbf{X}_A)\right)^2\right] \\ &= \sum_{S\subseteq A}\sum_{U\subseteq A}\hat{f}(S)\hat{f}(U)\mathbb{E}[\Phi_S(\mathbf{X}_A)\Phi_U(\mathbf{X}_A)] \\ &= 1 - \sum_{S\subseteq A}\hat{f}(S)^2, \qquad (19) \end{aligned}$$

where (19) follows from the orthogonality of the basis functions.

We start with proving the lower bound in Theorem 2. Applying the lower bound on the binary entropy function $h(p) \geq 4p(1-p)$, given in Theorem 1.2 of [26], on (18) yields

$$H(f(\mathbf{X})|\mathbf{X}_A) = \mathbb{E}[\,h(q(\mathbf{X}_A))] \geq \mathbb{E}[\,4q(\mathbf{X}_A)(1 - q(\mathbf{X}_A))],$$

and the lower bound in Theorem 2 follows using (19).

Next, we prove the upper bound in Theorem 2. Applying the upper bound on the binary entropy function $h(p) \leq (p(1-p))^{1/\ln(4)}$, given in Theorem 1.2 of [26], on (18) yields

$$\begin{aligned} H(f(\mathbf{X})|\mathbf{X}_A) &= \mathbb{E}[\,h(q(\mathbf{X}_A)] \\ &\leq \mathbb{E}[\,(\underbrace{4q(\mathbf{X}_A)(1 - q(\mathbf{X}_A))}_{Y})^{1/\ln(4)}]. \qquad (20) \end{aligned}$$

The term Y in (20) is a random variable, and the function $(Y)^{1/\ln(4)}$ is concave in Y. An application of Jensen's inequality (see e.g. [20]) yields $\mathbb{E}[\,(Y)^{1/\ln(4)}] \leq (\mathbb{E}[\,Y])^{1/\ln(4)}$; hence, the right-hand side of (20) can be lower as

$$H(f(\mathbf{X})|\mathbf{X}_A) \leq (\mathbb{E}[\,4q(\mathbf{X}_A)(1 - q(\mathbf{X}_A))])^{1/\ln(4)}. \tag{21}$$

Finally, the upper bound in Theorem 2 follows from combining (21) and (19).

Appendix 4

Proof of Theorem 3

According to Proposition 2,

$$\begin{aligned} I_A(f) &= \sum_{S\subseteq[n]}\hat{f}(S)^2\sum_{i\in S\cap A}\frac{1}{\sigma_i^2} \\ &\geq \sum_{S\subseteq[n]\setminus\emptyset}\hat{f}(S)^2|S\cap A|\min_{i\in A}\left(\frac{1}{\sigma_i^2}\right) \\ &\geq \min_{i\in A}\left(\frac{1}{\sigma_i^2}\right)\sum_{S\subseteq A\setminus\emptyset}\hat{f}(S)^2. \qquad (22) \end{aligned}$$

Next, we rewrite the lower bound on $H(f(\mathbf{X})|\mathbf{X}_A)$ given by Theorem 2 as

$$\sum_{S\subseteq A\setminus\emptyset} \hat{f}(S)^2 \geq 1-\hat{f}(\emptyset)^2 - H(f(\mathbf{X})|\mathbf{X}_A). \quad (23)$$

By adding $H(f(\mathbf{X})) - H(f(\mathbf{X}))$ on the right-hand side of (23) and using the definition of mutual information, (23) becomes

$$\sum_{S\subseteq A\setminus\emptyset} \hat{f}(S)^2 \geq \mathrm{MI}(f(\mathbf{X});\mathbf{X}_A) - H(f(\mathbf{X})) + 1 - \hat{f}(\emptyset)^2. \quad (24)$$

With $\mathrm{Var}\left(f(\mathbf{X})\right) = 1-\hat{f}(\emptyset)^2$ and by using the inequality $H(f(\mathbf{X})) \leq \left(\mathrm{Var}\left(f(\mathbf{X})\right)\right)^{1/\ln(4)}$, given in Theorem 1.2 of [26], (24) becomes

$$\sum_{S\subseteq A\setminus\emptyset} \hat{f}(S)^2 \geq \mathrm{MI}(f(\mathbf{X});\mathbf{X}_A) - \Psi\left(\mathrm{Var}\left(f(\mathbf{X})\right)\right), \quad (25)$$

with $\Psi(\cdot)$ as defined in (10). Finally, Theorem 3 follows by combining (22) and (25).

Appendix 5
Proof of Theorem 4

For notational convenience, let $A = [n]\setminus\{i\}$. By definition of the conditional entropy,

$$\begin{aligned} H(f(\mathbf{X})|\mathbf{X}_A) &= \sum_{\mathbf{x}_A\in\{-1,1\}^{|A|}} \mathrm{P}[\mathbf{X}_A = \mathbf{x}_A]\, H(f(\mathbf{X})|\mathbf{X}_A = \mathbf{x}_A) \\ &= \sum_{\mathbf{x}_A\in\{-1,1\}^{|A|}} \mathrm{P}[\mathbf{X}_A = \mathbf{x}_A]\, h\left(\mathrm{P}\left[f(\mathbf{X}) = 1|\mathbf{X}_A = \mathbf{x}_A\right]\right), \end{aligned} \quad (26)$$

where $h(\cdot)$ is the binary entropy function as defined in (6). Observe that

$$h(\mathrm{P}\left[f(\mathbf{X}) = 1|\mathbf{X}_A = \mathbf{x}_A\right]) = h(\mathrm{P}[X_i = 1])$$

if

$$\begin{aligned} & f(X_1 = x_1, ..., X_i = 1, ..., X_n = x_n) \\ & \neq f(X_1 = x_1, ..., X_i = -1, ..., X_n = x_n) \end{aligned}$$

and

$$h(\mathrm{P}\left[f(\mathbf{X}) = 1|\mathbf{X}_A = \mathbf{x}_A\right]) = 0$$

otherwise. Hence, (26) becomes

$$H(f(\mathbf{X})|\mathbf{X}_A) = \sum_{\mathbf{x}_A\in\{-1,1\}^{|A|}} \mathrm{P}[\mathbf{X}_A = \mathbf{x}_A]\, h(p_i) \mathbf{1}_{\{f(\mathbf{X})\neq f(\mathbf{X}\oplus e_i)\}},$$

where $\mathbf{x}\oplus e_i$ is the vector obtained from $\mathbf{x}$ by flipping its ith entry, and Theorem 4 follows by using the definition of the influence.

Appendix 6
Proof of Theorem 5

By definition, $f(\mathbf{X})$ and $\mathbf{X}_A$ are statistically independent if and only if for all $\mathbf{x}_A \in \{-1,+1\}^{|A|}$

$$\mathrm{P}\left[f(\mathbf{X}) = 1|\mathbf{X}_A = \mathbf{x}_A\right] = \mathrm{P}\left[f(\mathbf{X}) = 1\right]. \quad (27)$$

With

$$\mathrm{P}\left[f(\mathbf{X}) = 1|\mathbf{X}_A = \mathbf{x}_A\right] = \frac{1}{2} + \frac{1}{2}\mathbb{E}[f(\mathbf{X})|\mathbf{X}_A = \mathbf{x}_A]$$

and application of Lemma 1 given in Appendix 1, (27) becomes

$$\begin{aligned} & \sum_{S\subseteq A} \hat{f}(S)\Phi_S(\mathbf{x_A}) = \hat{f}(\emptyset) \\ \Leftrightarrow & \sum_{S\subseteq A\setminus\emptyset} \hat{f}(S)\Phi_S(\mathbf{x_A}) = 0. \end{aligned} \quad (28)$$

It follows from the Fourier expansion (3) that (28) holds for all $\mathbf{x}_A \in \{-1,+1\}^{|A|}$ if and only if $\hat{f}(S) = 0$ for all $S \subseteq A\setminus\emptyset$, which proves the theorem.

Competing interest

The authors declare that they have no competing interests.

Acknowledgements

We would like to thank Sara Al-Sayed and Dejan Lazich for their helpful discussions and careful reading of the manuscript.

Author details

[1] Department of Information Technology and Electrical Engineering, ETH Zürich, Zürich, Switzerland. [2] Institute of Telecommunications and Applied Information Theory, University of Ulm, Ulm, Germany.

References

1. S Kauffman, Metabolic stability and epigenesis in randomly constructed genetic nets. J. Theor. Biol. **22**(3), 437–467 (1969)
2. S Kauffman, Homeostasis and differentiation in random genetic control networks. Nature. **224**(5215), 177–178 (1969)
3. S Davidich, MI Bornholdt, Boolean network model predicts cell cycle sequence of fission yeast. PLoS ONE. **3**(2), e1672 (2008)
4. J Saez-Rodriguez, L Simeoni, JA Lindquist, R Hemenway, U Bommhardt, B Arndt, U Haus, R Weismantel, ED Gilles, S Klamt, B Schraven, logical model provides insights into T cell receptor signaling. PLoS Comput Biol. **3**(8), e163 (2007)
5. F Li, T Long, Y Lu, Q Ouyang, C Tang, The yeast cell-cycle network is robustly designed. Proc. Natl. Acad. Sci. USA. **101**(14), 4781–4786 (2004)
6. BO Covert, MW Knight, EM Reed, JL Herrgard, MJ Palsson, Integrating high-throughput and computational data elucidates bacterial networks. Nature. **429**(6987), 92–96 (2004)
7. P J Kesseli, O Rämö, Yli-Harja, On spectral techniques in analysis of Boolean networks. Physica D: Nonlinear Phenomena. **206**(1–2), 49–61 (2005)
8. J Kesseli, P Rämö, O Yli-Harja, Tracking perturbations in Boolean networks with spectral methods. Phys. Rev. E. **72**(2), 026137 (2005)
9. L Ribeiro, AS Kauffman, SA loyd-J Price, B Samuelsson, JES Socolar, Mutual information in random Boolean models of regulatory networks. Phys. Rev. E. **77**(011901) (2008)
10. R Heckel, S Schober, M Bossert, Determinative power and tolerance to perturbations in Boolean networks. Paper presented at the 9th international workshop on computational systems biology, Ulm, Germany, 4–6 June 2012
11. G Xiao, J Massey, A spectral characterization of correlation-immune combining functions. Inf Theory IEEE Trans. **34**(3), 569–571 (1988)
12. S Liang, S Fuhrman, R Somogyi, Reveal, a general reverse engineering algorithm for inference of genetic network architectures. Pacific Symposium on Biocomputing. **3**, 18–29 (1998)
13. J Grefenstette, S Kim, S Kauffman, An analysis of the class of gene regulatory functions implied by a biochemical model. Bio. Syst. **84**(2), 81–90 (2006)
14. B Derrida, Y Pomeau, Random networks of automata: a simple annealed approximation. Europhysics Lett. **1**(2), 45–49 (1986)

15. RR Bahadur, in *Studies in Item Analysis and Prediction*, ed. by H Solomon. A representation of the joint distribution of responses to n dichotomous items (Stanford University Press Stanford, 1961), pp. 158–168
16. M Ben-Or, N Linial, Collective coin flipping, robust voting schemes, and minima of Banzhaf values. Paper presented at the 26th annual symposium on foundations of computer science, Portland, Oregon, USA, 21–23 October 1985
17. C Bshouty, NH Tamon, On the Fourier spectrum of monotone functions. J. ACM. **43**(4), 747–770 (1996)
18. S Schober, About Boolean networks with noisy inputs. Paper presented at the fifth international workshop on computational systems biology, Leipzig, Germany, 11–13 June 2008
19. V Matache, MT Matache, On the sensitivity to noise of a Boolean function. J. Math. Phys. **50**(10), 103512 (2009)
20. JA Cover, TM Thomas, *Elements of Information Theory*, 2nd edn. (Wiley-Interscience, New York, 2006)
21. R Forre, Methods and instruments for designing S-boxes. J. Cryptology. **2**(3), 115–130 (1990)
22. B Rosell, L Hellerstein, S Ray, Why skewing works: learning difficult Boolean functions with greedy tree learners. Paper presented at the 22nd international conference on machine learning, Bonn, Germany, 7–11 August 2005
23. A Diskin, M Koppel, Voting power: an information theory approach. Soc Choice Welfare. **34**, 105–119 (2010)
24. L Raeymaekers, Dynamics of Boolean networks controlled by biologically meaningful functions. J. Theor. Biol. **218**(3), 331–341 (2002)
25. S Schober, *Analysis and Identification of Boolean Networks using Harmonic Analysis*. (Der Andere Verlag, Germany, 2011)
26. F Topsoe, Bounds for entropy and divergence for distributions over a two-element set. Inequalities Appl. Pure Math. **2**, Art, 25 (2001)

8

Properties of Boolean networks and methods for their tests

Johannes Georg Klotz[1*], Ronny Feuer[2], Oliver Sawodny[2], Martin Bossert[1], Michael Ederer[2] and Steffen Schober[1]

Abstract

Transcriptional regulation networks are often modeled as Boolean networks. We discuss certain properties of Boolean functions (BFs), which are considered as important in such networks, namely, membership to the classes of unate or canalizing functions. Of further interest is the average sensitivity (AS) of functions. In this article, we discuss several algorithms to test the properties of interest. To test canalizing properties of functions, we apply spectral techniques, which can also be used to characterize the AS of functions as well as the influences of variables in unate BFs. Further, we provide and review upper and lower bounds on the AS of unate BFs based on the spectral representation. Finally, we apply these methods to a transcriptional regulation network of *Escherichia coli*, which controls central parts of the *E. coli* metabolism. We find that all functions are unate. Also the analysis of the AS of the network reveals an exceptional robustness against transient fluctuations of the binary variables.[a]

Keywords: Regulatory Boolean networks, Boolean networks, Linear threshold functions, Unate functions, Canalizing function, Sensitivity, Average sensitivity, Restricted functions, *Escherichia coli*

1 Introduction

Boolean modeling is often used to describe signal transduction and regulatory networks [1-3]. Over the last years random Boolean models received much attention to find some generic properties that characterize regulatory networks. In addition to the study of topological features (e.g., [4]), the choice of Boolean functions in such networks is an important question to consider. Many results indicate the importance of functions with a low average sensitivity. For example, it is well known that a low expected average sensitivity is a prerequisite for non-chaotic behavior of random Boolean networks, e.g., [5,6]. Further, so called *canalizing* functions have been conjectured to be characteristic for biological networks [7]. These functions have a stabilizing effect on the network dynamics [1] and many functions occurring in (non-random) regulative networks are canalizing [7].

In this work we follow a non-random approach to find properties characterizing regulatory networks. Namely, we focus on the properties of Boolean functions in a large scale Boolean regulatory network model. Our goal is also to provide efficient algorithms to test these properties.

First, we consider the membership of the regulatory functions to certain classes of functions. We first consider unate functions, which are monotone in each of their variables and were shown to be implied by a biochemical model [2].

Next, we present a test using Fourier analysis to test canalizing properties of functions. Canalizing functions are used in signal processing for certain classes of filters [8] and play an important role in random and regulatory Boolean networks, as already mentioned. Interestingly, it has been shown in [9] that a subclass of canalizing functions, namely the nested canalizing functions, is identical to the class of unate-cascade functions, a subclass of the unate functions. The test presented in this work is inspired by [10], where the so-called forcing transform was introduced to test the membership of a function to the class of canalizing functions. Here, we generalize this approach to the Fourier transform, which is a more intuitive and natural approach and furthermore some spectral properties of canalizing functions have already been investigated in [11].

*Correspondence: johannes.klotz@uni-ulm.de
[1] Institute of Communications Engineering, Ulm University, Albert-Einstein-Allee 43, 89081 Ulm, Germany
Full list of author information is available at the end of the article

It is well known that the average sensitivity can be directly obtained from the Fourier spectral coefficients. Further, the Fourier transform turns out to be useful to prove bounds on the average sensitivity. We derive an upper bound for unate functions similar to known results for monotone functions and recall a well-known lower bound on the average sensitivity.

Finally, we apply our tests to a large-scale Boolean model of the transcriptional network of *Escherichia coli*. We extended the network model of the transcriptional network of *E. coli* (Covert et al. [3]) by mapping genes to their corresponding fluxes in the flux-balance model presented by [12]. The network has a layered feed-forward structure and shows characteristic topological features, such as a long-tail like out-degree distribution.

Throughout this article we use Fourier analysis to investigate the mentioned properties. In particular we use the concept of restricted functions. Therefore we derived both-way relations between the Fourier coefficients of a Boolean function and its restriction. A very general one-way approach of this relation can be found in [13].

The remainder of this article is organized as follows: In Section 2 we give a short introduction to Boolean functions and networks, discuss some fundamentals of Fourier analysis and investigate the spectra of restricted functions. In Section 3 we discuss certain classes and properties of Boolean functions and show efficient ways to check these properties. We also introduce the average sensitivity and prove an upper bound on it for unate functions. In Section 4 we finally introduce Boolean networks and apply our methods and tests to the regulatory network of *E.coli*. Some final remarks are given in Section 5.

2 BFs

A BF $f : \{-1,1\}^n \rightarrow \{-1,1\}$ maps n-ary binary *input* tuples to a binary *output*. In general, not all variables of a function f are *relevant*. A variable i is called relevant, if there exits at least one argument $\mathbf{x} \in \{-1,1\}^n$ such that $f(\mathbf{x}) \neq f(\mathbf{x} \oplus e_i)$, where the argument $\mathbf{x} \oplus e_i$ is obtained from $\mathbf{x}$ by changing its i-th entry. In the following, we denote the number of relevant variables by k.

For the sake of simplicity we assume throughout this article, that $k = n$, i.e., all variables are relevant, but note that the expositions in Section 2.1 are valid in general. The assignment of $+1$ and -1 chosen to represent the binary in and outputs is somewhat arbitrary. One can interpret the value -1 as "ON" or "TRUE" and $+1$ as "OFF" or "FALSE".

2.1 Fourier analysis

Here we will give a short introduction to the concepts of Fourier analysis so far used in this article. Let us consider $\mathbf{x} = (x_1, x_2, \ldots, x_N)$ as an instance of a product distributed random vector $\mathbf{X} = (X_1, X_2, \ldots, X_N)$ with probability density function

$$P_{\mathbf{X}}(\mathbf{x}) = \prod_i P_{X_i}(x_i).$$

Furthermore, let μ_i be the expected value of X_i , i.e., $\mu_i = \mathbb{E}[X_i]$ and let $\sigma_i = \sqrt{1 - \mu_i^2}$ be the standard deviation of X_i . It can easily be seen that

$$P_{X_i}(a_i) = \frac{1 + a_i \cdot \mu_i}{2}. \quad (1)$$

It is well known that any BF f can be expressed by the following sum, called Fourier-expansion [14,15],

$$f(\mathbf{x}) = \sum_{\mathbf{U} \subseteq [n]} \hat{f}(\mathbf{U}) \cdot \Phi_{\mathbf{U}}(\mathbf{x}), \quad (2)$$

where $[n] = \{1, 2, \ldots, n\}$ and

$$\Phi_{\mathbf{U}}(\mathbf{x}) = \prod_{i \in \mathbf{U}} \frac{x_i - \mu_i}{\sigma_i}. \quad (3)$$

For $\mathbf{U} = \emptyset$ we define $\Phi_{\emptyset}(\mathbf{x}) = 1$. The *Fourier coefficients* $\hat{f}(\mathbf{U})$ can be recovered by

$$\hat{f}(\mathbf{U}) = \sum_{\mathbf{x}} P_{\mathbf{X}}(\mathbf{x}) \cdot f(\mathbf{x}) \cdot \Phi_{\mathbf{U}}(\mathbf{x}). \quad (4)$$

Further, let $\mathbf{A} \subset \mathbf{U}$ and $\bar{\mathbf{A}} = \mathbf{U} \setminus \mathbf{A}$, then

$$\Phi_{\mathbf{U}}(\mathbf{x}) = \Phi_{\mathbf{A}}(\mathbf{x}) \cdot \Phi_{\bar{\mathbf{A}}}(\mathbf{x}), \quad (5)$$

which directly follows from the definition of $\Phi_{\mathbf{U}}$ (Equation 3).

If the input variables X_i are uniformly distributed, i.e., $\mu_i = 0$ and $\sigma_i = 1$, Equation (3) reduces to

$$\Phi_{\mathbf{U}}(\mathbf{x}) = \prod_{i \in \mathbf{U}} x_i,$$

and consequently, as $P_{\mathbf{X}}(\mathbf{x}) = 2^{-n}$ for all $\mathbf{x}$, Equation (4), reduces to

$$\hat{f}(\mathbf{U}) = 2^{-n} \sum_{\mathbf{x}} f(\mathbf{x}) \cdot \prod_{i \in \mathbf{U}} x_i.$$

2.2 Restricted functions

A function is called restricted, if some of the input variables are set to constants, i.e., variables $i \in \mathbf{K}$ are set to a constant $x_i = a_i$. Hence, the number of relevant variables is reduced by $|\mathbf{K}|$. First, we consider the case that only one variable is restricted ($\mathbf{K} = \{i\}$). The function obtained in this way is denoted as

$$f|_{x_i = a_i} : \{-1,1\}^{n-1} \rightarrow \{-1,1\}. \quad (6)$$

The following lemma gives a relation between the Fourier coefficients of the original function and its restriction.

Proposition 1. *Let the function $f(\mathbf{x})$ be a function in n variables. Consider the restricted function obtained by setting $x_i = a_i$, further, let $\hat{f}|_{x_i=a_i}$ be denoted as $\hat{f}_{a_i}$ then*

$$\hat{f}_{a_i}(\mathbf{U}) = \hat{f}(\mathbf{U}) + \Phi_{\{i\}}(a_i) \cdot \hat{f}(\mathbf{U} \cup \{i\}) \quad (7)$$

where $\mathbf{U} \subseteq [n] \setminus \{i\}$ and $\Phi_{\{i\}}(a_i) = \frac{a_i - \mu_i}{\sigma_i}$.

Proof. Using Equation (4) we can rewrite (7) as

$$\hat{f}_{a_i}(\mathbf{U}) = \sum_{\mathbf{x}} P_{\mathbf{X}}(\mathbf{x}) f(\mathbf{x}) \cdot \Phi_{\mathbf{U}}(\mathbf{x}) + \Phi_{\{i\}}(a_i) \cdot \sum_{\mathbf{x}} P_{\mathbf{X}}(\mathbf{x}) f(\mathbf{x}) \cdot \Phi_{\mathbf{U} \cup \{i\}}(\mathbf{x}). \quad (8)$$

By applying (5) and (3) we get

$$\Phi_{\mathbf{U} \cup \{i\}}(\mathbf{x}) = \Phi_{\mathbf{U}}(\mathbf{x}) \cdot \Phi_{\{i\}}(\mathbf{x}) = \Phi_{\mathbf{U}}(\mathbf{x}) \cdot \frac{x_i - \mu_i}{\sigma_i}.$$

Hence, we can combine the two sums in (8) and obtain:

$$\hat{f}_{a_i}(\mathbf{U}) = \sum_{\mathbf{x}} \left(P_{\mathbf{X}}(\mathbf{x}) f(\mathbf{x}) \cdot \Phi_{\mathbf{U}}(\mathbf{x}) \cdot \Xi_i \right), \quad (9)$$

where

$$\Xi_i = \left(1 + \frac{x_i - \mu_i}{a_i + \mu_i}\right) = \frac{a_i + x_i}{a_i + \mu_i},$$

due to $\Phi_{\{i\}}(a_i) = \frac{a_i - \mu_i}{\sigma_i} = \frac{\sigma_i}{a_i + \mu_i}$.

Further, with $a_i = \frac{1}{a_i}$ and Equation (1) we get

$$\Xi_i = \begin{cases} \frac{2}{1 + a_i \cdot \mu_i} = \frac{1}{P_{X_i}(a_i)} & \text{, if } x_i = a_i \\ 0 & \text{, if } x_i = -a_i \end{cases}.$$

Thus, the sum in Equation (9) can be simplified to

$$\hat{f}_{a_i}(\mathbf{U}) = \sum_{\mathbf{x}|x_i = a_i} \frac{P_{\mathbf{X}}(\mathbf{x})}{P_{X_i}(a_i)} \cdot f(\mathbf{x}) \cdot \Phi_{\mathbf{U}}(\mathbf{x})$$

and finally

$$\hat{f}_{a_i}(\mathbf{U}) = \sum_{\mathbf{x}|x_i = a_i} P_{\mathbf{X}|x_i}(\mathbf{x}|a_i) \cdot f(\mathbf{x}) \cdot \Phi_{\mathbf{U}}(\mathbf{x}),$$

which is the definition of the Fourier coefficients from Equation (4) and concludes the proof. □

A closely related property is given by the following proposition. Please note that this result for uniform distributed input variables can also be retrieved using ([13], Lemma 2.17).

Proposition 2. *Let $i \in [n]$ be fixed and denote $f|_{x_i=a}$ with f_a. For any n-ary BF f,*

$$\hat{f}(\mathbf{U}) = \frac{1 + \mu_i}{2} \left(\left(\Phi_{\{i\}}(+1) \right)^{|\mathbf{U} \cap \{i\}|} \hat{f}_{+1}(\mathbf{U} \setminus \{i\}) \right) + \frac{1 - \mu_i}{2} \left(\left(\Phi_{\{i\}}(-1) \right)^{|\mathbf{U} \cap \{i\}|} \hat{f}_{-1}(\mathbf{U} \setminus \{i\}) \right).$$

Proof. Starting from the definition we obtain

$$\begin{aligned} \hat{f}(\mathbf{U}) &= \mathbb{E}\left[f(\mathbf{X}) \Phi_{\mathbf{U}}(\mathbf{X})\right] \\ &= P_{X_i}(+1) \mathbb{E}\left[f(\mathbf{X}) \Phi_{\mathbf{U}}(\mathbf{X}) | X_i = +1\right] \\ &\quad + P_{X_i}(-1) \mathbb{E}\left[f(\mathbf{X}) \Phi_{\mathbf{U}}(\mathbf{X}) | X_i = -1\right] \\ &= P_{X_i}(+1) \Phi_{\{i\}}(+1) \mathbb{E}\left[f_{+1}(\mathbf{X}) \Phi_{\mathbf{U} \setminus \{i\}}(\mathbf{X})\right] \\ &\quad + P_{X_i}(-1) \Phi_{\{i\}}(-1) \mathbb{E}\left[f_{-1}(\mathbf{X}) \Phi_{\mathbf{U} \setminus \{i\}}(\mathbf{X})\right]. \end{aligned}$$

Note that for $a = +1$ or $a = -1$

$$\mathbb{E}\left[f_a(\mathbf{X}) \Phi_{\mathbf{U} \setminus \{i\}}(\mathbf{X})\right] = \hat{f}_a(\mathbf{U} \setminus \{i\})$$

by definition, hence, the proposition follows from Equation (1). □

For the general case, that a BF is restricted to more than one input, the following Corollary to Proposition 1 applies:

Corollary 1. *Let $f(\mathbf{x})$ be a BF and $\hat{f}(\mathbf{U})$ its Fourier coefficients. Furthermore, let $\mathbf{K}$ be a set containing the indices i of the input variables x_i, which are fixed to certain values a_i. The Fourier coefficients of the restricted function are then given as*

$$\hat{f}|_{\mathbf{K}}(\mathbf{U}) = \sum_{\mathbf{T} \subseteq \mathbf{K}} \left(\Phi_{\mathbf{T}}(\mathbf{a}) \cdot \hat{f}(\mathbf{U} \cup \mathbf{T}) \right),$$

where $\mathbf{U}$ contains the indices for the Fourier coefficients of the restricted functions, i.e., $\mathbf{U} \subseteq [n] \setminus \mathbf{K}$ and $\mathbf{a}$ is a vector containing all a_i, $i \in \mathbf{K}$.

3 Classes and properties of functions

In this section, we will present and discuss some classes of BFs, namely unate and canalizing functions. Further, we will discuss properties of functions characterizing their *robustness*, like for example the AS.

3.1 Unate functions

A BF is unate if it is monotone (either increasing or decreasing) in each of its variables, a precise definition will be given below. The class of unate functions is a simple extension of the class of monotone functions defined as follows

Definition 1. *A BF $f : \{-1, 1\}^n \rightarrow \{-1, 1\}$ is called monotone, if for each $i \in \{1, \ldots, n\}$ it holds that $f(x_1, \ldots, x_i = -1, \ldots, x_n) \leq f(x_1, \ldots, x_i = 1, \ldots, x_n)$.*

Now unate functions can be defined as follows.

Definition 2. *A BF f is unate, if there exists a vector $\mathbf{a} \in \{-1, 1\}^n$ such that the function $f(a_1 \cdot x_1, \ldots, a_n \cdot x_n)$ is monotone.*

The class of unate functions is closed with respect to restriction, since every restriction of a locally monotone function yields again in a locally monotone function.

To test whether a function is unate or not it is sufficient to use the definition, however, a necessary condition for a function to be unate is given by the following proposition:

Proposition 3 (for example [16]). *Iff is a unate function, then for each relevant variable i*

$$\hat{f}(\{i\}) \neq 0.$$

3.2 Canalizing functions

A BF is called canalizing, if there exists a canalizing variable x_i and a Boolean value $a_i \in \{-1,1\}$ such that the function

$$f|_{x_i=a_i}(\mathbf{x}) = b_i, \tag{10}$$

for all $x_1, \ldots x_{i-1}, x_{i+1} \ldots x_n$, where $b_i \in \{0,1\}$ is a constant. If the restricted function, which is obtained by setting $x_i = 1 - a_i$, is again canalizing and so on, the function is called nested canalizing.

The following propositions give a relation between the Fourier coefficients and the canalizing property.

Proposition 4. *A BF f is canalizing in variable i, if for any constants $a_i, b_i \in \{-1,1\}$ the Fourier coefficients $\hat{f}(\mathbf{U})$ fulfill the following condition.*

$$\hat{f}(\emptyset) + \Phi_{\{i\}}(a_i) \cdot \hat{f}(\{i\}) = b_i, \tag{11}$$

where μ_i is the expected value of x_i and σ_i the corresponding standard derivation.

Proof. Obviously, if a function is canalizing, $\mathbb{E}[f|_{x_i=a_i}(\mathbf{x})] = b_i$ holds. Since the expected value of a BF can be expressed as $\mathbb{E}[f(x)] = \hat{f}(\emptyset)$ we obtain

$$\mathbb{E}[f|_{x_i=a_i}(\mathbf{x})] = \hat{f}|_{x_i=a_i}(\emptyset).$$

Using Proposition 1, we get

$$\mathbb{E}[f|_{x_i=a_i}(\mathbf{x})] = \hat{f}(\emptyset) + \Phi_{\{i\}}(a_i) \cdot \hat{f}(\{i\}),$$

and the proposition follows from Equation (11). □

A similar result namely the calculation of the Fourier coefficients of a canalizing BF from the coefficients of the restricted functions $\hat{f}|_{x_i=a_i}(\mathbf{U})$ is addressed in [11]. These results can also be achieved using Proposition 2.

Proposition 4 can easily be extended for nested canalizing functions:

Proposition 5. *Assume $f(x)$ is canalizing for variables $x_i = -a_i, i \in \mathbf{K}$, then $f(x)$ is canalizing for $x_j = a_j, j \notin \mathbf{K}$, i.e., $\mathbb{E}[f_{\mathbf{K}\cup\{j\}}(x)] = b_j$, if*

$$\sum_{\mathbf{T}\subseteq\mathbf{K}\cup\{j\}} \left(\prod_{i\in\mathbf{T}} \left(\Phi_{\{i\}}(a_i)\right) \cdot \hat{f}(\mathbf{T}) \right) = b_j.$$

Proof. The proof follows from Corollary 1 and Proposition 4. □

From Proposition 4 it is clear that the canalizing property can be tested by considering all Fourier coefficients of order one. Using the Fast Walsh Transform [17] this test is as fast as the one presented in [10], however, once we have retrieved the spectra of a function, we can easily compute other properties, such as the AS (see next section).

3.3 AS of functions

The AS [18] gives the influence of random disturbance at the input on the output of a BF. This can be interpreted as an indicator for the robustness of this BF and finally for the whole Boolean network.

To define the as we first have to look at the sensitivity $s_{\mathbf{x}}(f)$ of an input argument $\mathbf{x} \in \{0,1\}^n$. It is defined as the number of single bit-flips in $\mathbf{x}$ so that the output of the function will change, i.e., $s_{\mathbf{x}}(f)$ is number of variables i for which $f(\mathbf{x}) \neq f(\mathbf{x} \oplus e_i)$. The AS $as(f)$ is the expected value over all arguments $\mathbf{x}$:

$$as(f) = \mathbb{E}_{\mathbf{x}}[s_{\mathbf{x}}(f)]. \tag{12}$$

It is worth noting that the as depends on the distribution of the input vector. For example, a function having a low AS for the uniform distribution may have a large AS for other distributions. In general, the AS can be as large as the number of relevant variables k, i.e.,

$$0 \leq as(f) \leq k.$$

Figure 1 explains the concepts defined above at an example.

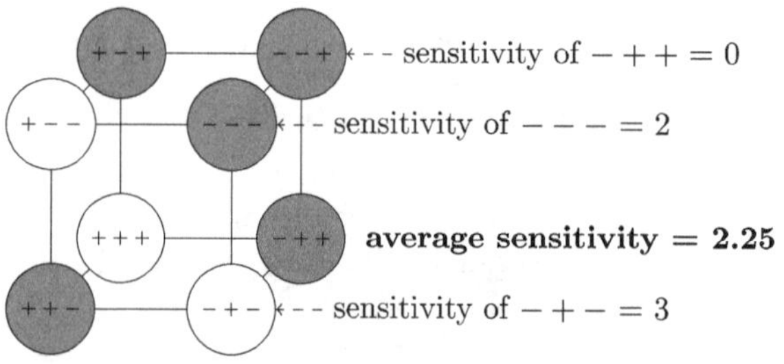

Figure 1 Sensitivities and AS of an exemplary BF. Each node represents an argument of a BF with $n = 3$ variables, where + stands for +1 and − represents a −1. A blank node indicates that the corresponding output of the function is 1 while a shaded node represents a −1. The sensitivity of a node is then the number of neighbor-nodes with a different shading. The expected value of these sensitivities is the AS.

Alternatively, the AS can be defined using the notion of *influence*. The influence $I_i(f)$ of a single input variable i on the functions f is defined as

$$I_i(f) = \text{Prob}[f(\mathbf{X}) \neq f(\mathbf{X} \oplus e_i)]\,. \tag{13}$$

The AS can then be defined as the sum of all influences [19]

$$as(f) = \mathbb{E}_{\mathbf{X}}[s_{\mathbf{X}}(f)] = \sum_i I_i(f). \tag{14}$$

The influence $I_i(f)$ for a unate function f is directly related to the corresponding Fourier coefficient:

$$I_i(f) = \frac{|\hat{f}(\{i\})|}{\sigma_i}, \tag{15}$$

as it was shown for monotone functions in ([16], Lemma 4.5) and can easily be extended to unate functions. Note that Equation (15) directly gives a proof for Proposition 3. Hence, for unate functions we can write

$$as(f) = \sum_{i=1}^{n} \frac{|\hat{f}(\{i\})|}{\sigma_i} = \sqrt{\left(\sum_{i=1}^{n} \frac{|\hat{f}(\{i\})|}{\sigma_i}\right)^2}, \tag{16}$$

and from the Cauchy-Schwarz inequality it follows that

$$\begin{aligned} as(f) &\leq \sqrt{\sum_{i=1}^{n} \left(|\hat{f}(\{i\})|\right)^2} \sqrt{\sum_{i=1}^{n} \left(\frac{1}{\sigma_i}\right)^2} \\ &\leq \sqrt{\left(1 - \hat{f}(\emptyset)^2\right)} \sqrt{\sum_{i=1}^{n} \left(\frac{1}{\sigma_i}\right)^2}. \end{aligned} \tag{17}$$

Together with a lower bound as presented in [19,20] and since $1 - \hat{f}(\emptyset)^2 = 1 - \mathbb{E}[f]^2 = \text{Var}(f)$ we obtain the following proposition.

Proposition 6. *Let f be an unate BF with in-degree n, further let σ_i be the standard derivation of the i-th input, then the AS of f ($as(f)$) is bounded by*

$$Var(f) \leq as(f) \leq \sqrt{Var(f)} \sqrt{\sum_{i=1}^{n} \left(\frac{1}{\sigma_i}\right)^2}, \tag{18}$$

where $Var(f)$ denotes the variance of f.

It can be shown that some functions get close to the upper bound. Assuming uniform distribution the upper bound in Equation (18) is smaller than $\sqrt{n}$. But it is well known that the AS of the majority function behaves like $O(\sqrt{n})$ (see for example [21]).

4 Application to a regulatory network of *E. coli*

In the previous sections, we only considered BFs. Now we will focus on BNs. A synchronous BN of N nodes can be described by a graph $G = G(V, E)$ with nodes $V \subseteq [N]$, $|V| = N$, and edges $E \subseteq V \times V$, and a set of ordered BFs $F = (f_1, f_2, \ldots, f_N)$, where we also allow a *dummy* function (see below). Each f_i has $n_i = k_i =$ in-deg(i) relevant variables where in-deg(i) is the in-degree of node i, i.e., the number of edges (j, i) with $j \in V$. In this case a node j is called a *controlling* node of i. If a node i has in-degree zero, the dummy function is attached and we call it an in-node. Consequently, the number of edges emerging from i is called the out-degree of node i. Usually to each node a binary state variable is assigned, i.e., for node i we assign $x_i(t) \in \{-1, +1\}$. For in-nodes the state can be set by some external process at some time t_0. The state of all other nodes at time t depend on its BF and the states of all controlling nodes at time instant $t - 1$.

In this article, we are only considering feed forward networks, i.e., networks without *feedback loops*. In such feed-forward BNs, the set of nodes is partitioned in layers $L_1, L_2, \ldots, L_l$. If a node i is an element of layer L_h all controlling nodes are element of layers L_m with $m < h$. The first (highest) layer L_1 consists of the input nodes (in-nodes), while the lowest layer L_l consists of the output nodes (out-nodes). In Figure 2 a sample network is depicted.

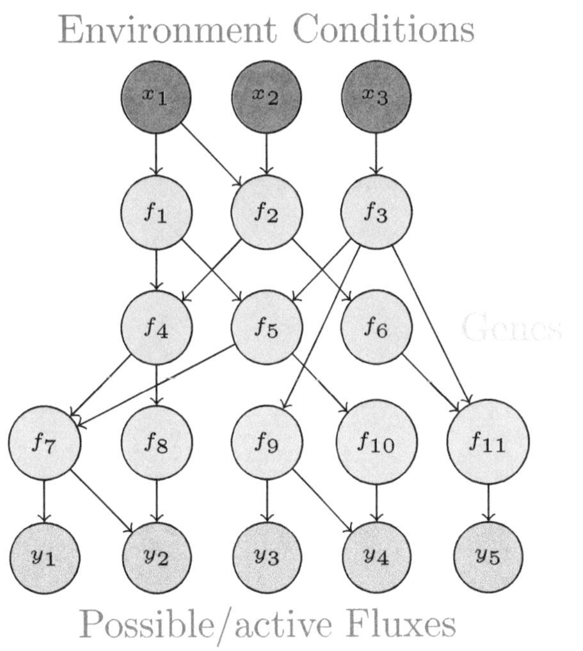

Figure 2 Example of a layered feed-forward Boolean network. The picture shows an example network. The upper layer (in red) consists of the inputs. These are fed forward through the middle layers (representing the regulation of the genes, in green) to the lowest layer. This layer is the output of the network (in blue). In our case it represents the fluxes of the metabolism.

4.1 Structural properties

We applied the tests described in the previous sections to the regulatory network of *E. coli* [3]. The model provides Boolean formulas that describe how environmental conditions act on gene expression via a transcriptional regulatory network. We extended this network by the mapping of the genes to their corresponding fluxes in the flux-balance model [12]. The network as described in the literature contains functions with irrelevant variables, respectively, redundant edges, which are removed. A list of the affected nodes and the removed edges can be found in the Additional file 1.

The resulting network has a total of $N = 3915$ nodes and $|E| = 4874$ edges, where $1,386$ of these nodes are in layer L_1, i.e., are inputs, hence, $2,529$ nodes have a non-dummy function attached. The in-degree and out-degree distributions can be found in Figures 3 and 4. The average in-degree is 1.92724. The out-degree distribution shows a typical long tail behavior [4].

We found that all functions attached to the nodes are unate. Furthermore 2499 functions (98.8%) are canalizing An overview of the functions, which are not canalizing, can be found in the Additional file 1.

4.2 Robustness

To evaluate the robustness of the network we assume in general that the state of nodes can be described by binary random variables. In a first step we assumed that each random variable of each nodes is uniformly distributed. This implies that we consider each node independently, i.e., the topology of the network is ignored. We calculated the AS for all functions in the network. In Figure 5, the resulting AS is plotted versus the *bias*, which is the probability that the output of the function equals one (a similar analysis

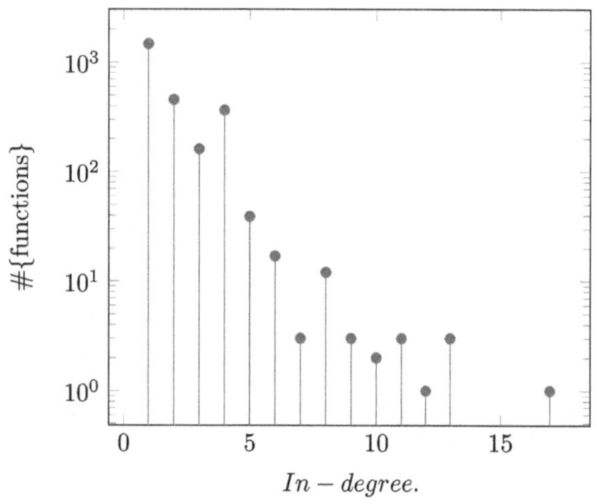

Figure 3 In-degree distribution of the investigated network ([3] extended by [12]).

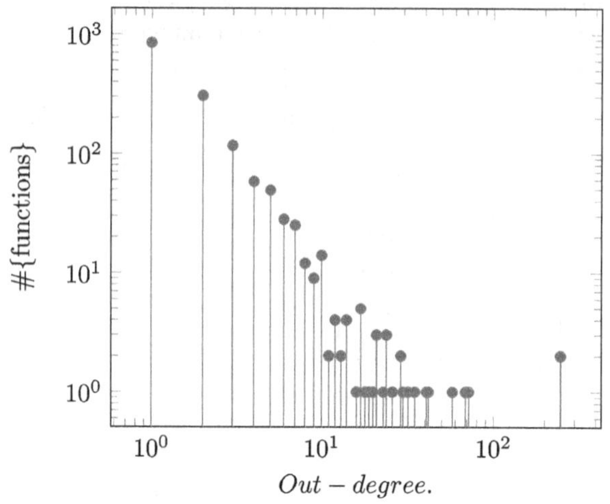

Figure 4 Out-degree distribution of the investigated network ([3] extended by [12]).

appears in [22]). Each color represents a BF with a certain in-degree n. We also included the lower bond and two exemplary upper bounds for $n = 5$ and $n = 8$ (Equation (18)). For increasing n the upper bounds will grow, i.e., the bound will move further to the right.

Obviously, functions with a strong bias, i.e., with a high probability to be either -1 or 1, have a low AS. Further it can be seen that the average sensitivities of all functions are very close to the lower bound. The mean value of the AS is 0.918874 . Hence, it can be stated that the AS of this network is rather low. Similar results can be obtained considering the network without the extension as originally defined by Covert et al. [3] and Samal and Jain [23].

In a second step we want to take the topology of the network into account. Therefore, we now assume that only the in-nodes of the network are equally distributed. However, the output of these functions will most certainly not be uniform, i.e., the functions have a bias unequal zero. Since the outputs of these functions serve as inputs of the functions of the next layer, we assume that their input distributions follow the output distribution of the first-layer functions. The output distributions of the second-layer functions serve then as input distributions of the third layer and so on. Obviously this has an impact on the *as* of the functions.

The results are shown in Figure 6. We did not include any upper bounds in this figure since these now depend on each input distribution (see Proposition 6). It can be seen that the AS is still very close to the lower bound. However, a few functions have a rather large AS, e.g., it can be seen in Figure 6 that two types of functions with in-degree $K = 2$ are very close to their upper bound (which is in this case at $as(f) = 2$). These functions have an argument with a sensitivity of 2. Due to the input distribution

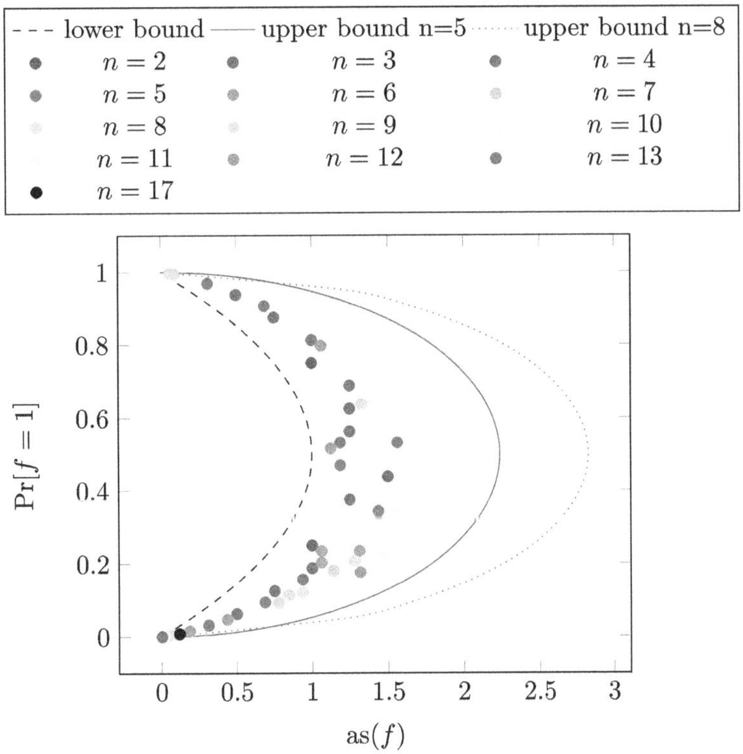

Figure 5 AS of functions plotted versus bias of functions (equally distributed inputs).

of these functions this argument has a very large probability (> 98%) which leads to a very high AS close to 2. Such high AS are normally observed for XOR and related functions. The average value of the AS is 0.908445 , hence the AS of the network further decreases when applying product distributions at the inputs of the functions.

4.3 Comparison with random ensembles

The network appears to be more *robust* against transient errors as for example certain randomly constructed networks. The in-degree distributions of all controlled nodes (in-degree larger zero) is shown in Figure 3. For all nodes with in-degree k we choose a random function out of the set of functions with k relevant variables. For $k = 1$ this results in $\mathbb{E}[as(f)] = 1$, for $k > 1$ we can at least state that $\mathbb{E}[as(f)] > \frac{k}{2}$, as it is well known that if we choose randomly from functions, we expect an AS of $\frac{k}{2}$. Taking the in-degree distribution into account this implies that the expectation of the AS of all BFs chosen in this way is larger than 1.25.

It is well known that random function ensembles with lower expected AS can be constructed, if functions with a higher bias have higher probability to be chosen [24]. To test if the observed robustness can be explained due to the bias of the functions, we proceeded as follows. Again, a random function is chosen for each node with in-degree k. We determine the frequency distribution for the bias $b = P[f = 1]$ for all functions of the original network model with a certain in-degree k. The random network is generated by replacing the original functions of the network with functions drawn from an ensemble of functions with the same distribution. For example, if $k = 2$, roughly 32% of all functions have $b = 0.25$, while all others have $b = 0.75$. Hence, with probability 32% we choose a function with $b = 0.25$, and $b = 0.75$ otherwise. The data can be found in the Additional file 1. As shown in [25,26], the expectation of the AS is then given by

$$\mathbb{E}(as(f)) = 2kb(1-b)\frac{2^k}{2^k-1}. \qquad (19)$$

The results obtained are shown in Table 1 sorted according to the in-degree k. For $k = 1$ and $k = 2$ the observed mean of $as(f)$ and the expectation of the random function coincides as only identity functions, respectively, AND or OR functions are chosen. For larger k, the observed mean is always smaller as the expectation of the random function. For some values of k, for example $k = 9$, both values are close to each other. This is due to the fact that the corresponding functions are highly biased, which means that there are three existing functions with the values for b being 0.00195312, 0.0917969 and 0.994141. In contrast, for $k = 11$ the mean of the observed values and the

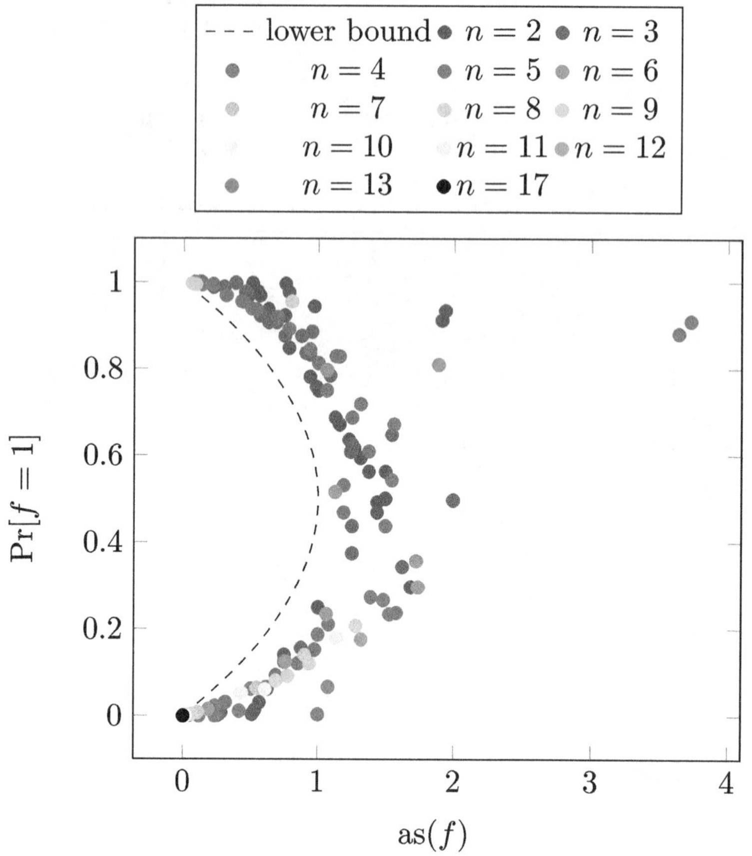

Figure 6 AS of functions plotted versus bias of functions (product distributed inputs).

expectation are far from each other. Indeed out of three functions, there is one function with $b = 0.354004$ for which, according to Equation (19), the expectation of the AS is 5.03353147.

It should be noted that in random BNs the expectation of the AS is an *order parameter* [5,6]. That is, if the expectation is less or equal to one many random networks show the so-called ordered behavior. Namely, single transient errors introduced in network nodes (by flipping their state) do not spread through the network with high probability. This ordered behavior is in sharp contrast to the so-called disordered behavior of random networks which is characterized by an expectation of the AS larger one. Indeed, it has been conjectured that biological relevant networks should be ordered (or critical) but not disordered [27]. A further investigation on how canalizing and nested canalizing functions influence the average sensitivity can be found in [7,11].

4.4 Impact of mutations on the metabolism

When investigating a regulatory network, the impact of the network on the metabolism is of major interest. Hence, only the stability of nodes in the bottom layer, i.e.,

Table 1 Fraction of functions with in-degree *k*, the mean of the AS of all functions with in-degree *k*, and the expectation of an accordingly chosen random function with same in-degree and same bias distribution (see text and Equation 19)

k	Fraction of functions	av(*f*)	$\mathbb{E}(\mathrm{av}(f))$
1	0.579905	1.000000	1.000000
2	0.179984	1.000000	1.000000
3	0.063291	0.887500	0.985714
4	0.143987	0.572115	0.623077
5	0.015427	0.491987	0.659895
6	0.006725	0.933824	1.737920
7	0.001187	0.796872	1.423026
8	0.004747	0.760416	1.641421
9	0.001187	0.300781	0.547935
10	0.000791	0.312500	0.587713
11	0.001187	1.009441	2.984577
12	0.000396	1.318360	3.481815
13	0.001187	0.003174	0.003174

the output of the network, is relevant. In regulatory networks, mutations are a source for errors. We consider two possible types of mutations. First we assume that a part of promoter region of a gene is mutated or deleted. In terms of our network this means that a edge is removed and the corresponding input is set to false (+1). The gene may still be transcribed, hence, the node itself remains functional. The second type of mutation is the deletion of a gene or a mutation which leads to disfunctional gene. In this case, the node is constantly set to false. In both cases, the value of one node may change (error). This error is now fed through the out-going edges of this node to other nodes. However, due to the low sensitivity of all functions in the network, the error has no impact on many nodes and, therefore, will in most cases not reach the bottom layer, which is, as mentioned above, the only part of the network, whose stability is crucial. From that point of view it can be stated that these permanent errors behave similar to the transient errors described above and that networks with a low mean AS are robust against such errors.

5 Summary

It is an important problem to characterize BFs that appear in Boolean models of regulatory networks. This will help to understand the constraints underlying such networks, but can, for example, also help to improve network inference algorithms (see for examples [28,29] for algorithms that utilize the membership to the class of unate functions). In this study, we focused on several properties that have been shown to be of interest in the context of Boolean regulatory networks. Namely, we discussed different classes of BFs such as unate and canalizing functions. Further, sensitivity measures of BFs, like the influence of variables, or the AS are considered. We devised simple algorithms to test these properties. To test canalizing properties of BFs we applied the Fourier representation of BFs where functions are represented as multivariate, multilinear real polynomials. To this end, we introduced two spectral relationships between the so-called *restricted* BFs and their unrestricted counter part. The Fourier representation is further useful as many interesting properties such as the influence of unate functions or the AS of BFs can easily be characterized in the spectral domain. For example, we show how to obtain theoretical upper bounds on the AS for unate functions using spectral techniques.

As an application of our results, we analyzed an extended [30] regulatory Boolean network model of the central metabolism of *E. coli*. It turned out that most functions are within the classes of unate functions. Further, the AS of most functions is close to a theoretical lower bound and far from the new upper bound. Especially, functions with large in-degree have low AS even if their so-called bias is close to 0.5 (see Figure 5). We compared our findings to random BNs with similar parameters and find that the investigated networks has an even lower AS. From that we conclude that the whole network is stable, and robust to small changes, e.g., mutations.

6 Endnote

[a]Preliminary results of this study have been presented at the 8th International Workshop on Computational Systems Biology (WCSB 2011) and the 3rd International Conference on Bioinformatics and Computational Biology (BICoB 2011).

Additional file

Additional file 1: This .xls file contains 3 sheets with listings of:

- **all nodes having pseudoedges**
- **all canalizing functions**
- **average sensitivities of all functions**

Competing interests
The authors declare that they have no competing interests.

Acknowledgements
The authors would like to thank Georg Sprenger and Katrin Gottlieb from the Institute for Microbiology at the University of Stuttgart for fruitful collaboration and discussions. Further we thank Reinhard Heckel for creating large parts of the software. This study was supported by the German Research Foundation "Deutsche Forschungsgemeinschaft" (DFG) under Grants Bo 867/25-1 and Sa 847/11-1.

Author details
[1]Institute of Communications Engineering, Ulm University, Albert-Einstein-Allee 43, 89081 Ulm, Germany. [2]Institute for System Dynamics, University of Stuttgart, 70569 Stuttgart, Germany.

References

1. S Kauffman, C Peterson, B Samuelsson, C Troein, Genetic networks with canalyzing Boolean rules are always stable. Proc. Natl Acad. Sci. USA. **101**(49), 17102–17107 (2004)
2. J Grefenstette, S Kim, S Kauffman, An analysis of the class of gene regulatory functions implied by a biochemical model. Biosystems. **84**(2), 81–90 (2006). http://www.sciencedirect.com/science/article/B6T2K-4HWXP4R-3/2/61a3092f98470e99a2c33786416697d0
3. MW Covert, EM Knight, JL Reed, MJ Herrgard, BO Palsson, Integrating high-throughput and computational data elucidates bacterial networks. Nature. **429**(6987), 92–96 (2004). http://dx.doi.org/10.1038/nature02456
4. M Aldana, Boolean dynamics of networks with scale-free topology. Physica D. **185**, 45–66 (2003)
5. I Shmulevich, SA Kauffman, Activities and sensitivities in Boolean network models. Phys. Rev. Lett. **93**(4), 048701 (2004)
6. JF Lynch, *Dynamics of random Boolean networks*. (byK Mahdavi, R Culshaw, J Boucher, eds.) (World Scientific Publishing Co, Singapore, 2007), pp. 15–38
7. SE Harris, BK Sawhill, A Wuensche, S Kauffman, A model of transcriptional regulatory networks based on biases in the observed regulation rules. Complexity. **7**(4), 23–40 (2002)
8. M Gabbouj, PT Yu, EJ Coyle, Convergence behavior and root signal sets of stack filters. Circuits Syst. Signal Process. **11**, 171–193 (1992)
9. AS Jarrah, B Raposa, R Laubenbacher, Nested Canalyzing, Unate Cascade, and Polynomial Functions. Physica D. **233**(2), 167–174 (2007)

10. I Shmulevich, H Lahdesmaki, K Egiazarian, Spectral methods for testing membership in certain post classes and the class of forcing functions. Signal Process. Lett. IEEE. **11**(2), 289–292 (2004)
11. J Kesseli, P Rämö, O Yli-Harja, in *Proceedings of the 2005 International TICSP Workshop on Spectral Methods and Multirate Signal Processing (SMMSP 2005)*. Analyzing dynamics of Boolean networks with canalyzing functions using spectral methods, (Riga, Latvia, 20-22 June 2005), pp. 151–158
12. AM Feist, CS Henry, JL Reed, M Krummenacker, AR Joyce, PD Karp, LJ Broadbelt, VBO Hatzimanikatis, V Palsson, A genome-scale metabolic reconstruction for Escherichia coli K-12 MG1655 that accounts for 1260 ORFs and thermodynamic information. Mol. Syst. Biol. **3**, 121 (2007). 10.1038/msb4100155
13. A Bernasconi, *Mathematical techniques for the analysis of Boolean functions. PhD thesis.* (University of Pisa, Italy, 1998)
14. RR Bahadur, in *Studies on Item Analysis and Prediction, no. 6 in Stanford Mathematical Studies in the Social Sciences*, ed. by byH Solomon. A representation of the joint distribution of responses to n dichotomous items (Stanford University Press, Stanford, CA, 1961), pp. 158–176
15. ML Furst, JC Jackson, SW Smith, in *Proceedings of the Fourth Annual Workshop on Computational Learning Theory*. Improved learning of AC0 functions (Morgan Kaufmann Publishers Inc., Santa Cruz, 1991), pp. 317–325
16. NH Bshouty, C Tamon, On the Fourier spectrum of monotone functions. J. ACM. **43**(4), 747–770 (1996)
17. J Shanks, Computation of the fast Walsh-Fourier transform. IEEE Trans. Comput. **C-18**(5), 457–459 (1969)
18. I Benjamini, G Kalai, O Schramm, Noise sensitivity of Boolean functions and applications to percolation. Publications mathematiques de l'IHES. **90**, 5–43 (1999)
19. J Kahn, G Kalai, N Linial, in *Proceedings of the 29th Annual Symposium on Foundations of Computer Science*. The influence of variables on Boolean functions (White Plains, (New York, USA, 24-26 Oct 1988), pp. 68–80
20. E Friedgut, Boolean functions with low average sensitivity depend on few coordinates. Combinatorica. **18**, 27–35 (1998). 10.1007/PL00009809
21. R O'Donnell, in *Proceedings of the 40th annual ACM symposium on Theory of computing*. Some topics in analysis of boolean functions (ACM, Victoria, 2008), pp. 569–578. http://portal.acm.org/citation.cfm?id=1374458
22. R Heckel, S Schober, M Bossert, Harmonic analysis of Boolean networks: determinative power and perturbations (2011). arXiv:1109.0807
23. A Samal, S Jain, The regulatory network of E. coli metabolism as a Boolean dynamical system exhibits both homeostasis and flexibility of response. BMC Syst. Biol. **2**, 21 (2008). doi:10.1186/1752-0509-2-21
24. B Derrida, Y Pomeau, Random networks of automata—a simple annealed approximation. Europhys. Lett. **2**, 45–49 (1986)
25. S Schober, *Analysis and identifiation of Boolean networks using harmonic analysis*. (Dissertation, Ulm University, Ulm, Germany, 2011)
26. S Schober, M Bossert, Analysis of random Boolean networks using the average sensitivity (2007). arXiv:nl.cg/0704.0197
27. SA Kauffman, Metabolic stability and epigenesis in randomly constructed nets. J. Theor. Biol. **22**, 437–467 (1969)
28. S Schober, D Kracht, M Heckel, R Bossert, Detecting controlling nodes of Boolean regulatory networks. EURASIP J. Bioinf. Syst. Biol. **27**(11), 1529–1536 (2011). http://www.ncbi.nlm.nih.gov/pubmed/21989141
29. M Maucher, B Kracher, M Kühl, HA Kestler, Inferring Boolean network structure via correlation. Bioinformatics (2011). http://bioinformatics.oxfordjournals.org/content/early/2011/04/05/bioinformatics.btr166.abstract
30. R Feuer, K Gottlieb, JG Klotz, S Schober, M Bossert, O Sawodny, G Sprenger, M Ederer, in *Proceedings of the 8th International Workshop on Computational Systems Biology (WCSB)*. Model-based analysis of adaptive evolution, (Zuerich, Switzerland, 2011), pp. 108-111

Integrating multi-platform genomic data using hierarchical Bayesian relevance vector machines

Sanvesh Srivastava[1], Wenyi Wang[2], Ganiraju Manyam[2], Carlos Ordonez[3] and Veerabhadran Baladandayuthapani[4*]

Abstract

Background: Recent advances in genome technologies and the subsequent collection of genomic information at various molecular resolutions hold promise to accelerate the discovery of new therapeutic targets. A critical step in achieving these goals is to develop efficient clinical prediction models that integrate these diverse sources of high-throughput data. This step is challenging due to the presence of high-dimensionality and complex interactions in the data. For predicting relevant clinical outcomes, we propose a flexible statistical machine learning approach that acknowledges and models the interaction between platform-specific measurements through nonlinear kernel machines and borrows information within and between platforms through a hierarchical Bayesian framework. Our model has parameters with direct interpretations in terms of the effects of platforms and data interactions within and across platforms. The parameter estimation algorithm in our model uses a computationally efficient variational Bayes approach that scales well to large high-throughput datasets.

Results: We apply our methods of integrating gene/mRNA expression and microRNA profiles for predicting patient survival times to The Cancer Genome Atlas (TCGA) based glioblastoma multiforme (GBM) dataset. In terms of prediction accuracy, we show that our non-linear and interaction-based integrative methods perform better than linear alternatives and non-integrative methods that do not account for interactions between the platforms. We also find several prognostic mRNAs and microRNAs that are related to tumor invasion and are known to drive tumor metastasis and severe inflammatory response in GBM. In addition, our analysis reveals several interesting mRNA and microRNA interactions that have known implications in the etiology of GBM.

Conclusions: Our approach gains its flexibility and power by modeling the non-linear interaction structures between and within the platforms. Our framework is a useful tool for biomedical researchers, since clinical prediction using multi-platform genomic information is an important step towards personalized treatment of many cancers. We have a freely available software at: http://odin.mdacc.tmc.edu/~vbaladan.

Keywords: Bayesian modeling; Multiple kernel learning; Genomics; High-dimensional data analysis; Prediction; Variational inference

*Correspondence: veera@mdanderson.org
[4]Department of Biostatistics, Division of Quantitative Sciences, The University of Texas MD Anderson Cancer Center, 1515 Holcombe Blvd, Unit 1411, Houston, Texas, USA
Full list of author information is available at the end of the article

1 Introduction

Recent advances in genome technologies such as microarrays and next-generation sequencing have enabled the measurement of genomic activity at a very detailed resolution (e.g., base pair, single-nucleotide polymorphisms) as well as across multiple molecular levels: the epigenome, transcriptome and proteome. The collection of genomic information at various resolutions holds promise to accelerate the amalgamation of discovery science and clinical medicine [1]. One of the overarching goals of such studies is to relate these genomic data to relevant (patient-specific) clinical outcomes, not only to find significant biomarkers of disease progression/evolution but also to use the biomarkers to develop prediction models for deployment in future therapeutic studies. Furthermore, genomic data are now available from multiple platforms and resolutions for the same individual, thus allowing a researcher to simultaneously query these multiple sources of data to achieve these goals. Such motivating data have been collected under the aegis of The Cancer Genome Atlas (TCGA) project, wherein data from multiple genomic platforms such as gene/mRNA expression, DNA copy number, methylation and microRNA expression profiles are available for multiple tumor types (see http://cancergenome.nih.gov for more details). In addition, the available clinical information, such as stage of disease and survival times, motivates the analytic frameworks that integrate patient-specific data.

One of the main challenges in modeling the statistical dependence between such high-throughput studies is that a large number of measurements (usually in thousands) is available for a relatively small number (usually in tens or hundreds) of patient samples; therefore, classical statistical approaches based on linear models and hierarchical clustering are prone to over-fitting [2,3]. In these situations, [3] recommends accounting for high-dimensionality by using approaches that borrow information across covariates to compensate for the limited information available across samples, which leads to better and more reliable inference. Several approaches have been developed to address these challenges in various contexts. Some examples include linear parametric models and hierarchical clustering for inferring the relation between phenotypes and genomic features [4], hierarchical Bayesian modeling approaches based on linear shrinkage estimators [5], linear canonical correlation analysis [6], intensity-based approaches for merging datasets [7], and regularized linear regression approaches [8].

Although these approaches are computationally efficient, interpretable, and simple, they make two unrealistic assumptions for practical data analysis. First, due to the parametric and linear assumptions, they might miss the underlying non-linear patterns in the data. Second, and more importantly, these non-linear patterns are further amplified in the presence of complex interactions within and between the different platforms that must be modeled while integrating data from these platforms. In this paper, we present a statistical machine learning approach called the hierarchical relevance vector machines (H-RVM) to address these modeling and inferential challenges. Briefly, the framework presented here: (a) models the relation between a relevant clinical outcome (scalar) and high-dimensional covariates/features through a data-adaptive and flexible nonparametric approach,(b) borrows information within and between platforms through a hierarchical Bayesian framework, (c) acknowledges and models the interaction between platforms through nonlinear kernel-based functionals, (d) has parameters that have explicit interpretation as the effects of the platforms and their interactions on the outcome, and (e) uses a computationally efficient variational Bayes approach that can be readily scaled to large datasets.

Our methods are motivated by and applied to a TCGA based glioblastoma multiforme (GBM) dataset, for which we integrate gene (mRNA) and microRNA (miRNA) expression profiles to predict patient survival times[a]. There is an increasing interest in identifying subtypes of GBM based on its gene expression data. The ultimate goal of subtyping GBM is to identify gene expression profiles that are prognostic or predictive of treatment outcomes. The known subtypes of GBM samples in TCGA include pro-neural, neural, classical, and mesenchymal; with the first two classes of which are suspected to differ from the other two in the cell of origin, which is a critical determinant of effective treatment regimens [9]. Differential expressions of miRNAs were recently found to be associated with many diseases, including cancers [10,11]. Previous studies have shown that combining multiple types of data, such as mRNA and miRNA expressions, could significantly improve the accuracy of detecting GBM subtypes, and thereby potentially predict the clinical outcomes [12]. However, methods are lacking to accurately model the effect of interactions between these data types directly on clinical outcomes. Here we show that our non-linear and interaction-based integrative methods have better prediction accuracy than linear alternatives and non-integrative methods that do not account for the interactions between the platforms. We also find several prognostic mRNAs and microRNAs that are related to tumor invasion and that are known to drive tumor metastasis and severe inflammatory response in GBM. In addition, our analysis reveals several interesting mRNA-miRNA interactions that have known implications in the etiology of GBM. The paper is structured as follows. The basic construction of H-RVM is detailed in Section 2. The analysis of GBM data is presented in Section 3, and concluding remarks about the H-RVM framework are presented in Section 4.

2 Hierarchical Relevance Vector Machine model

For ease of exposition, we illustrate the model building process of H-RVM using data from two sources: gene/mRNA and miRNA expression measurements. The framework is easily extended to multiple platforms as discussed in Section 4. Suppose, we have data for N patients, and $\mathbf{X}$ and $\mathbf{Y}$ represent mean-centered and -standardized gene and miRNA expression matrices, with rows corresponding to patients and columns representing the G genes and M miRNAs, respectively [b]. Centering and standardizing the gene and miRNA expression matrices remove any systematic mean or scaling effects caused by the use of different data sources, and make them compatible for model fitting. We denote the gene and miRNA expression for the i-th patient as row vectors $\mathbf{x}_i^T = (x_{i1}, \ldots, x_{iG})$ and $\mathbf{y}_i^T = (y_{i1}, \ldots, y_{iM})$. These covariates are high-dimensional, that is, both G and M are much larger than N; for example, in the GBM data $G \approx 12000, M \approx 540, N \approx 250$. Based on these measurements, our aim is to predict a relevant clinical outcome, which in our case is the (log-transformed) survival time measured from time of diagnosis to death, denoted by the column vector $\mathbf{t} = (t_1, \ldots, t_N)$ for the N patients.

2.1 Basic construction

A basic (conceptual) model can be written in a high-dimensional regression setting as,

$$t_i = \alpha_0 + f_{\mathbf{x}}(\mathbf{x}_i, \boldsymbol{\alpha}_1) + f_{\mathbf{y}}(\mathbf{y}_i, \boldsymbol{\alpha}_2) + f_{(\mathbf{x}\otimes\mathbf{y})}(\mathbf{x}_i, \mathbf{y}_i, \boldsymbol{\alpha}_3) + \epsilon_i, \quad (1)$$

where α_0 is the overall mean effect and ϵ_i is the random error; $f(\bullet)$'s, generally referred to as *basis functions*, are chosen to achieve a desired level of flexibility for modeling the effects of $\mathbf{X}, \mathbf{Y}$, and their functions on $\mathbf{t}$. Of these functions, $f_{(\mathbf{x}\otimes\mathbf{y})}$ models the *interactions* between $\mathbf{X}$ and $\mathbf{Y}$, and the remaining basis functions, $f_{\mathbf{x}}$ and $f_{\mathbf{y}}$, respectively, model the main effects of $\mathbf{X}$ and $\mathbf{Y}$ for predicting $\mathbf{t}$. In most situations the regression coefficients, $\boldsymbol{\alpha} = (\alpha_0, \boldsymbol{\alpha}_1, \boldsymbol{\alpha}_2, \boldsymbol{\alpha}_3)$, linearly relate the covariate effects (i.e., values of the basis functions evaluated at the covariates) to the response. Linear regression is a special case of (1) when all the basis functions are linear, and the response for the i-th patient,

$$t_i = \mathbf{x}_i^T \boldsymbol{\alpha}_1 + \mathbf{y}_i^T \boldsymbol{\alpha}_2 + (\mathbf{x}_i \otimes \mathbf{y}_i)^T \boldsymbol{\alpha}_3 + \epsilon_i, \quad (2)$$

where $(\mathbf{x}_i \otimes \mathbf{y}_i) = (x_{i1}y_{i1}, \ldots, x_{i1}y_{iM}, \ldots, x_{iG}y_{i1}, \ldots, x_{iG}y_{iM})$ models the first order interactions between genes and miRNAs and $\alpha_0 = 0$ because of the centered covariates. Further, due to the high-dimensional covariates $\mathbf{x}_i$'s and $\mathbf{y}_i$'s, a penalty is imposed on the regression coefficients $\boldsymbol{\alpha} = (\boldsymbol{\alpha}_1, \boldsymbol{\alpha}_2, \boldsymbol{\alpha}_3)$ to avoid overfitting. The most popular of such penalties is the Lasso because it has many desirable properties for high-dimensional linear regression and variable selection [13,14]. Although (2) with a Lasso penalty is a popular choice for high-dimensional regression, the linearity of the basis functions imposes serious restrictions on the flexibility of the model. For example, (2) does not model nonlinear covariate effects as well as second or higher order interactions between genes and miRNAs.

Through H-RVM, we propose a regression model as a special case of (1), using kernel-based functions to respectively model $f_{\mathbf{x}}, f_{\mathbf{y}}$, and $f_{(\mathbf{x}\otimes\mathbf{y})}$. The kernel functions incorporate nonlinear effects of possible interactions within and between high-dimensional gene and miRNA expression measurements. Further, H-RVM estimates the respective contributions of genes, miRNAs, and their interactions in predicting survival times, which is of primary importance in developing novel drug targets. H-RVM posits the following regression of $\mathbf{t}$ on $\mathbf{X}$ and $\mathbf{Y}$ for the i-th patient:

$$t_i = \beta_1 f_{\mathbf{x}}\{\mathbf{x}_i, \boldsymbol{\alpha}_1\} + \beta_2 f_{\mathbf{y}}\{\mathbf{y}_i, \boldsymbol{\alpha}_2\} + \beta_3 f_{(\mathbf{x}\otimes\mathbf{y})}\{(\mathbf{x}\otimes\mathbf{y})_i, \boldsymbol{\alpha}_3\} + \epsilon_i, \quad (3)$$

where $(\mathbf{x} \otimes \mathbf{y})_i = (x_{i1}, \ldots, x_{iG}, y_{i1}, \ldots, y_{iM})$ is a vector of length $G + M$ and $\boldsymbol{\beta} = (\beta_1, \beta_2, \beta_3)$ is such that its components lie on a probability simplex i.e. $\beta_m > 0$ for $m = 1, 2, 3$ and $\sum_{m=1}^{3} \beta_m = 1$. H-RVM posits different kernels for the data sources and combines them through weights $\boldsymbol{\beta}$. The model parameters have the following interpretation:

- The kernel functions $f_{\mathbf{x}}(\bullet)$ and $f_{\mathbf{y}}(\bullet)$ model all possible interactions among genes and among miRNAs, respectively, and $f_{(\mathbf{x}\otimes\mathbf{y})}(\bullet)$ models all possible interactions between genes and miRNAs. The three kernels together account for the high-dimensionality and non-linearity of the covariate effects of $\mathbf{X}$ and $\mathbf{Y}$ by embedding them in the space of kernels.
- The m-th component of $\boldsymbol{\beta}$, β_m, denotes the influence of the m-th source on predicting the log survival time and has the following interpretation: if $\boldsymbol{\beta} = \{1, 0, 0\}$, then (3) corresponds to a functional regression model that predicts $\mathbf{t}$ (log survival time) with only $\mathbf{x}$ (gene expressions) as covariates. Conversely, if $\boldsymbol{\beta} = \{1/3, 1/3, 1/3\}$, then (3) corresponds to a regression model, with the platforms and their interactions contributing equally to the prediction of the survival time. In reality, we expect (and show) different contributions from each platform and estimate these weights from the data.

The task now remains to explicitly characterize the functions $f_{\mathbf{x}}(\bullet), f_{\mathbf{y}}(\bullet)$ and $f_{(\mathbf{x}\otimes\mathbf{y})}(\bullet)$ using multiple kernels, as detailed below.

2.2 Multiple kernel learning

Kernel learning (KL) is an approach for nonparametric classification and regression that can be used for predicting $\mathbf{t}$ based on $\mathbf{X}$ and $\mathbf{Y}$ [14]. First, for simplicity, assume that we want to predict $\mathbf{t}$ based on $\mathbf{X}$. KL posits the following relation between $\mathbf{t}$ and $\mathbf{X}$

$$t_i = \alpha_0 + \sum_{j=1}^{N} \alpha_j \mathbf{K}(\mathbf{x}_j, \mathbf{x}_i|\sigma^2) + \epsilon_i \Rightarrow \mathbf{t} = \mathbf{K}^T\boldsymbol{\alpha} + \boldsymbol{\epsilon}, \quad (4)$$

where σ^2 is a kernel-specific "bandwidth" parameter and depends on the choice of kernel, $K(\bullet)$ (detailed later in the section) and $\boldsymbol{\epsilon} = (\epsilon_1, \ldots, \epsilon_N)$ is the (white-noise) error. The primary parameter of interest is $\boldsymbol{\alpha} = (\alpha_0, \ldots, \alpha_N)^T$, and $\alpha_1, \ldots, \alpha_N$ correspond to weights assigned to the features for N $\mathbf{x}_j$'s. Support Vector Machine (SVM) and Relevance Vector Machine (RVM) are canonical examples of KL [14]. We prefer RVM because of its probabilistic interpretation and other optimal properties compared to those of SVM [15]. There are cases, however, where one feature matrix may not fit the data well. Based on this observation, Multiple Kernel Learning (MKL) extends (4) and replaces $\mathbf{K}$ by a weighted average of L feature matrices $\{\mathbf{K}_l\}_{l=1}^L$,

$$\begin{aligned} t_i &= \alpha_0 + \sum_{j=1}^{N} \alpha_j \sum_{l=1}^{L} \beta_l \mathbf{K}_l(\mathbf{x}_j, \mathbf{x}_i|\sigma_l^2) + \epsilon_i \implies \\ \mathbf{t} &= \beta_1 \mathbf{K}_1^T\boldsymbol{\alpha} + \ldots + \beta_l \mathbf{K}_l^T\boldsymbol{\alpha} + \ldots + \beta_L \mathbf{K}_L^T\boldsymbol{\alpha} + \boldsymbol{\epsilon}. \end{aligned} \quad (5)$$

MKL improves the flexibility of KL by introducing L bandwidth parameters $\{\sigma_l^2\}_{l=1}^L$ and L weights for feature matrices $\boldsymbol{\beta} = (\beta_1, \ldots, \beta_L)^T$. A variety of approaches exist to learn $\{\sigma_l^2\}_{l=1}^L$, $\boldsymbol{\beta}$, and $\boldsymbol{\alpha}$ for MKL (for details see [14,16,17]). Note that in all these works the data source (i.e., $\mathbf{X}$) remains the same for both KL and MKL. The H-RVM framework developed in this article extends KL to include multiple data sources and their interactions, and uses a learning algorithm similar to the MKL framework.

Because the three data sources (gene expressions, miRNA expressions, and their interactions) can be used separately for predicting the log survival time, it is reasonable to combine their predictions to obtain more reliable estimates. To this end, H-RVM combines respective predictions obtained from different sources obtained using KL (4) through a weighted average, and chooses appropriate weights using MKL (5). Similar to (4), $\mathbf{K}_1^T\boldsymbol{\alpha}, \mathbf{K}_2^T\boldsymbol{\alpha}$, and $\mathbf{K}_3^T\boldsymbol{\alpha}$ are the predicted values of $\mathbf{t}$ that correspond to genes, miRNAs, and their interactions, respectively. Using (5), we combine the predictions $\{\mathbf{K}_i^T\boldsymbol{\alpha}\}_{i=1}^3$ through the weight vector $\boldsymbol{\beta} = (\beta_1, \beta_2, \beta_3)$ to model $\mathbf{t}$ as

$$\mathbf{t} = (\beta_1\mathbf{K}_1^T + \beta_2\mathbf{K}_2^T + \beta_3\mathbf{K}_3^T)\boldsymbol{\alpha} + \boldsymbol{\epsilon} = \mathbf{K}_{\boldsymbol{\beta}}^T\boldsymbol{\alpha} + \boldsymbol{\epsilon}. \quad (6)$$

We further constrain $\boldsymbol{\beta}$ such that its components lie on a probability simplex, i.e., $\sum_{m=1}^3 \beta_m = 1$. This constraint ensures that the joint (convolved) kernel, $\mathbf{K}_{\boldsymbol{\beta}}$, is positive definite and that β_m denotes the influence of the m-th source in predicting the log survival time. Note that H-RVM is a special case of (3) with $f_{\mathbf{X}}(\mathbf{x}_i, \boldsymbol{\alpha}) \equiv \mathbf{k}_{1,i}^T\boldsymbol{\alpha}$, $f_{\mathbf{Y}}(\mathbf{y}_i, \boldsymbol{\alpha}) \equiv \mathbf{k}_{2,i}^T\boldsymbol{\alpha}$, and $f_{(\mathbf{X}\otimes\mathbf{Y})}((\mathbf{x}\otimes\mathbf{y})_i, \boldsymbol{\alpha}) \equiv \mathbf{k}_{3,i}^T\boldsymbol{\alpha}$, where $\mathbf{k}_{m,i}$ is the i-th column of $\mathbf{K}_m$. Given $\{\mathbf{K}_i\}_{i=1}^3$, MKL can be used to learn $\boldsymbol{\alpha}$ and $\boldsymbol{\beta}$.

Although similar to (5), (6) differs in two important ways. First, (6) obtains kernels using (4) for different data sources, namely gene expression, miRNA expression, and their interaction. Second, we allow for dependence between data sources via the interaction kernel ($\mathbf{K}_3$), but MKL does not; instead MKL uses a convex combination of the different kernels from the same data source to aid prediction.

The learning algorithm of H-RVM is independent of the choice of kernels, but in this work we use a Gaussian radial basis function (RBF) kernel (denoted by $\mathbf{K}$) [14]. The RBF kernel maps the m-th high-dimensional covariate to its feature space that is represented as feature matrix $\mathbf{K}_m$. The feature matrices $\mathbf{K}_1, \mathbf{K}_2$, and $\mathbf{K}_3$ correspond to genes, miRNAs, and interactions, and their (i,j)-th entries are as follows:

$$\begin{aligned} (\mathbf{K}_1)_{ij} &= e^{-\frac{\|\mathbf{x}_i - \mathbf{x}_j\|^2}{2\sigma_1^2}} = \mathbf{K}(\mathbf{x}_i, \mathbf{x}_j|\sigma_1^2), \\ (\mathbf{K}_2)_{ij} &= e^{-\frac{\|\mathbf{y}_i - \mathbf{y}_j\|^2}{2\sigma_2^2}} = \mathbf{K}(\mathbf{y}_i, \mathbf{y}_j|\sigma_2^2), \\ (\mathbf{K}_3)_{ij} &= e^{-\frac{\|(\mathbf{x}\otimes\mathbf{y})_i - (\mathbf{x}\otimes\mathbf{y})_j\|^2}{2\sigma_3^2}} = \mathbf{K}((\mathbf{x}\otimes\mathbf{y})_i, (\mathbf{x}\otimes\mathbf{y})_j|\sigma_3^2), \end{aligned} \quad (7)$$

where σ_m^2 is the "bandwidth" parameter of the m-th kernel matrix and is chosen *a priori* through cross-validation (see [14] for details). The other choices of kernels include polynomial kernels and matern kernels [18]. To account for the overall mean (or intercept) in (1), an extra row of 1's is appended to the feature matrices in (7); therefore, $\{\mathbf{K}_i\}_{i=1}^3$ hereafter have dimensions $(N+1) \times N$.

2.3 Generative Bayesian model for H-RVM

H-RVM reformulates (6) as a hierarchical Bayesian model for greater flexibility and better interpretation of its parameters. This reformulation serves two important purposes. First, H-RVM is interpreted as a hierarchical Bayesian extension of RVM [15], which is a special case of Bayesian KL. Second, instead of using MKL methods, H-RVM learns parameters $\boldsymbol{\alpha}$ and $\boldsymbol{\beta}$ from $\mathbf{t}$, $\mathbf{X}$, and $\mathbf{Y}$ using the variational learning algorithm of hierarchical kernel learning (HKL) [14,16].

H-RVM posits the following generative model for the (noisy) log survival time measurements $\mathbf{t}$. Similar to MKL, $\mathbf{K}_{\boldsymbol{\beta}}^T\boldsymbol{\alpha}$ represents the mean of $\mathbf{t}$. The error distribution is Gaussian with mean 0 and precision parameter γ (8). Further, we impose a Gamma prior on γ such that

$$\mathbf{t}|\boldsymbol{\alpha}, \boldsymbol{\beta}, \gamma, \mathbf{X}, \mathbf{Y} \sim \mathcal{N}(\mathbf{t}|\mathbf{K}_{\boldsymbol{\beta}}^T\boldsymbol{\alpha}, \gamma^{-1}\mathbf{I}), \quad (8)$$

$$\gamma \sim \text{Gamma}(\gamma|c_\gamma, d_\gamma), \quad (9)$$

where $\mathcal{N}(.|\boldsymbol{\mu}, \boldsymbol{\Sigma})$ represents a multivariate Gaussian distribution with mean $\boldsymbol{\mu}$ and covariance matrix $\boldsymbol{\Sigma}$ and Gamma$(.|c_{\bullet}, d_{\bullet})$ represents a Gamma distribution with respective shape and rate parameters $c_{\bullet}$ and $d_{\bullet}$.

Motivated by the "automatic relevance determination" idea of RVM, we impose independent Gaussian priors on the α_j's with the same mean 0 and different precision parameters ϕ_j's (10), where ϕ_j controls (*a priori*) predictive power of the j-th feature vector from the three data sources for the log survival time. A large ϕ_j indicates low predictive power. We also impose independent Gamma priors on the ϕ_j's,

$$\boldsymbol{\alpha}|\boldsymbol{\phi} \sim \mathcal{N}(\boldsymbol{\alpha}|\mathbf{0}, diag(\boldsymbol{\phi}^{-1})), \tag{10}$$

$$\boldsymbol{\phi} \sim \prod_{j=0}^{N} \text{Gamma}(\phi_j|c_{\phi}, d_{\phi}), \tag{11}$$

where $\boldsymbol{\phi} = (\phi_0, \phi_1, \ldots, \phi_n)$. This setting forces many α_j's *a posteriori* to be near 0 with high precision. Most of the variance in $\mathbf{t}$ is explained by a small number of feature vectors that correspond to nonzero α_j's. These feature vectors are the "relevance vectors" of H-RVM that have the following three characteristics: they prevent over-fitting, represent a parsimonious description of the data, and correspond to feature vectors that are most predictive of the log survival time. An equivalent prior setting is found by marginalizing the ϕ_j's from the joint distribution of $\boldsymbol{\alpha}$ and $\boldsymbol{\phi}$ above, which imposes a multivariate Student's t prior on $\boldsymbol{\alpha}$ with mean $\mathbf{0}$.

Finally, we impose a Dirichlet prior on $\boldsymbol{\beta}$ to ensure that its components lie on a probability simplex:

$$\boldsymbol{\beta} = (\beta_1, \beta_2, \beta_3) \sim \text{Dirichlet}(\boldsymbol{\beta}|a_1, a_2, a_3), \tag{12}$$

where the m-th component of $\boldsymbol{\beta}$, β_m, denotes the influence of m-th source in predicting the log survival time.

The hierarchical Bayesian model (8) – (12) specifies a complete sampling model for the H-RVM framework. It can also be interpreted as a probabilistic approach for combining the predictions of log survival times from the three RVMs respectively corresponding to gene expressions, miRNA expressions, and their interactions. H-RVM introduces an additional hierarchy and combines the predictions of these three RVMs as a weighted average, with the weights generated from a Dirichlet distribution (12). The increased flexibility of H-RVM over RVM comes at the cost of analytic intractability of the posterior distributions of the H-RVM parameters. Estimation of the posterior distributions of the H-RVM's parameters can proceed via either simulation-based Markov chain Monte Carlo (MCMC) approaches or deterministic variational Bayes approaches. Given the complexity and size of high-throughput data in general and GBM data in particular, MCMC approaches tend to be computationally expensive and slow. We employ variational Bayes methods from HKL [16] and obtain the analytically tractable variational posterior distribution, $q(\boldsymbol{\alpha}, \boldsymbol{\beta}, \boldsymbol{\phi}, \gamma|\mathbf{t}, \mathbf{X}, \mathbf{Y}, c_{\phi}, d_{\phi}, c_{\gamma}, d_{\gamma}, a_1, a_2, a_3)$, that approximates analytically intractable true posterior distribution, $p(\boldsymbol{\alpha}, \boldsymbol{\beta}, \boldsymbol{\phi}, \gamma|\mathbf{t}, \mathbf{X}, \mathbf{Y}, c_{\phi}, d_{\phi}, c_{\gamma}, d_{\gamma}, a_1, a_2, a_3)$. This approximation achieves analytic tractability by assuming that $\boldsymbol{\alpha}, \boldsymbol{\beta}, \boldsymbol{\phi}$, and γ are independent under the variational posterior distribution. The analytic tractability leads to improved computational efficiency of the variational Bayes approach over sampling-based MCMC approaches. The derivations for variational posterior distributions are provided in Appendix A.

3 Data analysis

We apply the H-RVM approach to the GBM data as introduced in Section 1. GBM was one of the first cancers evaluated by the TCGA. GBM data have multiple molecular measurements on over 500 samples that include gene expression, copy number, methylation and microRNA expression. TCGA datasets are available at http://tcga-data.nci.nih.gov/tcga/. The dataset we analyze here includes information about the gene expressions (11972 probes), miRNA expressions (534 probes), and (uncensored) survival times for matched patient samples (248).

To remove the irrelevant noise variables before model fitting, we prescreened the gene and miRNA probes as follows. We performed univariate regression of the log survival times on the gene expression values, obtained p-values, and retained gene and miRNA probes that cross a liberal p-value threshold ($\leq$ 0.05 here) – to balance the practical and statistical significance. This pre-selection identifies 1747 and 43 gene expression and miRNA probes, respectively, for downstream modeling. All our analyses and comparisons were based on these selected gene and miRNA probes.

We compare the predictions of H-RVM and three linear methods: penalized regressions (2) with the Lasso penalty [13] and with the following covariates: *i.* gene expressions (Gene-Lasso), *ii.* miRNA expressions (MiRNA-Lasso), and *iii.* both gene and miRNA expressions, and their first order interactions (Interaction-Lasso). We randomly split the GBM survival data into a training data and a test data with 223 (90%) and 25 (10%) patients, respectively. H-RVM, Gene-Lasso, MiRNA-Lasso, and Interaction Lasso are fit using the gene and miRNA expressions and log survival times in the training data. The variational inference algorithm is used for fitting H-RVM (see Appendix A). The R package `glmnet` is used for the three penalized linear regressions [19,20]. The log survival times of the test data are predicted for the four methods using the model fits on the training data. The mean squared prediction errors (MSPEs) are respectively calculated for the four models as the average of the squared difference between the observed and predicted values for the test data. This process of randomly splitting the GBM survival data into training+test data and fitting the four models is repeated 50 times. The results are summarized below.

Figure 1 shows the prediction results for H-RVM, Gene-Lasso, MiRNA-Lasso, and Interaction-Lasso using the kernel density estimates (KDEs) of the MSPEs for the 50 random splits. The KDEs of the MSPEs for H-RVM is shifted to lower values than those for the three penalized linear regressions. The KDEs of the MSPEs for Gene-Lasso, MiRNA-Lasso, and Interaction-Lasso are close to each other, which implies that the MSPEs for these models are fairly similar. Two observations arise from these results. First, the results indicate that penalized linear regression with the Lasso penalty does not lead to improved performance after accounting for interactions among covariates, which has been well-established in literature [19]. Second, the prediction results of the penalized linear regressions do not improve after modeling the first order interactions among genes and miRNAs, thus indicating the presence of non-linear genomic effects and second or higher order interactions among them. For this case study, we see that H-RVM performs better than the penalized linear regression methods. This may be because of H-RVM accounts for the nonlinear effects of genes and miRNAs and models the interactions within genes, within miRNAs, and between genes and miRNAs. Further, because we model the log survival time, the gain for survival time predictions is, in fact, *exponentially higher* for H-RVM compared to those for the other methods.

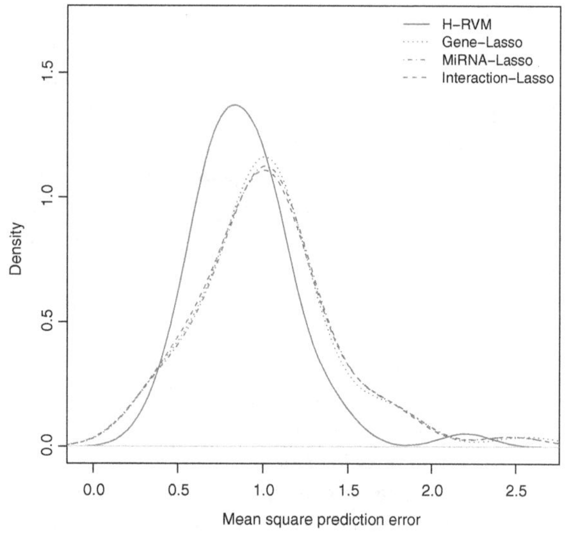

Figure 1 Kernel density estimates. Kernel density estimates (KDEs) of mean square prediction errors (MSPEs) for H-RVM, Gene-Lasso, MiRNA-Lasso, and Interaction-Lasso. The GBM survival data is randomly split 50 times into training and test data, all four models are fit on the training data, and MSPEs for log survival times are calculated for the test data using the model fit on training data. The x-axis represents the MSPEs and the y-axis represents the respective KDEs for H-RVM (in solid red), Gene-Lasso (in dotted blue), MiRNA-Lasso (in dotted and dashed blue), and Interaction-Lasso (in dashed blue).

We compared the performance of the predictions of the log survival times from H-RVM and the observed survival times using Kaplan-Meier estimates of the survival curves. We used the R package `survival` to perform the log rank test and estimate the Kaplan-Meier survival curves [21]. Figure 2 compares the survival probability curves of the log survival times of patients predicted to be in the long and short survival groups by H-RVM. The patients are assigned to the long and short survival groups based on a median cut-off of the predicted log survival times obtained from H-RVM. The p-value of the log rank test that the two survival curves are the same is close to 0, indicating that the survival group predictions of H-RVM closely agree with the observed survival groups of the patients. In addition, Figure 3 compares the actual survival probability curves of the observed and predicted log survival times of patients in the test data with the minimum MSPE. The p-values and the survival probability curves indicate that the log survival time predictions of H-RVM agree closely agree with the observed log survival times, as well.

One of the additional gains of our modeling framework is the determination of which platform has a more profound influence on predicting the response, as captured by the weight parameter $\boldsymbol{\beta}$. Figure 4 shows the estimates of the weights $\boldsymbol{\beta}$ for predicting the log survival time of the patients for gene expression, miRNA expressions, and their interactions obtained from H-RVM. The medians of the weights (25% and 75% quartiles) for the three data sources are 0.239 (0.113 and 0.360), 0.504 (0.408 and 0.583), and 0.201 (0.108 and 0.404), respectively. Interestingly, H-RVM shows that miRNAs have better predictive power than genes in predicting the log survival times of patients in the GBM data. The nonzero weight for interactions between gene and miRNA expressions further confirms the presence of nonlinear interactions.

To gain biological insights into our results, we performed a functional analysis of our model fitting results. We used Ingenuity Pathway Analysis software to perform functional analysis on selected significant genes used in fitting H-RVM. We used targetHub [22] to find the known and predicted interactions between significant genes and miRNAs. mirTarBase, a curated database of experimentally validated miRNA targets, was our choice as a source of known gene and miRNA interactions [23]. To identify the predicted gene and miRNA interactions, we used targetScan data [24] to filter out miRNA-gene interactions

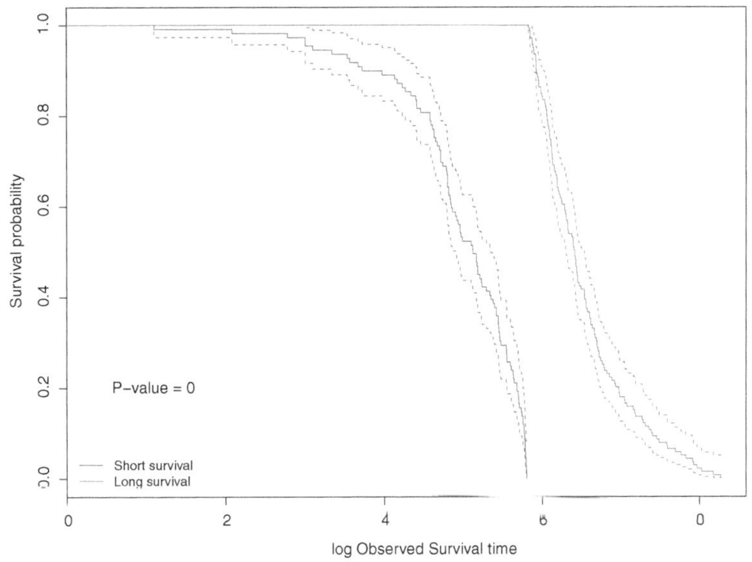

Figure 2 Survival probability curves for TCGA data. Survival probability curves for log survival time in the TCGA GBM data. The solid lines are the Kaplan-Meier estimates of survival probabilities for the patients predicted to have long survival times (in blue) and for the patients predicted to have short survival times (in red), respectively. The patients are assigned to the long and short survival groups based on the estimates of log survival times obtained from H-RVM. The dotted lines indicate point-wise 95% confidence intervals for the survival probabilities. The p-value of the log rank test is 0.

in which the miRNA and gene effects on survival were concordant, since discordant behavior is expected in biological systems for a direct interaction between miRNA and its targets.

Pathway analyses indicates that the anti-survival genes (i.e., genes with negative effects on survival times) are enriched with signaling pathways related to tumor invasion (see Figure 5). HMGB1 and TWEAK signaling pathways, which are known to drive tumor metastasis and severe inflammatory responses in GBM and other cancers, are associated with these genes [25-28]. Pro-survival genes are represented by PDGF, PTEN and other signaling pathways. It is well-established that the PDGF signaling pathway dominates the proneural subgroup, which correlates with a good survival time for patients with GBM [29]. The functional terms cellular movement

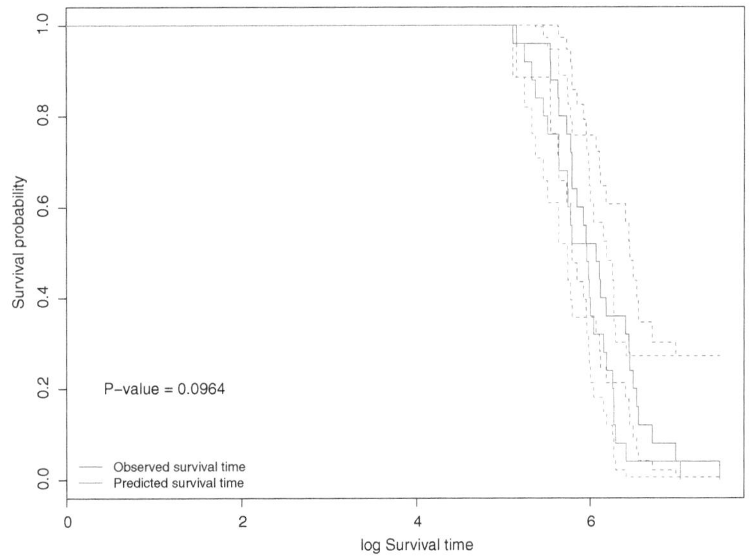

Figure 3 True and predicted survival probability curves. Survival probability curves for the observed log survival time and predicted log survival time (using H-RVM) of the patients in the test data with minimum mean square prediction error. The solid lines are the Kaplan-Meier estimates of survival probabilities for the predicted (in blue) and observed (in red) log survival times in the test data. The dotted lines indicate point-wise 95% confidence intervals for the survival probabilities. The p-value of the log rank test is 0.0964.

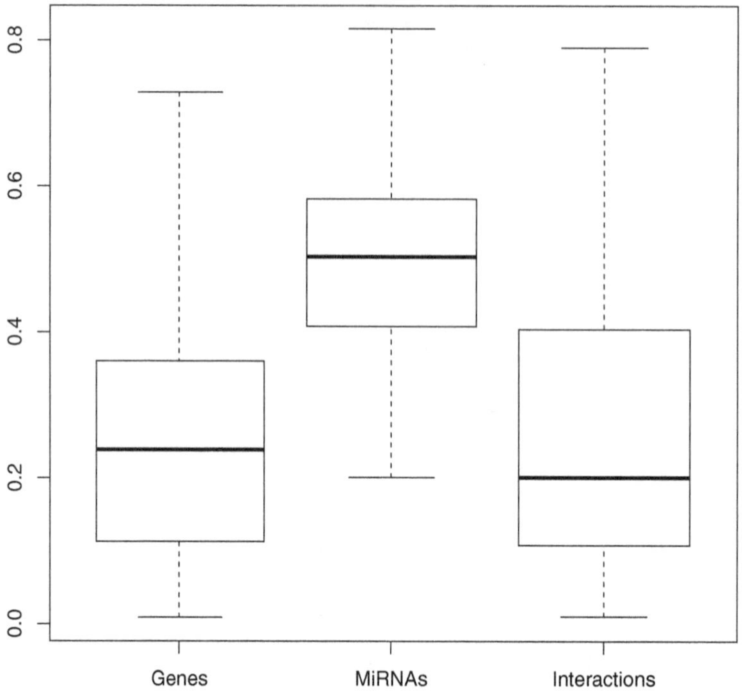

Figure 4 Boxplots of weights. Boxplots of weights $\boldsymbol{\beta} = (\beta_1, \beta_2, \beta_3)$ of gene expressions, miRNA expressions, and their interactions in predicting log survival time. The GBM survival data is randomly split 50 times into training and test data, H-RVM is fit on the training data, and $\boldsymbol{\beta}$ is obtained from the fit on training data. The y-axis shows the distributions of respective weights for gene expressions, miRNA expressions, and their interactions in predicting log survival time of patients across 50 random splits of the GBM survival data.

and cell-to-cell signaling and interaction pathways are enriched for anti-survival genes, reinforcing their role in invasive GBM.

The target analysis of miRNA revealed 22 known interactions between 8 miRNAs and 20 genes, as shown in Table 1. Four of these eight miRNAs (hsa-miR-31, hsa-miR-146b, hsa-miR-221 and hsa-miR-222) were previously identified as anti-survival markers of GBM [30]. Mir-21 is an established marker of GBM and is known to target many tumor suppressor genes [31]. Mir-34a expression is higher in other GBM subtypes compared to that in the pro-survival proneural glioma subtype [32]. The anti-survival patterns of all these miRNAs indicate that these gene and miRNA interactions can be targeted for therapy of GBM subgroups with expected poor survival. We also identified 1006 predicted interactions

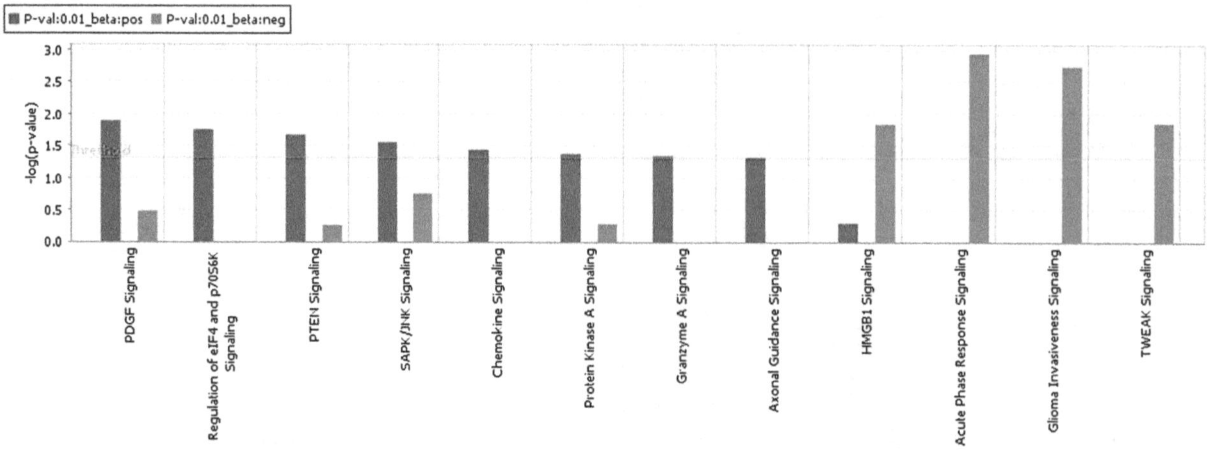

Figure 5 Comparison of the signaling pathways. Comparison of the signaling pathways associated with significant prognostic genes in Glioblastoma multiforme.

Table 1 List of known gene-microRNA interactions identified as significant in the H-RVM model using target analysis

Gene symbols	microRNA
FOXP3, YY1, KLF13, ETS1	hsa-mir-31
FOXO3, DDIT4	hsa-mir-221
ATAT1	hsa-mir-23a
FOXO3	hsa-mir-222
FGG , CPEB3, FGB, PIK3R1	hsa-mir-29a
PDGFB	hsa-mir-146b
PDCD4, TOPORS, BASP1, MARCKS, TP53BP2	hsa-mir-21
SIRT1, YY1, E2F3, CDC25C	hsa-mir-34a

(by TargetScan) between 31 miRNA and 484 genes that are significant (see Additional file 1).

4 Conclusions and future work

We have presented an integrative framework, H-RVM, that generalizes the multiple kernel learning framework for integrating high-dimensional data from multiple sources, incorporating within and between platform interactions to develop a prediction model for clinical outcomes. We applied H-RVM to a high-dimensional TCGA GBM data to predict patient survival times using two data sources: gene and miRNA expressions, and found that the predictive performance of H-RVM is better than those of linear methods that do not model nonlinear effects and interactions. We hypothesize that H-RVM gains flexibility and power by modeling the non-linear interaction structures between gene and miRNA expressions. H-RVM will be a useful tool for biomedical researchers, as clinical prediction using multi-platform genomic information is an important step towards identifying personalized treatments for many cancers. We have code for fitting H-RVM that is freely available at the corresponding author's website (see Additional file 2).

Although we have presented the application of H-RVM in the context of two platforms, the framework is general and can be extended and adapted to data from multiple platforms with different distributional assumptions. This will essentially entail a generalization of the H-RVM model by assuming additional terms for the different platforms. One key issue that warrants further investigation is an increase in the number of (multiplicative) between-platform interaction terms. We used the computationally efficient variational Bayes methods, which are extremely useful for handling large datasets from projects such as TCGA. In addition, [17] presents more scalable versions of HKL and MKL that can be adapted to our framework. Our future work will concentrate on extending the H-RVM framework using Bayesian spike and slab priors to select variables from the interacting covariates before embedding the data in the space of kernels, as well as incorporating uncertainty estimations of the scale parameters – thus aiding the joint model building process.

Endnotes

[a] We use gene and mRNA interchangeably to mean transcript-level expression.

[b] We use bold lowercase and uppercase alphabets to denote column vectors and matrices, respectively.

A Appendix: Variational inference for H-RVM

Following the hierarchic kernel learning algorithm (HKL) of [16], we provide the derivation for the variational inference algorithm that estimates the variational posterior distributions for the parameters of H-RVM. Our interest lies in the posterior distributions of $\boldsymbol{\alpha}$ and $\boldsymbol{\beta}$ that are obtained using the Bayesian model (8) – (12). Unlike RVM, the posterior distributions of $\boldsymbol{\alpha}$ and $\boldsymbol{\beta}$ in H-RVM are analytically intractable. There are several techniques that can be used to obtain these posteriors distributions. We employ the variational Bayes methods from HKL [16] and obtain analytically tractable variational posterior distribution, $q(\boldsymbol{\alpha}, \boldsymbol{\beta}, \boldsymbol{\phi}, \gamma \mid \mathbf{t}, \mathbf{X}, \mathbf{Y}, c_\phi, d_\phi, c_\gamma, d_\gamma, a_1, a_2, a_3)$, that approximates analytically intractable true posterior distribution, $p(\boldsymbol{\alpha}, \boldsymbol{\beta}, \boldsymbol{\phi}, \gamma \mid \mathbf{t}, \mathbf{X}, \mathbf{Y}, c_\phi, d_\phi, c_\gamma, d_\gamma, a_1, a_2, a_3)$. The variational approach minimizes the Kullback-Liebler (KL) divergence between $q(\boldsymbol{\alpha}, \boldsymbol{\beta}, \boldsymbol{\phi}, \gamma \mid \mathbf{t}, \mathbf{X}, \mathbf{Y}, c_\phi, d_\phi, c_\gamma, d_\gamma, a_1, a_2, a_3)$ and $p(\boldsymbol{\alpha}, \boldsymbol{\beta}, \boldsymbol{\phi}, \gamma \mid \mathbf{t}, \mathbf{X}, \mathbf{Y}, c_\phi, d_\phi, c_\gamma, d_\gamma, a_1, a_2, a_3)$. This approximation achieves analytic tractability by assuming that $\boldsymbol{\alpha}, \boldsymbol{\beta}, \boldsymbol{\phi}$, and γ are independent under $q(\boldsymbol{\alpha}, \boldsymbol{\beta}, \boldsymbol{\phi}, \gamma \mid \mathbf{t}, \mathbf{X}, \mathbf{Y}, c_\phi, d_\phi, c_\gamma, d_\gamma, a_1, a_2, a_3)$. Therefore,

$$q(\boldsymbol{\alpha}, \boldsymbol{\beta}, \boldsymbol{\phi}, \gamma \mid \mathbf{t}, \mathbf{X}, \mathbf{Y}, c_\phi, d_\phi, c_\gamma, d_\gamma, a_1, a_2, a_3) = q(\boldsymbol{\alpha})q(\boldsymbol{\beta})q(\boldsymbol{\phi})q(\gamma), \tag{13}$$

where we have suppressed the conditioning on the data and hyperparameters for the variational posteriors on the right. Notice that the factorization (13) alone guarantees the analytic tractability of $q(\boldsymbol{\alpha}, \boldsymbol{\beta}, \boldsymbol{\phi}, \gamma \mid \mathbf{t}, \mathbf{X}, \mathbf{Y}, c_\phi, d_\phi, c_\gamma, d_\gamma, a_1, a_2, a_3)$, and we do not assume any distributional form for the q's. Following [16] and [14], the variational posterior distributions are derived as

$$\log q(\boldsymbol{\alpha}) \propto \mathbb{E}_{\boldsymbol{\beta},\boldsymbol{\phi},\gamma}\left[p(\boldsymbol{\alpha}, \boldsymbol{\beta}, \boldsymbol{\phi}, \gamma, \mathbf{t}, \mathbf{X}, \mathbf{Y} \mid c_\phi, d_\phi, c_\gamma, d_\gamma, a_1, a_2, a_3)\right], \tag{14}$$

$$\log q(\boldsymbol{\beta}) \propto \mathbb{E}_{\boldsymbol{\alpha},\boldsymbol{\phi},\gamma}\left[p(\boldsymbol{\alpha}, \boldsymbol{\beta}, \boldsymbol{\phi}, \gamma, \mathbf{t}, \mathbf{X}, \mathbf{Y} \mid c_\phi, d_\phi, c_\gamma, d_\gamma, a_1, a_2, a_3)\right], \tag{15}$$

$$\log q(\boldsymbol{\phi}) \propto \mathbb{E}_{\boldsymbol{\alpha},\boldsymbol{\beta},\gamma}\left[p(\boldsymbol{\alpha}, \boldsymbol{\beta}, \boldsymbol{\phi}, \gamma, \mathbf{t}, \mathbf{X}, \mathbf{Y} \mid c_\phi, d_\phi, c_\gamma, d_\gamma, a_1, a_2, a_3)\right], \tag{16}$$

$$\log q(\gamma) \propto \mathbb{E}_{\boldsymbol{\alpha},\boldsymbol{\beta},\boldsymbol{\phi}}\left[p(\boldsymbol{\alpha}, \boldsymbol{\beta}, \boldsymbol{\phi}, \gamma, \mathbf{t}, \mathbf{X}, \mathbf{Y} \mid c_\phi, d_\phi, c_\gamma, d_\gamma, a_1, a_2, a_3)\right], \tag{17}$$

where all expectations are with respect to the variational posterior distributions. Hereafter, we will denote $\mathbb{E}_\bullet[f]$ as $\langle f \rangle_\bullet$ for notational simplicity.

Following [16] and using (14), the variational posterior distribution of $\boldsymbol{\alpha}$,

$$q(\boldsymbol{\alpha}) = \mathcal{N}(\boldsymbol{\mu}_\alpha, \Sigma_\alpha);$$
$$\Sigma_\alpha = \left[\langle\gamma\rangle_\gamma \langle \mathbf{K}_\beta \mathbf{K}_\beta^T \rangle_\beta + diag(\langle \boldsymbol{\phi} \rangle_\phi)\right]^{-1}, \quad (18)$$
$$\boldsymbol{\mu}_\alpha = \langle\gamma\rangle_\gamma \boldsymbol{\Sigma}_\alpha \langle \mathbf{K}_\beta \rangle_\beta \mathbf{t}.$$

Following [16] and using (16), the variational posterior distribution of $\boldsymbol{\phi}$,

$$q(\boldsymbol{\phi}) = \prod_{j=0}^{N} q(\phi_j), \text{where}$$
$$q(\phi_j) = \text{Gamma}\left(\frac{1}{2} + c_\phi, \frac{1}{2}\langle \alpha_i^2 \rangle_\alpha + d_\phi\right), \text{for } j = 1, \ldots, N. \quad (19)$$

Following [16] and using (17), the variational posterior distribution of γ,

$$q(\gamma) = \text{Gamma}\left(\frac{N}{2} + c_\gamma, \frac{1}{2}\langle \|\mathbf{e}\|^2 \rangle_{\alpha,\beta} + d_\gamma\right), \text{where}$$
$$\|\mathbf{e}\|^2 = \|\mathbf{t} - \mathbf{K}_\beta^T \boldsymbol{\alpha}\|^2. \quad (20)$$

All the expectations above are determined using $\langle \boldsymbol{\alpha} \rangle_\alpha$, $\langle \boldsymbol{\alpha}\boldsymbol{\alpha}^T \rangle_\alpha$, $\langle \boldsymbol{\phi} \rangle_\phi$, and $\langle\gamma\rangle_\gamma$, which are available from the distributional forms of $q(\boldsymbol{\alpha})$, $q(\boldsymbol{\phi})$, and $q(\gamma)$ in (18) – (20). Specifically,

$$\langle \boldsymbol{\alpha} \rangle_\alpha = \boldsymbol{\mu}_\alpha, \ \langle \boldsymbol{\alpha}\boldsymbol{\alpha}^T \rangle_\alpha = \Sigma_\alpha + \boldsymbol{\mu}_\alpha \boldsymbol{\mu}_\alpha^T,$$
$$\langle \phi_j \rangle_{\phi_j} = \frac{\frac{1}{2} + c_\phi}{\frac{1}{2}((\Sigma_\alpha)_{jj} + (\boldsymbol{\mu}_\alpha \boldsymbol{\mu}_\alpha^T)_{jj}) + d_\phi},$$
$$\langle\gamma\rangle_\gamma = \frac{\frac{N}{2} + c_\gamma}{\frac{1}{2}\langle \|\mathbf{e}\|^2 \rangle_{\alpha,\beta} + d_\gamma},$$
$$\langle \|\mathbf{e}\|^2 \rangle_{\alpha,\beta} = \sum_{n=1}^{N} t_n^2 - 2\sum_{n=1}^{N} t_n \sum_{m=1}^{3} \langle \beta_m \rangle_\beta \langle \boldsymbol{\alpha}^T \rangle_\alpha \mathbf{k}_{mn} + \sum_{m=1}^{3}\sum_{l=1}^{3} \langle \beta_m \beta_l \rangle_\beta \Omega_{ml},$$
$$\Omega_{ml} = \sum_{n=1}^{N} \mathbf{k}_{mn}^T \langle \boldsymbol{\alpha}\boldsymbol{\alpha}^T \rangle_\alpha \mathbf{k}_{ln}.$$

Instead of $q(\boldsymbol{\beta})$, its non-normalized version $q^*(\boldsymbol{\beta})$ is available from [16] as

$$q^*(\boldsymbol{\beta}) = \prod_{m=1}^{3} \beta_m^{a_m - 1} \exp\left(-\frac{\langle\gamma\rangle_\gamma}{2}(\boldsymbol{\beta}^T \boldsymbol{\Omega} \boldsymbol{\beta} - 2\boldsymbol{\beta}^T \mathbf{b})\right), \text{where}$$
$$\Omega_{ml} = \sum_{n=1}^{N} \mathbf{k}_{mn}^T \langle \boldsymbol{\alpha}\boldsymbol{\alpha}^T \rangle_\alpha \mathbf{k}_{ln}, \text{for } m, l = 1, 2, 3 \text{ and}$$
$$b_m = \langle \boldsymbol{\alpha}^T \rangle_\alpha \mathbf{K}_m \mathbf{t}, \ \text{for } m = 1, 2, 3. \quad (21)$$

Following [16], calculate $\langle \boldsymbol{\beta} \rangle_\beta$, $\langle \log \boldsymbol{\beta} \rangle_\beta$, and $\langle \boldsymbol{\beta}\boldsymbol{\beta}^T \rangle_\beta$, as follows. Sample S $\boldsymbol{\beta}$'s from Dirichlet(a_1, a_2, a_3) and estimate the expectations as $\langle f(\boldsymbol{\beta}) \rangle_\beta \approx \sum_{s=1}^{S} f(\boldsymbol{\beta}_s) w(\boldsymbol{\beta}_s)$ where $f(\boldsymbol{\beta}) \equiv \boldsymbol{\beta}, \log \boldsymbol{\beta}$, and $\boldsymbol{\beta}\boldsymbol{\beta}^T$, respectively, and

$$w(\boldsymbol{\beta}_s) = \frac{\exp\left(-\frac{\langle\gamma\rangle_\gamma}{2}(\boldsymbol{\beta}_s^T \boldsymbol{\Omega} \boldsymbol{\beta}_s - 2\boldsymbol{\beta}_s^T \mathbf{b})\right)}{\sum_{i=1}^{S} \exp\left(-\frac{\langle\gamma\rangle_\gamma}{2}(\boldsymbol{\beta}_i^T \boldsymbol{\Omega} \boldsymbol{\beta}_i - 2\boldsymbol{\beta}_i^T \mathbf{b})\right)}.$$

The analytic tractability of $q(\boldsymbol{\alpha}, \boldsymbol{\beta}, \boldsymbol{\phi}, \gamma \,|\, \mathbf{t}, \mathbf{X}, \mathbf{Y}, c_\phi, d_\phi, c_\gamma, d_\gamma, a_1, a_2, a_3)$ in variational inference guarantees that the marginal variational distribution (or likelihood) of the data $q(\mathbf{t}, \mathbf{X}, \mathbf{Y} | c_\phi, d_\phi, c_\gamma, d_\gamma, a_1, a_2, a_3)$ is also analytically tractable. Estimate hyperparameters $c_\phi, d_\phi, c_\gamma, d_\gamma, a_1, a_2$, and a_3 as

$$\underset{c_\phi, d_\phi, c_\gamma, d_\gamma, a_1, a_2, a_3}{\arg\max} \quad \log q(\mathbf{t}, \mathbf{X}, \mathbf{Y} | c_\phi, d_\phi, c_\gamma, d_\gamma, a_1, a_2, a_3),$$

which is the type II maximum likelihood procedure as recommended in [16]. The kernel parameters $\{\sigma_i^2\}_{i=1}^3$ are learned respectively from three RVMs for each of the three sources using cross-validation as recommended by [15].

Additional files

Additional file 1: mRNA-miRNA-predicted-interactions.xlsx. Excel file containing all predicted mRNA and microRNA interactions flagged as significant in our analysis. The file is available at: http://odin.mdacc.tmc.edu/~vbaladan/Veera_Home_Page/Software_files/mRNA-miRNA-predicted-interactions.xlsx.

Additional file 2: hrvm-0.1.1.tar.gz. R package for fitting H-RVM available at: http://odin.mdacc.tmc.edu/~vbaladan/Veera_Home_Page/Software_files/hrvm_0.1.1.tar.gz.

Competing interests

The authors declare that they have no competing interests.

Authors' contributions

VB conceived the research. SS and VB worked out the detailed algorithms and derivations. SS implemented the software and conducted the data analysis. WW and VB oversaw the entire research. WW and GM provided the biological insights into the findings. CO provided insights into the predictive analysis. All authors contributed towards writing the manuscript.

Acknowledgements

VB's research is partially supported by NIH grant R01 CA160736; NSF grant IIS-915196 and the Cancer Center Support Grant (CCSG) (P30 CA016672). WW's work is in part funded by 5U24 CA143883-04 and P30 CA016672. CO is supported by NSF grant IIS-914861. The content is solely the responsibility of the authors and does not necessarily represent the official views of the U.S. National Cancer Institute, the National Institutes of Health, or the National Science Foundation. We also thank LeeAnn Chastain for editorial assistance with the manuscript.

Author details

[1]Department of Statistics, Purdue University, 250 N. University Street, West Lafayette, IN 47907, USA. [2]Department of Bioinformatics and Computational Biology, Division of Quantitative Sciences, The University of Texas MD Anderson Cancer Center, 1515 Holcombe Blvd, Unit 1411, Houston, Texas, USA. [3]Department of Computer Science, University of Houston, 4800 Calhoun, Houston, Texas, USA. [4]Department of Biostatistics, Division of Quantitative Sciences, The University of Texas MD Anderson Cancer Center, 1515 Holcombe Blvd, Unit 1411, Houston, Texas, USA.

References

1. L Chin, JN Andersen, PA Futreal, Cancer genomics: from discovery science to personalized medicine. Nature Med. **17**(3), 297–303 (2011)
2. D Witten, R Tibshirani, A framework for feature selection in clustering. J. Am. Stat. Assoc. **105**(490), 713–726 (2010)
3. B Efron, *Large-Scale Inference: Empirical Bayes Methods for Estimation, Testing, and Prediction*. (Cambridge University Press, New York, USA, 2010)
4. M Diehn, C Nardini, M Kuo, Identification of noninvasive imaging surrogates for brain tumor gene-expression modules. Proc. Natl. Acad. Sci. **105**(13), 5213 (2008)
5. W Wang, V Baladandayuthapani, JS Morris, BM Broom, G Manyam, KA Do, iBAG: integrative Bayesian analysis of high-dimensional multiplatform genomics data. Bioinformatics. **29**(2), 149–159 (2013). http://bioinformatics.oxfordjournals.org/content/29/2/149.abstract
6. DM Witten, RJ Tibshirani, *et al*, Extensions of sparse canonical correlation analysis with applications to genomic data. Stat. Appl. Genet. Mol. Biol. **8**, 28 (2009)
7. AA Shabalin, H Tjelmeland, C Fan, CM Perou, AB Nobel, Merging two gene-expression studies via cross-platform normalization. Bioinformatics. **24**(9), 1154–1160 (2008)
8. S Ma, Y Zhang, J Huang, Y Huang, Q Lan, N Rothman, T Zheng, Integrative analysis of cancer prognosis data with multiple subtypes using regularized gradient descent. Genet. Epidemiol. **36**(8), 829–838 (2012). http://dx.doi.org/10.1002/gepi.21669, doi:10.1002/gepi.21669
9. RGx Verhaak, RG Hoadley, CM Perou, DN Hayes, Integrated genomic analysis identifies clinically relevant subtypes of glioblastoma characterized by abnormalities in PDGFRA , IDH1, EGFR , and NF1. Cancer Cell. **17**, 98–110 (2010)
10. MV Iorio, M Ferracin, M Negrini, CM Croce, MicroRNA gene expression deregulation in human breast cancer. Cancer Res. **65**(16), 7065–7070 (2005)
11. P Fasanaro, S Greco, M Ivan, MC Capogrossi, F Martelli, microRNA: emerging therapeutic targets in acute ischemic diseases. Pharmacol. Ther. **125**, 92–104 (2010)
12. W Tang, J Duan, JG Zhang, YP Wang, Subtyping glioblastoma by combining miRNA and mRNA expression data using compressed sensing-based approach. EURASIP J. Bioinformatics Syst. Biol. **2013**, 2 (2013)
13. R Tibshirani, Regression shrinkage selection via the lasso. J. R. Stat. Soc. Ser. B (Methodological). **58**(1), 267–288 (1996)
14. CM Bishop, *Pattern Recognition and Machine Learning*, vol. 4. (Springer, New York, 2006)
15. M Tipping, Sparse Bayesian learning and the relevance vector machine. J. Mach. Learn. Res. **1**, 211–244 (2001)
16. M Girolami, S Rogers, in *Proceedings of the 22nd International Conference on Machine Learning (ICML-05)*. Hierarchic Bayesian models for kernel learning (ACM, New York, USA, Bonn, Germany, 2005), pp. 241–248. http://doi.acm.org/10.1145/1102351.1102382, doi:10.1145/1102351.1102382
17. M Gönen, in *Proceedings of the 29th International Conference on Machine Learning (ICML-12)*, ed. by J Langford, J Pineau. Bayesian efficient multiple kernel learning (Omnipress, Edinburgh, Scotland, 2012), pp. 1–8
18. J Shawe-Taylor, N Cristianini, *Kernel Methods for Pattern Analysis*. (Cambridge university press, New York, USA, 2004)
19. J Friedman, T Hastie, R Tibshirani, Regularization paths for generalized linear models via coordinate descent. J. Stat. Softw. **33**, 1 (2010)
20. R Development Core Team, *R: A Language and Environment for Statistical Computing*. (R Foundation for Statistical Computing, Vienna, 2013). http://www.R-project.org/
21. TM Therneau, *Modeling Survival Data: Extending the Cox Model*. (Springer-Verlag New York, Inc., New York, USA, 2000)
22. targetHub, targetHub (2013). http://app1.bioinformatics.mdanderson.org/tarhub/_design/basic/index.html
23. SD Hsu, FM Lin, WY Wu, C Liang, WC Huang, WL Chan, WT Tsai, GZ Chen, CJ Lee, CM Chiu, *et al*, miRTarBase: a database curates experimentally validated microRNA–target interactions. Nucleic Acids Res. **39**(suppl 1), D163—D169 (2011)
24. RC Friedman, KKH Farh, CB Burge, DP Bartel, Most mammalian mRNAs are conserved targets of microRNAs. Genome Res. **19**, 92–105 (2009)
25. D Tang, R Kang, HJ Zeh, MT Lotze, High-mobility group box 1 and cancer. Biochimica et Biophysica Acta (BBA)-Gene Regul. Mech. **1799**, 131–140 (2010)
26. NL Tran, WS McDonough, BA Savitch, TF Sawyer, JA Winkles, ME Berens, The tumor necrosis factor-like weak inducer of apoptosis (TWEAK)-fibroblast growth factor-inducible 14 (Fn14) signaling system regulates glioma cell survival via NFκB pathway activation and BCL-XL/BCL-W expression. J. Biol. Chem. **280**(5), 3483–3492 (2005)
27. M Huang, S Narita, N Tsuchiya, Z Ma, K Numakura, T Obara, H Tsuruta, M Saito, T Inoue, Y Horikawa, *et al*, Overexpression of Fn14 promotes androgen-independent prostate cancer progression through MMP-9 and correlates with poor treatment outcome. Carcinogenesis. **32**(11), 1589–1596 (2011)
28. L Dai, L Gu, C Ding, L Qiu, W Di, TWEAK promotes ovarian cancer cell metastasis via NF-Î°B pathway activation and VEGF expression. Cancer Lett. **283**(2), 159–167 (2009). http://www.sciencedirect.com/science/article/pii/S0304383509002286
29. JT Huse, E Holland, LM DeAngelis, Glioblastoma: molecular analysis and clinical implications. Ann. Rev. Med. **64**, 59–70 (2012). doi:10.1146/annurev-med-100711-143028
30. S Srinivasan, IRP Patric, K Somasundaram, A ten-microRNA expression signature predicts survival in glioblastoma. PLoS One. **6**(3), e17438 (2011)
31. T Papagiannakopoulos, A Shapiro, KS Kosik, MicroRNA-21 targets a network of key tumor-suppressive pathways in glioblastoma cells. Cancer Res. **68**(19), 8164–8172 (2008)
32. J Silber, A Jacobsen, T Ozawa, G Harinath, A Pedraza, C Sander, EC Holland, JT Huse, miR-34a repression in proneural malignant gliomas upregulates expression of its target PDGFRA and promotes tumorigenesis. PLoS ONE. **7**(3), e33844 (2012). http://dx.doi.org/10.1371

10

A sequential Monte Carlo framework for haplotype inference in CNV/SNP genotype data

Alexandros Iliadis, Dimitris Anastassiou and Xiaodong Wang*

Abstract

Copy number variations (CNVs) are abundant in the human genome. They have been associated with complex traits in genome-wide association studies (GWAS) and expected to continue playing an important role in identifying the etiology of disease phenotypes. As a result of current high throughput whole-genome single-nucleotide polymorphism (SNP) arrays, we currently have datasets that simultaneously have integer copy numbers in CNV regions as well as SNP genotypes. At the same time, haplotypes that have been shown to offer advantages over genotypes in identifying disease traits even though available for SNP genotypes are largely not available for CNV/SNP data due to insufficient computational tools. We introduce a new framework for inferring haplotypes in CNV/SNP data using a sequential Monte Carlo sampling scheme 'Tree-Based Deterministic Sampling CNV' (TDSCNV). We compare our method with polyHap(v2.0), the only currently available software able to perform inference in CNV/SNP genotypes, on datasets of varying number of markers. We have found that both algorithms show similar accuracy but TDSCNV is an order of magnitude faster while scaling linearly with the number of markers and number of individuals and thus could be the method of choice for haplotype inference in such datasets. Our method is implemented in the TDSCNV package which is available for download at www.ee.columbia.edu/~anastas/tdscnv.

Introduction

Copy number variations (CNVs) are a form of a structural genomic variation referring to duplications and deletions of DNA segments larger than 1 kilobase in size. CNVs are abundant in the human genome, and it is estimated that they can occupy as much as 4% to 6%.

Recently, large-scale genome-wide studies have shed light in many aspects and characteristics of CNVs providing unique insights into the origins, mechanisms, formation, and population genetics of CNVs [1-3]. At the same time, CNVs have been associated with complex traits unexplained by recent genome wide association studies (GWAS) [2] and are believed to make a substantial contribution in uncovering the mechanisms and etiology of disease phenotypes that result from complex patterns of inheritance [2,4].

A variety of techniques exist for CNV detection. Initially, experimental studies have been performed primarily by array CGH, but lately due to improved resolution and genome coverage of genotyping arrays, a number of methods have been developed relying on whole-genome single-nucleotide polymorphism (SNP) genotyping arrays which offer a more sensitive approach and are more suitable for high-resolution CNV detection. As a result, there is currently simultaneously information on the integer copy number (CN) genotypes along a CNV region and on SNPs outside these regions, in which we will refer in the following as CNV-SNP genotypes.

For diploid organisms, theoretical and empirical arguments have been made for the use of haplotypes as opposed to genotypes. It has been shown that the study of haplotypes can improve the power of detecting associations with diseases, and a variety of methods exist in the literature that use haplotypes to detect causal relationships between a genetic region and a phenotype. Furthermore, haplotypes enable unique insides in the study of populations and are required for many population genetics analyses. Specifically, methods for inferring selection [5] for studying recombination [6,7] as well as historical migration [8,9] build their subsequent analysis on existing haplotype data.

The statistical determination of haplotype phase from genotype data is thus potentially very valuable if the estimation can be done accurately and has received an increasing

* Correspondence: xw2008@columbia.edu
Department of Electrical Engineering, Center for Computational Biology Bioinformatics and Columbia University, New York, NY 10027, USA

amount of attention over recent years. A number of well-known algorithms have been developed based on coalescent theory [10], imperfect phylogeny [11], Markov chain Monte Carlo [10,12], Gibbs sampler [13], hidden Markov models [14], expectation minimization algorithm [15], etc. However, only recently, this problem has drawn attention when haplotypes are inferred in a CNV-SNP region.

If we focus within a specific CNV region in a sample of individuals and assume that the ploidy is fixed for each individual along the region, then the problem of inferring the haplotypes is identical to the problem of inferring the haplotypes in polyploid organisms or estimating haplotypes from pooling data. A number of algorithms have been proposed for frequency estimation and inference on these settings, and not surprisingly, many have been applied to the associated CNV haplotype inference problem described above.

Apart from the previous scenarios, a number of methodologies have been specifically developed and tailored for CNV data. Kato et al. [16] have developed a methodology MOCSphaser based on the EM algorithm to assign copy numbers in their respective chromosomes in regions that include CN and SNPs. A core limitation of MOCSphaser as described above is that it takes into consideration only the total CN and not the alleles themselves, assigning on each chromosome a raw CN. As a consequence, even though it provides information about the total copies on a chromosome that could be potentially useful, it does not provide information on the diplotypes themselves.

Another algorithm recently proposed by Kato et al. [17], CNVphaser uses an EM approach to perform inference. The core limitation of that method is that the inference is performed within a CNV region and that the ploidy is considered fixed for an individual within the region. To address these problems and thus enabling the phasing of regions where the ploidy of an individual varies along the region and each individual can have different breakpoints, Su et al. [18] suggested polyHap(v2.0) in which they extended the functionality of their original methodology for pooling data [19]. In their study, they discern the phasing within a CNV into non-internal phasing in which the CNV in a chromosome is inferred as a diplotype and internal phasing in which the specific haplotypes comprising the CNV in a chromosome are further identified. We will use these definitions in our current work.

In their algorithm, Su et al. use an HMM methodology that has separate emission states for the internal and non-internal phasing. They treat the transition between states conceptually in a hierarchical two-level model where the first level is for the transition among CN states and the second for the transition among the haplotype states given the CN states. polyHap(v2.0) is the only currently available method that can phase complex CNV regions by allowing arbitrary changes of CN within individuals and along the genomic sequence.

In this paper, we propose a related new sequential Monte Carlo algorithm for haplotype phasing of CNV-SNP data. In our method, samples are processed sequentially and our method scales linearly with the number of samples as well as the number of individuals. We demonstrate that using our methodology, we can achieve state-of-the-art performance while our method is an order of magnitude faster than polyHap (v2.0).

Methods

The structure of this section is as follows. In the beginning of the section, we introduce some notation that we will use throughout the remaining manuscript. In the subsections that follow, we present the modified version of our TDS methodology for the case of CNV-SNP data. For completeness, we develop again our framework in detail as presented in [20,21]. We first present some modeling results for the prior and posterior distributions for the population haplotype frequencies given the observed data. We then present the TDS methodology for the cases of known population frequencies and subsequently extend it to the case of unknown frequencies. In the derivation of the later, we use the previously derived results for the prior and posterior distributions for the haplotype frequencies. We end the exposition of our method by deriving the state update equations for the 'Tree-Based Deterministic Sampling CNV' (TDSCNV) estimator and presenting the modified partition-ligation procedure adjusted for the CNV-SNP dataset scenario. In the end of the section, we describe the procedure for creating the datasets which we have used in the 'Results' section to evaluate our methodology.

Definitions and notation

Suppose we are given a set of CNV-SNP genotypes on L diallelic loci. We denote the two alleles at each locus by 0 and 1. In the following, we will use the counts of allele 1 as the provided measurement for each allele on each sample. In our method, we allow in a specific position a single amplification or deletion. Therefore, if we are within a CNV region in a chromosome, the allele counts could range from 0 to 2 but could range from 0 to 1 outside these regions.

Suppose that we have T individuals and we denote $c_t = \{c_t^1, \ldots, c_t^L\}$ to be the observed genotype of the t-th sample where $c_t^i \in \{0, 1, 2, 3, 4\}$ are the observed counts on the ith position. Suppose also that $C_t = \{c_1, \ldots, c_t\}$ is a set of individuals up to and including individual t and let C denote the full set of individuals.

In terms of haplotypes, we make an initial distinction in the values that alleles take in internal and non-internal phasing. The framework that follows however will be described generically and will be the same in both cases.

For non-internal phasing, our purpose is to infer haplotypic phase on diploid chromosomes as we are interested in the total copies of an allele at a specific position on a chromosome. Therefore, the possible values for an allele at each position are {–,0,1,01,00,11}. On the contrary for internal phasing, we infer haplotypic phase on polyploid chromosomes and the possible alleles at each position are {–,0,1}.

For individual t, we denote the haplotypes occurring in that individual as h_t. In the case of non-internal phasing, $h_t = \{h_{t,1}, h_{t,2}\}$. For internal phasing, $h_t = \{h_{t,1}, \ldots, h_{t,p}\}$, where p is the ploidy of the organism, and $p \in \{1, 2, 3, 4\}$ as in our methodology, we only consider a single deletion or a single amplification. Therefore, for the case of non-internal phasing $h_{t,1}$, $h_{t,2}$ are strings of length L in which $h_{t,i,j} \in \{-, 0, 1, 01, 00, 11\}$ and for internal phasing, $h_{t,i}$ are strings of length L in which $h_{t,i,j} \in \{-, 0, 1\}$.

We further denote $H_t = \{h_1, \ldots, h_t\}$, similarly to C_t as the set of haplotypes for each individual up to and including individual t.

Let us also define $z = \{z_1, \ldots, z_M\}$ as the set containing all haplotype vectors of length L that are consistent with any genotype in the set C. To obtain Z from the given dataset C, we first enumerate for each c_i the subset $\psi_i = \{h_i^1, \ldots, h_i^Y\}$ $i = 1,\ldots,T$ that contains all possible haplotype assignments which are consistent with c_i. The set Z is then given simply as $Z = \mathrm{U}_{i=1}^{T}\psi_i$. A set of population haplotype frequencies $\theta = \{\theta_1, \ldots, \theta_M\}$ is also associated with the set Z of all possible haplotype vectors, where θ_m is the probability with which the haplotype z_m occurs in the total population. We note here once again that we have given the definitions of Z and θ generically for both internal and not internal phasing, respectively.

Prior and posterior distribution for θ

Assuming random mating in the population, it is clear that the number of each unique haplotype in H is drawn from a multinomial distribution based on the haplotype frequency θ [22]. This leads us to the use of the Dirichlet distribution as the prior distribution for θ so that $\theta \sim D(\rho_1, \ldots, \rho_M)$. It is well known in Bayesian statistics that the Dirichlet distribution is the conjugate prior of the multinomial distribution. This implies in our case that if we assume that the prior distribution for θ is Dirichlet and we draw haplotypes based on their frequencies (multinomial distribution), then the posterior distribution for θ is again a Dirichlet distribution. We prove this fact below.

$$\begin{aligned} p(\theta|C_t, H_t, Z) &\propto p(c_t|h_t = (h_{t,1}, \ldots, h_{t,p}), \theta, C_{t-1}, H_{t-1})p \\ &\times (h_t = (h_{t,1}, \ldots, h_{t,p})|\theta, C_{t-1}, H_{t-1}, Z)p(\theta|C_{t-1}, H_{t-1}) \\ &\propto p(h_t = (h_{t,1}, \ldots, h_{t,p})|\theta, Z)p(\theta|C_{t-1}, H_{t-1}, Z) \\ &\propto \prod_{i=1}^{p}\theta_{h_{t,i}}\prod_{m=1}^{M}\theta_m^{\rho_m(t-1)-1} \propto \prod_{m=1}^{M}\theta_m^{\rho_m(t-1)-1+\sum_{i=1}^{p}I(z_m-h_{t,i})} \\ &\propto D\left(\rho_1(t-1) + \sum_{i=1}^{p}I(z_1-h_{t,i}), \ldots, \rho_M(t-1) + \sum_{i=1}^{p}I(z_M-h_{t,i})\right) \end{aligned} \tag{1}$$

where we denote $\rho_m(t)$ $m = 1,\ldots,M$ as the parameters of the distribution of θ after the t-th pool and $I(z_m - h_{t,i})$ is the indicator function which equals 1 when $z_m - h_{t,i}$ is a vector of zeros, and 0 otherwise. We note here once again that the number of haplotypes (i.e., the index p in the assignment) depends on the phasing and is 2 for non-internal phasing while it ranges for internal phasing. Furthermore, in the previous calculations for θ, for each genotype vector, we only consider haplotype configurations that are consistent with that genotype.

We have shown that the posterior distribution for θ is also Dirichlet with parameters as given in (1) and depends only on the sufficient statistics, $T_t = \{\rho_m(t), 1 \le m \le M\}$ which can be easily updated based on T_{t-1}, h_t, c_t as given by (1) i.e., $T_t = T_t(T_{t-1}, h_t, c_t)$.

TDS estimator with known system parameters θ

Similar to traditional sequential Monte Carlo (SMC) methods, we assume that by the time we have processed genotype c_{t-1}, we have a set of K potential solution streams (commonly termed as 'particles') $H_{t-1}^{(k)}$ $(k = 1, \ldots, K)$ each associated with its corresponding weight $w_{t-1}^{(k)}$, as $\{(H_{t-1}^{(k)}|w_{t-1}^{(k)}), k = 1, \ldots, K\}$.

At point t-1, we approximate the real continuous distribution $p(H_{t-1}|C_{t-1})$ as a discrete distribution as follows:

$$\hat{p}(H_{t-1}|C_{t-1}) = \frac{1}{W_{t-1}}\sum_{k=1}^{K}w_{t-1}^{(k)}I(H_{t-1}-H_{t-1}^{(k)}) \tag{2}$$

where $W_{t-1} = \sum_{k=1}^{K}w_{t-1}^{(k)}$,

and $I(\bullet)$ is the indicator function such that $I(x - y) = 1$ for $x = y$ and $I(x - y) = 0$ otherwise.

Processing the next individual t, we would like to make an online inference of the haplotypes H_t based on the genotypes C_t. From Bayes' theorem, we have $p_\theta(H_t|C_t) \propto p_\theta(c_t|H_t, C_{t-1})p_\theta(H_t|C_{t-1}) \propto p_\theta(c_t|H_t, C_{t-1})p_\theta(h_t|H_{t-1}, C_{t-1})p_\theta(H_{t-1}|C_{t-1}) \propto p_\theta(h_t|H_{t-1}, C_{t-1})p_\theta(H_{t-1}|C_{t-1})$ where for our purposes, we only consider haplotype assignments for individual t that are compatible to its observed genotype.

Assume further that there are K^{ext} such assignments. From previous relationships, if we knew the system parameters θ, we would be able to approximate the distribution of $p_\theta(H_t|C_t)$ as follows:

$$\hat{p}_\theta(H_t|C_t) = \frac{1}{W_t^{ext}} \sum_{k=1}^{K} \sum_{i=1}^{Kext} w_t^{(k,i)} I\left(H_t - \left[H_{t-1}^{(k)}, h_i^{(i)}\right]\right) \quad (3)$$

where $\left[H_{t-1}^{(k)}, h_t^{(i)}\right]$ represents the vector obtained by appending the element $h_t^{(i)}$ to the vector $H_{t-1}^{(k)}$ and $W_t^{ext} = \sum_{i,k} w_t^{(k,i)}$ with

$$w_t^{(k,i)} \propto w_{t-1}^{(k)} p_\theta(c_t|h_t = i) p_\theta(h_t = i|H_{t-1}^{(k)}).$$

TDS estimator with unknown system parameters θ

However, the system parameters are not known. In our model, we use a Dirichlet distribution, as the prior for θ and as shown, we obtain a posterior distribution for θ (given H_t and C_t) that is Dirichlet and only depends on a set of sufficient statistics.

Using Bayes' theorem and similarly to the previous subsection, we have:

$$\begin{aligned} &p_\theta(H_t|C_t, Z) \propto p_\theta(c_t|H_t, C_{t-1}) p_\theta \\ &\times (h_t|H_{t-1}, C_{t-1}) p_\theta(H_{t-1}|C_{t-1}, Z) \propto p_\theta(H_{t-1}|C_{t-1}, Z) p_\theta \\ &\times (c_t|H_t, C_{t-1}) \int p(h_t|H_{t-1}, \theta, Z) p(\theta|T_{t-1}, Z) d\theta \propto p_\theta \\ &\times (H_{t-1}|C_{t-1}, Z) \int p(h_t|H_{t-1}, \theta, Z) p(\theta|T_{t-1}, Z) d\theta \end{aligned} \quad (4)$$

where again we only consider haplotype assignments that are compatible with the observed genotype.

Taking into consideration as argued before that if we know the system parameters θ, then the $p(h_t|H_{t-1}, \theta, Z)$ term represents sampling from a multinomial distribution and that the mean of the Dirichlet distribution with respect to an element θ_k of the vector θ is as follows:

$$E\{\theta_k\} = \frac{\rho_k}{\sum_{j=1}^{M} \rho_j}$$

we have from (4) that:

$$\begin{aligned} &p_\theta(H_t|C_t, Z) \propto p_\theta(H_{t-1}|C_{t-1}, Z) \int p(h_t|H_{t-1}, \theta, Z) p \\ &\times (\theta|T_{t-1}, Z) d\theta \propto p(H_{t-1}|C_{t-1}, Z) \int \Big(\prod_{i=1}^{M} \theta_k^{\sum_{i=1}^{p} I(z_k - h_{t,i})}\Big) p \\ &\times (\theta|T_{t-1}, Z) d\theta \propto p(H_{t-1}|C_{t-1}, Z) \int \Big(\prod_{i=1}^{M} \theta_k^{r_k}\Big) \frac{1}{B(\rho(t-1))} \prod_{i=1}^{M} \theta_i^{\rho_i(t-1)-1} d\theta \propto p \\ &\times (H_{t-1}|C_{t-1}, Z) \frac{B(\rho(t-1)+r)}{B(\rho(t-1))} \int \frac{1}{B(\rho(t-1)+r)} \prod_{i=1}^{M} \theta_i^{\rho_i(t-1)+r_i-1} d\theta \propto p \\ &\times (H_{t-1}|C_{t-1}, Z) \frac{B(\rho(t-1)+r)}{B(\rho(t-1))} \end{aligned} \quad (5)$$

where $r = \left[\sum_{i=1}^{p} I(z_1 - h_{t,i}), \ldots, \sum_{i=1}^{p} I(z_M - h_{t,i})\right]$ and $B(\rho(t-1)) = \frac{\prod_{i=1}^{M} \Gamma(\rho_i(t-1))}{\Gamma\left(\sum_{i=1}^{M} \rho_i(t-1)\right)}$.

Assuming that we have approximated $p(H_{t-1}|C_{t-1})$ as in (2), we can approximate $p(H_t|C_t)$ using (5) as follows:

$$\hat{p}^{ext}(H_t|C_t) = \frac{1}{W_t^{ext}} \sum_{k=1}^{K} \sum_{i=1}^{Kext} w_i^{(k,i)} I\left(H_t - \left[H_{t-1}^{(k)}, \left(h_{t,1}^i, \ldots, h_{t,p}^i\right)\right]\right)$$

where the weight update formula is given by:

$$w_t^{(k,i)} \propto w_{t-1}^{(k)} \frac{\mathrm{B}(\rho^{(\mathrm{k})}(\mathrm{t-1}) + \mathrm{r})}{\mathrm{B}(\rho^{(\mathrm{k})}(\mathrm{t-1}))} \quad (6)$$

where again $r = \left[\sum_{i=1}^{p} I\left(z_1 - h_{t,i}^j\right), \ldots, \sum_{i=1}^{p} I\left(z_M - h_{t,i}^j\right)\right]$ and $\rho^{(k)}(t-1)$ is the parameter vector of the assumed Dirichlet prior which represents how many times we have encountered each haplotype in stream k in the solutions up to individual $t-1$.

Partition-ligation

In the partition phase, the dataset is divided into small segments of consecutive loci and each of the individual blocks is phased separately. To ligate the individual blocks, we have adjusted the original partition-ligation (PL) method for the case of CNV-SNP data.

In our current implementation, to be able to derive all possible solution combinations for each pool genotype efficiently, we have decided to keep the maximum block length to 5 SNPs. Clearly, the more SNPs are included in a block, the more information about the LD patterns we can capture but at the same time, the number of possible combinations increases and becomes prohibitive for more than 5 SNPs. For our experiments in a dataset with L loci, we have considered $L/5$ blocks of 5 consecutive loci and the remaining SNPs were treated as a separate block.

The result of phasing for each block is a set of haplotype solutions for each genotype. Two neighboring blocks are ligated by creating merged solutions for each genotype from combinations of the block solutions, each associated with the product of the individual solution weights called the *ligation weight.*

Depending on which haplotypes one from each block are going to be assigned on the same chromosome for each individual, a different number of changes in the ploidy of that individual will occur. In our method, we consider only the assignments that will produce the minimum number of such changes. Therefore, if both haplotypes in any block have the same CN, we examine both alternative assignments but we otherwise ligate solutions that have the same CN. The TDS algorithm is then repeated in the same manner as it was for the individual blocks with the weights of the solutions scaled by the associated ligation weight for that solution.

Summary of the proposed algorithm

Routine 1:

- Set the current number of solution streams $m = 1$. Define K as the maximum number of solution streams allowed. Define $H_0^1 = \{\}$.
- Find all possible haplotype assignments for each genotype and rearrange the genotypes in ascending order according to the number of distinct haplotype solutions each one of them has.
- For $t = 1, 2, \ldots$
    - Find the K^{ext} possible haplotype configurations compatible with the genotype of the t-th sample.
    - For $k = 1, 2, \ldots, m, j = 1, \ldots, K^{ext}$.
        - Enumerate all possible solution stream extensions $H_t^{(k,j)} = \left[H_{t-1}^{(k)}, \left(h_{t,1}^j, \ldots, h_{t,p}^j\right)\right]$.
        - $\forall j$ compute the weights $w_t^{(k,j)}$ according to (6).
    - Select and preserve $M = min\,(K, m \cdot K^{ext})$ distinct sample streams $\{H_t^{(k)}, k = 1, \ldots, M\}$ with the highest importance weights $\{w_t^{(k)}, k = 1, \ldots, M\}$ from the set $\{H_t^{(k,j)}, w_t^{(k,j)}, k = 1, \ldots, m, j = 1, \ldots, K^{ext}\}$.
    - Update the number of counts of each encountered haplotype in each stream.
    - Set $m = M$.

TDSCNV algorithm

- Partition the genotype dataset C into B subsets.
- For $b = 1, \ldots, B$, apply Routine 1 so that all segments are phased, and for each one, keep all the solutions contained in the top K particles.
- Until all blocks are ligated, repeat the following:
    - Find the blocks that if ligated would produce the minimum entropy.
    - Ligate the blocks, following the procedure described in the Partition-Ligation section.

Dataset creation

Our datasets consisted of SNPs from chromosomes 1 and 2 from HapMap CEU population (HapMap3 release 2 - phasing data). For our purposes, we have considered only the parents in each trio which are the unrelated individuals in our dataset thus resulting in a total of 88 individuals. We have initially filtered out SNPs with minor allele frequencies less than 5%, and we have then considered non-overlapping datasets with a fixed number of SNPs. To create artificial CNV regions within each dataset, we have used the following procedure.

First, in each dataset, we have found all the different haplotypes appearing in the dataset. In order to retain as much of the LD structure and also the property that most of the CNVs could be flagged by neighboring SNPs [2], we have randomly replaced specific areas of randomly chosen haplotypes with a CNV haplotype. To perform that procedure, we randomly selected haplotypes based on their frequency in the population and modified them inserting CNV regions sequentially as follows. Each position was considered as the beginning of a CNV region with a probability of 0.1. For each position flagging the beginning of a CNV, we assigned the length of the CNV region uniformly between three to eight SNPs. We then progressed along the haplotype from the end of the CNV region in a similar fashion until we reached the end of a given haplotype.

Table 1 Switch error rate Switch error rates for non-internal phasing

	Number of markers		
	30	50	100
TDSCNV	0.115	0.127	0.14
polyHap(v2.0)	0.128	0.135	0.138

The switch error rate presented for each number of markers is the average on 100 datasets.

Results

Measurement of phasing accuracy

We have used a number of different measures to evaluate the performance of our methodology. First, the switch error rate [23,24] is defined as the percentage of switches among all possible switches in haplotype orientation used to recover the correct phase in an individual.

In the case of a small number of loci where haplotype vectors can be expected to be reconstructed exactly, we have used two figures of merit namely the χ^2 and l_1 distance to evaluate the accuracy of frequency estimation. Suppose that f are the predicted haplotype frequencies from an algorithm and g are the gold standard population level haplotype frequencies. The χ^2 distance between the two distributions is simply the result of the χ^2 statistic, i.e., $\chi^2(f,g) = \sum_{i=1}^{d} (f_i - g_i)^2 / g_i$ where d is the number of gold standard haplotypes whereas the l_1 distance between the two distributions is defined as $l_1(f,g) = \sum_{i=1}^{d} |f_i - g_i|$ [25].

Switch error rate

We have compared the performance of our method with polyHap(v2.0) for haplotypic phase inference using the switch error rate. In this section, the evaluation was done on non-internal haplotypes. In the evaluation of the switch error rate, we consider only CN and SNP positions that are ambiguous. For a marker genotype to have ambiguous phasing, there should be at least two alternative orientation assignments. As an example, all 3CN genotypes are ambiguous positions. This is easy to see, as the choice alone of the chromosome that would have the duplication creates two distinct possible assignments.

The performance of our method when considering the full set of individuals in each dataset is shown in Table 1. We have considered three marker sizes namely 30, 50, and 100 markers. For each marker size, we have simulated 100 datasets and the result presented is the average error rate on these 100 datasets. We can see that for 30 and 50 markers, our method was marginally better than polyHap(v2.0), whereas for the 100 marker datasets, it was marginally worse.

We further demonstrate the accuracy of our approach when ranging the number of individuals in each dataset. The results for a fixed number of 30 and 50 markers are shown in Figure 1. As expected, the performance for both methods improves with increasing number of individuals per dataset.

Finally, we have broken down and calculated the switch error rates based on the CN of the 'from' and 'to' sites as shown in Table 2. Similarly, to Su et al., we observe the

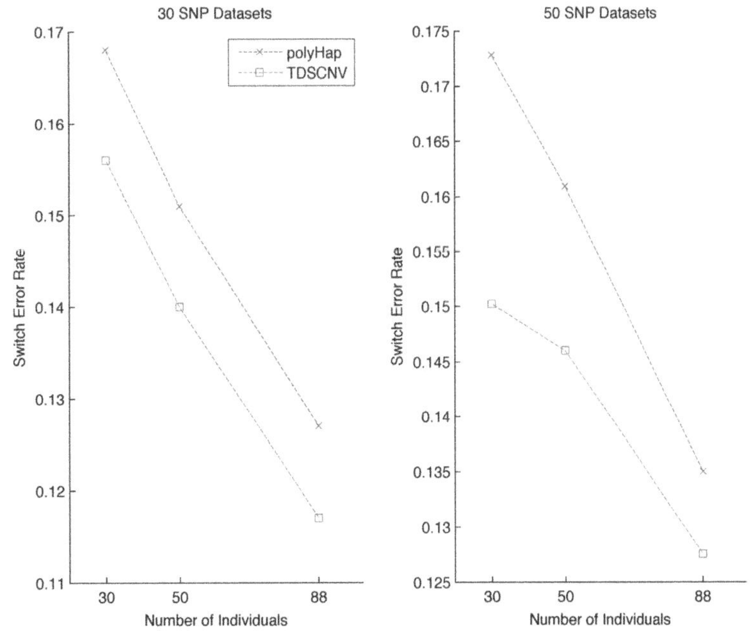

Figure 1 Switch error rate. Estimating the switch error rate for non-internal phasing on datasets having a varying number of individuals with polyHap(v2.0) and TDSCNV.

Table 2 Switch error rate for non-internal phasing according to the CN of the respective consecutive ambiguous markers

	CN on second site	
CN on first site	**1**	**2**
1	0.117	0.227
2	0.229	0.012

Table 3 Timing results

	Number of markers		
	30	**50**	**100**
TDSCNV	2.1	3.7	5.7
polyHap (v2.0)	262.3	431.5	892.1

For each method and each marker size, the computational time is the average time on the 100 datasets used in the switch error rate calculation. Time is given in seconds.

highest switch error rates appearing when the transitions happen between different CNs.

Haplotype frequency estimation

We have examined the accuracy of our method and compared it against polyHap(v2.0) on datasets of 8 and 10 markers in which individuals had a fixed ploidy. We have evaluated two appropriate figures of merit as described above, the χ^2 and l_1 distance. We should note here that in order to determine how good frequency estimations with a given method are, a small number of markers should be used. The reason is that for a large number of markers, it would be unlikely that the exact same haplotypes would appear or reconstructed with appreciable frequency. The results for both figures of merit on an increasing number of individuals are shown in Figure 2. Our method demonstrates superior performance for both figures of merit, and again as expected, both methods produced superior performance with an increasing number of individuals.

Internal phasing

We have further evaluated the performance of our method using the switch error rate inside duplicated regions. In this subsection, the evaluation was done on internal phasing and particularly in duplicated segments of a chromosome as the scope was to detect how good the specific haplotypes comprising the duplicated chromosomal region could be recovered. The switch error rate evaluation within such duplicated regions is exactly the same as the evaluation on a genotype with only SNPs.

We have used the same 100 datasets for each of the three dataset sizes, namely 30, 50, and 100 markers, as in the evaluation of the switch error rate for non-internal phasing described in a previous subsection. We found, as expected, that the results were similar irrespectively of the dataset size, and the average across all datasets was 0.183.

Timing results

The computational times for the 30, 50, and 100 marker datasets used for the calculation of the switch error rate are displayed in Table 3. We can see that TDSCNV is an

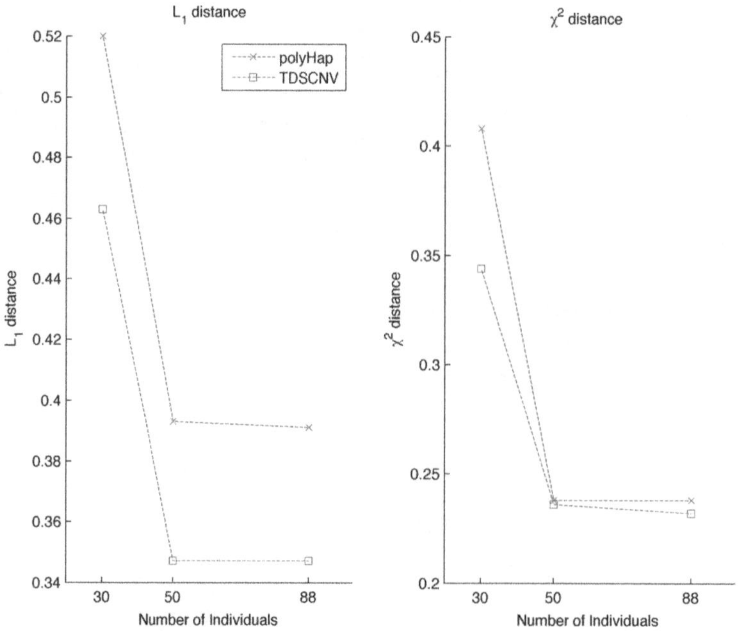

Figure 2 Frequency estimation. Estimating the χ^2 and l_1 distance on datasets having a varying number of individuals with polyHap (v2.0) and TDSCNV.

order of magnitude faster than polyHap(v2.0) for all marker sizes examined.

Discussion

We present an algorithm for haplotypic inference in regions of CNV-SNP genotypes. We compare our method with polyHap(v2.0) on a variety of marker sizes and evaluate the accuracy and computational time of each method. Our method has similar accuracy to polyHap(v2.0) but is an order of magnitude faster in all datasets examined.

In all instances of haplotype inference problems, it becomes increasingly significant that methods are able to incorporate prior knowledge in the form of haplotypes or genotypes from the same population as that from which the target samples were drawn. HapMap is a striking example of such database knowledge that could be used for haplotype inference. Furthermore, it is also important for researchers that samples that are phased at some point in time could be used efficiently for the phasing of samples presented at some later point. Our methodology offers a unique framework that can easily incorporate such prior knowledge. Haplotypes can be introduced in the form of a prior for the counts in the TDSCNV algorithm. From our experience with our framework and as expected, the presence of the extra information will improve the phasing accuracy of the target samples.

Conclusions

In this paper, we propose a new sequential Monte Carlo algorithm for haplotype phasing of CNV-SNP data. In our method, samples are processed sequentially and our method scales linearly with the number of samples as well as the number of individuals.

To demonstrate the performance of our method, we have compared it against polyHap(v2.0), the only currently available software able to perform inference in CNV/SNP genotypes, on datasets of varying number of markers. We have initially compared the accuracy of both methods for haplotypic phase inference on non-internal haplotypes, on datasets of 30, 50, and 100 markers. We have then examined the accuracy of frequency estimation with both methods on datasets with a small number of markers (8 and 10 markers). Finally, we have evaluated the performance of our methodology inside duplicated regions for internal phasing.

We have found that our method demonstrates comparable or better accuracy than polyHap(v2.0) and at the same time is an order of magnitude faster in all datasets and marker sizes examined while scaling linearly with the number of markers and number of individuals. We therefore believe that our method could be the method of choice for haplotype inference in such datasets.

Competing interests

All authors declare they have no competing interests.

References

1. DF Conrad, ME Hurles, The population genetics of structural variation. Nat Genet **39**(7 Suppl), S30–S36 (2007)
2. DF Conrad, D Pinto, R Redon, L Feuk, O Gokcumen, Y Zhang, J Aerts, TD Andrews, C Barnes, P Campbell, T Fitzgerald, M Hu, CH Ihm, K Kristiansson, DG Macarthur, RJ Macdonald, I Onyiah, AW Pang, S Robson, K Stirrups, A Valsesia, K Walter, J Wei, C Tyler-Smith, NP Carter, C Lee, SW Scherer, ME Hurles, The Wellcome Trust Case Control Consortium, Origins and functional impact of copy number variation in the human genome. Nature **464**(7289), 704–712 (2010)
3. R Redon, S Ishikawa, KR Fitch, L Feuk, GH Perry, TD Andrews, H Fiegler, MH Shapero, AR Carson, W Chen, EK Cho, S Dallaire, JL Freeman, JR González, M Gratacòs, J Huang, D Kalaitzopoulos, D Komura, JR MacDonald, CR Marshall, R Mei, L Montgomery, K Nishimura, K Okamura, F Shen, MJ Somerville, J Tchinda, A Valsesia, C Woodwark, F Yang et al., Global variation in copy number in the human genome. Nature **444**(7118), 444–454 (2006)
4. SA McCarroll, DM Altshuler, Copy-number variation and association studies of human disease. Nat Genet **39**(7 Suppl), S37–S42 (2007)
5. PC Sabeti, DE Reich, JM Higgins, HZ Levine, DJ Richter, SF Schaffner, SB Gabriel, JV Platko, NJ Patterson, GJ McDonald, HC Ackerman, SJ Campbell, D Altshuler, R Cooper, D Kwiatkowski, R Ward, ES Lander, Detecting recent positive selection in the human genome from haplotype structure. Nature **419**(6909), 832–837 (2002)
6. P Fearnhead, P Donnelly, Estimating recombination rates from population genetic data. Genetics **159**(3), 1299–1318 (2001)
7. SR Myers, RC Griffiths, Bounds on the minimum number of recombination events in a sample history. Genetics **163**(1), 375–394 (2003)
8. M Bahlo, RC Griffiths, Inference from gene trees in a subdivided population. Theor Popul Biol **57**(2), 79–95 (2000)
9. P Beerli, J Felsenstein, Maximum likelihood estimation of a migration matrix and effective population sizes in n subpopulations by using a coalescent approach. Proc Natl Acad Sci U S A **98**(8), 4563–4568 (2001)
10. M Stephens, P Scheet, Accounting for decay of linkage disequilibrium in haplotype inference and missing-data imputation. Am J Hum Genet **76**(3), 449–462 (2005)
11. E Halperin, E Eskin, Haplotype reconstruction from genotype data using Imperfect Phylogeny. Bioinformatics **20**(12), 1842–1849 (2004)
12. S Lin, A Chakravarti, DJ Cutler, Haplotype and missing data inference in nuclear families. Genome Res **14**(8), 1624–1632 (2004)
13. T Niu, ZS Qin, X Xu, JS Liu, Bayesian haplotype inference for multiple linked single-nucleotide polymorphisms. Am J Hum Genet **70**(1), 157–169 (2002)
14. SR Browning, Missing data imputation and haplotype phase inference for genome-wide association studies. Hum Genet **124**(5), 439–450 (2008)
15. ZS Qin, T Niu, JS Liu, Partition-ligation-expectation-maximization algorithm for haplotype inference with single-nucleotide polymorphisms. Am J Hum Genet **71**(5), 1242–1247 (2002)
16. M Kato, Y Nakamura, T Tsunoda, MOCSphaser: a haplotype inference tool from a mixture of copy number variation and single nucleotide polymorphism data. Bioinformatics **24**(14), 1645–1646 (2008)
17. M Kato, Y Nakamura, T Tsunoda, An algorithm for inferring complex haplotypes in a region of copy-number variation. Am J Hum Genet **83**(2), 157–169 (2008)
18. SY Su, JE Asher, MR Jarvelin, P Froguel, AI Blakemore, DJ Balding, LJ Coin, Inferring combined CNV/SNP haplotypes from genotype data. Bioinformatics **26**(11), 1437–1445 (2010)
19. SY Su, J White, DJ Balding, LJ Coin, Inference of haplotypic phase and missing genotypes in polyploid organisms and variable copy number genomic regions. BMC Bioinform **9**, 513 (2008)
20. A Iliadis, D Anastassiou, X Wang, Fast and accurate haplotype frequency estimation for large haplotype vectors from pooled DNA data. BMC Genet **13**, 94 (2012)
21. A Iliadis, J Watkinson, D Anastassiou, X Wang, A haplotype inference algorithm for trios based on deterministic sampling. BMC Genet **11**, 78 (2010)

22. L Excoffier, M Slatkin, Maximum-likelihood estimation of molecular haplotype frequencies in a diploid population. Mol Biol Evol **12**(5), 921–927 (1995)
23. S Lin, DJ Cutler, ME Zwick, A Chakravarti, Haplotype inference in random population samples. Am J Hum Genet **71**(5), 1129–1137 (2002)
24. J Marchini, D Cutler, N Patterson, M Stephens, E Eskin, E Halperin, S Lin, ZS Qin, HM Munro, GR Abecasis, P Donnelly, International HapMap Consortium, A comparison of phasing algorithms for trios and unrelated individuals. Am J Hum Genet **78**(3), 437–450 (2006)
25. B Kirkpatrick, CS Armendariz, RM Karp, E Halperin, HAPLOPOOL: improving haplotype frequency estimation through DNA pools and phylogenetic modeling. Bioinformatics **23**(22), 3048–3055 (2007)

11

Fastbreak: a tool for analysis and visualization of structural variations in genomic data

Ryan Bressler[1], Jake Lin[1], Andrea Eakin[1], Thomas Robinson[1], Richard Kreisberg[1], Hector Rovira[1], Theo Knijnenburg[1,2], John Boyle[1] and Ilya Shmulevich[1*]

Abstract

Genomic studies are now being undertaken on thousands of samples requiring new computational tools that can rapidly analyze data to identify clinically important features. Inferring structural variations in cancer genomes from mate-paired reads is a combinatorially difficult problem. We introduce *Fastbreak*, a fast and scalable toolkit that enables the analysis and visualization of large amounts of data from projects such as The Cancer Genome Atlas.

Keywords: Cancer genomics, Structural variation, Translocation

Introduction

Genomic analysis of cancer and other genetic diseases is changing from the study of individuals to the study of large populations. This is exemplified by large scale projects such as The Cancer Genome Atlas (TCGA), a multi-institution consortium working to build a comprehensive compendium of genomic information that promises to reveal the molecular basis of cancer, and lead to new discoveries and therapies. Currently, TCGA centers are targeted to undertake the integrated analysis of 20-25 cancer types using more than twenty thousand samples [1,2]. This endeavor provides investigators with an unprecedented view of the genomic aberrations that define many human cancers [3]. Cancer cells display diverse genetic structure even within a single individual [4]. Analysis of these structural variations (SVs) across thousands of individuals requires tools that must execute quickly and minimize systematic bias and errors.

Structural variants can be inferred from mapped mate-pair sequencing data by analyzing read pairs that have unlikely positions or orientations relative to each other and several methods and applications for this purpose have been presented [5,6]. However, identifying groups of unlikely reads that support a particular structural variation can involve computations that become combinatorially complex as the number of reads increases. Algorithms such as BreakDancer [6] that make pairwise comparisons between reads have running times that scale nonlinearly with input size and are thus expensive to apply to large data sets consisting of many high coverage genomes. We present *Fastbreak*, a toolset that has been designed to enable efficient and parallelizable SV analysis of next-generation sequencing data. The algorithm and associated tools are available as open source software at http://code.google.com/p/fastbreak/ and incorporates several features:

Scalable rule-based approach: The system uses a set of rules designed to detect the signatures of SVs in a single pass over the data and accumulate this information in efficient, parallelizable data structures. These rules can be further tailored to focus on the signature of cancer-associated SVs, greatly reducing false positives (see Rules used in sample analysis).
Robust analysis: Because of variations in coverage and quality in the large amounts of data available, the software chains together different tools and statistical methods to identify both statistically anomalous files and those sections of the data that are free from systematic bias (see Robustness of analysis and quality assurance of data).
Visual data mining: The tool incorporates a set of novel visualizations allowing for interactive exploration and the presentation of the results at different scales (see Interaction visual representation).

* Correspondence: ilya.shmulevich@systemsbiology.org
[1]Institute for System Biology, 401 Terry Avenue North, Seattle, WA 98109-5234, USA
Full list of author information is available at the end of the article

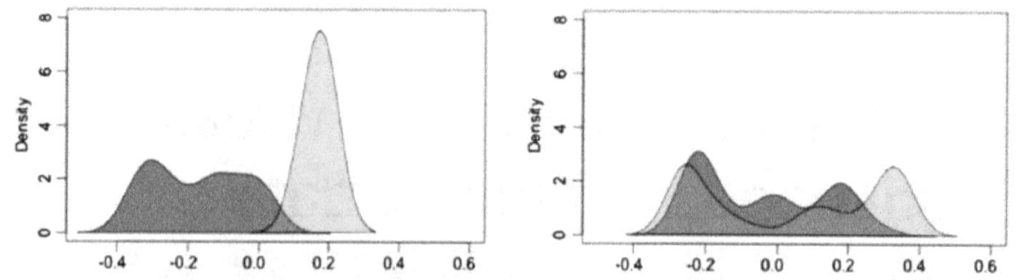

Figure 1 Separation of tumor from blood by *Fastbreak* (left) and BreakDancer (right). The separation of the tissue type (cancer versus blood), showing kernel density estimates along the first coordinate of a multidimensional scaling (MDS) solution derived from the mutual information distance [7] between samples, demonstrates that *Fastbreak* is robust against sample collection and instrumentation biases. The blood sample densities are shown in green, while the pooled cancer samples are shown in grey. For *Fastbreak* (left) the blood samples show a high c-index [8] for the blood cluster (0.97) and no significant correlation (−0.01) between SVs detected in genes and their corresponding coverage; for BreakDancer [6], the blood samples show a lower c-index for the blood cluster (0.68) and a weak correlation (0.28) between SVs detected in genes and their corresponding coverage, an undesired confounding property. Both applications were run only on samples and regions that passed our QA process. Without this restriction, variation along the primary coordinate of MDS is dominated by batch effects unrelated to tissue type.

By incorporating these features, *Fastbreak* has been used for detecting SVs in hundreds of TCGA samples and found to execute quickly and produce conservative results (Figures 1 and 2).

Fastbreak's rule based approach both allows the running time to scale linearly with input size and is linearizable in the sense that the analysis of a single file can be distributed across a number of commodity servers enabling rapid analysis of large datasets. Analysis of a single sample can take hours on a single machine. The analysis of a large data set can be distributed by sample, producing linear speedups. In our own testing we were able to efficiently utilize approximately 80 cores in this manner, allowing us to process hundreds of files in days. Beyond this point, we found that the analysis was bottlenecked by the speed of our file server. If more machines are available, the linearizable nature of the analysis allows it to be further distributed using Google's MapReduce paradigm (as implemented by Apache Hadoop) providing further log-linear speedups and eliminating the bottleneck of a single file server. Running times for various files and a comparison to BreakDancer are provided in Table 1.

The linear scaling and linearizability of the *Fastbreak* algorithm are both due to the use of efficient spatial data structures to accumulate counts of the read pairs that satisfy a set of rules in a single pass over the data. A second set of rules is then applied to all of the regions in the spatial data structure to calculate the confidence that structural variation has affected that region. The data structures are implemented for accumulating both one dimensional (the position of a single read) and two dimensional (such as the positions of two paired reads) genetic data in coarse (1000 bp) bins. The first set of rules describes what may be considered an abnormal read pair and the data structure accumulates both the density of normal and abnormal read pairs in one and two dimensions. The second set of rules identifies, classifies and scores possible structural variations based on the size of abnormal read pair clusters and the local coverage as represented in these densities. The rules are described in detail in Rules used in sample analysis.

Prior to analysis, a QA procedure is applied, which also produces a nonparametric estimate of the distribution of read pair distances (Figure 3) that can be used

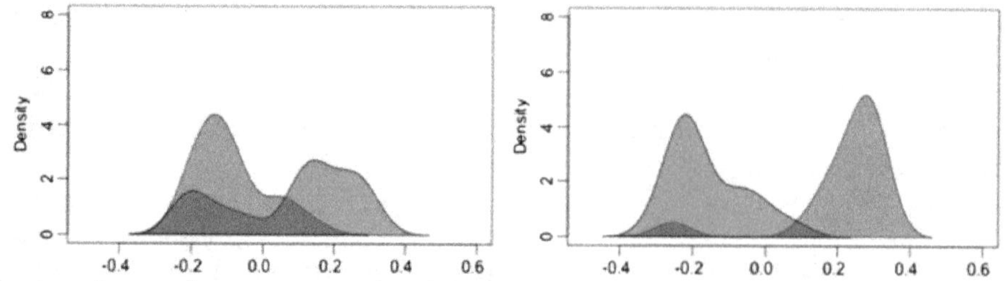

Figure 2 Kernel density estimates of cancer type samples (glioblastoma versus ovarian cancer) along the first coordinate of a multidimensional scaling solution derived from the mutual information distance between samples as analyzed by *Fastbreak* (left) and BreakDancer (right). The GBM cancer patient distribution is shown in red (with a c-index of 0.8 for *Fastbreak* and 0.94 for BreakDancer [8]), and the ovarian distribution (with a c-index of 0.7 for *Fastbreak* and 0.95 BreakDancer) in blue. The results show that *Fastbreak* can distinguish cancer types without exhibiting strong batch effects. Some of BreakDancer's separation of samples can be attributed to batch effects, as shown in Figure 1, due to differential coverage between the two cancers.

Table 1 Running times in minutes for fastbreak, fastbreak on hadoop on a 9 server cluster, and BreakDancer

Bam file	Fastbreak (both passes)	Fastbreak on hadoop (pass1 + pass2)	BreakDancer
9 gb Tumor	80	4 + 25	785
20 gb Tumor	91	8 + 40	812
40 gb Blood	163	9 + 110	449

Hadoop running times are dominated by the time it takes the longest reducer to finish, meaning most of the cluster is unused for most of the time allowing greater throughput when processing many files. BreakDancer running times appear to scale with the number of abnormal reads, not the file size; it performs faster on the larger "blood" files than it does on the smaller "tumor" files.

to fine-tune the rule system. Common problems identified by this process involve issues of erroneous read groups within samples and coverage depth discrepancies (see Robustness of analysis and quality assurance of data) due to changes in protocol and platforms (e.g., during the early stages of TCGA). The rule-based system can then be optimized by executing a first pass analysis to identify which parameters give reasonable differences between paired normal/cancer samples or across other sets of related samples (see Robustness of analysis and quality assurance of data). To remove biases due to coverage differences across a large sample set, a biclustering algorithm [9] is used to select subgroups of genes/patients for direct comparison. An analysis of the genes disrupted across hundreds of ovarian cancer and glioblastoma samples (Figure 4) shows that the *Fastbreak* results can be used to distinguish between tumor and blood samples and, to a lesser extent, disease types and to identify strong similarities in the types of gene function and pathways that

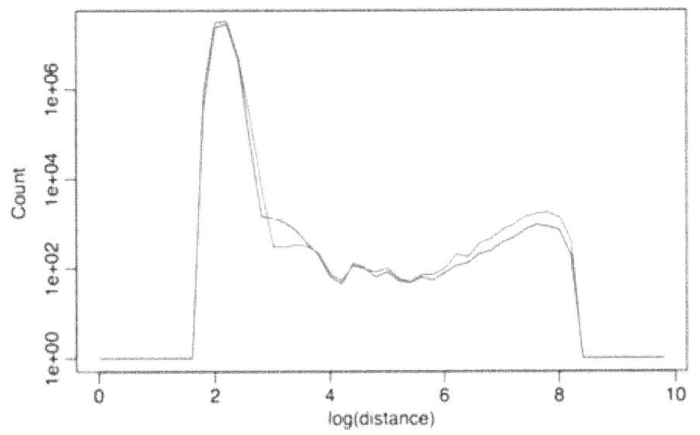

Figure 3 Example output from *Fastbreak* showing a density plot of the distances between paired-end read mapped positions. The red line represents cancer samples while blue represents the blood samples from the same patients. Across all the samples, distances between mate pairs of 1000 and 7000 base pairs were found to be more highly prevalent in tumor samples than in corresponding blood samples.

are disrupted by structural variation (Robustness of analysis and quality assurance of data).

Because it is difficult to represent such a large data set statically, we developed a dynamic web application that visualizes the results of *Fastbreak* at different scales, using a set of custom visualization components. This allows researchers to explore the effects of structural variation on a genetic level across the entire data set. The local genetic topology of a disrupted gene is a hierarchical structure of contiguous regions that may be visualized as a tree branching to different regions and chromosomes (Figure 5). The similarity (as measured by mutual information) of SVs between genes within a disease defines a network that can be visualized using an interactive circular plot (Figure 6). Comparisons between the most frequently disrupted genes in different diseases can be explored dynamically using an interactive parallel coordinates plot (Figure 5).

Rules used in sample analysis

The *Fastbreak* system uses sets of rules, designed to detect genetic structural variations in high throughput sequence data. For analysis of glioblastoma (GBM) and ovarian cancer, these rules have been further refined to detect features that occur prevalently in disease (cancer) samples. To detect these structural variations, rules have been developed to identify three different sorts of abnormal read pairs: those with an abnormal distance between mapped positions; those with inconsistent orientation; and those mapped to different chromosomes. The algorithm compiles a list of such abnormal ("odd") reads in a linear time pass over the data. These reads are stored in a spatial data structure allowing us to identify groups of similar odd read pairs that meet our criteria in a second linear time pass over the filtered data. This data structure uses a system of bins that limits the resolution of the data, but provides significant speed advantages.

In mate pair sequence data, the resolution at which breakpoints can be confidently detected is dictated by the longest distance between mate-paired reads that can be considered normal. In the non-disease (blood) samples that were analyzed, only 0.1% of the reads had mapped distances of more than 1000 base pairs. *Fastbreak* uses this length to define the size of the bins in its internal data structure so that most normal read pairs will fall within a single bin. This eliminates the combinatorial difficulty of identifying clusters of abnormal read pairs and is one of the key optimizations that allow the algorithm's running time to scale linearly with data size.

The rule set used in the analysis of the cancer samples was developed to identify clusters of abnormal read pairs that appear as part of a signature present in the majority of tumor samples within a set of matched (from the

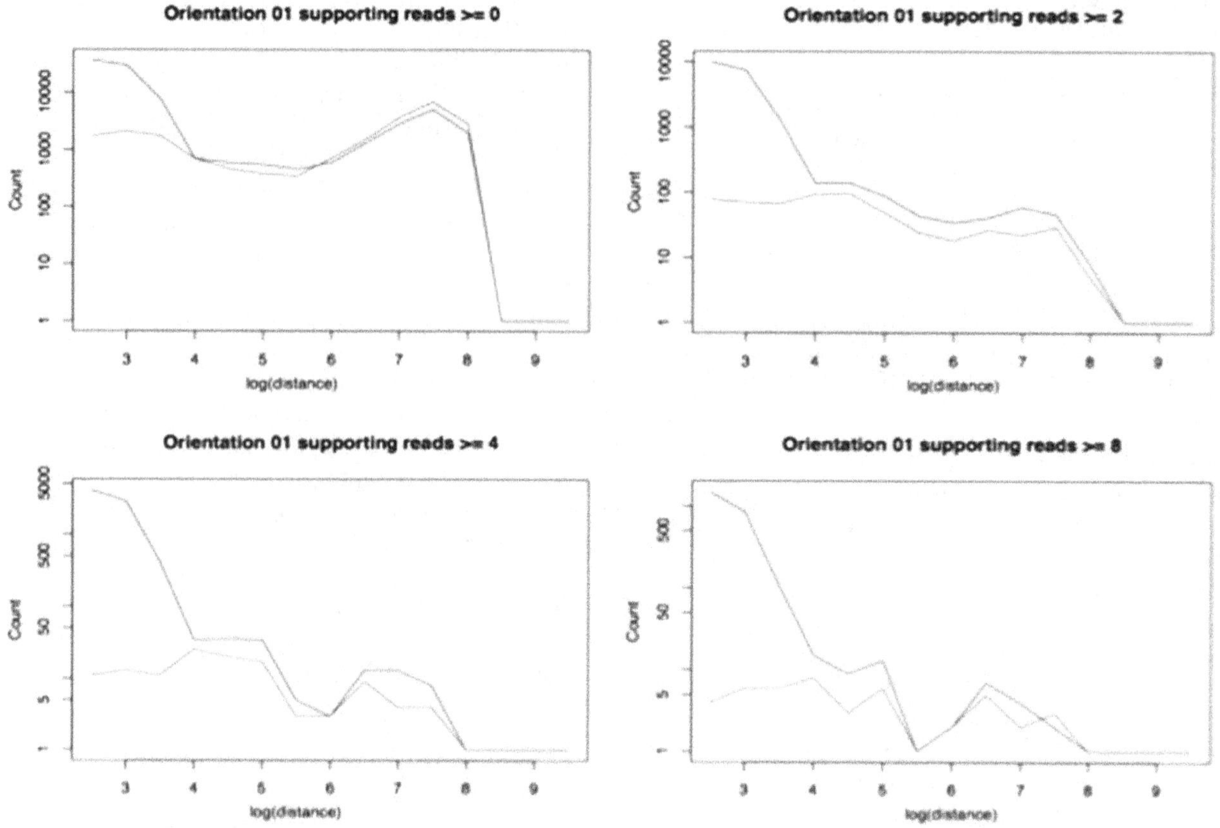

Figure 4 Distance distributions of clusters of read pairs of varying sizes. *Fastbreak* also generates statistics that can be used to determine thresholds for the minimum number of supported reads required to identify features. The plots above show how larger clusters of abnormal read pairs are significantly more prevalent in tumor samples. This information is used to define the rule that a minimum of two supporting reads is required to identify abnormal behavior.

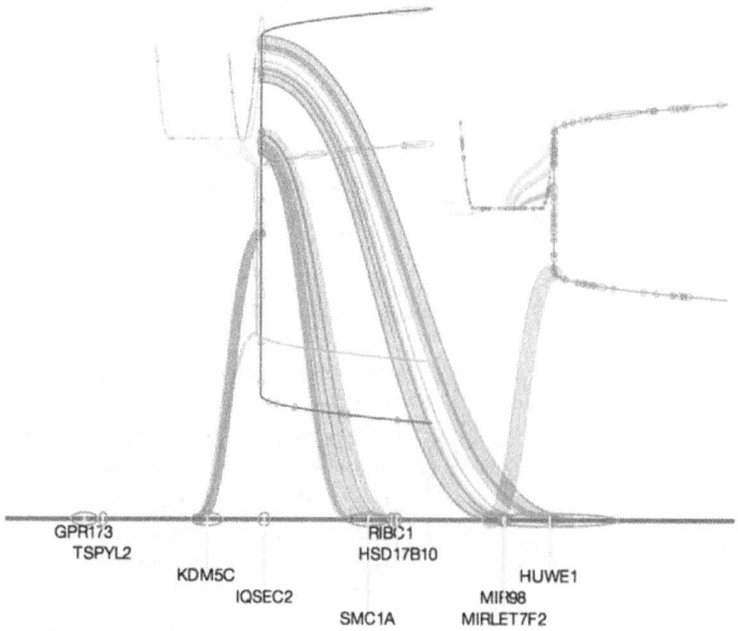

Figure 5 Screen shot of interactive visualization of the local genetic topology of a gene in a single sample highlights links between regions and chromosomes.

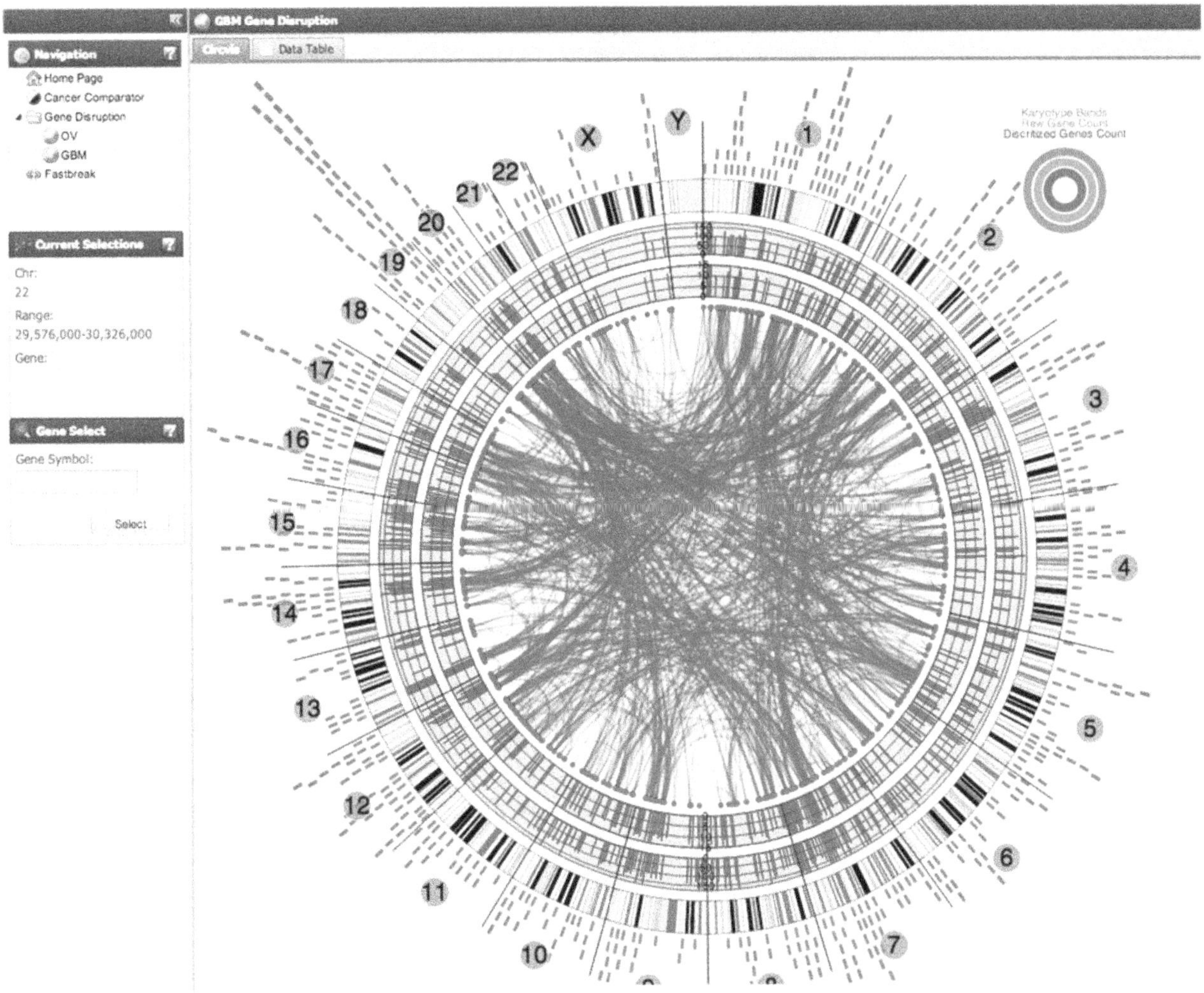

Figure 6 GBM plot highlights genes with informative occurrences of structural variation across the entire cancer as measured by mutual information. The plot is rendered using Visquick [10] which allows interactive exploration of the data.

same patient) tumor and blood samples. *Fastbreak* was used to identify the common signature of abnormal read pairs found in tumor samples. The analysis to determine the best rule set is run separately for each disease, and across all the tumors there was found to be an enrichment of mate-pair distances between 1000-7000 bp (see Figure 3). Pair distances greater than 7000 bp are not significantly enriched in tumor samples, indicating that they are caused primarily by random noise or by structural variations present in the normal tissue relative to the reference genome used for mapping. This upper limit of this window is on the same order as the fall off of structural variations longer than 2000 bp observed by Clark *et al.* Through the deep sequencing of a GBM cell line [11].

For the comparative cancer analysis, the rule system was designed to detect structural variations supported by orientation chromosome or pair distance in this 1000-7000 bp window. Because some of these reads will be the product of random noise, an additional analysis is done to determine how many reads and what percent of the total coverage of a region are needed to conservatively identify a structural variation. These rules can be shown to maximize the difference between the distance distributions of tumor and blood samples (Figure 4).

To account for differences in mapping quality of reads, each inferred feature is assigned a score which aggregates the mapping quality assigned to all supporting reads using a probabilistic interpretation, so that the score assigned to the feature is the probability that not all of the reads were mismapped. This provides a score for each identified feature that increases with both the number of supporting reads and their mapping quality. For the analysis presented, we specified that, for us to consider a cluster of abnormal reads a structural variation, the number of reads that show unusual characteristics must be greater than two, and must account for more than 5% of the local coverage. We found that these rules are well suited to the exome sequenced samples that we analyzed, but more or less conservative rules can be used depending on the quality and coverage of the data available.

Robustness of analysis and quality assurance of data

Fastbreak helps to formulate rules for the identification of biologically relevant features that are robust against false positives due to differences in coverage and other batch effects. In addition to sequencing errors, automated analyses need to remove coverage bias and sample anomalies. To minimize the effects of disparate coverage levels between samples and genes, a biclustering method has been integrated to identify a subgroup of genes and samples with relatively consistent coverage. Erroneous individual samples are removed by use of an internal QA process that analyses different read groups within a sample to find anomalies. Matched pairs that pass the QA tests are then processed for secondary analysis.

The example analysis here involves the identification of structural variants across different cancer types. The analysis used a data set of 172 GBM patients and 132 ovarian cancer patients. Of these, fewer than 50% (96 GBM samples and 38 ovarian samples) passed the QA test process (see below). The parameters of the tests can be changed to include more patients, either through analysis of fewer chromosome regions, or by lowering the quality/coverage thresholds.

The QA process is designed to identify biases across and within samples, and identify chromosome regions across patients that can be compared. The system identifies regions that have sufficient coverage across patients, so that biases due to coverage depth are minimized. Batch effects can be studied by looking for correlations between coverage and identified features (a generally undesired property), and by comparing across samples (see Figures 1 and 2). As *Fastbreak* can be optimized to identify features using rules specific to the system under study, and can compensate for differences in coverage, it shows some robustness to changes in conditions and corresponding batch effects.

The functional significance of the analysis is suggested by the enrichment of genes related to functions such as extracellular matrix and focal adhesion in the list of most disrupted genes (see Tables 2 and 3). Complete details of the samples used and a complete list of disrupted genes are given on the accompanying web site. The functional significance of the disrupted genes identified is shown in Table 3. The gene disruptions can be mined using the interactive web application outlined in Interaction visual representation (http://fastbreak.systemsbiology.net). All code associated with the web application, and analysis systems, is made freely available under an open source public license.

Table 2 Most disrupted genes across the ovarian cancer and glioblastoma cancer data sets

Gene name	Number of disrupted GBM samples	Gene name	Number of disrupted ovarian cancer samples
DNAH9	43	KALRN	17
SYNE1	42	MTOR	17
SYNE2	40	TG	16
TG	40	PAPPA2	15
KALRN	38	SYNE1	15
TRRAP	38	TRIO	15
MLL3	37	CACNA2D3	14
PKHD1	27	TECTA	14
RELN	37	ANK1	13
DNAH8	36	CIT	13

Interactive visual representation

A web application providing visualizations of *Fastbreak* analysis results was developed to enable an end-user to explore the data in an intuitive manner. The application allows a user to view data at three different levels, as well as search specific regions by chromosome coordinates or gene names. To explore similarities or differences between cancers, genes that have high structural variation are visualized in a parallel coordinates plot on the cancer comparator tab (see Figure 7). Mouse-over events and an alternate table view allow the user to view specific information regarding points on the plot and number of disruptions found for a particular gene.

Gene behaviors within a cancer type can be explored by selecting the OV (ovarian) or GBM (glioblastoma) tab on the left side of the application (see Figure 6). The cancer specific visualization level shows mutual information distances between genes across all patients as a circular plot. Again, mouse-over events and alternate table views can be used to view the data in more detail.

The third level of visualization allows a user to view structural variations at a specific location for a selected

Table 3 Functional enrichment of most structurally disrupted genes in pooled GBM and ovarian cancer samples

Functional group	Enrichment
Extracellular matrix	7e-6
Focal Adhesion	2e-5
Phospoprotein	3e-5
Guanyl-nucelotide exchange factor	5e-4
Cell morphogensis	7e-4
Axonogenesis	1e-3

The analysis was performed using the NIH DAVID tool [12,13] (March 2011), with the background population being those identified through the biclustering step of the *Fastbreak* analysis. The p-values are multi-test corrected using the default NIH David method (Benjamini–Hochberg correction).

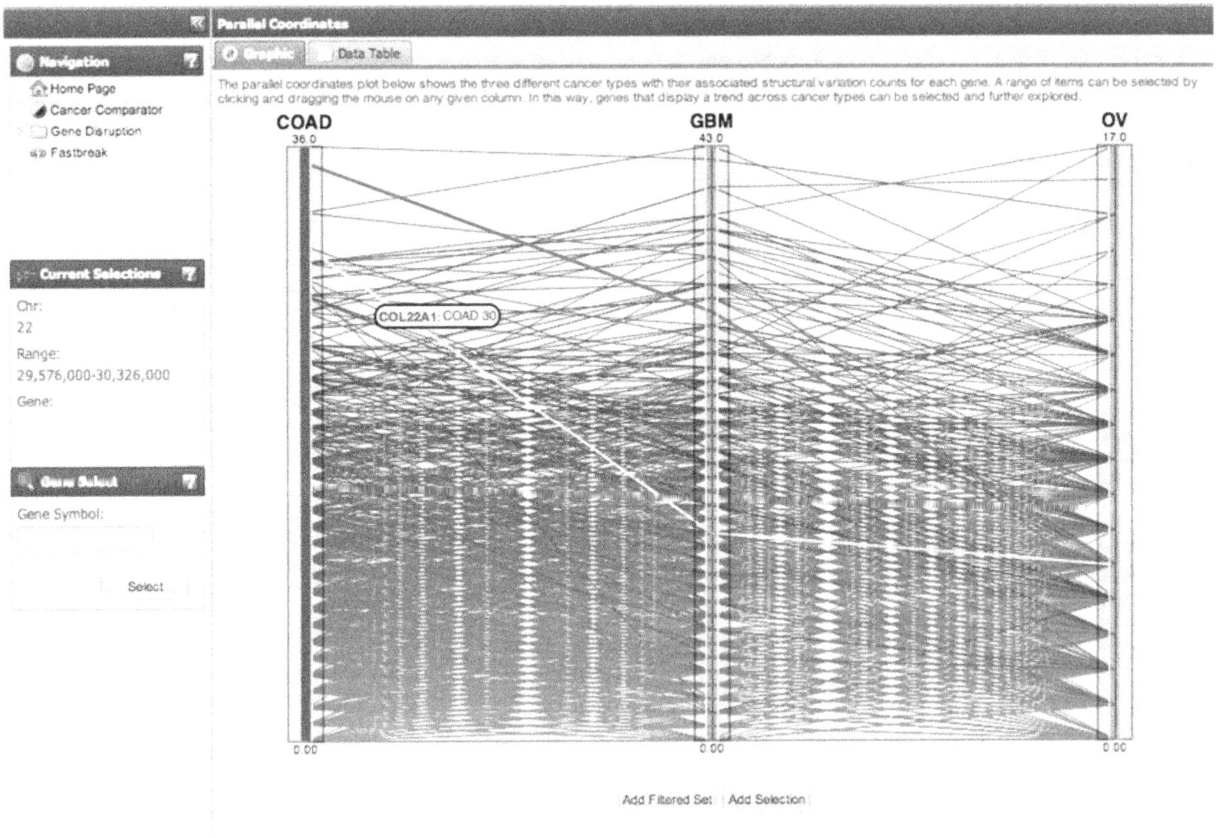

Figure 7 Cancer Comparator Interactive Parallel Coordinates Plot allows the user to explore the relative rank of genes with structural variations across colon adenocarcinoma (COAD), glioblastoma multiforme (GBM) and ovarian cancer (OV).

patient sample. Comparisons between tissues (tumor and blood) and patients can be done at this level of the application. Selection of patients and chromosome location can be done in the "data and range selection" window, while selection of parameters specific to the visualization can be altered in the "advanced parameters" window. A depth-first graph traversal of the structural variant data is used as the underlying data of the visualization. Results are drawn as a cyclic tree such that each contiguous region is represented by a pair of orthogonal branches. Gene location is shown along the base and branches of the trees while coverage information is displayed below the tree. The thickness of the branches indicates the number of supporting reads for the particular structural variation event. Mouse-over and click events are also implemented to view more

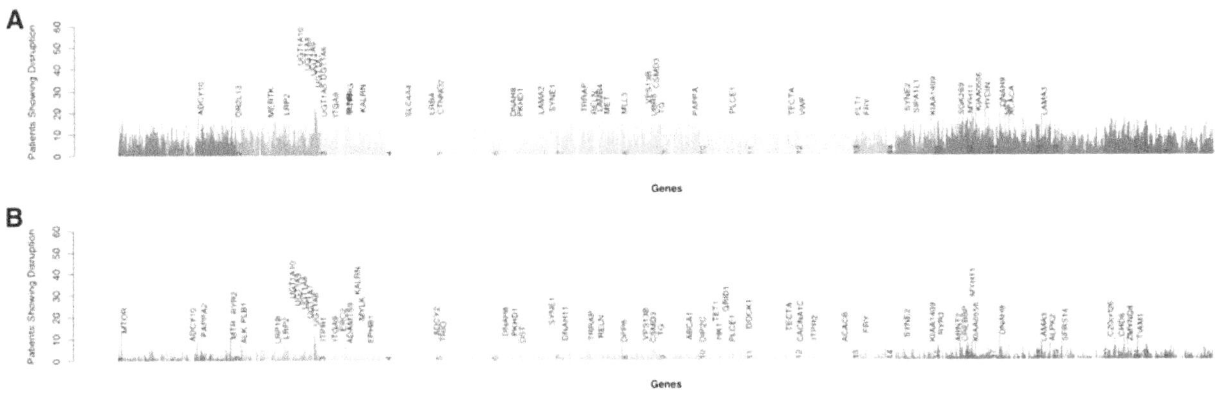

Figure 8 The genes that are most commonly disrupted in glioblastoma (A) and ovarian cancer (B). Genes are arranged in order by chromosome and position and only well covered genes are indicated.

information regarding a specific SV event. The organic structure of this visualization allows the viewer to quickly distinguish between different topologies based on qualitative differences in tree appearances (Figure 5).

The web application described above may be viewed and explored at http://fastbreak.systemsbiology.net. A download of the underlying data and web application are also available on the site.

Conclusions

The approach implemented has several advantages over existing approaches. *Fastbreak*'s rule-based algorithm can be used to reliably and conservatively identify structural variants of biological significance in the TCGA data set. In terms of resistance to bias correlated with the diverse levels of coverage seen in the exome data, our results improve upon those produced by BreakDancer [5], which was not designed with exome data in mind (see Figures 1 and 2). We have further shown that this approach can be easily parallelized across commodity servers, allowing the rapid analysis of petabyte-scale data sets and provided a new tool for dynamically visualizing and exploring the genetic topology of cancer samples inferred by *Fastbreak*. The combination of these approaches allows one to produce a novel population-scale view of genetic structural variation within and across cancers (Figure 8).

However, *Fastbreak* provides only a coarse view of structural variation. It can be used to identify the regions that have been affected by structural variation, but does not attempt to describe precisely what variation has occurred. It is our hope that future tools might use *Fastbreak*-like data structures and approaches to parallelization to accelerate more precise algorithms.

Competing interests

The author(s) declare that they have no competing interests.

Acknowledgements

The algorithm was developed with input and advice from Sheila Reynolds and Jared Roach. All data were acquired from The Cancer Genome Atlas at http://cancergenome.nih.gov/. This work was supported by the National Cancer Institute [U24CA143835]. The funders had no role in study design, data collection and analysis, decision to publish, or preparation of the manuscript.

Author details

[1]Institute for System Biology, 401 Terry Avenue North, Seattle, WA 98109-5234, USA. [2]Division of Molecular Carcinogenesis, Netherlands Cancer Institute, Plesmanlaan 121, 1066CX, Amsterdam, The Netherlands.

References

1. Cancer Genome Atlas Research Network, Comprehensive genomic characterization defines human glioblastoma genes and core pathways. Nature **455**, 1061–1068 (2008)
2. Cancer Genome Atlas Research Network, Integrated genomic analyses of ovarian carcinoma. Nature **474**, 609–615 (2011)
3. F.S. Collins, A.D. Barker, Mapping the cancer genome. Pinpointing the genes involved in cancer will help chart a new course across the complex landscape of human malignancies. Sci. Am. **296**(3), 50–57 (2007)
4. M.A. Nowak, N.L. Komarova, A. Sengupta, P.V. Jallepalli, L. Shih, B. Vogelstein, C. Lengauer, The role of chromosomal instability in tumor initiation. PNAS **99**(25), 16226–16231 (2002)
5. L. Feuk, A.R. Carson, S.W. Scherer, Structural variation in the human genome. Nat Reviews Genetics **7**, 85–97 (2006)
6. K. Chen, J.W. Wallis, M.D. McLellan, D.E. Larson, J.M. Kalicki, C.S. Pohl, S.D. McGrath, M.C. Wendl, Q. Zhang, D.P. Locke, X. Shi, R.S. Fulton, T. Ley, R.K. Wilson, D. Li, E.R. Mardis, BreakDancer: an algorithm for high-resolution mapping of genomic structural variation. Nat. Methods **6**, 677–681 (2009)
7. M.J. Clark, N. Homer, B.D. O'Connor, Z. Chen, A. Eskin, H. Lee, B. Merriman, S.F. Nelson, *bioDist: Different distance measures* (,). R package version 1.16.0
8. L. Hubert, J. Schultz, Quadratic assignment as a general data-analysis strategy. Br. J. Math. Stat. Psychol. **29**, 190–241 (1976)
9. M. van Uitert, W. Meuleman, L. Wessels, Biclustering sparse binary genomic data. J. Comput. Biol. **10**, 1329–1345 (2008)
10. R. Kreisberg, *Visquick, Javascript project providing a library of configurable SVG and Canvas-based visual tools*. http://code.google.com/p/visquick/
11. M.J. Clark, N. Homer, B.D. O'Connor, Z. Chen, A. Eskin et al., U87MG decoded: the genomic sequence of a cytogenetically aberrant human cancer cell line. PLoS Genet. **6**(1), e1000832 (2010). doi:10.1371/journal.pgen.1000832
12. D.W. Huang, B.T. Sherman, R.A. Lempicki, Systematic and integrative analysis of large gene lists using DAVID Bioinformatics Resources. Nature Protoc **4**(1), 44–57 (2009)
13. D.W. Huang, B.T. Sherman, R.A. Lempicki, Bioinformatics enrichment tools: paths toward the comprehensive functional analysis of large gene lists. Nucleic Acids Res. **37**(1), 1–13 (2009)

12

Regularized EM algorithm for sparse parameter estimation in nonlinear dynamic systems with application to gene regulatory network inference

Bin Jia[1] and Xiaodong Wang[2*]

Abstract

Parameter estimation in dynamic systems finds applications in various disciplines, including system biology. The well-known expectation-maximization (EM) algorithm is a popular method and has been widely used to solve system identification and parameter estimation problems. However, the conventional EM algorithm cannot exploit the sparsity. On the other hand, in gene regulatory network inference problems, the parameters to be estimated often exhibit sparse structure. In this paper, a regularized expectation-maximization (rEM) algorithm for sparse parameter estimation in nonlinear dynamic systems is proposed that is based on the maximum *a posteriori* (MAP) estimation and can incorporate the sparse prior. The expectation step involves the forward Gaussian approximation filtering and the backward Gaussian approximation smoothing. The maximization step employs a re-weighted iterative thresholding method. The proposed algorithm is then applied to gene regulatory network inference. Results based on both synthetic and real data show the effectiveness of the proposed algorithm.

Keywords: Nonlinear dynamic system; Parameter estimation; Sparsity; Expectation-maximization; Forward-backward recursion; Gaussian approximation; Gene regulatory network

1 Introduction

The dynamic system is a widely used modeling tool that finds applications in many engineering disciplines. Techniques for state estimation in dynamic systems have been well established. Recently, the problem of *sparse* state estimate has received significant interest. For example, various approaches to *static* sparse state estimation have been developed in [1-4], where the problem is essentially an underdetermined inverse problem, i.e., the number of measurements is small compared to the number of states. Extensions of these methods for *dynamic* sparse state estimation have been addressed in [5-7].

The expectation-maximization (EM) algorithm has also been applied to solve the sparse state estimate problem in dynamic systems [8-12]. In particular, in [8-10], the EM algorithm is employed to update the parameters of the Bernoulli-Gaussian prior and the measurement noise. These parameters are then used in the generalized approximate message passing algorithm [8-10]. In [12,13], the EM algorithm is used to iteratively estimate the parameters that describe the prior distribution and noise variances. Moreover, in [14], the EM algorithm is used for blind identification, where the sparse state is explored. Note that in the above works, only *linear* dynamic systems are considered.

In this paper, we focus on the *sparse parameter* estimation problem instead of the sparse state estimation problem. We consider a general *nonlinear* dynamic system, where both the state equation and the measurement equation are parameterized by some unknown parameters which are assumed to be sparse. One particular application is the inference of gene regulatory networks. The gene regulatory network can be modeled by the state-space model [15], in which the gene regulations are represented by the unknown parameters. The gene regulatory network

*Correspondence: wangx@ee.columbia.edu
[2]Department of Electrical Engineering, Columbia University, New York, NY 10027, USA
Full list of author information is available at the end of the article

is known to be sparse due to the fact that a gene directly regulates or is regularized by a small number of genes [16-19]. The EM algorithm has been applied to parameter estimation in dynamic systems [20]. However, the EM algorithm cannot exploit the sparsity of the parameters. Here, we propose a regularized expectation-maximization (rEM) algorithm for sparse parameter estimation in nonlinear dynamic systems. Specifically, the sparsity of the parameters is imposed by a Laplace prior and we consider the approximate maximum *a posteriori* (MAP) estimate of the parameters. It should be emphasized that the proposed method is an approximate MAP-EM algorithm based on various Gaussian assumptions and quadrature procedures for approximating Gaussian integrals. Note that the MAP-EM algorithm may get stuck at local minima or saddle points. Similar to the conventional EM algorithm, the rEM algorithm also consists of an expectation step and a maximization step. The expectation step involves the forward Gaussian approximation filtering and the backward Gaussian approximation smoothing. The maximization step involves solving an ℓ_1 minimization problem for which a re-weighted iterative thresholding algorithm is employed. To illustrate the proposed sparse parameter estimation method in dynamic systems, we consider the gene-regulatory network inference based on gene expression data.

The unscented Kalman filter has been used in the inference of gene regulatory network [15,21,22]. However, the methods proposed in [15,21,22] are fundamentally different with the method proposed in this paper. Firstly, the unscented Kalman filter is only used once in [15,21,22], while it is used in each iteration of the rEM algorithm in this paper. Secondly, not only the unscented Kalman filter but also the unscented Kalman smoother is used in our proposed rEM algorithm. In essence, only the observation before time k is used to the estimation at time k in the unscented Kalman filter. However, in our rEM algorithm, all observation data is used to the estimation at time k (by the unscented Kalman smoother). The fundamental difference between the proposed work and that of [9] is that the proposed work is for the sparse parameter estimation problem of the dynamic system, while that of [9] is only for the sparse parameter estimation of the static problem. In addition, a general nonlinear dynamic system is involved in our work and only linear system is involved in the work of [9]. The main difference between the proposed work and that of [23] is that the sparsity constraint is enforced. The main contribution of this paper is to use the sparsity-enforced EM algorithm to solve the sparse parameter estimation problem. In addition, the reweighted iterative threshold algorithm is proposed to solve the ℓ_1 optimization algorithm. To the best knowledge of the authors, the proposed rEM with the reweighted iterative threshold optimization algorithm is innovative. Furthermore, we have systematically investigated the performance of the proposed algorithm and compared the results with other conventional algorithms.

The remainder of this paper is organized as follows. In Section 2, the problem of the sparse parameter estimation in dynamic systems is introduced and the regularized EM algorithm is formulated. In Section 3, the E-step of rEM that involves forward-backward recursions and Gaussian approximations is discussed. Section 4 discusses the ℓ_1 optimization problem involved in the maximization step. Application of the proposed rEM algorithm to gene regulatory network inference is discussed in Section 5. Concluding remarks are given in Section 6.

2 Problem statement and the MAP-EM algorithm

We consider a general discrete-time nonlinear dynamic system with unknown parameters, given by the following state and measurement equations:

$$\boldsymbol{x}_k = \boldsymbol{f}(\boldsymbol{x}_{k-1}, \boldsymbol{\theta}) + \boldsymbol{u}_k, \tag{1}$$

$$\text{and } \boldsymbol{y}_k = \boldsymbol{h}(\boldsymbol{x}_k, \boldsymbol{\theta}) + \boldsymbol{v}_k, \tag{2}$$

where $\boldsymbol{x}_k$ and $\boldsymbol{y}_k$ are the state vector and the observation vector at time k, respectively; $\boldsymbol{\theta}$ is the unknown parameter vector; $\boldsymbol{f}(\cdot)$ and $\boldsymbol{h}(\cdot)$ are two nonlinear functions; $\boldsymbol{u}_k \sim \mathcal{N}(\boldsymbol{0}, \boldsymbol{U}_k)$ is the process noise, and $\boldsymbol{v}_k \sim \mathcal{N}(\boldsymbol{0}, \boldsymbol{R}_k)$ is the measurement noise. It is assumed that both $\{\boldsymbol{u}_k\}$ and $\{\boldsymbol{v}_k\}$ are independent noise processes and they are mutually independent. Note that the nonlinear functions $\boldsymbol{f}$ and $\boldsymbol{h}$ are assumed to be differentiable.

Define the notation $\boldsymbol{Y}^k \triangleq [\boldsymbol{y}_1, \cdots, \boldsymbol{y}_k]$. The problem considered in this paper is to estimate the unknown system parameter vector $\boldsymbol{\theta}$ from the length-K measurement data $\boldsymbol{Y}^K$. We assume that $\boldsymbol{\theta}$ is *sparse*. In particular, it has a Laplacian prior distribution which is commonly used as a sparse prior,

$$p(\boldsymbol{\theta}) = \prod_{i=1}^{m} \frac{\lambda_i}{2} e^{-\lambda_i |\theta_i|}. \tag{3}$$

In the EM algorithm and the MAP-EM algorithm [23], given an estimate $\boldsymbol{\theta}'$, a new estimate $\boldsymbol{\theta}''$ is given by

$$\boldsymbol{\theta}'' = \arg\max_{\boldsymbol{\theta}} Q(\boldsymbol{\theta}, \boldsymbol{\theta}'), \tag{4}$$

and

$$\boldsymbol{\theta}'' = \arg\max_{\boldsymbol{\theta}} \left[Q(\boldsymbol{\theta}, \boldsymbol{\theta}') + \log p(\boldsymbol{\theta}) \right], \tag{5}$$

respectively.

Note that the regularized EM can be viewed as a special MAP-EM. To differentiate the sparsity-enforced EM algorithm from the general MAP-EM algorithm, rEM is used. In this paper, the following assumptions are made. (1) The probability density function of the state is assumed to be Gaussian. The Bayesian filter is optimal; however, exact finite-dimensional solutions do not exist. Hence, numerical approximation has to be made. The Gaussian approximation is frequently assumed due to the relatively low complexity and high accuracy [24-26]. (2) The integrals are approximated by various quadrature methods. Many numerical rules, such as Gauss-Hermite quadrature [25], unscented transformation [27], cubature rule [24], and the sparse grid quadrature [26], as well as the Monte Carlo method [28], can be used to approximate the integral. However, the quadrature rule is the best when computational complexity and accuracy are both considered [29].

We next consider the expression of the Q-function in (5). Due to the Markovian structure of the state-space model (1) to (2), we have

$$p(X^K, Y^K|\boldsymbol{\theta}) = p(\boldsymbol{x}_1|\boldsymbol{\theta}) \prod_{k=2}^{K} p(\boldsymbol{x}_k|\boldsymbol{x}_{k-1}, \boldsymbol{\theta}) \prod_{k=1}^{K} p(\boldsymbol{y}_k|\boldsymbol{x}_k, \boldsymbol{\theta}). \tag{6}$$

Therefore,

$$\begin{aligned} Q(\boldsymbol{\theta},\boldsymbol{\theta}') &= \int \log p(X^K, Y^K|\boldsymbol{\theta}) p(X^K|Y^K,\boldsymbol{\theta}')\mathrm{d}X^K \\ &= \int \log p(\boldsymbol{x}_1|\boldsymbol{\theta}) p(\boldsymbol{x}_1|Y^K,\boldsymbol{\theta}')\mathrm{d}\boldsymbol{x}_1 \\ &+ \sum_{k=2}^{K} \int \underbrace{\log p(\boldsymbol{x}_k|\boldsymbol{x}_{k-1},\boldsymbol{\theta})}_{-\frac{1}{2}(\boldsymbol{x}_k-\boldsymbol{f}(\boldsymbol{x}_{k-1},\boldsymbol{\theta}))^T \boldsymbol{U}_k^{-1}(\boldsymbol{x}_k-\boldsymbol{f}(\boldsymbol{x}_{k-1},\boldsymbol{\theta}))-c_k} p(\boldsymbol{x}_k,\boldsymbol{x}_{k-1}|Y^K,\boldsymbol{\theta}')\mathrm{d}\boldsymbol{x}_{k-1}\mathrm{d}\boldsymbol{x}_k \\ &+ \sum_{k=1}^{K} \int \underbrace{\log p(\boldsymbol{y}_k|\boldsymbol{x}_k,\boldsymbol{\theta})}_{-\frac{1}{2}(\boldsymbol{y}_k-\boldsymbol{h}(\boldsymbol{x}_k,\boldsymbol{\theta}))^T \boldsymbol{R}_k^{-1}(\boldsymbol{y}_k-\boldsymbol{h}(\boldsymbol{x}_k,\boldsymbol{\theta}))-d_k} p(\boldsymbol{x}_k|Y^K,\boldsymbol{\theta}')\mathrm{d}\boldsymbol{x}_k, \end{aligned} \tag{7}$$

where $c_k \triangleq \frac{1}{2}[\log|\boldsymbol{U}_k| + \dim(\boldsymbol{x}_k)\log(2\pi)]$ and $d_k \triangleq \frac{1}{2}[\log|\boldsymbol{R}_k| + \dim(\boldsymbol{y}_k)\log(2\pi)]$. We assume that the initial state $\boldsymbol{x}_1$ is independent of the parameter $\boldsymbol{\theta}$. Hence, with the prior given in (3), the optimization in (5) can be rewritten as

$$\begin{aligned} \boldsymbol{\theta}'' &= \arg\max_{\boldsymbol{\theta}} \left[Q(\boldsymbol{\theta},\boldsymbol{\theta}') + \log p(\boldsymbol{\theta})\right] \\ &= \arg\min_{\boldsymbol{\theta}} \sum_{k=2}^{K} \Big\{ 2c_k + \int \Big[(\boldsymbol{x}_k - \boldsymbol{f}(\boldsymbol{x}_{k-1},\boldsymbol{\theta})^T \boldsymbol{U}_k^{-1} (\boldsymbol{x}_k - \boldsymbol{f}(\boldsymbol{x}_{k-1},\boldsymbol{\theta}) \Big] \\ &\quad \times p\,(\boldsymbol{x}_k,\boldsymbol{x}_{k-1}|Y^K,\boldsymbol{\theta}')\mathrm{d}\boldsymbol{x}_{k-1}\mathrm{d}\boldsymbol{x}_k \Big\} \\ &+ \sum_{k=1}^{K} \Big\{ 2d_k + \int \Big[(\boldsymbol{y}_k - \boldsymbol{h}(\boldsymbol{x}_k,\boldsymbol{\theta})^T \boldsymbol{R}_k^{-1} (\boldsymbol{y}_k - \boldsymbol{h}(\boldsymbol{x}_k,\boldsymbol{\theta}) \Big] p(\boldsymbol{x}_k|Y^K,\boldsymbol{\theta}')\mathrm{d}\boldsymbol{x}_k \Big\} \\ &+ 2\|\boldsymbol{\lambda} \circ \boldsymbol{\theta}\|_1, \end{aligned} \tag{8}$$

where $\boldsymbol{\lambda} = [\lambda_1, \lambda_2, \cdots, \lambda_m]^T$, and '∘' denotes the point-wise multiplication.

Note that in many applications, the unknown parameters $\boldsymbol{\theta}$ are only related to the state equation, but not to the measurement equation. Therefore, the second term in (8) can be removed. In the next section, we discuss the procedures for computing the densities $p(\boldsymbol{x}_k, \boldsymbol{x}_{k-1}|Y^K, \boldsymbol{\theta}')$ and $p(\boldsymbol{x}_k|Y^K, \boldsymbol{\theta}')$, the integrals, and the minimization in (8).

3 The E-step: computing the Q-function

We first discuss the calculation of the probability density functions of the states $p(\boldsymbol{x}_k, \boldsymbol{x}_{k-1}|Y^K, \boldsymbol{\theta}')$ and $p(\boldsymbol{x}_k|Y^K, \boldsymbol{\theta}')$ in (8), which involves a forward recursion of a point-based Gaussian approximation filter to compute $p(\boldsymbol{x}_k|Y^k, \boldsymbol{\theta}')$ and $p(\boldsymbol{x}_{k+1}|Y^k, \boldsymbol{\theta}')$, $k = 1, 2, ..., K$, and a backward recursion of a point-based Gaussian approximation smoother to compute $p(\boldsymbol{x}_k, \boldsymbol{x}_{k-1}|Y^K, \boldsymbol{\theta}')$ and $p(\boldsymbol{x}_k|Y^K, \boldsymbol{\theta}')$, $k = K, K-1, ..., 1$. For notational simplicity, in the remainder of this section, we drop the parameter $\boldsymbol{\theta}'$.

3.1 Forward recursion

The forward recursion is composed of two steps: prediction and filtering. Specifically, given the prior probability density function (PDF) $p(\boldsymbol{x}_{k-1}|Y^{k-1})$ at time $k-1$, we need to compute the predicted conditional PDF $p(\boldsymbol{x}_k|Y^{k-1})$; then, given the measurement $\boldsymbol{y}_k$ at time k, we update the filtered PDF $p(\boldsymbol{x}_k|Y^k)$. These PDF recursions are in general computationally intractable unless the system is linear and Gaussian. The Gaussian approximation filters are based on the following two assumptions: (1) Given Y^{k-1}, $\boldsymbol{x}_{k-1}$ has a Gaussian distribution, i.e., $\boldsymbol{x}_{k-1}|Y^{k-1} \sim \mathcal{N}(\hat{\boldsymbol{x}}_{k-1|k-1}, \boldsymbol{P}_{k-1|k-1})$; and (2) $(\boldsymbol{x}_k, \boldsymbol{y}_k)$ are jointly Gaussian, given Y^{k-1}.

It then follows that the predictive PDF is Gaussian, i.e., $\boldsymbol{x}_k|Y^{k-1} \sim \mathcal{N}(\hat{\boldsymbol{x}}_{k|k-1}, \boldsymbol{P}_{k|k-1})$, with [24,26,27]

$$\hat{\boldsymbol{x}}_{k|k-1} \triangleq \mathbb{E}\{\boldsymbol{x}_k|Y^{k-1}\} = \mathbb{E}_{\boldsymbol{x}_{k-1}|Y^{k-1}}\left\{\boldsymbol{f}(\boldsymbol{x}_{k-1})\right\}, \tag{9}$$

$$\boldsymbol{P}_{k|k-1} \triangleq \mathrm{Cov}\{\boldsymbol{x}_k|Y^{k-1}\} = \mathbb{E}_{\boldsymbol{x}_{k-1}|Y^{k-1}} \left\{(\boldsymbol{f}(\boldsymbol{x}_{k-1}) - \hat{\boldsymbol{x}}_{k|k-1})(\boldsymbol{f}(\boldsymbol{x}_{k-1} - \hat{\boldsymbol{x}}_{k|k-1})^T\right\} + \boldsymbol{U}_{k-1}, \tag{10}$$

where $\mathbb{E}_{\boldsymbol{x}_{k-1}|Y^{k-1}}\left\{\boldsymbol{g}(\boldsymbol{x}_{k-1})\right\} = \int \boldsymbol{g}(\boldsymbol{x})\phi(\boldsymbol{x}; \hat{\boldsymbol{x}}_{k-1|k-1}, \boldsymbol{P}_{k-1|k-1})\mathrm{d}\boldsymbol{x}$, and $\phi\left(\boldsymbol{x}; \hat{\boldsymbol{x}}, \boldsymbol{P}\right)$ denotes the multivariate Gaussian PDF with mean $\hat{\boldsymbol{x}}$ and covariance $\boldsymbol{P}$.

Moreover, the filtered PDF is also Gaussian, i.e., $\boldsymbol{x}_k|Y^k \sim \mathcal{N}(\hat{\boldsymbol{x}}_{k|k}, \boldsymbol{P}_{k|k})$ [24,26,27], where

$$\hat{\boldsymbol{x}}_{k|k} \triangleq \mathbb{E}\{\boldsymbol{x}_k|Y^k\} = \hat{\boldsymbol{x}}_{k|k-1} + \boldsymbol{L}_k(\boldsymbol{y}_k - \hat{\boldsymbol{y}}_{k|k-1}), \tag{11}$$

$$\text{and } \boldsymbol{P}_{k|k} \triangleq \mathrm{Cov}\{\boldsymbol{x}_k|Y^k\} = \boldsymbol{P}_{k|k-1} - \boldsymbol{L}_k\boldsymbol{P}_k^{xy}, \tag{12}$$

with

$$\hat{\boldsymbol{y}}_{k|k-1} = \mathbb{E}_{\boldsymbol{x}_k|Y^{k-1}}\left\{\boldsymbol{h}(\boldsymbol{x}_k)\right\}, \tag{13}$$

$$\boldsymbol{L}_k = \boldsymbol{P}_k^{xy}(\boldsymbol{R}_k + \boldsymbol{P}_k^{yy})^{-1}, \tag{14}$$

$$P_k^{xy} = \mathbb{E}_{x_k|Y^{k-1}}\left\{(x_k - \hat{x}_{k|k-1})(h(x_k) - \hat{y}_{k|k-1})^T\right\}, \tag{15}$$

$$P_k^{yy} = \mathbb{E}_{x_k|Y^{k-1}}\left\{(h(x_k) - \hat{y}_{k|k-1})(h(x_k) - \hat{y}_{k|k-1})^T\right\}. \tag{16}$$

3.2 Backward recursion

In the backward recursion, we compute the smoothed PDFs $p(x_k, x_{k+1}|Y^K)$ and $p(x_k|Y^K)$. Here, the approximate assumption made is that conditioned on y^k, x_k and x_{k+1} are jointly Gaussian [30], i.e.,

$$\begin{bmatrix} x_k \\ x_{k+1} \end{bmatrix} \mid Y^k \sim \mathcal{N}\left(\begin{bmatrix} \hat{x}_{k|k} \\ \hat{x}_{k+1|k} \end{bmatrix}, \times \begin{bmatrix} P_{k|k} & C_k \\ C_k^T & P_{k+1|k} \end{bmatrix}\right), \tag{17}$$

$$\text{with } C_k \triangleq \mathrm{Cov}\{x_k, x_{k+1}|Y^k\} = \mathbb{E}_{x_k|Y_k}\left\{(x_k - \hat{x}_{k|k})(f(x_k) - \hat{x}_{k+1|k})^T\right\}. \tag{18}$$

Due to the Markov property of the state-space model, we have $p(x_k|x_{k+1}, Y^K) = p(x_k|x_{k+1}, Y^k)$. Therefore, we can write [30]

$$\begin{aligned} p(x_k, x_{k+1}|Y^K) &= p(x_k|x_{k+1}, Y^K)p(x_{k+1}|Y^K) \\ &= p(x_k|x_{k+1}, Y^k)p(x_{k+1}|Y^K). \end{aligned} \tag{19}$$

Now, assume that

$$x_{k+1}|Y^K \sim \mathcal{N}(\tilde{x}_{k+1}, \tilde{P}_{k+1}), \text{ with } \tilde{x}_K = \hat{x}_{K|K}, \ \tilde{P}_K = P_{K|K}. \tag{20}$$

It then follows from (17) and (19) that [30]

$$\begin{bmatrix} x_k \\ x_{k+1} \end{bmatrix} |Y^K \sim \mathcal{N}\left(\begin{bmatrix} \tilde{x}_k \\ \tilde{x}_{k+1} \end{bmatrix}, \begin{bmatrix} \tilde{P}_k & D_k\tilde{P}_{k+1} \\ \tilde{P}_{k+1}D_k^T & \tilde{P}_{k+1} \end{bmatrix}\right), \tag{21}$$

where

$$\tilde{x}_k = \hat{x}_{k|k} + D_k(\tilde{x}_{k+1} - \hat{x}_{k+1|k}), \tag{22}$$

$$\tilde{P}_k = P_{k|k} + D_k(\tilde{P}_{k+1} - P_{k+1|k})D_k^T, \tag{23}$$

$$D_k = C_k P_{k+1|k}^{-1}. \tag{24}$$

3.3 Approximating the integrals

The integrals associated with the expectations in the forward-backward recursions for computing the approximate state PDFs, i.e., (9), (10), (13), (15), (16), and (18), as well as the integrals involved in computing the function $Q(\theta, \theta')$ in (8), are integrals of Gaussian type that can be efficiently approximated by various quadrature methods. Specifically, if a set of weighted points $\{(\gamma_i, w_i), i = 1, \ldots, N\}$ can be used to approximate the integral

$$\mathbb{E}_{\mathcal{N}(0,I)}\{g(x)\} = \int g(x)\phi\,(x; 0, I)\,\mathrm{d}x \approx \sum_{i=1}^{N} w_i g(\gamma_i), \tag{25}$$

then the general Gaussian-type integral can be approximated by

$$\mathbb{E}_{\mathcal{N}(\hat{x},P)}\{g(x)\} = \int g(x)\phi\left(x; \hat{x}, P\right)\mathrm{d}x \approx \sum_{i=1}^{N} w_i g(S\gamma_i + \hat{x}), \tag{26}$$

where $P = SS^T$ and S can be obtained by Cholesky decomposition or singular value decomposition (SVD).

By using different point sets, different Gaussian approximation filters and smoothers can be obtained, such as the Gauss-Hermite quadrature (GHQ) [25], the unscented transform (UT) [27], the spherical-radial cubature rule (CR) [24], the sparse grid quadrature rule (SGQ) [26], and the quasi Monte Carlo method (QMC) [28]. Both the UT and the CR are the third-degree numerical rules which means the integration can be exactly calculated when $g(x)$ is a polynomial with the degree up to three. In addition, the form of the CR is identical to the UT with a specific parameter. The main advantage of the UT and the CR is that the number of points required by the rule increases linearly with the dimension. However, one problem of the UT and the CR is that the high-order information of the nonlinear function is difficult to capture so that the accuracy may be low when $g(x)$ is a highly nonlinear function. The GHQ rule, in contrast, can capture arbitrary degree information of $g(x)$ by using more points. It has been proven that GHQ can provide more accurate results than the UT or the CR [25,26]. Similarly, the QMC method can also obtain more accurate results than the UT. However, both the GHQ rule and the QMC method require a large number of points for the high-dimensional problem. Specifically, the number of points required by the GHQ rule increases exponentially with the dimension. To achieve a similar performance of the GHQ with a small number of points, the SGQ is proposed [26], where the number of points increases only polynomially with the dimension.

For the numerical results in this paper, the UT is used in the Gaussian approximation filter and smoother, where we have $N = 2n + 1$, with n being the dimension of the state vector x_k. The quadrature points and the corresponding weights are given, respectively, by

$$\boldsymbol{\gamma}_i = \begin{cases} \mathbf{0}, & i = 1, \\ \sqrt{(n+\kappa)}\boldsymbol{e}_{i-1}, & i = 2, \cdots, n+1, \\ -\sqrt{(n+\kappa)}\boldsymbol{e}_{i-n-1}, & i = n+2, \cdots, 2n+1, \end{cases} \quad (27)$$

and

$$w_i = \begin{cases} \dfrac{\kappa}{n+\kappa}, & i = 1, \\ \dfrac{1}{2(n+\kappa)}, & i = 2, \cdots, 2n+1, \end{cases} \quad (28)$$

where κ is a tunable parameter, and $\boldsymbol{e}_i$ is the ith n dimensional unit vector. Note that $\kappa = 0$ is used as the default value in this paper, as in the cubature Kalman filter [24]. In addition, $\kappa = -3$ can also be used as in the unscented Kalman filter [27].

4 The M-step: solving the ℓ_1 optimization problem

Solving the ℓ_1 optimization problems in (8) is not trivial since $|\theta_i|$ is nondifferentiable at $\theta_i = 0$. The ℓ_1 optimization is a useful tool to obtain sparse solutions. Methods for solving linear inverse problems with sparse constraints are reviewed in [1]. Some more recent developments include the projected scaled subgradient [31] method, the gradient support pursuit method [32], and the greedy sparse-simplex method [33]. In this paper, for the maximization step in the proposed rEM algorithm, due to the simplicity of implementation, we will employ a modified version of the iterative thresholding algorithm.

4.1 Iterative thresholding algorithm

Denote $\tilde{Q}(\boldsymbol{\theta}, \boldsymbol{\theta}')$ as the two summation terms in (8). We consider the optimization problem in (8)

$$\arg\min_{\boldsymbol{\theta}} J(\boldsymbol{\theta}) = \tilde{Q}(\boldsymbol{\theta}, \boldsymbol{\theta}') + 2\|\boldsymbol{\lambda} \circ \boldsymbol{\theta}\|_1. \quad (29)$$

The solution to (29) can be iteratively obtained by solving a sequence of optimization problems [34]. As in the Newton's method, the Taylor series expansion of the $\tilde{Q}(\boldsymbol{\theta}, \boldsymbol{\theta}')$ around the solution $\boldsymbol{\theta}^t$ at the tth iteration is given by

$$\tilde{Q}(\boldsymbol{\theta}^t + \Delta\boldsymbol{\theta}, \boldsymbol{\theta}') \cong \tilde{Q}(\boldsymbol{\theta}^t, \boldsymbol{\theta}') + \Delta\boldsymbol{\theta}^T \nabla\tilde{Q}(\boldsymbol{\theta}^t, \boldsymbol{\theta}') + \frac{\alpha_t}{2}\|\Delta\boldsymbol{\theta}\|_2^2, \quad (30)$$

where $\nabla\tilde{Q}$ is the gradient of the negative Q-function and α_t is such that $\alpha_t \boldsymbol{I}$ mimics the Hessian $\nabla^2\tilde{Q}$. Then, $\boldsymbol{\theta}^{t+1}$ is given by

$$\boldsymbol{\theta}^{t+1} = \arg\min_{\boldsymbol{z}} (\boldsymbol{z} - \boldsymbol{\theta}^t)^T \nabla\tilde{Q}(\boldsymbol{\theta}^t, \boldsymbol{\theta}') + \frac{\alpha_t}{2}\|\boldsymbol{z} - \boldsymbol{\theta}^t\|_2^2 + 2\|\boldsymbol{\lambda} \circ \boldsymbol{z}\|_1, \quad (31)$$

where $\boldsymbol{z}$ denotes the variable to be optimized in the objective function.

The equivalent form of (31) is given by

$$\boldsymbol{\theta}^{t+1} = \arg\min_{\boldsymbol{z}} \frac{1}{2}\|\boldsymbol{z} - \boldsymbol{u}^t\|_2^2 + \frac{2}{\alpha_t}\|\boldsymbol{\lambda} \circ \boldsymbol{z}\|_1, \quad (32)$$

$$\text{with } \boldsymbol{u}^t = \boldsymbol{\theta}^t - \frac{1}{\alpha_t}\nabla\tilde{Q}(\boldsymbol{\theta}^t, \boldsymbol{\theta}'), \quad (33)$$

$$\alpha_t \approx \frac{(\boldsymbol{s}^t)^T \boldsymbol{r}^t}{\|\boldsymbol{s}^t\|^2}, \quad (34)$$

$$\boldsymbol{s}^t = \boldsymbol{\theta}^t - \boldsymbol{\theta}^{t-1}, \quad (35)$$

$$\boldsymbol{r}^t = \nabla\tilde{Q}(\boldsymbol{\theta}^t, \boldsymbol{\theta}') - \nabla\tilde{Q}(\boldsymbol{\theta}^{t-1}, \boldsymbol{\theta}'). \quad (36)$$

Note that Equation 34 is derived as follows. Because we require that $\alpha_t \boldsymbol{I}$ mimics the Hessian $\nabla^2\tilde{Q}$, i.e., $\alpha_t \boldsymbol{s}^t \approx \boldsymbol{r}^t$, solving α_t in the least-squares sense, we have

$$\alpha_t \approx \arg\min_{\alpha} \|\alpha \boldsymbol{s}^t - \boldsymbol{r}^t\|_2^2 = \frac{(\boldsymbol{s}^t)^T \boldsymbol{r}^t}{\boldsymbol{s}^t)^T \boldsymbol{s}^t}. \quad (37)$$

The solution to (32) is given by $\boldsymbol{\theta}^{t+1} = \eta^S(\boldsymbol{u}^t, \frac{2\boldsymbol{\lambda}}{\alpha_t})$, where

$$\eta^S(\boldsymbol{u}^t, \boldsymbol{a}) = \text{sign}(\boldsymbol{u}^t)\max\left\{|\boldsymbol{u}^t| - \boldsymbol{a}, \mathbf{0}\right\} \quad (38)$$

is the soft thresholding function with $\text{sign}(\boldsymbol{u}^t)$ and $\max\left\{|\boldsymbol{u}^t| - \boldsymbol{a}, \mathbf{0}\right\}$ being component-wise operators.

Finally, the iterative procedure for solving (29) is given by

$$\boldsymbol{\theta}^{t+1} = \text{sign}\left(\boldsymbol{\theta}^t - \frac{1}{\alpha_t}\nabla\tilde{Q}(\boldsymbol{\theta}^t, \boldsymbol{\theta}')\right) \max\left\{\left|\boldsymbol{\theta}^t - \frac{1}{\alpha_t}\nabla\tilde{Q}(\boldsymbol{\theta}^t, \boldsymbol{\theta}')\right| - \frac{2\boldsymbol{\lambda}}{\alpha_t}, \mathbf{0}\right\}. \quad (39)$$

And the iteration stops when the following condition is met:

$$\frac{|J(\boldsymbol{\theta}^{t+1}) - J(\boldsymbol{\theta}^t)|}{|J(\boldsymbol{\theta}^t)|} \le \epsilon, \quad (40)$$

where ϵ is a given small number.

4.2 Adaptive selection of $\boldsymbol{\lambda}$

So far, the parameters λ_i in the Laplace prior are fixed. Here, we propose to adaptively tune them based on the output of the iterative thresholding algorithm. The algorithm consists of solving a sequence of weighted ℓ_1-minimization problems. λ_i used for the next iteration are computed from the value of the current solution. A good choice of λ_i is to make them counteract the influence of the magnitude of the ℓ_1 penalty function [35]. Following this idea, we propose an iterative re-weighted thresholding algorithm. At the beginning of the maximization step, we set $\lambda_i = 1, \forall i$. Then, we run the iterative thresholding algorithm to obtain $\boldsymbol{\theta}$. Next, we update λ_i as $\lambda_i = \frac{1}{|\theta_i| + \epsilon}, \forall i$, where ϵ is a small positive number, and run the iterative thresholding algorithm again using the new $\boldsymbol{\lambda}$. The above process is repeated until it converges at the point where the maximization step completes. Note that for the iterative re-weighted thresholding algorithm, the assumption that θ has a Laplacian prior no longer holds.

5 Application to gene regulatory network inference

The gene regulatory network can be described by a graph in which genes are viewed as nodes and edges depict causal relations between genes. By analyzing collected gene expression levels over a period of time, one can find some regulatory relations between different genes. Under the discrete-time state-space modeling, for a gene regulatory network with n genes, the state vector $\boldsymbol{x}_k = [x_{1,k}, \ldots, x_{n,k}]^T$, where $x_{i,k}$, denotes the gene expression level of the ith gene at time k.

In this case, the nonlinear function $\boldsymbol{f}(\boldsymbol{x})$ in the general dynamic Equation (1) is given by [15]

$$\boldsymbol{f}(\boldsymbol{x}_{k-1}, \boldsymbol{\theta}) = \boldsymbol{A}\boldsymbol{g}(\boldsymbol{x}_{k-1}), \tag{41}$$

with

$$\boldsymbol{g}(\boldsymbol{x}) = \begin{bmatrix} g(x_1) \\ \vdots \\ g(x_n) \end{bmatrix}, \tag{42}$$

and

$$g_i(x) = \frac{1}{1+e^{-x}}, \qquad \forall i = 1, \cdots, n. \tag{43}$$

In (41), $\boldsymbol{A}$ is an $n \times n$ regulatory coefficient matrix with the element a_{ij} denoting the regulation coefficient from gene j to gene i. A positive coefficient a_{ij} indicates that gene j activates gene i, and a negative θ_{ij} indicates that gene j represses gene i. The parameter to be estimated is $\boldsymbol{\theta} = \boldsymbol{A}$ which is sparse.

For the measurement model, we have

$$\boldsymbol{y}_k = \boldsymbol{x}_k + \boldsymbol{v}_k. \tag{44}$$

5.1 Inference of gene regulatory network with four genes

In the simulations, we consider a network with four genes. The true gene regulatory coefficients matrix is given by

$$\boldsymbol{A} = \begin{bmatrix} 3 & 0 & 0 & -4.5 \\ -2.9 & 0 & 5 & 0 \\ -6 & 4 & 0 & 0 \\ 0 & -5 & 2 & 0 \end{bmatrix}. \tag{45}$$

To compare the EM algorithm with the proposed rEM algorithm, the simulation was conduced ten times. In each time, the initial value of $\boldsymbol{A}(\boldsymbol{\theta})$ is randomly generated from a Gaussian distribution with mean 0 and variance 2. The EM, rEM, and rEM$_w$, as well as the basis pursuit de-noising dynamic filtering (BPDN-DF) method and the ℓ_1 optimization method, are tested. Here, rEM$_w$ denotes the version of the rEM algorithm with the iterative re-weighted thresholding discussed in Section 4.2.

As a performance metrics, the receiver operating characteristic (ROC) curve is frequently used. However, for this specific example, with the increasing of the false-positive rate, the true-positive rate given by rEM and EM is always high (close to 1) which makes the distinguishment of the performance of rEM algorithm and EM algorithm difficult. Hence, the root mean-squared error (RMSE) and the sparsity factor (SF) are used in this section. The RMSE is defined by

$$\text{RMSE} = \sqrt{\frac{1}{N^2}\sum_{i=1}^{N}\sum_{j=1}^{N}(\text{A}_{\text{ij}} - \bar{\text{A}}_{\text{ij}})^2}, \tag{46}$$

where $\bar{\boldsymbol{A}}$ denotes the estimated $\boldsymbol{A}$. The SF is given by

$$\text{SF} = \frac{\phi_0}{\phi}, \tag{47}$$

where ϕ_0 and ϕ are the number of zero values of the estimated parameter and the number of zero values of true parameter, respectively. It can be seen that the estimation is over sparse if the sparsity factor is greater than 1.

In addition, to test the effectiveness of the proposed method at finding the support of the unknown parameters, the number of matched elements is used and can be obtained by the following procedures: (1) Compute the support of $\boldsymbol{A}$ using the true parameters (denoted by $\boldsymbol{A}_s$) and the support of $\boldsymbol{A}$ using the estimated parameters (denoted by $\bar{\boldsymbol{A}}_s$). Note that we assign $[\boldsymbol{A}_s]_{ij} = 1$ if $A_{ij} \neq 0$ and $[\boldsymbol{A}_s]_{ij} = 0$ if $A_{ij} = 0$. Similarly, we assign $[\bar{\boldsymbol{A}}_s]_{ij} = 1$ if $\bar{A}_{ij} \neq 0$ and $[\bar{\boldsymbol{A}}_s]_{ij} = 0$ if $\bar{A}_{ij} = 0$. (2) Compute the number of zero elements of $\boldsymbol{A}_s - \bar{\boldsymbol{A}}_s$ as the matched elements. It is easy to see that it is effective at finding the support of the unknown parameters when the number of matched elements is large.

5.1.1 *The effect of different λ*

The performance of rEM using different λ $(10, 5, 1, 0.5, 0.1)$ is compared with the EM algorithm and the rEM$_w$. The RMSE and SF are shown in Figures 1 and 2, respectively. The RMSE does not increase monotonously with the decreasing of parameter λ. It can be seen that the rEM with $\lambda = 5$ has better performance than that using other λ. In addition, the rEM with all λ except $\lambda = 10$ outperforms the EM algorithm. It provides smaller RMSE and sparser result. The rEM$_w$ provides the smallest RMSE and sparsest parameter estimation. The number of matched elements of test algorithms with different λ is given in Figure 3. It can also be seen that rEM$_w$ provides more matched elements than the EM algorithm.

5.1.2 *The effect of noise*

Two different cases are tested. In the first case, the covariance of the process noise and measurement noise are chosen to be 0.01. In the second case, they are chosen to be 0.1. The performance of two test cases is shown in

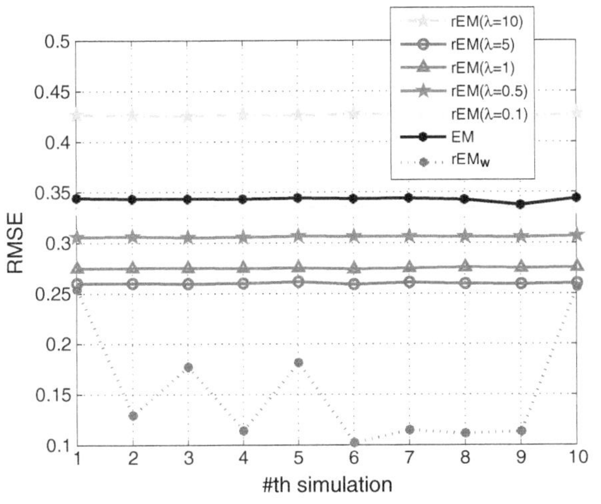

Figure 1 RMSE of rEM with different λ and rEM_w.

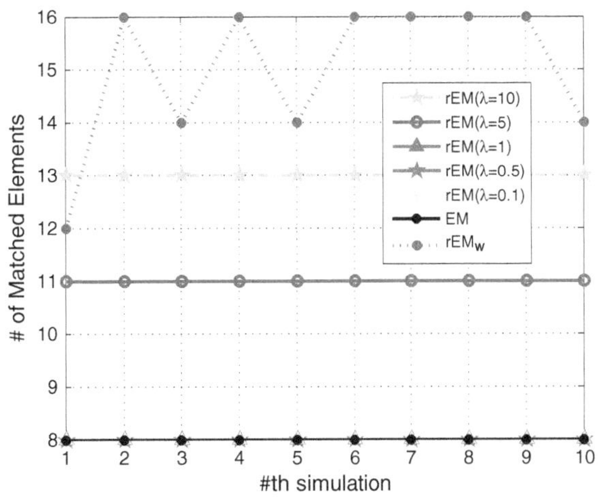

Figure 3 The number of matched elements of rEM with different λ and rEM_w.

Figures 4, 5, 6. It can be seen that the RMSE of rEM_w with $\boldsymbol{U}, \boldsymbol{R} = 0.01\boldsymbol{I}$ is smaller than that with $\boldsymbol{U}, \boldsymbol{R} = 0.1\boldsymbol{I}$. In addition, the rEM_w with $\boldsymbol{U}, \boldsymbol{R} = 0.01$ provides a larger number of matched elements than that with $\boldsymbol{U}, \boldsymbol{R} = 0.1$ as shown in Figure 6. Hence, the estimation accuracy is better when the process noise and measure noise are small.

5.1.3 *The effect of the number of observations*

In order to test the effect of the number of observations, the rEM_w algorithm with 10 and 20 observations are tested. The simulation results are shown in Figures 7, 8, 9. It can be seen that rEM_w with more observations gives less RMSE. In addition, as shown in Figure 9, rEM_w with more observations gives slightly better result for finding the support of the unknown parameters.

5.1.4 *The effect of* κ

In order to test the performance of κ, the rEM_w algorithm with different κ (0,-1,-3) is tested. The performance results are shown in Figures 10, 11, 12. Note that the cubature rule corresponds to $\kappa = 0$, and the unscented transformation corresponds to $\kappa = -1$. Roughly speaking, the performance of rEM_w with different κ is close. Specifically, it can be seen that the RMSE of rEM_w using $\kappa = -1$ and rEM_w using $\kappa = -3$ is less than that of rEM_w using $\kappa = 0$. The sparsity factor of rEM_w using $\kappa = -1$ is more close to 1 than that of rEM_w using $\kappa = -3$ and $\kappa = 0$. Moreover, the number of matched elements of rEM_w using $\kappa = -1$ is more than that of rEM_w using $\kappa = -3$ and $\kappa = 0$. Hence, the performance of rEM using $\kappa = -1$ is the best in this case.

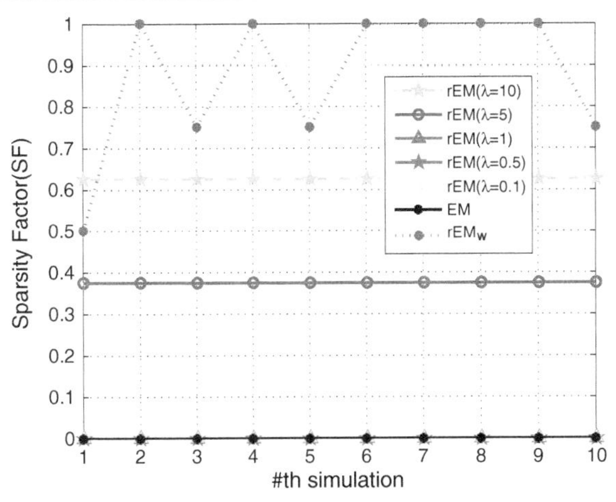

Figure 2 SF of rEM with different λ and rEM_w.

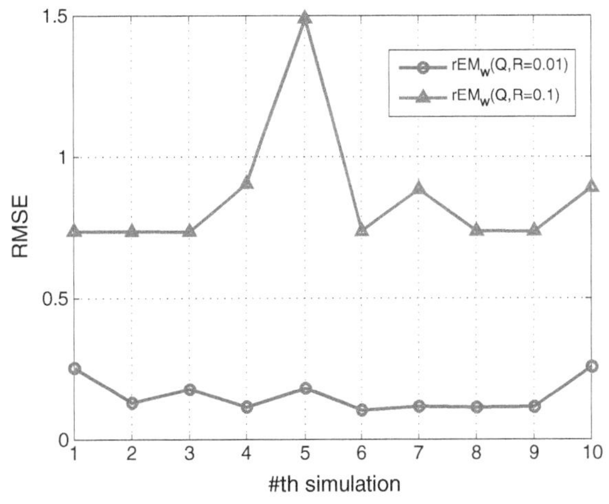

Figure 4 RMSE of rEM_w with different noise levels.

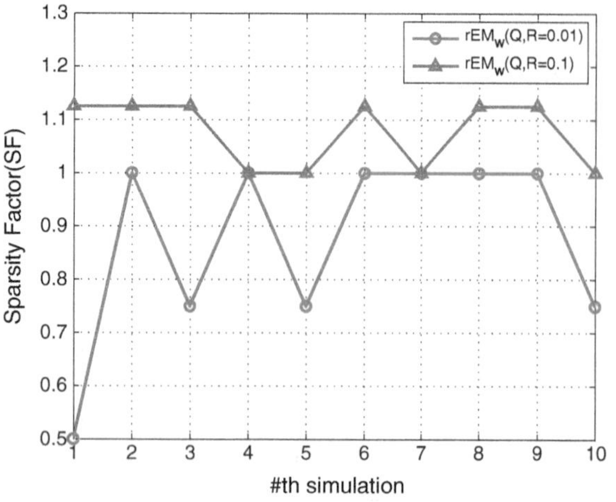

Figure 5 SF of rEM_w with different noise levels.

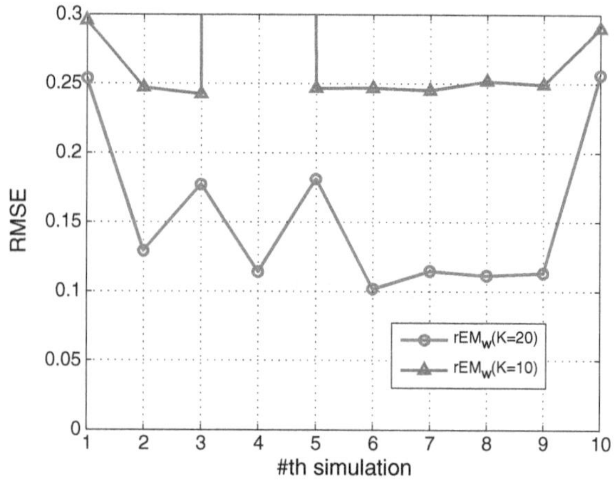

Figure 7 RMSE of rEM_w with different lengths of observations.

5.1.5 Effect of sparsity level

The performance comparison of the rEM_w and the conventional EM with different sparsity levels of $\boldsymbol{A}$ is shown in Figures 13, 14, 15. In this subsection, another $\boldsymbol{A}$ which is denser than the previously used $\boldsymbol{A}$ is given by

$$\boldsymbol{A} = \begin{bmatrix} 3 & -1 & 0 & -4.5 \\ -2.9 & 0 & 5 & 1 \\ -6 & 4 & 0 & -1 \\ 1 & -5 & 2 & 0 \end{bmatrix}. \quad (48)$$

Note that '(Denser)' is used to denote the result using $\boldsymbol{A}$ shown in Equation 48. It can be seen that the RMSE of rEM_w(Denser) is comparable to that of the EM(Denser). However, the sparsity factor of rEM_w(Denser) is closer to 1 than that of the EM(Denser) which means that the rEM_w(Denser) is better. In addition, the number of matched elements of the rEM_w(Denser) is large than that of the EM(Denser), which means that the rEM_w(Denser) is better than the EM(Denser) in finding the support of the unknown parameters. The performance of the rEM_w(Denser), however, is worse than that of the rEM_w in terms of the improvement of the RMSE. Hence, the rEM algorithm may have close performance with the EM algorithm when the sparsity is not obvious.

5.1.6 Comparison with ℓ_1 optimization

We compare the proposed rEM algorithm and the ℓ_1 optimization-based method, as well as the conventional EM algorithm. The ℓ_1 optimization is a popular approach to obtain the sparse solution. For the problem under consideration, it obtains an estimate of $\boldsymbol{\theta}$ by solving the following optimization problem:

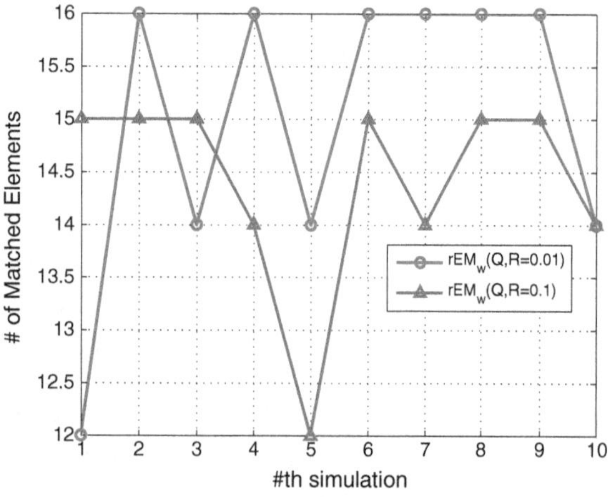

Figure 6 The number of matched elements of rEM_w with different noise levels.

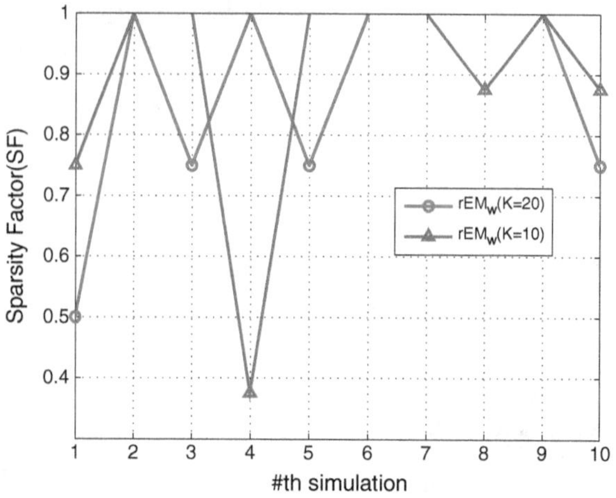

Figure 8 SF of rEM_w with different lengths of observations.

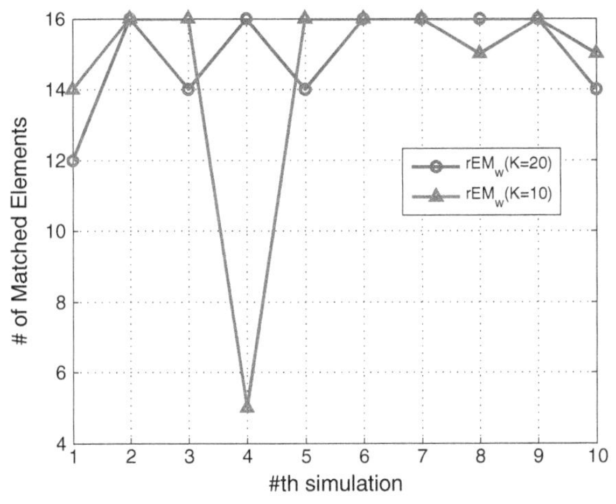

Figure 9 The number of matched elements of rEM_w with different lengths of observations.

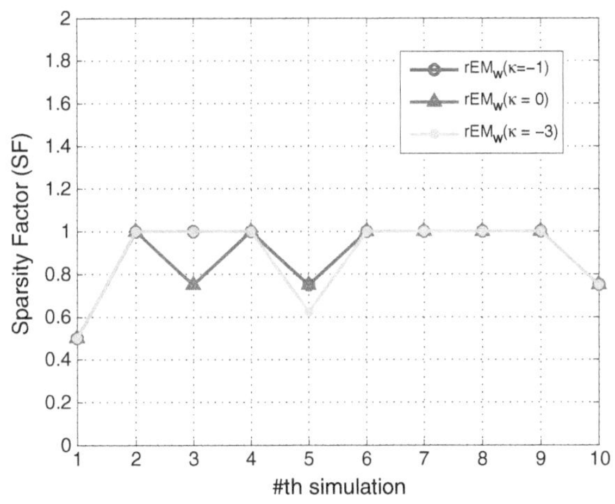

Figure 11 SR of rEM_w with different κ.

$$\hat{\theta} = \arg\min_{\theta} \sum_{k=2}^{K} [y_k - A(\theta) g(\hat{x}_{k-1})]^T [y_k - A(\theta) g(\hat{x}_{k-1})] + \lambda \|\theta\|_1, \quad (49)$$

where $\hat{x}_1 = x_1$ and $\hat{x}_{k+1} = g(\hat{x}_k)$.

We also compare the ℓ_1 optimization method with the proposed rEM_w algorithm, and the results are shown in Figures 16, 17, 18. Seven different λ (5, 2, 1, 0.5, 0.1, 0.05, and 0.01) are used in the ℓ_1 optimization method. The RMSE does not decrease monotonously with the decreasing of the parameter λ. Among all tested values, the ℓ_1 optimization method with $\lambda = 0.1$ gives the smallest RMSE. However, the sparsity factor of the ℓ_1 optimization with $\lambda = 0.1$ is far from the ideal value 1. The ℓ_1 optimization with $\lambda = 5$ gives the best support detection as shown in Figure 18. The re-weighted ℓ_1 optimization algorithm is also used in the simulation. However, all ℓ_1 optimization-based methods cannot achieve better performance than that of using the rEM_w.

5.1.7 Comparison with BPDN-DF

To solve the problem using BPDN-DF, the model in (41) and (44) are modified as

$$\tilde{x}_k = \tilde{f}(\tilde{x}_{k-1}) \begin{bmatrix} A(\theta_{k-1}) g(x_{k-1}) \\ \theta_{k-1} \end{bmatrix} + \begin{bmatrix} v_k \\ 0 \end{bmatrix} \quad (50)$$

and

$$h(\tilde{x}_k) = \tilde{H}_k + n_k = \begin{bmatrix} I_4 & 0_{16} \end{bmatrix} \tilde{x}_k + n_k, \quad (51)$$

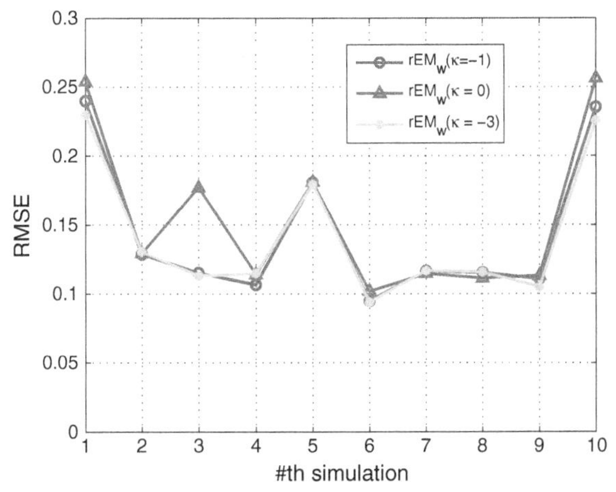

Figure 10 RMSE of rEM_w with different κ.

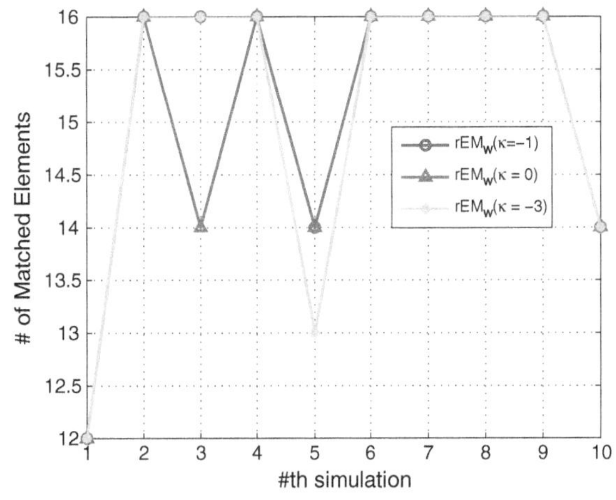

Figure 12 The number of matched elements of rEM_w with different κ.

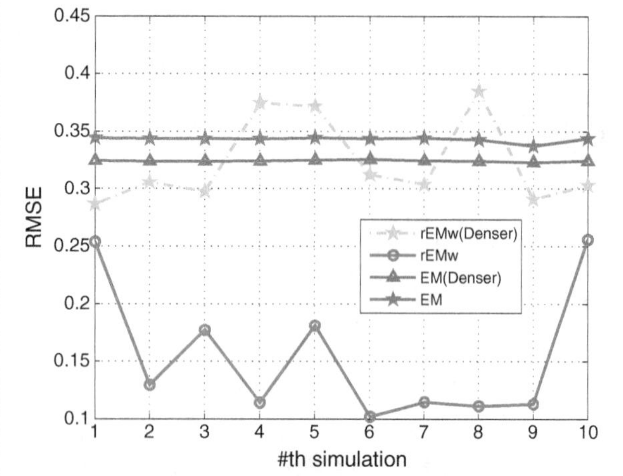

Figure 13 RMSE of the EM and rEM$_w$ for normal and denser A.

respectively. Note that $\tilde{x}_k = \left[x_k^T, \theta_k^T\right]^T$. Then, $\hat{\tilde{x}}_k$ is given by [36]

$$\hat{\tilde{x}}_k = \arg\min_{\tilde{x}} \left[\|y_k - \tilde{H}_k\tilde{x}\|_2^2 + \lambda\|\tilde{x}\|_1 + \|\tilde{x} - \tilde{f}(\tilde{x}_{k-1})\|_2^2\right], \tag{52}$$

where $\lambda = [\lambda_1, \cdots, \lambda_{20}]$ with $\lambda_i = 0$, $i = 1, 2, 3, 4$ since our objective is to explore the sparsity of the parameter θ. The exact same initial values used in testing EM and rEM are used to test the performance of the BPDN-DF. The simulation results are shown in Figures 19, 20, 21. It can be seen that although the sparsity factor of BPDN-DF is comparable with that of the rEM$_w$, the RMSE of the BPDN-DF is much larger than that of the rEM$_w$. In addition, as shown in Figure 21, the rEM$_w$ is better than the BPDN-DF in finding the support of the unknown parameters. The possible reason is that the BPDN-DF does not consider the noise in the dynamic system, and the measurement matrix $\tilde{H}_k$ is an ill-conditioned matrix. In the simulation, $\lambda_j = 0.1, j = 5, \cdots, 20$. Based on our tests by using other values of λ, there is no obvious improvement.

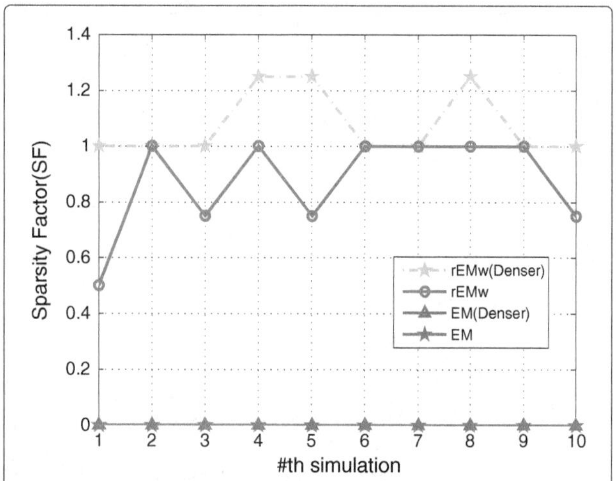

Figure 14 SF of the EM and rEM$_w$ for normal and denser A.

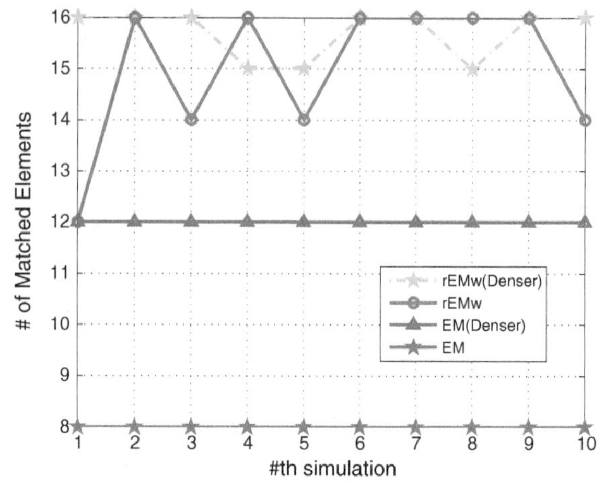

Figure 15 The number of matched elements of the EM and rEM$_w$ for normal and denser A.

5.2 Inference of gene regulatory network with eight genes

In this section, we test the proposed algorithm using a larger gene regulatory network which includes eight genes; the performances of the EM, the rEM, the rEM$_w$, the ℓ_1 optimization method, and BPDN-DF are given. Forty data points are collected to infer the structure of the network. The system noise and measurement noise are assumed to be Gaussian-distributed with means $\mathbf{0}$ and covariances $U_k = 0.01I_8$ and $R_k = 0.01I_8$, respectively.

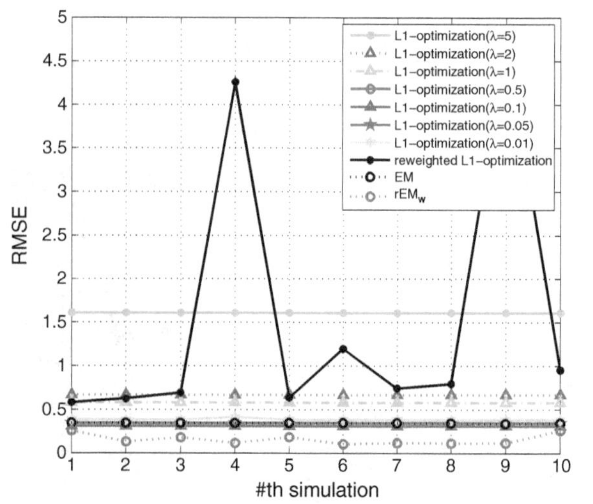

Figure 16 RMSE of the ℓ_1 optimization with different λ, reweighted ℓ_1 optimization, EM, and rEM$_w$.

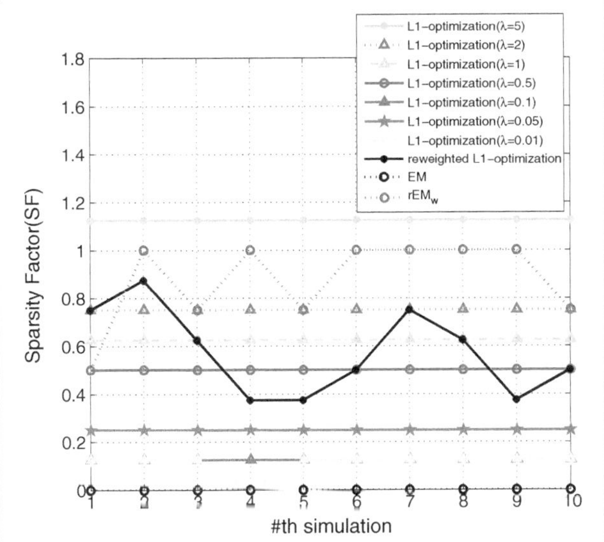

Figure 17 SF of the ℓ_1 optimization with different λ, reweighted ℓ_1 optimization, EM, and rEM$_w$.

The connection coefficient matrix is given by

$$A = \begin{pmatrix} 0 & 0 & 0 & 0 & 0 & 0 & 2.4 & 3.2 \\ 0 & 0 & 0 & 4.1 & 0 & -2.4 & 0 & 4.1 \\ -5.0 & 2.1 & -1.5 & 0 & 4.5 & 0 & 2.1 & 0 \\ 0 & 1.3 & 2.5 & -3.7 & 1.8 & 0 & 0 & -3.1 \\ 0 & 0 & 0 & -2.6 & -3.2 & 0 & -1 & 4 \\ -1.5 & -1.8 & 0 & 3.4 & 1.4 & 1.1 & 0 & 1.7 \\ -1.8 & 0 & 0 & -3 & 1.1 & 2.4 & 0 & 0 \\ -1.3 & 0 & -1 & 0 & 2.1 & 0 & 0 & 2.2 \end{pmatrix}. \tag{53}$$

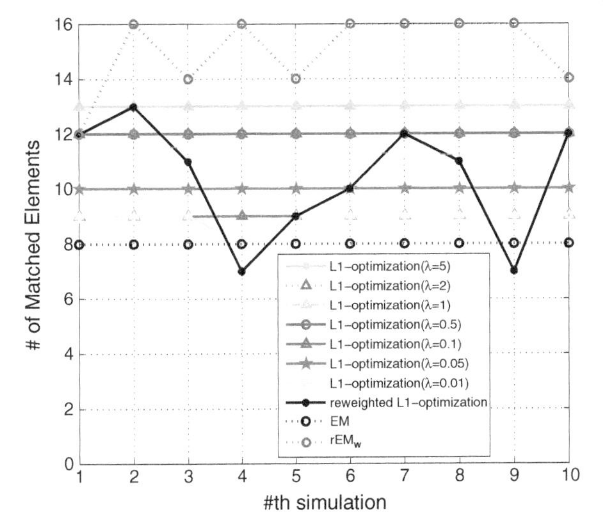

Figure 18 The number of matched elements of the ℓ_1 optimization with different λ, reweighted ℓ_1 optimization, EM, and rEM$_w$.

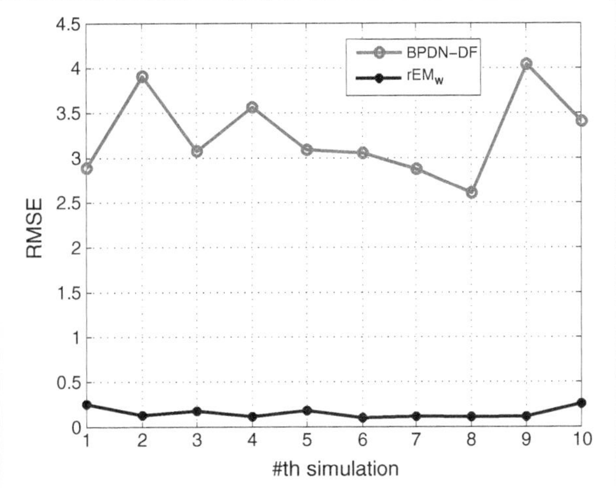

Figure 19 RMSE of BPDN-DF and rEM$_w$.

For testing, each coefficient in $\hat{A}$ is initialized from a Gaussian distribution with mean 0 and variance 1. The system state is initialized using the first measurement.

The metric used to evaluate the inferred GRN is the ROC curve, in which the true-positive rate (TPR) and the false-positive rate (FPR) are involved. They are given by

$$\text{TPR} = \frac{\text{TP\#}}{\text{TP\#} + \text{FN\#}}, \tag{54}$$

$$\text{FPR} = \frac{\text{FP\#}}{\text{FP\#} + \text{TN\#}}, \tag{55}$$

where the number of true positives (TP#) denotes the number of links correctly predicted by the inference algorithm, the number of false positives (FP#) denotes the number of incorrectly predicted links. The number of true negatives (TN#) denotes the number of correctly predicted non-links, and the number of false negatives

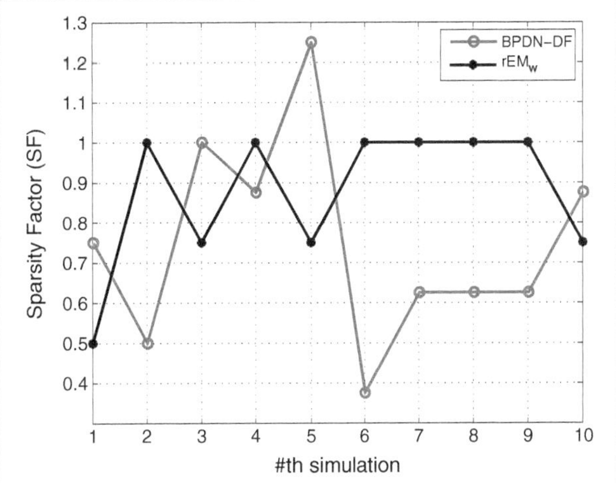

Figure 20 SF of BPDN-DF and rEM$_w$.

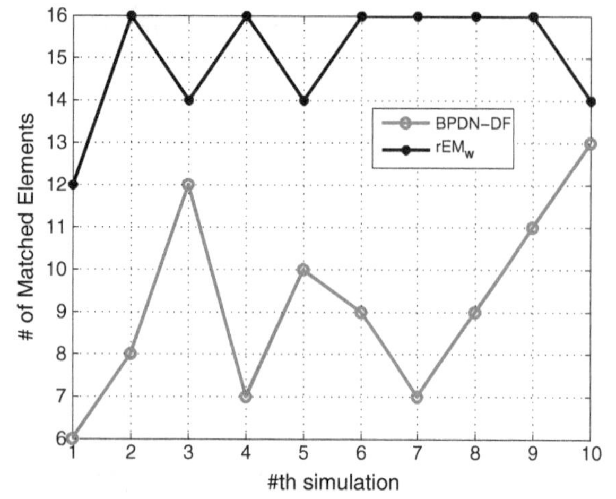

Figure 21 The number of matched elements of BPDN-DF and rEM$_w$.

(FN#) denotes the number of missed links by the inference algorithm [15].

The ROC curves of the EM, the rEM, and the rEM$_w$ are compared in Figure 22. The rEM with different λ is tested. In Figure 22, the curves of rEM with four typical values of λ are shown. There is no obvious improvement by using other λ. From the figure, it can be seen that the rEM$_w$ performs better than the rEM and the convectional EM algorithms.

In addition, the sparse solution is obtained by using rEM and rEM$_w$ while it cannot be obtained by using the EM algorithm. The sparsity factor of rEM and rEM$_w$ is shown in Figure 23; the sparsity of the solution given by rEM$_w$ is closer to the ground truth than that given by the EM algorithm.

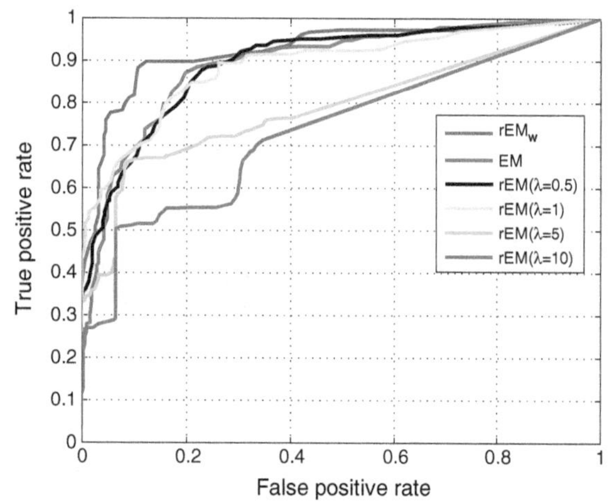

Figure 22 ROCs of the EM, the rEM, and the rEM$_w$.

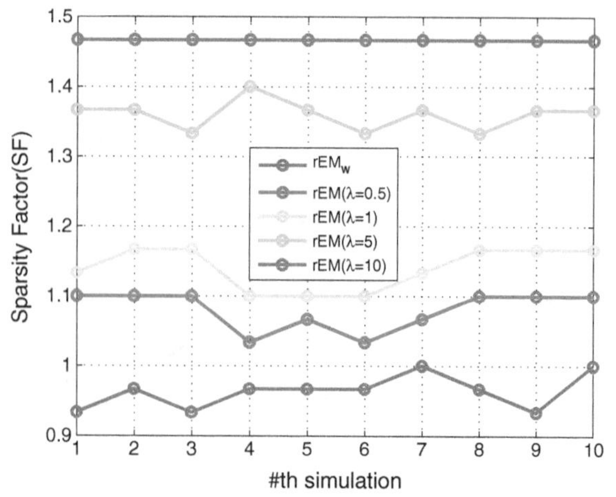

Figure 23 Sparsity factor of the rEM and the rEM$_w$.

In Figure 24, the ROC curves of the rEM$_w$, ℓ_1 optimization method, and BPDN-DF are compared. Similarly, the ℓ_1 optimization method with different λ is tested, and only four curves are shown in the figure. By using other values, there is no obvious improvement. The BPDN-DF with different λ has no obvious difference in the test. From Figure 24, it can be seen that the rEM$_w$ performs much better than the ℓ_1 optimization method and BPDN-DF algorithm. Hence, the sparsity factor of ℓ_1 optimization method and BPDN-DF is not shown.

5.3 Inference of gene regulatory network from malaria expression data

The dataset with the first six gene expression data of malaria is given in reference [37] and is used in this section. The initial covariance for the algorithm is $\boldsymbol{P}_0 = 0.5\boldsymbol{I}$. The process noise and measurement noise are

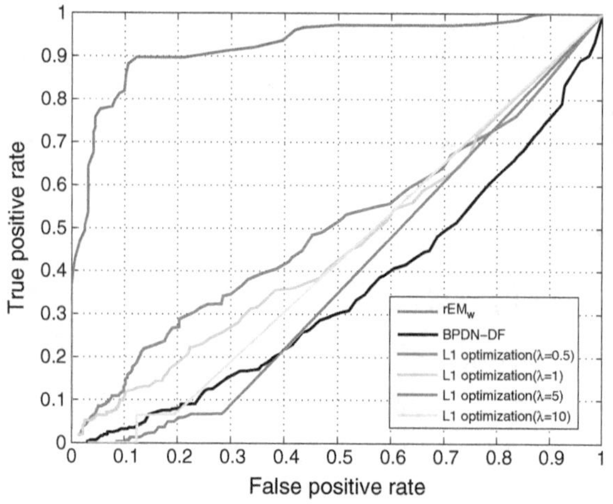

Figure 24 ROCs of the rEM$_w$, ℓ_1 optimization method, and BPDN-DF.

assumed to be Gaussian noise with zero mean and covariance $0.3^2\boldsymbol{I}$ and $0.4^2\boldsymbol{I}$, respectively. In the following, we show the inference results of the parameter and the state estimation provided by the unscented Kalman filter (UKF) based on the model using the inferred parameters.

The inferred $\boldsymbol{A}$ by the EM algorithm is

$$\bar{A} = \begin{bmatrix} 2.2120 & -7.9443 & 2.3843 & 6.1800 & -3.5269 & 2.8300 \\ -0.6585 & -0.5319 & 0.5987 & 4.0023 & -2.8684 & 1.1167 \\ 1.9022 & -9.1935 & 3.0504 & 7.9274 & -5.0037 & 3.4825 \\ 1.8157 & -8.8003 & 3.4441 & 9.4813 & -7.1284 & 3.4345 \\ 1.8413 & -8.3515 & 2.2789 & 5.3726 & -1.6722 & 2.5999 \\ 2.1053 & -3.3850 & 3.4007 & 10.2753 & -12.3170 & 2.1100 \end{bmatrix}. \tag{56}$$

The inferred $\boldsymbol{A}$ by the rEM with $\lambda = 1$ is

$$\bar{A} = \begin{bmatrix} 0.8448 & -6.3169 & 0.8943 & 3.9423 & 0 & 2.8387 \\ 0 & -0.2422 & 0 & 0.5051 & 0 & 1.3407 \\ 0.1424 & -7.1799 & 0.7461 & 5.2535 & 0.3607 & 2.9298 \\ 0.0048 & -8.1010 & 0.7851 & 5.3300 & 0 & 4.2157 \\ 0.4022 & -6.9358 & 2.0375 & 4.0332 & 0 & 2.7372 \\ 0 & -5.6613 & 0 & 4.3934 & -2.9426 & 6.3350 \end{bmatrix}. \tag{57}$$

The inferred $\boldsymbol{A}$ by the rEM_w is

$$\bar{A} = \begin{bmatrix} 0.3662 & -7.5033 & 0 & 9.6020 & 0 & 0 \\ -2.0531 & -1.1905 & 0 & 5.1439 & -0.0011 & 0 \\ 0 & -9.0526 & 0 & 11.6504 & 0 & 0 \\ 0 & -9.3419 & 0 & 14.4056 & -3.5361 & 1.0739 \\ 0.0034 & -8.5250 & 0 & 11.0732 & 0 & 0 \\ 0 & -3.8773 & 0.0025 & 13.1848 & -8.3610 & 1.4877 \end{bmatrix}. \tag{58}$$

The state estimation provided by the UKF based on the model using the inferred parameters of the EM, the rEM, the rEM_w, and the true gene expression is shown in Figure 25. The left top and right top panels are the expression of the first gene and the second gene, respectively. The left center and right center panels are the expression of the third gene and the fourth gene, respectively. The left bottom and right bottom panels are the expression of the fifth gene and the sixth gene, respectively. It can be seen that the estimate gene expression using the UKF and parameters given by the EM, the rEM, and the rEM_w is close to the true gene expression data. In addition, The rEM_w algorithm provide sparser

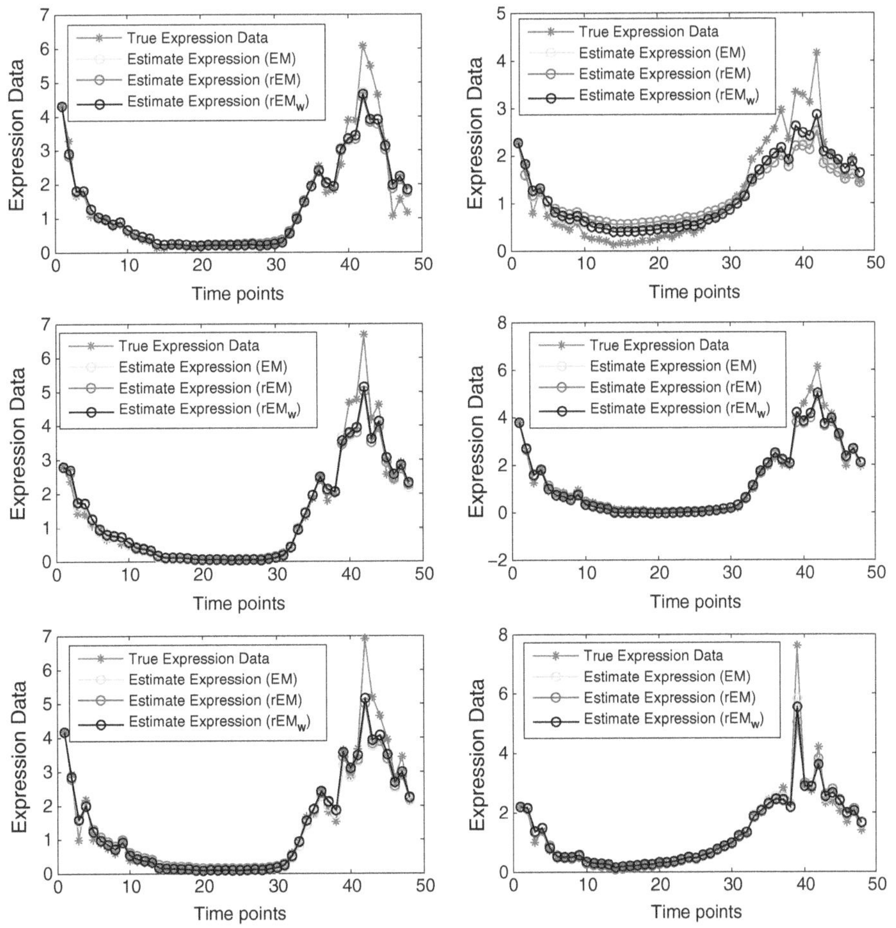

Figure 25 True malaria gene expression and estimated gene expression by different algorithms.

solution than the rEM algorithm. Both the rEM and the rEM_w algorithms give sparser solutions than the EM algorithm which validates the effectiveness of the proposed method.

6 Conclusions

In this paper, we have considered the problem of sparse parameter estimation in a general nonlinear dynamic system, and we have proposed an approximate MAP-EM solution, called the rEM algorithm. The expectation step involves the forward Gaussian approximation filtering and the backward Gaussian approximation smoothing. The maximization step employs a re-weighted iterative thresholding method. We have provided examples of the inference of gene regulatory network based on expression data. Comparisons with the traditional EM algorithm as well as with the existing approach to solving sparse problems such as the ℓ_1 optimization and the BPDN-DF show that the proposed rEM algorithm provides both more accurate estimation result and sparser solutions.

Competing interests

The authors declare that they have no competing interests.

Author details

[1]Intelligent Fusion Technology, Germantown, Inc., MD 20876, USA.
[2]Department of Electrical Engineering, Columbia University, New York, NY 10027, USA.

References

1. J Tropp, S Wright, Computational methods for sparse solution of linear inverse problems. Proc. IEEE. **98**(6), 948–958 (2010)
2. S Ji, Y Xue, L Carin, Bayesian compressive sensing. IEEE Trans. Signal Processing. **56**(6), 2346–2356 (2008)
3. EG Larsson, Y Selen, Linear regression with a sparse parameter vector. IEEE Trans. Signal Processing. **55**(2), 451–460 (2007)
4. M Figueiredo, R Nowak, S Wright, Gradient projection for sparse reconstruction: application to compressed sensing and other inverse problems. IEEE J. Sel. Top. Sign. Process. **1**(4), 586–597 (2007)
5. D Zachariah, S Chatterjee, M Jansson, Dynamic iterative pursuit. IEEE Trans. Signal Processing. **60**(9), 4967–4972 (2012)
6. C Qiu, W Lu, N Vaswani, Real-time dynamic MR image reconstruction using Kalman filtered compressed sensing. Paper presented in the IEEE international conference on acoustics, speech and signal processing (ICASSP), Taipei, 19–24 April 2009, pp. 393–396
7. J Ziniel, P Schniter, Efficient high-dimensional inference in the multiple measurement vector problem. IEEE Trans. Signal Processing. **61**(2), 340–354 (2013)
8. J Vila, P Schniter, Expectation-maximization Bernoulli-Gaussian approximate message passing. Paper presented at the forty-fifth Asilomar conference on signals, systems and computers (ASILOMAR), Pacific Grove, CA USA, 6–9 Nov 2011, pp. 799–803
9. J Vila, P Schniter, Expectation-maximization Gaussian-mixture approximate message passing. Paper presented in the 46th annual conference on information sciences and systems (CISS), Princeton, NJ USA, 21–23 March 2012, pp. 1–6
10. U Kamilov, S Rangan, A Fletcher, M Unser, Estimation, Approximate Message Passing with Consistent Parameter and Applications to Sparse Learning. Paper presented at the 26th annual conference on neural information processing systems, Lake Tahoe, NV, USA, 3–8 Dec 2012
11. A Gurbuz, M Pilanci, O Arikan, Expectation maximization based matching pursuit. Paper presented at the in IEEE international conference on acoustics, speech and signal processing (ICASSP), Kyoto, 25–30 March 2012, pp. 3313–3316
12. A Charles, C Rozell, *Re-weighted l_1 Dynamic Filtering for Time-Varying Sparse Signal Estimation* (Cornell University, Ithaca, 2012). arXiv:1208.0325
13. J Ziniel, P Schniter, Efficient high-dimensional inference in the multiple measurement vector problem. IEEE Trans. Signal Processing. **61**(2), 340–354 (2013)
14. S Barembruch, E Moulines, A Scaglione, A sparse EM algorithm for blind and semi-blind identification of doubly selective OFDM channels. Paper presented at the IEEE eleventh international workshop on signal processing advances in wireless communications (SPAWC), Marrakech, 20–23 June 2010, pp. 1–5
15. A Noor, E Serpedin, M Nounou, H Nounou, Inferring gene regulatory networks via nonlinear state-space models and exploiting sparsity. IEEE/ACM Trans. Comput. Biol. Bioinform. **9**(4), 1203–1211 (2012)
16. TS Gardner, D Di Bernardo, D Lorenz, JJ Collins, Inferring genetic networks and identifying compound mode of action via expression profiling. Science **301**(5629), 102–105 (2003)
17. J Tegner, MS Yeung, J Hasty, JJ Collins, Reverse engineering gene networks: integrating genetic perturbations with dynamical modeling. Proc. Natl. Acad. Sci. **100**(10), 5944–5949 (2003)
18. X Cai, JA Bazerque, GB Giannakis, Inference of gene regulatory networks with sparse structural equation models exploiting genetic perturbations. PLoS Comput. Biol. **9**(5), e1003068 (2013)
19. D Thieffry, AM Huerta, E Pérez-Rueda, J Collado-Vides, From specific gene regulation to genomic networks: a global analysis of transcriptional regulation in *Escherichia coli*. Bioessays. **20**(5), 433–440 (1998)
20. Z Wang, F Yang, D Ho, S Swift, A Tucker, X Liu, Stochastic dynamic modeling of short gene expression time-series data. IEEE Trans. Nanobioscience. **7**(1), 44–55 (2008)
21. A Noor, E Serpedin, M Nounou, H Nounou, Reverse engineering sparse gene regulatory networks using cubature Kalman filter and compressed sensing. Adv. Bioinformatics. **2013**, 205763 (2013)
22. L Wang, X Wang, AP Arkin, MS Samoilov, Inference of gene regulatory networks from genome-wide knockout fitness data. Bioinformatics. **29**(3), 338–346 (2013)
23. G McLachlan, T Krishnan, *The EM Algorithm and Extensions* (Wiley-Interscience, Hoboken, 2008)
24. I Arasaratnam, S Haykin, Cubature Kalman filters. IEEE Trans. Automat. Contr. **54**(6), 1254–1269 (2009)
25. K Ito, K Xiong, Gaussian filters for nonlinear filtering problems. IEEE Trans. Automat. Contr. **45**(5), 910–927 (2000)
26. B Jia, M Xin, Y Cheng, Sparse-grid quadrature nonlinear filtering. Automatica. **48**(2), 327–341 (2012)
27. SJ Julier, JK Uhlmann, Unscented filtering and nonlinear estimation. Proc. IEEE. **92**(3), 401–422 (2004)
28. D Guo, X Wang, Quasi-Monte Carlo filtering in nonlinear dynamic systems. IEEE Trans. Signal Processing. **54**(6), 2087–2098 (2006)
29. B Jia, M Xin, Y Cheng, High-degree cubature Kalman filter. Automatica. **49**(2), 510–518 (2013)
30. S Sarkka, Unscented Rauch–Tung–Striebel smoother. IEEE Trans. Automat. Cont. **53**(3), 845–849 (2008)
31. M Schmidt, Graphical model structure learning with L1-regularization. Ph.D. Dissertation, University of British Columbia, 2010
32. S Bahmani, B Raj, P Boufounos, Greedy sparsity-constrained optimization. J. Mac. Learn. Res. **14**, 807–841 (2013)
33. A Beck, YC Eldar, Sparsity constrained nonlinear optimization: optimality conditions and algorithms. SIAM J. Optim. **23**(3), 1480–1509 (2013)
34. S Wright, R Nowak, M Figueiredo, Sparse reconstruction by separable approximation. IEEE Trans. Signal Processing. **57**(7), 2479–2493 (2009)
35. EJ Candes, MB Wakin, S Boyd, Enhancing sparsity by reweighted l1 minimization. J. Fourier. Anal. Appl. **14**, 877–905 (2008)

36. A Charles, MS Asif, J Romberg, C Rozell, Sparsity penalties in dynamical system estimation. Paper presented at the 45th annual conference on information sciences and systems (CISS), Baltimore, 23–25 March 2011, pp. 1–6
37. Z Wang, X Liu, Y Liu, J Liang, V Vinciotti, An extended kalman filtering approach to modeling nonlinear dynamic gene regulatory networks via short gene expression time series. IEEE/ACM Trans. Comput. Biol. Bioinform. **6**(3), 410–419 (2009)

Bayesian methods for expression-based integration of various types of genomics data

Elizabeth M Jennings[1], Jeffrey S Morris[2], Raymond J Carroll[1], Ganiraju C Manyam[3] and Veerabhadran Baladandayuthapani[2*]

Abstract

We propose methods to integrate data across several genomic platforms using a hierarchical Bayesian analysis framework that incorporates the biological relationships among the platforms to identify genes whose expression is related to clinical outcomes in cancer. This integrated approach combines information across all platforms, leading to increased statistical power in finding these predictive genes, and further provides mechanistic information about the manner in which the gene affects the outcome. We demonstrate the advantages of the shrinkage estimation used by this approach through a simulation, and finally, we apply our method to a Glioblastoma Multiforme dataset and identify several genes potentially associated with the patients' survival. We find 12 positive prognostic markers associated with nine genes and 13 negative prognostic markers associated with nine genes.

Keywords: Bayesian modeling; Genomics; Hierarchical models; Integrative analysis; Shrinkage priors

1 Introduction

The central dogma of molecular biology summarizes the steps involved in the passage of genetic information at a molecular level: DNA is transcribed to messenger RNA (mRNA), which is then translated to a protein, which carries out a specific action in an organism. In addition, there are also other alterations and interferences, such as epigenetic factors, that can occur at the DNA and/or mRNA levels which affect the ultimate expression of a given gene. In this paper, we consider methylation (which occurs at the DNA level and typically results in a silencing of the gene), copy number (which describes an attribute at the DNA level that affects mRNA expression), and mRNA expression (which affects protein expression); these subsequently affect a clinical phenotype (e.g., survival) (see Figure 1). In addition, it is believed that the mechanism of cancer development is complex and involves multiple genes [1]. It is known that genes interact and are related through certain pathways, and in this paper, we focus on genes from important signaling pathways that influence cancer progression and development [2].

Current technologies allow us to obtain data from the above-mentioned platforms (and many others) for each gene involved in the investigations. The Cancer Genome Atlas (TCGA) is a project that began in 2006 to gather comprehensive genomic data using multiple platforms on over 20 types of cancer [3]. The increasing availability of such data has motivated the development of methods that seek to improve estimation and prediction regarding genomic effects on cancer outcomes by integrating data from multiple platforms in a single analysis. The incorporation of information from more than one platform has the potential to increase power and lower false discovery rates in identifying markers related to clinical outcomes for cancer patients [4]; such improvements would deepen our understanding of how cancer develops and spreads, offering researchers valuable insight regarding the development of drugs and procedures intended to prevent or inhibit cancer development.

Some integration techniques consider different platforms sequentially and then draw conclusions from the combination of results. For example, the TCGA Research Network performed a large-scale study of ovarian cancer

*Correspondence: veera@mdanderson.org
[2]Department of Biostatistics, UT M.D. Anderson Cancer Center, Houston, TX 77030, USA
Full list of author information is available at the end of the article

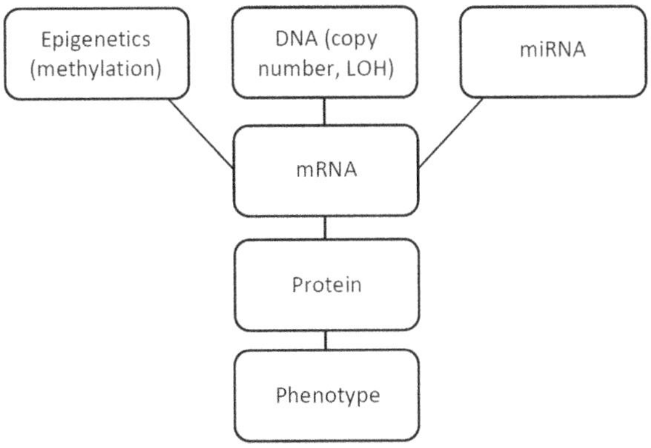

Figure 1 Platform relationships. Schematic representation of the multiple molecular platforms and their biological relationships.

data, including specific platforms such as gene mutations, copy number, mRNA expression, miRNA expression, and DNA methylation. Within each platform, they compared normal and tumor cells to identify significant genes and combined the information obtained from different platforms to understand the deeper biology behind the cancer mechanisms, including gene interactions. Using the prevalence of significant genes, they also identified influential pathways, including the RB1 and PI3K/RAS pathways [5]. TCGA Research Network conducted a similar style study on Glioblastoma Multiforme (GBM) data and, among other things, discovered a previously unknown link between MGMT methylation and the mutation spectra of mismatch repair genes through the integration of mutation, methylation, and clinical treatment data [6]. These methods provide insight into the roles and interactions of genes as related to the development and outcome of the disease.

Another type of integrative method proposes incorporating multiple platforms in a single model. Such approaches must face the challenges of high dimensionality and complex biological relationships both within and between platforms. One such approach is iCluster, proposed by Shen et al., which is a joint latent variable model-based clustering method that integrates data from multiple genomic platforms to cluster samples into subtypes. iCluster achieves reduced dimension of the data, and it is shown to identify potentially novel subtypes of breast cancer and lung cancer [7]. However, this method does not directly model the biological relationships among platforms; in addition, it is an unsupervised method, while our approach is supervised. Tyekucheva et al. suggest a method that includes multiple platforms as predictors in a logistic regression model (with phenotype as the response), and they show that incorporating multiple platforms yields more power to detect differentially expressed genes than approaches that only use a single platform [8]. As with iCluster, this approach accounts for dependence between platforms, but it does not directly take into account their biological relationships.

Another method, proposed by Lanckriet et al., first represents data from each platform (such as primary protein sequence, protein-protein interaction, and mRNA expression) via a kernel function and then combines the kernels in a classification model (predicting, for example, protein type). It is shown that this method outperforms methods based on a single kernel from any one data platform [9]. However, this method does not directly model the relationships among the platforms, and kernel representations of the marker effects on the clinical outcomes are not directly interpretable. Liu et al. suggest another approach that integrates clinical covariates and multiple gene expressions (from a common pathway) to predict a continuous outcome through a semiparametric model; the covariates are modeled parametrically, and the pathway effect is modeled through least squares kernel machines (LSKM) (either parametrically or not). The covariate as well as pathway effects can be estimated, and the pathway effect can be tested for significance. The nonparametric LSKM regression allows for complicated interactions between genes [10], but this method only incorporates a single genomic platform (and accounts for its internal biological relationships). Recently, Wang et al. proposed an integrative Bayesian analysis of genomics data (iBAG) framework that models the biological relationships between two platforms [4]. This approach involves a global gene search and uses variable selection via the Bayesian lasso-based shrinkage priors to deal with the high dimensionality of the data.

In this paper, we introduce a generalized version of iBAG that integrates data from an arbitrary (multiple) number of genomic platforms using a hierarchical model that incorporates the biological relationships among them. We focus our analysis on genes from several important cancer signaling pathways and integrate mRNA, methylation, and copy number data to predict survival in GBM patients. In addition, we reduce dimension by regressing the clinical outcome on latent scores of the platforms (see Section 2.1 for details). To improve effect size estimation and to achieve sparsity, we use a Normal-Gamma (NG) prior for the effects, which increases flexibility in the estimation as compared to the Laplace prior of the Bayesian lasso [11] (see Section 2.2 for further discussion). Section 3 illustrates our methodology on a synthetic example; analysis of GBM data is presented in Section 4; and conclusions are drawn in Section 5.

2 A multivariate iBAG model

Our construction of a multivariate iBAG model employs a two-component hierarchical model where the first component can be considered as the *mechanistic model* and the second can be considered as the *clinical model*. In the first stage mechanistic model, we partition each gene's expression into the factors explained by methylation, copy number, and other (unknown/unmeasured) causes using a principal component-based regression model. Subsequently, we include these factors as predictors in the second stage clinical model, thus finding not only those genes whose expression is directly related to clinical outcome, but also expression effects driven by methylation, copy number, or other mechanisms. We explain the construction of each of these components below.

2.1 Mechanistic model

Let $n =$ number of patients, $J =$ number of platforms being integrated, and $p_j =$ number of genes from platform j. The mechanistic model for each gene can be expressed as:

$$\mathrm{mRNA}_i = \mathrm{M}_i + \mathrm{CN}_i + \mathrm{O}_i,$$

where each of the terms are defined as follows:

- mRNA_i is the level of gene expression for gene i (where $i = 1, \ldots, \max(p_j)$; $j = 1, \ldots, J$) and is of dimension $(n \times 1)$.
- M_i is the part of gene$_i$ expression that is attributed to methylation, and is of dimension $(n \times 1)$. Specifically, M_i is the product of some methylation predictor and a fitted coefficient. Details are below.
- CN_i is the part of gene$_i$ expression that is attributed to changes in copy number, and is of dimension $(n \times 1)$. Specific calculation is similar to M_i – see below.
- O_i represents the 'other' (remaining) part of the gene expression that is explained by something other than methylation or copy number, and is of dimension $(n \times 1)$.

Since the raw methylation and copy number data for any given gene can contain multiple (up to 40 in our data) values from different markers within that gene, to estimate each of the components M_i, CN_i, and O_i, we first carry out two principal component analyses (PCA) for gene$_i$: one each for the methylation and copy number data, and in each case, we keep the number of principal components that retain $\geq 90\%$ of the total variation. We then regress mRNA_i on the methylation and copy number PC scores. We use the estimated pieces and the corresponding residuals from this regression to estimate the vectors $\mathrm{M}_i = \sum_{k=1}^{K} X_{i,k}^{M} B_k^{M}$ (where $X_{i,k}^{M}$ is the methylation value for gene i with $K = 1$ if there is only one methylation marker for that gene, or the methylation score for principal component k for gene i if there are multiple methylation markers for gene i, and B_k^{M} is the vector of regression coefficients), $\mathrm{CN}_i = \sum_{r=1}^{R} X_{i,r}^{CN} B_r^{CN}$ (where $X_{i,r}^{CN}$ is the copy number value for gene i with $R = 1$ if there is only one copy number marker for that gene, or the copy number score for principal component r for gene i if there are multiple copy number markers for gene i, and B_r^{CN} is the vector of regression coefficients), and O_i = residuals. This process is repeated for each gene independently.

2.2 Clinical model

The clinical model component of our construction relates the effect of the mechanistic parts of the genes (as estimated above) to a clinical outcome of interest (e.g., survival, in our context) and can be written as:

$$Y = \mathrm{M}\boldsymbol{\beta}_1 + \mathrm{CN}\boldsymbol{\beta}_2 + \mathrm{O}\boldsymbol{\beta}_3 + \boldsymbol{\epsilon},$$

where Y denotes the clinical outcome, $\boldsymbol{\beta}_j$ are the effects of platform j on Y, and $\boldsymbol{\epsilon}$ is the error term. The covariates in the model $\{\mathrm{M}, \mathrm{CN}, \mathrm{O}\}$ are the vectorized gene expression effects attributed to methylation, copy number, and other sources, respectively, and are estimated from the mechanistic model. In essence, our clinical component jointly (additively) models the effects of all the gene expressions and their components - derived from different sources (methylation/copy number) - in a unified manner. When the clinical response is survival, we use an accelerated failure time (AFT) model, taking Y to be log(survival) [12].

Our goal is to find a list of significant genes that affect the outcome via the various mechanisms; hence, efficient estimation of $\boldsymbol{\beta} = \{\boldsymbol{\beta}_1, \boldsymbol{\beta}_2, \boldsymbol{\beta}_3\}$ is of primary interest. One route would be to simply fit a least squares regression to estimate the parameters. However, the number of predictors is large compared to the number of samples, and, more importantly, we expect our solution to be very sparse since only a few genes will be related to clinical response; hence, least squares would overfit the data and yield less accurate results as compared to approaches that induce sparsity by shrinkage/penalization. We illustrate this fact in our simulation in Section 3.

To induce shrinkage/penalization, we follow a Bayesian approach and specify particular prior distributions for each model parameter in the clinical model and sample from the posterior distribution using Markov Chain

Monte Carlo (MCMC). There are several priors known to achieve sparsity and facilitate Bayesian variable selection, which we will discuss briefly. One option is to simply put vague Normal(0, ∞) priors on each regression coefficient. This is equivalent to doing least squares regression and is impossible in cases where there are more variables than data points, because singular solutions arise. A natural extension is to place proper mean-zero Normal priors on the coefficients, which is equivalent to ridge regression. Although accommodating more predictors than data points and facilitating shrinkage, the type of shrinkage is linear which is not desirable in the current settings. This linear shrinkage leads to more shrinkage and thus greater bias for larger coefficients, while in this setting, we desire the opposite: less shrinkage for large (significant) coefficients and greater shrinkage for smaller (non-significant) ones. This type of non-linear shrinkage can be accomplished by various priors. One is the 'spike and slab' prior consisting of a mixture of a point mass at zero (the spike) and a Normal (the slab). Although this can accommodate a large number of predictors and avoids linear shrinkage, the shrinkage asymptotes to a constant which still results in attenuation of the truly large effects, something we want to avoid. In addition, computational complications and difficulties accompany the use of spike and slab priors. As we show below, all but one of our complete conditional distributions are in closed form, so we can avoid the computational difficulties associated with the spike and slab method, as well as the attenuation of large effects, by utilizing continuous shrinkage priors.

A widely known method that places a continuous sparsity prior on the regression coefficients is the Bayesian lasso [13], which is incorporated by assigning a double exponential (i.e., Laplace) prior to $\boldsymbol{\beta}$. When posterior modes are used as the coefficent estimates, this process yields the same solutions as Tibshirani's lasso [14]. The Bayesian lasso has proven to perform well in conducting adaptive shrinkage-induced sparsity, but the single hyperparameter formulation does not allow for enough flexibility to estimate the true size of potentially large, non-zero effects. Instead, these effect estimates are shrunk toward zero along with the smaller effects [11]. An alternate class of priors we use and discuss is the Normal-Gamma (NG) prior distribution for $\boldsymbol{\beta}$. Incorporating this continuous prior not only provides shrinkage of the coefficients but the extra hyperparameter in the NG prior construction facilitates more adaptability in the estimated shrinkage relative to the Bayesian lasso [13] - with the NG, the larger effects are shrunk less than the smaller effects [15], thus leading to improved estimation [11]. In summary, the NG prior is extremely advantageous in our situation, since it delivers the sparsity we need, while leaving larger effects mostly unshrunk, thus aiding our estimation of the important effects.

For our method, we assign a Normal-Gamma (NG) prior distribution for each $\boldsymbol{\beta}_j$. Our complete hierarchical clinical model can be written as:

$$
\begin{aligned}
\mathbf{Y} &= \text{Normal}(X\boldsymbol{\beta}, \sigma^2\mathbf{I}_n);\\
\boldsymbol{\beta} &= \text{Normal}(\mathbf{0}_{\tilde{p}}, D_\psi) \text{ where}\\
D_\psi &= \text{diag}(\psi_{1,1}, \ldots, \psi_{1,p_1}, \ldots, \psi_{J,1}, \ldots \psi_{J,p_J});\\
\psi_{j,i} &= \text{Gamma}(\lambda_j, 1/(2\gamma_j^2))\\
\sigma^2 &= \text{InverseGamma}(a, b),\\
\lambda_j &= \text{Exponential}(c),\\
\gamma_j^{-2} &= \text{Gamma}(\tilde{a}, \tilde{b}/(2\lambda_j)),
\end{aligned}
$$

where $\tilde{p} = \sum_{j=1}^{J} p_j$ is the total number of predictors in the model. (Note that the double exponential prior of the Bayesian lasso would be constructed by assigning $\beta_{j,i}|\psi_{j,i} \sim \text{Normal}(0, \psi_{j,i})$ and $\psi_{j,i} \sim \text{Exponential}(\lambda_j)$. The single parameter in the exponential prior (λ_j) is the reason such a construction has limited flexibility as compared to the NG prior which is parameterized by both λ_j and γ_j.) With the NG formulation as given above, the complete conditionals for most parameters are available in closed form - we can use Gibbs sampling to update all parameters except λ_j, which we update using a Metropolis-Hastings random walk step. More details for drawing MCMC samples are available in Appendix B.

2.3 Gene selection

Given the posterior samples from the MCMC, we determine which genes are significantly related to clinical outcome using a method based on the median probability model [16]. First, we define a minimum effect size which is driven by practical considerations. Since we are analyzing survival data, we use AFT models using log(survival) as the response; thus, a δ-fold or larger change in survival for a unit increase in a predictor corresponds to a $\beta_{j,i}$ outside the region (log(1-δ), log(1+δ)), where $\beta_{j,i}$ is the regression coefficient for platform j of gene i. Denote this region (δ_-^*, δ_+^*). (In our following analyses, we use $\delta = 0.05$ which corresponds to a 5% change in survival time.) If S is the number of MCMC samples and $\beta_{j,i}^{(s)}$ is the $\beta_{j,i}$ sample from iteration s, then $p_+(x_{j,i}) = \sum_{s=1}^{S} \mathbf{I}(\beta_{j,i}^{(s)} > \delta_+^*)/S$ is the posterior probability that $\beta_{j,i}$ is higher than the practical cutoff δ_+^*. Similarly, $p_-(x_{j,i}) = \sum_{s=1}^{S} \mathbf{I}(\beta_{j,i}^{(s)} < \delta_-^*)/S$ is the posterior probability that $\beta_{j,i}$ is lower than the practical cutoff δ_-^*. We flag a gene as 'significant' if $p_+(x_{j,i}) > 0.5$ or if $p_-(x_{j,i}) > 0.5$.

Algorithm 1 provides a concise summary of implementing the multivariate iBAG model and conducting gene selection.

Algorithm 1 Method implementation

Input: Raw data matrices, one for outcome (survival) and one for each platform (mRNA, methylation, copy number) (Rows are patients, and columns are markers arranged by gene.), number of patients n, number of platforms J, number of genes in platform j p_j, number of MCMC samples S, number of MCMC samples to use as burn-in B, and practical effect size δ.

Output: Prognostic markers with high posterior probability of having prespecified practical effect size.

Prepare data:
- Impute missing data (see Appendix A).
- For methylation and copy number platforms:
  - For each gene i:
    - Perform principal component analysis (PCA) on platform j. Keep the number of components that account for $\geq 90\%$ of the variation.
    - Get PC scores associated with retained components. Call matrix of scores M^* for methylation and CN^* for copy number, where the number of columns is the number of score vectors.
- Repeat for any other platforms available upstream of mRNA.

Fit mechanistic model:
- For each gene i:
    - Use least squares to regress response platform (mRNA) on M^* and CN^*. (Note that the modeled relationship should reflect the biological relationships between platforms.)
    - Let M be the linear combination of predicted coefficients and M^*, CN be the linear combination of predicted coefficients and CN^*, and O be the residuals.

Standardize M_i's, CN_i's, and O_i's. There should be $\sum_{j=1}^{J} p_j$ of these predictors.

Log-transform survival responses and mean-center.

Fit clinical model:
- Draw S MCMC samples from the complete conditionals (see Appendix B), using the first B samples as burn-in, to fit the AFT model and obtain $S - B$ posterior samples of regression coefficients $\beta_{j,i}$.

Marker selection:
- Given practical threshold δ, compute $\delta^*_- = \log(1 - \delta)$ and $\delta^*_+ = \log(1 + \delta)$.
- For each marker:
    - Calculate $\Pr(\beta_{j,i} > \delta^*_+)$ and $\Pr(\beta_{j,i} < \delta^*_-)$ using posterior samples.
    - Flag marker if either calculated probability is greater than 0.5.

return: identified markers

3 Simulation

We investigate the shrinkage properties of our Bayesian penalized regression formulation of the clinical model as compared to least squares regression, Bayesan lasso, frequentist lasso, and frequentist elastic net through a simulation. We simulate a training dataset with 90 predictors ($J = 3$ platforms with $p_1 = p_2 = p_3 = 30$ predictors from each), where 30 randomly selected $\beta_{j,i}$'s are set exactly to 0 and the other 60 are sampled from a Laplace($\mu = 0$, $b = 1/7$) distribution; this reflects the effective sparsity we expect to see in our data. The other settings for the simulated data are $n = 100$, $\sigma^2 = 1$, each X entry is from Normal$(0, 1)$, and $\mathbf{Y} = \text{Normal}(X\boldsymbol{\beta}, \sigma^2\mathbf{I}_n)$. The test dataset used to assess performance is simulated with the same settings as the training data, but $n = 400$. We applied our method for estimating the parameters in the clinical model, using 10,000 iterations of the Gibbs sampler with 500 for a burn-in period. For both the frequentist lasso and elastic net, we ran the simulation with two standard choices for the penalty parameter λ: (1) '1 SE' where we used the largest λ with cross validation error within one standard error of the minimum cross validation error and (2) 'min' where we used the λ with minimum error (from cross validation). For elastic net, we set the mixing parameter (that controls the mixture of penalties) to 0.5. The results of our method are compared to those of the other methods in Table 1.

We see that our method gives a good estimate of σ^2 (recall $\sigma^2 = 1$). We also note that the least squares regression yields coverage probabilities that are too high, while the frequentist coverage probabilities of the Bayesian credible intervals are close to the nominal levels. (Note that for the frequentist lasso and elastic net, it is not possible to obtain standard errors for the coefficients set to 0, and therefore, we cannot construct the CI's.) For all methods (other than least squares), the MSE ratio is less than 1 for the training data but much greater than 1 for the test data; this is consistent with the idea that in this high dimensional setting with expected sparsity, least squares tends to overfit the training data, while methods that perform shrinkage lead to improved estimation on the test data and thus yield results more applicable to the overall population. Considering that the MSE ratio is the mean squared error from least squares divided by the MSE from the respective method, we see that our method has the best (largest) MSE ratio on test data, which for our purposes is the most relevant comparison criterion.

We also see excellent shrinkage properties of our method in Figure 2; most least squares coefficient estimates (which are the maximum likelihood estimates) are far from the true parameter values, while the posterior means from our method shrink these estimates closer to the true values. The non-linear shrinkage and flexibility provided by the NG prior facilitate more shrinkage near 0

Table 1 Simulation results

	$\widehat{\sigma^2}$	95% CI coverage	90% CI coverage	MSE ratio (train data)	MSE ratio (test data)
Our method	0.9073	0.9778	0.8889	0.2827	9.4630
Maximum likelihood	0.1181	1.00	0.9667	1	1
Bayesian lasso	0.6407	0.9667	0.9111	0.3727	8.858
Freq. lasso (1 SE)	1.2020	NA	NA	0.0983	8.1163
Freq. lasso (min)	0.6379	NA	NA	0.1851	8.8374
Freq. EN (1 SE)	0.9278	NA	NA	0.1273	8.4439
Freq. EN (min)	0.7012	NA	NA	0.1684	8.7154

Freq. EN means freqentist elastic net, which was run with mixing parameter (for penalty mixture) 0.5. The estimate of σ^2 is the posterior mean for our method and the Bayesian lasso. For the others, it is the mean sum of squared error. 'CI' is credible interval for Bayesian methods and confidence interval for frequentist methods. Note that for the frequentist lasso and elastic net, it is not possible to obtain standard errors for the coefficients set to 0, and therefore, we cannot construct the CI's. The penalty choice of '1 SE' means we used the largest parameter with error within one standard error of the minimum error, while 'min' means we used the parameter with minimum error (from cross validation). MSE ratio is the mean squared error from least squares divided by the MSE from the respective method. NA indicates not applicable.

without severe attenuation of the estimates for truly large regression coefficients.

4 Integrative analysis of GBM data

GBM is one of the most common and most malignant brain tumors. The American Cancer Society estimates that in the year 2013, there will be 23,130 new cases of brain and other nervous system cancers in the USA and that 14,080 Americans will die from such cancers [17]. GBM tumors make up 17% of all primary brain tumors [18], and prognosis is typically very poor; a study with 7,259 patients, each diagnosed with GBM from 2005 to 2008, found a median survival time of 14.6 months for patients who received tumor-directed surgery and radiation therapy and a median survival time of 2.9 months for patients who did not receive any radiation treatment [19]. Treatment options include surgery, radiation, and/or chemotherapy, but even for a patient receiving more than one of these treatments, the outlook is dismal at best. Finding prognostic biomarkers related to cancer development and patient survival is an important issue, and GBM was one of first cancers to be studied in TCGA. The data currently available contains information from multiple molecular platforms (genomic/epigenomic/transcriptomic) as well as clinical data on several hundred tumor samples (approximately 500).

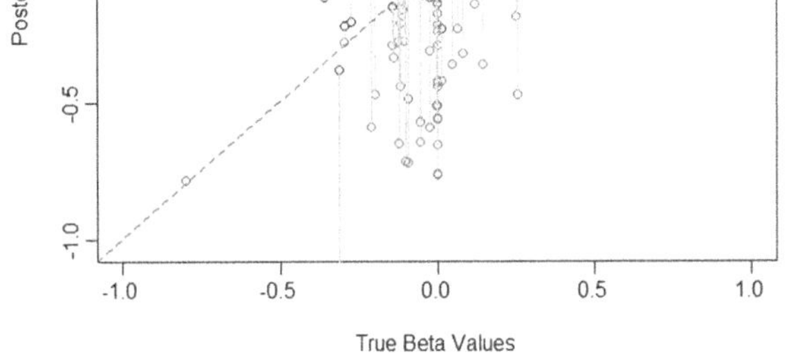

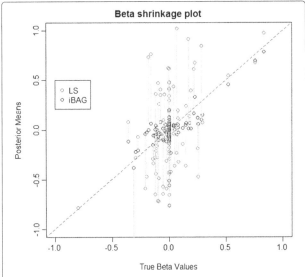

Figure 2 Simulation results. Least squares estimates and posterior means from our method are plotted against the true β values. The vertical lines denote the difference between the estimates from each method thus indicating the shrinkage properties of the NG prior.

The availability of such extensive genomic data has prompted several studies using the TCGA GBM data, and fortunately, there continue to be discoveries of biomarkers that aid in predicting survival and identifying subtypes of GBM. One such study conducted by Verhaak et al. combined gene expression data from multiple types of microarray assays to classify tumors into four distinct subtypes (each responding differently to therapy) and to discover which gene expression levels had a significant impact on the classification. Other platforms were also used, such as copy number and mutations, in separate analyses to test for associations with subtype [20]. Another study by Noushmehr et al. used the available GBM DNA methylation data to identify a subgroup of GBM tumors associated with a significantly longer survival time [21]. In our integrative analysis, we use 163 matched tumor samples that have been assayed by expression, methylation, and copy number platforms as described below. Each of these samples has an uncensored survival time (in days), and our aim is to identify prognostic biomarkers.

4.1 Description of data

Our copy number data is level 2 data from the HG_CGH_244A platform; it is the normalized signal for copy number alterations of aggregated regions per probe. Our methylation data is level 3 data from the HumanMethylation27K arrays; it is the methylated sites along a gene (probe level data). Our expression data is level 3 data (summarized per gene) from the Affymetrix profiled HT_HG_U133A platform [22].

We focus our analysis on data corresponding to 49 genes implicated in important signaling pathways in GBM (RTK/PI3K, P53, and RB pathways [2]), using the following structure:

1. *OurSurvival* (163 × 1), containing days of survival after diagnosis for each patient.
2. *OurMRNA* (163 × 49), containing mRNA expression levels for each gene (columns) for each patient (rows).
3. *OurMeth* (163 × 176), containing data on the methylation markers (columns) for each patient (rows). There can be multiple (ranging from 1 to 21) methylation markers per gene, and the columns are ordered by gene.
4. *OurCopyNumber* (163 × 524), containing copy number data (columns) for each patient (rows). Again, there are multiple (ranging from 1 to 43) values per gene, and the columns are ordered by gene.

One gene has no methylation data, so we remove that column from the X matrix, which essentially sets M_i to be 0 for that gene. Any effect that may be due to methylation for that gene would then be captured by the 'other' predictor in the clinical model. After standardizing the predictors and imputing the (few) missing values, we model the data using an AFT model with log survival times as the outcome and apply our method of estimating the parameters of the iBAG model.

4.2 Results using iBAG model

After applying our method to the GBM data, we then use the method discussed in Section 2.3 to determine the significant markers using $\delta = 0.05$ (corresponding to a 5% change in survival time). Figures 3 and 4 show the posterior probabilities of the effect ($\beta_{j,i}$) being greater than δ^*_+ and less than δ^*_-, respectively. Figure 5 depicts the posterior means of the $\beta_{j,i}$'s and also indicates which were flagged as significant. We find 25 markers to be significant, 12 with positive effects on survival (more expression attributed to that platform, better prognosis) and 13 with negative effects (more expression attributed to that platform, poorer prognosis). The genes with the 12 positive markers were PDGFRB, FGFR1, CCND2, PIK3R2, IRS1, CDKN2C, TP53, PIK3CA, and PDGFRA. The genes PDGFRB, FGFR1, and CCND2 were determined to be related to clinical outcome through methylation effects,

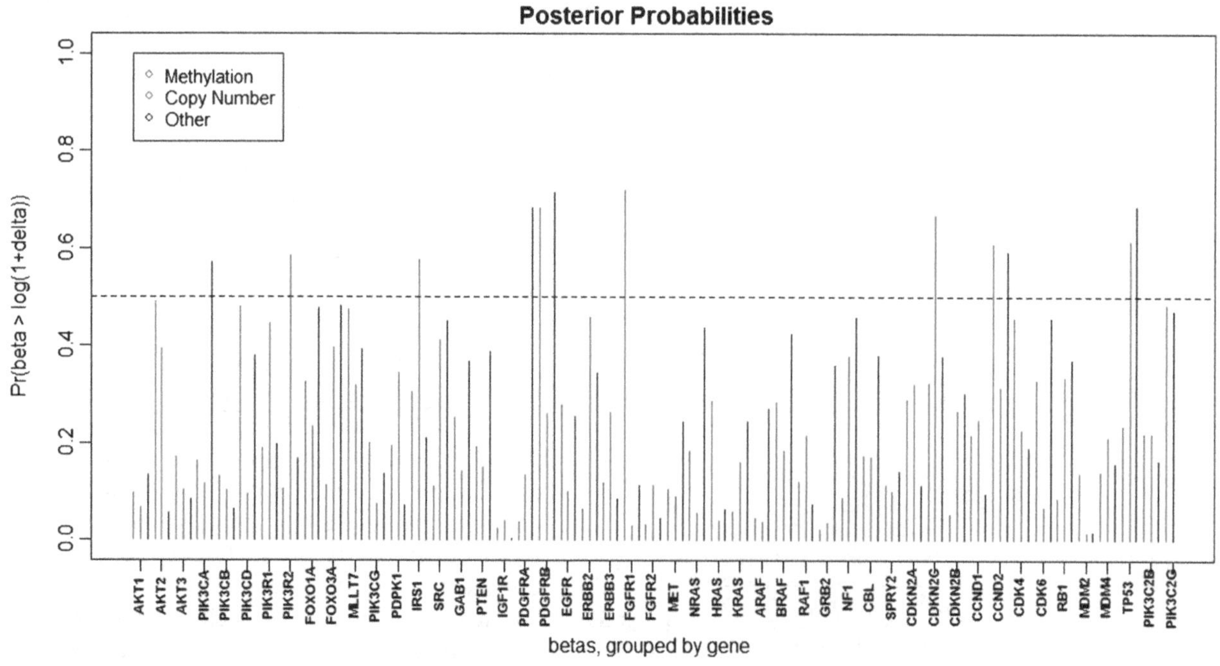

Figure 3 GBM data results. The posterior probabilities (based on MCMC samples) that $\beta_{j,i} > \delta^*_+$ is plotted, where $\beta_{j,i}$ is the clinical model regression coefficient for the marker associated with platform j of gene i, and $\delta^*_+ = \log(1+\delta)$ is the transformed upper practical cutoff. For our analysis, we use $\delta = 0.05$, which corresponds to a 5% change in survival time, so the posterior probability shown here indicates the probability that a one unit increase in the marker results in at least a 5% increase in survival time. We consider the marker j, i to be significant if this probability is greater than 0.5.

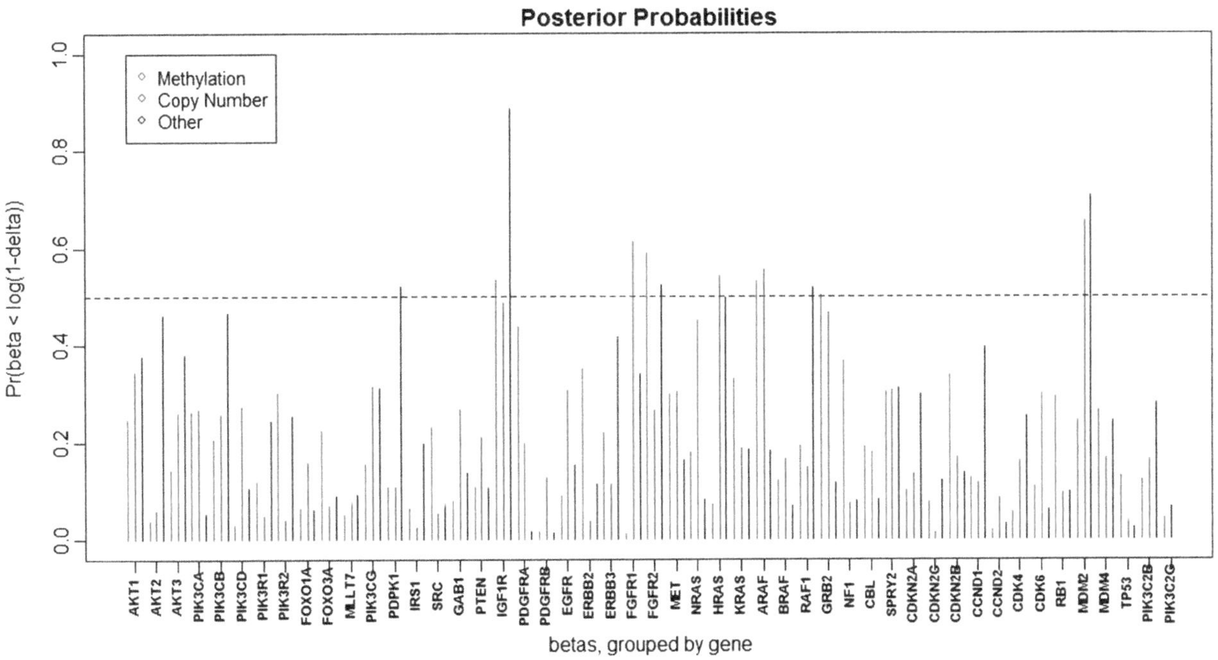

Figure 4 GBM data results. The posterior probabilities (based on MCMC samples) that $\beta_{j,i} < \delta^*_-$ is plotted, where $\beta_{j,i}$ is the clinical model regression coefficient for the marker associated with platform j of gene i, and $\delta^*_- = \log(1 - \delta)$ is the transformed lower practical cutoff. For our analysis, we use $\delta = 0.05$, which corresponds to a 5% change in survival time, so the posterior probability shown here indicates the probability that a one unit increase in the marker results in at least a 5% decrease in survival time. We consider the marker j, i to be significant if this probability is greater than 0.5.

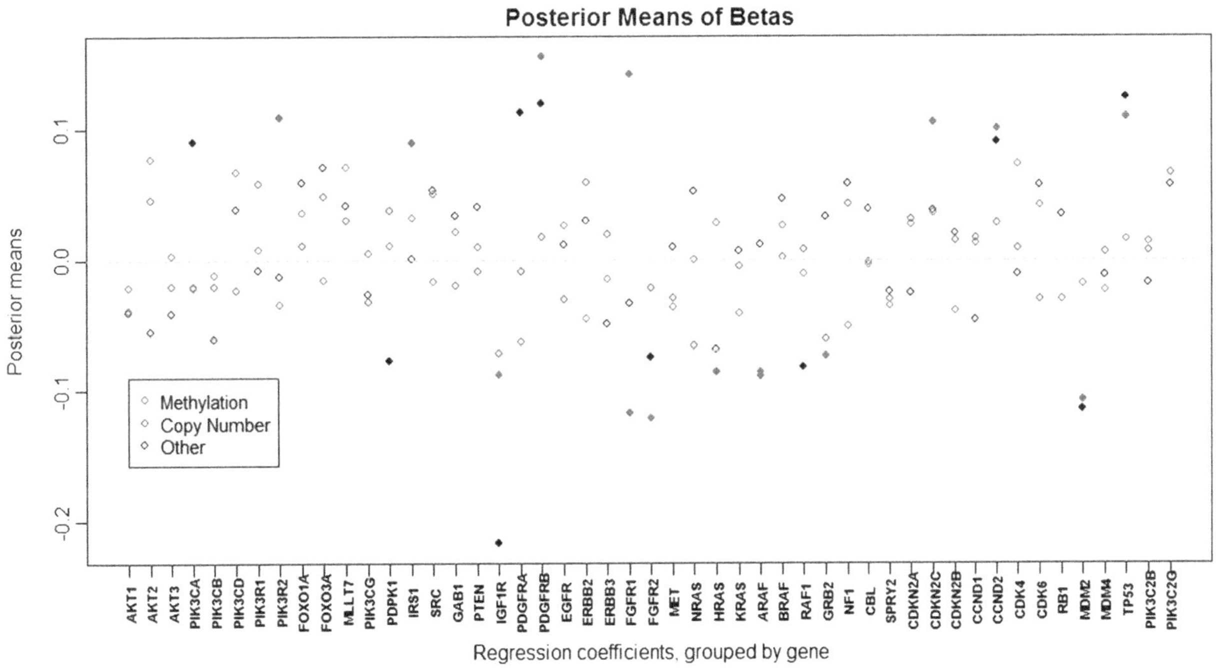

Figure 5 Regression coefficient posterior means. The estimates of the regression coefficients in the clinical model ($\beta_{j,i}$'s) are shown, where $\beta_{j,i}$ is the coefficient for the marker associated with platform j of gene i; the estimates are computed as the posterior means from our MCMC samples. The multiple platforms for each gene are labeled by color, and solid plot markers indicate that the effect was found to be significant, meaning that the posterior probability that a one unit increase in the marker results in at least a 5% change in survival time is at least 0.5.

while expressions of PIK3R2, IRS1, CDKN2C, and TP53 were related to clinical outcome through copy number. For PIK3CA, PDGFRA, PDGFRB, CCND2, and TP53, gene expression was related to clinical outcome through some other unspecified mechanism. The genes with the 13 negative markers were IGF1R, FGFR2, ARAF, GRB2, FGFR1, HRAS, MDM2, PDPK1, and RAF1. The first four were related to clinical response through methylation, while FGFR1, HRAS, ARAF, and MDM2 were related through copy number, and PDPK1, IGF1R, FGFR2, RAF1, and MDM2 were related through some mechanism other than methylation or copy number. Note that eight genes (IGF1R, PDGFRB, FGFR1, FGFR2, ARAF, CCND2, MDM2, and TP53) are found to be significant on two or more different platforms. We have not only identified 17 genes as having a significant effect on survival (Table 2), but we have also determined which platform(s) of those genes is (are) modulating the effect.

4.3 Biological interpretation

There are a total of 17 genes found to affect the expression of glioblastoma tumors significantly. Of these, nine genes are negatively affecting the survival and nine genes are affecting the survival positively. The positive and negative prognostic markers are reviewed within the context of glioblastoma biology in this section.

Negative prognostic markers: Fibroblast growth factor pathway signaling is associated with significant tumor enhancement in glioblastoma [23]. Fibroblast growth factor receptors FGFR1 and FGFR2 play an oncogenic role in various tumor types and can be targeted by multiple small molecules in cancer therapy [24]. FGFR1 expression can be regulated by methylation level of the upstream CpG island [25]. Hyper-methylation of FGFR1 would provide positive effects by reducing the expression level of FGFR1 and thus appear to be affecting the survival in both ways. Insulin-like growth factor receptor 1 (IGF1R) is a well-known target to treat GBM and has been found to be associated with astrocytoma and meningioma as well [26]. It is also associated with anti-EGFR resistance in GBM and is a pan-cancer biomarker connected with many different tumor types [27,28]. MDM2 is a well-known oncogene and inhibitor of the tumor suppressor TP53. Previous studies in glioblastoma using expression and copy number platforms indicated the abnormal over-expression and amplification of MDM2 [29,30]. ARAF is a serine/threonine protein kinase of RAF family, known to stabilize the hetero-dimerization of RAF proteins, BRAF and CRAF [31]. Its role and over-expression are observed in other tumors but are not explored in the context of glioblastoma [32]. Growth factor receptor-bound protein 2 (GRB2) is involved in RAS signaling pathway and known to be associated with EGFR [33]. GRB2 is an interacting partner of EGFRvIII, a common mutated variant of EGFR in the molecular signaling of EGFR-driven glioblastoma [34,35].

Table 2 Gene results

Gene names				
AKT1	MLLT7	EGFR	BRAF	*CCND2*
AKT2	PIK3CG	ERBB2	*RAF1*	CDK4
AKT3	*PDPK1*	ERBB3	*GRB2*	CDK6
PIK3CA	*IRS1*	*FGFR1*	NF1	RB1
PIK3CB	SRC	*FGFR2*	CBL	*MDM2*
PIK3CD	GAB1	MET	SPRY2	MDM4
PIK3R1	PTEN	NRAS	CDKN2A	*TP53*
PIK3R2	*IGF1R*	*HRAS*	*CDKN2C*	PIK3C2B
FOXO1A	*PDGFRA*	KRAS	CDKN2B	PIK3C2G
FOXO3A	*PDGFRB*	*ARAF*	CCND1	

All 49 genes appearing in the data are listed. Italic genes were identified by our method to have at least one significant marker.

Positive prognostic markers: The tumor suppressor gene TP53 is a positive prognostic marker as expected. The Cyclin-dependent kinase inhibitor CDKN2C, a known tumor suppressor of glioblastoma, is also identified as a positive marker [36]. Platelet-derived growth factors (PDGF) receptors PDGFRA and PDGFRB show positive survival effects, whose oncogenic role is well established in the context of glioma [37,38]. These PDGF receptors are the representative genes of the pro-neural subtype of glioblastoma [20,39]. Interestingly, the pro-neural subtype of glioblastoma is enriched in oligodendroglioma and has higher survival rates compared to other subtypes of glioblastoma [40]. The insulin receptor substrate gene IRS1 is shown to be one of the representative candidates for mesenchymal subtype of GBM with poor survival [41]. The role of IRS1 is not clear, given that we found it to be a positive marker in our analysis. Overall, the positive markers are generally enriched in the pro-neural subtype of glioblastoma, which was found to have prolonged survival [20].

5 Conclusions

In this article, we present a hierarchical Bayesian model that integrates data from multiple genomic platforms, incorporating information about the platforms' biological relationships in order to better identify genes that are critical to patient survival and to additionally provide mechanistic information on the manner of their effect. In summary, the key advantages of our method include (1) multiple platforms are integrated in a single model; (2) the biological relationships between platforms are taken into account by the model; (3) high dimensional data can be handled easily, with shrinkage priors; (4) the NG prior on the predictors allows for flexible shrinkage of the parameter estimates; (5) the model can be extended to incorporate more platforms, as long as the underlying biological relationships are well understood; and (6) we have the ability to not only identify genes significant to patient survival but also gain mechanistic information on the manner by which the gene expression is related to outcome.

Applying our methodology to a GBM dataset from TCGA, our method identified several genes with effects that have a significant impact on survival time. In addition, we identified whether each gene was related to clinical outcome through methylation, copy number, or some other mechanism. This is especially advantageous in investigating the biological mechanisms of cancer development and progression, and in subsequent development of novel therapeutic strategies.

Although beyond the scope of this paper, two areas of future investigation might include (1) relaxing the parametric assumptions by using generalized additive models instead of linear models or substituting specified parametric non-linear models if they are justified by the science, and (2) dynamic modeling, which would require different types of data and further modeling assumptions to capture complex patterns of feedback loops both within and between platforms.

Appendices

Appendix A Data imputation

Since the percentage of missing data is so low ($\sim$ 5% for methylation and $\sim$ 0.1% for copy number), we choose to do imputation using the following algorithm for both the methylation data and the copy number data: (1) For each marker, replace any NA's with the mean of the other patients. Call this resulting matrix Temp. (2) Use Temp to calculate a correlation matrix between markers. (3) For each marker with missing value(s), regress it on the three markers which it is most highly positively correlated with (using the Temp matrix for the predictors to avoid further complications from missing data). (4) Substitute this predicted value for the missing value in the original matrix.

Appendix B Complete conditionals

$$\begin{aligned}\boldsymbol{\beta}|\text{rest} &\sim \text{Normal}\{(X^{\mathrm{T}}X+\sigma^2 D_\tau^{-1})^{-1}X^{\mathrm{T}}\mathbf{Y}, \sigma^2(X^{\mathrm{T}}X\\ &\qquad +\sigma^2 D_\tau^{-1})^{-1}\}\\ \sigma^2|\text{rest} &\sim \text{Inv.Gamma}(a=a+n/2, b=b+\{(\mathbf{Y}\\ &\qquad -X\boldsymbol{\beta})^{\mathrm{T}}(\mathbf{Y}-X\boldsymbol{\beta})\}/2)\\ \psi_{j,i}|\text{rest} &\sim \text{Gen.Inv.Gaussian}(a=\gamma_j^{-2}, b=\beta_{j,i}^2, p=\lambda_j-1/2),\\ &\qquad \text{where } V=\text{Gen.Inv.Gaussian}(a,b,p)\\ &\qquad \text{has density}(a/b)^{p/2}v^{p-1}\exp\{-(av+b/v)/2\}/\\ &\qquad \{2K_p(\sqrt{ab})\}, \text{where } K_p(\cdot) \text{ is a modified}\\ &\qquad \text{Bessel function of the second kind.}\end{aligned}$$

$$\begin{aligned}\lambda_j|\text{rest} &\sim (1/\lambda_j)^{\tilde{a}}\exp\left\{-\tilde{b}\gamma_j^{-2}/(2\lambda_j)-c\lambda_j\right\}\\ &\quad\times\left(\prod_{i=1}^{p_j}\psi_{j,i}^{\lambda_j}\right)/\left[\{\Gamma(\lambda_j)\}^{p_j}(2\gamma_j^2)^{p_j\lambda_j}\right]\\ \gamma_j^{-2}|\text{rest} &\sim \text{Gamma}(a=p_j\lambda_j+\tilde{a}, b=(\tilde{b}/\lambda_j+\sum_{i=1}^{p_j}\psi_{j,i})/2)\end{aligned}$$

In the Metropolis-Hastings update step, the proposed value is $\lambda_j^* = \exp(\sigma_\lambda^2 z)\lambda_j$ where $z \sim \text{Normal}(0,1)$ and the tuning parameter σ_λ^2 is chosen to result in an acceptance rate between 20% and 30%. The acceptance probability is then $\min\left\{1, \frac{\pi(\lambda_j^*)}{\pi(\lambda_j)}\left(\frac{\Gamma(\lambda_j)}{\Gamma(\lambda_j^*)}\right)^{p_j}\left((2\gamma_j^2)^{-p_j}\prod_{i=1}^{p_j}\psi_{j,i}\right)^{\lambda_j^*-\lambda_j}\left(\frac{\lambda_j^*}{\lambda_j}\right)\right\}$ where $\pi(\lambda_j) = (1/\lambda_j)^{\tilde{a}}\exp\{-\tilde{b}\gamma_j^{-2}/(2\lambda_j)-c\lambda_j\}$, the prior for λ_j.

Initial values and hyperparameters

The initial values and hyperparameters are chosen as follows:

- The hyperparameters for σ^2 are $a = b = 0.001$, so as to be uninformative.
- The hyperparameter for λ_j is $c = 1$ [11].
- The hyperparamters for γ_j^{-2} are $\tilde{a} = 2$ and $\tilde{b}$ = the mean of the least squares $\widehat{\beta_{j,i}^2}$ [11].
- The initial $\boldsymbol{\beta}$ is the estimate from the frequentist lasso with a single shrinkage parameter.
- The initial σ^2 is the mean sum of squares from the frequentist lasso.
- Each initial λ_j, $\psi_{j,i}$, and γ_j^{-2} is set to 1.

Competing interests

The authors declared that they have no competing interests.

Acknowledgements

VB and JSM's research was partially supported by NIH grant R01 CA160736 and the Cancer Center Support Grant (CCSG) (P30 CA016672). The content is solely the responsibility of the authors and does not necessarily represent the official views of the National Cancer Institute or the National Institutes of Health.

Author details

[1]Department of Statistics, Texas A&M University, College Station, TX 77843, USA. [2]Department of Biostatistics, UT M.D. Anderson Cancer Center, Houston, TX 77030, USA. [3]Department of Bioinformatics and Computational Biology, UT M.D. Anderson Cancer Center, Houston, TX 77030, USA.

References

1. OO Kanu, B Hughes, C Di, N Lin, J Fu, DD Bigner, H Yan, C Adamson, Glioblastoma multiforme oncogenomics and signaling pathways. Clin. Med. Oncol. **3**, 39–52 (2009)
2. Pathway analysis of genetic alterations in glioblastoma (TCGA). http://cbio.mskcc.org/cancergenomics/gbm/pathways/ 2012. [Memorial Sloan-Kettering Cancer Center]. Accessed 9 August 2012 .
3. Program overview. http://cancergenome.nih.gov/abouttcga/overview 2012. [The Cancer Genome Atlas]. Accessed 9 August 2012
4. W Wang, V Baladandayuthapani, JS Morris, BM Broom, G Manyam, KA Do, iBAG: integrative Bayesian analysis of high-dimensional multiplatform genomics data. Bioinformatics. **29**(2), 149–159 (2013)

5. D Bell, A Berchuck, M Birrer, J Chien, D Cramer, F Dao, R Dhir, P DiSaia, H Gabra, P Glenn, A Godwin, J Gross, L Hartmann, M Huang, D Huntsman, M Iacocca, M Imielinski, S Kalloger, B Karlan, D Levine, G Mills, C Morrison, D Mutch, N Olvera, S Orsulic, K Park, N Petrelli, B Rabeno, J Rader, B Sikic, et al., Integrated genomic analyses of ovarian carcinoma. Nature. **474**(7353), 609–615 (2011)
6. L McR endon, A Friedman, D Bigner, EG Van Meir, DJ Brat, GM Mastrogianakis, JJ Olson, T Mikkelsen, N Lehman, K Aldape, WK Yung, O Bogler, JN Weinstein, S VandenBerg, M Berger, M Prados, D Muzny, M Morgan, S Scherer, A Sabo, L Nazareth, L Lewis, O Hall, Y Zhu, Y Ren, O Alvi, J Yao, A Hawes, S Jhangiani, G Fowler, et al., Comprehensive genomic characterization defines human glioblastoma genes and core pathways. Nature. **455**(7216), 1061–1068 (2008)
7. R Shen, AB Olshen, M Ladanyi, Integrative clustering of multiple genomic data types using a joint latent variable model with application to breast and lung cancer subtype analysis. Bioinformatics. **25**(22), 2906–2912 (2009)
8. S Tyekucheva, L Marchionni, R Karchin, G Parmigiani, Integrating diverse genomic data using gene sets. Genome Biol. **12**(10), R105 (2011)
9. GR Lanckriet, T De Bie, N Cristianini, MI Jordan, WS Noble, A statistical framework for genomic data fusion. Bioinformatics. **20**(16), 2626–2635 (2004)
10. D Liu, X Lin, D Ghosh, Semiparametric regression of multi-dimensional genetic pathway data: least squares kernel machines and linear mixed models. Biometrics. **63**, 1079–1088 (2007)
11. JE Griffin, PJ Brown, Inference with normal-gamma prior distributions in regression problems. Bayesian Anal. **5**, 171–188 (2010)
12. LJ Wei, The accelerated failure time model: A useful alternative to the cox regression model in survival analysis. Stat Med. **11**(14–15), 1871–1879 (1992) [http://dx.doi.org/10.1002/sim.4780111409].
13. T Park, G Casella, The Bayesian lasso. J Am. Stat. Assoc. **103**(482), 681–686 (2008)
14. R Tibshirani, Regression shrinkage and selection via the lasso. J. R. Stat Soc. Series B (Methodological). **58**, 267–288 (1996)
15. JE Griffin, PJ Brown, Structuring shrinkage: some correlated priors for regression. Biometrika. **99**(2), 481–487 (2012). [http://EconPapers.repec.org/RePEc:oup:biomet:v:99:y:2012:i:2:p:481-487].
16. MM Barbieri, JO Berger, Optimal predictive model selection. Ann. Stat. **32**(3), 870–897 (2004)
17. American Cancer Society, *American Cancer Society: Cancer Facts and Figures 2013*. (American Cancer Society, Atlanta, GA, 2013)
18. Glioblastoma. http://www.abta.org/understanding-brain-tumors/types-of-tumors/glioblastoma.html 2013. [American Brain Tumor Association]. Accessed 6 June 2013
19. DR Johnson, BP O'Neill, Glioblastoma survival in the United States before and during the temozolomide era. J. Neurooncol. **107**(2), 359–364 (2012)
20. RG Verhaak, KA Hoadley, E Purdom, V Wang, Y Qi, MD Wilkerson, CR Miller, L Ding, T Golub, JP Mesirov, G Alexe, M Lawrence, M O'Kelly, P Tamayo, BA Weir, S Gabriel, W Winckler, S Gupta, L Jakkula, HS Feiler, JG Hodgson, CD James, JN Sarkaria, C Brennan, A Kahn, PT Spellman, RK Wilson, TP Speed, JW Gray, et al., Integrated genomic analysis identifies clinically relevant subtypes of glioblastoma characterized by abnormalities in, PDGFRA, IDH1, EGFR, and NF1. Cancer Cell. **17**, 98–110 (2010)
21. H Noushmehr, DJ Weisenberger, K Diefes, HS Phillips, K Pujara, BP Berman, F Pan, CE Pelloski, EP Sulman, KP Bhat, RG Verhaak, KA Hoadley, DN Hayes, CM Perou, HK Schmidt, Ding L, RK Wilson, D Van Den Berg, H Shen, H Bengtsson, P Neuvial, LM Cope, J Buckley, JG Herman, SB Baylin, PW Laird, K Aldape, Identification of a CpG island methylator phenotype that defines a distinct subgroup of glioma. Cancer Cell. **17**(5), 510–522 (2010)
22. Data levels and data types. https://tcga-data.nci.nih.gov/tcga/tcgaDataType.jsp. [TCGA]. Accessed 22 August 2013
23. W Loilome, AD Joshi, CM ap Rhys, S Piccirillo, AL Vescovi, VL Angelo, GL Gallia, GJ Riggins, Glioblastoma cell growth is suppressed by disruption of Fibroblast Growth Factor pathway signaling. J. Neurooncol. **94**(3), 359–366 (2009)
24. M Katoh, H Nakagama, FGF Receptors: Cancer Biology and Therapeutics. Rev. Med. Res (2013). doi:10.1002/med.21288
25. M Goldstein, I Meller, A Orr-Urtreger, FGFR1 over-expression in primary rhabdomyosarcoma tumors is associated with hypomethylation of a 5′ CpG island and abnormal expression of the AKT1, NOG, and BMP4 genes. Genes Chromosomes Cancer. **46**(11), 1028–1038 (2007)
26. M Carapancea, O Alexandru, AS Fetea, L Dragutescu, J Castro, A Georgescu, A Popa-Wagner, ML Backlund, R Lewensohn, A Dricu, Growth factor receptors signaling in glioblastoma cells: therapeutic implications. J. Neurooncol. **92**(2), 137–147 (2009)
27. A Chakravarti, JS Loeffler, NJ Dyson, Insulin-like growth factor receptor I mediates resistance to anti-epidermal growth factor receptor therapy in primary human glioblastoma cells through continued activation of phosphoinositide 3-kinase signaling. Cancer Res. **62**, 200–207 (2002)
28. M Hewish, I Chau, D Cunningham, Insulin-like growth factor 1 receptor targeted therapeutics: novel compounds and novel treatment strategies for cancer medicine. Recent Pat. Anticancer Drug Discov. **4**, 54–72 (2009)
29. Y Ruano, M Mollejo, T Ribalta, C Fiano, FI Camacho, E Gomez, AR de Lope, JL Hernandez-Moneo, P Martinez, B Melendez, Identification of novel candidate target genes in amplicons of Glioblastoma multiforme tumors detected by expression and CGH microarray profiling. Mol. Cancer. **5**, 39 (2006)
30. D Yin, S Ogawa, N Kawamata, P Tunici, G Finocchiaro, M Eoli, C Ruckert, T Huynh, G Liu, M Kato, M Sanada, A Jauch, M Dugas, KL Black, HP Koeffler, High-resolution genomic copy number profiling of glioblastoma multiforme by single nucleotide polymorphism DNA microarray. Mol. Cancer Res. **7**(5), 665–677 (2009)
31. AP Rebocho, R Marais, ARAF acts as a scaffold to stabilize BRAF: CRAF heterodimers. Oncogene. **32**(26), 3207–3212 (2013)
32. DW Craig, JA O'Shaughnessy, JA Kiefer, J Aldrich, S Sinari, TM Moses, S Wong, J Dinh, A Christoforides, JL Blum, CL Aitelli, CR Osborne, T Izatt, A Kurdoglu, A Baker, J Koeman, C Barbacioru, O Sakarya, FM De La Vega, A Siddiqui, L Hoang, PR Billings, B Salhia, AW Tolcher, JM Trent, S Mousses, D Von Hoff, JD Carpten, Genome and transcriptome sequencing in prospective metastatic triple-negative breast cancer uncovers therapeutic vulnerabilities. Mol. Cancer Ther. **12**, 104–116 (2013)
33. EJ Lowenstein, RJ Daly, AG Batzer, W Li, B Margolis, R Lammers, A Ullrich, EY Skolnik, D Bar-Sagi, J Schlessinger, The SH2 and SH3 domain-containing protein GRB2 links receptor tyrosine kinases to ras signaling. Cell. **70**(3), 431–442 (1992)
34. GS Kapoor, DM O'Rourke, SIRPalpha1 receptors interfere with the EGFRvIII signalosome to inhibit glioblastoma cell transformation and migration. Oncogene. **29**(29), 4130–4144 (2010)
35. SA Prigent, M Nagane, H Lin, I Huvar, GR Boss, JR Feramisco, WK Cavenee, HS Huang, Enhanced tumorigenic behavior of glioblastoma cells expressing a truncated epidermal growth factor receptor is mediated through the Ras-Shc-Grb2 pathway. J. Biol. Chem. **271**(41), 25639–25645 (1996)
36. DA Solomon, JS Kim, S Jenkins, H Ressom, M Huang, N Coppa, L Mabanta, D Bigner, H Yan, W Jean, T Waldman, Identification of p18 INK4c as a tumor suppressor gene in glioblastoma multiforme. Cancer Res. **68**(8), 2564–2569 (2008)
37. I Nazarenko, SM Hede, X He, A Hedren, J Thompson, MS Lindstrom, M Nister, PDGF and PDGF receptors in glioma. Ups. J. Med. Sci. **117**(2), 99–112 (2012)
38. K Suzuki, H Momota, A Tonooka, H Noguchi, K Yamamoto, M Wanibuchi, Y Minamida, T Hasegawa, K Houkin, Glioblastoma simultaneously present with adjacent meningioma: case report and review of the literature. J. Neurooncol. **99**, 147–153 (2010)
39. Y Jiang, M Boije, B Westermark, L Uhrbom, PDGF-B Can sustain self-renewal and tumorigenicity of experimental glioma-derived cancer-initiating cells by preventing oligodendrocyte differentiation. Neoplasia. **13**(6), 492–503 (2011)
40. LA Cooper, DA Gutman, Q Long, BA Johnson, SR Cholleti, T Kurc, JH Saltz, DJ Brat, CS Moreno, The proneural molecular signature is enriched in oligodendrogliomas and predicts improved survival among diffuse gliomas. PLoS ONE. **5**(9), e12548 (2010)
41. C Brennan, H Momota, D Hambardzumyan, T Ozawa, A Tandon, A Pedraza, E Holland, Glioblastoma subclasses can be defined by activity among signal transduction pathways and associated genomic alterations. PLoS ONE. **4**(11), e7752 (2009)

14

Inferring Boolean network states from partial information

Guy Karlebach

Abstract

Networks of molecular interactions regulate key processes in living cells. Therefore, understanding their functionality is a high priority in advancing biological knowledge. Boolean networks are often used to describe cellular networks mathematically and are fitted to experimental datasets. The fitting often results in ambiguities since the interpretation of the measurements is not straightforward and since the data contain noise. In order to facilitate a more reliable mapping between datasets and Boolean networks, we develop an algorithm that infers network trajectories from a dataset distorted by noise. We analyze our algorithm theoretically and demonstrate its accuracy using simulation and microarray expression data.

Keywords: Boolean network; Inference; Conditional entropy; Gradient descent

Introduction

Boolean networks were introduced by Kauffman [1] several decades ago as a model for gene regulatory networks. In this model, every gene corresponds to a node in the network. Every node is assigned an initial Boolean value, which is its value at time 0. A Boolean value of 1 means that the gene is active; in other words, its product is present in the cell and can perform its designated role. A Boolean value of 0 means exactly the opposite - a gene is not active and its product is absent from the cell. Since the activity or inactivity of genes affects the activity or inactivity of other genes, the Boolean value of a node at time point $T + 1$ is determined by the Boolean values of other nodes at time T. More specifically, the Boolean value of a node is determined by a time-invariant Boolean function that takes as input the Boolean values of a set of network nodes at the preceding time point. The set of nodes that constitute the input to the Boolean function is called its regulators, and the output node is referred to as target. The vector of the Boolean values of all the network nodes is called the network state. A sequence of states that evolves from some initial state according to the Boolean functions is called a trajectory. The trajectories of network states can be complex, displaying chaos or order depending on the network structure and the initial state [2]. When the outputs of all the Boolean functions at state S produce the state S itself, S is called a steady state. Since in every state every node is set to one of two Boolean values, the number of possible network states is exponential to the number of nodes. Figure 1 illustrates a simple Boolean network.

In recent years, new experimental technologies in molecular biology enabled a broader examination of gene activity in cells [3-5] and consequently, significant efforts have been invested in the application of gene regulatory networks modeling [6]. However, experimental procedures produce continuous values that do not determine conclusively the activity or inactivity of a gene. Hence, these values cannot be mapped into states of Boolean networks unambiguously, and the resulting picture of the cell state contains errors. Computational methods address this problem in various ways, for example, by using additional data such as the genomic sequences of gene promoters [7], by mapping the continuous measurements into discrete values and then optimally fitting the transformed dataset to a network model [8,9], or by using a prior distribution on states [10]. It is well recognized that an improved ability to probe the state of a cell can lead to improvement in our understanding of a broad range of biological processes.

With this motivation in mind, we propose a novel algorithm for inferring the state of a Boolean network using a continuous noisy expression dataset and the network structure, i.e., the genes and their regulators. The

Correspondence: g.karlebach@dkfz-heidelberg.de
German Cancer Research Institute (DKFZ), Im Neuenheimer Feld 280, Heidelberg 69121, Germany

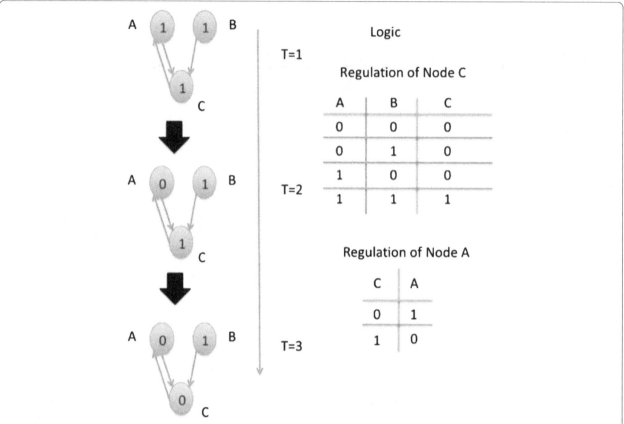

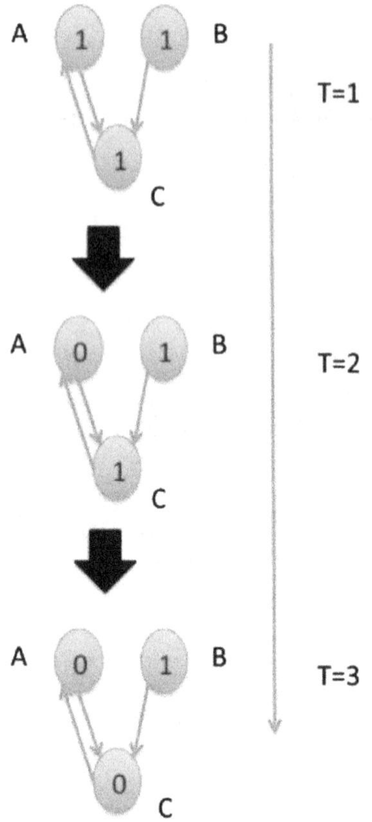

Logic

Regulation of Node C

A	B	C
0	0	0
0	1	0
1	0	0
1	1	1

Regulation of Node A

C	A
0	1
1	0

Figure 1 A simple Boolean network. The network has three nodes, denoted as **A**, **B**, and **C**. Nodes **A** and **B** can change the Boolean value of node **C**, according to the rules given at the right side of the figure. Similarly, node **C** can change the value of node **A**. At the left side of the figure, a trajectory of length 3 is illustrated. In the initial state ($T = 1$), all the nodes receive a Boolean 1. According to the logical rule by which **C** changes the value of **A**, the value of **A** changes to 0 at time $T = 2$. At time point $T = 3$, the node **C** changes its value, since the input to the logical rule that determines its value has changed.

algorithm is based on the following idea: High expression values are more likely to correspond to a Boolean 1, while low to a Boolean 0. By combining the network structure and the expression dataset, we can estimate the likelihood of each continuous value to correspond to a Boolean value of 1 or 0. We can then update the likelihood (equivalently the expression value) of each gene accordingly and repeat the process until any further change would either (a) change a gene towards a Boolean value that is less likely for it or (b) change a gene towards a Boolean value that is as likely as the opposite Boolean value (i.e., make an arbitrary guess). The update scheme should be such that if enough updates were possible, the final probability distribution will describe the states of a Boolean network.

The next section explains how to implement this idea using the conditional entropy [11] of the network. It will be shown that changing the gene probabilities in the opposite direction of the conditional entropy gradient is equivalent to executing the inference algorithm that we outlined above. The section begins by analyzing a simple network and then extends the results to general networks.

In the 'Testing' section, we use simulation and real data in order to test the performance of the algorithm. We generate noisy datasets for several Boolean network structures and use a microarray time-series dataset from a study of the *Saccharomyces cerevisiae* cell cycle. We find that using the simulated datasets, the algorithm infers a large proportion of the Boolean states correctly; and using the yeast dataset, it infers Boolean states that agree with the conclusion of the study. We conclude by summarizing our results and suggesting research directions that can lead to further progress in this domain.

Main text

Analysis

Consider the following simple network: gene X negatively regulates gene Y. In other words, when X is active Y is inactive, and vice versa. X is also said to be a repressor of Y or to repress Y. The Boolean function that controls the value of Y is called NOT.

An experimental device can measure the states of X and Y. If a gene is active, it measures a value from a normal distribution with a large positive average μ and small standard deviation σ. If a gene is inactive, the device measures a value from a normal distribution with a negative average $-\mu$ and standard deviation σ.

The input to our problem is a series of N i.i.d. measurements of the genes X, Y (for example, under different stimulations given to the cells). X can be active or inactive in every measurement with equal probabilities. We are also given the structure of the network. We do not know the logic with which X regulates Y, but the values in the dataset will reflect this logic.

Our goal is to find the states of X and Y in each measurement. Clearly, we cannot always recover the 'true' states from every measurement, since there is a nonzero probability that the device will measure a large value for the inactive gene and, at the same time, a small value for the active gene. Nevertheless, the best strategy is to identify X as a repressor and then predict that in each pair of values the larger one corresponds to an active gene and the smaller to an inactive - the larger the difference, the higher our confidence. The inference algorithm, which we will shortly describe, will apply a generalization of this strategy. We will show that in the case of the simple network, the algorithm predicts the network states in the optimal way. Then, we will explain how it generalizes to more complex networks. Before we describe the algorithm, we need to define several random variables.

Denote the N measurements by $C_1, C_2, \ldots, C_N$, and the continuous values of X and Y in measurement C_i as x_i and y_i, respectively. As a convention, we will use uppercase and lowercase letters to define variables that assume discrete values and continuous values, respectively. The terms measurement i and C_i are used interchangeably.

We define the following continuous values:

$$\lambda(x_i) = \frac{1}{1+e^{-x_i}} \text{ (the logistic function of } x_i\text{)}$$
$$\bar{\lambda}(x_i) = 1 - \lambda(x_i) = 1 - \frac{1}{1+e^{-x_i}}.$$

The role of the logistic function is to map continuous values to probabilities. For example, if x_i is close to the average of its distribution μ, it will have a high probability to correspond to a Boolean 1, because μ is a large positive number. The use of the logistic function will also enable us to implement the update step in our algorithm, in which we update the probabilities of the previous iteration.

Similarly we define

$$\lambda(y_i) = \frac{1}{1+e^{-y_i}}$$
$$\bar{\lambda}(y_i) = 1 - \frac{1}{1+e^{-y_i}}.$$

Using these values, we define the discrete random variable $[X;Y]_i \in \{00, 10, 01, 11\}$:

$$P([X;Y]_i = 11) = \lambda(x_i)\cdot\lambda(y_i)$$
$$P([X;Y]_i = 00) = \bar{\lambda}(x_i)\cdot\bar{\lambda}(y_i)$$
$$P([X;Y]_i = 10) = \lambda(x_i)\cdot\bar{\lambda}(y_i)$$
$$P([X;Y]_i = 01) = \bar{\lambda}(x_i)\cdot\lambda(y_i).$$

The probability distribution of $[X;Y]_i$ is well defined, since all probabilities are in (0,1) and sum to 1.

Since each of x_i and y_i is from one of the normal distributions $N(\mu,\sigma^2)$, $N(-\mu,\sigma^2)$ with a small σ^2, the probabilities $P([X;Y]_i = 11)$ and $P([X;Y]_i = 00)$ will be small.

Similar to $[X;Y]_i$, we can define the discrete random variable X_i with probability function:

$$P(X_i = 1) = \lambda(x_i) \text{ and } P(X_i = 0) = \bar{\lambda}(x_i).$$

We define the discrete random variable Y_i by replacing $\lambda(x_i), \bar{\lambda}(x_i)$ with $\lambda(y_i), \bar{\lambda}(y_i)$ in the definition of X_i.

The discrete random variables that we defined so far correspond to specific experiments. We also need to define discrete random variables that correspond to the set of experiments as a whole. For example, such variables would answer the question: What is the probability of seeing $X = 1$ and $Y = 0$ in the whole dataset? In order to do that, note that as σ^2 becomes smaller and the number of measurements N larger, by the law of large numbers:

$$\frac{\Sigma_{i=1}^{N} P([X;Y]_i = 10)}{N} \approx \frac{1}{2}, \frac{\Sigma_{i=1}^{N} P([X;Y]_i = 01)}{N} \approx \frac{1}{2}$$
$$\frac{\Sigma_{i=1}^{N} P([X;Y]_i = 11)}{N} \approx 0, \frac{\Sigma_{i=1}^{N} P([X;Y]_i = 00)}{N} \approx 0,$$

which is what one expects intuitively - either X is active and Y is inactive, or vice versa, but they cannot both be active or inactive in the same measurement, because X represses Y. Although it is possible to have a high probability $P([X;Y]_i = 00)$ for some i, such deviations will have little effect on the average of the N samples. Hence, we define a variable $[X;Y] \in \{00, 01, 10, 11\}$ with a distribution that is an average of the probabilities of the variables $[X;Y]_i$.

Since X can be inactive or active in any measurement with equal probabilities, similarly to $[X;Y]$ we define the variable X using the distribution

$$\frac{\Sigma_{i=1}^{N} P(X_i = 1)}{N} \approx \frac{\Sigma_{i=1}^{N} P(X_i = 0)}{N} \approx \frac{1}{2}$$

and in a similar way a discrete random variable Y. Note that the probability of $[X;Y]$ is an estimation of the joint probabilities of X and Y, $P(X,Y)$.

How can we infer the probabilities of variables that do not conform to the $X \rightarrow Y$ network, for example, when

x_i and y_i are both positive? We can use the average of all the samples, which is rather accurate, and estimate the probabilities of $X_i = 1$ and $Y_i = 1$. Then we will correct the values of x_i and y_i accordingly. This estimation and correction process is in fact equivalent to changing x_i and y_i in the opposite direction of the gradient of the conditional entropy $H(Y|X)$. We have defined the probability distributions $P(X)$, $P(Y)$, $P(X,Y)$ as functions of the continuous values x_i, y_i. We can therefore partially derive the conditional entropy $H(Y|X)$ according to each continuous value and obtain the gradient $\nabla H(Y|X)$. This leads to the following algorithm:

Algorithm 1: State Inference

1. Find the gradient $\nabla H(Y/X)$
2. Add $-\delta \cdot \nabla H(Y/X)$ to the continuous values, where δ is some constant
3. If the change in $H(Y/X)$ is greater than a threshold τ, go back to 1
4. For every continuous value c predict Boolean 1 if $\lambda(c) > 0.5$, otherwise 0

We now show that the algorithm obtains the desired solution for our simple network. More specifically, if $y_i > x_i$, then $\lambda(x_i)$ will approach 0 and $\lambda(y_i)$ will approach 1 and vice versa.

First, in order to compute the gradient, we use the chain rule for conditional entropy: $H(Y|X) = H(Y,X) - H(X)$.

It is easy to see [12] that

$$\frac{\partial H(Y,X)}{\partial x_i} = \sum_{(X,Y)\in\{00,01,10,11\}} \frac{\partial P(X,Y)}{\partial x_i} \cdot \log\left(P(X,Y)^{-1}\right) - \sum_{(X,Y)\in\{00,01,10,11\}} \frac{\partial P(X,Y)}{\partial x_i} = \sum_{(X,Y)\in\{00,01,10,11\}} \frac{\partial P(X,Y)}{\partial x_i} \cdot \log\left(\frac{P(X,Y)^{-1}}{e}\right)$$

$(\text{for } \log_e)$.

Expanding the partial derivative we have

$$\frac{1}{N}\left[\begin{array}{l} (\lambda(x_i)\cdot(1-\lambda(x_i))\cdot\lambda(y_i))\cdot\log\frac{P((X,Y)=(1,1))^{-1}}{e} + \\ {[\lambda(x_i)\cdot(1-\lambda(x_i))\cdot(1-\lambda(y_i))]}\cdot\log\frac{P((X,Y)=(1,0))^{-1}}{e} \\ -(\lambda(x_i)\cdot(1-\lambda(x_i))\cdot\lambda(y_i))\cdot\log\frac{P((X,Y)=(0,1))^{-1}}{e} \\ -[\lambda(x_i)\cdot(1-\lambda(x_i))\cdot(1-\lambda(y_i))]\cdot\log\frac{P((X,Y)=(0,0))^{-1}}{e} \end{array}\right]$$

$$= \frac{1}{N}\left[[\lambda(x_i)\cdot(1-\lambda(x_i))]\cdot\left(\log\prod_{X=1,Y\in\{0,1\}}\left(\frac{P(X,Y)}{e}\right)^{-P(Y_i=Y)} - \log\prod_{X=0,Y\in\{0,1\}}\left(\frac{P(X,Y)}{e}\right)^{-P(Y_i=Y)}\right)\right]$$

$$= \frac{1}{N}\left[[\lambda(x_i)\cdot(1-\lambda(x_i))]\cdot\log\left(\frac{\prod_{X=0,Y\in\{0,1\}}P(X,Y)^{P(Y_i=Y)}}{\prod_{X=1,Y\in\{0,1\}}P(X,Y)^{P(Y_i=Y)}}\right)\right] \quad (*).$$

The direction of change in x_i (positive or negative, i.e., towards Boolean 1 or Boolean 0) will be determined by the ratio within the log. If this ratio is greater than 1, the direction of change will be negative (because the change is in the opposite direction of the gradient). If it is smaller than 1, the change will be positive.

The expression (*) expresses three properties of the data:

1. How certain we are in x_i. If x_i is very high or very low, the whole expression, and the change it implies to x_i, will be small. This is a result of the factor $[\lambda(x_i) \cdot (1 - \lambda(x_i))]$ that has its maximum at $\lambda(x_i) = 0.5$ and approaches 0 when $\lambda(x_i)$ approaches 1 or 0.
2. The more likely Boolean value to assign to y_i. The exponent of $P(X,Y)^{P(Y_i = Y)}$) will decrease the weight of the probability $P(X,Y)$ in the ratio if $P(Y_i = Y)$ is low, and vice versa.
3. The more likely Boolean (X,Y) vectors. For example, if $P(Y_i = 0) \approx 0$, we will have within the log a ratio between $P(X = 0, Y = 1)$ and $P(X = 1, Y = 1)$. If $P(X = 0, Y = 1)$ is more likely, the ratio will be greater than 1; and if $P(X = 1, Y = 1)$ is more likely, it will be smaller than 1.

A symmetric expression can be developed for y_i. Note that since all regulator values are equally likely, the term $\frac{\partial H(X)}{\partial x_i}$ is 0 (otherwise it negates the bias).

Now assume that $P((X,Y) = (1,0)) = P((X,Y) = (0,1)) = 0.49$; and $P((X,Y) = (0,0)) = P((X,Y) = (1,1)) = 0.01$. We look at measurement i in which $x_i = 2$ and $y_i = 1$ and plot the changes to x_i, y_i in eight consecutive steps of the algorithm (Figure 2). We choose $\delta = N$ and therefore the constant $1/N$ is canceled out. As can be seen in the figure, x_i does not change significantly, while y_i is reduced sharply to a negative value. This is in agreement with our optimal solution scheme for the simple $X \rightarrow Y$ network.

We used a very simple network in order to explain the principles of our algorithm, and we now turn to more

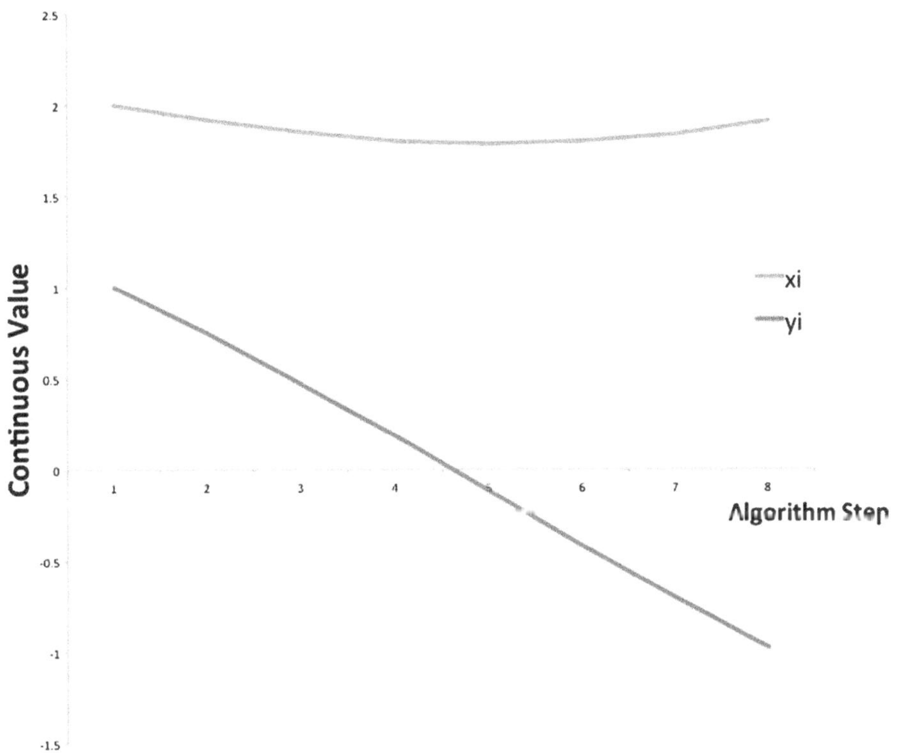

Figure 2 Changes in x_i, y_i in eight consecutive gradient descent steps. We set $P(XY = 01) = P(XY = 10) = 0.49$; and $P(XY = 11) = P(XY = 00) = 0.01$. Since x_i is larger than y_i in the beginning, it is hardly reduced. In contrast, y_i is reduced sharply to a negative value. The inferred states for measurement *i* are gene X is active gene Y is inactive.

complex networks. Any network can be described by a directed graph G(V,E), where the set of nodes V contains a node for every gene, and the set of edges E contains edges from every regulator to each of its targets. The entropy of every node Y_i is conditional on its set of regulators $\mathbf{X}_{Y_i}$. The conditional entropy of the network becomes $\sum_{i=1}^{|V|} H(Y_i|\mathbf{X}_{Y_i})$.

The dataset of more complex networks may contain steady states, like in the case of the simple network, but it may also include longer trajectories. In the latter case, if two measurements i, $i + 1$ correspond to two consecutive states in a trajectory, the value of y_{i+1} should be taken from C_{i+1} and the values x_i of its regulators from C_i.

In the simple network that we discussed so far, V contains two nodes, one for gene X and one for gene Y, and E contains one directed edge from the node of X to the node of Y. Each measurement is a vector of size 2, (x_i, y_i). For calculating (*), we needed to find the probability $P(X,Y)$ of vectors of size 2.

In the general case, in order to derive the conditional entropy of the network by the value x_i of one of the regulators X at the measurement i, we need to find the probability of a Boolean assignment to vectors of arbitrary size. We can do this in the same way as we did for $P([X;Y]_i)$ - by multiplying the individual probabilities of the vector entries. The probability of seeing a Boolean vector in the dataset as a whole is again an average of its probabilities in the N measurements.

Denote by M_x the number of targets that X regulates. Denote by $\vec{Z}_j$, a Boolean assignment to $\mathbf{X}_{Yj} \cup \{Y_j\}/\ X$, where Y_j is the jth target of X, and $\mathbf{X}_{Yj}$ is the set of regulators of Y_j, at the ith measurement. Denote as $\vec{Z}$ any Boolean vector of size $\left|\vec{Z}_j\right|$. We generalize the derivative by x_i given by (*) as follows:

$$\frac{1}{N}\cdot\left[(\lambda(x_i)\cdot(1-\lambda(x_i)))\cdot\log\left(\frac{\prod_{X=0,\vec{Z}\in\{0,1\}^{\left|\vec{Z}_j\right|},1\le j\le M_X} P(X,\vec{Z})^{P(\vec{Z}_j=\vec{Z})}}{\prod_{X=1,\vec{Z}\in\{0,1\}^{\left|\vec{Z}_j\right|},1\le j\le M_X} P(X,\vec{Z})^{P(\vec{Z}_j=\vec{Z})}}\right)\right]. \quad (**)$$

The expression (**) determines the change to x_i in the same way as (*), taking into account all the targets of gene X in the network. If X is itself a target of other regulators, then M_x increases by 1, and $\vec{Z}_{M_x+1}$ will correspond to a Boolean assignment to the regulators of X at measurement i.

Note that if we decrease the step size of the gradient descent δ by a factor C, the change in the x_i

values $-\delta \cdot \nabla \sum_{i=1}^{|V|} H(Y_i|\mathbf{X}_{Y_i})$ will decrease by a factor of C. However, since the logistic function maps the x_i values to the finite interval (0,1), equal probabilities $\lambda(x_i) = P(X_i = 1)$ may not change by the same factor. For a ratio within the log in (**) that is very large for some x_i, and smaller for another x_j, the change in $P(X_j)$ as a result of decreasing δ can remain large while the change in $P(X_i)$ becomes small. In addition, if the change in the total entropy becomes very small as a result of decreasing δ, the algorithm will proceed to step 4.

It may be the case that the dataset is not sufficiently informative for inferring all the states. For example, if in the simple $X \rightarrow Y$ network $x_i = y_i$, the algorithm will change both values to 0. On the other hand, if all x_i and y_i are different, there are always parameters τ, δ for which the algorithm will change all x_i and y_i to have opposite signs, and $H(Y|X)$ will approach 0. A situation as the former can also occur in more complex networks. We would like to prove that if it does not occur, i.e., if the dataset is informative enough, our algorithm will infer the states of a Boolean network. This is shown by the following theorem:

Theorem 1: *Let G = (V,E) be a graph that describes the structure of a Boolean network and D a dataset of N measurements.*

Let X_Y be a set of nodes that regulate some node Y, i.e., $\forall X' \in X_Y, (X' \rightarrow Y) \in E$

Denote by $\vec{X}_{Y_i}$ an assignment of Boolean values to the nodes in X_Y at measurement i. Similarly, Y_i is a Boolean assignment to Y at measurement i.

If the algorithm converges to a global minimum and updates dataset D to become D′, then for any two measurements i,j in D′: $P\left(\vec{X}_{Y_i} = \vec{X}_{Y_j} \wedge Y_i \neq Y_j\right) = 0.$

Proof The conditional entropy of the network is a sum of conditional entropies. Since conditional entropy is always nonnegative, the global minimum is reached when the conditional entropy of the network is 0, and every term in the sum is also 0.

The conditional entropy of gene Y and its set of regulators X_Y can be written as

$$H(Y|X_Y) = -\sum_{Y\in\{0,1\},\vec{X}_Y\in\{0,1\}^{|X_Y|}} P\left(\vec{X}_Y\right) \cdot P\left(Y|\vec{X}_Y\right) \cdot \log\left(P\left(Y|\vec{X}_Y\right)\right).$$

Since the log is non-positive and the probabilities are non-negative, $H(Y|X_Y)$ reaches its minimum when for every $\left(Y, \vec{X}_Y\right)$ either $P\left(\vec{X}_Y\right) = 0$, $P\left(Y|\vec{X}_Y\right) = 0$, or $P\left(Y|\vec{X}_Y\right) = 1$.

If $P\left(\vec{X}_Y\right) = 0$, the value $\vec{X}_Y$ of the regulators never occurs in the data.

Otherwise, if $P\left(Y = 1|\vec{X}_Y\right) = 0$, then since $\sum_{Y\in\{0,1\}} P\left(Y|\vec{X}_Y\right) = 1$ it must hold that $P\left(Y = 0|\vec{X}_Y\right) = 1$. Similarly, if $P\left(Y = 1|\vec{X}_Y\right) = 1$ then $P\left(Y = 0|\vec{X}_Y\right) = 0$.

Hence, for a specific assignment $\vec{X}_Y$ of the regulators, the target Y is either 0 or 1 but never both. □

To summarize the analysis section, we showed that the algorithm infers the states of a simple network optimally if the dataset is informative enough. We then generalized the inference process to general networks, and showed that if the algorithm converges it will infer the states of a Boolean network.

In the 'Testing' section, we test the algorithm using simulation and real microarray expression data.

Testing

Boolean networks with two regulators per node

We can evaluate the accuracy of the algorithm without bias by using a known Boolean network structure. We use the Boolean network that is illustrated in Figure 3 and generate our dataset according to the following procedure:

1. Assign logic rules to all the nodes. We use the same logic function for all the nodes - XOR in the first experiment and NOR in the second experiment. XOR's output is 1 if and only if the values of the

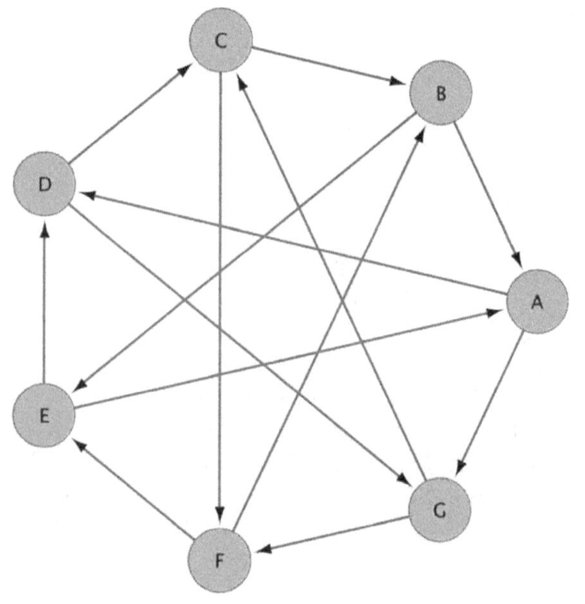

Figure 3 The structure of the Boolean network used in the simulation. For example, the regulator set of node A contains nodes B and E. The figure was generated using Cytoscape [13].

regulator nodes differ. NOR's output is 1 if and only if the values of the regulator nodes are both 0

2. Randomly choose an initial state
3. Generate a trajectory of length 400 states
4. Convert the Boolean trajectory to a continuous trajectory as follows:
   (a) Replace every Boolean 1 by a value from a normal distribution with an average of 1 and a standard deviation of 1.1
   (b) Replace every Boolean 0 by a value from a normal distribution with an average of −1 and a standard deviation of 1.1

We use a C implementation of the algorithm as described in [12], without normalizing the continuous values. The process is illustrated in Figure 4. A trajectory of length 400 corresponds to the size of biological datasets that are available in public databases [14].

In [15] Shmulevich and Zhang describe a mapping of continuous values to Boolean values that maps every value above some threshold to 1 and below that threshold to 0. We will compare the results of our inference process to this method, which we will refer to as 'maximal probability reconstruction.' The threshold that we will use is 0. Figure 5 illustrates this comparison. As can be seen in the figure, the gradient descent makes significantly less mistakes in its reconstructed trajectory. Its mistakes tend to cluster at consecutive time points, since if it makes a mistake in a regulator at time T, it is more likely to make mistakes in its target at time $T + 1$.

Boolean networks with imperfect structure

In the previous experiment, we assumed that we know the regulator set of each node. However, it is often the case that the network structure is not perfectly known, for example, some regulator set may contain incorrect nodes. Therefore, we now use the same continuous dataset, but give the algorithm an incorrect structure as input. We perform two experiments. In the first we add an incorrect node to one of the regulator sets, and in the

Original Network Trajectory

Time	A	B	C	D	E	F	G
1	1	0	1	0	1	0	1
2	1	1	1	0	0	0	1
3	1	1	1	1	1	0	1
4	0	1	0	0	1	0	0
5	0	0	0	1	1	0	0
6	1	0	1	1	0	0	1
7	0	1	0	1	0	0	0
8	1	0	1	0	1	0	1

Logical Rules:

A(t+1)= XOR(B(t),E(t))
E(t+1)= XOR(F(t)B(t))
B(t+1)= XOR(C(t),F(t))
F(t+1)= XOR(G(t),C(t))
C(t+1)= XOR(D(t),G(t))
G(t+1)= XOR(A(t),D(t))
D(t+1)= XOR(E(t),A(t))

Time	A	B	C	D	E	F	G
1	1.04751	-1.27844	1.41795	-0.665863	2.45957	-0.609037	2.71929
2	2.67914	1.3075	3.81133	-3.0713	-1.03547	-2.08456	-0.306087
3	1.27626	1.71614	1.22564	1.63595	0.263287	-1.92094	1.88821
4	-1.60686	0.527762	-0.270363	0.26825	0.172525	0.0397375	0.118338
5	-2.09162	-1.13789	0.070675	1.0346	0.626737	-2.48894	-2.2126
6	0.959313	0.2957	1.658	0.016825	-0.804675	-1.77702	2.5443
7	-4.92401	1.29964	-2.24825	0.978588	0.437325	-0.996525	-0.980662
8	0.278962	-1.09064	1.51266	0.196187	0.719313	0.0228875	1.37037

Continuous values, normally distributed around -1 (for Boolean 0) or 1 (for Boolean 1)

Time	A	B	C	D	E	F	G
1	1	0	1	0	1	1	1
2	1	1	1	0	0	0	1
3	1	1	1	1	1	0	1
4	0	1	0	0	1	0	0
5	0	0	0	1	1	1	0
6	1	0	1	1	0	1	1
7	0	1	0	1	0	0	0
8	1	0	1	0	1	1	1

Reconstructed Boolean values – errors are highlighted in yellow

Figure 4 The process by which datasets are generated in the simulation. A Boolean trajectory is generated using a Boolean network and a set of logical rules (top). The Boolean values are translated into normally distributed continuous values (middle). The continuous values are reconstructed into Boolean values that are then compared to the original Boolean trajectory (bottom).

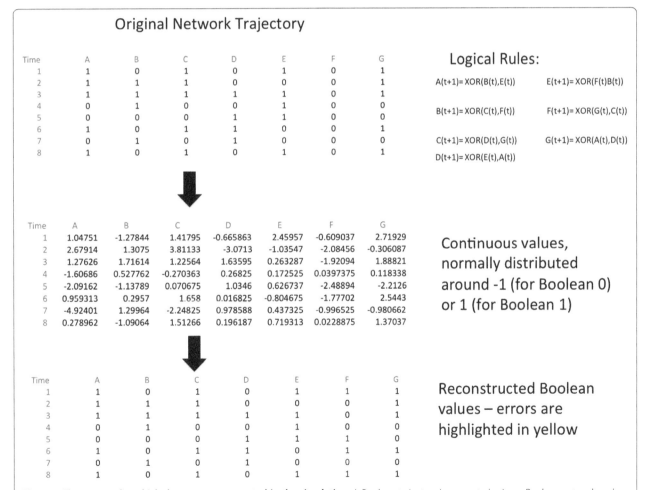

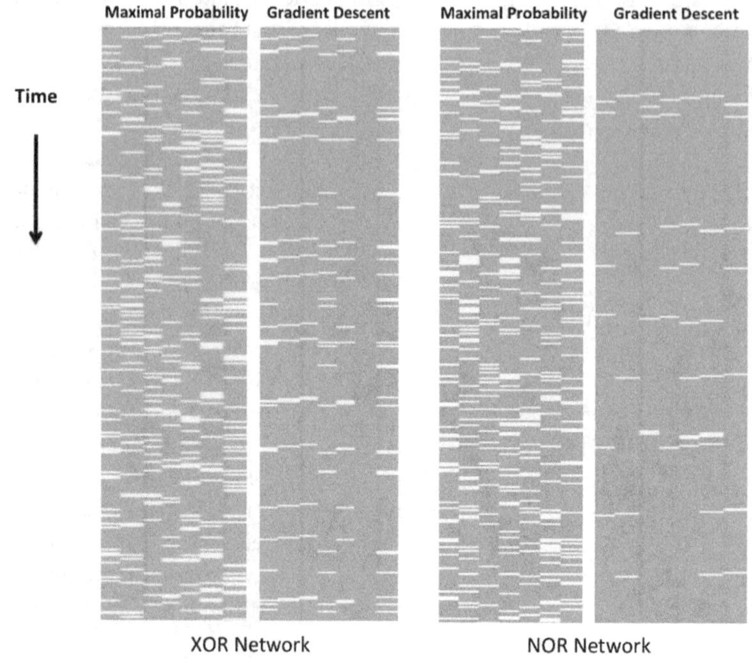

Figure 5 Maximal probability reconstruction vs. gradient descent reconstruction. Maximal probability reconstruction vs. gradient descent reconstruction of trajectories of the Boolean XOR (left) and Boolean NOR (right) networks. Rows correspond to the time points and columns to network nodes. For display purposes, only a prefix of the trajectory is shown. The yellow color represents mistakes, i.e., values which are different than the real Boolean values, and orange represents a correct value. In each of the two comparisons, the maximal probability reconstruction is presented to the left of the gradient descent reconstruction. Overall, the gradient descent is more accurate than the maximal probability reconstruction. The percentages of incorrect reconstructed values for the latter method are 17.6% (XOR) and 18% (NOR), and for the gradient descent reconstruction, 6.7% (XOR) and 2.2% (NOR).

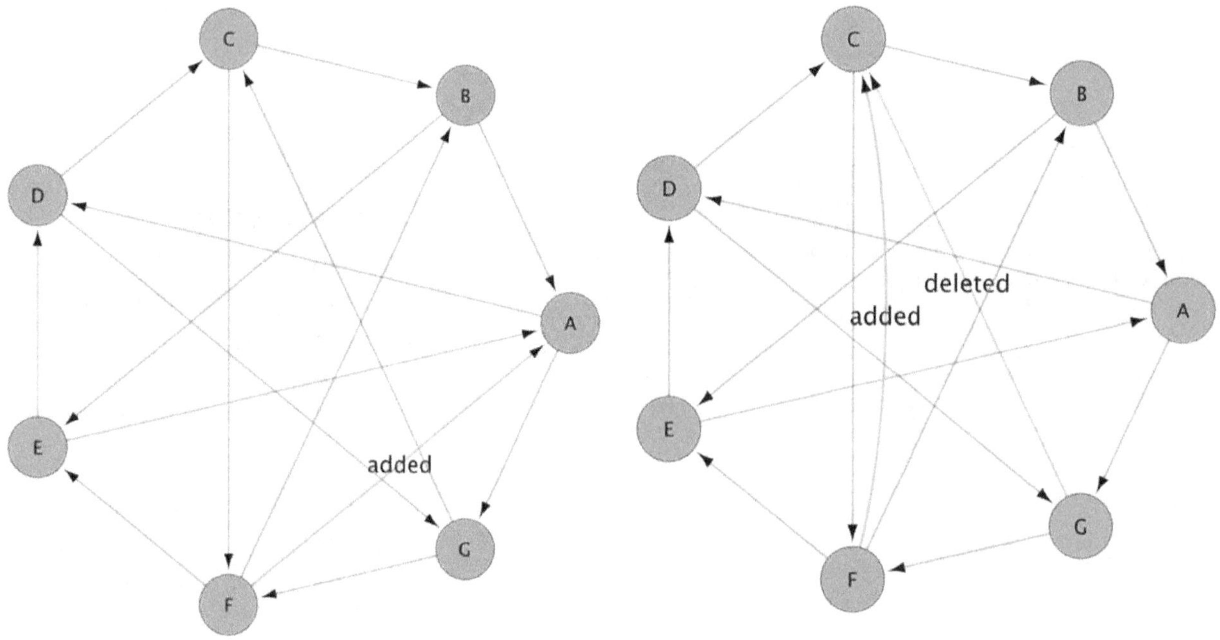

Figure 6 Incorrect structures that were given to the algorithm as input. Incorrect structures that were given to the algorithm as input with the dataset generated by the network in Figure 2. The wrong structure on the left was given as input with the dataset generated for the XOR network (see text). The wrong structure on the right was given as input with the dataset generated for the NOR network (see text). Edges that were removed (regulator sets that were changed) are colored in faded red and marked 'deleted'. Edges that were added are colored in green and marked 'added'. The figure was generated using Cytoscape [13].

second experiment we replace a node in a regulator set by a node that does not belong to that set. These changes are illustrated in Figure 6. As can be seen in Figure 7 when using a wrong structure, the algorithm can make more mistakes in the reconstruction of the network trajectories. However, even with an imperfect network structure, the trajectories reconstructed by the algorithm are more accurate than the maximal probability trajectories.

The cell cycle network of Li et al.

The cell cycle is a process by which cells grow and multiply. It constitutes several distinct phases through which the cell grows and divides. Its daughter cells start the cycle from the first phase and so on. A gene regulatory network controls this process. Li et al. [16] created a Boolean network model of the yeast cell cycle. In their model, every node in the regulator set is assigned a repressing or an activating role and is referred to as a repressor or an activator, respectively. A node is activated by its regulator set if the sum of active activators is greater than the sum of active repressors and repressed if the former sum is lesser than the latter sum. If the sums are equal, a node either remains unchanged or is assigned a Boolean 0, meaning that without sufficient activation the gene product is degraded. Li et al. showed that the trajectories of their model converge to the first phase of the yeast cell cycle, and given an external trigger the network resumes the cycle. The network is illustrated in Figure 8.

We repeated our data generation procedure for the cell cycle network of Li et al. Since this network converges to the first phase of the cell cycle and awaits a trigger to continue cycling, we provided that trigger repeatedly and generated a trajectory of length 400. The results of reconstructing the Boolean states are illustrated in Figure 9. As in the previous experiments, the reconstructed trajectory is more accurate than the maximal probability trajectory. The mistakes in this case were mainly concentrated to the node Cln3 and its direct target MBF. The reason is that when we generated the dataset, we repeatedly changed Cln3 to provide a

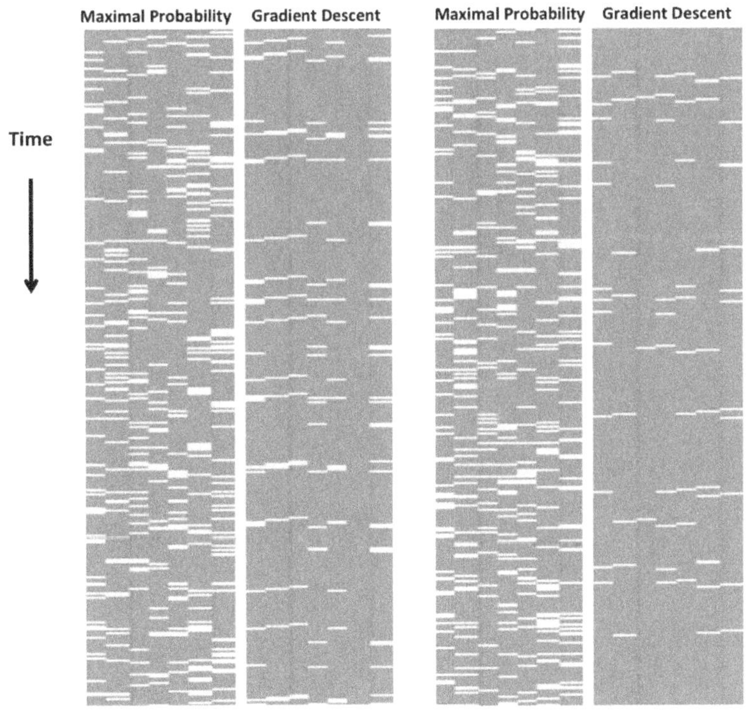

Figure 7 Maximal probability reconstruction vs. gradient descent reconstruction. Maximal probability reconstruction vs. gradient descent reconstruction of trajectories of the Boolean XOR (left) and Boolean NOR (right) networks. The gradient descent algorithm is given an inaccurate structure. The rows correspond to the time points and columns to the network nodes. For display purposes, only a prefix of the trajectory is shown. The yellow color represents mistakes, i.e., values different than the real Boolean values, and orange represents a correct value. In each of the two comparisons, the maximal probability reconstruction is presented to the left of the gradient descent reconstruction. Overall, the gradient descent is more accurate than the maximal probability reconstruction despite the imperfect structures that are given to it as input. The XOR network's trajectory reconstruction is not affected by the error in structure, while the NOR network's reconstruction is slightly less accurate. The percentages of incorrect reconstructed values for maximal probability reconstruction are 17.6% (XOR) and 18% (NOR), and for the gradient descent reconstruction, 6.7% (XOR) and 3% (NOR).

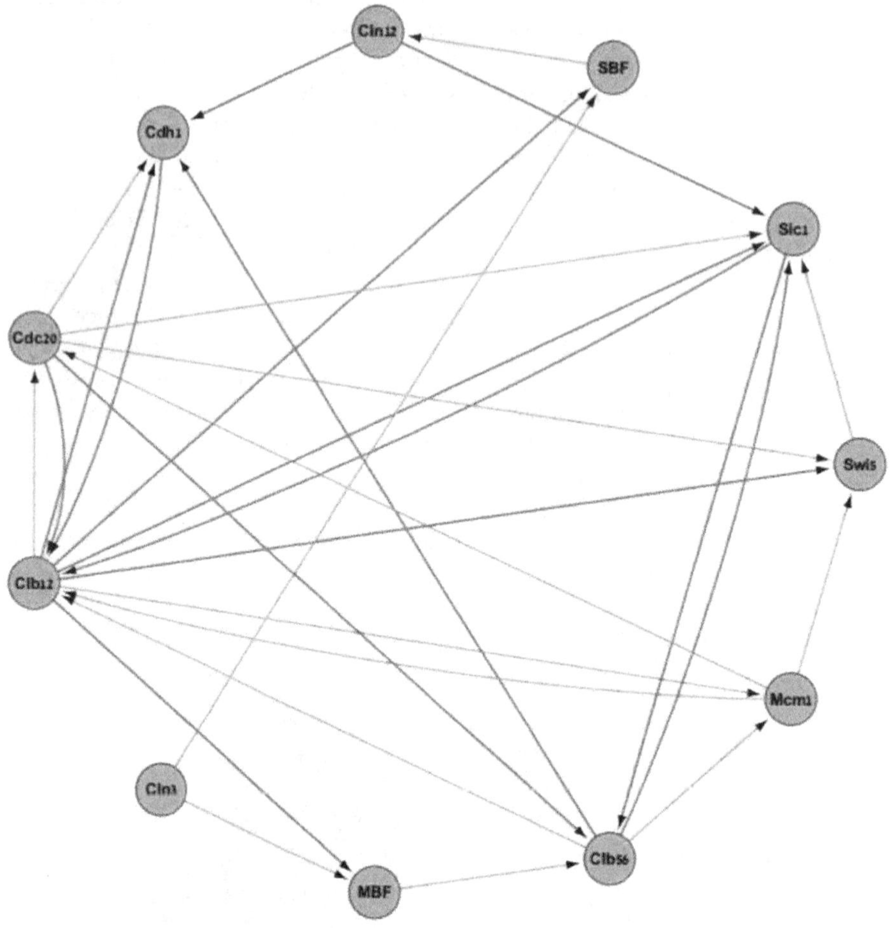

Figure 8 The structure of the yeast cell cycle network of Li et al. [16]. Edges in green correspond to activators (see text), and red edges to repressors (see text). The node Cln3 has no regulators but receives an external signal that causes the network to go through the phases of the cell cycle. The figure was generated using Cytoscape [13].

trigger for cycling, but we did not include any regulators for Cln3 in the network structure. This creates a discrepancy between the input that we provided to the algorithm and the network behavior - the algorithm does not expect Cln3 to change its value along the trajectory if it does not have regulators.

Conway's game of life

Conway's game of life is composed of a square grid of cells in which each cell's Boolean value is controlled by the values of neighboring cells, and changes over time [17]. The grid can generate complex patterns that may vary significantly depending on the initial values. We modeled the game of life with grid size 7×7 as a Boolean network. Each node has 3 to 8 regulators, depending on the number of grid neighbors, and the initial state is chosen randomly. The results of reconstructing a trajectory of length 100 with the same level of noise as in previous experiments are displayed in Additional file 1: Movie 1. The left frame is the real trajectory, the middle frame is a maximal probability reconstruction, and the right frame is the gradient descent reconstruction. Boolean 1 is represented by a black cell and Boolean 0 by a white cell. As can be observed in the movie, the reconstruction algorithm makes more mistakes in the early states than in the later states. The reason for this is most likely the fact that at later states, the network enters a 3-cycle, i.e., a trajectory in which three states occur in the same order repeatedly. Since the relationships between the nodes occur more than once, the algorithm can learn these relationships and use them in reconstruction. The algorithm also identifies the existence of a 3-cycle, in the sense that it predicts a repetitive sequence of three patterns that are similar to the real patterns of the 3-cycle. In contrast, in the early time points, the states vary and do not reoccur, which makes it harder to learn some of the dependencies that play a role in generating these states. Note that most nodes have eight regulators, which means that their logic function has 256 different inputs. The number of possible network states is 2^{49}.

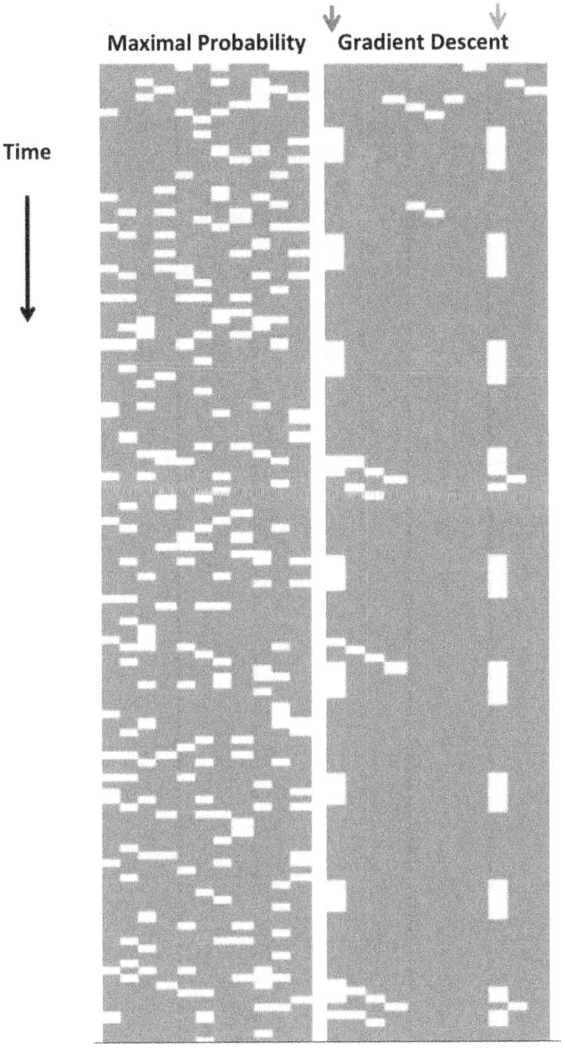

Figure 9 Maximal probability reconstruction vs. gradient descent reconstruction. Maximal probability reconstruction vs. gradient descent reconstruction of the trajectory of the yeast cell cycle network of Li et al. [16]. Rows correspond to the time points and columns to network nodes. For display purposes only a prefix of the trajectory is shown. The yellow color represents mistakes, i.e., values different than the real Boolean values, and orange represents a correct value. The maximal probability reconstruction is presented to the left of the gradient descent reconstruction. Overall, the gradient descent is more accurate than the maximal probability reconstruction. The percentages of wrongly reconstructed values for the latter method are 17.9%, and for the gradient descent reconstruction, 7.4%. The gradient descent algorithm makes more mistakes for the node Cln3 that has no regulators and receives an external input (red arrow) and for the MBF that has Cln3 in its regulator set (green arrow).

The maximal probability reconstruction makes an error on 18.6% of the nodes. In the initial 50 states, it errs on 18.2% of the nodes, and in the last 50 states, on 19% of the nodes. The gradient descent reconstruction assigns the wrong values to 8.8% of the nodes. In the initial 50 states, its error rate is 12.8%, and in the last 50 states, 4.8%.

Microarray expression data

Orlando et al. [18] compared gene expression patterns in wild type yeast compared to a cyclin mutant strain. They observed that many genes are expressed in a cyclic pattern in both strains. In order to explain this observation, they suggested a Boolean network of nine transcription factors and transcription complexes. They showed that for logic functions of their choice and most initial states, the network traverses the cell cycle stages and, therefore, can explain their observation. We will use the expression data of the transcription factors and the network structure from [18] and infer the network states in wild type and mutant cells. If the states represent the cell cycle in both strains, then our analysis will support the conclusion of the study.

For the MBF, SBF, and SFF complexes, we use the expression profiles of their members STB1, SWI4, and FKH1, respectively. The dataset of [18] contains four time series of 15 microarrays for time points from 30 to 260 min, two replicates for the wild type and two for the mutant. Since all expression values are positive values, we need to map them to a symmetric range centered at 0, as the input of the simulations. However, different arrays will typically contain biases; for example, a gene can have a higher value in an array that has a higher mean expression value. Therefore, mapping two identical values from two different arrays to the same value may result in a bad estimation of the initial probabilities.

Shmulevich and Zhang [15] showed that bias in different arrays can be eliminated by applying a normalization process. We use the following normalization: The network is expected to perform about two cell cycles during the measured time points. The expression levels of a gene at the 2 cycles should correlate. Based on this observation, we normalize in every replicate the genes on the first set of seven arrays and the second set of eight arrays to average 0 and unit standard deviation. Using the resulting initial probability estimates and the network structure, we apply our inference process and compare the resulting set of Boolean states with the pattern hypothesized in the study (Figure 10). As can be seen in the figure, the network performs a cyclic trajectory in both strains, while the trajectory of the mutant corresponds to a slower cell cycle. This finding is in agreement with a slower cell cycle for the mutant as reported in [18]. It also indicates that the network structure may not account for all the regulatory interactions in the network, since both networks start from the same initial state.

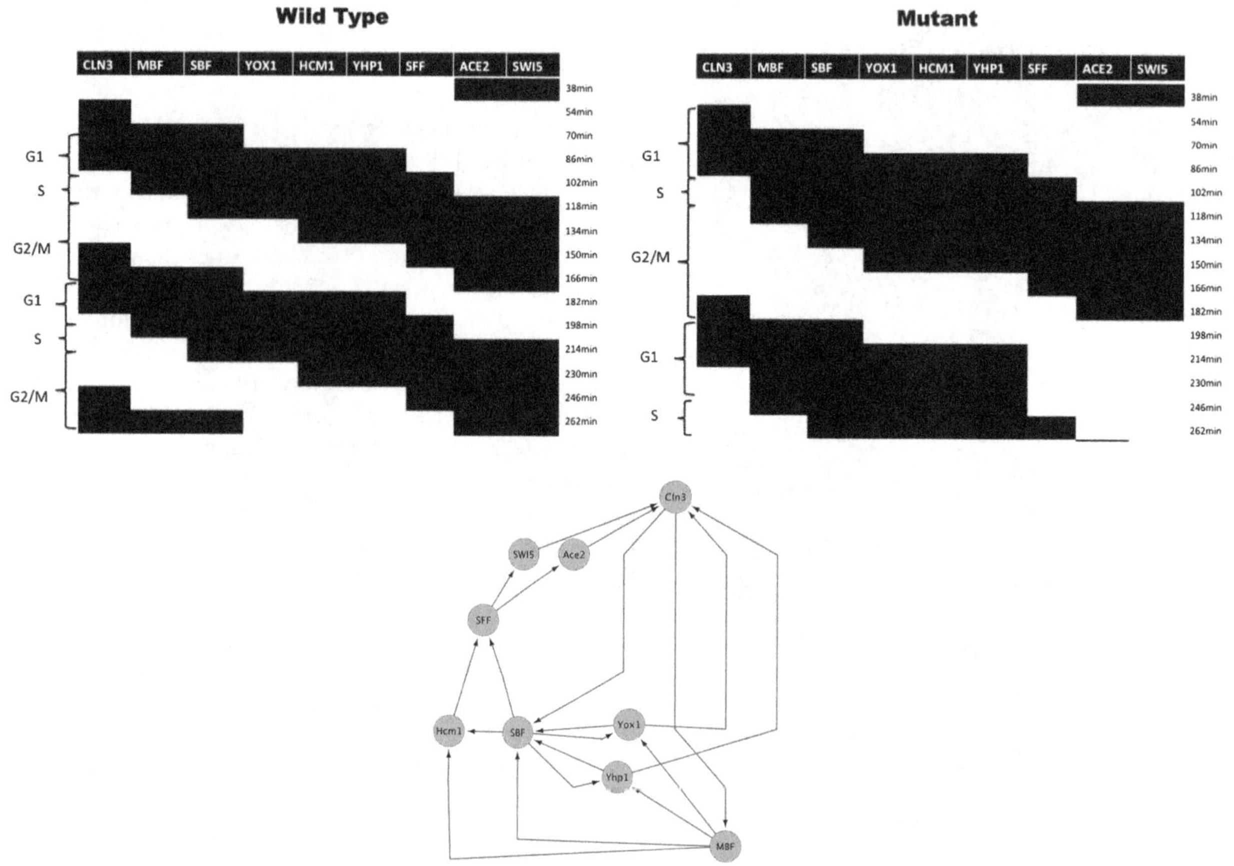

Figure 10 Inferred trajectories of the Boolean network for wild type and mutant strains. Inferred trajectories of the Boolean network from [18] for the wild type and mutant strains (one replicate is shown for each). The network structure is displayed at the bottom. Black cells correspond to a Boolean 1 and white cells to a Boolean 0. The corresponding cell cycle stages are marked at the left side of each trajectory. Both trajectories start with active ACE2 and SWI5, which are the last active factors at the completion of the previous cycle, followed activation of CLN3 and an initiation of a new cycle. The network seems to cycle a little faster in the wild type. The network structure was generated using Cytoscape [13].

Conclusions

In this study we presented a problem that arises in molecular biology, namely, that of inferring the activity of cellular network components given noisy measurements, and defined it as mapping continuous measurements to Boolean network states. We developed an algorithm that given a network structure infers its Boolean states from a dataset of continuous measurements. Our results show that the algorithm can successfully reconstruct Boolean states from inaccurate continuous data. The algorithm performs reasonably well even if the relations between the nodes of the network contain errors. We also showed that it can be used to interpret real microarray data and examine experimental hypotheses.

Our approach is highly dependent on a network structure, and when that is not available, methods that rely solely on expression should be used [15,19]. We did not define a concept of prior knowledge, which has been used in various works to integrate information into Bayesian models [20,21]. While this makes our method arguably less flexible, it also exempts us from the need to define prior distributions. Finally, the algorithm is defined for deterministic Boolean networks, in contrast to probabilistic Boolean networks that may better express biological noise [22].

Further research could improve inference accuracy and explore various aspects of the problem. One such aspect is the amount of information about the network trajectory that is lost due to noise. In the simple network that we described in the analysis section, the proportion of information that will be lost is the sum of probabilities of two events:

$$P\left(x_i \sim N(\mu, \sigma^2) \wedge y_i \sim N(-\mu, \sigma^2) \wedge x_i \leq y_i\right) + P\left(x_i \sim N(-\mu, \sigma^2) \wedge y_i \sim N(\mu, \sigma^2) \wedge x_i \geq y_i\right).$$

When one of these two events occurs, it is impossible to reconstruct the original states of X and Y. In more complex networks, information loss is a more complex. Determining an upper limit on the number of Boolean values that can be recovered given a certain amount of noise may prove insightful.

Another aspect that should be investigated is how to choose parameters that optimize the performance of the algorithm, such as the parameters of the logistic function or the step size δ and threshold τ of the gradient descent.

As Boolean networks can generate a diverse range of dynamic behaviors, the accuracy of reconstructing trajectories that arise in different dynamic regimes should also be characterized. For example, are chaotic trajectories harder to reconstruct then those that display order? More simulation tests can better define the relationships between the quality of data and different classes of networks.

Current experimental techniques produce an ever-greater number of measurements, and there is a pressing need for methods that will enable researchers to interpret it accurately and without bias. An accurate method for inferring the state of a cell can translate this richness of data into important discoveries.

Additional file

Additional file 1: Movie 1. Reconstruction of a trajectory of Conway's Game of Life. The left frame is the real trajectory, the middle frame is a maximal probability reconstruction, and the right frame is the gradient descent reconstruction. Boolean 1 is represented by a black cell and Boolean 0 by a white cell.

Competing interests
The author declares that he has no competing interests.

References

1. SA Kauffman, Metabolic stability and epigenesis in randomly constructed genetic nets. J. Theor. Biol. **22**, 437–467 (1969)
2. SA Kauffman, *The Origins of Order, Self-Organization and Selection in Evolution* (Oxford University Press, Oxford, 1993)
3. X Yu, N Schneiderhan-Marra, TO Joos, Protein microarrays and personalized medicine. Ann. Biol. Clin. **69**(1), p17–p29 (2011)
4. F Liu, WPTK Kuo Jenssen, E Hovig, Performance comparison of multiple microarray platforms for gene expression profiling. Methods Mol. Biol. **802**, 141–155 (2012)
5. NC Roy, E Alterman, ZA Park, WC McNabb, A comparison of analog and next-generation transcriptomic tools for mammalian studies. Brief. Funct. Genomics **10**(3), p135–p150 (2011)
6. G Karlebach, R Shamir, Modeling and analysis of gene regulatory networks. Nat. Rev. Mol. Cell Biol. **9**, 770–780 (2008)
7. Y Pan, T Durfee, J Bockhorst, M Craven, Connecting quantitative regulatory-network models to the genome. Bioinformatics **23**, p367–p376 (2007)
8. T Akutsu, S Miyano, S Kuhara, Identification of genetic networks from a small number of gene expression patterns under the Boolean network model. Pac. Symp. Biocomput. **1999**, 17–28 (1999)
9. R Sharan, RM Karp, Reconstructing Boolean models of signaling. J. Comput. Biol. **3**, p1–p9 (2013)
10. I Gat-Viks, A Tanay, D Raijman, R Shamir, A probabilistic methodology for integrating knowledge and experiments on biological networks. J. Comput. Biol. **13**, p165–p181 (2006)
11. CE Shannon, A mathematical theory of communication. Bell Syst. Tech. J. **27**(379–423), 623–656 (1948)
12. G Karlebach, R Shamir, Constructing logical models of gene regulatory networks by integrating transcription factor-DNA interactions with expression data: an entropy-based approach. J. Comput. Biol. **19**, p30–p41 (2012)
13. P Shannon, A Markiel, O Ozier, NS Baliga, JT Wang, D Ramage, N Amin, B Schwikowski, T Ideker, Cytoscape: a software environment for integrated models of biomolecular interaction networks. Genome Res. **13**, p2498–p2504 (2003)
14. R Edgar et al., Gene expression omnibus: NCBI gene expression and hybridization array data repository. Nucleic Acids Res. **30**(1), p207–p210 (2002)
15. I Shmulevich, W Zhang, Binary analysis and optimization-based normalization of gene expression data. Bioinformatics **18**(4), 555–565 (2002)
16. F Li, T Long, Y Lu, Q Ouyang, C Tang, The yeast cell-cycle network is robustly designed. Proc. Natl. Acad. Sci. U. S. A. **101**, p4781–p4786 (2004)
17. M Gardner, Mathematical games - the fantastic combinations of John Conway's new solitaire game "life". Scientific Am. **223**, 120–123 (1970)
18. DA Orlando, CY Lin, A Bernard, JY Wang, JES Socolar, ES Iversen, AJ Hartemink, SB Haase, Global control of cell-cycle transcription by coupled CDK and network oscillators. Nature **453**, 944–948 (2008)
19. X Zhou, X Wang, E Dougherty, Binarization of microarray data based on a mixture model. Mol Cancer Therap **2**(7), 679–684 (2003)
20. I Gat-Viks, A Tanay, D Raijman, R Shamir, A probabilistic methodology for integrating knowledge and experiments on biological networks. J. Comput. Biol. **13**, 165–181 (2006)
21. N Friedman, M Linial, I Nachman, D Pe'er, Using Bayesian networks to analyze expression data. J. Comput. Biol. **7**, 601–620 (2000)
22. I Shmulevich, ER Dougherty, S Kim, W Zhang, Probabilistic Boolean networks: a rule-based uncertainty model for gene regulatory networks. Bioinformatics **18**, 261–274 (2002)

A 2D graphical representation of the sequences of DNA based on triplets and its application

Sai Zou, Lei Wang* and Junfeng Wang

Abstract

In this paper, we first present a new concept of 'weight' for 64 triplets and define a different weight for each kind of triplet. Then, we give a novel 2D graphical representation for DNA sequences, which can transform a DNA sequence into a plot set to facilitate quantitative comparisons of DNA sequences. Thereafter, associating with a newly designed measure of similarity, we introduce a novel approach to make similarities/dissimilarities analysis of DNA sequences. Finally, the applications in similarities/dissimilarities analysis of the complete coding sequences of β-globin genes of 11 species illustrate the utilities of our newly proposed method.

Keywords: Graphical representation; Similarities/dissimilarities analysis; Triplet; DNA sequence

1. Introduction

In the recent years, an exponential growth of sequence data in DNA databases has been observed by biologists; the importance of understanding genetic sequences coupled with the difficulty of working with such immense volumes of DNA sequence data underscores the urgent need for supportive visual tools. Recently, graphical representation is well regarded which can offer visual inspection of data and provide a simple way to facilitate the similarity analysis and comparison of DNA sequences [1-5]. Because of its convenience and excellent maneuverability, currently, all kinds of methods based on graphical representation have been extensively applied in relevant realms of bioinformatics.

Until now, there are many different graphical representation methods having been proposed to numerically characterize DNA sequences on the basis of different multiple-dimension spaces. For example, Liao et al. [6-9], Randic et al. [10-13], Guo et al. [14,15], Qi et al. [16], Dai et al. [17,18], and Dorota et al. [19] proposed different 2D graphical representation methods of DNA sequences, respectively. Liao et al. [20-23], Randic et al. [24,25], Qi et al. [26], Yu et al. [27], and Aram et al. [28] proposed different 3D graphical representation methods of DNA sequences, respectively. Liao et al. [29], Tang et al. [30], and Chi et al. [31] proposed different 4D graphical representation methods of DNA sequences, respectively. In addition, Liao et al. [32] also proposed a kind of 5D representation method of DNA sequences and so on.

In these approaches mentioned above, most of them adopt the leading eigenvalues of some matrices, such as L/L matrices, M/M matrices, E matrices, covariance matrices, and D/D matrices, to weigh the similarities/dissimilarities among the complete coding sequences of β-globin genes of different species. Because the matrix computation is needed to obtain the leading eigenvalues, these methods are usually computationally expensive for long DNA sequences. Furthermore, in some of these approaches, their results of similarities/dissimilarities analysis are not quite reasonable, and there are some results that do not accord with the fact [7,9].

To degrade the computational complexity and obtain more reasonable results of similarities/dissimilarities analysis of DNA sequences, in this article, we propose a new 2D graphical representation of DNA sequences based on triplets, in which, we present a new concept of 'weight' for 64 triplets and a new concept of 'weight deviation' to weigh the similarities/dissimilarities among the complete coding sequences of β-globin genes of different species. Compared with some existing graphical representations of the DNA sequences, our new scheme has the following advantages: (1) no matrix computation is needed, and (2) it can characterize the graphical representations for DNA sequences exactly and obtain reasonable results of similarities/dissimilarities analysis of DNA sequences.

* Correspondence: phd.leiwang@gmail.com
School of Software Engineering, Chongqing College of Electronic Engineering, Chongqing 401331, People's Republic of China

2. Proposed 2D graphical representation of DNA sequence

Codon is a specific sequence of three adjacent nucleotides on the mRNA that specifies the genetic code information for synthesizing a particular amino acid. As illustrated in Table 1, there are total 20 amino acids and 64 codons in the natural world, and each of these codons has a specific meaning in protein synthesis: 64 codons represent amino acids and the other 3 codons cause the termination of protein synthesis.

For the 64 codons illustrated in Table 1, their corresponding triplets of DNA are illustrated in Table 2.

Based on the above 64 triplets of DNA illustrated in Table 2, we define a new mapping Ψ to map each of these triplets into a different weight. Obviously, the mapping Ψ shall satisfy the following rule: for any two pairs of triplets (X_1, Y_1) and (X_2, Y_2), where X_1, Y_1, X_2, and Y_2 are all triplets, if the corresponding codons of X_1 and Y_1 code the same amino acid but the corresponding codons of X_2 and Y_2 code two different amino acids, then there shall be $|\Psi(X_1) - \Psi(Y_1)| < |\Psi(X_2) - \Psi(Y_2)|$. So, according to the above rule and for the sake of convenience, weights consist of amino acid and codon. Amino acid is the integer part of weight, and codon is the fractional part of weight. Alanine is defined as 1, arginine is defined as 2, and the rest can be done in the same manner. Codons of every amino acid are reordered, so the first codon of alanine's (GCT) weight value is 1.1. We design the detailed mapping rules of Ψ as illustrated in Table 3.

Table 1 Relationship between 20 different kinds of most common amino acids and 64 different kinds of mRNA codons

Codons	Amino acid	Codons	Amino acid
GCU, GCC, GCA, GCG	Alanine	CUU, CUC, CUA, CUG, UUA, UUG	Leucine
CGU, CGC, CGA, CGG, AGA, AGG	Arginine	AAA, AAG	Lysine
GAU, GAC	Aspartic acid	AUG	Methionine
AAU, AAC	Asparagine	UUU, UUC	Phenylalanine
UGU, UGC	Cysteine	CCU, CCC, CCA, CCG	Proline
GAA, GAG	Glutamic acid	UCU, UCC, UCA, UCG, AGU, AGC	Serine
CAA, CAG	Glutamine	ACU, ACC, ACA, ACG	Threonine
GGU, GGC, GGA, GGG	Glycine	UGG	Tryptophan
CAU, CAC	Histidine	UAU, UAC	Tyrosine
AUU, AUC, AUA	Isoleucine	GUU, GUC, GUA, GUG	Valine
UAA, UAG, UGA			

Table 2 The corresponding triplets of 64 codons

Codons	Corresponding triplets	Codons	Corresponding triplets
GCU, GCC, GCA, GCG	GCT, GCC, GCA, GCG	CUU, CUC, CUA, CUG, UUA, UUG	CTT, CTC, CTA, CTG, TTA, TTG
CGU, CGC, CGA, 0020CGG, AGA, AGG	CGT, CGC, CGA, CGG, AGA, AGG	AAA, AAG	AAA, AAG
GAU, GAC	GAT, GAC	AUG	ATG
AAU, AAC	AAT, AAC	UUU, UUC	TTT, TTC
UGU, UGC	TGT, TGC	CCU, CCC, CCA, CCG	CCT, CCC, CCA, CCG
GAA, GAG	GAA, GAG	UCU, UCC, UCA, UCG, AGU, AGC	TCT, TCC, TCA, TCG, AGT, AGC
CAA, CAG	CAA, CAG	ACU, ACC, ACA, ACG	ACT, ACC, ACA, ACG
GGU, GGC, GGA, GGG	GGT, GGC, GGA, GGG	UGG	TGG
CAU, CAC	CAT, CAC	UAU, UAC	TAT, TAC
AUU, AUC, AUA	ATT, ATC, ATA	GUU, GUC, GUA, GUG	GTT, GTC, GTA, GTG
UAA, UAG, UGA	TAA, TAG, TGA		

For example, from Table 3, we will have Ψ (GCT) = 1.1, Ψ (GCC) = 1.2, Ψ (ATG) = 20.1, etc., and in addition, we can propose a novel 2D graphical representation of DNA sequences as follows:

Let $G = g_1, g_2, g_3 \ldots g_N$ be an arbitrary DNA primary sequence, where $g_i \in \{A, T, G, C\}$ for any $i \in \{1, 2, \ldots, N\}$, and then, we can transform G into a sequence of triplets such as $G = t_1, t_2, t_3 \ldots t_M$, where $M = [N/3]$ and t_i is a triplet of DNA for any $i \in \{1, 2, \ldots, M\}$. Thereafter, we can define a new mapping Θ to map G into a plot set as illustrated in the formula (1).

$$\Theta(G) = \{(1, \Psi(t_1)), (2, \Psi(t_2)), \ldots, (M, \Psi(t_M))\} \quad (1)$$

As for the complete coding sequences of β-globin genes of 11 species illustrated in the Table 4, each of them can be mapped into a plot set by using the new given mapping Θ, and the 2D graphical representations corresponding to the complete coding sequences of β-globin genes of human, chimpanzee, and opossum are shown in Figures 1, 2, and 3, respectively.

3. Similarity analysis of DNA sequence

Let $G = g_1, g_2, g_3 \ldots g_N$ be an arbitrary complete coding sequence, where $g_i \in \{A, T, G, C\}$ for any $i \in \{1, 2, \ldots, N\}$, and $G = t_1, t_2, t_3 \ldots t_M$ be its corresponding sequence of triplets, where $M = [N/3]$ and t_i is a triplet of DNA for any $i \in \{1, 2, \ldots, M\}$. Then, we define a function δ and let $\delta(t_i)$ represent the total number of times that the triplet

Table 3 The mapping rules of Ψ

Triplet	Corresponding weight	Triplet	Corresponding weight
GCT	1.1	CTT	11.1
GCC	1.2	CTC	11.2
GCA	1.3	CTA	11.3
GCG	1.4	CTG	11.4
		TTA	11.5
		TTG	11.6
CGT	2.1	AAA	12.3
CGC	2.2	AAG	12.4
CGA	2.3		
CGG	2.4		
AGA	2.5		
AGG	2.6		
GAT	3.3	TTT	13.1
GAC	3.4	TTC	13.2
AAT	4.1	CCT	14.1
AAC	4.2	CCC	14.2
		CCA	14.3
		CCG	14.4
TGT	5.1	TCT	15.1
TGC	5.2	TCC	15.2
		TCA	15.3
		TCG	15.4
		AGT	15.5
		AGC	15.6
GAA	6.1	ACT	16.3
GAG	6.2	ACC	16.4
		ACA	16.5
		ACG	16.6
CAA	7.1	TGG	17.3
CAG	7.2		
GGT	8.1	TAT	18.1
GGC	8.2	TAC	18.2
GGA	8.3		
GGG	8.4		
CAT	9.1	GTT	19.1
CAC	9.2	GTC	19.2
		GTA	19.3
		GTG	19.4
ATT	10.1	ATG	20.1
ATC	10.2		
ATA	10.3		
TAA	21.1		
TAG	21.2		
TGA	21.3		

t_i repeats in the sequence of triplets $G = t_1, t_2, t_3 \ldots t_M$ for any $i \in \{1, 2,\ldots, M\}$.

Let T_1 = GCT, T_2 = GCC, T_3 = GCA, T_4 = GCG, T_5 = CGT, T_6 = CGC, T_7 = CGA, T_8 = CGG, T_9 = AGA, T_{10} = AGG, T_{11} = GAT, T_{12} = GAC, T_{13} = AAT, T_{14} = AAC, T_{15} = TGT, T_{16} = TGC, T_{17} = GAA, T_{18} = GAG, T_{19} = CAA, T_{20} = CAG, T_{21} = GGT, T_{22} = GGC, T_{23} = GGA, T_{24} = GGG, T_{25} = CAT, T_{26} = CAC, T_{27} = ATT, T_{28} = ATC, T_{29} = ATA, T_{30} = CTT T_{31} = CTC, T_{32} = CTA, T_{33} = CTG, T_{34} = TTA, T_{35} = TTG, T_{36} = AAA, T_{37} = AAG, T_{38} = TTT, T_{39} = TTC, T_{40} = CCT, T_{41} = CCC, T_{42} = CCA, T_{43} = CCG, T_{44} = TCT, T_{45} = TCC, T_{46} = TCA, T_{47} = TCG, T_{48} = AGT, T_{49} = AGC, T_{50} = ACT, T_{51} = ACC, T_{52} = ACA, T_{53} = ACG, T_{54} = TGG, T_{55} = TAT, T_{56} = TAC, T_{57} = GTT, T_{58} = GTC, T_{59} = GTA, T_{60} = GTG, T_{61} = ATG, T_{62} = TAA, T_{63} = TAG, and T_{64} = TGA.

Thereafter, according to Table 2, since there are a total of 64 triplets of DNA, then we can construct a set of 64 vectors $\{<T_1, \delta(T_1)>, <T_2, \delta(T_2)>,\ldots, <T_{64}, \delta(T_{64})>\}$ for the given sequence of triplets $G = t_1, t_2, t_3 \ldots t_M$ as follows: if $T_i = t_j \in \{t_1, t_2, t_3,\ldots t_M\}$, then $\delta(T_i) = \delta(t_j)$, else $\delta(T_i) = 0$, for any $i \in \{1, 2,\ldots, 64\}$ and $j \in \{1, 2,\ldots, M\}$.

For convenience, we call $\{<T_1, \delta(T_1)>, <T_2, \delta(T_2)>,\ldots, <T_{64}, \delta(T_{64})>\}$ as the triplet-repeat model set of G.

For any two given complete coding sequences A and B, suppose that their triplet-repeat model sets are $\{<T_1, X_1>, <T_2, X_2>,\ldots, <T_{64}, X_{64}>\}$ and $\{<T_1, Y_1>, <T_2, Y_2>,\ldots, <T_{64}, Y_{64}>\}$, respectively. Then, on the basis of the 2D graphical representation given in the previous Section 2, we can define the weight deviation between the two DNA sequences A and B as the following formula (2) to measure the similarity between A and B.

$$\mathrm{WD}(A,B) = \frac{\sum_{i=1}^{64} |X_i - Y_i| * \Psi(T_i)}{64} \qquad (2)$$

Obviously, the above formula (2) satisfies the fact that the smaller the weight deviation between the two DNA sequences A and B, the higher the degree of similarity of A and B. According to formula (2), the detailed similarity/dissimilarity matrix obtained for the coding sequences listed in Table 4 is illustrated in Table 5. Basing on the similarity matrix (Table 5) constructs a phylogenetic tree, which is shown in Figure 4.

Observing Table 5, it is easy to find out that human, gorilla, and chimpanzee are most similar to each other, and the pairs like gorilla-chimpanzee (with weight deviation of 1.1266), human-gorilla (with weight deviation of 4.3359), and human-chimpanzee (with weight deviation of 5.2500) are the most similar species pairs, but *Gallus* and opossum are the most dissimilar to the others (with weight deviation bigger than 11). It is consistent with the fact that *Gallus* is not a mammal, whereas the others

Table 4 The complete coding sequences of β-globin genes of 11 species

Species	Complete coding sequence
Human	ATGGTGCACCTGACTCCTGAGGAGAAGTCTGCCGTTACTGCCCTGTGGGGCAAGGTGAACGTGGATGAAGTTGGTGGTGAGGCCCTGGGCAGGCTGCTGGTGGTCTACCCTTGGACCCAGAGGTTCTTTGAGTCCTTTGGGGATCTGTCCACTCCTGATGCTGTTATGGGCAACCCTAAGGTGAAGGCTCATGGCAAGAAAGTGCTCGGTGCCTTTAGTGATGGCCTGGCTCACCTGGACAACCTCAAGGGCACCTTTGCCACACTGAGTGAGCTGCACTGTGACAAGCTGCACGTGGATCCTGAGAACTTCAGGCTCCTGGGCAACGTGCTGGTCTGTGTGCTGGCCCATCACTTTGGCAAAGAATTCACCCCACCAGTGCAGGCTGCCTATCAGAAAGTGGTGGCTGGTGTGGCTAATGCCCTGGCCCACAAGTATCACTAA
Chimpanzee	ATGGTGCACCTGACTCCTGAGGAGAAGTCTGCCGTTACTGCCCTGTGGGGCAAGGTGAACGTGGATGAAGTTGGTGGTGAGGCCCTGGGCAGGTTGGTATCAAGGCTGCTGGTGGTCTACCCTTGGACCCAGAGGTTCTTTGAGTCCTTTGGGGATCTGTCCACTCCTGATGCTGTTATGGGCAACCCTAAGGTGAAGGCTCATGGCAAGAAAGTGCTCGGTGCCTTTAGTGATGGCCTGGCTCACCTGGACAACCTCAAGGGCACCTTTGCCACACTGAGTGAGCTGCACTGTGACAAGCTGCACGTGGATCCTGAGAACTTCAGGCTCCTGGGCAACGTGCTGGTCTGTGTGCTGGCCCATCACTTTGGCAAAG
Gorilla	ATGGTGCACCTGACTCCTGAGGAGAAGTCTGCCGTTACTGCCCTGTGGGGCAAGGTGAACGTGGATGAAGTTGGTGGTGAGGCCCTGGGCAGGCTGCTGGTGGTCTACCCTTGGACCCAGAGGTTCTTTGAGTCCTTTGGGGATCTGTCCACTCCTGATGCTGTTATGGGCAACCCTAAGGTGAAGGCTCATGGCAAGAAAGTGCTCGGTGCCTTTAGTGATGGCCTGGCTCACCTGGACAACCTCAAGGGCACCTTTGCCACACTGAGTGAGCTGCACTGTGACAAGCTGCACGTGGATCCTGAGAACTTCAAGCTCCTGGGCAATGTGCTGGTCTGTGTGCTGGCCCATCACTTTGGCAAAG
Black lemur	ATGACTTTGCTGAGTGCTGAGGAGAATGCTCATGTCACCTCTCTGTGGGGCAAGGTGGATGTAGAGAAAGTTGGTGGCGAGGCCTTGGGCAGGCTGCTGGTCGTCTACCCATGGACCCAGAGGTTCTTCGAGTCCTTTGGGGACCTGTCCTCTCCTTCTGCTGTTATGGGGAACCCTAAGGTGAAGGCCCATGGCAAGAAGGTGCTGAGTGCCTTTAGTGAAGGTCTGCATCACCTGGACAACCTCAAGGGCACCTTTGCTCAACTGAGTGAGCTGCACTGTGACAAGTTGCACGTGGATCCTCAGAACTTCACTCTCCTGGGCAACGTGCTGGTGGTTGTGCTGGCTGAACACTTTGGCAATGCATTCAGCCCGGCGGTGCAGGCTGCCTTTCAGAAGGTGGTGGCTGGTGTGGCCAATGCTCTGGCTCACAAGTACCACTGA
Norway rat	ATGGTGCACCTAACTGATGCTGAGAAGGCTACTGTTAGTGGCCTGTGGGGAAAGGTGAATGCTGATAATGTTGGCGCTGAGGCCCTGGGCAGGCTGCTGGTTGTCTACCCTTGGACCCAGAGGTACTTTTCTAAATTTGGGGACCTGTCCTCTGCCTCTGCTATCATGGGTAACCCCCAGGTGAAGGCCCATGGCAAGAAGGTGATAAATGCCTTCAATGATGGCCTGAAACACTTGGACAACCTCAAGGGCACCTTTGCTCATCTGAGTGAACTCCACTGTGACAAGCTGCATGTGGATCCTGAGAACTTCAGGCTCCTGGGCAATATGATTGTGATTGTGTTGGGCCACCACCTGGGCAAGGAATTCACCCCCTGTGCACAGGCTGCCTTCCAGAAGGTGGTGGCTGGAGTGGCCAGTGCCCTGGCTCACAAGTACCACTAA
House mouse	ATGGTGCACCTGACTGATGCTGAGAAGTCTGCTGTCTCTTGCCTGTGGGCAAAGGTGAACCCCGATGAAGTTGGTGGTGAGGCCCTGGGCAGGCTGCTGGTTGTCTACCCTTGGACCCAGCGGTACTTTGATAGCTTTGGAGACCTATCCTCTGCCTCTGCTATCATGGGTAATCCCAAGGTGAAGGCCCATGGCAAAAAGGTGATAACTGCCTTTAACGAGGGCCTGAAAAACCTGGACAACCTCAAGGGCACCTTTGCCAGCCTCAGTGAGCTCCACTGTGACAAGCTGCATGTGGATCCTGAGAACTTCAGGCTCCTAGGCAATGCGATCGTGATTGTGCTGGGCCACCACCTGGGCAAGGATTTCACCCCTGCTGCACAGGCTGCCTTCCAGAAGGTGGTGGCTGGAGTGGCCACTGCCCTGGCTCACAAGTACCACTAA
Goat	ATGCTGACTGCTGAGGAGAAGGCTGCCGTCACCGGCTTCTGGGGCAAGGTGAAAGTGGATGAAGTTGGTGCTGAGGCCCTGGGCAGGCTGCTGGTTGTCTACCCCTGGACTCAGAGGTTCTTTGAGCACTTTGGGGACTTGTCCTCTGCTGATGCTGTTATGAACAATGCTAAGGTGAAGGCCCATGGCAAGAAGGTGCTAGACTCCTTTAGTAACGGCATGAAGCATCTTGACGACCTCAAGGGCACCTTTGCTCAGCTGAGTGAGCTGCACTGTGATAAGCTGCACGTGGATCCTGAGAACTTCAAGCTCCTGGGCAACGTGCTGGTGGTTGTGCTGGCTCGCCACCTTGGCAGTGAATTCACCCCGCTGCTGCAGGCTGAGTTTCAGAAGGTGGTGGCTGGTGTTGCCAATGCCCTGGCCCACAGATATCACTAA
Bovine	ATGCTGACTGCTGAGGAGAAGGCTGCCGTCACCGCCTTTTGGGGCAAGGTGAAAGTGGATGAAGTTGGTGGTGAGGCCCTGGGCAGGCTGCTGGTTGTCTACCCCTGGACTCAGAGGTTCTTTGAGTCCTTTGGGGACTTGTCCACTGCTGATGCTGTTATGAACAACCCTAAGGTGAAGGCCCATGGCAAGAAGGTGCTAGATTCCTTTAGTAATGGCATGAAGCATCTCGATGACCTCAAGGGCACCTTTGCTGCGCTGAGTGAGCTGCACTGTGATAAGCTGCATGTGGATCCTGAGAACTTCAAGCTCCTGGGCAACGTGCTAGTGGTTGTGCTGGCTCGCAATTTTGGCAAGGAATTCACCCCGGTGCTGCAGGCTGACTTTCAGAAGGTGGTGGCTGGTGTGGCCAATGCCCTGGCCCACAGATATCATTAA
Rabbit	ATGGTGCATCTGTCCAGTGAGGAGAAGTCTGCGGTCACTGCCCTGTGGGGCAAGGTGAATGTGGAAGAAGTTGGTGGTGAGGCCCTGGGCAGGCTGCTGGTTGTCTACCCATGGACCCAGAGGTTCTTCGAGTCCTTTGGGGACCTGTCCTCTGCAAATGCTGTTATGAACAATCCTAAGGTGAAGGCTCATGGCAAGAAGGTGCTGGCTGCCTTCAGTGAGGGTCTGAGTCACCTGGACAACCTCAAAGGCACCTTTGCTAAGCTGAGTGAACTGCACTGTGACAAGCTGCACGTGGATCCTGAGAACTTCAGGCTCCTGGGCAACGTGCTGGTTATTGTGCTGTCTCATCATTTTGGCAAAGAATTCACTCCTCAGGTGCAGGCTGCCTATCAGAAGGTGGTGGCTGGTGTGGCCAATGCCCTGGCTCACAAATACCACTGA
Opossum	ATGGTGCACTTGACTTCTGAGGAGAAGAACTGCATCACTACCATCTGGTCTAAGGTGCAGGTTGACCAGACTGGTGGTGAGGCCCTTGGCAGGATGCTCGTTGTCTACCCCTGGACCACCAGGTTTTTTGGGAGCTTTGGTGATCTGTCCTCTCCTGGCGCTGTCATGTCAAATTCTAAGGTTCAAGCCCATGGTGCTAAGGTGTTGACCTCCTTCGGTGAAGCAGTCAAGCATTTGGACAACCTGAAGGGTACTTATGCCAAGTTGAGTGAGCTCCACTGTGACAAGCTGCATGTGGACCCTGAGAACTTCAAGATGCTGGGGAATATCATTGTGATCTGCCTGGCTGAGCACTTTGGCAAGGATTTTACTCCTGAATGTCAGGTTGCTTGGCAGAAGCTCGTGGCTGGAGTTGCCCATGCCCTGGCCCACAAGTACCACTAA
Gallus	ATGGTGCACTGGACTGCTGAGGAGAAGCAGCTCATCACCGGCCTCTGGGGCAAGGTCAATGTGGCCGAATGTGGGGCCGAAGCCCTGGCCAGGCTGCTGATCGTCTACCCCTGGACCCAGAGGTTCTTTGCGTCCTTTGGGAACCTCTCCAGCCCCACTGCCATCCTTGGCAACCCCATGGTCCGCGCCCACGGCAAGAAAGTGCTCACCTCCTTTGGGGATGCTGTGAAGAACCTGGACAACATCAAGAACACCTTCTCCCAACTGTCCGAACTGCATTGTGACAAGCTGCATGTGGACCCCGAGAACTTCAGGCTCCTGGGTGACATCCTCATCATTGTCCTGGCCGCCCACTTCAGCAAGGACTTCACTCCTGAATGCCAGGCTGCCTGGCAGAAGCTGGTCCGCGTGGTGGCCCATGCCCTGGCTCGCAAGTACCACTAA

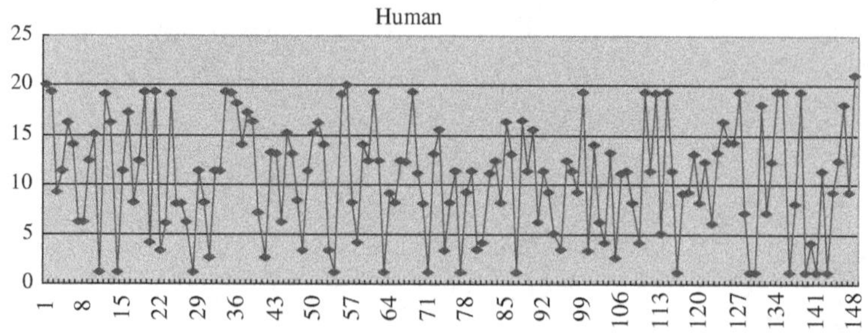

Figure 1 The 2D graphical representations of the complete coding sequences of β-globin genes of human.

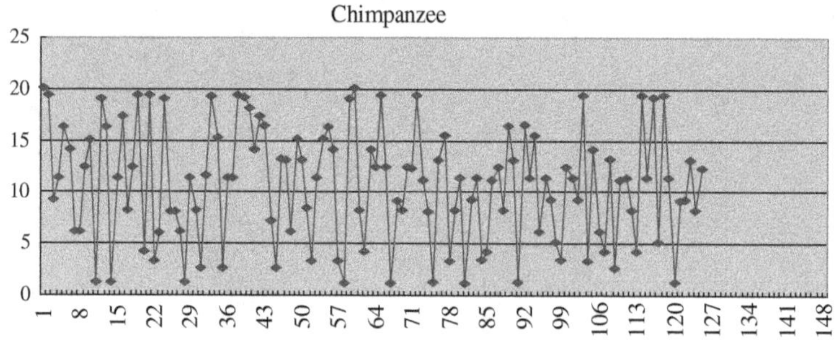

Figure 2 The 2D graphical representations of the complete coding sequences of β-globin genes of chimpanzee.

are mammals, and opossum is the most remote species from the remaining mammals. Similar results have been obtained in other papers by different approaches [2,5,7,9,33].

For testing the validity of our method, the existing results of the examination of the degree of similarity/dissimilarity of the coding sequences of β-globin genes of several species with the coding sequence of the human β-globin gene by means of approaches using alternative DNA sequence descriptors [2,5,7,9] are listed in Table 6 for comparison.

From Table 6, we can find that the pairs like human-gorilla and human-chimpanzee are the two most similar species pairs when adopting (A) the method of our work, (B) the method of [2], (C) the method of [5], and (D) the method of [7], which is in accordance with the fact that gorilla and chimpanzee are the two most closest species of human, but when adopting (E) the method of [9], the most similar species pair is human-goat, which is obviously not correct. In addition, the pairs like human-*Gallus* and human-opossum are the two most dissimilar species pairs when adopting (A) the method of our work, (C) the method of [5], and (E) the method of [9], which is in accordance with the fact that *Gallus* is not a mammal, whereas the others are mammals, and opossum is the most remote species from the remaining mammals. However, when adopting (D) the method of [7], the two most dissimilar species pairs are human-opossum and human-lemur, which is obviously not reasonable also.

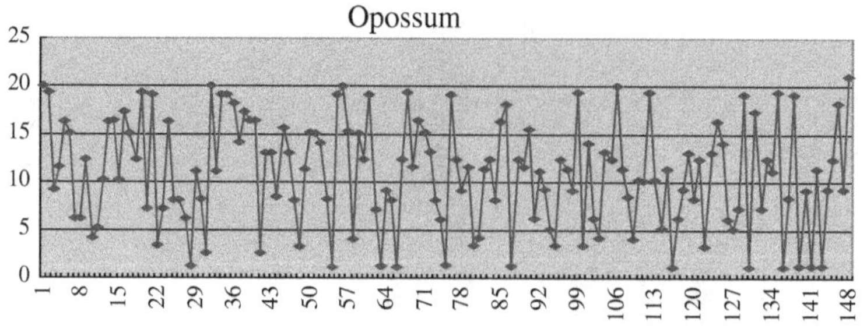

Figure 3 The 2D graphical representations of the complete coding sequences of β-globin genes of opossum.

Table 5 The similarity/dissimilarity matrix for the coding sequences of Table 1 based on the weight deviation

	Human	Chimpanzee	Gorilla	Lemur	Rat	Mouse	Goat	Bovine	Rabbit	Opossum	*Gallus*
Human	0	5.2500	4.3359	8.5891	10.670	9.7047	8.2219	8.1438	7.8281	15.6078	16.7109
Chimpanzee		0	1.1266	8.0297	10.645	9.6016	8.4375	9.3219	9.6000	14.2578	15.8734
Gorilla			0	7.8688	9.9625	8.6063	7.6734	8.5578	8.5547	13.9719	14.8781
Lemur				0	8.7219	9.5500	7.1328	9.3891	5.6891	12.9281	15.2000
Rat					0	6.0750	7.0484	9.3641	9.6578	13.5906	14.1219
Mouse						0	9.4953	9.2641	10.7984	12.3406	12.3688
Goat							0	5.2625	8.7219	11.9703	14.5359
Bovine								0	9.2906	12.5922	15.0234
Rabbit									0	14.8984	15.6953
Opossum										0	14.2750
Gallus											0

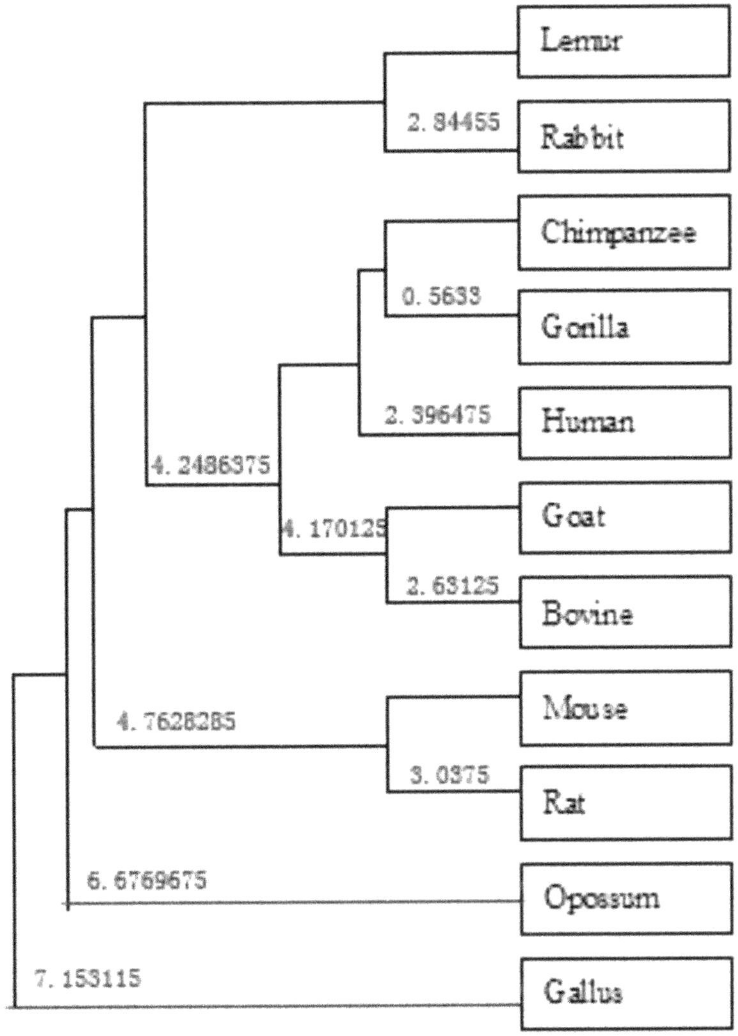

Figure 4 Phylogenetic tree based on the similarity matrix (Table 5).

Table 6 The similarity/dissimilarity of the coding sequences

Species	A	B	C	D	E
Chimpanzee	5.2500	0.0144	14.00	0.005069	0.863
Gorilla	4.3359	0.0125	13.63	0.006611	0.339
Lemur	8.5891	-	31.75	0.030894	1.188
Rat	10.670	0.1377	41.65	0.015539	1.966
Mouse	9.7047	0.1427	30.27	0.015700	0.735
Goat	8.2219	0.1161	31.39	0.020980	0.311
Bovine	8.1438	0.0773	30.68	0.017700	2.489
Rabbit	7.8281	0.1332	35.575	0.015788	1.372
Opossum	15.6078	-	48.701	0.033363	6.322
Gallus	16.7109	-	70.46	0.025801	7.170

4. Conclusion

In this paper, we propose a new 2D graphical representation for DNA sequences based on triplets, and associating with a newly introduced concept of weight of triplets and a newly designed measure of similarity named weight deviation, we propose a new method to make similarity analysis of DNA sequences, in which no matrix computation is needed and reasonable and useful approaches for both computational scientists and molecular biologists to effectively analyze DNA sequences can be provided at the same time.

Competing interests

The authors declare that they have no competing interests.

Acknowledgements

This work is supported by the Chongqing Education Science Project of China in 2014, Chongqing "Twelfth Five Year plan" educational programming projects of China (2013-ZJ-077), program for university youth backbone teachers of Chongqing in 2014.

References

1. W Chen, B Liao, Y Liu, W Zhu, Z Su, A numerical representation of DNA sequences and its applications. MATCH: Commun Math Comput Chem. **60**, 291–300 (2008)
2. N Jafarzadeh, A Iranmanesh, A novel graphical and numerical representation for analyzing DNA sequences based on codons. MATCH: Commun Math Comput Chem. **68**, 611–620 (2012)
3. B Liao, BY Liao, XM Sun, QG Zeng, A novel method for similarity analysis and protein sub-cellular localization prediction. Bioinformatics **26**, 2678–2683 (2010)
4. XQ Qi, Q Wu, Y Zhang, E Fuller, CQ Zhang, A novel model for DNA sequence similarity analysis based on graph theory. J Evol Bioinform **7**, 149–158 (2011)
5. JF Yu, JH Wang, X Sun, Analysis of similarities/dissimilarities of DNA sequences based on a novel graphical representation. MATCH: Commun Math Comput Chem. **63**, 493–512 (2010)
6. Y Li, G Huang, B Liao, Z Liu, H-L curve: a novel 2D graphical representation of protein sequences. MATCH: Commun Math Comput Chem. **61**, 519–532 (2009)
7. B Liao, TM Wang, New 2D graphical representation of DNA sequences. J. Comput. Chem. **25**, 1364–1368 (2004)
8. B Liao, XY Xiang, W Zhu, Coronavirus phylogeny based on 2D graphical representation of DNA sequence. J. Comput. Chem. **27**, 1196–1202 (2006)
9. ZB Liu, B Liao, W Zhu, GH Huang, A 2D graphical representation of DNA sequence based on dual nucleotides and its application. Int. J. Quantum Chem. **109**, 948–958 (2009)
10. M Randic, M Vracko, J Zupan, M Novic, Compact 2D graphical representation of DNA. Chem. Phys. Lett. **373**, 558–562 (2003)
11. M Randic, M Vracko, N Lers, D Plavsic, Analysis of similarity/dissimilarity of 2D graphical representation. Chem. Phys. Lett. **371**, 202–207 (2003)
12. M Randic, M Vracko, N Lers, D Plavsic, Novel 2-D graphical representation of DNA sequences and their numerical characterization. Chem. Phys. Lett. **368**, 1–6 (2003)
13. M Randic, Graphical representations of DNA as 2-D map. Chem. Phys. Lett. **386**, 468–471 (2004)
14. XF Guo, M Randic, SC Basak, A novel 2-D graphical representation of DNA sequences of low degeneracy. Chem. Phys. Lett. **350**, 106–112 (2001)
15. XF Guo, A Nandy, Numerical characterization of DNA sequences in a 2-D graphical representation scheme of low degeneracy. Chem. Phys. Lett. **369**, 361–366 (2003)
16. ZH Qi, XQ Qi, Novel 2D graphical representation of DNA sequence based on dual nucleotides. Chem Phys Lett. **440**, 139–144 (2007)
17. Q Dai, ZL Xiu, TM Wang, A novel 2D graphical representation of DNA sequences and its application. J Mol Graph Model. **25**, 340–344 (2006)
18. XQ Liu, Q Dai, ZL Xiu, TM Wang, PNN-curve: a new 2D graphical representation of DNA sequences and its application. J. Theor. Biol. **243**, 555–561 (2006)
19. BW Dorota, C Timothy, W Piotr, 2D-dynamic representation of DNA sequences. Chem. Phys. Lett. **442**, 140–144 (2007)
20. CX Yuan, B Liao, TM Wang, New 3D graphical representation of DNA sequences and their numerical characterization. Chem. Phys. Lett. **379**, 412–417 (2003)
21. B Liao, TM Wang, 3-D graphical representation of DNA sequences and their numerical characterization. J. Mol. Struct. (THEOCHEM) **681**, 209–212 (2004)
22. B Liao, TM Wang, A 3D graphical representation of RNA secondary structure. J Biomol Struct Dynam. **21**, 827–832 (2004)
23. Z Cao, B Liao, RF Li, A group of 3D graphical representation of DNA sequences based on dual nucleotides. Int. J. Quantum Chem. **108**, 1485–1490 (2008)
24. M Randic, M Vracko, A Nandy, SC Basak, On 3D graphical representation of DNA primary sequences and their numerical characterization. J. Chem. Inf. Comput. Sci. **40**, 1235–1244 (2000)
25. M Randic, J Zupan, M Novic, On 3D graphical representation of proteomics maps and their numerical characterization. J. Chem. Inf. Comput. Sci. **41**, 1339–1344 (2001)
26. XQ Qi, TR Fan, PN-curve: a 3D graphical representation of DNA sequences and their numerical characterization. Chem. Phys. Lett. **442**, 434–440 (2007)
27. JF Yu, X Sun, JH Wang, TN curve: a novel 3D graphical representation of DNA sequence based on trinucleotides and its applications. J. Theor. Biol. **261**, 459–468 (2009)
28. V Aram, A Iranmanesh, 3D-dynamic representation of DNA sequences. MATCH: Commun Math Comput Chem. **67**, 809–816 (2012)
29. B Liao, MS Tan, KQ Ding, A 4D representation of DNA sequences and its application. Chem. Phys. Lett. **402**, 380–383 (2005)
30. XC Tang, PP Zhou, WY Qiu, On the similarity/dissimilarity of DNA sequences based on 4D graphical representation. Chin. Sci. Bull. **55**, 701–704 (2010)
31. R Chi, KQ Ding, Novel 4D numerical representation of DNA sequences. Chem. Phys. Lett. **407**, 63–67 (2005)
32. B Liao, XY Xiang, RF Li, W Zhu, On the similarity of DNA primary sequences based on 5D representation. J. Math. Chem. **42**, 47–57 (2007)
33. P He, J Wang, Characteristic sequences for DNA primary sequence. J. Chem. Inf. Comput. Sci. **42**, 1080–1085 (2002)

16

A novel cost function to estimate parameters of oscillatory biochemical systems

Seyedbehzad Nabavi* and Cranos M Williams

Abstract

Oscillatory pathways are among the most important classes of biochemical systems with examples ranging from circadian rhythms and cell cycle maintenance. Mathematical modeling of these highly interconnected biochemical networks is needed to meet numerous objectives such as investigating, predicting and controlling the dynamics of these systems. Identifying the kinetic rate parameters is essential for fully modeling these and other biological processes. These kinetic parameters, however, are not usually available from measurements and most of them have to be estimated by parameter fitting techniques. One of the issues with estimating kinetic parameters in oscillatory systems is the irregularities in the least square (LS) cost function surface used to estimate these parameters, which is caused by the periodicity of the measurements. These irregularities result in numerous local minima, which limit the performance of even some of the most robust global optimization algorithms. We proposed a parameter estimation framework to address these issues that integrates temporal information with periodic information embedded in the measurements used to estimate these parameters. This periodic information is used to build a proposed cost function with better surface properties leading to fewer local minima and better performance of global optimization algorithms. We verified for three oscillatory biochemical systems that our proposed cost function results in an increased ability to estimate accurate kinetic parameters as compared to the traditional LS cost function. We combine this cost function with an improved noise removal approach that leverages periodic characteristics embedded in the measurements to effectively reduce noise. The results provide strong evidence on the efficacy of this noise removal approach over the previous commonly used wavelet hard-thresholding noise removal methods. This proposed optimization framework results in more accurate kinetic parameters that will eventually lead to biochemical models that are more precise, predictable, and controllable.

1 Introduction

Oscillatory biochemical pathways are an important class of biochemical systems [1,2] that play significant roles in living systems. For instance, "circadian rhythms" are fundamental daily time-keeping mechanisms in a wide range of species from unicellular organisms to complex eukaryotes [3]. One of their most important roles is in regulating physiological processes such as the sleep-wake cycle in mammals [4]. "Cell cycles" are also another vital class of biochemical oscillations. The cell cycle is the sequence of events by which a growing cell replicates all its components and divides into two daughter cells [5]. Inappropriate cell proliferation due to malfunctioning cell cycle control mechanisms can cause development of certain types of cancers [5]. There are also other classes of biochemical rhythms such as cardiac rhythms [6], ovarian cycles [7] and cAMP oscillations [8] that have their own significance in systems biology.

A complete modeling of a biochemical system includes characterization of all nonlinear structures of the network along with the associated kinetic rates. In other words, without fully identifying all the kinetic parameter values, these models are still incomplete even if the full structure of the model has been determined. Few kinetic rates are available directly from experimentation or literature. Most of them, however, have to be estimated by parameter fitting techniques to complete the modeling of the biochemical pathway. Thus, a mathematical framework is needed to fit the kinetic parameters using the observables. Optimization frameworks that focus specifically on estimating parameters

* Correspondence: snabavi@ncsu.edu
Department of Electrical and Computer Engineering, North Carolina State University, Raleigh, NC, USA

associated with biochemical pathways have received much attention in recent years [9-14].

Two main issues in estimating kinetic parameters in biochemical systems are data related issues and computational issues [14]. The measurement dataset used to fit these parameters are usually noisy and incomplete. Measurement datasets are also affected by uncertainties related to experimental conditions such as temperature and light [14]. Much study is done recently to reduce noise for different biochemical signals [15-17]. Mostacci et al. [15] proposed a denoising method for mass spectrometry data by integrating wavelet soft thresholding and principal component analysis. Weng et al. [16] suggested a noise removal approach for oscillatory ECG signals based on a recently developed method known as empirical mode decomposition. Ren et al. [17] also developed a method of denoising biochemical spectra by introducing a new thresholding function integrated with the "translation invariant" approach to lower the root mean square error (RMSE) in the measurements in comparison to the traditional soft and hard thresholding methods.

The computational issues include the challenges optimization algorithms face when identifying an optimal fit to measurement data. There are problems with optimization methods such as slow convergence toward global optima, complicated error surfaces and lack of convergence proofs [14]. Much study has been done to address these issues in parameter estimation in biochemical systems [12,13,18-21]. Zhan et al. proposed a method to reduce the computational time of each trial by integrating the spline functions theory with nonlinear programming to eliminate the need of solving the system of ordinary differential equations (ODEs) [21]. Rodriguez-Fernandez et al. [12] suggested a hybrid optimization method to speed up the convergence toward the global optima. A variety of different algorithms has also been adapted to perform the inverse problem. A comprehensive list of such studies is provided in [14].

Furthermore, heuristic approaches have been developed to address the optimization problem in fitting parameters in oscillatory systems [9-11]. These methods improved the optimization by constructing error functions based on the features extracted from the data. Locke et al. [11] proposed a cost function based on the comparison of entrained period, phase and strength of oscillation for the circadian clock in *Arabidopsis thaliana*. Also, Zeilinger et al. [10] performed another parameter estimation approach for the *A. thaliana* model by investigating amplitudes of some species in dark/light cycles, periods under dark and light conditions and the period of one mutant phenotype under constant light. In [9], Bagheri et al. built up an optimization process to model *Drosophila melanogaster* circadian clock by defining three cost functions based on free running period, light/dark entrained period, differences in amplitude and differences in the phase of the components in the system. These methods are more applicable for problems where characteristics in the system and/or data can be exploited to improve the performance of the parameter estimation. These methods, however, require more information about the system than purely data-driven comparison methods. For instance, the cost function proposed in [9] needs the period information of both the light and dark cycles of their investigated model, which requires a greater level of first principles knowledge. These methods are also model specific, which makes it difficult to apply them to general oscillatory systems. For example, the dark/light cycle characteristics that were introduced in parameter fitting problem of [10] may not be a suitable feature for parameter fitting of non-circadian biorhythms.

This article focuses on the problem of estimating the kinetic parameters in oscillatory biochemical systems. We show that periodicity in the measurements of oscillatory systems results in irregularly surface properties of the LS cost function leading to numerous local minima. These multiple local optima cause premature convergence of even robust optimization algorithms. This eventually results in incorrect estimates, bad predictions of dynamics, and incorrect acceptance of functional hypotheses. This, compounded with uncertainties or noisy measurements leads to a difficult estimation problem to solve.

We develop a parameter estimation framework to address these issues by integrating information of oscillatory systems in the modeling process (parameter estimation and denoising). This periodic information is used to build a cost function with better surface properties. Our proposed cost function takes advantage of the basic properties of these oscillatory systems, which allows us to generalize our cost function to a variety of biochemical systems with sustained oscillations. The proposed cost function also needs less first principles knowledge to generate the cost function in comparison to the previous methods that was developed for oscillatory systems [9-11]. We verified for three oscillatory biochemical systems that our proposed cost function results in increased ability to estimate accurate kinetic parameters as compared to the traditional LS cost function. We combined this cost 6 function with an improved denoising method that also leverages periodic characteristics embedded in the measurements to effectively reduce noise. The results provide strong evidence on the efficacy of this noise removal approach over the previous commonly used wavelet hard-thresholding noise removal method. This proposed optimization framework results in more accurate kinetic parameters that will eventually lead to biochemical models that are more accurate, predictable, and controllable.

2 Methodology

This study considers deterministic, nonlinear oscillatory biochemical pathways described by ODEs as shown in (1):

$$\begin{aligned}\dot{\mathbf{x}}(t) &= \mathbf{f}(\mathbf{x}(t), \mathbf{p}) \quad t_0 < t < t_e, \\ \mathbf{x}_0 &= \mathbf{x}(t_0).\end{aligned} \tag{1}$$

Here, $\mathbf{x} \in \mathbb{R}^{m\times1}$ is the state vector of the m components of the pathway, $\mathbf{p} \in \mathbb{R}^{n\times1}$ is the vector of n kinetic parameters, $\mathbf{f}$: $\mathbb{R}^{m\times1} \to \mathbb{R}^{m\times1}$ is a nonlinear vector function, $\mathbf{x}_0 \in \mathbb{R}^{m\times1}$ is the vector of the initial component concentrations at time t_0 and $t_0 < t < t_e$ represents the time of interest.

Optimization describes the approach of estimating the kinetic parameters ($\mathbf{p}$) of the system described in (1) that cannot be measured directly using a set of experimental data. The criteria for verifying the quality of the estimates is often an error function such as Φ as shown in (2). This function quantifies the ability of the estimates to reproduce the same results as the measurements. This objective function is minimized such that $\mathbf{p} = \hat{\mathbf{p}}$results in the minimum value of Φ. In that way, $\hat{\mathbf{p}}$ is called the estimated point.

$$\hat{\mathbf{p}} = \arg\min_{\mathbf{p}} \Phi(\mathbf{p}) \tag{2}$$

One of the most common cost functions is the *least square (LS) estimator* [22]. This estimator is based on the sum of the squares of the point by point errors between measured experimental data and the simulated measurements from the estimated model as described in (3):

$$\Phi(\mathbf{p}) = \sum_{i=1}^{N_x}\sum_{j=1}^{N_m}(x_{ij} - \hat{x}_{ij}(\mathbf{p}))^2. \tag{3}$$

Here, x_{ij}, is the measurement at time j of the ith state of the system, $\hat{x}_{ij}$ is the reproduced data at time j for the ith state of the system given some parameter $\mathbf{p}$, N_m is the number of time points where measurements are obtained and N_x is the number of measured outputs (in this manuscript, they are considered to be the measured states of the system).

The objective of this article is to propose a method to estimate the kinetic parameters for a given oscillatory biochemical system of the form (1) using the noisy measurements of the system states. We first captured periodic information of the measurements. This information is used to improve noise reduction and generate an error cost function with better optimization properties. The next step implements a modified wavelet hard thresholding denoising approach that uses the previously obtained periodic information of the measurements to further reduce uncertainties in noisy data. We then generate our proposed cost function by integrating the periodic information obtained in the first step with the simulated data and measurements. We searched the surface of the proposed cost function with a series of optimizers in a hybrid manner. Hybrid methods use global optimization followed by local 8 [24]. We used a frequency-based method called optimization [12,23]. Global and local optimization algorithms were used in succession to further improve optimization results. A block diagram of our approach for parameter estimation of oscillatory systems is shown in Figure 1. The following sections outline each of the blocks of this diagram.

2.1 Fundamental frequency estimation

The fundamental frequency is an essential metric for assessing the underlying oscillatory characteristics in a signal and is a critical step in developing our proposed cost function and noise removal method. The fundamental frequency is the oscillation frequency of the continuous data. The measurements are samples of this continuous-time signal. If one assumes a periodic waveform of $x(t)$ such that:

$$x(t) = x(t + kT) \quad \forall k \in \mathbb{Z}, \tag{4}$$

the smallest value of $T \neq 0$ for which (4) is valid is the *"fundamental period"* of oscillation. The inverse of the fundamental period is the fundamental frequency (f_0). Several approaches has been proposed to estimate f_0 [24]. We used a frequency-based method called *component frequency ratio* [24] to extract the fundamental frequency of the measured data due to the fact that the time-series methods may not be adequate for biochemical measurements due to their low rate of sampling and low temporal resolution. This method starts with transforming the data to the Fourier domain by taking their Fourier transform. The locations of the peaks in the spectrum are then identified. The peaks in the frequency spectrum are the harmonics of the fundamental frequency. The final step is to find the greatest common factor of these frequencies in which peaks occur.

Figure 1 The implemented process of parameter estimation for oscillatory biochemical systems.

2.1.1 Effect of noise on estimation of f_0

This section investigates the effect of noise on estimation of f_0. We considered three model systems identified from the literature: the two-state Tyson model [25], the two-state Brusselator model [26] and the five-state Golbeter model [27]. We considered the measurements of the states of these models with the sampling rate equal to 1 (sample/hour). Then, we added AWGN noise with various SNRs to these signals and we estimate their fundamental period using the method *component frequency ratio.* Figure 2 shows the absolute error between the estimated and the nominal fundamental period of the three models for various amount of additive noise.

Figure 2 shows that the method used to estimate the fundamental period is robust enough to the additive noise.

2.2 Removing noise

One common approach to reduce noise in measurements is wavelet hardthresholding [28], which employs a thresholding function over the wavelet coefficients of the noisy data samples. The motivation of using wavelets is that it provides an appropriate basis to separate noise from signal in the wavelet domain. The small wavelet coefficients are more likely to be noise and large coefficients are more likely to be components of the original signal. Thus, noise could be eliminated approximately from the signal by thresholding the wavelet coefficients [29]. The steps of the noise removal procedure using this method are shown in Figure 3:

2.2.1 Improving the hard-thresholding method in oscillatory systems

Samples of oscillatory signals contain repetitive patterns if they are taken over multiple periods. Thus, we hypothesized that is possible to take advantage of data oscillation to improve the denoising of the samples provided that their fundamental frequency is given or can be estimated. We modified the denoising procedure of oscillatory signals by adding two additional steps to the traditional hardthresholding method as depicted in Figure 4. Two assumptions have been made about the noisy oscillatory data. First, the fundamental period of the data is not an integer multiple of the sampling rate. Otherwise, it is not possible to increase the resolution of the data by shifting them in this method. Second, we assumed to have the measurements of more than one period of the data. Otherwise, there will be no way to estimate the fundamental period of the measurements.

The first step in Figure 4 is shifting all samples to the first period of the data. This is based on the following steps:

1. Partition the measurements $X(nT_s)$ based on their calculated fundamental period to the sets of X_k according to (5)

$$X_k(nT_s) = X(nT_s) \quad k\mathcal{T} \leq nT_s < (k+1)\mathcal{T},\ 0 \leq k < m, \quad (5)$$

where T_s is the sampling period and $\mathcal{T}$ is the fundamental period of the measurements X.

2. Shift each x_k by the value of $k\mathcal{T}$. This will result in a single period of the measurements with higher resolution. The shifted versions of x_k's are calculated based on (6)

$$\bigcup_{k=0}^{N-1} x_k(nt - k\mathcal{T}) \quad (6)$$

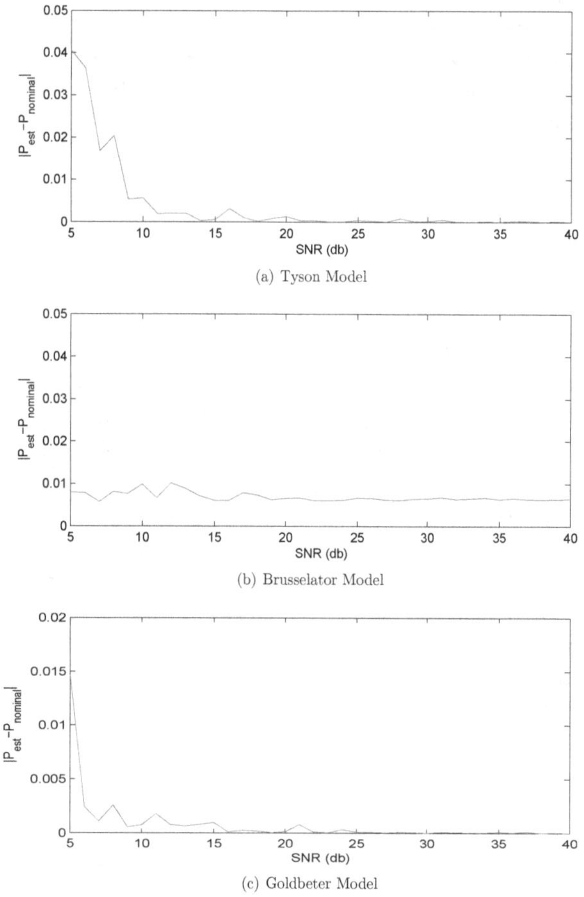

Figure 2 The error in estimating of the fundamental period versus the amount of noise in measurements for (a) Tyson model [25], **(b) Brusselator model** [26], **(c) Goldbeter model** [27].

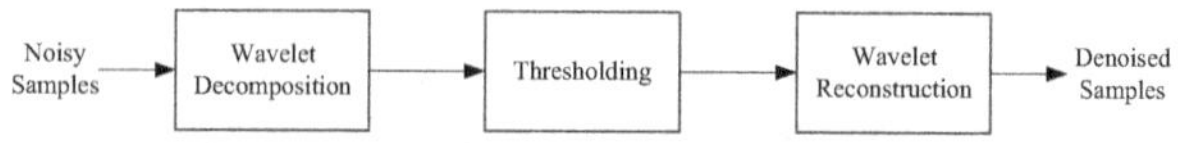

Figure 3 The commonly used thresholding algorithm to remove noise.

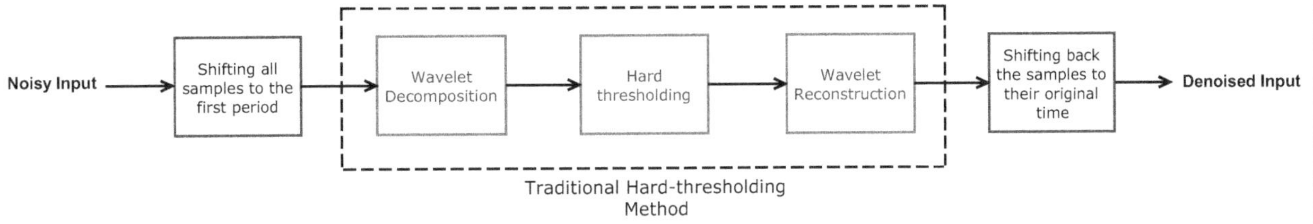

Figure 4 **The proposed noise removal steps.**

Figure 5 illustrates the samples of a sine function of $x(t) = \sin 2\pi t$ with the rate of 2 (sample/sec) and its shifted version. We see that Figure 5b shows only the first period of the sine function but with higher resolution.

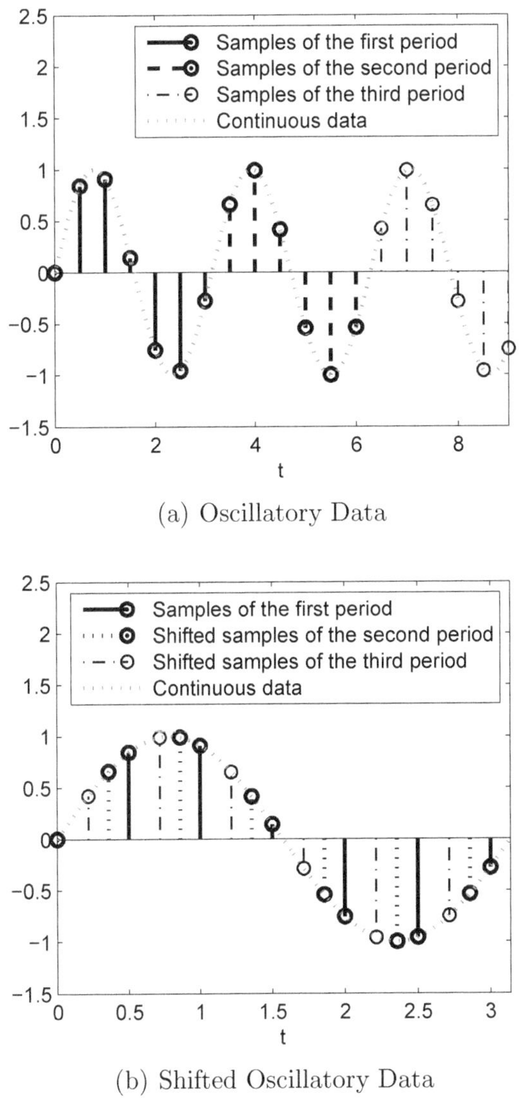

Figure 5 **The samples of three periods of the function $x(t) = \sin 2\pi t$ with the rate of 2 (sample/sec) and their shifted version based on the procedure outlined in (5) and (6).**

Figure 6 shows the denoising process for the *in-silico* measurements of the [*M*] component with sampling rate = 1 (sample/hour) in the model of the circadian clock in *D. melanogaster* proposed by Tyson [25]. The noise in the measurements is additive white Gaussian noise (AWGN) with SNR = 20 dB. Figure 6b shows the shifted version of the noisy measurements of Figure 6a using a calculated fundamental period of 24.21.

Wavelet decomposition, thresholding and reconstruction are then applied to this "shifted version" of the noisy data. MATLAB was used to implement a three level wavelet decomposition using the *"Daubechies 6"* wavelet and the threshold value equaling 0.3. The wavelet type, number of levels, and the threshold value were chosen empirically and may vary from system to system. The results are shown in Figure 6c. The final step is to reconstruct the original signal by shifting the samples back to their respective periods (Figure 6d).

We compared the performance of the proposed denoising method and the traditional wavelet hardthresholding by taking the samples of the [*Pt*] component with sampling rate = 1 (sample/hour) in the Tyson model of circadian clock in *D. Melanogaster* [25]. Then, we added AWGN noise with SNR = 20 to the dataset in 200 trials. We then removed noise using two approaches: the traditional wavelet hardthresholding method [29] and our proposed 12 method. Figure 7 compares three errors for each of the 200 trials. (1) The RMSE between the noisy data and the original dataset (the original error), (2) the RMSE between the denoised data resulting from the traditional thresholding method and the original dataset (Approach 1), and (3) the RMSE between the denoised data resulting from the proposed denoising method and the original dataset (Approach 2). This figure shows that our proposed method of denoising is more effective at removing noise than the wavelet hardthresholding method, consistently lowering the RMSE between the original signal and the denoised signal.

2.2.2 The effect of error in estimating f_0 on proposed denoising method

This section investigates the impact of the inaccuracies of the fundamental period estimate on the proposed denoising method. We considered the samples of the

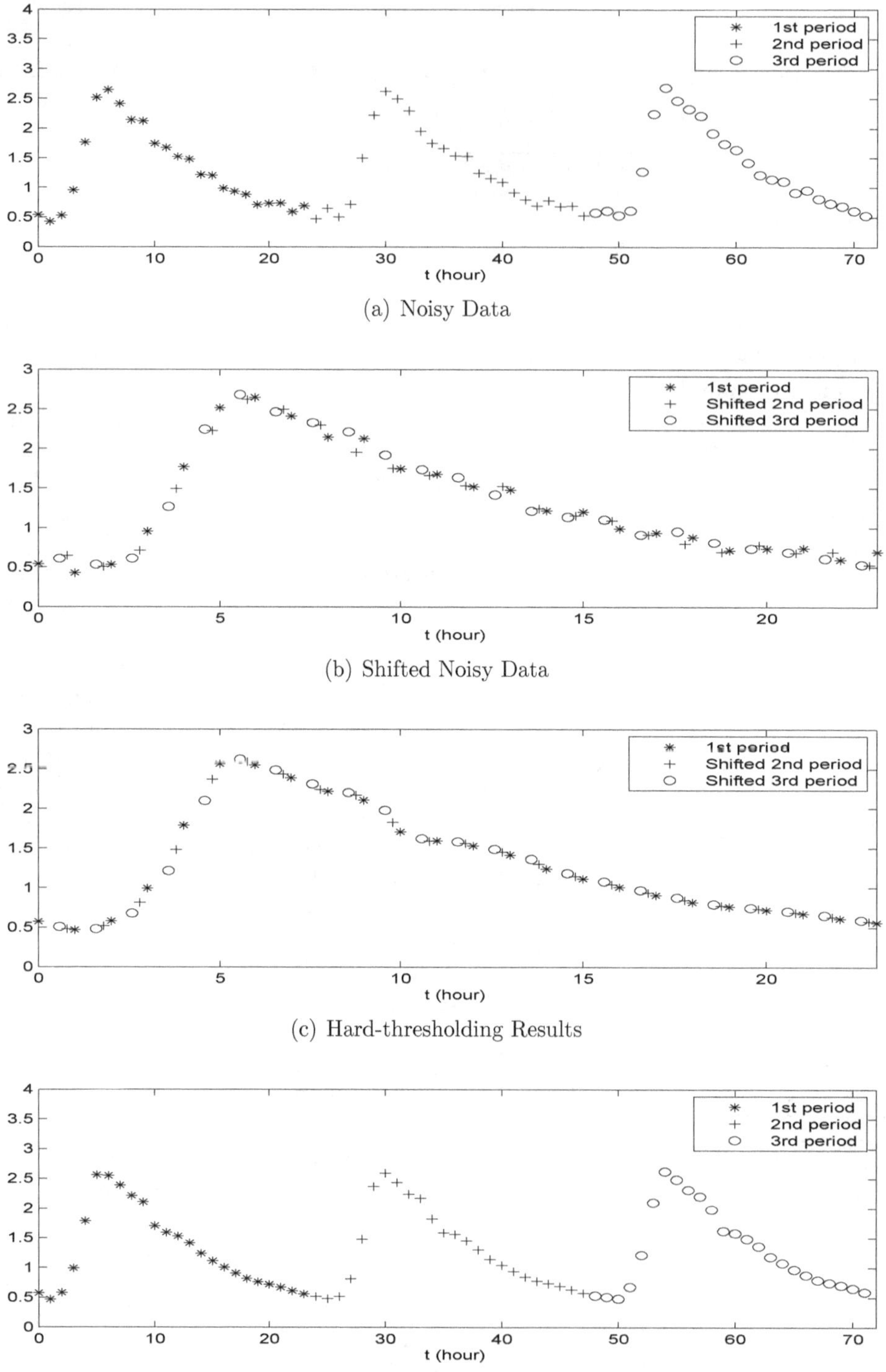

(a) Noisy Data

(b) Shifted Noisy Data

(c) Hard-thresholding Results

(d) Denoised Data

Figure 6 **The proposed noise removal steps (a) the original noisy measurements, (b) shifted version of the noisy data based on fundamental period, (c) the thresholding results over shifted version of the data, (d) moving back all samples to their original time.**

components of the Tyson [25], Brusselator [26], and Goldbeter model [27] with sampling rate = 1 (sample/hour) and AWGN noise with SNR = 20. Then, we denoised the data with using the traditional wavelet thresholding (Approach 1) and the proposed denoising method (Approach 2) assuming inaccurate estimated fundamental period. Figure 8 compares the RMSEs of the results of these two methods and the noisy data

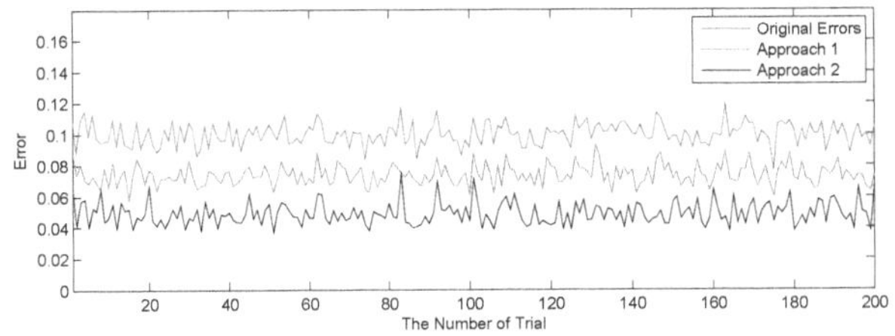

Figure 7 Comparison of the two noise removing methods for an oscillatory biochemical dataset ($[P_t]$ in the Tyson model). Original errors: sum of the squared errors between noisy data and the original data, Approach 1: sum of the squared errors between the original data and the denoised data using the traditional thresholding method, Approach 2: sum of the squared errors between the original data and the denoised data using the proposed noise removing method.

for ranges of inaccurate estimated fundamental periods.

Figure 8 shows that the results of the proposed denoising method has lower RMSEs than the traditional wavelet thresholding with small errors in the estimation fundamental period. However, if the fundamental period is estimated with errors approximately more than 0.25 for these models, the proposed method does not yield lower RMSEs. However, Figure 2 shows that the error in fundamental period estimation due to noise is much smaller than the order of error that is considered in Figure 8.

2.3 Optimization

2.3.1 Forming cost function

One big disadvantage of comparing point by point samples to build the LS cost function of (3) for oscillatory systems is the introduction of surface irregularities and numerous local optima. Let us consider a simple example of a sine function described in (7):

$$y(n) = 1 + \sin(2\pi fn/1000 + \phi), \tag{7}$$

where $f = 1$ is the frequency and $\varphi = 0$ is the initial phase. Figure 9 illustrates the surface of the LS cost function (3) for ranges of the signal parameters, f and Φ.

Figure 9 shows significant rippling especially along the f direction of the LS cost function. This happens due to the varying degree of overlap between various periods of two oscillatory signals in the LS objective function along the f axis. This potentially results in numerous local basins of attractions that hinder the optimizer's ability to find the global optimum. These ripples are fundamental characteristics of the LS cost function for systems with oscillatory dynamics. This phenomenon can be observed for a large class of oscillatory systems especially along the parameter axes to which the fundamental frequency is more sensitive.

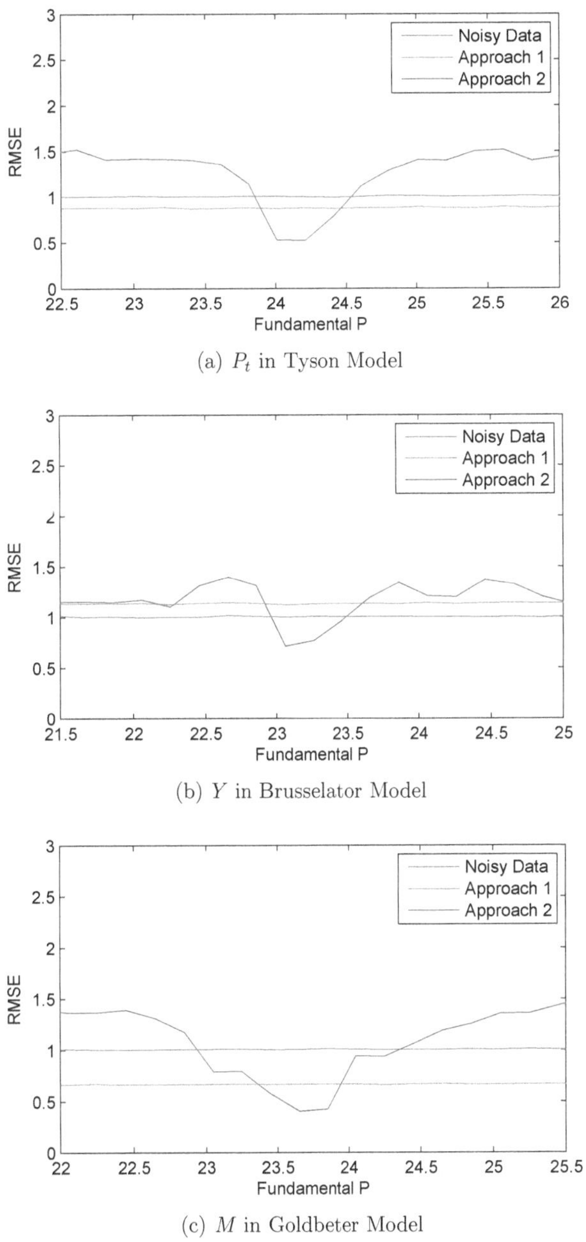

Figure 8 The comparison of the RMSEs of noisy signal, the traditional hardthresholding method, and the proposed denoising method for various estimations of the fundamental period for three models of (a) Tyson with fundamental period of 24.17, (b) Brusselator with the fundamental period of 23.06, (c) Goldbeter with fundamental period of 23.65.

Thus, we hypothesize that we can leverage information embedded in the data to produce a cost function with better surface properties, resulting in fewer local minima. This function is constructed in a piecewise manner based on the oscillatory characteristics of the simulated data at various parameter values. These characteristics are divided into two cases: sustained

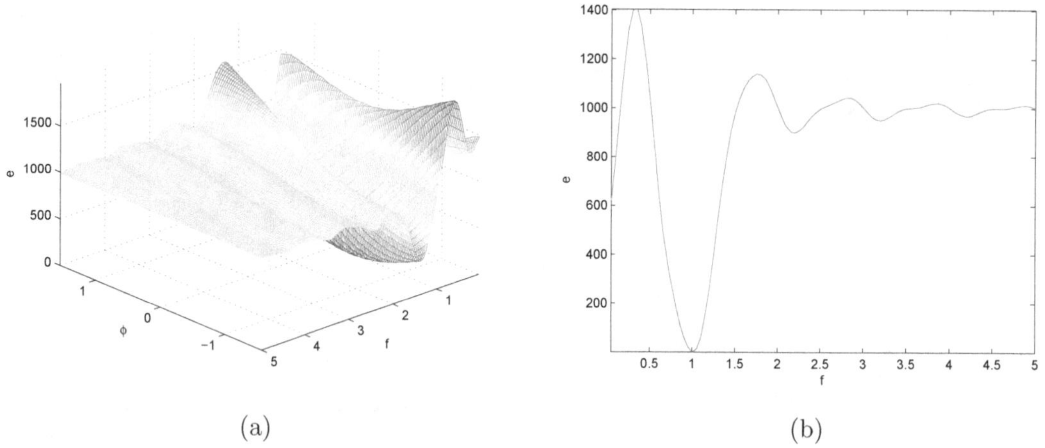

Figure 9 The surface of LS cost function for the function shown in (7) versus the variation in parameters φ and f and its cross section for $\varphi = 0$.

oscillations in the simulated data and no sustained oscillations in the simulated data. Sustained oscillation for a specific value of the parameter k is characterized by the fundamental period of the oscillations. A plot describing this is shown in Figure 10. All the parameter values for k in "area 1" produces sustained oscillations. This figure shows that the fundamental period of the sustained oscillation over this range may change. The values in "area 2", on the other hand, lead to dynamics that are not sustained oscillations.

If the simulated data are periodic, we introduced only the samples of one period of the data into the cost function. Likewise, only the samples of one period of the measurements will also be incorporated into this cost function. If the fundamental period of the measured data is not equal to the fundamental period of the simulated data, the signal with the smallest period is padded with zeros until the lengths of the signals are equal. This results in monotonic changes in error with respect to changes in fundamental period of the simulated data.

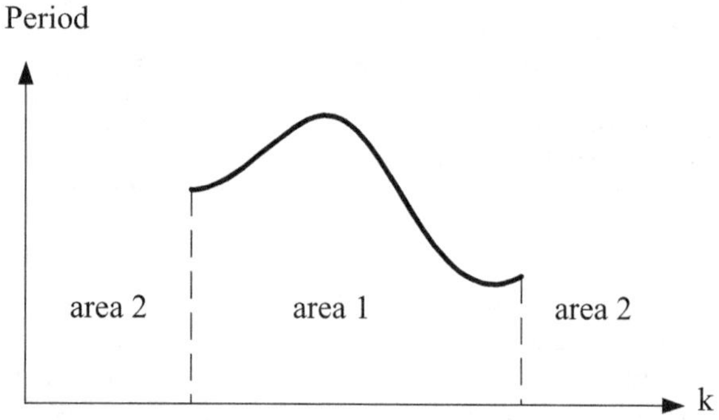

Figure 10 Changes of the fundamental period of the sustained oscillation for ranges of values of a certain kinetic parameter for a hypothetical oscillatory system.

If the simulated data are nonperiodic as in area two of Figure 10, all time point measurements and the simulated data will be included in the cost function, resulting in the same cost function as the traditional LS objective function. Equation (8) describes the new proposed cost function for the ODE-based model of an oscillatory biochemical pathway (1).

$$e(\mathbf{p}) = \sum_{i=1}^{N_x} \sum_{j=1}^{N_{z_i}} (z_{ij} - \hat{z}_{ij}(\mathbf{p}))^2, \tag{8}$$

where z_{ij} and $\hat{z}_{ij}$ for periodic $\hat{x}_i$ are calculated as:

$$z_{ij} = \begin{cases} x_{ij} & 0 \le t_j < T_i \\ 0 & T_i < t_j \le \max(T_i, \hat{T}_i) \end{cases}, \tag{9a}$$

$$\hat{z}_{ij} = \begin{cases} \hat{x}_{ij} & 0 \le t_j \le \hat{T}_i \\ 0 & \hat{T}_i < t_j \le \max(T_i, \hat{T}_i) \end{cases}. \tag{9b}$$

Otherwise, z_{ij} and $\hat{z}_{ij}$ for non-periodic $\hat{x}_i$ are calculated as:

$$z_{ij} = x_{ij} \tag{10a}$$

$$\hat{z}_{ij} = \hat{x}_{ij}. \tag{10b}$$

Here, x_{ij} is the measurement at time t_j of the ith state of the system, $\hat{x}_{ij}$ is the simulated data at time t_j for the ith state of the system. z_{ij} and $\hat{z}_{ij}$ are the truncated and zero padded x_{ij} and $\hat{x}_{ij}$, respectively, for the oscillatory $\hat{x}_i$. For non oscillatory $\hat{x}_i$, z_{ij}, and $\hat{z}_{ij}$ are equal to x_{ij} and $\hat{x}_{ij}$, respectively. N_{z_i} is the length of the z_i and $\hat{z}_i$. N_x is the number of states of the system, T_i is the fundamental period of the measurements (x_i), which was computed using the component frequency ratio approach and $\hat{T}_i$ is the fundamental period of the simulated data $(\hat{x}_i)$, which is estimated for each candidate parameter value. $\hat{T}_i$ was estimated using the YIN approach [30], which is a modified version of the time-domain autocorrelation method.

Figure 11 illustrates how the proposed cost function compares two signals with different fundamental periods.

Figure 12 shows the surface of the proposed cost function of (8) for the sine function of (7). The global minimum of the proposed cost function also occurs at $f = 1$ and $\varphi = 0$ similar to the LS cost function of (3) shown in Figures 9. However, visual inspection of these two figures shows that the surface of proposed cost function is smoother than the surface of the LS cost function for the example of (7). We hypothesize that this improvement of the cost function surface will improve the performance of the optimization search algorithm.

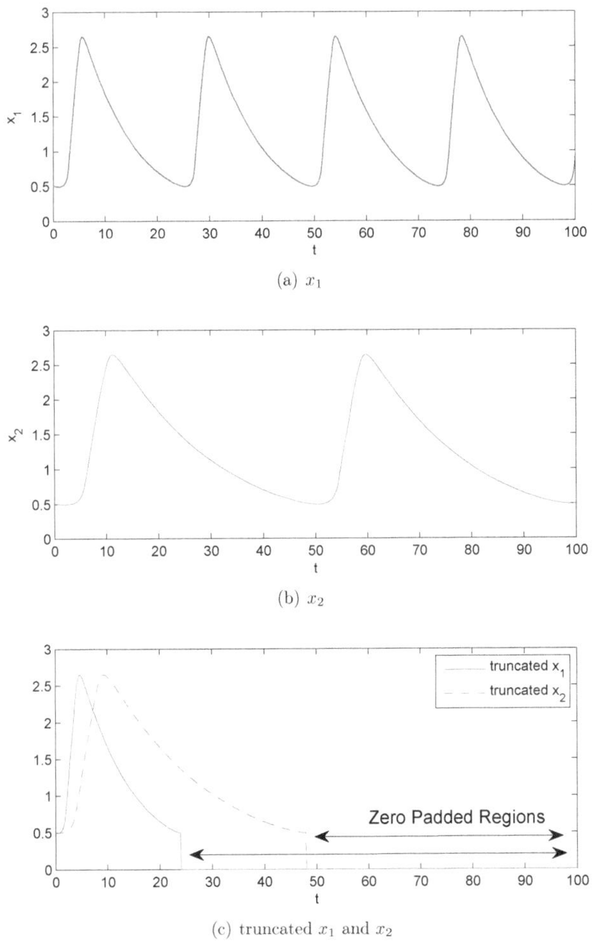

Figure 11 Illustrating the two data sets with two different periods and the way the new cost function compares them; (a) the first data set with a period 24, (b) the second data set with period 48, (c) their truncated version to be compared by the cost function.

The effect of error in estimating f_0 on the performance of the cost function The performance of the proposed cost function (8) is not affected significantly by errors in the estimation of the fundamental frequency of the measurements. This is because of the fact that the measurements used in (8) have a certain sampling rate. Basically, if the error of the estimated fundamental period is small with respect to this sampling rate, it will not affect the number of samples that lies in one fundamental period of the data. Also, adding or reducing one sample in the summation of (8) obviously will not change the performance of the proposed cost function dramatically.

2.3.2 The optimization method

The optimization of the proposed cost function was performed using a hybrid approach. Hybrid methods, i.e. the combinations of global and local search methods, have been shown to yield results with smaller errors than global searches individually [12,23]. The global search algorithm that we adopt in this study is the "Genetic Algorithm", which is a widely-used approach of a class of global search methods called *evolutionary strategies* [31]. We used two consecutive local search methods of MATLAB [32] in this research. The first one was the derivative-based, constrained routine of fmincon, and the second one was the derivative-free `routine of fminsearch` that is based on the simplex algorithm [33].

3 Results

This section shows the results of the optimization process that was illustrated in Figures 1 using two cost functions: the LS cost function of (3) and our proposed cost function of (8). We used three model of Tyson [25], Brusselator [26], and Goldbeter [27]. We compare 15 independent runs of the optimization process for parameter estimation for each oscillatory model. We add AWGN noise with SNR = 20 to the data. We use our proposed noise removal method to remove noise. The surface of the two cost functions will be shown and compared for these three systems. Results at all the intermediate steps of the optimization will be presented for each of the 15 runs:

1. The global optimization (MATLAB ga routine).
2. The first local optimization (MATLAB fmincon routine)
3. The second local optimization (MATLAB fminsearch routine)

3.1 Comparison of two different cost function

The two cost functions of (3) and (8) are two different functions of the kinetic parameters which do not

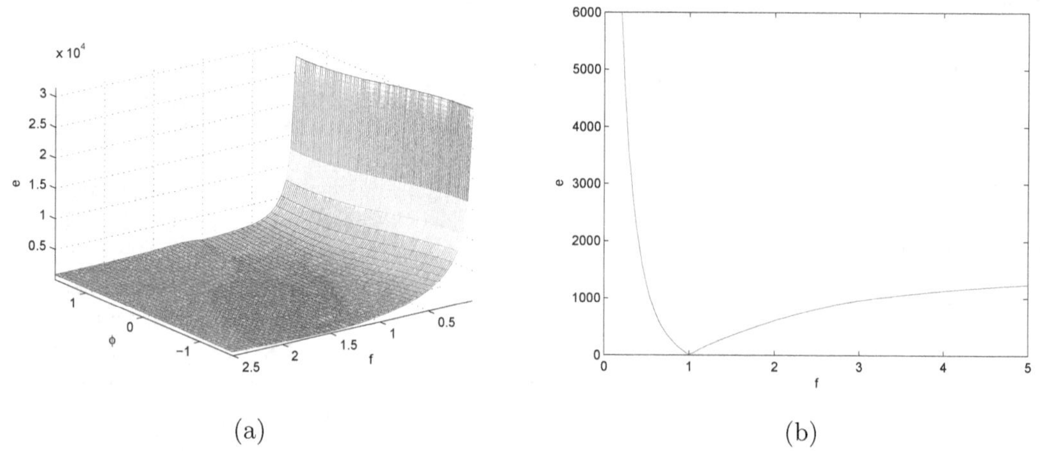

Figure 12 The surface of the new cost function for the function shown in (7) versus changes in φ and f and its cross section for $\varphi = 0$.

necessarily yield the same value for a given parameter set. Thus, a true comparison of the estimated parameters obtained from the two objective functions will require the LS score shown in (11) to equate the quality of the respective estimates. Equation (11) is basically the LS cost function summed only over the samples taken from the first fundamental period of the measurements. Introducing the measurements of only one period in computing the score creates a fair metric that shows the quality of estimated parameter sets.

$$\text{score}(\mathbf{k}) = \sum_{i=1}^{Nx} \sum_{j=1}^{N_{T_i}} (\hat{x}_{ij}(\mathbf{k}) - x_{ij})^2. \tag{11}$$

Here, N_x, x_{ij}, and $\hat{x}_{ij}$ are defined as (3) and N_{T_i} is the number of samples that are extracted in $(0 < t < T_i)$ assuming T_i is the fundamental period of the x_i.

3.2 Parameter estimation results for two-state Tyson model

The two-state Tyson model (BIOMD0000000036 in BioModels database [34]) is a mathematical model of the circadian clock in wild-type fruit flies, *D. melanogaster*. This organism has circadian clocks similar to mice and bread molds. This model, shown in (12), consists of two states and nine kinetic parameters. The nominal values of the parameters of this system are shown in Table 1.

$$\frac{dM}{dt} = \frac{v_m}{1 + (P_t(1-q)/2P_{crit})^2} - k_m M \tag{12a}$$

$$\frac{dPt}{dt} = v_p M - \frac{k_{p1} P_t q + k_{p2} P_t}{J_p + P_t} - k_{p3} P_t \tag{12b}$$

$$q = \frac{2}{\sqrt{1 + 8K_{eq} P_t}} \tag{12c}$$

Figure 13 shows the surfaces of the LS cost function and the proposed cost function of (8) for pairwise combinations of parameters k_m and J_p and k_{p3} and P_{crit} over specific ranges. Characteristics of these parameters are representative of the characteristics of all kinetic parameters of the Tyson model (results are not shown). The values of the remaining parameters are held constant at their nominal values in all figures.

We see through visual inspection that our proposed cost function produces a smoother surface than that of the LS cost function for different values of the parameters k_m, k_{p3}, P_{crit}, and J_p. Figure 14 shows the cross-sections of the cost functions above (dashed lines) together with the fundamental period of the data (solid line) for ranges of values in the same order of magnitude as the nominal value.

Figure 14a shows that the system produces sustained oscillations only for k_m in the range [0.03 0.44]. The fundamental period of the sustained oscillations falls from 58 to 6.6 along this range. This radical change in the fundamental period produces irregularities in the LS cost function over this interval. However, the proposed cost function maintains good surface properties in spite of this extreme change in the fundamental period of the system. This emphasizes that our proposed cost function addresses the issue of surface irregularities of the LS cost function caused by introducing multiple periods of the data in calculating the error. Figure 14b shows similar results.

Figure 14c, d shows that the fundamental period for different values of P_{crit} is between 15.4 and 25.4 which is less than the changes in fundamental period that

Table 1 The results of optimization with minimum score for Tyson model.

Parameter	Nominal value	Estimation of the proposed cost function	Estimation of the LS cost function
v_m	1	**1.1372**	0.9472
k_m	0.1	0.1049	0.1097
v_p	0.5	0.4668	0.4740
k_{p1}	10	**15.88**	**21.48**
k_{p2}	0.03	**0.0936**	**0.0927**
k_{p3}	0.1	**0.0766**	**0.0615**
K_{eq}	200	**692.64**	**922.16**
P_{crit}	0.1	0.1076	**0.1477**
J_p	0.05	0.0511	**0.0738**
Score	0.1378	0.1084	0.2441

The values of kinetic parameters with minimum score derived from optimization using the proposed cost function and the LS cost function for the Tyson model. The bold values are the ones that are estimated incorrectly (error more than 10%). The score values are calculated based on (11)

shown in Figure 14a, b. The LS cost function still shows varying levels of surface irregularities particularly along the P_{crit} axis. The proposed cost function again shows smoother surface characteristics under these conditions as well.

3.2.1 Results of parameter estimation

We assumed the measurements to be 100 samples of both $[M]$ and $[P_t]$ components with the rate of one sample per hour and the AWGN noise of SNR = 20. We removed the noise using the proposed approach before the optimization step. The RMSE between the noisy samples and their real values of the samples were 0.0989. This was suppressed to 0.0413 after denoising. The population size was set to 200 and number of generations equals 50 for the ga routine. We calculated N_{T_i} from (11) to be 24 for the Tyson model. The computed

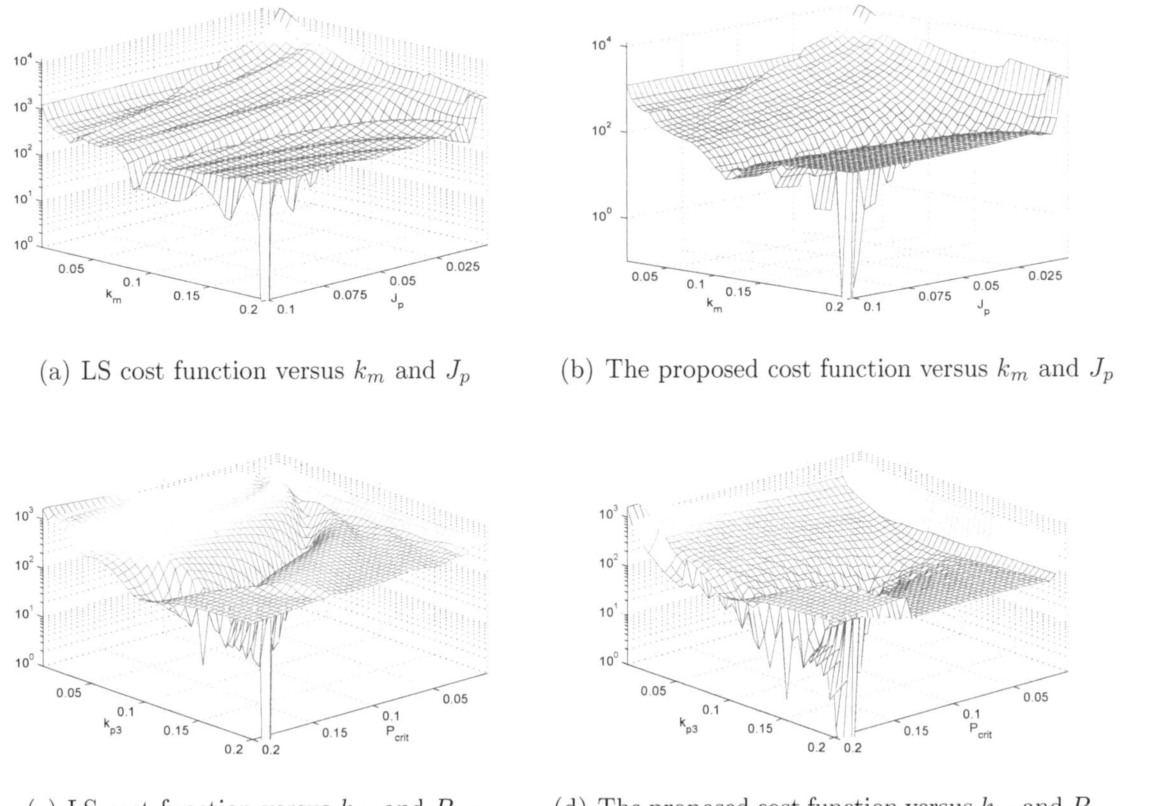

(a) LS cost function versus k_m and J_p (b) The proposed cost function versus k_m and J_p

(c) LS cost function versus k_{p3} and P_{crit} (d) The proposed cost function versus k_{p3} and P_{crit}

Figure 13 The comparison of the surface of the two cost functions, left column: LS cost function, right column: the proposed cost function, for different values of k_m, J_p, k_{p3} and P_{crit} in Tyson system, while changing two values of parameters, the rest of parameters are locked in their nominal value.

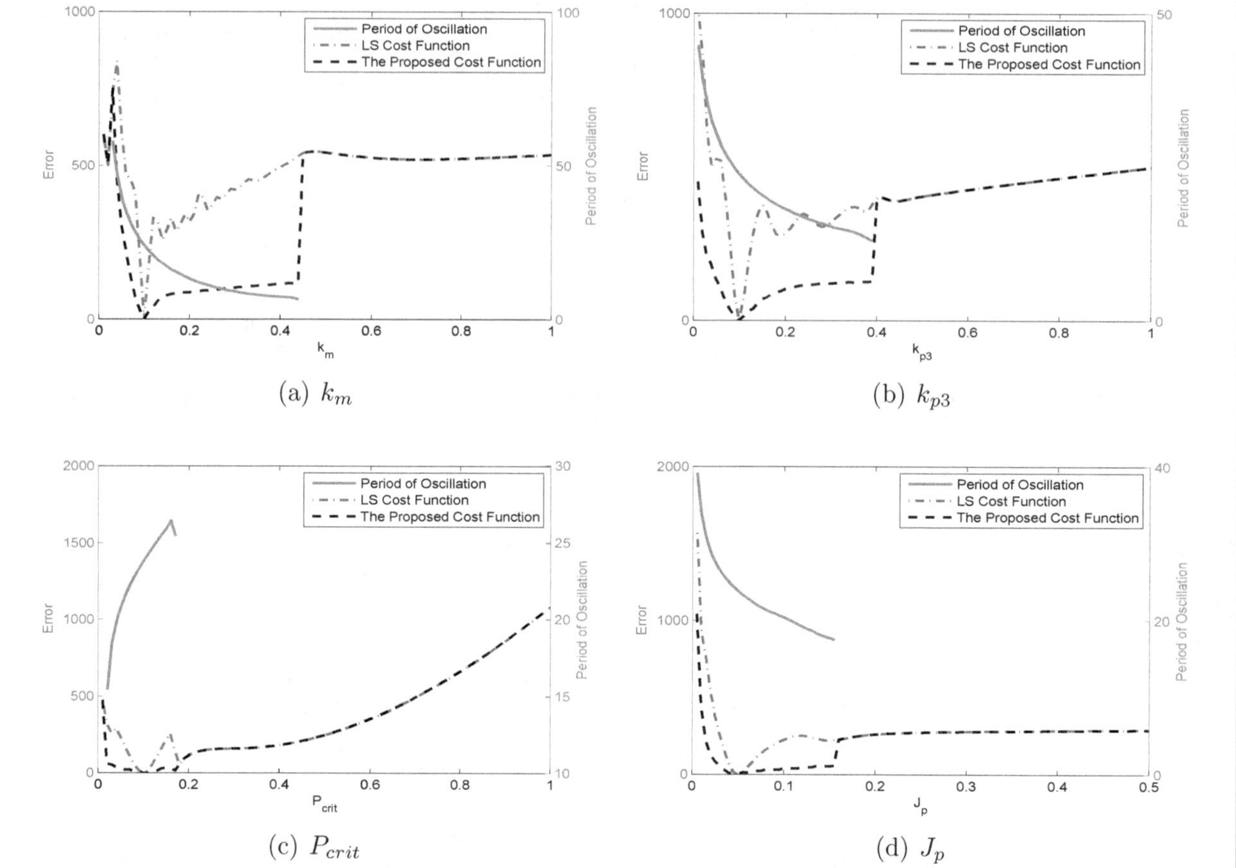

Figure 14 The values of the LS cost functions, the proposed cost function and the fundamental period of the data for different values of 4 parameters of Tyson model k_m, k_{p3}, P_{crit} and J_p.

scores for the estimated parameters from the 15 runs of optimization are shown in Figure 15 at the three steps of the hybrid optimization process. The mean, median and the minima of the computed scores at each level for the two cost functions are also shown in Table 2. Figure 15 and Table 2 show visually and numerically that the optimization routine performs better using the proposed cost function than the LS cost function at all steps. These results are also consistent with our visual inspections of the cost functions in Figures 13 and 14.

The optimized results with the lowest score out of 15 runs for the LS cost function and the proposed cost function are shown in Table 1.

The estimate results in the lowest score using noise-free measurements produces six of nine kinetic parameters with less than 10% errors (results not shown). Table 1 shows that the noisy case results in four of nine estimated parameters with more than 10% error. In both cases, proposed cost function yields more accurate

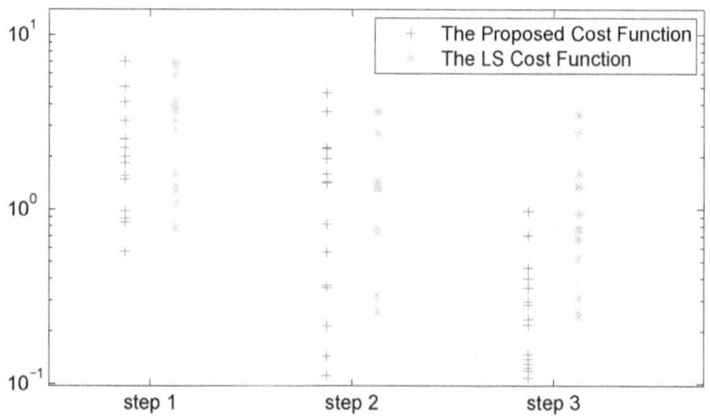

Figure 15 The comparison of the computed scores resulted from the cost functions in 3 steps of optimization: Step 1: results of ga routine. Step 2: results of fmincon routine. Step 3: results of fminsearch routine.

Table 2 Statistics of optimization results for Tyson model.

	Step 1		Step 2		Step 3	
	Proposed	**LS**	**Proposed**	**LS**	**Proposed**	**LS**
Mean	2.4497	3.5838	1.4465	1.7760	0.3131	1.1116
Median	1.9998	3.5731	1.4117	1.3595	0.2354	0.7788
Min	0.5706	0.7788	0.1118	0.2589	0.1084	0.2441

Mean, median, and minimum of the score values shown in Figure 15 results in comparison to the LS cost function. The large number of inaccuracies for the noisy case is more a result of system sloppiness versus inaccuracies of the estimation procedure [35,36], which results in 21 a wide range of parameters with similar system dynamics. It is evident that our proposed cost function was able to produce better overall system dynamics than the traditional LS cost function, which is clearly conveyed by the lower overall error. Our proposed method, similar to the LS cost function, only takes into account the accuracy of dynamics. Thus, the sloppiness can results in moderate level of parameter accuracy. Recently, Apgar et al. proposed an experiment design framework to improve estimates of sloppy parameters in biochemical models [37]. This, however, is beyond the scope of this article.

3.3 Parameter estimation for two-state Brusselator model

The Brusselator model was proposed by Prigogine for theoretical analysis of autocatalytic reactions [26]. This model consists of two states and four kinetic parameters as shown in (13). The nominal values of the parameters of this system are shown in Table 3.

$$\frac{dX}{dt} = k_1A + k_2X^2Y - k_3BX - k_4X, \quad (13a)$$

$$\frac{dY}{dt} = -k_2X^2Y + k_3BX, \quad (13b)$$

$$A = 0.5, \quad B = 3. \quad (13c)$$

Figure 16 shows the values of the two cost functions together with the fundamental period of the data (the green trajectories) for different values of four parameters of the system.

Figure 16a shows the fundamental period of sustained oscillation falls from 45.9 to 4.3 for k_1 in the range [0.7 2.8]. This change in the fundamental period again produce irregularities in the LS cost function over this interval. The proposed cost function, on the other hand, maintains good surface properties in spite of this change in the fundamental period of the 22 system. This further verifies that the proposed cost function is able to address the irregularities of the LS cost function resulting from sustained dynamics embedded in the dynamics used to evaluate the cost function.

3.3.1 Results of parameter estimation

This section shows the results of 15 runs of optimization for the Brusselator model using 100 samples of only [Y] component with sampling rate = 1 (sample/hour) and AWGN noise with SNR = 20. We removed the noise using the proposed denoising approach. The RMSE between the noisy samples and their real values was 0.0971, which was suppressed to 0.0570 after denoising. The population size was set to 100 and the number of generations equals 50. The computed scores for the estimated parameters from the 15 runs of optimization are shown in Figure 17 and Table 4. We calculate $N_{T_i} = 23$ for calculating the score of (11) for the Brusselator model. The results again demonstrate visually and numerically that the optimization routine performs better using the proposed cost function than the LS cost function in all steps even in presence of noise. These results are also consistent with our visual inspections of the cost functions in Figure 16.

The derived results with the lowest score out of 15 runs for the LS cost function and the proposed cost function are in Table 3.

Table 3 shows that the resulting overall error for the proposed cost function is lower than that of the LS cost function. All four parameters were estimated incorrectly using the LS cost function, while they were estimated almost accurately using the proposed cost function.

3.4 Parameter estimation results for five-state Goldbeter model

The *D. melanogaster* circadian model of Goldbeter [27] was investigated in the third study. This model is also available in BioModels database [34] (BIOMD0000000016). Here, the circadian oscillations of PER is modeled with five states: PER mRNA [M], PER protein [P0], the mono-phosphorylated form [P1], the bi-phosphorylated form [P2] and nuclear PER [PN]. This five-state model has 18 kinetic parameters. The ODE model of the system is shown in 14. The nominal values of the 18 kinetic parameters of this system are available in Table 5.

Table 3 The results of optimization with minimum score for Brusselator model.

Parameter	Nominal value	Estimation of the proposed cost function	Estimation of the LS cost function
k_1	1	0.9912	**1.4064**
k_2	1	0.9112	**0.8492**
k_3	1	0.9526	**0.8944**
k_4	1	0.9335	**1.6732**
Score	0.3128	0.2763	0.7619

The values of kinetic parameters with minimum score derived from optimization using the proposed cost function and the LS cost function for the Brusselator model. The bold values are the ones that are estimated incorrectly (error more than 10%)

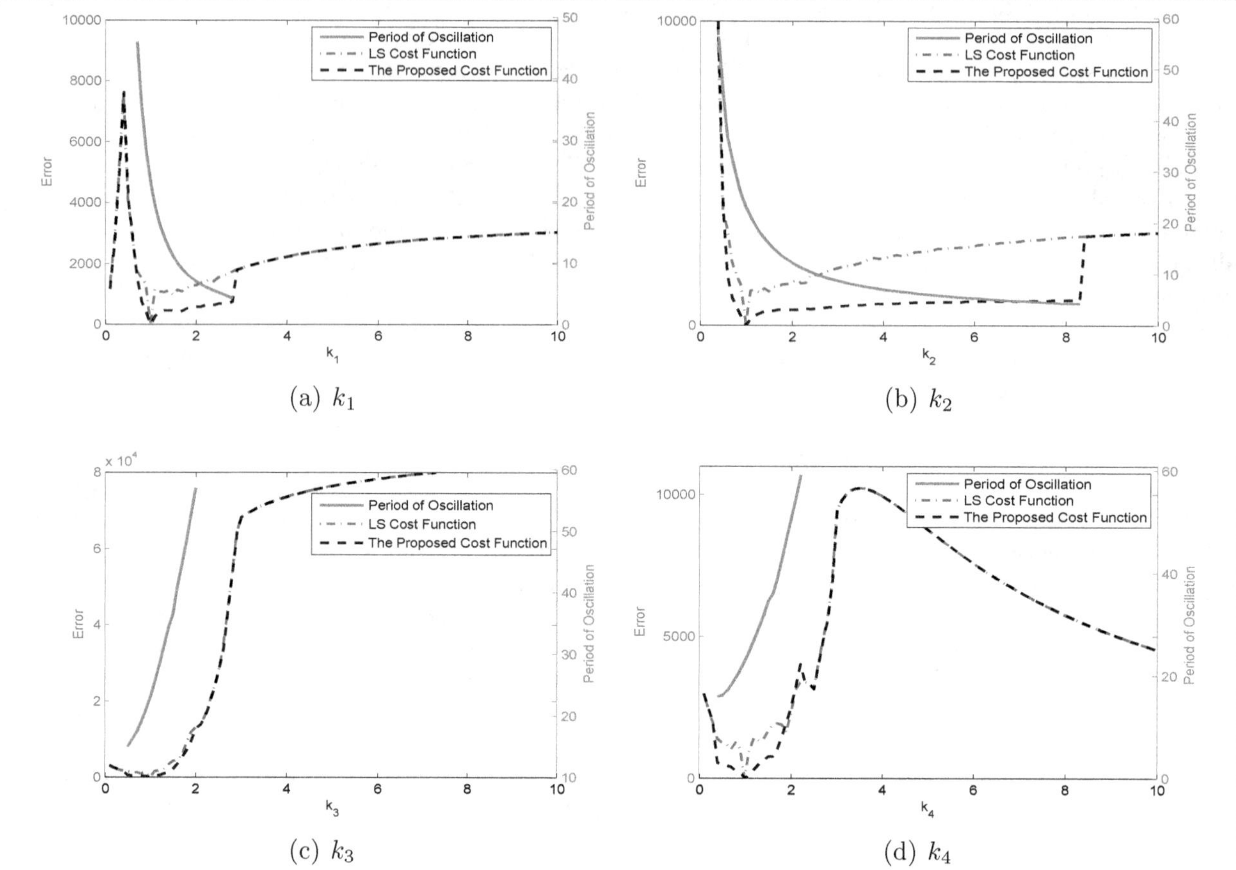

Figure 16 The values of the LS cost functions, the proposed cost function and the fundamental period of the data for different values of 4 parameters of Brusselator model k_1, k_2, k_3, and k_4.

$$\frac{dM}{dt} = v_s \frac{K_I^n}{K_I^n + P_N^n} - v_m \frac{M}{K_m + M} \quad (14a)$$

$$\frac{dP_0}{dt} = k_s M - V_1 \frac{P_0}{K_1 + P_0} + V_2 \frac{P_1}{K_2 + P_1} \quad (14b)$$

$$\frac{dP_1}{dt} = V_1 \frac{P_0}{K_1 + P_0} - V_2 \frac{P_1}{K_2 + P_1} - V_3 \frac{P_1}{K_3 + P_1} - V_4 \frac{P_2}{K_4 + P_2} \quad (14c)$$

$$\frac{dP_2}{dt} = V_3 \frac{p_1}{K_3 + p_1} - V_4 \frac{P_2}{K_4 + P_2} - k_1 P_2 + k_2 P_N - v_d \frac{P_2}{K_d + P_2} \quad (14d)$$

$$\frac{dPN}{dt} = k_1 P_2 - k_2 P_N \quad (14e)$$

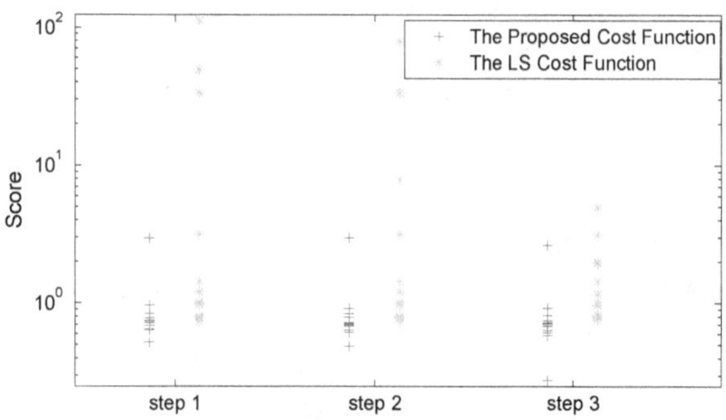

Figure 17 The comparison of the computed scores resulted from the cost functions in 3 steps of optimization: Step 1: results of ga routine. Step 2: results of fmincon routine. Step 3: results of fminsearch routine.

Figure 18 shows the values of the two cost function together with the fundamental period of the data (the green trajectories) along different values of four parameters of the system.

Table 4 Statistics of optimization results for Brusselator model.

	Step 1		Step 2		Step 3	
	Proposed	LS	Proposed	LS	Proposed	LS
Mean	0.8857	14.8167	0.8688	9.4746	0.8177	1.5517
Median	0.7336	1.0179	0.7116	1.0179	0.7107	1.0179
Min	0.5207	0.7323	0.4879	0.7323	0.2763	0.7619

Mean, median, and minimum of the score values shown in Figure 17

Table 5 The Result of Optimization with Minimum Score for Goldbeter Model.

Parameter	Nominal value	Estimation of the proposed cost function	Estimation of the LS cost function
v_s	0.76	0.6980	**0.6275**
K_I	1	0.9996	0.9400
n	4	**4.9920**	**5.7232**
v_m	0.65	0.5972	**0.5559**
K_m	0.5	0.5056	**0.7412**
k_s	0.38	0.3677	0.3732
V_1	3.2	**3.8093**	3.1552
K_1	2	**2.6488**	1.8288
V_2	1.58	**3.1221**	**1.2836**
K_2	2	**4.4760**	**1.1952**
V_3	5	**8.8000**	4.5100
K_3	2	**4.6696**	2.0120
V_4	2.5	**5.6410**	**2.8120**
K_4	2	**7.0128**	**3.0704**
v_d	0.95	0.9713	0.9814
K_d	0.2	**0.2413**	**0.2250**
k_1	1.9	1.7541	**2.1944**

The values of kinetic parameters with minimum score derived from optimization using the proposed cost function and the LS cost function for the five-state Goldbeter model. The bold values are the ones that are estimated incorrectly (error more than 10%)

It could be seen in all figures that the changes in period of the oscillation does not produce significant irregularities in the LS cost function surface, which is different than previous examples. Figure 18b, for instance, shows the changes of period for k_2 in the interval [0.4 2]. However, there are not multiple basins of attractions along the k_2 direction in spite of these changes in fundamental period. This is due to the fact that the LS cost function changes over orders of magnitudes along this parameter direction in a way that the produced ripples has little effect on the monotonicity of the LS cost function. This extreme change in the LS cost function (approximately from 400 to 2200 for k_2 over the interval [0.4 2]) happens because the peak to peak magnitude of the sustained oscillations of the simulated data also increases in order of magnitudes along this parameter direction. For example, the peak of the $[P_2]$ increases from 0.25 to 1.5 for k_2 over the interval [0.4 2].

The proposed cost function still shows good surface characteristics although it was not much different than the already favorable characteristics of the LS cost function. Thus, it is expected that both of these cost functions would perform almost similar in the optimization process.

3.4.1 Parameter estimation results

This section shows the results of 15 optimization runs using 100 samples of $[M]$, $[P_0]$, $[P_1]$, $[P_2]$, and $[P_N]$ components with the sampling rate = 1 (sample/hour) and AWGN noise with SNR = 20. We suppressed the noise using the proposed denoising approach. The RMSE between the noisy samples and their real values were 0.1012, which was suppressed to 0.04906 after denoising. We calculated $N_{T_i} = 23$ for the score in (11). The results of 15 optimization runs are shown in Figure 19 and Table 6. This shows that the performances of the LS cost function and the proposed cost function are almost the same in all steps. These results are also consistent with our visual inspections of the cost functions in Figure 18.

The derived results with the minimum score out of 15 runs for the LS cost function and the proposed cost function are shown in Table 5.

Table 5 shows that 8 out of 18 parameters were estimated within 10% of their nominal value for the proposed cost function as opposed to 7 out of 18 for the LS cost function. This shows a wide range of parameters have similar dynamics. This is due to system sloppiness that was also mentioned for the Tyson model. Our proposed cost function takes into account the accuracy of dynamics, which is similar to the LS cost function. Therefore, this may results in moderate accuracy in parameter values because of the sloppiness.

4 Conclusions

This article addresses the issue of kinetic parameter estimation in oscillatory biochemical systems. We showed that the LS cost function for oscillatory systems results in surface characteristics that potentially hinder the performance of optimization routines used to estimate kinetic parameters. Thus, we suggested a new cost function with more favorable surface properties which leads

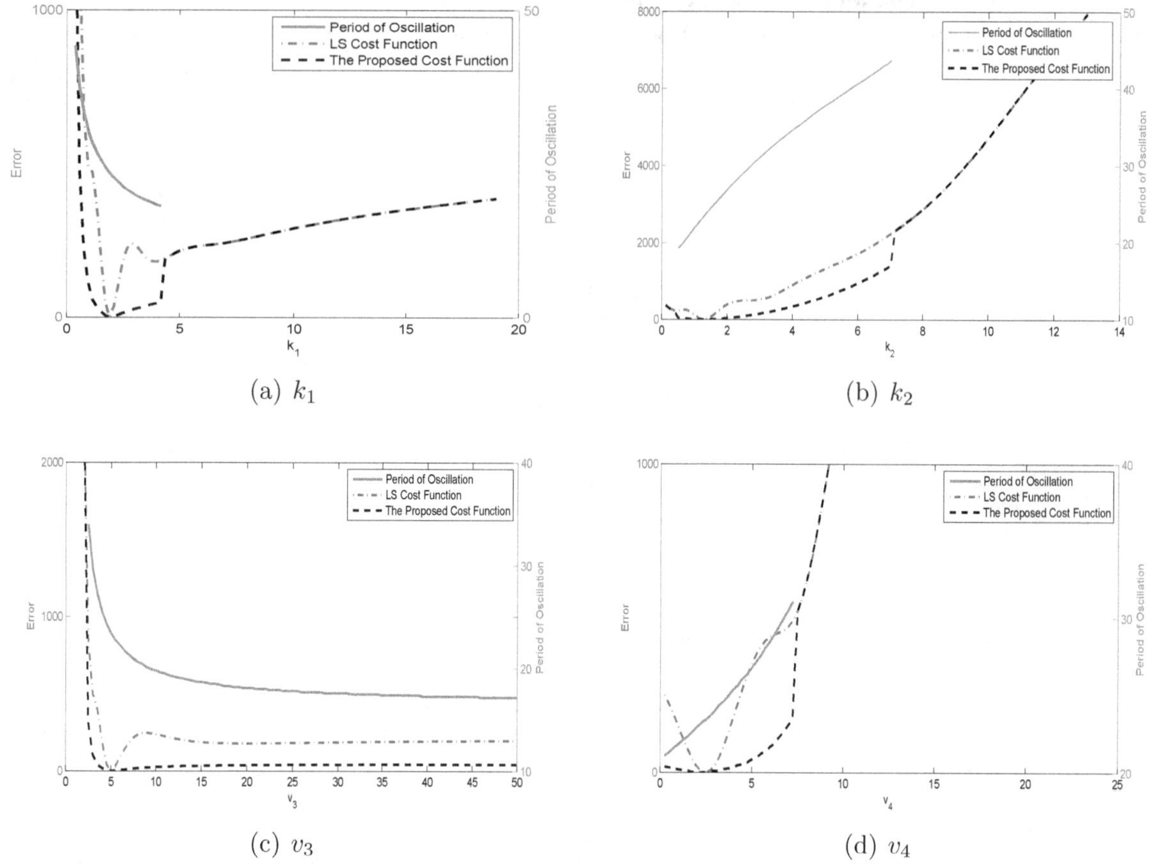

Figure 18 The values of the LS cost functions, the proposed cost function and the fundamental period of the data for different values of 4 parameters of Goldbeter model k_1, k_2, v_3, and v_4.

to improved results for parameter estimation. This cost function integrates temporal information with periodic information embedded in measurements used to estimate these parameters. This generalized cost function also needs less first principles knowledge to generate the cost function in comparison to the previous developed methods for oscillatory systems. We tested our cost function using three benchmark oscillatory biochemical pathways and compared our proposed objective function with the traditional LS cost function in several optimization runs using noisy measurements. The comparison of the results verified that the optimization performed more effectively using our 26 proposed cost function as compared to the traditional LS cost function. Furthermore, we introduced a wavelet hardthresholding approach for noise removal. This modified approach is able to suppress noise in oscillatory data better than the traditional wavelet thresholding approach. This, together with the proposed objective function will result in more

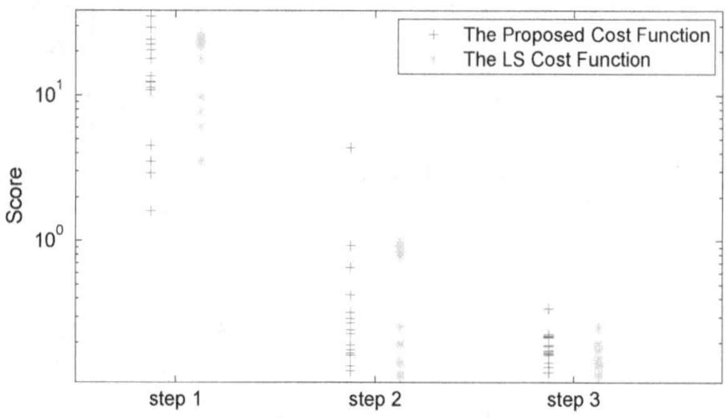

Figure 19 The comparison of the computed scores resulted from the cost functions in 3 steps of optimization: Step 1: results of ga routine. Step 2: results of fmincon routine. Step 3: Results of fminsearch routine.

Table 6 Statistics of optimization results for Goldbeter model.

	Step 1		Step 2		Step 3	
	Proposed	**LS**	**Proposed**	**LS**	**Proposed**	**LS**
Mean	14.7428	18.8913	0.5812	0.4939	0.1914	0.1585
Median	12.3454	22.7683	0.2456	0.2553	0.1778	0.1446
Min	1.5970	3.5281	0.1282	0.1183	0.1255	0.1183

Mean, median and minimum of the score values shown in Figure 19 accurate kinetic parameters that will eventually lead to biochemical models that are more precise, predictable and controllable. There are, however, unsolved issues with sloppiness of biochemical pathways [35,36], which require further investigation especially for oscillatory biochemical pathways.

Competing interests

The authors declare that they have no competing interests.

References

1. A Goldbeter, *Biochemical Oscillations and Cellular Rhythms the Molecular Bases of Periodic and Chaotic Behaviour*, (Cambridge University Press, Cambridge, 1996)
2. C Fall, F Marland, J Tyson, *Computational Cell Biology*, (Springer, New York, 2002)
3. J Perez-Martin, Growth and development eukaryotes. Current Opinion Microbiol. **13**(6), 661–662 (2010). doi:10.1016/j.mib.2010.10.007
4. J Yan, H Wang, Y Liu, C Shao, Analysis of gene regulatory networks in the mammalian circadian rhythm. PLos Comput Biol. **4**(10), e1000193 (2008). doi:10.1371/journal.pcbi.1000193
5. K Collins, T Jacks, N Pavletich, The cell cycle and cancer. PNAS: Proc Natl Acad Sci. **94**(7), 2776–2778 (1997). doi:10.1073/pnas.94.7.2776
6. J Boullin, JM Morgan, The development of cardiac rhythm. Heart. **91**(7), 874–875 (2005). doi:10.1136/hrt.2004.047415
7. J Perry, *The Ovarian Cycle of Mammals*, (Oliver and Boyd, Edinburgh, 1971)
8. M Zaccolo, T Pozzan, cAMP and Ca2+ interplay: a matter of oscillation patterns. Trends Neurosci. **26**(2), 53–55 (2003). doi:10.1016/S0166-2236(02)00017-6
9. N Bagheri, M Lawson, J Stelling, F Doyle, Modeling the Drosophila melanogaster circadian oscillator via Phase optimization. J Biol Rhythms. **23**(6), 525–537 (2008). doi:10.1177/0748730408325041
10. M Zeilinger, E Farre, S Taylor, S Kay, F Doyle, A novel computational model of the circadian clock in Arabidopsis that incorporates PRR7 and PRR9. Mol Syst Biol. **2**(58) (2006)
11. J Locke, A Millar, M Turner, Modelling genetic networks with noisy and varied experimental data the circadian clock in Arabidopsis thaliana. J Theor Biol. **234**(3), 383–393 (2005). doi:10.1016/j.jtbi.2004.11.038
12. M Rodriguez-Fernandez, P Mendes, J Banga, A hybrid approach for efficient and robust parameter estimation in biochemical pathways. BioSystems. **83**, 248–265 (2005)
13. V Vyshemirsky, M Girolami, Bayesian ranking of biochemical system models. Bioinformatics. **24**(6), 833–839 (2008). doi:10.1093/bioinformatics/btm607
14. IC Chou, E Voit, Recent developments in parameter estimation and structure identification of biochemical and genomic systems. Math Biosci. **219**(2), 57–83 (2009). doi:10.1016/j.mbs.2009.03.002
15. E Mostacci, C Truntzer, H Cardot, P Ducoroy, Multivariate denoising methods combining wavelets and principal component analysis for mass spectrometry data. Proteomics. **10**(14), 2564–2572 (2010). doi:10.1002/pmic.200900185
16. G Tang, A Qin, ECG de-noising based on empirical mode decomposition. *The 9th International Conference for Young Computer Scientists, 2008. ICYCS* 903–906 (2008)
17. Z Ren, G Liu, L Zeng, Z Huang, S Huang, Research on biochemical spectrum denoising based on a novel wavelet threshold function and an improved translation-invariance method. Proc SPIE. **7280**, 72801Q (2008)
18. M Sugimoto, S Kikuchi, M Tomita, Reverse engineering of biochemical equations from time-course data by means of genetic programming. Biosystems. **80**(2), 155–164 (2005). doi:10.1016/j.biosystems.2004.11.003
19. O Gonzalez, C Kuper, K Jung, JP Naval, E Mendoza, Parameter estimation using simulated annealing for S-system models of biochemical networks. Bioinformatics. **23**(4), 480–486 (2007). doi:10.1093/bioinformatics/btl522
20. P Flaherty, M Radhakrishnan, T Dinh, R Rebres, T Roach, M Jordan, A Arkin, A dual receptor crosstalk model of g-protein-coupled signal transduction. PLoS Comput Biol. **4**(9), e1000185 (2008). doi:10.1371/journal.pcbi.1000185
21. C Zhan, L Yeung, Parameter estimation in systems biology models using spline approximation. BMC Syst Biol. **5**(14) (2011)
22. D Marquardt, An algorithm for least squares estimation of nonlinear parameters. SIAM J Appl Math. **11**(2), 431–441 (1963). doi:10.1137/0111030
23. J Renders, S Flasse, Hybrid methods using genetic algorithms for global optimization. IEEE Trans Syst Man Cybernet Part B, Cybernet. **26**(2), 243–258 (1996). doi:10.1109/3477.485836
24. D Gerhard, Pitch extraction and fundamental frequency history and current techniques. Department of Computer Science, University of Regina, Regina, Canada (2003)
25. J Tyson, C Hong, D Thron, B Novak, A simple model of circadian rhythm based on dimerization and proteolysis of PER and TIM. Biophys J. **77**, 2411–2417 (1999). doi:10.1016/S0006-3495(99)77078-5
26. D Kondepudi, I Prigogine, *Modern Thermodynamics from Heat Engines to Dissipative Structures*, (Wiley, Chichester, 1998)
27. A Goldbeter, A model for circadian oscillations in the drosophila period protein (PER). Proc Royal Soc B, Biol Sci. **261**(1362), 319–324 (1995). doi:10.1098/rspb.1995.0153
28. S Mallat, *A Wavelet Tour of Signal Processing*, (American Press, San Diego, 1998)
29. S Mallat, A theory for multiresolution signal decomposition: the wavelet representation. IEEE Pattern Anal Mach Intell. **11**(7), 674–693 (1989). doi:10.1109/34.192463
30. A Cheveigne, H Kawahara, Yin, a fundamental frequency estimator for speech and music. J Acoust Soc Am. **111**(4), 1917–1930 (2002). doi:10.1121/1.1458024
31. C Moles, P Mendes, J Banga, Parameter estimation in biochemical pathways: a comparison of global optimization methods. Genome Res. **13**(11), 2467–2474 (2003). doi:10.1101/gr.1262503
32. Inc TM, MATLAB: version 7.6.0. Natick Massachusetts (2008)
33. J Lagarias, J Reeds, M Wright, P Wright, Convergence properties of the Nelder-Mead simplex method in low dimensions. SIAM J Optim. **9**, 112–147 (1998). doi:10.1137/S1052623496303470
34. N Le Novère, B Bornstein, A Broicher, M Courtot, M Donizelli, H Dharuri, L Li, H Sauro, M Schilstra, B Shapiro, JL Snoep, M Hucka, BioModels Database: a free, centralized database of curated, published, quantitative kinetic models of biochemical and cellular systems. Nucleic Acids Res. **34**(suppl 1), D689–D691 (2006)
35. R Gutenkunst, J Waterfall, F Casey, K Brown, C Myers, J Sethna, Universally Sloppy Parameter Sensitivities in Systems Biology Models. PLos Comput Biol. **3**(10), 1871–1878 (2005)
36. J Waterfall, F Casey, R Gutenkunst, K Brown, C Myers, P Brouwer, V Elser, J Sethna, Sloppy-model universality class and the Vandermonde matrix. Phys Rev Lett. **97**(15), 150601 (2006)
37. J Apgar, D Witmer, F Whitead, B Tidor, Sloppy models, parameter uncertainty, and the role of experimental design. Mol BioSyst. **6**(10), 1890–1900 (2010). doi:10.1039/b918098b

Learning restricted Boolean network model by time-series data

Hongjia Ouyang[1], Jie Fang[1], Liangzhong Shen[1], Edward R Dougherty[2,3] and Wenbin Liu[1,2*]

Abstract

Restricted Boolean networks are simplified Boolean networks that are required for either negative or positive regulations between genes. Higa et al. (BMC Proc 5:S5, 2011) proposed a three-rule algorithm to infer a restricted Boolean network from time-series data. However, the algorithm suffers from a major drawback, namely, it is very sensitive to noise. In this paper, we systematically analyze the regulatory relationships between genes based on the state switch of the target gene and propose an algorithm with which restricted Boolean networks may be inferred from time-series data. We compare the proposed algorithm with the three-rule algorithm and the best-fit algorithm based on both synthetic networks and a well-studied budding yeast cell cycle network. The performance of the algorithms is evaluated by three distance metrics: the normalized-edge Hamming distance μ_{ham}^{e}, the normalized Hamming distance of state transition μ_{ham}^{st}, and the steady-state distribution distance μ^{ssd}. Results show that the proposed algorithm outperforms the others according to both μ_{ham}^{e} and μ_{ham}^{st}, whereas its performance according to μ^{ssd} is intermediate between best-fit and the three-rule algorithms. Thus, our new algorithm is more appropriate for inferring interactions between genes from time-series data.

Keywords: Restricted Boolean network; Inference; Budding yeast cell cycle

1 Introduction

A key goal in systems biology is to characterize the molecular mechanisms governing specific cellular behaviors and processes. This entails selecting a model class for representing the system structure and state dynamics, followed by the application of computational or statistical inference procedures to reveal the model structure from measurement data. The models of gene regulatory networks run the gamut from coarse-grained discrete networks to the detailed description of stochastic differential equations [1]. They provide a uniform way to study biological phenomena (e.g., cell cycle) and diseases (e.g., cancer) and ultimately lead to systems-based therapeutic strategies [2].

Boolean networks, and the more general class of probabilistic Boolean networks, are one of the most popular approaches for modeling gene networks. The inference of gene networks from high-throughput genomic data is an ill-posed problem. There exists more than one model that can explain the data. The search space for potential regulator sets and their corresponding Boolean functions generally increases exponentially with the number of genes in the network and the number of regulatory genes. It is particularly challenging in the face of small sample sizes, because the number of genes typically is much greater than the number of observations. Thus, estimates of modeling errors, which themselves are determined from the measurement data, can be highly variable and untrustworthy. Many inference algorithms have been proposed to elucidate the regulatory relationships between genes. Mutual information (MI) is an information-theoretic approach that can capture the nonlinear dependence between random variables. REVEAL is the first information-based algorithm to infer the regulatory relationships between genes [3]. However, a small MI does not necessarily mean that no regulatory relationship exists between genes (false negative). Conversely, a large MI does not necessarily mean a real regulatory relationship. 'False-positive' relationships often result from indirect interactions between two genes. The data processing inequality (DPI) and conditional mutual information (CMI) are two methods used to reduce the problem of false positives [4,5]. Another information-

* Correspondence: wbliu6910@126.com
[1]Department of Physics and Electronic Information Engineering, Wenzhou University, Wenzhou, Zhejiang 325035, China
[2]Department of Electrical and Computer Engineering, Texas A&M University, College Station, TX 33101, USA
Full list of author information is available at the end of the article

based method is the minimum description length principle (MDL), which achieves a good trade-off between model complexity and fit to the data [6–10]. The coefficient of determination (CoD) selects a set of predictors whose expression levels can be used to better predict the expression of a target gene relative to the best possible prediction in the absence of observations [11,12]. The best-fit extension incorporates inconsistencies generated from measurements or other unknown latent factors by constructing a network that makes as few misclassifications as possible [13,14]. Any prior knowledge about the network structure or dynamics likely improves inference accuracy, especially for small sample sizes. Theoretical considerations and computational studies suggest that gene regulatory networks might operate close to a critical phase transition between ordered and disordered dynamical regimes [15,16]. Liu et al. proposed a method to embed such a criticality assumption into the inference procedure. Such regularization of the sensitivity can both improve the inference and move the inferred networks closer to criticality [17].

A restricted Boolean network is a simplified Boolean model that has been used to study dynamical behavior of the yeast cell cycle [18–24]. In this model, the regulatory relationship between genes is either upregulation or downregulation. The output of the target gene is mainly dominated by the summation of its input genes. When the input summation is zero, the output state will remain as the current state of the target gene. The inference algorithm mentioned above generally cannot deal with this situation, and thus may not be appropriate to infer such network models. Recently, Higa et al. proposed a 'three-rule algorithm' to construct a restricted Boolean network from time-series data [25]. Their idea is that the consecutive state transitions of the system must be driven by some constraints, which can be induced from the small perturbations between two similar system states (detailed rules are provided in Section 3.1). However, the perturbations in microarry data sometimes may be caused by stochastic biological randomness or measurement process instead of real changes in gene expression level. This makes the three-rule algorithm inevitably lead to some incorrect constraints. In this paper, we propose a systematic method to infer a restricted Boolean network based on the state transitions of the target gene. Results of simulated networks and a modeled yeast cell cycle show that the proposed algorithm is more robust to noise than the three-rule method.

This paper is organized as follows: Background information and definitions are given in Section 2. Section 3 presents a brief introduction to the three rules; after which, we systematically analyze the regulatory relationships between input genes and their target gene and propose an inference algorithm. Section 4 and Section 5 present results for the simulated networks and for the cell cycle model of budding yeast. Concluding remarks are given in Section 6.

2 Background

2.1 Boolean networks

A Boolean network $G(V, F)$ is defined by a set of nodes $V = \{x_1, \ldots, x_n\}$, $x_i \in \{0, 1\}$ and a set of Boolean functions $F = \{f_1, \ldots, f_n\}$ and $f_i : \{0,1\}^{k_i} \rightarrow \{0,1\}$. Each node x_i represents the expression state of gene x_i, where $x_i = 0$ means that the gene is off, and $x_i = 1$ means it is on. Each node x_i is assigned a Boolean function $f_i(x_1, \ldots, x_{k_i})$ with k_i specific input nodes, which is used to update its value. Under the synchronous updating scheme, all genes are updated simultaneously according to their corresponding update functions. The network's state at time t is represented by a binary vector $x(t) = (x_1(t), \ldots, x_n(t))$. In the absence of noise, the state of the system at the next time step is

$$x(t+1) = F(x_1(t), \ldots, x_n(t)) \tag{1}$$

The long-run behavior of a deterministic Boolean network (BN) depends on the initial state, and the network will eventually settle down and cycle endlessly through a set of states called an attractor cycle. The set of all initial states that reach a particular attractor cycle forms the basin of attraction (BOA) for the cycle. Following a perturbation, the network in the long run may randomly escape an attractor cycle, be reinitialized, and then begin its transition process anew. For a BN with perturbation probability p, its corresponding Markov chain possesses a steady-state distribution. It has been hypothesized that attractors or steady-state distributions in Boolean formalisms correspond to different cell types of an organism or to cell fates. In other words, the phenotypic traits are encoded in the attractors [1]. There are two ways to define the perturbation probability p. One is that each gene can flip its state according to an i.i.d random perturbation vector $\gamma = (\gamma_1, \cdots, \gamma_n)$, where $\gamma_i \in \{0, 1\}$, the ith gene flips if and only $\gamma_i = 1$, and $p = P(\gamma_i = 1)$ for $i = 1, 2, \cdots, n$. The other is each state $x(t)$ can transit to any other state with the same probability p. In this situation, at each time step, state $x(t)$ will transit to the next state according to F with probability $1 + p - 2^n * p$ and other states with probability p. In this paper, we adopt the later definition of the perturbation probability p.

2.2 Restricted Boolean networks

Restricted Boolean networks are simplified Boolean networks in which the regulatory relationships between genes obey the following convention: $a_{ij} = 1$ represents a positive regulation from gene x_j to x_i (activation); $a_{ij} = -1$ represents a negative regulation from gene x_j to x_i (inhibition);

and $a_{ij} = 0$ means that x_j has no effect on x_i. The Boolean function $f_i(x_1, \ldots, x_{k_i})$ is defined as [18]

$$x_i(t+1) = \begin{cases} 1, & \text{if } \sum_{j \in \{1,\ldots,k_i\}} a_{ij}x_i(t) > 0 \\ 0, & \text{if } \sum_{j \in \{1,\ldots,k_i\}} a_{ij}x_i(t) < 0 \\ x_i(t), & \text{if } \sum_{j \in \{1,\ldots,k_i\}} a_{ij}x_i(t) = 0. \end{cases} \quad (2)$$

This model is 'restricted' in the sense that functions satisfying formula (2) constitute a subset of the class of all Boolean functions. The number of restricted functions decreases dramatically as the input degree k_i increases. For example, there are 12 ($< 2^{2^2} = 16$) restricted functions for $k_i = 2$, and only 60 functions ($<< 2^{2^3} = 256$) for $k_i = 3$. The restricted model significantly reduces the model space, which is beneficial for inference, given a limited number of noisy high-throughput data.

3 Methods

3.1 Three-rule method

A time-series observation can be treated as a trajectory (or random walk) of the state space of the network used to model a real biological system. The three-rule method proposed by Higa et al. is to induce the constraints between genes from the small difference between two similar states and the difference between their next states [25]. Given an m-point time series S = {$S(1), S(2), \ldots, S(m)$} of gene expression profiles, where $S(t) \in \{0, 1\}^n$ for $t = 1, 2, \ldots, m$, the three rules are as follows:

Rule 1: Let $S(t-1)$, $S(t)$, and $S(t+1)$ be three consecutive states. If $S(t-1)$ and $S(t)$ differ by a single gene x_k, then for each gene x_i such that $x_i(t) \neq x_i(t+1)$, we have x_k directly regulates x_i; that is, $a_{ik} \neq 0$.

Rule 2: Only the active genes at time t can possibly regulate genes at time $t+1$.

Rule 3: Given two similar states $S(t_1)$ and $S(t_2)$, the difference between $S(t_1+1)$ and $S(t_2+1)$ must result from the genes in their predecessors $S(t_1)$ and $S(t_2)$ that are expressed differently.

Both rules 1 and 3 can also be extended to situations where $S(t-1)$ and $S(t)$ or $S(t_1)$ and $S(t_2)$ differ in more than one gene. Cyclically applying these rules to any two states may lead to a group of constraint inequalities between variables a_{ij}. Many available constraint satisfaction problem solvers (CSPs) [26] can be used to solve the possible regulatory relationships of one gene to the target gene.

Rules 1 and 3 may give incorrect relationships if applied to noisy data; in other words, they are very sensitive to the noise inherent in data. We demonstrate this by using a small network that contains only four genes (see Figure 1). An arrow represents positive regulation, a line segment with a bar at the end represents negative regulation, and the dotted loop on x_2 indicates that this gene downregulates itself. The time-series data at the right in Figure 1 are extracted from the network in Figure 1. Between $S(1)$ and $S(2)$, only x_2 changes from 1 to 0, and only x_3 flips from 0 to 1 in the successive states $S(2)$ and $S(3)$. We can conclude that x_2 must inhibit x_3 by applying rule 1, which means $a_{32} = -1$ because turning off x_2 turns on x_3. If $S(2)$ becomes 100$\underline{1}$ owing to noise, then we will also have that gene x_4 inhibiting x_2, which means $a_{24} = -1$.

3.2 Analysis of regulatory relationships based on constraints

In this section, we study the regulatory relationships based on the constraint inequalities in formula (2) and how the target gene switches from one state to another. The target gene can switch in one of four ways: $0 \rightarrow 0$, $0 \rightarrow 1$, $1 \rightarrow 0$, or $0 \rightarrow 1$. Given an input state, inactive genes have no effect on the target gene, which may help reduce the constraint inequalities of the summation $\sum_j a_{ij}x_j(t)$ $(1 \leq j \leq k_i)$. Because the null input provides no constraints between a_{ij}, we only need to investigate the non-null input situations.

First, consider the simplest situation where there is only one regulatory gene x_{j_1}. If gene x_{j_1} is active and the target gene x_i switches from 0 to 1, then gene x_{j_1} must activate the target gene x_i (which means $a_{ij_1} = 1$). On the contrary, if the target gene x_i switches from 1 to 0, then it must be

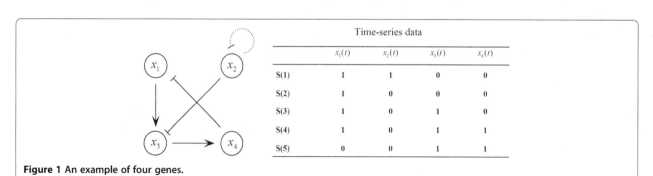

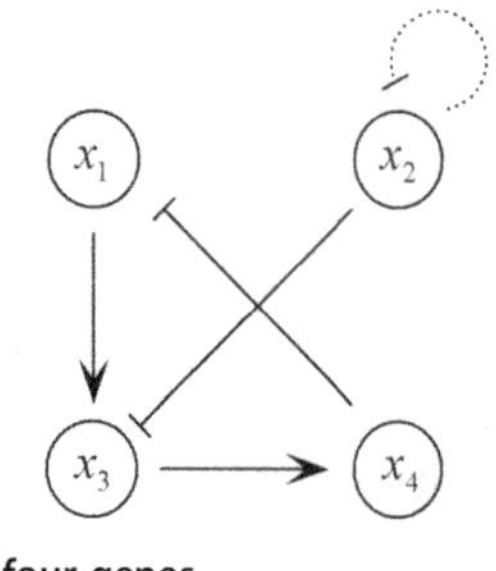

Time-series data

	$x_1(t)$	$x_2(t)$	$x_3(t)$	$x_4(t)$
S(1)	1	1	0	0
S(2)	1	0	0	0
S(3)	1	0	1	0
S(4)	1	0	1	1
S(5)	0	0	1	1

Figure 1 An example of four genes.

inhibited by x_{j_1} (which means $a_{ij_1} = -1$). When the target gene x_i remains in state 1, we have $a_{ij_1}x_{j_1} \geq 0$ (which means $a_{ij_1} = 1$). When the target gene x_i remains in state 0, we have $a_{ij_1}x_{j_1} \leq 0$ (which means $a_{ij_1} = -1$). We present the four possible regulatory relationships a_{ij_1} in Table 1.

When there are two regulatory genes x_{j_1} and x_{j_2}, we only consider the input states 01, 10, and 11. If only one input gene is active, such as $x_{j_1}x_{j_2} = 01$, then we can directly determine a_{ij_2} from Table 1, whereas a_{ij_1} remains totally nondeterminant because it has no effect on the target gene. If both gene x_{j_1} and gene x_{j_2} are active, then we need to know whether or not the target gene x_i switches its state. First, if x_i switches from 1 to 0, then we have $a_{ij_1} = a_{ij_2} = -1$ to satisfy the constraint $a_{ij_1} + a_{ij_2} < 0$. Similarly, if x_i switches from 0 to 1, then we have $a_{ij_1} = a_{ij_2} = 1$ to satisfy the constraint $a_{ij_1} + a_{ij_2} > 0$. Second, if x_i remains in state 0, then we have $a_{ij_1} = a_{ij_2} = -1$ or $a_{ij_1} = -a_{ij_2}$ because $a_{ij_1} + a_{ij_2} \leq 0$. Similarly, if x_i remains in state 1, then we have $a_{ij_1} = a_{ij_2} = 1$ or $a_{ij_1} = -a_{ij_2}$ because $a_{ij_1} + a_{ij_2} \leq 0$. We call these later cases 'semi-determined' because there are two possible combinations of a_{ij_1} and a_{ij_2} in each case. In Table 2, we present the 12 possible regulatory relationships of a_{ij_1} and a_{ij_2} for two input genes.

Analogously, the regulatory relationships for three input genes are shown in Table 3. There are 10 semi-determined cases, and most of them occur when the target gene x_i does not change. Some of the semi-determined cases in Tables 2 and 3 may become determined if some a_{ij} are determined. For example, given $a_{ij_1} + a_{ij_2} \leq 0$ for (3) in Table 2, we can determine $a_{ij_2} = 1$ if a_{ij_1} is determined to be 1. However, a_{ij_1} still remains semi-determined (either 1 or −1) if a_{ij_1} is determined to be −1. As the number of regulatory genes increases, the proportion of semi-determined cases increases significantly. We will not extend the above analysis to situations of more than three input genes. In most reference studies, the limit $k_i \leq 3$ is generally respected to mitigate model complexity, particularly for small sample sizes.

Given a target gene x_i and its predictor genes x_j ($1 \leq j \leq k_i$), we may determine the value of a_{ij} at each time point t ($1 \leq t \leq m-1$) by searching Tables 1, 2, or 3 across the whole time series $S = \{S(1), S(2), \ldots, S(m)\}$. Let N_{ij}^{-1}, N_{ij}^{1}, and $N_{ij}^{-1,1}$ denote the number of $a_{ij} = -1$, $a_{ij} = 1$, and $a_{ij} = -1$ or 1, respectively. The *degree of determination* of a regulatory relationship a_{ij} is defined as

$$d_{ij} = \left|N_{ij}^{-1} - N_{ij}^{1}\right|. \tag{3}$$

If $N_{ij}^{-1} > N_{ij}^{1}$, then a_{ij} is likely to be −1; otherwise, it is likely to be 1. The larger the value of d_{ij}, the greater the determination of a_{ij}. In order to reduce the semi-determined cases, we first find the one with the largest determination, say, a_{ij}, and determine its value by the majority rule. Then, we apply the value of a_{ij} to those inequalities including it to solve other semi-determined a_{ip} ($p \neq j$, $1 \leq p, j \leq k_i$). By repeating this process, we can reduce the number of semi-determined cases and determine the values of other a_{ip} accordingly.

Table 1 Regulatory relationships for one input gene

Number	$x_{j_1}(t)$	$x_i(t) \to x_i(t+1)$	a_{ij_1}
1	1	$0 \to 0$	−1
2	1	$0 \to 1$	1
3	1	$1 \to 0$	−1
4	1	$1 \to 1$	1

Table 2 Regulatory relationships for two input genes

Number	$x_{j_1}(t)$	$x_{j_2}(t)$	$x_i(t) \to x_i(t+1)$	a_{ij_1}	a_{ij_2}	Constraint
1	0	1	$0 \to 0$	No	−1	
2	1	0		−1	No	
3	1	1		−1 or 1	−1 or 1	$a_{ij_1} + a_{ij_2} \leq 0$
4	0	1	$0 \to 1$	No	1	
5	1	0		1	No	
6	1	1		1	1	
7	0	1	$1 \to 0$	No	−1	
8	1	0		−1	No	
9	1	1		−1	−1	
10	0	1	$1 \to 1$	No	1	
11	1	0		1	No	
12	1	1		−1 or 1	−1 or 1	$a_{ij_1} + a_{ij_2} \geq 0$

No, totally undetermined; −1 or 1, semi-determined.

3.3 Error analysis

Given a predictor set for gene x_i, the basic inconsistency is the discrepancy in the determination of a_{ij}, and we define the error resulting from such an inconsistency by $\varepsilon_{ij}^{-1,1} = \min\left(N_{ij}^{-1}, N_{ij}^{1}\right)$. A second kind of inconsistency arises from the null input. Specifically, the target gene x_i cannot flip its state under null input situations. Moreover, if it is negatively self-regulated (self-degradation), it cannot be active when its input genes are null. The number of such inconsistencies defines the error $\varepsilon_i^{\text{null}}$, which is listed in Table 4 for self-degradation and no self-degradation, respectively. The *total error* of a predictor set is defined by $\varepsilon = \varepsilon_i^{\text{null}} + \sum_j \varepsilon_{ij}^{-1,1}$. Generally, a consistent predicator set should have the minimal error and the minimal number of regulatory genes simultaneously.

Table 3 Regulatory relationships for three input genes

Number	$x_{j_1}(t)$	$x_{j_2}(t)$	$x_{j_3}(t)$	$x_i(t) \to x_i(t+1)$	a_{ij_1}	a_{ij_2}	a_{ij_3}	Constraint
1	0	0	1	$0 \to 0$	No	No	−1	
2	0	1	0		No	−1	No	
3	1	0	0		−1	No	No	
4	0	1	1		No	−1 or 1	−1 or 1	$a_{ij_2} + a_{ij_3} \leq 0$
5	1	0	1		−1 or 1	No	−1 or 1	$a_{ij_1} + a_{ij_3} \leq 0$
6	1	1	0		−1 or 1	−1 or 1	No	$a_{ij_1} + a_{ij_2} \leq 0$
7	1	1	1		−1 or 1	−1 or 1	−1 or 1	$a_{ij_1} + a_{ij_2} + a_{ij_3} < 0$
8	0	0	1	$0 \to 1$	No	No	1	
9	0	1	0		No	1	No	
10	1	0	0		1	No	No	
11	0	1	1		No	1	1	
12	1	0	1		1	No	1	
13	1	1	0		1	1	No	
14	1	1	1		−1 or 1	−1 or 1	−1 or 1	$a_{ij_1} + a_{ij_2} + a_{ij_3} > 0$
15	0	0	1	$1 \to 0$	No	No	−1	
16	0	1	0		No	−1	No	
17	1	0	0		−1	No	No	
18	0	1	1		No	−1	−1	
19	1	0	1		−1	No	−1	
20	1	1	0		−1	−1	No	
21	1	1	1		−1 or 1	−1 or 1	−1 or 1	$a_{ij_1} + a_{ij_2} + a_{ij_3} < 0$
22	0	0	1	$1 \to 1$	No	No	1	
23	0	1	0		No	1	No	
24	1	0	0		1	No	No	
25	0	1	1		No	−1 or 1	−1 or 1	$a_{ij_2} + a_{ij_3} \geq 0$
26	1	0	1		−1 or 1	No	−1 or 1	$a_{ij_1} + a_{ij_3} \geq 0$
27	1	1	0		−1 or 1	−1 or 1	No	$a_{ij_1} + a_{ij_2} \geq 0$
28	1	1	1		−1 or 1	−1 or 1	−1 or 1	$a_{ij_1} + a_{ij_2} + a_{ij_3} > 0$

No, totally undetermined; −1 or 1, semi-determined.

3.4 A small example

We now apply the above analysis to infer the predicator set for gene x_3 in Figure 1. Based on Tables 1,2,3,4, the results for all possible one- and two-input genes at each time point are presented in Tables 5,6,7,8, respectively. In those six possible predictor sets, the minimal error is achieved by x_1 and x_2, which are just the regulatory genes of x_3.

Table 4 Errors in the null-input situations

Number	$x_{j_1}(t) = \cdots = x_{j_{ki}}(t)$	$x_i(t) \to x_i(t+1)$	$\varepsilon_i^{\text{null}}$	
			Self-degradation regulated	No self-degradation
1	0	$0 \to 0$	0	0
2	0	$0 \to 1$	1	1
3	0	$1 \to 0$	0	1
4	0	$1 \to 1$	1	0

3.5 Inference algorithm

Given a time series $S = \{S(1), S(2), \ldots, S(m)\}$, the minimal error predictor sets may not be unique. Each of them can be viewed as fitting the target gene in a different way. We employ the heuristic that if one gene occurs

Table 5 Regulatory relationships a_{3j} for one input x_1 (or x_2 or x_4) at each time step

t	$x_1(t)$	$x_2(t)$	$x_4(t)$	$x_3(t) \to x_3(t+1)$	a_{31}	$\varepsilon_3^{\text{null}}$	a_{32}	$\varepsilon_3^{\text{null}}$	a_{34}	$\varepsilon_3^{\text{null}}$
1	1	1	0	$0 \to 0$	−1	0	−1	0		0
2	1	0	0	$0 \to 1$	1	0		1		1
3	1	0	0	$1 \to 1$	1	0		0		1
4	1	0	1	$1 \to 1$	1	0		0	1	0

Table 6 Regulatory relationships a_{3j} for two inputs x_1 and x_2 at each time step

t	$x_1(t)$	$x_2(t)$	$x_3(t) \rightarrow x_3(t+1)$	a_{31}	a_{32}	Constraint	ε_3^{null}
1	1	1	$0 \rightarrow 0$	−1,1	*−1,1*	$a_{31} + a_{32} \leq 0$	0
2	1	0	$0 \rightarrow 1$	1	No		0
3	1	0	$1 \rightarrow 1$	1	No		0
4	1	0	$1 \rightarrow 1$	1	No		0

The italicized value is solved from the determination $a_{31} = 1$.

frequently in those sets, then it is highly probably to be a true regulatory gene. Combining them may give a more reliable prediction and can also help alleviate the constraint of using at most three input genes for a target gene. Given a target gene x_i, we propose the following algorithm to infer its regulatory gene set:

1. Calculate the total error of each combination of one, two, or three regulatory gene sets $P(x_i)$.
2. Sort the predictor sets in ascending order of their errors.
3. If a gene appears in the first l sets with a frequency greater than or equal to 50%, then it is selected as a regulatory gene.

4 Implementation

As mentioned in the introduction, many algorithms have been proposed to infer gene regulatory networks. A recent study shows that the best-fit algorithm appears to give the best results for the recovery of regulatory relationships among REVEAL, BIC, MDL, uMDL, and Best-Fit [27]. In this paper, we compare the performance of the three-rule algorithm, the best-fit algorithm and the proposed algorithm based on both synthetic networks as well as on a well-studied budding yeast cell cycle network.

We have implemented the three-rule algorithm and our proposed algorithm based on the PBN Toolbox (http://code.google.com/p/pbn-matlab-toolbox/), which includes the implementation of best-fit algorithm and the calculation of the steady state distribution and other intervention modules for Boolean networks. Genetic regulatory networks are commonly believed to have sparse connectivity topology. To evaluate the inference algorithms based on simulated time series of network states, we have restricted the random BNs to resemble this property of biological networks. Specifically, we have generated random BNs with a scale-free topology, and each gene has at most five predictors: $= max_{i=1}^{n} k_i \leq 5$. We uniformly assign each gene 1 to K regulators that upregulate (1) or downregulate (−1) it. The average connectivity of random networks is $(1+K)/2$.

Table 7 Regulatory relationships a_{3j} for two inputs x_1 and x_4 at each time step

t	$x_1(t)$	$x_4(t)$	$x_3(t) \rightarrow x_3(t+1)$	a_{31}	a_{34}	Constraint	ε_3^{null}
1	1	0	$0 \rightarrow 0$	−1	No		0
2	1	0	$0 \rightarrow 1$	1	No		0
3	1	0	$1 \rightarrow 1$	1	No		0
4	1	1	$1 \rightarrow 1$	−1,1	−1,1	$a_{31} + a_{34} \geq 0$	0

Table 8 Regulatory relationships a_{3j} for two inputs x_2 and x_4 at each time step

t	$x_2(t)$	$x_4(t)$	$x_3(t) \rightarrow x_3(t+1)$	a_{32}	a_{34}	Constraint	ε_3^{null}
1	1	0	$0 \rightarrow 0$	−1	No		0
2	0	0	$0 \rightarrow 1$				1
3	0	0	$1 \rightarrow 1$				0
4	0	1	$1 \rightarrow 1$	No	1		0

In order to compare the performance of the three algorithms with the ground-truth network, we use the following three distances [28,29]:

(1) The normalized-edge Hamming distance,

$$\mu_{ham}^{e} = \frac{FN + FP}{P + N},$$

where FN and FP represent the number of false-negative and false-positive wires, respectively. P and N represent the total number of positive and negative wires, respectively.

Table 9 Average number of true-positive and false-positive connections for three algorithms

K	Noise (%)	Algorithm	$m = 10$		$m = 20$		$m = 30$		$m = 40$	
			TP	FP	TP	FP	TP	FP	TP	FP
3	0	Three-rule	6.2	0	8.7	0.6	11.3	1.6	13.3	3.0
		New	8.7	3.1	10.5	3.1	11.8	3.3	12.5	3.3
		Best-fit	8.1	4.6	10.2	5.4	12.2	6.4	13.3	7.0
	5	Three-rule	2.6	2.7	7.3	11.5	10.6	20.7	12.5	30.3
		New	7.0	7.5	8.7	6.9	10.1	6.3	10.7	6.3
		Best-fit	7.1	11.1	9.2	15.1	10.8	15.7	11.6	15.9
	10	Three-rule	1.8	3.6	6.5	17.6	10.5	31.6	12.4	39.8
		New	5.5	10.0	6.9	9.5	8.1	9.2	8.4	9.1
		Best-fit	6.0	15.2	8.1	19.1	9.2	19.3	9.9	19.0
5	0	Three-rule	6.7	0.1	8.9	0.6	11.0	1.3	12.6	2.3
		New	8.3	2.7	9.9	3.0	10.9	3.4	11.4	3.9
		Best-fit	8.2	4.6	10.1	5.4	11.8	6.4	12.7	6.9
	5	Three-rule	3.0	3.2	7.86	11.8	10.7	20.5	12.8	28.6
		New	6.7	7.6	8.4	7.0	9.3	6.7	9.8	6.3
		Best-fit	7.1	11.5	9.2	15.4	10.4	15.7	11.1	16.1
	10	Three-rule	2.7	2.8	6.9	16.5	10.6	31.6	12.4	39.4
		New	5.3	9.9	7.0	9.5	7.5	9.3	8.1	9.1
		Best-fit	7.2	11.5	8.2	18.9	9.0	19.3	9.4	19.4

This Hamming distance reflects the accuracy of the recovered regulatory relationships.

(2) The normalized Hamming distance of state transitions,

$$\mu_{\mathrm{ham}}^{\mathrm{st}} = \frac{1}{n*2^n}\sum_{i=1}^{n}\sum_{k=1}^{2^n}\left[f_i(\mathrm{x_k})\oplus f_i'(\mathrm{x_k})\right],$$

where $f_i(\bullet)$ and $f_i'(\bullet)$ represent the Boolean function of gene i in the ground-truth network and the inferred network, respectively; $\mathrm{x_k}$ represents a binary state vector, and $\oplus$ denotes modulo-2 addition. This Hamming distance indicates the accuracy of the inferred network for predicting the next state of the ground-truth network.

(3) The steady-state distribution distance,

$$\mu^{\mathrm{ssd}} = \sum_{k=1}^{2^n}\left|\pi_k - \pi_k'\right|,$$

where π_k and π_k' are the steady-state distribution of state x_k in the ground-truth network and the inferred network, respectively. The steady-state distribution distance reflects the degree of an inferred network approaching the long-run behavior of the ground-truth network.

5 Results and discussion

5.1 Simulated results

Owing to the computational complexity and the network state space, which increases exponentially with the number of genes or the network size, all our simulations are based on networks with $n = 10$ genes. We generate 300 random Boolean networks respectively with maximal input degree $K = 3$ and $K = 5$. For each simulated network, we generate about 4 time series so that the total time points add up to 40. Given a specific sample data, the noise is added by flipping the value of each bit with probability 0.05 and 0.10, respectively. The steady-state distribution is calculated by a perturbation parameter $p = 0.\ 0001$. For the proposed algorithm, we selected the first $l = 10$ minimal error predictor sets. For best fit, we selected the minimal error predictor sets from $k = 1, 2, 3$. In Table 9, we list the average number of true-positive and false-positive connections for $K = 3$ and $K = 5$ in different noise intensities.

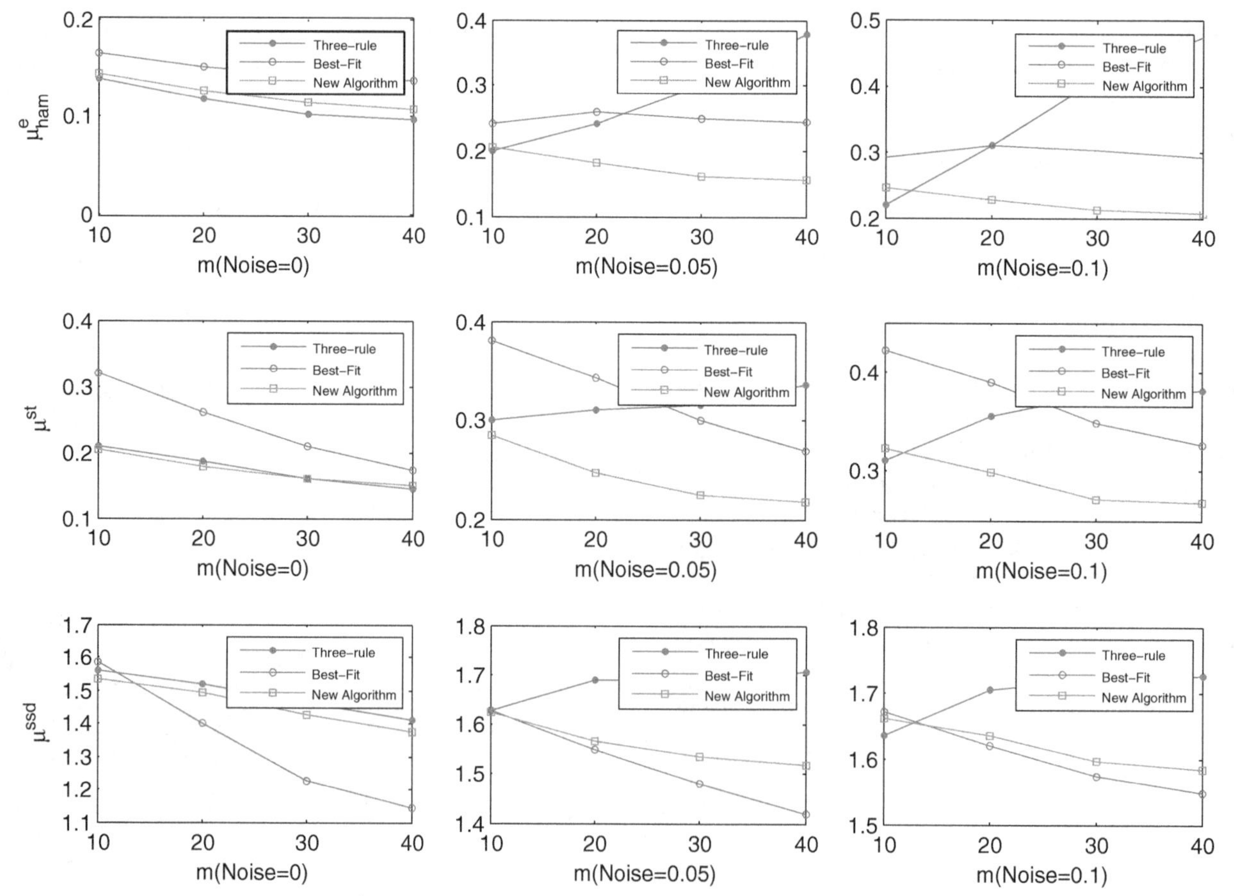

Figure 2 Comparison of $\mu_{\mathrm{ham}}^{\mathrm{e}}$, $\mu_{\mathrm{ham}}^{\mathrm{st}}$, μ^{ssd} for the three algorithms with 0%, 5%, and 10% noises ($K = 3$).

Figure 2 shows the performance of three algorithms on networks with $K=3$ under different noise intensities according to three distance metrics: the normalized-edge Hamming distance $\mu_{\text{ham}}^{\text{e}}$, the normalized Hamming distance of state transition $\mu_{\text{ham}}^{\text{st}}$, and the steady-state distribution distance μ^{ssd}. The performance of the three-rule algorithm and the proposed algorithm is very close when there is no noise. However, it differs dramatically in noisy data. Specifically, the performance of the proposed algorithm increases as the sample size increases while that of the three-rule algorithm decreases. The main reason lies in the fact that the proposed algorithm infers the regulatory relation based on the entire time series instead of on a small perturbation between two time points, which makes it more robust against noise than the three-rule algorithm. Given a specific noise intensity η, with more samples, there are more noisy perturbed bits, so, more incorrect connections will be inferred by the three-rule algorithm. Table 9 shows that the number of the false positives of the three-rule algorithm increases more quickly than that of the true positives as the sample size increases. This is the main factor which makes its performance deteriorate even though the sample size increases. Consequently, the three-rule algorithm is very sensitive to noise in the data, and increasing sample size makes no improvement in its performance.

Compared with the best-fit algorithm, the proposed algorithm performs better with respect to $\mu_{\text{ham}}^{\text{e}}$ and $\mu_{\text{ham}}^{\text{st}}$. In a restricted Boolean network model, the output of states with $\sum_j a_{ij}x_i(t)=0$ is determined by the current state of the target gene x_i. This means that given the same input state, x_i may be 1 at one time and be 0 at another time. The best-fit algorithm does not allow such situation, and it will treat such a case in the data as an error. If the target gene x_i has three regulators and one downregulates it, then there will be 3 such states out of the 8 possible input states. The influence of such cases on the performance of best fit algorithm can not be neglected. Additionally, the best-fit algorithm cannot deal with the inconsistency listed in Figure 3. These two factors hurt its performances as compared to the proposed algorithm on $\mu_{\text{ham}}^{\text{e}}$ and $\mu_{\text{ham}}^{\text{st}}$. Table 9 shows that the number of the true positives of both algorithms is

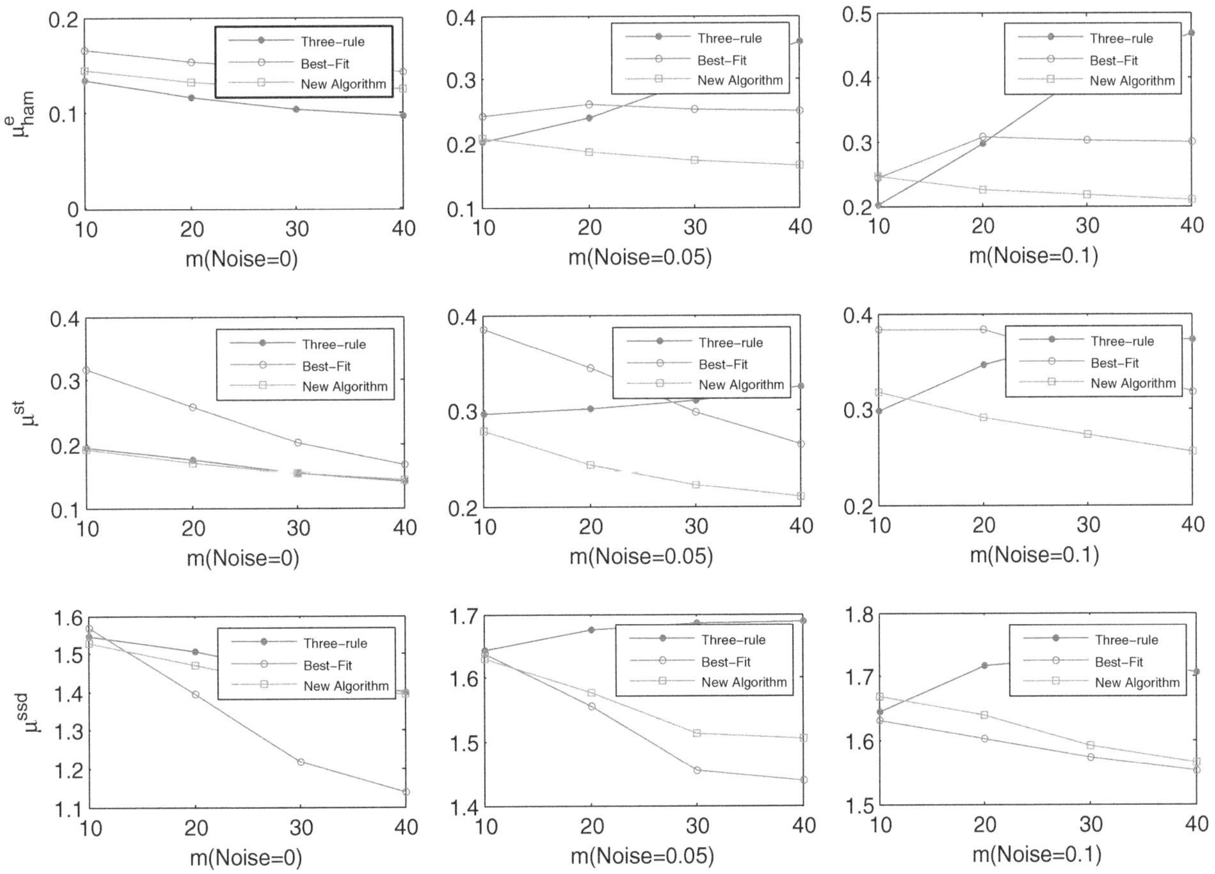

Figure 3 Comparison of $\mu_{\text{ham}}^{\text{e}}$, $\mu_{\text{ham}}^{\text{st}}$, μ^{ssd} for the three algorithms with 0%, 5%, and 10% noises ($K=5$).

almost the same, but the number of false positives of the best-fit algorithm is larger than that of the proposed algorithm.

Concerning the steady state distribution distance μ^{ssd}, the proposed algorithm performs not so well as the best-fit algorithm. However, their difference decreases as the noise intensity increases. As pointed in [27], the inferred networks with relative more connections can explain the observed data better with respect to steady-state distribution distance μ^{ssd}, even though some are incorrect connections. Because the best-fit algorithm infers more connection than the proposed algorithm (see Table 9), it performs better on μ^{ssd} than the latter. On the other hand, the proposed algorithm is more robust than the best-fit algorithm as it combines those minimal error sets to determine the regulatory gene instead of selecting one. When noise intensity increases, the performance of the best-fit algorithm will drop more quickly than that of the proposed algorithm, which leads to their performance on μ^{ssd} converges.

Figure 4 shows the performance of three algorithms on networks with $K = 5$, which are analogous to the trends observed in Figure 2. The only difference is that the performance of the three algorithms decreases because the networks' complexity makes them hard to infer. In summary, the proposed algorithm performs better than the three-rule algorithm on the three distance metrics in noisy

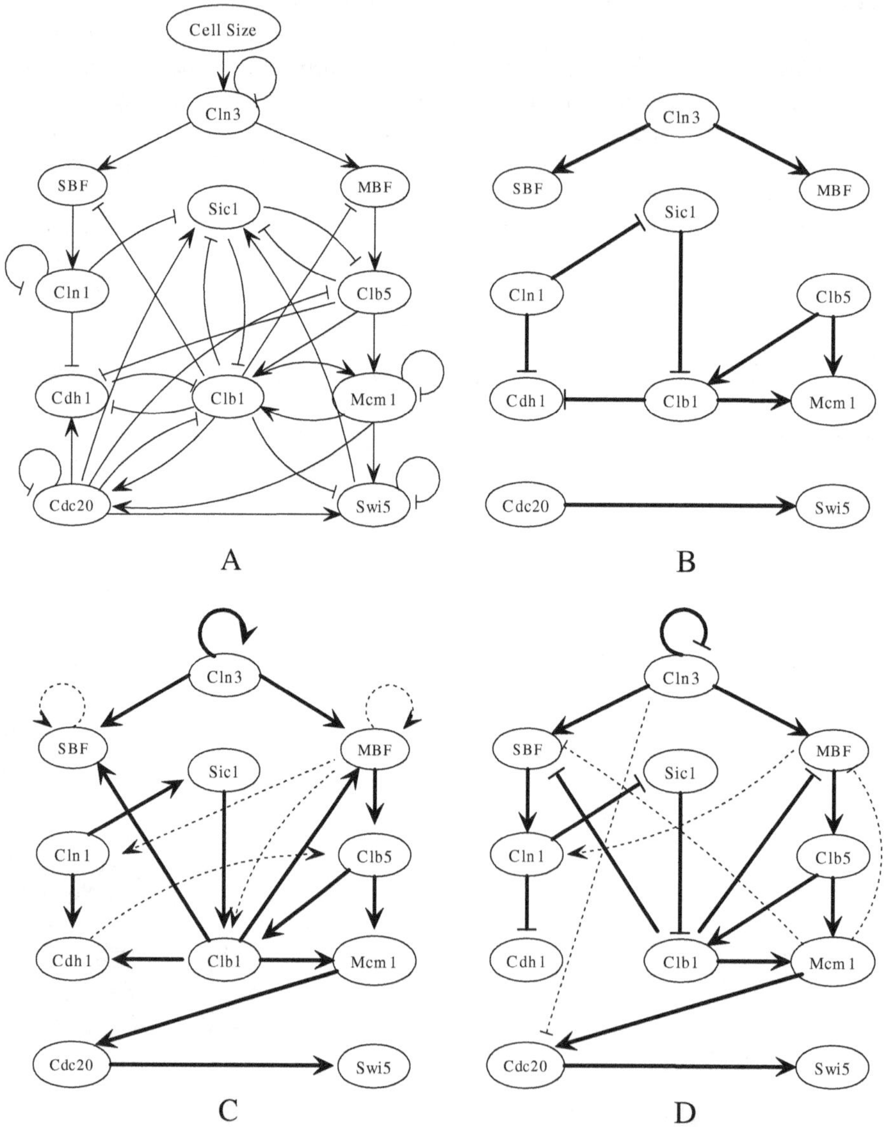

Figure 4 The original and inferred cell cycle networks of budding yeast. (A) Original network. **(B)** Network inferred by three-rule method. **(C)** Network inferred by the best-fit algorithm. **(D)** Network inferred by the proposed algorithm. In **(A)**, **(B)**, and **(D)**, arrows denote positive regulation; 'T' lines are negative regulation; and 'T loops are self-degradation. In **(B)**, **(C)**, and **(D)**, bold solid lines denote the correct inferred regulatory relationships, and the light dashed lines denote the incorrectly inferred regulatory relationships.

Table 10 Temporal evolution of state for cell cycle

Time	Cln3	MBF	SBF	Cln1	Cdh1	Swi5	Cdc20	Clb5	Sic1	Clb1	Mcm1	Phase
1	1	0	0	0	1	0	0	0	1	0	0	Start
2	0	1	1	0	1	0	0	0	1	0	0	G1
3	0	1	1	1	0	0	0	0	1	0	0	G1
4	0	1	1	1	0	0	0	0	0	0	0	G1
5	0	1	1	1	0	0	0	1	0	0	0	S
6	0	1	1	1	0	0	0	1	0	1	1	G2
7	0	0	0	1	0	0	1	1	0	1	1	M
8	0	0	0	0	0	1	1	0	0	1	1	M
9	0	0	0	0	0	1	1	0	1	1	1	M
10	0	0	0	0	0	1	1	0	1	0	1	M
11	0	0	0	0	1	1	1	0	1	0	0	M
12	0	0	0	0	1	1	0	0	1	0	0	M
13	0	0	0	0	1	0	0	0	1	0	0	G1

situations, whereas it performs less well than the best-fit algorithm on the steady-state distribution distance. This suggests that it is more feasible to infer the structure of restricted Boolean network model than the three-rule algorithm and best-fit algorithm.

5.2 Cell cycle model of budding yeast

The cell cycle is a vital biological process in which one cell grows and divides into two daughter cells. It consists of four phases, G1, S, G2, and M, and is regulated by a highly complex network that is highly conserved among the eukaryotes. From the 800 genes involved in the cell cycle process of budding yeast, Li et al. constructed a network of 11 key regulators: Cln3, MBF, SBF, Cln1, Cdh1, Swi5, Cdc20, Clb5, Sic1, Clb1, and Mcm1 [18]. This restricted Boolean network model (shown in Figure 4A) has an attractor whose biggest basin corresponds to the biological G1 stationary state. The temporal sequence in Table 10 is a pathway from this basin, which follows the biological trajectory of the cell cycle network.

We have applied the three algorithms to the above artificial time-series data and show the inferred networks in Figure 4. In the simplified model of the budding yeast cell cycle, there are a total of 34 regulatory relationships (or connections). The three-rule algorithm inferred 10 relationships, all correct (see Figure 4B). The best-fit algorithm inferred 15 correct and 5 incorrect relationships (see Figure 4C). The proposed algorithm inferred 15 correct and 4 incorrect relationships (see Figure 4D). Both best-fit and the proposed algorithms inferred more true regulatory relationships than the three-rule algorithm with some incorrect connections. For studying regulatory relationships, this may be more advantageous because more potential regulatory relationships are made available for biologists to check in the wet lab.

We also ran 100 simulations with 5% and 10% noises for this pathway. Even for the same pathway data, the result of each noisy pathway data differs dramatically. This is not surprising because noise significantly influences the determination of regulatory relations for all algorithms. The performance of the three algorithms on μ^{e}_{ham}, μ^{st}_{ham}, and μ^{ssd} is listed Table 11. The relative performance of the three algorithms for this pathway data is also consistent with the previous simulation results.

5.3 Computational issues

When inferring real networks with moderate size, the time complexity of algorithms is a key issue. Almost all

Table 11 The performance of the three algorithms for the yeast-pathway data

	Noise								
	0%			5%			10%		
	Distance								
	μ^{e}_{ham}	μ^{st}_{ham}	μ^{ssd}	μ^{e}_{ham}	μ^{st}_{ham}	μ^{ssd}	μ^{e}_{ham}	μ^{st}_{ham}	μ^{ssd}
Three-rule	0.198	0.313	1.394	0.27	0.378	1.454	0.29	0.402	1.472
New algorithm	0.19	0.250	1.372	0.252	0.304	1.386	0.292	0.334	1.438
Best-fit	0.198	0.229	1.245	0.298	0.341	1.263	0.365	0.403	1.298

Table 12 Algorithm timings (seconds)

n	$N = 20$			$N = 40$			SSD
	Three-rule	Best-fit	Proposed	Three-rule	Best-fit	Proposed	
11	1.04	0.09	1.11	2.7	0.14	1.67	25
12	2.5	0.11	2.63	4.1	0.18	2.15	160
13	6.3	0.15	3.55	7.5	0.23	4.11	1,500

algorithms proposed to date possess exponential complexity. The time complexity of the proposed algorithm and best-fit algorithm is $\left(n \cdot C_n^k \cdot m\right)$. The most time-consuming process for the three-rule algorithm is to solve the constraint inequalities, and its time complexity is $O(n \cdot c^n \cdot m^2)$ $(1 < c < 2)$. From this point of view, the three-rule algorithm is more time consuming than the other two.

The proposed algorithm is similar in workflow to the best-fit algorithm; however, additional computation time results from three factors: (1) determination of the possible regulatory relationships, (2) determination during error estimation if an output state is correct for a given model according to Equation (2), and (3) combination of the first ten least-error models in the last step.

In practice, however, algorithm complexity is not the limiting factor. As shown in Table 12, for 11, 12, and 13 genes, and for $N = 20$ and $N = 40$, the proposed algorithm's computation time is between the best-fit and the three-rule algorithms, but the overriding computational issue is computation of the steady-state distribution, which is often required for application. It is for this reason that interest has focused on reducing network complexity [29–31].

6 Conclusion

The model space of Boolean networks is huge and from the point of view of evolution, it is unimaginable for nature to select its operational mechanisms from such a large space. Restricted Boolean networks, as a simplified model, have recently been extensively used to study the dynamical behavior of the yeast cell cycle process. In this paper, we propose a systematic method to infer the restricted Boolean network from time-series data. We compare the performance of the three-rule, best-fit, and the proposed algorithms both on simulated networks and on an artificial model of budding yeast. Results show that our algorithm performs better than the three-rule and best-fit algorithms according to the distance metrics μ^{e}_{ham} and μ^{st}_{ham}, but slightly less well than the best-fit algorithm according to μ^{ssd}. This result indicates that the proposed algorithm may be more appropriate for recovering regulatory relationships between genes under the restricted Boolean network model.

The main advantage of the proposed algorithm is that it is more robust to noise than both the three-rule algorithm and best-fit algorithm. The proposed algorithm infers the regulatory relationships according to the consecutive state transitions of the target gene, instead of the small perturbations between two similar states in the three-rule algorithm. Simulation results show that noise in the data may induce many incorrect constraints by the three-rule algorithm. This hinders its application to noisy samples. Moreover, the proposed algorithm can capture the intrinsic state transition defined in Equation 2, whereas the best-fit algorithm cannot. Hence, because the inference processes of both algorithms try to find the minimal-error predictor set, the proposed algorithm can distinguish error in the data more accurately than the best-fit algorithm. Additionally, combination of the minimal error predictor sets in the proposed algorithm also improves its robustness.

In the Boolean formalism, a single time series (or trajectory) can be treated as a random walk across state space. It is not possible to recover the complex biological system from just one short trajectory by any method. Using heterogeneous data and some *a priori* knowledge is typically a necessity. *A priori* knowledge can be incorporated into the proposed algorithm and helps by reducing the search space. For instance, an algorithm might assume a prescribed attractor structure [32]. In our case, if we know that x regulates y, then we only consider those combinations containing x, thereby reducing the search space. Additionally, different methods may focus on different aspects of the inference process. For example, the best-fit algorithm and CoD are mainly concerned with the fitness of the data, whereas MDL-based methods intend to reduce structural risks. Future work will involve combining MDL with the proposed algorithm to reduce the rate of false positives.

Competing interests

The authors declare that they have no competing interests.

Acknowledgements

This work was funded in part by the National Science Foundation of China (Grant No. 61272018, No. 60970065, and No. 61174162) and the Zhejiang Provincial Natural Science Foundation of China (Grant No. R1110261 and No. LY13F010007) and support from China Scholarship Council.

Author details

[1]Department of Physics and Electronic Information Engineering, Wenzhou University, Wenzhou, Zhejiang 325035, China. [2]Department of Electrical and Computer Engineering, Texas A&M University, College Station, TX 33101, USA. [3]Computational Biology Division, Translational Genomics Research Institute, Phoenix, AZ 77843, USA.

References

1. S Ilya, ER Dougherty, *Genomic Signal Processing (Princeton Series in Applied Mathematics)* (Princeton University Press, Princeton, 2007)
2. S Ilya, ER Dougherty, *Probabilistic Boolean Networks: The Modeling and Control of Gene Regulatory Networks* (Siam, Philadelphia, 2010)
3. L Shoudan, F Stefanie, S Roland, *REVEAL, a general reverse engineering algorithm for inference of genetic network architectures, in Pacific Symposium on Biocomputing* (World Scientific, Hawaii, 1998), p. 2
4. AA Margolin, N Ilya, B Katia, W Chris, S Gustavo, DF Riccardo, C Andrea, ARACNE: an algorithm for the reconstruction of gene regulatory networks in a mammalian cellular context. BMC Bioinforma **7**, S7 (2006)
5. W Zhao, E Serpedin, ER Dougherty, Recovering genetic regulatory networks from chromatin immunoprecipitation and steady-state microarray data. EURASIP J. Bioinforma. Syst. Biol. (2008). doi:10.1155/2008/248747
6. C Vijender, G Preetam, P Edward, GP Gong, Y Deng, C Zhang, A novel gene network inference algorithm using predictive minimum description length approach. BMC Syst. Biol. **4**, S7 (2010)
7. C Vijender, Z Chaoyang, G Preetam, EJ Perkins, P Gong, Y Deng, Gene regulatory network inference using predictive minimum description length principle and conditional mutual information, in *International Joint Conference on Bioinformatics, Systems Biology and Intelligent Computing (IJCBS)*, ed. by J Zhang, G Li, JY Yang (IEEE Computer Society, Piscataway, 2009), pp. 487–490
8. J Dougherty, I Tabus, J Astola, A universal minimum description length-based algorithm for inferring the structure of genetic networks, in *IEEE International Workshop on Genomic Signal Processing and Statistics (GENSIPS)*, ed. by Y Huang (IEEE, Piscataway, 2007), pp. 1–2
9. I Tabus, J Astola, On the use of MDL principle in gene expression prediction. EURASIP J Appl Signal Process **2001**, 297–303 (2001)
10. W Zhao, S Erchin, ER Dougherty, Inferring gene regulatory networks from time series data using the minimum description length principle. Bioinformatics **22**, 2129–2135 (2006)
11. RE Dougherty, K Seungchan, C Yidong, Coefficient of determination in nonlinear signal processing. Signal Process. **80**, 2219–2235 (2000)
12. S Kim, ER Dougherty, ML Bittner, Y Chen, K Sivakumar, P Meltzer, JM Trent, General nonlinear framework for the analysis of gene interaction via multivariate expression arrays. J. Biomed. Opt. **5**, 411–424 (2000)
13. I Shmulevich, ER Dougherty, K Seungchan, W Zhang, Probabilistic Boolean networks: a rule-based uncertainty model for gene regulatory networks. Bioinformatics **18**, 261–274 (2002)
14. H Lähdesmäki, I Shmulevich, O Yli-Harja, Learning gene regulatory networks under the Boolean network model. Mach. Learn. **52**, 147–167 (2003)
15. I Shmulevich, SA Kauffman, A Maximino, Eukaryotic cells are dynamically ordered or critical but not chaotic. Proc. Natl. Acad. Sci. U. S. A. **102**, 13439–13444 (2005)
16. M Nykter, ND Price, A Maximino et al., Gene expression dynamics in the macrophage exhibit criticality. Proc. Natl. Acad. Sci. **105**, 1897–1900 (2008)
17. W Liu, H Lähdesmäki, ER Dougherty, I Shmulevich, Inference of Boolean networks using sensitivity regularization. EURASIP J. Bioinforma. Syst. Biol. (2008). doi:10.1155/2008/780541
18. F Li, T Long, L Ying, Q Ouyang, C Tang, The yeast cell-cycle network is robustly designed. Proc. Natl. Acad. Sci. U. S. A. **101**, 4781–4786 (2004)
19. Y Zhang, M Qian, Q Ouyang, M Deng, F Li, C Tang, Stochastic model of yeast cell-cycle network. Physica D: Nonlinear Phenomena **219**, 35–39 (2006)
20. L Kai-Yeung, G Surya, T Chao, Function constrains network architecture and dynamics: a case study on the yeast cell cycle Boolean network. Phys. Rev. E. **75**, 051907 (2007)
21. S Bornholdt, Boolean network models of cellular regulation: prospects and limitations. J. R. Soc. Interface **5**, S85–S94 (2008)
22. MI Davidich, B Stefan, Boolean network model predicts cell cycle sequence of fission yeast. PLoS One **3**, e1672 (2008)
23. H Ronaldo Fumio, S Henrique, H Carlos HA, Budding yeast cell cycle modeled by context-sensitive probabilistic Boolean network, in *IEEE International Workshop on Genomic Signal Processing and Statistics (GENSIPS)*, ed. by U Braga-Neto (IEEE, Piscataway, 2009), pp. 1–4
24. RG Todd, H Tomáš, Ergodic sets as cell phenotype of budding yeast cell cycle. PLoS One **7**, e45780 (2012)
25. CHA Higa, VHP Louzada, TP Andrade, RF Hashimoto, Constraint-based analysis of gene interactions using restricted Boolean networks and time-series data. BMC Proc. **5**(Suppl 2), S5 (2011). doi:10.1186/1753-6561-5-S2-S5
26. E Niklas, S Niklas, An extensible SAT-solver, in *Theory and Applications of Satisfiability Testing*, ed. by E Giunchiglia, A Tacchella (Springer, New York, 2004), pp. 502–518
27. ER Dougherty, Validation of gene regulatory networks: scientific and inferential. Brief. Bioinform. **12**, 245–252 (2011)
28. Q Xiaoning, ER Dougherty, Validation of gene regulatory network inference based on controllability. Front. Genet. **4**, 272 (2013). doi:10.3389/fgene.2013.00272
29. N Ghaffari, I Ivanov, X Qian, ER Dougherty, A CoD-based reduction algorithm for designing stationary control policies on Boolean networks. Bioinformatics **26**, 1556–1563 (2010)
30. I Ivanov, P Simeonov, N Ghaffari, Q Xiaoning, ER Dougherty, Selection policy-induced reduction mappings for Boolean networks. Signal Process. IEEE Trans. **58**, 4871–4882 (2010)
31. X Qian, N Ghaffari, I Ivanov, ER Dougherty, State reduction for network intervention in probabilistic Boolean networks. Bioinformatics **26**, 3098–3104 (2010)
32. R Pal, I Ivanov, A Datta, ML Bittner, ER Dougherty, Generating Boolean networks with a prescribed attractor structure. Bioinformatics **21**, 4021–4025 (2005)

Using the minimum description length principle to reduce the rate of false positives of best-fit algorithms

Jie Fang[1], Hongjia Ouyang[1], Liangzhong Shen[1], Edward R Dougherty[2,3] and Wenbin Liu[1,2*]

Abstract

The inference of gene regulatory networks is a core problem in systems biology. Many inference algorithms have been proposed and all suffer from false positives. In this paper, we use the minimum description length (MDL) principle to reduce the rate of false positives for best-fit algorithms. The performance of these algorithms is evaluated *via* two metrics: the normalized-edge Hamming distance and the steady-state distribution distance. Results for synthetic networks and a well-studied budding-yeast cell cycle network show that MDL-based filtering is more effective than filtering based on conditional mutual information (CMI). In addition, MDL-based filtering provides better inference than the MDL algorithm itself.

Keywords: Boolean network; Best-fit; Minimum description length principle; Conditional mutual information

1 Introduction

A key goal in systems biology is to characterize the molecular mechanisms that govern specific cellular behavior and processes. Models of gene regulatory networks run the gamut from coarse-grained discrete networks to detailed descriptions of such networks by stochastic differential equations [1]. Boolean networks and the more general class of probabilistic Boolean networks are among the most popular approaches for modeling gene networks because they provide a structured way to study biological phenomena (e.g., the cell cycle) and diseases (e.g., cancer), ultimately leading to systems-based therapeutic strategies. The inference of gene networks from high-throughput genomic data is an ill-posed problem known as reverse engineering. It is particularly challenging when dealing with small sample sizes because the number of variables in the system (e.g., the number of genes) typically is much greater than the number of observations [2]. Many inference algorithms have been proposed to elucidate the regulatory relationships between genes, such as Reveal [3], ARACNE [4], the minimum description length principle (MDL) [5-9], the coefficient of determination (CoD) [10,11], and the best-fit extension [12,13].

False positives are a common problem in inference, especially when dealing with small sample sizes and noisy conditions. In fact, false positives are a kind of structural redundancy. Given three genes, x_1, x_2, and x_3, they may interact in a chain-like manner, such as $x_1 \rightarrow x_2 \rightarrow x_3$ or $x_1 \leftarrow x_2 \leftarrow x_3$; or in a hub-based way, such as $x_1 \rightarrow x_2 \leftarrow x_3$ or $x_1 \leftarrow x_2 \rightarrow x_3$. Indirect interactions between two genes may produce some correlation in their expression data, which can lead to a false regulation detection by inference algorithms. The data-processing inequality (DPI) was first used in ARACNE, which aims to reduce the false positives produced by chain interaction [4]. Later, conditional mutual information (CMI) was proposed to tackle the false positives produced by both the chain-like and hub-based interactions [14]. Because the conditioning gene, x_2, is usually not known, a greedy search strategy was adopted to check if the CMI between x_1 and x_3 conditioned on some other genes was below a given threshold. To check the CMI on other unrelated genes is problematic. Not only is it computationally burdensome, it also suffers from an enormous multiple-comparisons problem. Moreover, since the interaction strength between genes generally varies a lot, their being

* Correspondence: wbliu6910@126.com
[1]Department of Physics and Electronic information engineering, Wenzhou University, Wenzhou, Zhejiang 325035, China
[2]Department of Electrical and Computer Engineering, Texas A&M University, College Station, TX 33101, USA
Full list of author information is available at the end of the article

both strong and weak interactions, how to set an appropriate threshold is a key problem.

A recent study shows that the best-fit algorithm appears to give the best results for recovering regulatory relationships in comparison to the aforementioned algorithms [15]. In the present paper, we propose to reduce the false positives of the best-fit algorithm by using the MDL principle. Simulation results show that it is more effective than the CMI-based method and can reduce the false positives in the MDL algorithm in [5]. In effect, the false-positive reducing procedure acts as a filter for removing false positives.

The aim of filtering in the present framework is to reduce the number of false positive connections. As with any false-positive reducing algorithm, this will invariably increase the number of false negatives, meaning more missing connections. Thus, two questions must be addressed. First, what benefits accrue from reducing the number of false positives? Second, does the increase in false negatives significantly impact inference performance?

A salient problem in translational genomics is the utilization of gene regulatory networks in determining therapeutic intervention strategies [2,16,17]. A big obstacle in deriving optimal treatment strategies from networks is the computational complexity arising directly from network complexity. Hence, significant effort has been focused on network reduction [18,19]. As with any compression scheme, reduction methods sacrifice information in return for computational tractability. Because genes are removed from the network based upon their regulatory relations with other genes, false positives are particularly troublesome. First, they increase the amount of reduction necessary and second, they compete with true positive connections for retention in the reduced network. While it is true that an increase in false negatives is not beneficial, a missing connection creates no additional computational burden (in fact, reduces computation) and plays no role in the reduction procedure.

Now, for the caveat, all of this is fine, so long as the accuracy of the original inference algorithm is not adversely impacted. Practically, this means that, relative to some distance function between a ground-truth network and an inferred network (which quantifies inference accuracy), the distance is not increased when using the modified false-positive reducing algorithm in place of the original algorithm. In this paper, we will consider two distance functions, one based on the hamming distance between the ground-truth and inferred networks and the other based on the difference between the steady-state distributions of the ground-truth and inferred networks.

This paper is organized as follows: Background information and necessary definitions are given in Section 2. The implementation of MDL, the best-fit algorithm, and CMI- and MDL-based filtering is then introduced in Section 3. Results from simulated networks and from the cell cycle model of budding yeast are presented in Section 4. Finally, concluding remarks are given in Section 5.

2 Background

2.1 Boolean networks

A Boolean network $G(V, F)$ is defined by a set of nodes $V = \{x_1, \dots, x_n\}$, $x_i \in \{0, 1\}$, and a set of Boolean functions $F = \{f_1, \dots, f_n\}$, $f_i : \{0,1\}^{k_i} \rightarrow \{0,1\}$ Each node x_i represents the expression state of a gene, where $x_i = 0$ means that the gene is off and $x_i = 1$ means it is on. To update its value, each node x_i is assigned a Boolean function f_i $(x_{i1}, \dots, x_{ik_i})$ with k_i specific input nodes. Under the synchronous updating scheme, all genes are updated simultaneously according to their corresponding update functions. The network's state at time t is represented by a binary vector $x(t) = (x_1(t), \dots, x_n(t))$. In the absence of noise, the state of the system at the next time step is

$$x(t+1) = F(x_1(t), \dots, x_n(t)). \quad (1)$$

The long-term behavior of a deterministic Boolean network depends on the initial state. The network will eventually settle down and cycle endlessly through a set of states called an *attractor cycle*. The set of all initial states that reach a particular attractor cycle forms the *basin of attraction* for the cycle. Following a random perturbation, the network may escape an attractor cycle, be reinitialized, and then begin its transition process anew. For a Boolean network with perturbation, its corresponding Markov chain possesses a steady-state distribution. It has been hypothesized that attractors or steady-state distributions in Boolean formalisms correspond to different cell types of an organism or to cell fates. In other words, the phenotypic traits are encoded in the attractors or steady-state distribution [1].

2.2 Best-fit extension

One approach to infer Boolean networks is to search a consistent rule from examples, the so-called consistency problem [20]. Owing to noise in gene-expression profiles, we relax it to the called best-fit extension problem, which has been extensively studied for many function classes [21]. We briefly introduce the best-fit extension problem for Boolean functions. A partially defined Boolean function (pdBf) is defined by two sets, T, $F \subseteq \{0, 1\}^n$, where T and F represent the set of true and false vectors, respectively. A function f is called an *extension* of pdBf(T, F) if $T \subseteq T(f) = \{x \in \{0,1\}^n : f(x) = 1\}$ and $F \subseteq F(f) = \{x \in \{0,1\}^n : f(x) = 0\}$. The magnitude of the error of function f is

$$\varepsilon(f) = T \cap F(f) + F \cup T(f). \quad (2)$$

The best-fit extension aims to find two subsets T^* and F^* such that $T^* \cap F^* = \phi$ and $T^* \cup F^* = T \cup F$, for which the function pdBf(T*, F*) has an extension in some class C of Boolean functions such that $T^* \cap F + F^* \cup T$ is minimized. Clearly, any extension $f \in C$ of pdBf (T*, F*) has minimum error magnitude [12,13].

2.3 Conditional mutual information

Mutual information (MI) is a general measurement that can detect nonlinear dependence between two random variables X and Y. For discrete-valued random variables, the one-time-lag MI from X_t to Y_{t+1} is given by

$$I(Y_{t+1};X_t) = H(Y_{t+1}) - H(Y_{t+1}|X_t) \quad (3)$$

where $H(\bullet)$ denotes entropy and X_t and Y_{t+1} are two equal-length vectors. The conditional mutual information (CMI) from X_t to Y_{t+1} given Z_t is

$$I(Y_{t+1};X_t|Z_t) = H(Y_{t+1}|Z_t) - H(Y_{t+1}|X_t, Z_t), \quad (4)$$

and quantifies the reduction in the uncertainty of Y_{t+1} due to knowledge of X_t given Z_t. In the chain-like or hub-based scenarios, genes X_t and Y_{t+1} should be independent given the intermediate or hub gene Z_t, which means that $I(X_t; Y_{t+1}|Z_t) = 0$.

2.4 Minimum description length principle

A fundamental principle in model selection is the minimum description length (MDL) principle, which states that we should choose the model that gives the shortest description of the data. The 'two-part MDL' developed by Rissanen consists of writing the description length of a given model applied to a data set as the sum of the code length for describing the model and the code length for describing the data set fit by the model [22]

$$L = L_M + L_D. \quad (5)$$

There are various ways to encode the model-coding length L_M and the data-coding length L_D. Given a time series of length m, Zhao et al. proposed to encode L_M and L_D as [5]

$$L_M = \tau \sum_{i=1}^{n} \{d_i * k_i + d_f * 2^{k_i}\}, \quad (6)$$

$$L_D = -\sum_{i=1}^{n} \sum_{t=1}^{m-1} \log p(x_i(t+1)|x_{i1}(t) \cdots x_{ik_i}(t)), \quad (7)$$

where τ is a free parameter to balance the model- and data-coding lengths, n and m are the number of genes and time points. $d_i = \lceil \log_2 n \rceil$ and $d_f = \lceil \log_2 m \rceil$ denote the number of bits needed to code an integer and a floating-point number, respectively.

3 Implementation

Based on the common assumption that genetic regulatory networks are sparsely connected, we restrict simulated Boolean networks to a scale-free topology with maximal connectivity $K = 4$ and average connectivity $k = 2$. The best-fit algorithm searches for the best-fit function for each gene by exhaustively searching for all combinations of potential regulator sets. The search space grows exponentially with the number of genes. In practice, the limit $k_i \leq 3$ is generally applied to mitigate model complexity. In this paper, we restrict best-fit-algorithm searches to combinations of 1, 2, or 3 possible regulators. The combinatorial set with the smallest error is then selected as the regulatory set. We call this best-fit-I. In practice, the minimal error predictor set may not unique. We employ the heuristic that each of them can be viewed as fitting the target gene in a different way and if one gene occurs frequently in those sets, then it is highly likely to be a true regulatory gene. Thus, we can determine the regulatory set by applying the majority rule in these sets. Here, we refer to this algorithm as best-fit-II.

Then CMI and MDL criteria are used to filter false-positive connections. For each regulatory connection, if the CMI for one of the remaining genes is less than 0.005, then the gene is deleted; otherwise, it remains. The MDL criterion is applied to each target gene x_i. Given its parent set, $Pa(x_i)$, we delete the regulatory gene $x_j \in Pa(x_i)$ that can maximally reduce its coding length L_i for each point in time, repeating this process until the deletion of one regulatory gene causes L_i to increase. We implement an MDL inference algorithm by directly searching the combination of 1, 2, or 3 possible regulators with minimal coding length L_i. The free parameter τ in Equation 6 is set to 0.2.

We have analyzed CMI- and MDL-based filtering by using both synthetic networks as well as the well-studied cell-cycle model known as the budding-yeast network. We compare them with the ground-truth network according to the following two distances [15,23]:

(1) The normalized-edge Hamming distance:

$$\mu^{e}_{ham} = \frac{FN + FP}{P}, \quad (8)$$

where FN and FP represent the number of false-negative and false-positive wires, respectively, and P represents the total number of positive wires. This Hamming distance reflects the accuracy of the recovered regulatory relationships.

(2) The steady-state distribution distance:

$$\mu^{ssd} = \sum_{k=1}^{2n} |\pi_k - \pi'_k|, \quad (9)$$

where π_k and π'_k are the steady-state probabilities state x_k in the ground-truth and inferred network, respectively. The steady-state distribution distance reflects the degree to which an inferred network approximates the long-run behavior of the ground-truth network.

4 Results and discussion

4.1 Simulation on synthetic networks

We generated 1,000 random $n = 10$ genes and for each network generated a random sample of $m = 10, 20, 30, 40,$ and 50 time points. As it is hard to obtain one time series with required length, we adopt the following sampling strategy: (1) select several start states which are the farthest from their attractor; (2) run each start state to its attractor; (3) select one path as a time series, if its length is shorter than required, add another path in it until we have required length of time points. We added 5% and 10% noise to these samples to investigate the effect of noise. The perturbation probability to calculate the steady state distribution was set to $p = 0.0001$. In Table 1, we list the average number of true-positive and false-positive connections for various noise intensities. Figure 1 shows the average performance of the MDL, best-fit-I, and best-fit-II filtered by CMI and MDL for 0%, 5%, and 10% noise. As a whole, the performance of these algorithms increases as sample size increases from 10 to 50. This result is easy to understand: the more data we have, the better the inferred results.

Examination of the table reveals several trends. First, MDL-based filtering (dashed lines in Figure 1) always performs better than CMI-based filtering (dotted lines in Figure 1). MDL-based filtering aims to reduce the redundancy of a model according to the MDL principle, whereas CMI-based filtering attains reduction by blindly checking if the CMI of a connection conditioned on all other genes is below a given threshold. The results indicate that the former approach is superior to the latter. According to Table 1, on the whole, MDL-based filtering retains more true connections and deletes more false connections than CMI-based filtering.

Second, the performances of MDL, best-fit-I, and best-fit-II are very similar when used with noiseless data. In this case, the MDL algorithm gives a model with $L_D = 0$, which also corresponds to the zero-error model obtained by best-fit-I. In addition, MDL-based filtering results in little improvement over the best-fit algorithms. However, their performance is strongly related to sample size when the data are noisy. Specifically, for sample size less

Table 1 Average number of true-positive and false-positive connections for MDL, best-fit-I, and best-fit-II filtered by CMI and MDL

Noise (%)	Algorithm	$m = 10$		$m = 20$		$m = 30$		$m = 40$		$m = 50$	
		TP	FP	TP	FP	TP	FP	TP	FP	TP	FP
0	MDL	10.9	3.0	15.4	1.1	17.0	0.5	17.5	0.3	17.7	0.1
	BF-I	11.4	3.8	15.8	1.6	17.1	0.7	17.4	0.4	17.5	0.3
	BF-I-CMI	10.4	3.2	14.8	1.3	15.9	0.6	16.2	0.4	16.3	0.3
	BF-I-MDL	11.0	2.6	15.4	1.2	16.9	0.6	17.3	0.4	17.5	0.2
	BF-II	11.7	2.8	16.1	1.5	17.3	0.7	17.6	0.6	17.7	0.3
	BF-II-CMI	10.9	2.3	15.2	1.3	16.1	0.6	16.4	0.4	16.4	0.2
	BF-II-MDL	10.8	1.9	15.3	0.9	16.9	0.4	17.5	0.3	17.6	0.2
5	MDL	9.5	5.8	14.1	5.8	16.2	5.5	17.0	5.9	17.4	6.4
	BF-I	10.0	9.1	14.5	8.9	16.4	6.5	17.0	4.3	17.3	2.7
	BF-I-CMI	9.1	6.7	13.5	7.1	15.2	5.2	15.7	3.8	15.9	2.5
	BF-I-MDL	9.4	6.8	14.2	6.0	16.3	5.0	16.9	3.1	17.3	2.0
	BF-II	10.4	7.3	14.9	8.5	16.6	6.8	17.3	4.6	17.5	3.0
	BF-II-CMI	9.7	5.9	14.0	7.1	15.4	5.3	16.0	3.5	16.0	2.4
	BF-II-MDL	9.3	4.9	14.0	5.3	16.2	4.7	17.0	3.4	17.3	2.2
10	MDL	8.3	8.1	12.8	10.4	15.1	10.6	16.2	10.7	16.9	11.0
	BF-I	8.8	12.9	13.0	13.7	15.1	11.1	16.3	8.6	16.8	6.4
	BF-I-CMI	7.9	9.4	12.1	11.0	13.9	9.7	14.9	7.7	15.3	4.5
	BF-I-MDL	8.1	9.6	12.6	10.7	15.0	8.4	16.2	6.3	16.8	5.8
	BF-II	9.2	10.9	13.5	13.1	15.6	11.4	16.6	9.2	17.1	7.0
	BF-II-CMI	8.4	8.5	12.6	10.8	14.4	8.9	15.1	7.2	15.5	5.0
	BF-II-MDL	8.1	7.5	12.6	9.0	15.1	8.5	16.3	6.9	16.9	5.6

BF, best-fit.

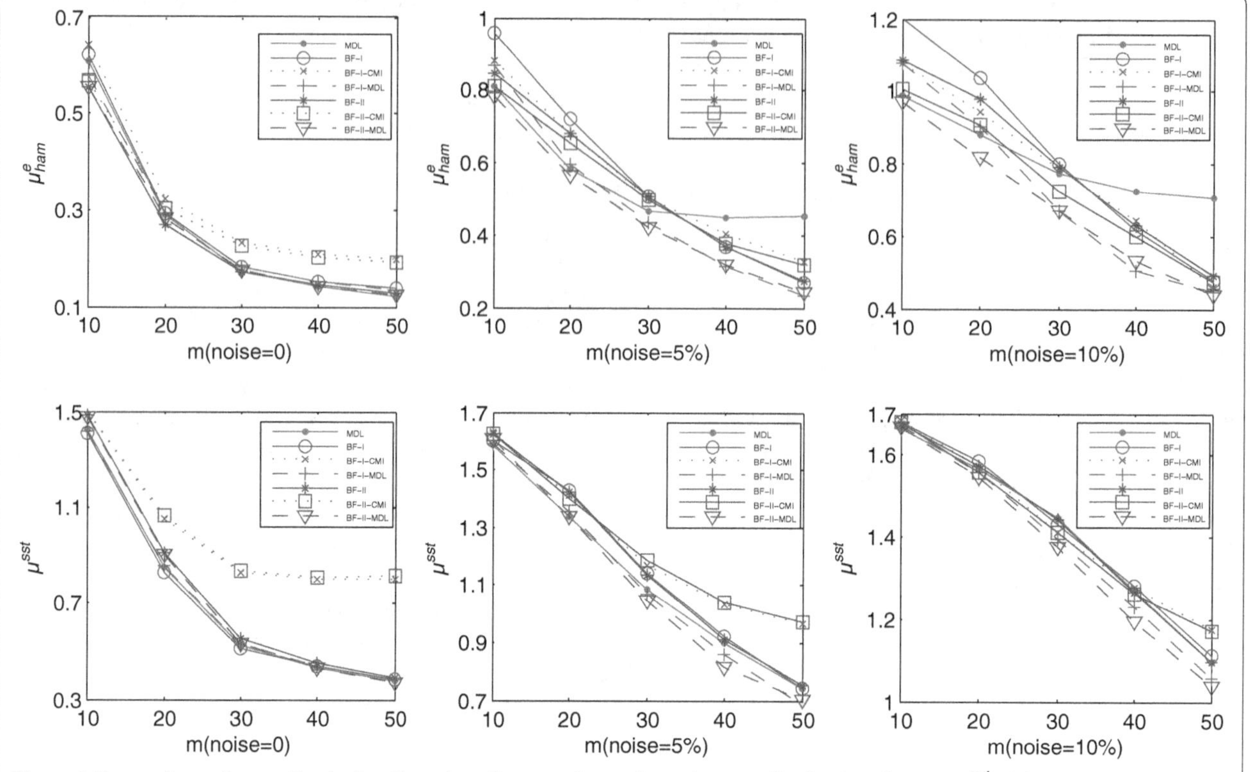

Figure 1 Comparison of normalized-edge Hamming distance μ^{e}_{ham} and steady-state distribution distance μ^{ssd} with 0%, 5%, and 10% noise for MDL, best fit I, and best-fit-II filtered by CMI and MDL.

than 30, MDL performs better than best-fit-I and best-fit-II based on the average Hamming-edge distance μ^{e}_{ham}. But MDL performs worse than best-fit-I and best-fit-II for sample sizes lager than 30, because the structural regularization of MDL is beneficial only for small sample sizes whereas it leads to overfitting for large sample sizes. From Table 1, we see that, compared with best-fit-I and best-fit-II, the rate of false positives is relatively low for MDL with small sample sizes and relatively high for MDL with large sample sizes. Concerning the steady-state distribution distance μ^{ssd}, MDL performs better than best-fit-I and best-fit-II for data with 5% noise, but the performance of these algorithms becomes equivalent for data with 10% noise. This result may be due to the noise not only deteriorating the inference of the regulatory relationships, but also deteriorating the interaction Boolean functions, which strongly influence μ^{ssd}.

Third, for noisy situations, based on μ^{e}_{ham} and μ^{ssd}, not only does MDL-based filtering not degrade performance, it improves the performance of best-fit-I and best-fit-II, with the performance for best-fit-II being slightly better than that of best-fit-I. One reason for this result may be that best-fit-II infers more true-positive connections and less false-positive connections in small-sample situations (see Table 1). It is interesting that, in noisy situations, MDL-based filtering can even outperform the MDL algorithm across all sample sizes. In essence, the two methods are totally different because the former aims to reduce the structural redundancy of the minimal-error model obtained by the best-fit algorithm, whereas the latter aims to search the model with the minimum coding length *L*. From the point of view of the MDL principle, the coding length *L* of MDL-based filtering may not be the minimum length. Because MDL-based filtering combines both the best-fit algorithm and the MDL principle, it reduces structural redundancy and overcomes the over-fitting in large-sample-size situations.

4.2 Cell cycle model of budding yeast

The cell cycle is a vital biological process in which one cell grows and divides into two daughter cells. It consists of four phases, G1, S, G2, and M, and is regulated by a highly complex network that is highly conserved among the eukaryotes. From the 800 genes involved in the cell cycle process of budding yeast, Li et al. constructed a network of 11 key regulators: Cln3, MBF, SBF, Cln1, Cdh1, Swi5, Cdc20, Clb5, Sic1, Clb1, and Mcm1 [24]. This Boolean network model, shown in Figure 2A, has an attractor whose biggest basin corresponds to the biological G1 stationary state. The temporal sequence in Table 2 is a pathway from this basin that follows the biological trajectory of the cell cycle network.

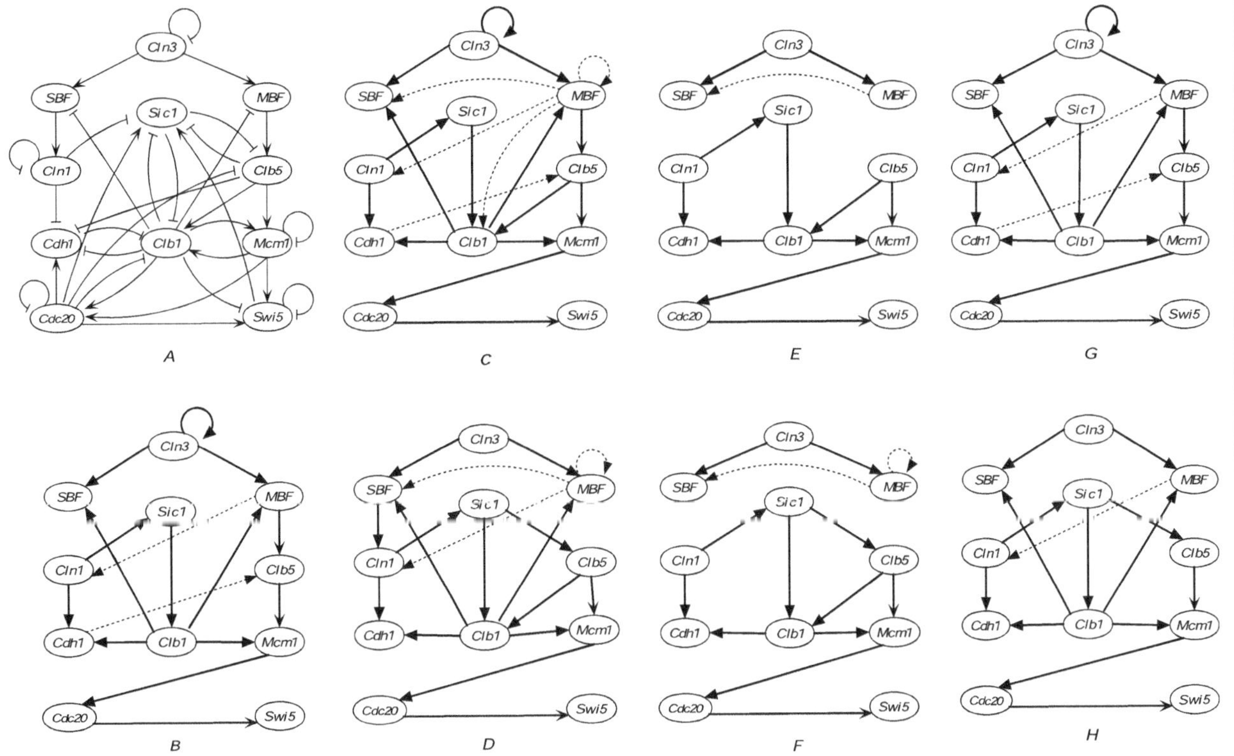

Figure 2 Simplified cell-cycle network of budding yeast and the inferred networks from time-series in Table 2. (A) Simplified cell-cycle network of budding yeast. Arrows are positive regulation, "T" lines are negative regulation, "T" loops are self-degradation. **(B)** Network inferred by MDL. **(C)** Network inferred by best-fit-I. **(D)** Network inferred by best-fit-II. **(E)** Network inferred by best-fit-I filtered by CMI. **(F)** Network inferred by best-fit-II filtered by CMI. **(G)** Network inferred by best-fit-I filtered by MDL. (H) Network inferred by best-fit-II filtered by MDL. From panel **(B)** to **(H)**, the bold solid lines are the correctly inferred regulatory relations, while the light dashed lines are the incorrectly inferred regulatory relations.

We applied MDL, best-fit-I, and best-fit-II filtered by CMI and MDL to the artificial time-series data in Table 2. The inferred networks are shown in Figure 2. Figure 2B shows the network inferred by the MDL algorithm, which is the best network. Figure 2C,D has the same number of true-positive connections, with the latter having fewer false-positive connections. This result demonstrates that the method of selecting regulatory genes in best-fit-II is superior to using best-fit-I. Compared with Figure 2E,F, which was filtered by CMI from Figure 2C,D, Figure 2G,H

Table 2 Temporal evolution of state for the cell cycle

Time	Cln3	MBF	SBF	Cln1	Cdh1	Swi5	Cdc20	Clb5	Sic1	Clb1	Mcm1	Phase
1	1	0	0	0	1	0	0	0	1	0	0	Start
2	0	1	1	0	1	0	0	0	1	0	0	G1
3	0	1	1	1	0	0	0	0	1	0	0	G1
4	0	1	1	1	0	0	0	0	0	0	0	G1
5	0	1	1	1	0	0	0	1	0	0	0	S
6	0	1	1	1	0	0	1	1	0	1	1	G2
7	0	0	0	1	0	1	1	1	0	1	1	M
8	0	0	0	0	0	1	1	0	0	1	1	M
9	0	0	0	0	0	1	1	0	1	1	1	M
10	0	0	0	0	0	1	1	0	1	0	1	M
11	0	0	0	0	1	1	0	0	1	0	0	M
12	0	0	0	0	1	0	0	0	1	0	0	M
13	0	0	0	0	1	0	0	0	1	0	0	G1

Table 3 Comparison of MDL, best-fit-I, and best-fit-II with CMI- and MDL-based filtering for yeast-pathway data

Algorithm	Noise = 0				Noise = 5%				Noise = 10%			
	TP	FP	μ^e_{ham}	μ^{ssd}	TP	FP	μ^e_{ham}	μ^{ssd}	TP	FP	μ^e_{ham}	μ^{ssd}
MDL	14	2	0.65	1.31	11.5	9	0.93	1.42	8.9	12.5	1.11	1.45
BF-I	15	5	0.71	1.25	12.2	11.9	0.99	1.44	9.8	18.4	1.25	1.49
BF-I-CMI	11	1	0.71	1.43	10.4	9	0.96	1.47	8.3	14	1.17	1.51
BF-I-MDL	14	2	0.65	1.17	10.8	8.5	0.93	1.43	8.6	13.1	1.13	1.48
BF-II	15	3	0.65	1.41	12.4	10.4	0.94	1.45	10.6	16.5	1.17	1.48
BF-II-CMI	12	2	0.71	1.46	11	8.7	0.93	1.47	8.3	12.4	1.12	1.50
BF-II-MDL	13	1	0.65	1.36	11.1	7.7	0.9	1.42	9.2	11.9	1.08	1.44

filtered by MDL have more true connections, whereas the number of false-positive connections are about the same. Furthermore, we can see that the networks resulting from CMI-based filtering have two disconnected subgraphs, whereas the network resulting from MDL is a connected graph. This result shows that MDL-based filtering is more effective than CMI-based filtering. In fact, Figure 2G shows the same result as in Figure 2B, which is the best result.

We also ran 100 simulations with 5% and 10% noise for the pathway under consideration. Table 3 lists the average number of true positives and false positives, the normalized Hamming-edge distance μ^e_{ham} and the steady-state distribution distance μ^{ssd}. The results are consistent with those of the simulated networks (Figure 1) and they demonstrate that MDL-based filtering is effective for samples containing a small amount of noise.

5 Conclusion

Reducing the rate of false positives is an important issue in network inference. In this paper, we address this question by using the minimum description length (MDL) principle. Specifically, we apply the MDL measurement technique proposed by Zhao et al. to filter the model obtained by two best-fit algorithms (best-fit-I and best-fit-II). We compare the performance of MDL, best-fit-I, and best-fit-II filtered by CMI and MDL both on simulated networks and on an artificial model of budding yeast. The results show that, as determined by the distance metrics μ^e_{ham} and μ^{ssd}, MDL-based filtering does not degrade inference performance, can improve inference performance, and is more effective than CMI-based filtering. Moreover, the combination of MDL filtering with the best-fit algorithm can even outperform the MDL algorithm alone. Additionally, applying MDL-based filtering is computationally less burdensome than using the MDL algorithm alone because calculating the data-coding length L_D is more complex than calculating the error estimate of the best-fit algorithm, and the complexity of the calculation increases dramatically as the sample size m increases. Last but not the least, MDL-based filtering can also be applied to the results of other minimal error algorithms such as CoD.

Competing interests

The authors declare that they have no competing interests.

Acknowledgements

This work was funded in part by the National Science Foundation of China (Grants No. 61272018, No. 60970065, and No. 61174162) and the Zhejiang Provincial Natural Science Foundation of China (Grants No. R1110261 and No. LY13F010007) and support from China Scholarship Council.

Author details

[1]Department of Physics and Electronic information engineering, Wenzhou University, Wenzhou, Zhejiang 325035, China. [2]Department of Electrical and Computer Engineering, Texas A&M University, College Station, TX 33101, USA. [3]Center for Bioinformatics and Genomics Systems, College Station, TX 33101, USA.

References

1. I Shmulevich, ER Dougherty, *Genomic Signal Processing (Princeton Series in Applied Mathematics)* (Princeton University Press, Princeton, 2007)
2. I Shmulevich, ER Dougherty, *Probabilistic Boolean Networks: The Modeling and Control of Gene Regulatory Networks* (SIAM, Philadelphia, 2010)
3. S Liang, S Fuhrman, R Somogyi, *REVEAL, a general reverse engineering algorithm for inference of genetic network architectures, in Pacific Symposium on Biocomputing* (World Scientific, Singapore, 1998), pp. 18–29
4. AA Adam, I Nemenman, K Basso, C Wiggins, G Stolovitzky, RF Dalla, A Califano, ARACNE: an algorithm for the reconstruction of gene regulatory networks in a mammalian cellular context. BMC Bioinformatics **7**, S7 (2006)
5. Z Wentao, S Erchin, ER Dougherty, Inferring gene regulatory networks from time series data using the minimum description length principle. Bioinformatics **22**, 2129–2135 (2006)
6. V Chaitankar, P Ghosh, E Perkins, G Ping, D Youping, Z Chaoyang, A novel gene network inference algorithm using predictive minimum description length approach. BMC Syst. Biol. **4**, S7 (2010)
7. CV Chaitankar, Z Chaoyang, G Preetam, P Ghosh, EJ Perkins, G Ping, D Youping, *Gene regulatory network inference using predictive minimum description length principle and conditional mutual information* (International Joint Conference on Bioinformatics, Systems Biology and Intelligent Computing, 2009), pp. 487–490. IJCBS'09, 2009
8. J Dougherty, I Tabus, J Astola, Inference of gene regulatory networks based on a universal minimum description length. EURASIP J. Bioinform. Syst. Biol. **2008**, 482090 (2008). doi:10.1155/2008/482090
9. I Tabus, J Astola, On the use of MDL principle in gene expression prediction. EURASIP J. Appl. Signal Proc. **2001**, 297–303 (2001)
10. ER Dougherty, S Kim, Y Chen, Coefficient of determination in nonlinear signal processing. Signal Process. **80**, 2219–2235 (2000)
11. S Kim, ER Dougherty, ML Bittner, Y Chen, K Sivakumar, P Meltzer, JM Trent, General nonlinear framework for the analysis of gene interaction via multivariate expression arrays. J. Biomed. Opt. **5**, 411–424 (2000)

12. I Shmulevich, A Saarinen, O Yli-Harja, J Astola, *Inference of genetic regulatory networks via best-fit extensions. Computational and Statistical Approaches to Genomics* (Springer, US, 2002)
13. H Lähdesmäki, I Shmulevich, O Yli-Harja, On learning gene regulatory networks under the Boolean network model. Mach. Learn. **52**, 147–167 (2003)
14. W Zhao, E Serpedin, ER Dougherty, Inferring connectivity of genetic regulatory networks using information-theoretic criteria. IEEE/ACM Trans. Comput. Biol. Bioinform. **5**(2), 262–274 (2008)
15. X Qian, ER Dougherty, Validation of gene regulatory network inference based on controllability. Front. Genet. **4**, 272 (2013). doi:10.3389/fgene.2013.00272
16. ER Dougherty, R Pal, X Qian, ML Bittner, A Datta, Stationary and structural control in gene regulatory networks: basic concepts. Int. J. Syst. Sci. **41**(1), 5–16 (2010)
17. MR Yousefi, ER Dougherty, Intervention in gene regulatory networks with maximal phenotype alteration. Bioinformatics. **29**(14), 1758–1767 (2013)
18. I Ivanov, P Simeonov, N Ghaffari, X Qian, ER Dougherty, Selection policy induced reduction mappings for boolean networks. IEEE Trans. Signal Process. **58**(9), 4871–4882 (2010)
19. N Ghaffari, I Ivanov, X Qian, ER Dougherty, A CoD-based reduction algorithm for designing stationary control policies on Boolean networks. Bioinformatics **26**, 1556–1563 (2010)
20. T Akutsu, S Miyano, S Kuhara, Identification of genetic networks from a small number of gene expression patterns under the boolean network model. Pac. Symp. Biocomput. **4**, 17–28 (1999)
21. E Boros, T Ibaraki, K Makino, Error-free and best-fit extensions of partially defined boolean functions. Inf. Comput. **140**, 254–283 (1998)
22. J Rissanen, Modeling by shortest data description. Automatica **14**, 465–471 (1978)
23. ER Dougherty, Validation of gene regulatory networks: scientific and inferential. Brief. Bioinform. **12**, 245–252 (2011)
24. F Li, T Long, L Ying, Q Ouyang, C Tang, The yeast cell-cycle network is robustly designed. Proc. Natl. Acad. Sci. USA **101**, 4781–4786 (2004)

Unbiased bootstrap error estimation for linear discriminant analysis

Thang Vu[1], Chao Sima[2], Ulisses M Braga-Neto[1,2*] and Edward R Dougherty[1,2]

Abstract

Convex bootstrap error estimation is a popular tool for classifier error estimation in gene expression studies. A basic question is how to determine the weight for the convex combination between the basic bootstrap estimator and the resubstitution estimator such that the resulting estimator is unbiased at finite sample sizes. The well-known 0.632 bootstrap error estimator uses asymptotic arguments to propose a fixed 0.632 weight, whereas the more recent 0.632+ bootstrap error estimator attempts to set the weight adaptively. In this paper, we study the finite sample problem in the case of linear discriminant analysis under Gaussian populations. We derive exact expressions for the weight that guarantee unbiasedness of the convex bootstrap error estimator in the univariate and multivariate cases, without making asymptotic simplifications. Using exact computation in the univariate case and an accurate approximation in the multivariate case, we obtain the required weight and show that it can deviate significantly from the constant 0.632 weight, depending on the sample size and Bayes error for the problem. The methodology is illustrated by application on data from a well-known cancer classification study.

Keywords: Bootstrap; Error estimation; Bias; Linear discriminant analysis; Gene expression classification

Introduction

The bootstrap method [1-7] has been used in a wide range of statistical problems. The asymptotic behavior of bootstrap has been studied [8-11], while small-sample properties have been studied under simplifying assumptions, such as considering the estimator based on all possible bootstrap samples (the 'complete' bootstrap) [12-14]. The small-sample properties of the usual bootstrap are not well understood, in particular when it comes to estimating the error rates of classification rules [15,16].

There has been, on the other hand, interest in the application of bootstrap to error estimation in classification problems and, in particular, gene expression classification studies [17-20]. Of particular interest is the issue of classifier error estimation [21,22]. Bootstrap methods have generally been shown to outperform more traditional error estimation techniques, such as resubstitution and cross-validation, in terms of root-mean-square (RMS) error [4,5,7,23-35]. Bootstrap error estimation is typically performed via a convex combination of the (generally) pessimistic basic bootstrap estimator, known as the zero bootstrap, and the (generally) optimistic resubstitution estimator. A basic problem is how to choose the weight that yields an unbiased estimator.

The problem of unbiased convex error estimation was previously considered in [36-38] for a convex combination of resubstitution and cross-validation estimators, and in [4,7,23] for a combination between resubstitution and the basic bootstrap estimator. In the former case, a fixed suboptimal weight of 0.5 was proposed in [36,38], while an asymptotic analysis to find the optimal weight was provided in [37]. In the latter case, our case of interest, a fixed suboptimal weight of 0.632 was proposed in [4], leading to the well-known 0.632 bootstrap estimator, while in [7], a suboptimal weight is computed by means of a sample-based procedure, which attempts to counterbalance the effect of overfitting on the bias, leading to the so-called 0.632+ bootstrap error estimator; the problem of finding the optimal weight for finite sample cases was addressed via a numerical approach in [23].

Here, we determine the optimal weight for finite sample cases analytically, in the case of linear discriminant analysis under Gaussian populations. In the univariate case, no

*Correspondence: ulisses@ece.tamu.edu
[1]Department of Electrical and Computer Engineering, Texas A&M University, 3128 TAMU, College Station, TX 77843, USA
[2]Center for Bioinformatics and Genomic Systems Engineering, Texas A&M University, 101 Gateway, Suite A, College Station, TX 77845, USA

other assumptions are made. In the multivariate case, it is assumed that the populations are homoskedastic and that the common covariance matrix is known and used in the discriminant. In either case, no simplifications are introduced to the bootstrap error estimator; it is the usual one, based on a finite number of random bootstrap samples.

The analysis in this paper follows in the steps of previous papers that have provided analytical representations for the moments of error-estimator distributions [39,40]. In the univariate case, exact expressions are given for the expectation of the zero bootstrap error estimator, in the general heteroskedastic (general-variance) Gaussian case. By using similar expressions for the expected true and resubstitution error [39], this allows the exact calculation of the required weight. In the multivariate case, the expectation of the zero bootstrap error estimator is expressed as a probability involving the ratio of two noncentral chi-square variables, in the homoskedastic Gaussian case, assuming that the true common covariance matrix is used in the discriminant. The resulting expression is exact but necessitates approximation for its numerical computation. This is done in this paper via the Imhof-Pearson three-moment method, which is accurate in small-sample cases [41]. Use of similar expressions for the expected true and resubstitution error [40] then allows the exact calculation of the required weight.

In the homoskedastic case, the required weight for unbiasedness is shown to be a function only of the Bayes error and sample size. Accordingly, plots and tables of the required weight for varying values of Bayes error and sample size are presented; if the Bayes error can be estimated for a problem, this provides a way to obtain the optimal weight to use. In the univariate case, it was observed that as the sample size increases, the optimal weight settles on an asymptotic value of around 0.675, thus slightly over the heuristic value 0.632; by contrast, in the multivariate case ($d = 2$), the asymptotic value appears to be strongly dependent on the Bayes error, being as a rule significantly smaller than 0.632, except for very small Bayes error.

This paper is organized as follows. The 'Bootstrap classification' section defines linear discriminant analysis as well as its application under bootstrap sampling. The 'Bootstrap error estimation' section reviews convex bootstrap error estimation. The 'Unbiased bootstrap error estimation' section contains the main theoretical results in the paper, providing the analytical expressions for the computation of the required convex bootstrap weight in the univariate and multivariate cases. The 'Gene expression classification example' section contains a demonstration of the usage of the optimal weight in bootstrap error estimation using data from the breast cancer classification study in [42,43]. Lastly, the 'Conclusions' section contains a summary and concluding remarks.

All the proofs are presented in the Appendix.

Bootstrap classification

Classification involves a predictor vector $X \in R^d$, also known as a *feature* vector, which represents an individual from one of two populations Π_0 and Π_1 (we consider here only this binary classification problem). The classification problem is to assign X correctly to its population of origin. The populations are coded into a discrete *label* $Y \in \{0, 1\}$. Therefore, given a feature vector X, classification attempts to predict the corresponding value of the label Y. We assume that there is a joint *feature-label distribution* F_{XY} for the pair (X, Y) characterizing the classification problem. In particular, it determines the probabilities $c_0 = P(X \in \Pi_0) = P(Y = 0)$ and $c_1 = P(X \in \Pi_1) = P(Y = 1)$, which are called the *prior probabilities*.

Given a fixed sample size n, the *sample data* is an i.i.d. sample $S_n = \{(X_1, Y_1), \ldots, (X_n, Y_n)\}$ from F_{XY}. The population-specific sample sizes are given by $n_0 = \sum_{i=1}^{n} I_{Y_i=0}$ and $n_1 = \sum_{i=1}^{n} I_{Y_i=1} = n - n_0$, which are random variables, with $n_0 \sim \text{Binomial}(n, c_0)$ and $n_1 \sim \text{Binomial}(n, c_1)$. When we need to emphasize that n_0 and n_1 are random variables, we will use capital letters N_0 and N_1, respectively. This sampling design, which is the most commonly found one in contemporary pattern recognition, is known as *mixture sampling* [44].

A *classification rule* Ψ_n is used to map the training data S_n into a designed classifier $\psi_n = \Psi_n(S_n)$, where ψ_n is a function taking on values in the set $\{0, 1\}$, such that X is assigned to population Π_0 or Π_1 according to whether $\psi_n(X) = 0$ or 1, respectively. The *classification error rate* ε_n of classifier ψ_n is the probability that the assignment is erroneous:

$$\varepsilon_n = c_0 \, P(\psi_n(X) = 1 \mid Y = 0) + c_1 \, P(\psi_n(X) = 0 \mid Y = 1) \stackrel{\text{def}}{=} c_0 \, \varepsilon_n^0 + c_1 \, \varepsilon_n^1, \tag{1}$$

where (X, Y) is an independent test point and $\varepsilon_n^i = P(\psi_n(X) = 1 - i \mid Y = i)$ is the error rate specific to population Π_i, for $i = 0, 1$. Since the training set S_n is random, ε_n is a random variable, with *expected classification error rate* $E[\varepsilon_n]$; this gives the average performance over all possible training sets S_n, for fixed sample size n.

Linear discriminant analysis (LDA) employs Anderson's W discriminant [45], which is defined as follows:

$$W(X) = \left(X - \frac{\hat{\mu}_0 + \hat{\mu}_1}{2}\right)^T \Sigma^{-1} \left(\hat{\mu}_0 - \hat{\mu}_1\right) \tag{2}$$

where

$$\hat{\mu}_0 = \frac{1}{n_0} \sum_{i=1}^{n} X_i I_{Y_i=0} \quad \text{and} \quad \hat{\mu}_1 = \frac{1}{n_1} \sum_{i=1}^{n} X_i I_{Y_i=1} \tag{3}$$

are the sample means relative to each population, and Σ is a matrix, which can be either (1) the true common covariance matrix of the populations, assuming it is known (this is the approach followed, for example, in [39,40,46]), or (2) the sample covariance matrix based on the pooled sample S_n, which leads to the general LDA case. In this paper, we will assume case (1) throughout.

The corresponding LDA classifier is given by

$$\psi_n(X) = \begin{cases} 1, & \text{if } W(X) < 0 \\ 0, & \text{if } W(X) \geq 0 \end{cases}, \tag{4}$$

that is, the sign of $W(X)$ determines the classification of X.

A *bootstrap sample* S_n^* contains n instances drawn uniformly, with replacement, from S_n. Hence, some of the instances in S_n may appear multiple times in S_n^*, whereas others may not appear at all. Let C be a vector of size n, where the ith component $C(i)$ equals the number of appearances in S_n^* of the ith instance in S_n. The vector C will be referred to as a *bootstrap vector.*

For a given S_n, the vector C uniquely determines a bootstrap sample S_n^*, which we denote by S_n^C. Note that the original sample itself is included: if $C = (1, \ldots, 1) \stackrel{\text{def}}{=} \mathbf{1}_n$, then $S_n^C = S_n$, since each original instance appears once in the bootstrap sample. Note also that the number of distinct bootstrap samples, i.e., values for C, is equal to $\binom{2n-1}{n}$; even for small n, this is a large number. For example, the total number of possible bootstrap samples of size $n = 20$ is larger than 6.8×10^{10}.

The vector C has a multinomial distribution with parameters $(n, 1/n, \ldots, 1/n)$,

$$P(C = (i_1, \ldots, i_n)) = \frac{1}{n^n} \frac{n!}{i_1! \cdots i_n!}, \quad i_1 + \cdots + i_n = n. \tag{5}$$

Starting from a classification rule Ψ_n, one may design a classifier $\psi_n^C = \Psi_n(S^C)$ on a bootstrap training set S^C. Its classification error ε_n^C is given as in (1), namely, $\varepsilon_n^C = c_0 \varepsilon_n^{C,0} + c_1 \varepsilon_n^{C,1}$ where $\varepsilon_n^{C,i} = P(\psi_n^C(X) = 1 - i \mid Y = i)$ is the error rate specific to population Π_i, for $i = 0, 1$. In this paper, we apply this scheme to the LDA classification rule defined previously. Notice the distinction between a bootstrap LDA classifier and a 'bagged' (bootstrap-aggregated) LDA classifier [47,48]; these correspond to distinct classification rules. The bootstrap LDA classifier is employed here as an auxiliary tool to analyze the problem of unbiased bootstrap error estimation for the plain LDA classifier.

Bootstrap error estimation

Since the feature-label distribution is typically unknown, the classification error rate ε_n has to be estimated by a sample-based statistic $\hat{\varepsilon}_n$, commonly referred to as an *error estimator.* Data in practice are often limited, and the training sample S_n has to be used for both designing the classifier ψ_n and as the basis for the error estimator $\hat{\varepsilon}_n$. The simplest and fastest way to estimate the error of a designed classifier ψ_n is to compute its error on the sample data itself:

$$\hat{\varepsilon}_n^{\,r} = \frac{1}{n} \sum_{i=1}^{n} \left(I_{\psi_n(X_i)=1} I_{Y_i=0} + I_{\psi_n(X_i)=0} I_{Y_i=1} \right). \tag{6}$$

This *resubstitution* estimator, or *apparent error,* is often optimistically biased, that is, it is often the case that $\text{Bias}(\hat{\varepsilon}_n^{\,r}) = E[\hat{\varepsilon}_n^{\,r}] - E[\varepsilon_n] < 0$, though this is not always so. The bias tends to worsen with more complex classification rules [49].

The basic bootstrap error estimator is the *zero bootstrap* error estimator [4], which is introduced next. Given the training data S_n, B bootstrap samples are randomly drawn from it. Denote the corresponding (random) bootstrap vectors by $\{C_1, \ldots, C_B\}$. The zero bootstrap error estimator is defined as the average error committed by the B bootstrap classifiers on sample points that do not appear in the bootstrap samples:

$$\hat{\varepsilon}_n^{\,\text{boot}} = \frac{1}{B} \sum_{i=1}^{B} \left[\frac{1}{n(C_i)} \sum_{j:\, C_i(j)=0} \left(I_{\psi_n^C(X_j)=1} I_{Y_j=0} + I_{\psi_n^C(X_j)=0} I_{Y_j=1} \right) \right], \tag{7}$$

where $n(C)$ is the number of zeros in C.

The bootstrap zero estimator tends to be pessimistically biased, since the amount of distinct training instances available for designing the classifier is on average $(1 - e^{-1})n \approx 0.632n < n$. Pessimistic bias in an error estimator can be mitigated by forming a convex combination with an optimistic error estimator [23]. In the case of bootstrap error estimation, the standard approach is to form a convex combination of the zero bootstrap with resubstitution,

$$\hat{\varepsilon}_n^{\,\text{conv}} = (1 - w)\, \hat{\varepsilon}_n^{\,r} + w\, \hat{\varepsilon}_n^{\,\text{boot}}. \tag{8}$$

Selecting the appropriate weight $w = w^*$ leads to an unbiased error estimator, $E[\hat{\varepsilon}_n^{\,\text{conv}}] = E[\varepsilon_n]$.

In [4], the weight w is heuristically set to $w = 0.632$ to reflect the average ratio of original training instances that appear in a bootstrap sample. This is known as the *.632 bootstrap estimator*

$$\hat{\varepsilon}_n^{\,\text{b632}} = (1 - 0.632)\, \hat{\varepsilon}_n^{\,r} + 0.632\, \hat{\varepsilon}_n^{\,\text{boot}}, \tag{9}$$

which has been heavily employed in the machine learning field.

Unbiased bootstrap error estimation

The 0.632 bootstrap error estimator reviewed in the previous section is not guaranteed to be unbiased. In this section, we will examine the necessary conditions for setting the weight $w = w^*$ in (8) to achieve unbiasedness. We will then particularize the analysis to the Gaussian linear discriminant case, where exact expressions for w^* will be derived, both in the univariate and multivariate cases.

The bias of the convex estimator in (8) is given by

$$E\left[\hat{\varepsilon}_n^{\,\text{conv}} - \varepsilon_n\right] = (1-w)E\left[\hat{\varepsilon}_n^{\,r}\right] + wE\left[\hat{\varepsilon}_n^{\,\text{boot}}\right] - E\left[\varepsilon_n\right]. \tag{10}$$

Setting this to zero yields the exact weight

$$w^* = \frac{E\left[\hat{\varepsilon}_n^{\,r}\right] - E\left[\varepsilon_n\right]}{E\left[\hat{\varepsilon}_n^{\,r}\right] - E\left[\hat{\varepsilon}_n^{\,\text{boot}}\right]} \tag{11}$$

that produces an unbiased error estimator.

Now, applying expectation on both sides of (7) produces

$$E\left[\hat{\varepsilon}_n^{\,\text{boot}}\right] = \sum_C E\left[\varepsilon_n^C \mid C\right] p(C), \tag{12}$$

where $p(C)$ is given by (5) and the sum is taken over all possible values of C (an efficient procedure for listing all multinomial vectors is provided by the NEXCOM routine given in [50], Chapter 5). Equations (11) and (12) allow the computation of the weight w^* given the knowledge of $E[\varepsilon_n]$, $E\left[\hat{\varepsilon}_n^{\,r}\right]$, and $E\left[\varepsilon_n^C \mid C\right]$. We will present next exact formulas for these expectations in the case of the LDA classification rule under Gaussian populations.

Univariate case

In the univariate case, the common variance term cancels and the W statistic and LDA classifier become greatly simplified, with

$$\psi_n(X) = \begin{cases} 1, & \text{if } \left(X - \frac{\hat{\mu}_0 + \hat{\mu}_1}{2}\right)(\hat{\mu}_0 - \hat{\mu}_1) < 0 \\ 0, & \text{otherwise} \end{cases}. \tag{13}$$

The following functions will be useful. Let $\Phi(u) = P(Z \leq u)$ and $\Phi(u, v; \rho) = P((Z_1, Z_2) \leq (u, v))$, where Z is a zero-mean, unit-variance Gaussian random variable, and Z_1, Z_2 are zero-mean, unit-variance random variables that are jointly Gaussian distributed, with correlation coefficient ρ.

Assume that population Π_i is distributed as $N(\mu_i, \sigma_i)$, for $i = 0, 1$, where $\sigma_0 \neq \sigma_1$ in general.

Under these conditions, John obtained in [39] an exact expression for the expectation of the true classification error for *fixed* sample sizes n_0 and n_1 (this is known as *separate* sampling [44]). John's result can be written as follows:

$$E\left[\varepsilon_n^0 \mid N_0 = n_0\right] = \Phi(a, b; \rho_e) + \Phi(-a, -b; \rho_e), \tag{14}$$

where

$$a = \frac{\mu_1 - \mu_0}{\sqrt{\frac{\sigma_0^2}{n_0} + \frac{\sigma_1^2}{n_1}}}, \quad b = \frac{\mu_0 - \mu_1}{\sqrt{\left(4 + \frac{1}{n_0}\right)\sigma_0^2 + \frac{\sigma_1^2}{n_1}}},$$

$$\rho_e = \frac{\frac{\sigma_0^2}{n_0} - \frac{\sigma_1^2}{n_1}}{\sqrt{\left(\frac{\sigma_0^2}{n_0} + \frac{\sigma_1^2}{n_1}\right)\left(\left(4 + \frac{1}{n_0}\right)\sigma_0^2 + \frac{\sigma_1^2}{n_1}\right)}}. \tag{15}$$

The corresponding result for $E[\varepsilon_n^1 \mid N_0 = n_0]$ is obtained by simply interchanging all indices 0 and 1 in the previous expressions. The expected error rate can then be found by using conditioning and Equation (1):

$$\begin{aligned} E[\varepsilon_n] &= \sum_{n_0=0}^{n} E[\varepsilon_n \mid N_0 = n_0]\, P(N_0 = n_0) \\ &= \sum_{n_0=0}^{n} \left(c_0 E\left[\varepsilon_n^0 \mid N_0 = n_0\right] + c_1 E\left[\varepsilon_n^1 \mid N_0 = n_0\right]\right) \\ &\quad \times P(N_0 = n_0). \end{aligned} \tag{16}$$

where

$$P(N_0 = n_0) = \binom{n}{n_0} c_0^{n_0} c_1^{n_1}. \tag{17}$$

As for resubstitution, Hills provided in [51] exact expressions for the expected error for fixed n_0 and n_1. However, his expression applies only to the case $\sigma_0 = \sigma_1$. Theorem 3 in [52] provides a generalization of this result to the case of populations of unequal variances. First, note that

$$\hat{\varepsilon}_n^{\,r} = \frac{n_0}{n}\hat{\varepsilon}_n^{\,r,0} + \frac{n_1}{n}\hat{\varepsilon}_n^{\,r,1}, \tag{18}$$

where

$$\hat{\varepsilon}_n^{\,r,0} = \frac{1}{n_0}\left[\sum_{i=1}^{n} I_{\psi(X_i)=1} I_{Y_i=0}\right] \quad \text{and}$$

$$\hat{\varepsilon}_n^{\,r,1} = \frac{1}{n_1}\left[\sum_{i=1}^{n} I_{\psi(X_i)=0} I_{Y_i=1}\right] \tag{19}$$

are the apparent error rates specific to class 0 and 1, respectively. The result in [52] can be written as

$$E\left[\hat{\varepsilon}_n^{\,r,0} \mid N_0 = n_0\right] = \Phi(c, d; \rho_r) + \Phi(-c, -d; \rho_r), \tag{20}$$

where

$$c = \frac{\mu_1 - \mu_0}{\sqrt{\frac{\sigma_0^2}{n_0} + \frac{\sigma_1^2}{n_1}}}, \quad d = \frac{\mu_0 - \mu_1}{\sqrt{\left(4 - \frac{3}{n_0}\right)\sigma_0^2 + \frac{\sigma_1^2}{n_1}}},$$

$$\rho_r = -\frac{\frac{\sigma_0^2}{n_0} + \frac{\sigma_1^2}{n_1}}{\sqrt{\left(\frac{\sigma_0^2}{n_0} + \frac{\sigma_1^2}{n_1}\right)\left(\left(4 - \frac{3}{n_0}\right)\sigma_0^2 + \frac{\sigma_1^2}{n_1}\right)}}. \tag{21}$$

The corresponding result for $E[\hat{\varepsilon}_n^{r,1} \mid N_0 = n_0]$ is obtained by interchanging all indices 0 and 1. The expected resubstitution error rate can then be found by using conditioning and Equation (18):

$$E\left[\hat{\varepsilon}_n^r\right] = \sum_{n_0=0}^{n} E\left[\hat{\varepsilon}_n^r \mid N_0 = n_0\right] P(N_0 = n_0)$$
$$= \sum_{n_0=0}^{n} \left(\frac{n_0}{n} E\left[\hat{\varepsilon}_n^{r,0} \mid N_0 = n_0\right] + \frac{n_1}{n} E\left[\hat{\varepsilon}_n^{r,1} \mid N_0 = n_0\right]\right) \times P(N_0 = n_0). \tag{22}$$

Finally, let us consider the expected bootstrap error. Given C, the bootstrap LDA classifier is obtained by replacing $\hat{\mu}_i$ by $\hat{\mu}_i^C$, $i = 0, 1$, in (13):

$$\psi_n^C(X) = \begin{cases} 1, & \text{if } \left(X - \frac{\hat{\mu}_0^C + \hat{\mu}_1^C}{2}\right)\left(\hat{\mu}_0^C - \hat{\mu}_1^C\right) < 0 \\ 0, & \text{otherwise} \end{cases}, \tag{23}$$

where

$$\hat{\mu}_0^C = \frac{\sum_{i=1}^{n} C(i) X_i I_{Y_i=0}}{\sum_{i=1}^{n} C(i) I_{Y_i=0}} \quad \text{and} \quad \hat{\mu}_1^C = \frac{\sum_{i=1}^{n} C(i) X_i I_{Y_i=1}}{\sum_{i=1}^{n} C(i) I_{Y_i=1}} \tag{24}$$

are *bootstrap sample means.*

Now, note that with $N_0 = n_0$ fixed, the training data labels Y_i, $i = 1, \ldots, n$, are no longer random. Since all classification rules of interest are invariant to reordering of the training data, we can, without loss of generality, reorder the sample points so that $Y_i = 0$ for $i = 1, \ldots, n_0$, and $Y_1 = 1$ for $i = n_0 + 1, \ldots, n$. Let the same reordering be applied to a given bootstrap vector C. The next theorem extends John's result to the classification error of the bootstrapped LDA classification rule defined by (23).

Theorem 1. *Assume that population Π_i is distributed as $N(\mu_i, \sigma_i^2)$, for $i = 0, 1$. Then the expected error rate of the bootstrap LDA classification rule defined by (23) is given by:*

$$E\left[\varepsilon_n^{C,0} \mid N_0 = n_0, C\right] = \Phi(e, f; \rho_c) + \Phi(-e, -f; \rho_c), \tag{25}$$

where

$$e = \frac{\mu_1 - \mu_0}{\sqrt{s_0\sigma_0^2 + s_1\sigma_1^2}}, \quad f = \frac{\mu_0 - \mu_1}{\sqrt{(4 + s_0)\sigma_0^2 + s_1\sigma_1^2}},$$

$$\rho_c = \frac{s_0\sigma_0^2 - s_1\sigma_1^2}{\sqrt{\left((4 + s_0)\sigma_0^2 + s_1\sigma_1^2\right)\left(s_0\sigma_0^2 + s_1\sigma_1^2\right)}}, \tag{26}$$

with

$$s_0 = \frac{\sum_{i=1}^{n_0} C(i)^2}{\left(\sum_{i=1}^{n_0} C(i)\right)^2} \quad \text{and} \quad s_1 = \frac{\sum_{i=1}^{n_1} C(n_0 + i)^2}{\left(\sum_{i=1}^{n_1} C(n_0 + i)\right)^2}, \tag{27}$$

The corresponding result for $E\left[\varepsilon_n^{C,1} \mid N_0 = n_0, C\right]$ is obtained by interchanging all indices 0 and 1.

Proof. See the Appendix.

It is easy to check that the result in Theorem 1 reduces to the one in (14) and (15) when $C = \mathbf{1}_n$. Following (16), we can then write

$$E\left[\varepsilon_n^C \mid C\right] = \sum_{n_0=0}^{n} E\left[\varepsilon_n^C \mid N_0 = n_0, C\right] P(N_0 = n_0)$$
$$= \sum_{n_0=0}^{n} \left(c_0 E\left[\varepsilon_n^{C,0} \mid N_0 = n_0, C\right] + c_1 E\left[\varepsilon_n^{C,1} \mid N_0 = n_0, C\right]\right) P(N_0 = n_0). \tag{28}$$

The expected bootstrap error rate $E[\hat{\varepsilon}_n^{\text{boot}}]$ can now be computed via (12).

The weight w^* for unbiased bootstrap error estimation can now be computed exactly by means of Equations (11), (12), (14) to (17), (20) to (22), and (25) to (28).

In the special case $\sigma_0 = \sigma_1 = \sigma$ (homoskedasticity), it follows easily from the previous expressions that $E[\varepsilon_n]$, $E[\hat{\varepsilon}_n^r]$, and $E[\hat{\varepsilon}_n^{\text{boot}}]$ depend only on the sample size n and on the Mahalanobis distance between the populations $\delta = |\mu_1 - \mu_0|/\sigma$, and therefore so does the weight w^*, through (11). Since the optimal (Bayes) classification error in this case is $\varepsilon^* = \Phi(-\delta/2)$, there is a one-to-one correspondence between Bayes error and the Mahalanobis distance. Therefore, in the homoskedastic case, the weight w^* *is a function only of the Bayes error ε^* and the sample size n.*

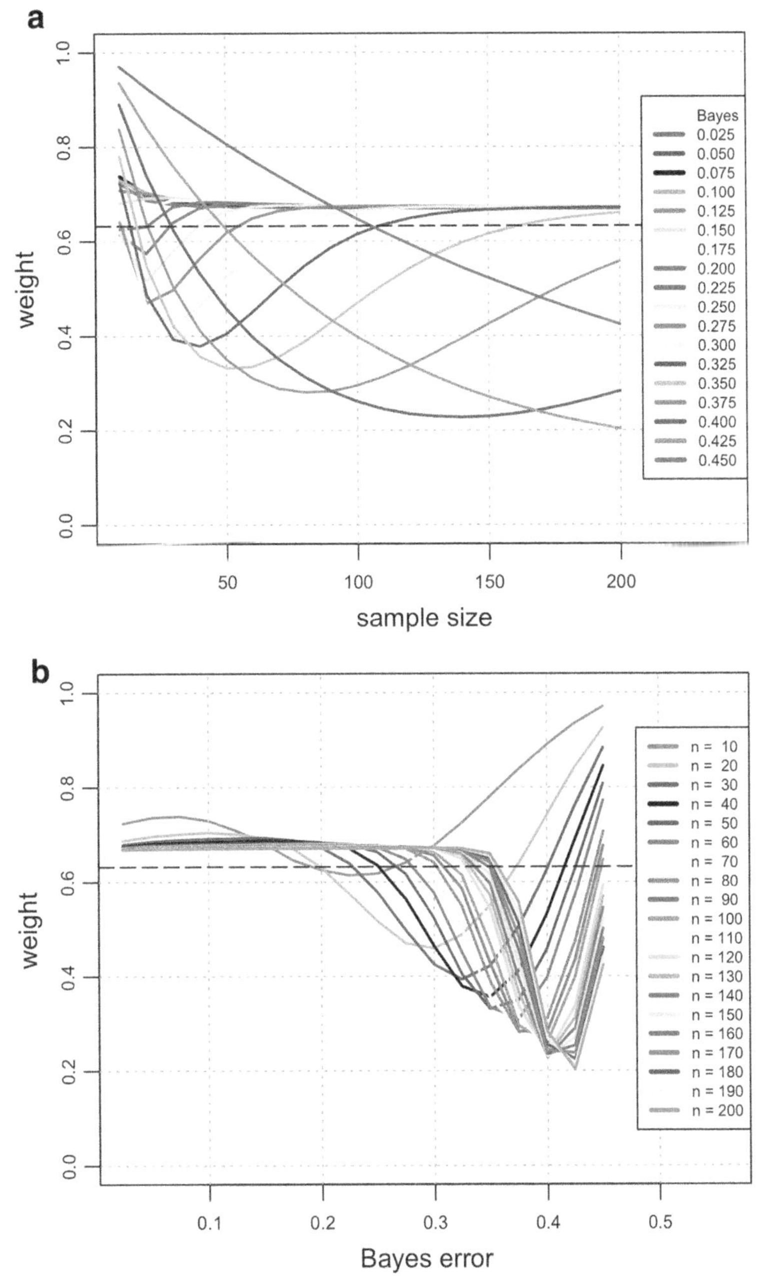

Figure 1 Univariate case. Required weight w^* for unbiased convex bootstrap estimation plotted against **(a)** sample size and **(b)** Bayes error.

Figure 1 and Table 1 display the value of w^* in the homoskedastic case, for several sample sizes and Bayes errors. In order to extend the plots up to $n = 200$, it is necessary to approximate $E[\hat{\varepsilon}_n^{\text{boot}}]$ in (12) by a Monte Carlo procedure; this is done by generating $M = 100 \times n^2$ independent random vectors $\{C_i \mid i = 1, \ldots, M\}$ and letting $E[\hat{\varepsilon}_n^{\text{boot}}] \approx (1/M) \sum_{i=1}^{M} E[\epsilon_n^{C_i} \mid C_i]$. We find that this value of M is large enough to obtain an accurate approximation. All other quantities are computed exactly, as described previously. One can see in Figure 1a that w^* varies wildly and can be very far from the heuristic 0.632 weight; however, as the sample size increases, w^* appears to settle around an asymptotic fixed value. This asymptotic value is approximately 0.675, being thus slightly larger than 0.632. In addition, Figure 1b allows one to see that convergence to the asymptotic value is faster for smaller Bayes errors. These facts help explain the good performance of the original convex 0.632 bootstrap error

Table 1 Univariate case: required weight w^* for unbiased convex bootstrap estimation

	$n = 10$	$n = 20$	$n = 30$	$n = 40$	$n = 50$	$n = 60$	$n = 70$	$n = 80$	$n = 90$	$n = 100$
$\epsilon^* = 0.025$	0.724	0.687	0.679	0.675	0.674	0.672	0.671	0.671	0.670	0.670
$\epsilon^* = 0.050$	0.736	0.696	0.685	0.680	0.678	0.676	0.674	0.673	0.672	0.672
$\epsilon^* = 0.075$	0.738	0.701	0.689	0.683	0.679	0.677	0.676	0.674	0.674	0.673
$\epsilon^* = 0.100$	0.729	0.704	0.691	0.684	0.681	0.678	0.677	0.675	0.674	0.673
$\epsilon^* = 0.125$	0.708	0.701	0.692	0.686	0.682	0.679	0.677	0.676	0.675	0.674
$\epsilon^* = 0.150$	0.681	0.692	0.693	0.687	0.683	0.680	0.678	0.677	0.676	0.675
$\epsilon^* = 0.175$	0.646	0.670	0.688	0.687	0.683	0.680	0.678	0.677	0.676	0.675
$\epsilon^* = 0.200$	0.625	0.631	0.673	0.683	0.683	0.681	0.679	0.677	0.676	0.675
$\epsilon^* = 0.225$	0.614	0.574	0.639	0.671	0.679	0.680	0.679	0.677	0.676	0.675
$\epsilon^* = 0.250$	0.617	0.516	0.579	0.635	0.663	0.673	0.676	0.677	0.676	0.675
$\epsilon^* = 0.275$	0.641	0.470	0.498	0.563	0.617	0.648	0.664	0.671	0.673	0.674
$\epsilon^* = 0.300$	0.676	0.459	0.425	0.464	0.523	0.577	0.616	0.641	0.656	0.665
$\epsilon^* = 0.325$	0.724	0.487	0.393	0.379	0.405	0.451	0.502	0.548	0.587	0.614
$\epsilon^* = 0.350$	0.780	0.549	0.422	0.356	0.331	0.334	0.356	0.389	0.428	0.469
$\epsilon^* = 0.375$	0.837	0.639	0.505	0.412	0.350	0.310	0.288	0.280	0.282	0.295
$\epsilon^* = 0.400$	0.890	0.741	0.626	0.533	0.458	0.398	0.350	0.312	0.283	0.261
$\epsilon^* = 0.425$	0.935	0.842	0.761	0.690	0.627	0.570	0.519	0.474	0.434	0.399
$\epsilon^* = 0.450$	0.971	0.925	0.884	0.845	0.808	0.772	0.739	0.707	0.676	0.647

	$n = 110$	$n = 120$	$n = 130$	$n = 140$	$n = 150$	$n = 160$	$n = 170$	$n = 180$	$n = 190$	$n = 200$
$\epsilon^* = 0.025$	0.669	0.669	0.669	0.669	0.669	0.669	0.669	0.668	0.668	0.668
$\epsilon^* = 0.050$	0.671	0.671	0.671	0.671	0.670	0.670	0.670	0.669	0.670	0.669
$\epsilon^* = 0.075$	0.672	0.672	0.671	0.671	0.671	0.671	0.670	0.670	0.670	0.670
$\epsilon^* = 0.100$	0.673	0.672	0.672	0.671	0.671	0.671	0.671	0.670	0.670	0.670
$\epsilon^* = 0.125$	0.673	0.673	0.672	0.672	0.672	0.671	0.671	0.671	0.670	0.670
$\epsilon^* = 0.150$	0.674	0.673	0.673	0.672	0.672	0.672	0.671	0.671	0.671	0.671
$\epsilon^* = 0.175$	0.674	0.673	0.673	0.672	0.672	0.672	0.672	0.671	0.671	0.671
$\epsilon^* = 0.200$	0.674	0.673	0.673	0.673	0.672	0.672	0.672	0.671	0.671	0.671
$\epsilon^* = 0.225$	0.675	0.674	0.673	0.672	0.672	0.672	0.672	0.672	0.671	0.671
$\epsilon^* = 0.250$	0.675	0.674	0.673	0.673	0.672	0.672	0.672	0.672	0.671	0.671
$\epsilon^* = 0.275$	0.674	0.674	0.673	0.673	0.673	0.673	0.672	0.671	0.671	0.671
$\epsilon^* = 0.300$	0.669	0.671	0.672	0.672	0.672	0.672	0.672	0.672	0.672	0.672
$\epsilon^* = 0.325$	0.635	0.648	0.657	0.663	0.666	0.668	0.669	0.670	0.671	0.671
$\epsilon^* = 0.350$	0.508	0.543	0.572	0.597	0.615	0.630	0.642	0.649	0.655	0.660
$\epsilon^* = 0.375$	0.313	0.337	0.365	0.394	0.425	0.455	0.484	0.511	0.536	0.557
$\epsilon^* = 0.400$	0.245	0.234	0.229	0.228	0.229	0.235	0.243	0.254	0.268	0.283
$\epsilon^* = 0.425$	0.367	0.338	0.313	0.290	0.270	0.253	0.238	0.224	0.213	0.203
$\epsilon^* = 0.450$	0.620	0.594	0.569	0.545	0.522	0.501	0.480	0.461	0.442	0.424

estimator with moderate sample sizes and small Bayes errors.

Multivariate case

Assume that population Π_i is distributed as a multivariate Gaussian $N(\mu_i, \Sigma)$, for $i = 0, 1$. Under these conditions, John obtained in [39] an exact expression for the expectation of the error of the LDA classification rule, defined by (2) to (4), for the case where $N_0 = n_0$ is fixed. This result is stated by Moran in [40] as follows:

$$E\left[\varepsilon_n^0 \mid N_0 = n_0\right] = P\left(\frac{W_1}{W_2} > \frac{1-\rho_e}{1+\rho_e}\right), \tag{29}$$

where W_1 and W_2 are independently distributed as non-central chi-square variables with d degrees of freedom

(d being the dimensionality) and noncentrality parameters λ_1 and λ_2, with

$$\lambda_1 = \frac{n_0 n_1}{2(1+\rho_e)}\left(\frac{1}{\sqrt{n_0+n_1}} - \frac{1}{\sqrt{n_0+n_1+4n_0n_1}}\right)^2 \delta^2,$$

$$\lambda_2 = \frac{n_0 n_1}{2(1-\rho_e)}\left(\frac{1}{\sqrt{n_0+n_1}} + \frac{1}{\sqrt{n_0+n_1+4n_0n_1}}\right)^2 \delta^2,$$

$$\rho_e = \frac{n_1 - n_0}{\sqrt{(n_0+n_1)(n_0+n_1+4n_0n_1)}}, \tag{30}$$

where $\delta^2 = (\mu_1 - \mu_0)^T \Sigma^{-1} (\mu_1 - \mu_0)$ is the squared Mahalanobis distance between the populations. The corresponding result for $E[\varepsilon_n^1 \mid N_0 = n_0]$ is obtained by interchanging n_0 and n_1. The expected true error rate can then be found by using (16).

Moran also provided the following expression for the expectation of the resubstitution error estimator in the multivariate case, for fixed $N_0 = n_0$ [40]:

$$E\left[\hat{\varepsilon}_n^{r,0} \mid N_0 = n_0\right] = P\left(\frac{W_3}{W_4} > \frac{1-\rho_r}{1+\rho_r}\right), \tag{31}$$

where W_3 and W_4 are independently distributed as noncentral chi-square variables with d degrees of freedom and noncentrality parameters λ_3 and λ_4, with

$$\lambda_3 = \frac{n_0 n_1}{2(1+\rho_r)}\left(\frac{1}{\sqrt{n_0+n_1}} - \frac{1}{\sqrt{n_0-3n_1+4n_0n_1}}\right)^2 \delta^2,$$

$$\lambda_4 = \frac{n_0 n_1}{2(1-\rho_r)}\left(\frac{1}{\sqrt{n_0+n_1}} + \frac{1}{\sqrt{n_0-3n_1+4n_0n_1}}\right)^2 \delta^2,$$

$$\rho_r = -\sqrt{\frac{n_0+n_1}{n_0-3n_1+4n_0n_1}}, \tag{32}$$

The corresponding result for $E[\hat{\varepsilon}_n^{r,1}]$ is obtained by interchanging n_0 and n_1. The expected resubstitution error rate can then be found by using (22).

The bootstrap LDA classifier in the multivariate case is given by

$$\psi_n^C(X) = \begin{cases} 1, & \text{if } \left(X - \frac{\hat{\mu}_0^C + \hat{\mu}_1^C}{2}\right)^T \Sigma^{-1}\left(\hat{\mu}_0^C - \hat{\mu}_1^C\right) < 0 \\ 0, & \text{otherwise} \end{cases}, \tag{33}$$

where $\hat{\mu}_0^C$ and $\hat{\mu}_1^C$ are defined in (24). The next theorem generalizes John's result for the multivariate classification error to the case of the bootstrapped LDA classification rule.

Theorem 2. *Assume that population Π_i is distributed as $N(\mu_i, \Sigma)$, for $i = 0, 1$. Then, the expected error rate of the bootstrap LDA classification rule defined by (33) is given by*

$$E\left[\varepsilon_n^{C,0} \mid N_0 = n_0, C\right] = P\left(\frac{W_5}{W_6} > \frac{1-\rho_c}{1+\rho_c}\right), \tag{34}$$

where W_5 and W_6 are independently distributed as noncentral chi-square variables with d degrees of freedom and noncentrality parameters λ_5 and λ_6, with

$$\lambda_5 = \frac{1}{2(1+\rho_c)}\left(\frac{1}{\sqrt{s_0+s_1}} - \frac{1}{\sqrt{s_0+s_1+4}}\right)^2 \delta^2,$$

$$\lambda_6 = \frac{1}{2(1-\rho_c)}\left(\frac{1}{\sqrt{s_0+s_1}} + \frac{1}{\sqrt{s_0+s_1+4}}\right)^2 \delta^2,$$

$$\rho_c = \frac{s_0 - s_1}{\sqrt{(s_0+s_1)(s_0+s_1+4)}}, \tag{35}$$

where s_0 and s_1 are defined in (27). The corresponding result for $E[\varepsilon_n^{C,1} \mid N_0 = n_0, C]$ is obtained by interchanging s_0 and s_1.

Proof. See the Appendix.

It is easy to check that the result in Theorem 2 reduces to the one in (29) and (30) when $C = \mathbf{1}_n$.

As in the univariate case, Theorem 2 can be used in conjunction with Equations (12) and (28) to compute $E[\hat{\varepsilon}_n^{\text{boot}}]$.

The weight w^* for unbiased bootstrap error estimation can now be computed exactly by means of Equations (11), (12), (16) to (17), (22), (28), (29) to (32), and (34) to (35).

An issue that arises in the multivariate case is the computation of the probabilities in (29), (31), and (34). This computation is very difficult since it involves the ratio of noncentral chi-square random variables, which has a doubly noncentral F distribution. Computation of this distribution is a hard problem. Moran proposes in [40] a complex procedure, based on work by Price [53], to compute this probability, which only applies to even dimensionality d. We employ a simpler procedure, namely, the Imhof-Pearson three-moment method, which is applicable to even and odd dimensionality [41]. This consists of approximating a noncentral $\chi_d^2(\lambda)$ random variable with a central χ_h^2 random variable, by equating the first three moments of their distributions. This approach was also employed in [52], where it was found to be very accurate. To fix ideas, we consider (29). The Imhof-Pearson three-moment approximation is given by

$$E[\varepsilon_n^0] = P\left(\frac{W_1}{W_2} > \frac{1-\rho_e}{1+\rho_e}\right) \simeq P\left(\chi_h^2 > y\right), \quad (36)$$

where χ_h^2 is a central chi-square random variable with h degrees of freedom, with

$$h = \frac{c_2^3}{c_3^2}, \qquad y = h - c_1\sqrt{\frac{h}{c_2}}, \quad (37)$$

and

$$c_i = (1+\rho_e)^i\,(d+i\lambda_1) + (-1)^i\,(1-\rho_e)^i\,(d+i\lambda_2), \quad i = 1,2,3. \quad (38)$$

The approximation is valid only for $c_3 > 0$ [41]. If $c_3 < 0$, one uses the approximation

$$E[\varepsilon_n^0] = P\left(\frac{W_1}{W_2} > \frac{1-\rho_e}{1+\rho_e}\right) \simeq P\left(\chi_h^2 < y\right), \quad (39)$$

where h and y are as in (37), and

$$c_i = (-1)^i\,(1+\rho_e)^i\,(d+i\lambda_1) + (1-\rho_e)^i\,(d+i\lambda_2), \quad i = 1,2,3. \quad (40)$$

The same approximation method applies to (31) and (34) by substituting the appropriate values.

As in the univariate case, the assumption of a common covariance matrix Σ makes the expectations $E[\,\varepsilon_n]$, $E[\,\hat{\varepsilon}_n^r]$, and $E[\,\hat{\varepsilon}_n^{\text{boot}}]$ and thus also the weight w^*, functions only of n and δ. Since $\varepsilon^* = \Phi(-\delta/2)$, this means that the weight w^* is a function only of the Bayes error ε^* and the sample size n.

Figure 2 and Table 2 display the value of w^* computed with the previous expressions in this section, for several sample sizes and Bayes errors. As in the univariate case, $E[\,\hat{\varepsilon}_n^{\text{boot}}]$ in (12) is approximated by a Monte Carlo procedure, with the same number $M = 100 \times n^2$ of MC vectors. All other quantities are computed exactly, as described previously, save for the Imhof-Pearson approximation. We can see in Figure 2 that there is considerable variation in the value of w^* and it can be far from the heuristic 0.632 weight; however, as the sample size increases, w^* appears to settle around an asymptotic fixed value. In contrast to the univariate case, these asymptotic values here appear to be strongly dependent on the Bayes error and are significantly smaller than the heuristic 0.632 except for very small Bayes errors. As in the univariate case, convergence to the apparent asymptotic value is faster for smaller Bayes errors. These facts again help explain the good performance of the original convex 0.632 bootstrap error estimator for moderate sample sizes and small Bayes errors.

Gene expression classification example

Here we demonstrate the application of the previous theory in comparing the performance of the bootstrap error estimator using the optimal weight versus the use of the fixed $w = 0.632$ weight, using gene expression data from the well-known breast cancer classification study in [42], which analyzed expression profiles from 295 tumor specimens, divided into $N_0 = 115$ specimens belonging to the 'good-prognosis' population (class 1 here) and $N_1 = 180$ specimens belonging to the 'poor-prognosis' population (class 0).

Our experiment was set up in the following way. We selected two genes among the previously published 70-gene prognosis profile [43]. These genes were selected for their approximate homoskedastic Gaussian distributions (see Figure 3). Since the real prior probabilities c_0 and c_1 for the good- and poor-prognosis populations are unknown, we assumed three different scenarios corresponding to $c_0 = 1/3$, $c_0 = 1/2$, and $c_0 = 2/3$ and *downsampled* randomly one or the other set of specimens to obtain new sample sizes $(90, 180)$, $(115, 115)$, and $(115, 68)$, respectively, so as to reflect the assumed prior probabilities. In each of the three cases, we then drew 2,000 random samples of size $n = 30$ from the pooled data, computed for each the true error, resubstitution, basic bootstrap, and convex bootstrap error rates. Bias and root-mean-square (RMS) error for each estimator were estimated by averaging over the 2,000 repetitions. We considered both the fixed 0.632 weight and the optimal weight prescribed by our analysis. For the latter, we estimated for each value of c_0 the Bayes error using the full data set and read off Table 2 the optimal weight corresponding to the estimated Bayes error and sample size $n = 30$. The results are displayed in Table 3. Despite the approximate nature of the results, given that the simulated training samples are not independent from each other, we can see that the bias and RMS were always smaller for the estimator using the optimal weight than using the fixed 0.632 weight (all bootstrap estimators vastly outperforming resubstitution).

Conclusions

Exact expressions were derived for the required weight for unbiased convex bootstrap error estimation in the finite sample case, for linear discriminant analysis of Gaussian populations. The results not only provide the practitioner with a recommendation of what weight to use

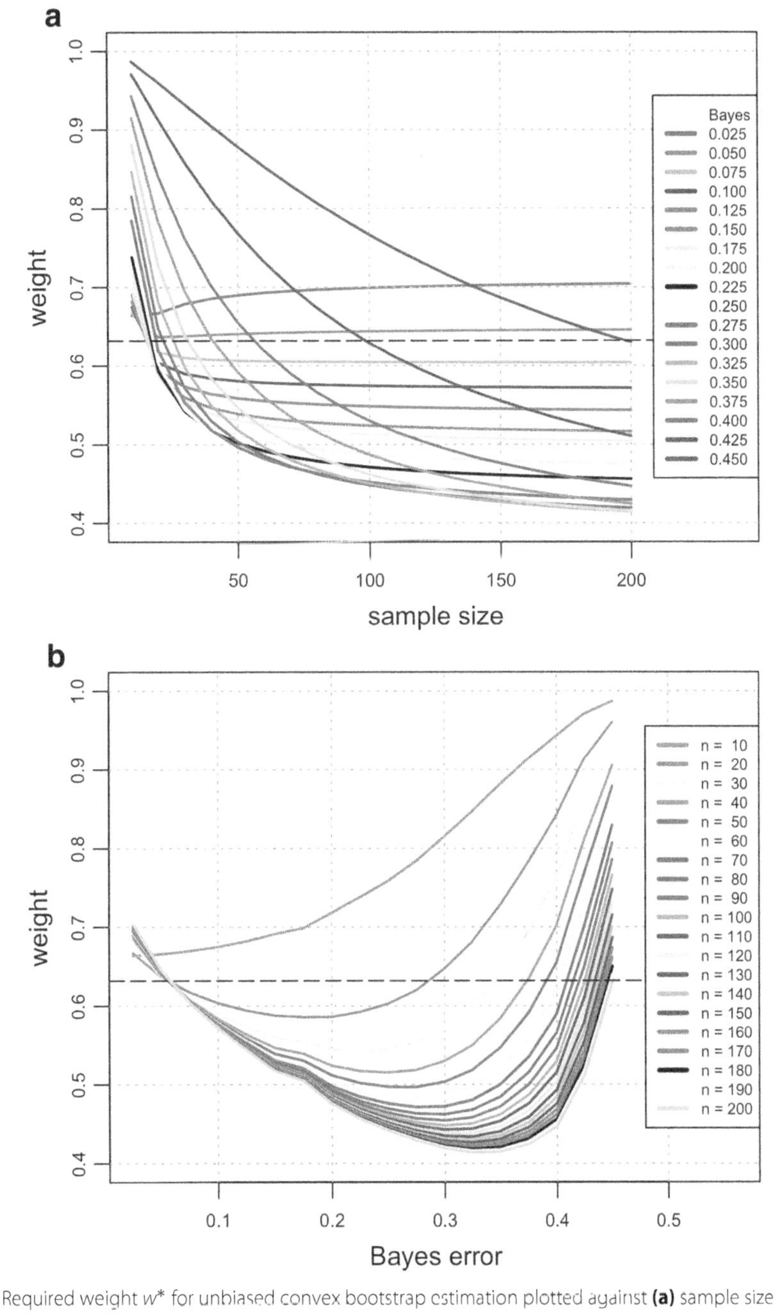

Figure 2 Bivariate case. Required weight w^* for unbiased convex bootstrap estimation plotted against **(a)** sample size and **(b)** Bayes error.

given the sample size and problem difficulty, but also offer insight into the choice of the 0.632 weight for the classic 0.632 bootstrap error estimator. It was observed that the required weight for unbiasedness can deviate significantly from the 0.632 weight, particularly in the multivariate case, where the required weight for unbiasedness appears to settle on an asymptotic value that is strongly dependent on the Bayes error, being as a rule smaller than 0.632. The results were illustrated by application to gene expression data from a well-known breast cancer study.

Appendix

Proof of Theorem 1

Following the same technique used in [40], we write

$$
\begin{aligned}
E\left[\varepsilon_C^0 | C\right] &= P\left(\psi_n^C(X) = 1 \mid X \in \Pi_0, C\right) \\
&= P\left(\widehat{\mu}_1^C > \widehat{\mu}_0^C, X > \frac{\widehat{\mu}_0^C + \widehat{\mu}_1^C}{2} \mid X \in \Pi_0, C\right) \\
&\quad + P\left(\widehat{\mu}_1^C \le \widehat{\mu}_0^C, X \le \frac{\widehat{\mu}_0^C + \widehat{\mu}_1^C}{2} \mid X \in \Pi_0, C\right) \\
&= P(UV > 0 \mid X \in \Pi_0, C), \qquad (41)
\end{aligned}
$$

Table 2 Bivariate case: required weight w^* for unbiased convex bootstrap estimation

	$n = 10$	$n = 20$	$n = 30$	$n = 40$	$n = 50$	$n = 60$	$n = 70$	$n = 80$	$n = 90$	$n = 100$
$\epsilon^* = 0.025$	0.664	0.667	0.679	0.685	0.690	0.693	0.695	0.697	0.698	0.699
$\epsilon^* = 0.050$	0.666	0.637	0.638	0.639	0.641	0.642	0.642	0.643	0.644	0.644
$\epsilon^* = 0.075$	0.670	0.617	0.610	0.608	0.606	0.606	0.605	0.605	0.605	0.605
$\epsilon^* = 0.100$	0.675	0.604	0.590	0.584	0.581	0.578	0.577	0.576	0.575	0.574
$\epsilon^* = 0.125$	0.682	0.594	0.573	0.564	0.559	0.555	0.553	0.551	0.550	0.548
$\epsilon^* = 0.150$	0.691	0.588	0.560	0.547	0.539	0.534	0.530	0.528	0.526	0.524
$\epsilon^* = 0.175$	0.699	0.586	0.554	0.539	0.530	0.524	0.520	0.517	0.515	0.513
$\epsilon^* = 0.200$	0.718	0.586	0.544	0.524	0.512	0.504	0.498	0.493	0.490	0.487
$\epsilon^* = 0.225$	0.738	0.592	0.542	0.517	0.502	0.492	0.485	0.479	0.475	0.471
$\epsilon^* = 0.250$	0.759	0.603	0.545	0.515	0.497	0.485	0.476	0.469	0.464	0.460
$\epsilon^* = 0.275$	0.784	0.620	0.553	0.518	0.497	0.482	0.471	0.463	0.457	0.452
$\epsilon^* = 0.300$	0.815	0.647	0.572	0.530	0.503	0.485	0.472	0.462	0.454	0.448
$\epsilon^* = 0.325$	0.847	0.681	0.598	0.550	0.518	0.496	0.480	0.468	0.458	0.450
$\epsilon^* = 0.350$	0.882	0.728	0.639	0.584	0.546	0.520	0.500	0.484	0.472	0.462
$\epsilon^* = 0.375$	0.915	0.784	0.695	0.635	0.592	0.560	0.535	0.516	0.500	0.487
$\epsilon^* = 0.400$	0.943	0.842	0.763	0.702	0.655	0.619	0.590	0.566	0.546	0.530
$\epsilon^* = 0.425$	0.971	0.914	0.859	0.811	0.769	0.732	0.701	0.673	0.650	0.629
$\epsilon^* = 0.450$	0.987	0.960	0.933	0.905	0.879	0.853	0.830	0.807	0.786	0.766

	$n = 110$	$n = 120$	$n = 130$	$n = 140$	$n = 150$	$n = 160$	$n = 170$	$n = 180$	$n = 190$	$n = 200$
$\epsilon^* = 0.025$	0.700	0.701	0.701	0.702	0.702	0.703	0.703	0.704	0.704	0.704
$\epsilon^* = 0.050$	0.644	0.645	0.645	0.645	0.645	0.645	0.645	0.646	0.646	0.646
$\epsilon^* = 0.075$	0.604	0.604	0.604	0.604	0.604	0.604	0.604	0.604	0.604	0.604
$\epsilon^* = 0.100$	0.574	0.573	0.573	0.573	0.573	0.572	0.572	0.572	0.572	0.572
$\epsilon^* = 0.125$	0.548	0.547	0.546	0.546	0.545	0.545	0.544	0.544	0.544	0.543
$\epsilon^* = 0.150$	0.523	0.522	0.521	0.520	0.519	0.518	0.518	0.517	0.517	0.517
$\epsilon^* = 0.175$	0.511	0.510	0.509	0.508	0.507	0.506	0.506	0.505	0.505	0.504
$\epsilon^* = 0.200$	0.485	0.483	0.482	0.480	0.479	0.478	0.477	0.477	0.476	0.475
$\epsilon^* = 0.225$	0.469	0.466	0.464	0.463	0.461	0.460	0.459	0.458	0.457	0.456
$\epsilon^* = 0.250$	0.457	0.454	0.452	0.449	0.448	0.446	0.445	0.443	0.442	0.441
$\epsilon^* = 0.275$	0.448	0.444	0.442	0.439	0.437	0.435	0.433	0.432	0.430	0.429
$\epsilon^* = 0.300$	0.443	0.438	0.435	0.432	0.429	0.426	0.424	0.422	0.420	0.419
$\epsilon^* = 0.325$	0.444	0.439	0.434	0.430	0.426	0.423	0.421	0.418	0.416	0.414
$\epsilon^* = 0.350$	0.454	0.447	0.441	0.435	0.431	0.427	0.423	0.420	0.417	0.415
$\epsilon^* = 0.375$	0.476	0.467	0.459	0.452	0.446	0.441	0.436	0.432	0.428	0.424
$\epsilon^* = 0.400$	0.516	0.504	0.493	0.484	0.476	0.469	0.462	0.457	0.451	0.447
$\epsilon^* = 0.425$	0.611	0.594	0.580	0.567	0.555	0.544	0.535	0.526	0.518	0.511
$\epsilon^* = 0.450$	0.748	0.731	0.715	0.700	0.687	0.674	0.662	0.650	0.640	0.630

where $U = \hat{\mu}_1^C - \hat{\mu}_0^C$ and $V = X - \frac{\hat{\mu}_0^C + \hat{\mu}_1^C}{2}$. From (303), it is clear that, given C, $\hat{\mu}_0^C$ and $\hat{\mu}_1^C$ are independent Gaussian random variables, such that $\hat{\mu}_i^C \sim N(\mu_i, s_i\sigma_i^2)$, for $i = 0, 1$, where s_1 and s_2 are defined in (27). It follows that U and V are jointly Gaussian random variables, with the following parameters:

$$
\begin{aligned}
&E[U \mid X \in \Pi_0, C] = \mu_1 - \mu_0, \mathrm{Var}(U \mid X \in \Pi_0, C) = s_0\sigma_0^2 + s_1\sigma_1^2,\\
&E[\,V \mid X \in \Pi_0, C] = \frac{\mu_0 - \mu_1}{2},\\
&\mathrm{Var}(V \mid X \in \Pi_0, C) = \left(1 + \frac{s_0}{4}\right)\sigma_0^2 + \frac{s_1}{4}\sigma_1^2,\\
&\mathrm{Cov}(U, V \mid X \in \Pi_0, C) = \frac{s_0\sigma_0^2 - s_1\sigma_1^2}{2}.
\end{aligned}
\tag{42}
$$

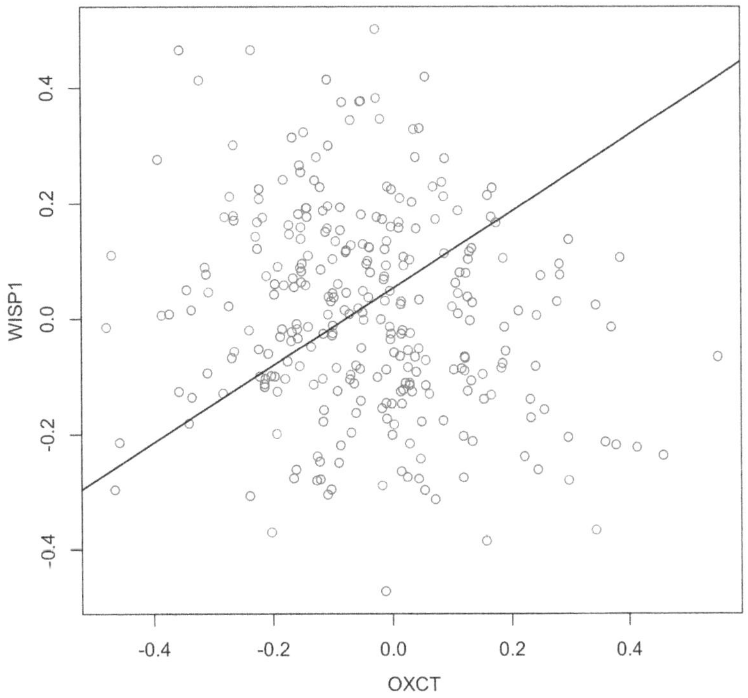

Figure 3 Data used in the gene expression experiment. The plot shows the optimal (linear) classifier superimposed on the sample for the genes OXCT and WISP1, from the breast cancer study in [42]. We can see that both populations are approximately Gaussian with equal dispersion. Bad prognosis = red. Good prognosis = blue.

The result then follows after some algebraic manipulation. By symmetry, to obtain $E[\varepsilon_C^1 \mid C]$, one needs only to interchange all indices 0 and 1. □

Proof of Theorem 2

Following the same technique used in [32], we write

$$E[\varepsilon_C^0 \mid C] = P(\psi_n^C(X) = 1 \mid X \in \Pi_0, C) = P\left((\hat{\mu}_1^C - \hat{\mu}_0^C)^T \Sigma^{-1}\left(X - \frac{\hat{\mu}_0^C + \hat{\mu}_1^C}{2}\right) > 0 \mid X \in \Pi_0, C\right) = P\left(U^T V > 0 \mid X \in \Pi_0, C\right)$$
$$= P((U+V)^T(U+V) - (U-V)^T(U-V) > 0 \mid X \in \Pi_0, C)$$
$$= P\left(\frac{(U+V)^T(U+V)}{(U-V)^T(U-V)} > 1 \mid X \in \Pi_0, C\right), \qquad (43)$$

where $U = (s_0+s_1)^{-\frac{1}{2}}\Sigma^{-\frac{1}{2}}(\widehat{\mu}_1^C - \widehat{\mu}_0^C)$ and $V = 2\,(s_0 + s_1 + 4)^{-\frac{1}{2}}\Sigma^{-\frac{1}{2}}\left(X - \frac{\widehat{\mu}_0^C + \widehat{\mu}_1^C}{2}\right)$. It can be readily checked that $U+V$ and $U-V$ are independent Gaussian random vectors, such that

$$E[U+V \mid X \in \Pi_0, C] = \left[(s_0+s_1)^{-\frac{1}{2}} - (s_0+s_1+4)^{-\frac{1}{2}}\right] \times \Sigma^{-1/2}(\mu_1 - \mu_0),$$
$$E[U-V \mid X \in \Pi_0, C] = \left[(s_0+s_1)^{-\frac{1}{2}} + (s_0+s_1+4)^{-\frac{1}{2}}\right] \times \Sigma^{-1/2}(\mu_1 - \mu_0),$$
$$\Sigma_{U+V} \mid X \in \Pi_0, C = 2(1+\rho_c)I, \quad \Sigma_{U-V} \mid X \in \Pi_0, C = 2(1-\rho_c)I, \qquad (44)$$

Table 3 Bias and RMS of estimators considered in the experiment with expression data from genes 'OXCT' and 'WISP1'

c_0	n	ε^*	$E[\varepsilon_n]$	Resub		Basic boot		Opt boot		0.632 boot	
				Bias	RMS	Bias	RMS	Bias	RMS	Bias	RMS
0.33	30	0.4043	0.4206	−0.0702	0.1061	0.0008	0.0820	−0.0161	0.0803	−0.0253	0.0817
0.50	30	0.3969	0.4266	−0.0719	0.1060	0.0072	0.0830	−0.0116	0.0798	−0.0219	0.0806
0.67	30	0.3893	0.4131	−0.0914	0.1185	−0.0181	0.0878	−0.0355	0.0885	−0.0451	0.0909

Also displayed are the assumed values for the prior probability c_0, sample size n, the estimated value of the Bayes error ε^*, and the expected classification error $E[\varepsilon_n]$.

where ρ_c is defined as in (35) and I denotes the identity matrix of dimension d. It follows that

$$W_5 = \frac{1}{2(1+\rho_c)}(U+V)^T(U+V),$$
$$W_6 = \frac{1}{2(1-\rho_c)}(U-V)^T(U-V) \quad (45)$$

are independent noncentral chi-squared random variables with d degrees of freedom and noncentrality parameters λ_5 and λ_6 defined in (35). The result then follows from (62). Following along the same lines, one can show that $E[\varepsilon_C^1 \mid C]$ is obtained by interchanging s_0 and s_1 in the result for $E[\varepsilon_C^0 \mid C]$ (the details are omitted for brevity). □

Competing interests
The authors declare that they have no competing interests.

Authors' contributions
TV proved Theorems 1 and 2. TV and SC conducted numerical experiments to compute Figures 1 and 2 and Tables 1 and 2. SC conducted the numerical experiments with gene expression data. UMB conceived the study and wrote the first draft of the manuscript. ERD contributed ideas on convex error estimation and revised the manuscript. All authors read and approved the final manuscript.

Acknowledgements
The authors acknowledge the support of the National Science Foundation, through NSF awards CCF-0845407 (Braga-Neto) and CCF-0634794 (Dougherty).

References
1. B Efron, Bootstrap methods: another look at the jackknife. Ann. Stat. **7**(1), 1–26 (1979). [Online]. http://projecteuclid.org/euclid.aos/1176344552
2. B Efron, Computers and the theory of statistics: thinking the unthinkable. SIAM Rev. **21**(4), 460–480 (1979). [Online]. http://www.jstor.org/stable/2030104
3. B Efron, Nonparametric standard errors and confidence intervals. Can. J. Stat. **9**(2), 139–158 (1981)
4. B Efron, Estimating the error rate of a prediction rule: improvement on cross-validation. J. Am. Stat. Assoc. **78**(382), 316–331 (1983). [Online]. http://dx.doi.org/10.2307/2288636
5. B Efron, G Gong, A leisurely look at the bootstrap, the jackknife, and cross-validation. Am. Stat. **37**(1), 36–48 (1983). [Online]. http://dx.doi.org/10.2307/2685844
6. B Efron, R Tibshirani, *An Introduction to the Bootstrap*. (Chapman & Hall, New York, 1993)
7. B Efron, R Tibshirani, Improvements on cross-validation: the .632+ bootstrap method. J. Am. Stat. Assoc. **92**(438), 548–560 (1997). [Online]. http://dx.doi.org/10.2307/2965703
8. K Singh, On the asymptotic accuracy of Efron's bootstrap. Ann. Stat. **9**, 1187–1195 (1981)
9. P Bickel, D Freedman, Some asymptotic theory for the bootstrap. Ann. Stat. **9**, 1196–1217 (1981)
10. R Beran, Estimated sampling distributions: the bootstrap and competitors. Ann. Stat. **10**(1), 212–225 (1982). [Online]. http://www.jstor.org/stable/2240513
11. P Hall, *The Bootstrap and Edgeworth Expansion*. (Springer, New York, 1992)
12. F Scholz, *The Bootstrap Small Sample Properties*. (University of, Washington, Seattle, 2007)
13. P Porter, S Rao, J-Y Ku, R Poirot, M Dakins, Small sample properties of nonparametric bootstrap t confidence intervals. J. Air Waste Manag. Assoc. **47**(11), 1197–1203 (1997)
14. K Chan, S Lee, An exact iterated bootstrap algorithm for small-sample bias reduction. Comput. Stat. Data Anal. **36**(1), 1–13 (2001)
15. G Young, Bootstrap: more than a stab in the dark? With discussion and a rejoinder by the author. Stat. Sci. **9**(3), 382–415 (1994)
16. J Shao, D Tu, *The Jackknife and Bootstrap*. (Springer, New York, 1995). [Online]. http://www.worldcat.org/isbn/0387945156
17. D Pils, D Tong, G Hager, E Obermayr, S Aust, G Heinze, M Kohl, E Schuster, A Wolf, J Sehouli, I Braicu, I Vergote, T Van Gorp, S Mahner, N Concin, P Speiser, R Zeillinger, A combined blood based gene expression and plasma protein abundance signature for diagnosis of epithelial ovarian cancer–a study of the OVCAD consortium. BMC Cancer. **13**(178) (2013). doi: 10.1186/1471-2407-13-178
18. S Paul, P Maji, muHEM for identification of differentially expressed miRNAs using hypercuboid equivalence partition matrix. BMC Bioinformatics. **14**(266) (2013). doi:10.1186/1471-2105-14-266
19. S Student, K Fujarewicz, Stable feature selection and classification algorithms for multiclass microarray data. Biol Direct. **7**, 33 (2012). doi:10.1186/1745-6150-7-33
20. T Hwang, CH Sun, T Yun, GS Yi, FiGS: a filter-based gene selection workbench for microarray data. BMC Bioinformatics. **11**(50) (2010). doi:10.1186/1471-2105-11-50
21. G McLachlan, *Discriminant Analysis and Statistical Pattern Recognition*. (Wiley, New York, 1992)
22. L Devroye, L Gyorfi, G Lugosi, *A Probabilistic Theory of Pattern Recognition*. (Springer, New York, 1996)
23. C Sima, E Dougherty, Optimal convex error estimators for classification. Pattern Recognit. **39**(6), 1763–1780 (2006)
24. M Chernick, V Murthy, C Nealy, Application of bootstrap and other resampling techniques: evaluation of classifier performance. Pattern Recognit. Lett. **3**(3), 167–178 (1985). [Online] http://www.sciencedirect.com/science/article/B6V15-48MPVCK-55/2/32754228bc17ac0655b9fa9a7a60ca90
25. K Fukunaga, R Hayes, Estimation of classifier performance. IEEE Trans. Pattern Anal. Mach. Intell. **11**(10), 1087–1101 (1989)
26. G McLachlan, Error rate estimation in discriminant analysis: recent advancesAdv. Multivariate Stat. Anal, 233–252 (1987)
27. A Davison, P Hall, On the bias and variability of bootstrap and cross-validation estimates of error rate in discrimination problems. Biometrika. **79**(2), 279–284 (1992). [Online] http://www.jstor.org/stable/2336839
28. M Chernick, *Bootstrap Methods: A Guide for Practitioners and Researchers (Wiley Series in Probability and Statistics)*, 2nd ed. (Wiley-Interscience, Hoboken, 2007). [Online]. http://www.worldcat.org/isbn/0471756210
29. S Chatterjee, S Chatterjee, Estimation of misclassification probabilities by bootstrap methods. Comput. **12**, 645–656 (1983)
30. A Jain, R Dubes, C Chen, Bootstrap techniques for error estimation. IEEE Trans. Pattern Anal. Mach. Intell. **9**(5), 628–633 (1987)
31. S Raudys, On the accuracy of a bootstrap estimate of the classification erro, in *Proceedings of Ninth International Joint Conference on Pattern Recognition*, (Rome 14–17 Nov 1988, p. 1230–1232(1988)
32. U Braga-Neto, E Dougherty, Bolstered error estimation. Pattern Recognit. **37**(6), 1267–1281 (2004). [Online] http://www.sciencedirect.com/science/article/B6V14-4BNMG7H-1/2/752fe2e9105d351b88850e48577ba182c
33. U Braga-Neto, R Hashimoto, E Dougherty, D Nguyen, R Carroll, Is cross-validation better than re-substitution for ranking genes? Bioinformatics. **20**(2), 253–258 (2004). [Online] http://bioinformatics.oxfordjournals.org/cgi/content/abstract/20/2/253
34. U Braga-Neto, E Dougherty, Is cross-validation valid for small-sample microarray classification? Bioinformatics. **20**(3), 374–380 (2004). [Online]. http://bioinformatics.oxfordjournals.org/cgi/content/abstract/20/3/374
35. R Kohavi, A study of cross-validation and bootstrap for accuracy estimation and model selection. (IJCAI), 1137–1145 (1995). [Online]. http://citeseerx.ist.psu.edu/viewdoc/summary?doi=10.1.1.48.529
36. G Toussaint, An efficient method for estimating the probability of misclassification applied to a problem in medical diagnosis. Comput. Biol. Med. **4**, 269 (1975)

37. G McLachlan, A note on the choice of a weighting function to give an efficient method for estimating the probability of misclassification. Pattern Recognit. **9**(2), 147–149 (1977)
38. S Raudys, A Jain, Small sample size effects in statistical pattern recognition: recommendations for practitioners. IEEE Trans. Pattern Anal. Mach. Intell. **13**(3), 4–37 (1991)
39. S John, Errors in discrimination. Ann. Math. Stat. **32**(4), 1125–1144 (1961). [Online]. http://www.jstor.org/stable/2237911
40. M Moran, On the expectation of errors of allocation associated with a linear discriminant function. Biometrika. **62**(1), 141–148 (1975). [Online]. http://www.jstor.org/stable/2334496
41. J Imhof, Computing the distribution of quadratic forms in normal variables. Biometrika. **48**(3/4), 419–426 (1961)
42. MJ van de Vijver, YD He, LJ van't Veer, H Dai, AAM Hart, DW Voskuil, GJ Schreiber, JL Peterse, C Roberts, MJ Marton, M Parrish, D Astma, A Witteveen, A Glas, L Delahaye, T van der Velde, H Bartelink, S Rodenhuis, ET Rutgers, SH Friend, R Bernards, A gene-expression signature as a predictor of survival in breast cancer. N. Engl. J. Med. **347**(25), 1999–2009 (2002)
43. LJ van't Veer, H Dai, MJ van de Vijver, YD He, AAM Hart, M Mao, HL Peterse, K van der Kooy, MJ Marton, AT Witteveen, GJ Schreiber, RM Kerkhoven, C Roberts, PS Linsley, R Bernards, SH Friend, Gene expression profiling predicts clinical outcome of breast cancer. Nature. **415**, 530–536 (2002)
44. UM Braga-Neto, A Zollanvari, ER Dougherty, Cross-validation under separate sampling: strong bias and how to correct it. Bioinformatics (2014). doi:10.1093/bioinformatics/btu527
45. T Anderson, Classification by multivariate analysis. Psychometrika. **16**, 31–50 (1951)
46. S Raudys, Comparison of the estimates of the probability of misclassification, in *Proc. 4th Int. Conf. Pattern Recognition* Kyoto, Japan, 1978), pp. 280–282
47. L Breiman, Bagging predictors. Mach. Learn. **24**(2), 123–140 (1996)
48. T Vu, U Braga-Neto, Is bagging effective in the classification of small-sample genomic and proteomic data?. URASIP J. Bioinformatics Syst. Biol. **2009**, Article ID 158368 (2009)
49. V Vapnik, *Statistical Learning Theory*. (Wiley, New York, 1998)
50. A Nijenhuis, H Wilf, *Combinatorial Algorithms*, 2nd ed. (Academic Press, New York, 1978)
51. M Hills, Allocation rules and their error rates. J. R. Stat. Soc. Series B (Methodological). **28**(1), 1–31 (1966). [Online]. http://www.jstor.org/stable/2984268
52. A Zollanvari, U Braga-Neto, E Dougherty, On the sampling distribution of resubstitution and leave-one-out error estimators for linear classifiers. Pattern Recognit. **42**(11), 2705–2723 (2009)
53. R Price, Some non-central f-distributions expressed in closed form. Biometrika. **51**, 107–122 (1964)

Permissions

All chapters in this book were first published in EURASIP-JBSB, by Springer; hereby published with permission under the Creative Commons Attribution License or equivalent. Every chapter published in this book has been scrutinized by our experts. Their significance has been extensively debated. The topics covered herein carry significant findings which will fuel the growth of the discipline. They may even be implemented as practical applications or may be referred to as a beginning point for another development.

The contributors of this book come from diverse backgrounds, making this book a truly international effort. This book will bring forth new frontiers with its revolutionizing research information and detailed analysis of the nascent developments around the world.

We would like to thank all the contributing authors for lending their expertise to make the book truly unique. They have played a crucial role in the development of this book. Without their invaluable contributions this book wouldn't have been possible. They have made vital efforts to compile up to date information on the varied aspects of this subject to make this book a valuable addition to the collection of many professionals and students.

This book was conceptualized with the vision of imparting up-to-date information and advanced data in this field. To ensure the same, a matchless editorial board was set up. Every individual on the board went through rigorous rounds of assessment to prove their worth. After which they invested a large part of their time researching and compiling the most relevant data for our readers.

The editorial board has been involved in producing this book since its inception. They have spent rigorous hours researching and exploring the diverse topics which have resulted in the successful publishing of this book. They have passed on their knowledge of decades through this book. To expedite this challenging task, the publisher supported the team at every step. A small team of assistant editors was also appointed to further simplify the editing procedure and attain best results for the readers.

Apart from the editorial board, the designing team has also invested a significant amount of their time in understanding the subject and creating the most relevant covers. They scrutinized every image to scout for the most suitable representation of the subject and create an appropriate cover for the book.

The publishing team has been an ardent support to the editorial, designing and production team. Their endless efforts to recruit the best for this project, has resulted in the accomplishment of this book. They are a veteran in the field of academics and their pool of knowledge is as vast as their experience in printing. Their expertise and guidance has proved useful at every step. Their uncompromising quality standards have made this book an exceptional effort. Their encouragement from time to time has been an inspiration for everyone.

The publisher and the editorial board hope that this book will prove to be a valuable piece of knowledge for researchers, students, practitioners and scholars across the globe.

List of Contributors

Chetan Kumar and Alok Choudhary
Department of Electrical Engineering and Computer Science, Northwestern University, Evanston, IL 60201, USA

Rajasekhar Kakumani and Omair Ahmad
Department of Electrical and Computer Engineering, Concordia University, 1455 de Maisonneuve Blvd. West Montreal, QC H3G1M8, Canada

Vijay Devabhaktuni
Department of Electrical Engineering and Computer Science, University of Toledo, MS 308, 2801 W. Bancroft St., Toledo, OH 43606, USA

Bin Jia
Intelligent Fusion Technology, Germantown, MD 20876, USA

Xiaodong Wang
Department of Electrical Engineering, Columbia University, New York, NY 10027, USA

Onder Suvak and Alper Demir
Department of Electrical and Electronics Engineering, College of Engineering, Koç University Rumeli Feneri Yolu 34450 Sariyer Istanbul, Turkey

Michael P Verdicchio
Department of Mathematics and Computer Science, The Citadel, Charleston, SC 29409, USA

Seungchan Kim
Integrated Cancer Genomics Division, Translational Genomics Research Institute, Phoenix, AZ 85004, USA

Yihua Liu and Peng Qiu
Department of Bioinformatics and Computational Biology, University of Texas MD Anderson Cancer Center, Houston, TX 77030, USA

Yuan Ji
Center for Clinical and Research Informatics, NorthShore University HealthSystem, Chicago, IL 60201, USA

Reinhard Heckel
Department of Information Technology and Electrical Engineering, ETH Zürich, Zürich, Switzerland

Steffen Schober and Martin Bossert
Institute of Telecommunications and Applied Information Theory, University of Ulm, Ulm, Germany

Johannes Georg Klotz, Steffen Schober and Martin Bossert
Institute of Communications Engineering, Ulm University, Albert-Einstein-Allee 43, 89081 Ulm, Germany

Ronny Feuer, Oliver Sawodny and Michael Ederer
Institute for System Dynamics, University of Stuttgart, 70569 Stuttgart, Germany

Sanvesh Srivastava
Department of Statistics, Purdue University, 250 N. University Street, West Lafayette, IN 47907, USA

Wenyi Wang and Ganiraju Manyam
Department of Bioinformatics and Computational Biology, Division of Quantitative Sciences, The University of Texas MD Anderson Cancer Center, 1515 Holcombe Blvd, Unit 1411, Houston, Texas, USA

Carlos Ordonez
Department of Computer Science, University of Houston, 4800 Calhoun, Houston, Texas, USA

Veerabhadran Baladandayuthapani
Department of Biostatistics, Division of Quantitative Sciences, The University of Texas MD Anderson Cancer Center, 1515 Holcombe Blvd, Unit 1411, Houston, Texas, USA

Alexandros Iliadis, Dimitris Anastassiou and Xiaodong Wang
Department of Electrical Engineering, Center for Computational Biology Bioinformatics and Columbia University, New York, NY 10027, USA

Ryan Bressler, Jake Lin, Andrea Eakin, Thomas Robinson, Richard Kreisberg, Hector Rovira John Boyle and Ilya Shmulevich
Institute for System Biology, 401 Terry Avenue North, Seattle, WA 98109-5234, USA

Theo Knijnenburg
Institute for System Biology, 401 Terry Avenue North, Seattle, WA 98109-5234, USA
Division of Molecular Carcinogenesis, Netherlands Cancer Institute, Plesmanlaan 121, 1066CX, Amsterdam, The Netherlands

Bin Jia
Intelligent Fusion Technology, Germantown, Inc., MD 20876, USA

Xiaodong Wang
Department of Electrical Engineering, Columbia University, New York, NY 10027, USA

Elizabeth M Jennings
Department of Statistics, Texas A&M University, College Station, TX 77843, USA

Jeffrey S Morris
Department of Biostatistics, UT M.D. Anderson Cancer Center, Houston, TX 77030, USA

Raymond J Carroll
Department of Statistics, Texas A&M University, College Station, TX 77843, USA

Ganiraju C Manyam
Department of Bioinformatics and Computational Biology, UT M.D. Anderson Cancer Center, Houston, TX 77030, USA

Veerabhadran Baladandayuthapani
Department of Biostatistics, UT M.D. Anderson Cancer Center, Houston, TX 77030, USA

Guy Karlebach
German Cancer Research Institute (DKFZ), Im Neuenheimer Feld 280, Heidelberg 69121, Germany

Sai Zou
School of Software Engineering, Chongqing College of Electronic Engineering, Chongqing 401331, People's Republic of China

Lei Wang
School of Software Engineering, Chongqing College of Electronic Engineering, Chongqing 401331, People's Republic of China

Junfeng Wang
School of Software Engineering, Chongqing College of Electronic Engineering, Chongqing 401331, People's Republic of China

Seyedbehzad Nabavi and Cranos M Williams
Department of Electrical and Computer Engineering, North Carolina State University, Raleigh, NC, USA

Hongjia Ouyang, Jie Fang and Liangzhong Shen
Department of Physics and Electronic Information Engineering, Wenzhou University, Wenzhou, Zhejiang 325035, China

Edward R Dougherty
Department of Electrical and Computer Engineering, Texas A&M University, College Station, TX 33101, USA
Computational Biology Division, Translational Genomics Research Institute, Phoenix, AZ 77843, USA

Wenbin Liu
Department of Physics and Electronic Information Engineering, Wenzhou University, Wenzhou, Zhejiang 325035, China
Department of Electrical and Computer Engineering, Texas A&M University, College Station, TX 33101, USA

Jie Fang, Hongjia Ouyang and Liangzhong Shen
Department of Physics and Electronic information engineering, Wenzhou University, Wenzhou, Zhejiang 325035, China

Edward R Dougherty
Department of Electrical and Computer Engineering, Texas A&M University, College Station, TX 33101, USA
Center for Bioinformatics and Genomics Systems, College Station, TX 33101, USA

Wenbin Liu
Department of Physics and Electronic information engineering, Wenzhou University, Wenzhou, Zhejiang 325035, China
Department of Electrical and Computer Engineering, Texas A&M University, College Station, TX 33101, USA

Thang Vu
Department of Electrical and Computer Engineering, Texas A&M University, 3128 TAMU, College Station, TX 77843, USA

Chao Sima
Center for Bioinformatics and Genomic Systems Engineering, Texas A&M University, 101 Gateway, Suite A, College Station, TX 77845, USA

Ulisses M Braga-Neto and Edward R Dougherty
Department of Electrical and Computer Engineering, Texas A&M University, 3128 TAMU, College Station, TX 77843, USA
Center for Bioinformatics and Genomic Systems Engineering, Texas A&M University, 101 Gateway, Suite A, College Station, TX 77845, USA

CPSIA information can be obtained
at www.ICGtesting.com
Printed in the USA
BVHW01*0957070918
526815BV00003B/6/P

9 781682 862346